AQA Business Studies for A2

Malcolm Surridge
Andrew Gillespie

4TH EDITION

DYNAMIC LEARNING

HODDER EDUCATION
AN HACHETTE UK COMPANY

GET BETTER RESULTS FOR AQA

Orders: please contact Bookpoint Ltd, 130 Milton Park, Abingdon, Oxon OX14 4SB. Telephone: (44) 01235 827720. Fax: (44) 01235 400454. Lines are open from 9.00–5.00, Monday to Saturday, with a 24-hour message answering service. You can also order through our website www.hoddereducation.co.uk

If you have any comments to make about this, or any of our other titles, please send them to educationenquiries@ hodder.co.uk

British Library Cataloguing in Publication Data

A catalogue record for this title is available from the British Library

ISBN: 978 1444 16820 4

First edition published 2001
Second edition published 2005
Third edition published 2009
This edition published 2012

Impression number   10 9 8 7 6 5 4 3 2 1
Year   2017, 2016, 2015, 2014, 2013, 2012

Hachette UK's policy is to use papers that are natural, renewable and recyclable products and made from wood grown in sustainable forests. The logging and manufacturing processes are expected to conform to the environmental regulations of the country of origin.

Cover photo © Damir Spanic/iStockphoto.com.

Typeset by DC Graphic Design Limited, Swanley, Kent.

Printed in Italy for Hodder Education, an Hachette UK Company, 338 Euston Road, London NW1 3BH.

CONTENTS

Unit 4

INTRODUCTION

Building on AS Business Studies

From studying AQA AS Business Studies last year you will know that there is a story that runs through AS Business Studies and on into the A2 specification. It is important that you understand this story because it sets out the philosophy of the specification and the extent of each part of the specification. It will help to guide you through your studies as well as helping you to prepare for the AS and A2 examinations.

AS Business Studies started with Unit 1, which considered the activities involved in starting a business. Therefore, it considered small businesses and the process of planning. Unit 2 continued the story to include medium-sized businesses and to focus on how managers of small to medium-sized businesses can use tactical decisions (such as increasing capacity utilisation or recruiting new staff) to improve the performance of their businesses.

The A2 specification continues this story.

The A2 story

Unit 3 is based on large businesses, normally public limited companies that are trading nationally and internationally. The focus of this unit is on examining the functional strategies (human resources, operations, marketing and finance) that such businesses may adopt in order to achieve success. The story encompasses the ways in which businesses measure their performance and the strategies they may adopt (such as relocating overseas or adopting lean production techniques) to achieve the objectives they set themselves.

Unit 4 concludes the story. It continues to be based on large (possibly multinational) businesses, but it examines the internal and external causes of change that can affect a business. Therefore the initial focus of this unit is outside the business; all the previous units have looked at the internal operations of a business. This part of the story invites you to think carefully about the impact that internal and external causes of change can have on different businesses and to make some attempt to assess the likely impact of the various causes of change. The latter part of this unit is entitled 'Managing change' and considers the ways in which businesses manage change, as well as important factors in such management, including leadership and culture.

A2 assessment

The A2 assessment package comprises two compulsory papers. These papers can be taken each January and June.

Unit 3 – Buss3 (Strategies for Success)

This paper is worth 25 per cent of the total marks for the A level. The examination's duration is 1 hour 45 minutes. It comprises approximately five questions based on a decision-making case study including at least two numerical appendices. The paper carries 80 marks maximum.

Unit 4 – Buss4 (The Business Environment and Change)

This paper is worth 25 per cent of the total marks for the A level. The examination's duration is 1 hour 45 minutes. It is presented in two sections.

- The first section is based on some research that you will have carried out prior to the examination. This research will have been based on a research brief, which is available to you at least five months before the examination. The paper then offers you a choice of two questions, from which you have to choose one.
- The second section is a choice of three essays from which you have to select one.

There are 80 marks in total for this paper – 40 for each section.

How AQA A2 Business Studies examinations are marked

Introduction

Both of the A2 Business Studies papers have been designed to test not only your knowledge but also the skills of application, analysis and evaluation. Examiners seek to reward knowledge as well as these skills when marking your answers. Most of the A2 questions require you to offer knowledge plus all of these skills. The command words used in questions to signify that evaluation is required are: evaluate, discuss, to what extent, justify and assess.

The same basic approach is used to mark candidates' responses to Buss3 and Buss4 papers. However, the examination skills tested by the two papers are different. as shown in Table 0.1.

Examination skill	Unit 3	Unit 4	A2
Knowledge	20	20	20
Application	30	20	25
Analysis	25	25	25
Evaluation	25	35	30

Table 0.1 A2 assessment objectives in percentages

Marking Buss3 responses

The normal structure of a Buss3 paper is a case study and appendices plus four questions. One of these questions is usually an analytical question; the other three require evaluative answers. Three marking grids are used to mark these questions. The marks are written with the highest number first to encourage examiners to use the full mark range at each level.

(a) Analytical questions

Table 0.2 is used to mark analytical questions on Buss3 and assumes that a maximum of ten marks is allocated to the question. This may not always be the case.

Level	Descriptor	Marks
L5	Good analysis **AND** good application	10–9
L4	Good analysis **or** good application **AND** reasonable application **or** reasonable analysis	8–7
L3	Good analysis **or** application **OR** reasonable application **and** reasonable analysis	6–5
L2	Knowledge **plus** reasonable application **OR** reasonable analysis	4–3
L1	Answer contains relevant knowledge – basic points and/or evidence of understanding of relevant term(s)	2–1

Table 0.2 Analytical questions

(b) Evaluative questions

Tables 0.3 and 0.4 show how the marks might be allocated for questions worth 18 marks in total and for those worth 34 marks. Note that these marks are spread across the two grids. Also the marks allocated to these two types of evaluative questions may not be exactly 18 and 34 marks, but are likely to be similar to this.

Level	Descriptor	Marks (18 mark question)	Marks (34 mark question)
L5	Good analysis **AND** good application	13–12	24–21
L4	Good analysis **or** good application **AND** reasonable application **or** reasonable analysis	11–9	20–16
L3	Good analysis **or** good application **OR** reasonable application **and** reasonable analysis	8–6	15–11
L2	Good knowledge **plus** reasonable application **OR** reasonable analysis	5–3	10–6
L1	Answer contains relevant knowledge – basic points and/or evidence of understanding of relevant term(s)	2–1	5–1

Table 0.3 Evaluative questions: first grid

Level	Descriptor	Marks (18 mark question)	Marks (34 mark question)
E3	Judgement with well supported justification. Answer has a logical structure throughout, with effective use of technical terms.	5–4	10–8
E2	Judgement with reasonable attempt at justification. Evidence of a logical structure and some use of technical terms.	3–2	7–4
E1	Assertion or judgement which is unsupported. Reasonable evidence of a logical structure and little use of technical terms.	1	3–1

Table 0.4 Evaluative questions: second grid

What do the terms in the marking schemes mean and how should I respond?

You will see firstly that knowledge only scores a small number of marks. Of course, knowledge is an essential starting point, but it alone will not get you high marks or a good grade. Your revision programme should be such as to give you thorough knowledge of the Buss3 specification, but this is only a starting point.

Application means relating your answer to the case study by drawing on ideas or facts from it or by using numbers. It is an important skill in responding to Buss3. If your answer contains application, the examiner will judge it to be reasonable or good. Clearly, it is better for you to provide good application. Good application means that you have applied your answer consistently, have carried out relevant calculations or have combined information from the case study in support of a theoretical point.

Analysis is the part of your answer where you develop relevant lines of argument in response to questions. This may involve the use of theory. Once again the terms 'reasonable' and 'good' are used to differentiate different quality responses. Good analysis requires you to develop one or more arguments fully, making sure you explain each link in your chain of reasoning and maintaining a good focus on the question. Too often students fail to develop arguments fully and receive 'reasonable analysis' awards as a result.

Evaluation is marked using a separate grid, but the principles are the same. This is an important part of the marking of the A2 papers. Most candidates make a judgement, usually in the final paragraph. The marks awarded for evaluation normally depend heavily on the quality of support given for your view. It is best to support your judgement with evidence from the case study.

How are these grids used by examiners?

The examiner will read through your answer and use these grids to annotate your answer using the levels. The highest level you achieve within your answer will be noted and then a decision made as to precisely what mark you would receive.

For example, if an examiner was marking your answer to a 34 mark question and they thought that it contained relevant knowledge as well as reasonable application and reasonable analysis at best, they would settle on a mark within level three. You would score between 11 and 15 marks from the first grid. Their decision over evaluation would be made separately and, assuming that they awarded level two (for a decision supported by reasonable justification), they would select a mark between 4 and 7. If they decided to award the top mark in each case you would receive 22 marks (out of 34) for your answer.

Level three in the main grid is probably the most complex level to understand. You can be awarded this for three different reasons:

- for offering knowledge plus evidence of reasonable application **and** reasonable analysis (as in our example above)
- for an answer which has knowledge plus good application, but no analysis
- for an answer which has knowledge plus good analysis, but no application.

Marking Buss4 responses

The general approach to marking answers to the research questions and essays is the same as described above for Buss3. The mark allocations tend to be higher, because each question on the Buss4 paper is worth 40 marks.

All the questions on the Buss4 paper are evaluative and worth 40 marks so, the grids shown below are relevant throughout.

Level	Descriptor	Marks
L5	Good analysis **AND** good application	26–23
L4	Good analysis **or** good application **AND** reasonable application **or** reasonable analysis	22–18
L3	Good analysis **or** application **OR** reasonable application **and** reasonable analysis	17–13
L2	Good knowledge **plus** reasonable application **OR** reasonable analysis	12–8
L1	Answer contains relevant knowledge – basic points and/or evidence of understanding of relevant term(s)	7–1

Table 0.5

Level	Descriptor	Marks
E3	Good evaluation. Answer has a logical structure throughout, with effective use of technical terms.	14–11
E2	Reasonable evaluation. Evidence of a logical structure and some use of technical terms.	10–6
E1	Limited evaluation. Reasonable evidence of a logical structure and little use of technical terms.	5–1

Table 0.6

Are there any differences in the way Buss4 papers are marked?

Although the general principles of marking are the same, there are several points you should be aware of, if you are to achieve the highest marks of which you are capable.

(a) The research question

- The research question requires you to undertake a study of a prescribed topic before the examination. To achieve high marks on this type of question your answer must include evidence of relevant research. It is a good idea to research a small number of contrasting businesses in relation to the research theme. This will make it easier for you to write evaluatively by comparing and contrasting your evidence.
- To achieve good marks for application your answer must include evidence of your research and use the stimulus material included in the examination paper. If you do not include any evidence of research, you will not receive any marks for application and will only be able to achieve level 3 on the main grid, as a maximum.

- Similarly, marks awarded for evaluation on research questions are restricted to E1 only if there is no evidence of your independent research included within the answer.

(b) Essays

- Essays provide only a limited amount of information for you to use as a basis for application. It is normal for the title to include one or two businesses or industries, though this is not always the case. You should seek to apply your answer to these examples **and/or** any others which you know about. Therefore, **you do not have to use the examples set out in the essay title**. Thus, when you study the various topics that comprise Buss4, do support your study with investigating how the material covered relates to a small number of diverse businesses.
- Focusing on the precise title throughout is essential in achieving good marks on essays. Examiners will only credit your answer if it is relevant and the best answers have a very precise focus. It is common for essays to ask whether something could be done quickly or whether it is always the case, or some similar angle. You must respond to the exact wording of the question throughout, and especially in your evaluation.

HOW TO USE THIS BOOK

This book gives you a comprehensive coverage of the AQA A2 specification. It builds on the AS specification that you have covered and cross-references the A2 materials with those that you studied at AS. This will help you to understand the relationships between the two specifications and to use AS material to underpin your study of the A2 subject matter when necessary.

This book is designed to help you to understand the key issues in each topic and the interrelationships between the various topics. Throughout the book we have introduced you to a range of theories and concepts which can be used to build arguments when responding to examination questions. These are not always mentioned directly in the specification but they will enable you to develop strong arguments and to make and support judgements. The book will also help you to learn how to use your knowledge effectively and to develop the right skills for success in the AQA A2 examinations.

Within each chapter there are also several features to help you understand the material. These are:

- Business in focus: this feature should help to bring a topic to life by showing it in action in a real business context. We hope to show you how the various theories and models can be applied to real business decisions. The questions have marks allocated if they are similar in style to exam questions.
- Key issues: this feature explores a business concept or issue in greater depth.
- One step further: this has been provided in some chapters in order to give you extension material that is useful if you want to go beyond the specification or add to your understanding of a topic.

At the end of each chapter we provide:

- Key terms: this feature gives you definitions of key terms.
- Examiner's advice: this feature highlights the type of questions that might be asked in the exam and the issues you should think about when revising.
- Progress questions: these are short questions to help you check whether you have understood the key points.
- Analysis and evaluation questions (Unit 3): these will help you to develop your examination skills. By answering these questions you can practise key skills such as applying your answers and evaluating the key points in your argument. The case study for the questions can be found at the beginning of the section.
- Essay questions (Unit 4): these will help you to develop the skills you need for the Unit 4 examination.
- Sample answers to some of the questions: these are designed to show examples of good technique in responding to exam questions, and to illustrate some of the more common errors found in candidates' responses. One way of using these answers may be to tackle the questions yourself before looking at the answers we have provided and the commentaries. This will help to sharpen your exam technique by giving a clearer understanding of what examiners are looking for.

Overall, we hope this book provides an interesting read and that you feel it provides good coverage of the AQA specification and helps prepare you effectively for your exams. If you have any suggestions for how we can improve the book in future editions, do not hesitate to contact us on wattgill@aol.com.

ACKNOWLEDGEMENTS

The authors would like to thank everyone at Hodder Education for all their support.

For my parents, Alan and Bennice, with love — Malcolm Surridge

All my love to Al, Clemmie, Romily and Seth, who now know more about business than they ever wanted or needed to! — Andrew Gillespie

Every effort has been made to trace the copyright holders of material reproduced here, and to credit the sources used in research. The authors and publishers would like to thank the following for permission to reproduce copyright illustrations:

Photo on page 1 © Yuri Arcurs – Fotolia; Figure 1.1 © PORNCHAI KITTIWONGSAKUL/AFP/Getty Images; Figure 4.1 © Diana Bier Mexico Paseo Angel/Alamy; Figure 4.2 © David Pearson/Alamy; Figure 6.2 © AP/ Press Association Images; Figure 8.4 © goodluz – Fotolia; Figure 10.4 © Justin Sullivan/Getty Images; Figure 10.6 © AP/Press Association Images; Figure 11.2 © BERND OTTEN/AFP/Getty Images; Figure 11.3 © Hulton Archive/Getty Images; Figure 12.1 © Petr Malyshev – Fotolia; Figure 12.2 © David Levenson/Getty Images; Figure 15.1 © Imagestate Media (John Foxx); Figure 17.5 © PA Wire/Press Association Images; Figure 18.2 © Nicholas Bailey/Rex Features; Figure 18.4 © Susannah Ireland/Rex Features; photo on page 235 © Yuri Arcurs – Fotolia; Figure 21.5 © Imagestate Media (John Foxx); Figure 23.1 © Photodisc/ Getty Images; Figure 25.2 © blue eye – Fotolia; Figure 28.4 © James Nielsen/Getty Images.

'Open the skies' (page 275) © The Economist Newspaper, London (2011).

UNIT 3

Functional objectives and corporate objectives

As we saw in Unit 2 of the AS specification, a business has a number of internal functions including marketing, finance, human resource management and operations. In a large business the managers or directors responsible for each of these functions will set functional objectives. This introduction looks at these functional objectives and considers how they can help the organisation to achieve its overall corporate objectives.

In this introduction we will examine:
- functional objectives and their relationship with corporate objectives
- the relationship between functional objectives and strategies.

Functional objectives and corporate objectives

Corporate objectives

Corporate objectives are the overall goals of the whole business. Corporate goals vary according to the size and history of the organisation, as well as the personal aims of the business's senior managers.

The 'Business in focus' here outlines Tesco's corporate objectives – from these it will derive its functional objectives. Achieving these will assist it in achieving its corporate objectives.

BUSINESS IN FOCUS

Tesco's objectives

In 1997, Tesco set out a strategy based on corporate objectives including to grow the core business (grocery retailing) and diversify with new products and services in existing and new markets. This strategy enabled us to deliver strong, sustained growth over the past 14 years.

We've followed customers into large expanding markets in the UK and new markets abroad.

Some elements of the strategy remain unchanged. The objective 'to grow the core UK business' is as relevant today as it was in 1997. The UK is the largest business in the group and a key driver of sales and profit.

Another of our original objectives was to be a 'successful international retailer'. In 1997, our international businesses generated 1.8 per cent of the group's profits. Today they represent 25 per cent.

Our services businesses have come a long way since we first included the objective 'to develop retailing services'. Today these parts of Tesco generate £583 million profit, representing 16 per cent of the group total.

In 2007, we added a fifth element to our strategy to underpin our commitment to communities and the environment. Our objective is to put our responsibilities to the communities we serve at the heart of what we do.

(Source: Adapted from Tesco Annual Report, 2011)

A business could pursue a number of corporate objectives, including the following:

- growth – to increase the overall scale of the business
- diversification – look to sell new products in new markets
- to achieve the maximum possible profits in the long term
- to develop innovative goods and services.

The setting and communication of clear corporate objectives allows senior managers to delegate authority to more junior employees while maintaining the organisation's overall sense of direction.

Functional objectives

A functional objective is a goal that is pursued by particular functions within the business, such as

Figure 0.1 Corporate and functional objectives

human resources (HR) or marketing. A functional objective is likely to have a numerical element and a stated timescale. Thus, a business might set a financial objective which is a specific profit figure in relation to the capital available to the business. The objective will also set out the timescale within which this financial objective is to be attained.

Once clear corporate objectives have been set it is possible for the business to set targets at functional levels. The achievement of their objectives by the various functional areas of the business will contribute to the overall business achieving its corporate objectives. For example, a business that has a corporate objective of growth will require its HR function to set and achieve objectives to increase the size or productivity (or both) of its workforce to enable it to increase its supplies of goods or services. At the same time, the finance function may be setting itself goals of increasing the funds available to the business to allow the objective of growth to be financed properly.

The relationship between functional objectives and strategies

A functional objective is a goal that is pursued by a particular function of the business. A functional strategy is the medium- to long-term plan used to achieve the objective. Vodafone has set itself a number of functional objectives relating to the finance function, for the period up to 2014, including those set out below.

- Revenue growth of 1 per cent–4 per cent every year.

- To focus on cost reductions resulting from the business's large size and using standardised technology.

For Vodafone to achieve these financial objectives other functions within the business will have to take appropriate decisions. For example, the company's marketing department may have to develop new products or enter new markets to gain the 1 per cent–4 per cent growth in sales revenue each year. So, although functional objectives are set independently, they do require cooperation between the various functions that comprise a business.

Functional objectives should also contribute to the achievement of the business's corporate objectives. Functional objectives should be set first (and should contribute to the achievement of corporate objectives) and then the strategy should be devised to achieve the functional objective.

A business such as Vodafone with a corporate strategy of growth, may set a functional objective within the HR department of developing a larger and more highly skilled workforce which will help the organisation to meet its corporate objectives.

Figure 0.2 Functional strategies and functional objectives

This will require the managers responsible for the HR function to devise a strategy or plan to meet its functional objectives. The key elements of such a plan may include training employees, recruiting new staff and possibly relocating certain staff.

Summary

A business sets itself corporate objectives, which are targets or goals for the entire business, to be achieved over the medium to long term. In turn, the various functions (for example, marketing, human resources, operations) of a business will set themselves functional objectives. The achievement of these functional objectives will assist the business in attaining its corporate objectives. To achieve their objectives the functions of the business will draw up functional strategies, which are medium- to long-term plans.

Progress questions

1 Which of the following might **not** be a corporate objective of a large business?
   a diversification
   b growth
   c profit maximisation
   d relocation *(1 mark)*

2 Explain the difference between a functional objective and a functional strategy. *(4 marks)*

3 Explain, using examples, why the setting of a functional objective by the operations department of producing high-quality products will impact upon the objectives set elsewhere in the business. *(8 marks)*

4 Outline why the achievement of functional objectives should assist a business in attaining its corporate objectives. *(6 marks)*

SECTION 1 *Financial strategies and accounts*

Introduction

As with all topics in A2 Business Studies, you will have studied some elements of this subject during your AS level course. The major elements you will have studied are:

- classifying costs (for example fixed and variable costs)
- the concept of contribution (selling price less variable costs)
- break-even analysis using calculations and charts
- the management of cash flow and the distinction between cash flow and profit
- sources of finance
- budgets and budgeting.

The A2 specification for business studies builds upon the subject knowledge and skills acquired during the AS programme. It is therefore worthwhile looking back over your AS materials before starting to study A2 Financial Strategies and Accounts. You will find more specific advice on any prior knowledge required at the beginning of each chapter.

During your A2 programme you will study:

- financial objectives that are pursued by businesses and the factors that influence the choice of these
- company accounts in detail, considering their structure and interrelationships, and topics such as depreciation and working capital
- ratio analysis – a technique used to analyse company accounts
- investment decision-making – looking at financial and non-financial factors considered by businesses before taking a decision on whether to undertake major investments.

Case study for Section 1: Invicta holdings plc

This case study relates to the analysis and evaluation questions at the end of each chapter in Section 1.

Invicta was established in July 1999 by Kevin Sergeant. The company was initially launched as an online fashion clothing and beauty retailer with the primary aim of rapid growth. In November 2001 the company was admitted to the AIM on the London Stock Exchange. It turned the latest fashion from the catwalk into good quality products; it termed this 'stylish quality' and acquired a positive image amongst fashion conscious customers.

Invicta has achieved rapid increases in online sales both in the UK and across many EU countries. It has made effective use of social networking sites such as Facebook, allowing customers to buy through such websites. The company's early success led to the opening of 42 stores across the UK by 2012 selling its own range of clothing and beauty products as well as famous fashion brands such as Diesel and Tommy Hilfiger. The success of these stores has been very variable – some in less-favoured locations are thought to be barely profitable.

A challenging market

From the outset Kevin Sergeant decided that the company's financial objective should be to achieve ROCE figures in excess of 25 per cent to fulfil his aims. During the prosperous years after the millennium incomes in the UK rose steadily and the company's sales soared, despite the company's high (and rising) prices. In 2008 its sales revenue exceeded £850 million, its ROCE figure was 28.2 per cent and shareholders were doubly satisfied as its share price hit an all time high of 324 pence.

In part, the increase in sales came from the launching of new Invicta brands such as 'Little Invicta' which caters for babies up to 24 months and girls and boys aged from 2 to 8 years. This has proved popular and successful. Although total UK online sales of clothing reached £4.3 billion in 2010 (a rise of 152 per cent in five years), consumers' tastes are difficult to predict and sales are also vulnerable to changes in consumers' incomes. The arrival of other strong competitors in the market (such as ASOS.com, who has launched new brands recently) means that the market is becoming increasingly competitive.

Kevin's proposal

Kevin Sergeant presented the company's 2011 accounts to the board of directors in January 2012. He argued that the company's income statements and balance sheets are the most important evidence in predicting the company's ability to continue to grow.

From this he developed his proposal to open 65 retail outlets in seven EU countries including Germany, Holland, France and Spain. The key elements of his plan were as follows:

- An investment of £350 million would be required to acquire suitable properties, stock, hire and train employees and to finance a major marketing campaign.
- The outlets would be located in wealthy cities such as Barcelona, Amsterdam, Berlin and Marseille where incomes are higher. (For example, average incomes in Paris are forecast to rise by 4.8 per cent in 2012.)
- Each of the new outlets (as well as existing ones in the UK) would operate as profit centres. Authority would be decentralised and a profit-sharing scheme would be introduced based on each stores individual performance.

The response to Kevin's proposal was mixed. Several directors were worried about the current weakness of the eurozone economy, where economic growth has been slow (the latest quarterly GDP growth figure was 0.2 per cent) and unemployment is rising. The marketing director argued that selling a relatively unknown premium brand in such economic circumstances would be very difficult. Kevin countered by saying the cost of the expansion would be much lower at this time (up to 20 per cent cheaper) and that the returns on the proposed investment were excellent, especially in the long run.

Some directors argued that it was not necessary for the company to invest in retail outlets in the EU. Online sales had been rising strongly in the EU – they increased by 22 per cent to £94 million in 2011.

Appendices

Appendix A: Invicta plc summarised financial accounts

Invicta plc – balance sheets for 2010 and 2011		
	31 December 2011 (£m)	31 December 2010 (£m)
Non-current assets	995.4	841.8
Current assets	214.1	200.5
Current liabilities	(310.9)	(297.4)
Non-current liabilities	(498.2)	(383.3)
Net assets	**400.4**	**361.6**
Share capital	211.2	180.2
Reserves & retained earnings	189.2	181.4
Total equity	**400.4**	**361.6**
Invicta plc – income statements for 2010 and 2011		
	2011 (£m)	2010 (£m)
Revenue (sales excluding VAT)	1,200.7	1,099.9
Cost of sales	(802.9)	(758.3)
Gross profit	**397.8**	**341.6**
Administrative & other expenses	(132.2)	(136.8)
Operating profit	**265.6**	**204.8**
Net finance income (costs)	(15.8)	1.1
Profit before tax	**249.8**	**205.9**

Table 1 Extracts from balance sheets and income statements for Invicta plc

Appendix B: selected ratios

Ratio	2011	2010
Acid test	0.48	0.40
Creditor days	55.1	37.4
Asset turnover	3.00	3.04
Operating cash flow	0.98	1.12

Table 2 Selected ratios for Invicta plc, 2010 and 2011

Appendix C: further data

- Invicta's labour turnover: 2010 – 9.1 per cent, 2011 – 17.3 per cent.
- Invicta plc's share price was 260 pence on 31 December 2010 and 280 pence on 31 December 2011.
- Estimated price elasticity of demand for Invicta's products: –0.4.
- Dividend per share: 2010 – 13.1 pence, 2011 – 14.6 pence.
- Employee numbers rose from 1,210 to 1,275 during 2011; average wages rose by 0.2 per cent.

Appendix D: investment data

Year 1	£36.6m
Year 2	£72.3m
Year 3	£99.1m
Year 4	£142.0m
Year 5	£179.9m

Table 3 Expected net return from Kevin's proposal over a five year period

Year 1	Year 2	Year 3	Year 4	Year 5
0.909	0.826	0.751	0.683	0.621

Table 4 Discounting factors

1 Understanding financial objectives

This chapter looks at the targets or goals that a finance department may set itself. The achievement of these targets or goals will assist the business in achieving its corporate goals or objectives. This chapter builds on some important topics from your study of AS Business Studies, not least costs, profit and cash flow. If you are unsure about the meaning of any of these terms and the distinction between cash flow and profit, you should look again at the relevant AS materials.

In this chapter we examine:

- the types of financial objectives that businesses pursue
- the external and internal influences on financial objectives.

The financial objectives of business

A financial objective is a goal or target pursued by the finance department (or function) within an organisation. It is likely that a financial objective will contain a specific numerical element and also a timescale within which it is to be achieved. The financial objective will be set by the managers responsible for finance in the business, but will be consistent with other functional objectives and will also contribute to the achievement of the business's corporate objectives.

A business might pursue a number of financial objectives including those discussed below.

Return on capital employed targets

The return on capital employed (commonly referred to as ROCE) is calculated by expressing the net profits made by a business as a percentage of the value of the capital employed in the business. Stakeholders in a business can compare its current ROCE figure with those achieved by other businesses or by the same business in previous years. We consider ROCE more fully as part of the chapter on ratio analysis (see pages 34–47).

A business might set itself a financial objective of achieving a ROCE figure of 25 per cent. This means that its net profits for the financial year will be 25 per cent of the capital employed in the business. This financial objective is very precise and has the advantage of being relatively simple to measure and compare with that achieved by other businesses and by the same business in previous years. To achieve such an objective (which is likely to be a higher figure than that achieved in previous years) can require actions to increase net profits as well as to minimise the value of assets used within the business. Aviva, one of the world's largest insurance companies set a ROCE target of 31.5 per cent for the financial year 2010-11. In part the bonuses of the company's senior managers depend upon achieving at least this level of ROCE.

As with other financial objectives, this has considerable implications for other functions within the business. The marketing function may set objectives in terms of market share to improve profitability. At the same time the operations department may outsource some production functions to reduce the amount of capital that the business requires to conduct its trading activities.

Shareholders' returns

Shareholders' returns can be defined in more than one way. One approach is to take a short-term view and define it as the current share price and any associated dividends that are due in the near future. It is also possible to have a longer-term view of shareholders' returns and define it as a combination of short-term returns (both share prices and dividends) as well as future share prices and dividends. However it is defined, shareholders' returns focus on generating profits and on increasing the value of the company as reflected in its share price.

Tesco sets itself tough financial targets

In April 2011 Tesco, Britain's biggest retailer, reported record profits of £3.8bn – more than £10m a day – but admitted that it needed to do better in its core UK operations. Results for the year to end February showed the bulk of Tesco's 12.3 per cent profit increase came from its growing Asian operations. Total group sales were £68bn and in Britain sales grew 5.5 per cent to £45bn, with trading profits ahead by 3.8 per cent to £2.5bn.

But the performance was not good enough, Tesco's new boss Philip Clarke admitted. 'We didn't achieve our planned growth in the year and this was only partly attributable to the deterioration in the consumer environment during the second half. We can do better and we are taking action in key areas – for example, to drive a faster rate of product innovation and to improve the sharpness of our communication to customers.'

Like-for-like sales in the UK, excluding VAT and petrol, declined by 0.7 per cent in the last three months of Tesco's financial year. General merchandise, clothing and electricals fared particularly badly. Tesco said, 'Our performance in electrical goods was below the market and the growth in clothing was also not as strong as we had planned.'

(Source: Alex Hawkes in The Guardian, *19 April 2011)*

In 2011 Tesco's ROCE rose to 12.9 per cent from 12.1 per cent in the previous year. However, the company has set itself a target of increasing ROCE to 14.6 per cent by the 2014–15 financial year.

Questions:

1 Analyse the actions that Tesco might take to achieve its ROCE target of 14.6 per cent by 2014–15. *(10 marks)*
2 To what extent do you agree with the view that the marketing function will have to undergo greater changes than Tesco's other functions if the ROCE target is to be achieved? *(18 marks)*

Increasing shareholders' returns requires the support of the other functions within the business. Minimising costs can be an important element of any strategy implemented to achieve this financial objective, and this could have significant consequences for the operations and human relations (HR) functions within the business. Equally, the marketing function may aim to improve the business's product range and to increase added value in support of the achievement of this financial objective.

Shareholders can clearly benefit from a business pursuing a financial target of maximising its shareholders' returns. However, other stakeholder groups such as employees may be disadvantaged. This financial objective is likely to result in a business seeking to cut its costs, which may involve a number of HR strategies that result in the loss of jobs (particularly the loss of full-time permanent jobs in relatively high-wage economies such as the UK). Equally, suppliers may suffer as businesses with this financial objective seek to drive down the cost of purchases of raw materials and fuel.

Cost minimisation

This financial objective has become better known over recent years due to the publicity given to low-cost airlines and easyGroup, and their strategies of cost minimisation. A financial strategy of cost minimisation entails seeking to reduce to the lowest possible level all the costs of production that a business incurs as part of its trading activities. In the case of low-cost or budget airlines this has extended to minimising labour costs (for example, some require employees to pay for their own uniforms), reducing administrative costs (for example by using the internet for booking) and using 'out of town and city' airports to reduce landing and take-off fees charged by airport authorities.

The financial objective of cost minimisation has clear implications for the objectives (and hence strategies) of other functional areas within the business. Clearly the managers responsible for the other functions should aim to operate with minimal expenditure in order to support the fulfilment of this financial objective. Such a financial objective is likely to support corporate objectives such as profit maximisation or growth.

Cash-flow targets

For many businesses cash flow is vital and an essential element of success. This is especially true of businesses that face long cash cycles. A cash cycle is the time that elapses between the outflow of cash to pay for labour and raw materials for a product or service and the receipt of cash from the sale of the product (for instance, house builders and pharmaceutical firms may face long cash cycles). In 2011 BP set itself a target of increasing its net cash flow by 50 per cent by 2014 (the company's cash position had been damaged by the clean-up and compensation costs arising from the accident in the Gulf of Mexico in 2010).

Banks require a steady inflow of cash from depositors to enable them to engage in lending activities. The recent crises surrounding banks in the UK and other countries has, in part, been due to a lack of cash (or liquidity) being available to these organisations. Without cash banks do not have the necessary funds to avail themselves of possible profitable lending opportunities.

Without cash a business is unable to meet its financial commitments as they fall due. If a business cannot meet its financial commitments it cannot continue trading.

Other businesses that may establish financial objectives in terms of cash flow include businesses that are growing and need regular inflows of cash to finance the purchase of increasing quantities of inputs (such as labour and raw materials). Failure to set such objectives may result in a business facing financial problems because it runs short of cash as its expenditure or outflow of cash 'runs ahead' of its inflows of cash. Such a situation is described as overtrading.

The internal and external influences on financial objectives

A management team will be subject to a range of influences when setting its financial objectives. Some of these influences arise from within the business, while others are external. In 2012 many economies in the world are performing poorly, with some slipping back into recession. This made external influences particularly important on financial objectives at this time.

Internal influences

- **The corporate objectives of the business**. This might be the most important internal influence on a business's financial objectives. As we saw earlier, a financial objective must assist the business in achieving its overall corporate objectives. The corporate objectives are set first, followed by functional objectives, which are designed to complement them. Thus, a business that has profit maximisation as its overriding corporate objective may operate a financial objective of cost minimisation. Reducing costs as a financial objective should assist the business in maximising its profits.

- **The nature of the product that is sold**. The type of product can be a major influence on financial objectives. Businesses with long cash cycles are much more likely to set cash-flow targets as this is particularly vital to the management of their finance. Alternatively, if a product's demand is sensitive to price (that is, if its demand is price elastic), managers may be more likely to implement and pursue a financial objective of cost minimisation. This financial objective may allow price reduction with a positive impact on future sales and the business's sales revenue.

- **The objectives of the business's senior managers.** If the managers of the business hold large numbers of shares (perhaps as part of a share option scheme or as a result of founding the business), then increasing the shares' value might be an attractive proposition, especially if a long-term view is taken of this financial objective. On the other hand, managers may seek the recognition that accompanies the successful achievement of a corporate objective of growth. In such circumstances a financial objective of cost minimisation may be more appropriate.

External influences

- **The actions of other businesses**. A business will be most unlikely to ignore the actions of its competitors when establishing its financial objectives. For example, a business operating in a highly price-competitive market might consider establishing an objective of cost minimisation to allow it more flexibility in pricing decisions. In contrast, a business that wants to achieve a higher ROCE target may seek to form alliances with its rivals or to develop a Unique Selling Point (USP) for its products to allow it to charge premium prices and to increase its profit margins.

- **The availability of external finance.** If a business is experiencing difficulty in raising capital then financial objectives are more likely to centre on profits and profitability. Achieving specific returns in terms of profit will assist in reassuring potential shareholders or investors of the safety of their investments and the level of expected returns. It will also provide a source of capital for future investments.

- **The state of the market.** If the market for the business's products is expanding it may lead a business's managers to set more expansive financial objectives, such as higher rates of shareholders' returns or higher targets for ROCE. In contrast, in a market in which sales figures are stable or declining, financial objectives may be more cautious. Financial objectives such as targets for cost minimisation or cash flow may be deemed more appropriate in these circumstances. The 'Business in focus' feature on Canon in this chapter highlights the impact of low rates of economic growth on a business's financial objectives.

BUSINESS IN FOCUS

Canon cuts profit forecasts due to weakening sales and floods in Thailand

In October 2011 Canon Inc., the world's largest camera maker, cut its annual profit forecast owing to disruptions to production because of floods in Thailand and weakening economic growth in the US and Europe (meaning that sales were likely to be below their original forecasts).

They stated that their full year profits may be 230 billion yen (£2 billion) compared with a previous forecast for 260 billion yen. They also cut their sales and operating profit forecasts.

Toshizo Tanaka, Canon's executive vice president, told reporters in Tokyo (where the company is based) that the floods may have reduced annual sales by 50 billion yen and operating profit by 20 billion yen. and that Canon planned to trim costs to overcome the impact on earnings from the floods and lower economic growth in wealthy economies such as the US.

Shares of the company fell 1.8 per cent to 3,490 yen at the close in Tokyo trading before the revision of earnings. The stock had declined by 17 per cent that year, while Nikon Corp., Canon's biggest rival in the market for single-lens reflex cameras, gained 1.8 per cent.

Figure 1.1 Floods at Canon factory in Thailand

(Source: Adapted from Bloomberg, 25 October 2011, www.bloomberg.com)

Question

1 Analyse the actions that Canon's senior managers may take in response to cutting its profits forecast by 30 billion yen. *(10 marks)*

Profit is the surplus of revenues over total costs at the end of a trading period.

Cash flow is the movement of cash into and out of a business over a period of time.

Return on capital employed (ROCE) is the net profits of a business expressed as a percentage of the value of the capital employed in the business.

Examiner's advice

Do link the functional financial objective to the overall corporate objectives of the business and the objectives set by other functions within the business. For instance, in the case of cash-flow targets the marketing function may set itself objectives such as increasing sales, and especially cash sales.

Remember that financial objectives are not set in isolation from the rest of the business. They will be a part of the creation of corporate objectives as well as the objectives of the remaining functions within the business. These are part of a complementary package.

Progress questions

1   Define, with the use of examples, the term 'financial objective'. *(3 marks)*

2   Distinguish between cash flow and profit. *(6 marks)*

3   Explain **two** reasons why a public limited company might use ROCE as a basis for a financial objective. *(8 marks)*

4   What types of businesses might use cash-flow targets as a financial objective? Why? *(5 marks)*

5   Explain why a business entering an established market might choose to operate cost minimisation as a financial target. *(6 marks)*

6   What is meant by the term 'shareholders' returns'? *(4 marks)*

7   Explain why a business's finance department should not set its objectives without consulting the other functions of the business. *(6 marks)*

8   JHG plc builds oil rigs for use in locations across the globe. Explain how the nature of the company's product might influence its corporate objectives. *(8 marks)*

9   Why might a business's corporate objectives be considered the most important influence on its financial objectives? *(6 marks)*

10 Outline how the state of the market in which a business is selling might influence the financial objectives that it chooses. *(6 marks)*

Analysis question

✗ These questions relate to the case study on page 5.

Analyse why Invicta plc may have chosen a financial objective of achieving ROCE figures 'in excess of 25 per cent'. *(10 marks)*

Candidate's answer:

ROCE is return on capital employed and compares operating profit with the amount invested into the business whether shares or loans.

Kevin has set Invicta the target of growing as quickly as possible in the future. Having a financial objective of ROCE (of over 25 per cent) will help the company to achieve this overall

aim. A high return in the form of profits provides funds for reinvestment in marketing campaigns (as well as shops) to help to increase sales. In 2011 the company grew quickly to sales of over £1,200 million but still managed to achieve a high profit providing more finance for expansion – perhaps into Europe.

High ROCE figures will help Invicta to attract more investment from both banks and shareholders over the next few years and thus provide capital for further growth. Its ROCE figure in 2011 is nearly 30 per cent and this will help to reassure lenders that the company will be able to repay loans. In addition this will help to attract new shareholders who will be impressed by the rising share prices (at a time when shares are not performing well) as well as the possibility of sharing in profits in terms of dividends. For this company, at this time, this is the correct financial objective.

Examiner's comments:

This is a very competent answer. The candidate has demonstrated clear understanding of ROCE and has selected two sound arguments to support its use as a financial objective in these circumstances. They have also applied their arguments very effectively to the case study using both numerical and non-numerical information. They have conducted a simple calculation to illustrate the company's success in achieving a high ROCE figure in support of their second argument. Each argument has been developed clearly and with a close focus on the demands of the question and their use of paragraphs is effective.

There are very few limitations to this answer. At times they could have written their responses more concisely to make more effective use of the time available to them. They could have developed a very strong argument using the nature of the product (and its inelastic demand) as possibly the strongest argument available. Despite this the answer is very strong.

Evaluation question

Analyse the possible reasons why the company decided not to adopt a financial objective of cost minimisation. *(10 marks)*

2 Using financial data to measure and assess performance

This chapter looks at the major documents that businesses in the UK use to report financial performance – the balance sheet and the income statement. These documents enable stakeholders to measure and analyse the performance of a business in financial terms. Stakeholders can use this information to assess an organisation's financial performance by making comparisons with the same business in earlier years or with similar businesses over the same financial year.

In this chapter we examine:
- how to analyse balance sheets
- how to analyse income statements
- how to use financial data for comparisons, trend analysis and decision-making
- the strengths and weaknesses of financial data in judging a business's performance.

How to analyse balance sheets

Since 2005 there have been significant changes to the way that public companies in the UK present their accounts. A European Union regulation required public companies to prepare financial statements complying with the International Financial Reporting Standards (IFRS) after 1 January 2005. This requirement has not yet been extended to private limited companies, although negotiations are taking place. As a consequence, different types of companies can present their balance sheets in different ways. This chapter will use the post-IFRS approach, but will use the old terminology alongside the new wherever possible. The key changes are set out in 'Business in focus' below.

BUSINESS IN FOCUS

IFRS changes to balance sheets

The implementation of International Financial Reporting Standards (IFRS) throughout the EU has required that listed public companies present their balance sheets in a format slightly different from that used in the past. There are a number of differences in the terminology used on the IFRS balance sheet:

- Fixed assets are called non-current assets but continue to include tangible and non-tangible assets.
- There are two changes within the current assets section of the balance sheet: stocks are renamed as 'inventories' and debtors are now termed 'trade and other receivables'.
- Under current liabilities, creditors are referred to as 'trade and other payables'.
- Long-term liabilities are renamed 'non-current liabilities'.
- Reserves in the final section of the balance sheet are supplemented by 'retained earnings'. Retained earnings are profits that a company has generated which have not been paid out to shareholders.
- Shareholders' funds are termed 'total equity' or 'total shareholders' equity'.

There are some differences between the balance sheets of public and private limited companies as, at the time of writing, private limited companies have not had to implement the IFRS changes. In this chapter we will concentrate on the balance sheets of public companies. Some public companies (for example Marks & Spencer) call their balance sheets 'statements of financial position'.

What is a balance sheet?

A balance sheet is a financial statement recording the assets (possessions) and liabilities (debts) of a business on a particular day at the end of an accounting period. The balance sheet only represents a picture of a business's assets and liabilities at a moment in time: it is commonly described as a 'snapshot' of the financial position of an organisation. Because of this, balance sheets always carry a date on which the valuation of assets and assessment of liabilities took place.

Key balance sheet relationships

1 ASSETS = LIABILITIES
   This is the fundamental relationship that helps to explain why the balance sheet 'always balances'.
2 TOTAL ASSETS = CURRENT ASSETS + NON-CURRENT ASSETS
   Businesses need to invest in a range of assets if they are to operate efficiently.
3 LIABILITIES = SHARE CAPITAL + BORROWINGS + RESERVES

By recording assets and liabilities the balance sheet sets out the ways in which the business has raised its capital and the uses to which this capital has been put. The balance sheet provides a great deal of information for those with an interest in a business, and is the primary financial document published by businesses.

Balance sheets are an essential source of information for a variety of business decisions and for a number of stakeholders.

- **Shareholders** (and potential shareholders) may use balance sheets to assess a business's potential to generate profits in the future. Thus, they may examine the extent and type of assets available to a business. A high proportion of assets such as machinery and property may signify a potential for profit, depending upon the type of business.
- **Suppliers** are more likely to use a balance sheet to investigate the short-term position of the company. Thus, they may consider cash and other liquid assets a business holds and make a judgement about whether the business is likely to be able to pay its bills over the coming months. This may help a supplier reach a decision on whether to offer credit to the business in question.
- **Managers** will be interested in a balance sheet as an indication of the performance of the business. Thus, they may extract information to help them reach a decision on how to raise further capital for future investment. The amount of existing loans may be one factor influencing this decision.

The precise information drawn from the balance sheet will depend upon the stakeholder and the nature of their enquiry. However, it is important to appreciate that this particular financial statement contains a great deal of information.

BUSINESS IN FOCUS

Weak balance sheet causes Saab shutdown

The Swedish motor vehicle manufacturer, which halted production of its cars in April 2011 because of a shortage of cash, admitted that its balance sheet was very weak and that it did not have short-term financing available to pay staff.

'This is really bad news and we are working intensely to do something about it. There are no guarantees but we are not giving up,' Saab spokeswoman Gunilla Gustavs told Reuters. Swedish Automobile, the owner of Saab, said it was in discussions with 'various parties to obtain short-term funding'.

The production shutdown followed a payment dispute with suppliers. Production restarted in late May after the group secured a cash advance from Chinese car sales company Pangda Automobile Trade Co, but was suspended again in June.

Saab continued to hold discussions with suppliers during June and hoped to reach agreement on payment terms and resume production. FKG, the Swedish trade organisation for car manufacturers, estimated that Saab owed the country's suppliers at least 300 million kroner (£29 million). The car maker was reported to have asked suppliers to accept 10 per cent of what they were owed immediately with the balance to be paid in September.

(*Source: Adapted from* The Daily Telegraph, *23 June 2011*)

Question:

Analyse the possible reason why Saab's cash position on its balance sheet may have become so weak. *(10 marks)*

Assets

An asset is simply something that a business owns. Thus assets are what a business uses its capital to purchase. There are two main categories of assets that appear on the balance sheet. The distinction between the two categories is based upon the time the assets are held within the business.

1 **Non-current assets** (previously called fixed assets). These are assets owned by a business that it expects to retain for one year or more. Such assets are used regularly by a business and are not bought for the purpose of resale. Examples of non-current assets include land, property, production equipment and vehicles.

2 **Current assets.** This category of asset is likely to be converted into cash before the next balance sheet is drawn up. Therefore, cash and inventories (previously called stock) are examples of current assets as they are only retained by the business for a short period of time.

There is another way to classify assets which, although it does not affect the balance sheet directly, is still important.

1 **Tangible assets.** These are assets that have a physical existence and have been traditionally included on a balance sheet. Tangible assets include:
- land and property, which are frequently the most valuable assets owned by a business
- machinery and equipment, a tangible asset that is likely to be of importance to manufacturing industries.

2 **Intangible assets.** These assets do not take a physical form. Examples include:
- Patents and other rights – for example, the mobile telephone companies have paid the UK government substantial sums for licences to operate cell phones. These licences represent a valuable intangible asset for companies such as Vodafone.
- Goodwill – this is the value of established custom and a good name to a business.
- Brands – these can be included on a balance sheet if they were purchased or can be separately valued. However, many brands can fluctuate in value as they may have a relatively short life.

Intangible assets are only recorded on the balance sheet if they can be separately identified and money was spent upon their acquisition. For example, it would be appropriate for mobile telephone companies to present their licences to supply services (sold to them by the government) as intangible assets.

Liabilities

A liability is a debt owed by the business to organisations or individuals. Another way of thinking of a liability is that it shows the sources of capital the business has raised in order to purchase its assets. As with assets there are a number of categories of liabilities.

1 **Current liabilities.** In many senses these are the equivalent of current assets. They represent debts owed by the business due for payment within one year or less. Examples of such short-term debt are overdrafts and tax due for payment. Trade and other payables (which were previously called creditors) are organisations such as suppliers to whom the business owes money. These are normally classified as a current liability because payment is normally due within a short period of time.

2 **Non-current liabilities** (previously called long-term liabilities). These are debts that a business does not expect to repay within the period of one year. Mortgages and bank loans repayable over several years are common examples of this type of liability.

3 **Total equity** (previously shareholders' funds). It may seem strange that the money invested into the business by its owners (shareholders in the case of a company) is a liability. However, if the company ceases trading, shareholders would hope for the repayment of their investment. Thus these funds (called total equity or total shareholders' equity) are liabilities.

BUSINESS IN FOCUS

The BBC's balance sheet

The BBC published its accounts on 31 March 2011, as it does each year. The net worth of the Corporation as measured by its net assets rose dramatically from £115.7 million in 2010 to £231.3 million in 2011. This was due principally to an increase in the value of assets the corporation plans to sell. In both years the organisation's balance sheet recorded net current assets. In 2011 this figure had risen to £367.4 million from £321.4 million. At the same time the corporation's long-term borrowing (non-current liabilities) fell from £134.2 million to £95.3 million.

(Source: BBC Annual Review 2010–11)

Question:

On the basis of this evidence, analyse the strength of the BBC's balance sheet in 2011. *(10 marks)*

Why does a balance sheet always balance?

The balance sheet is well named as at all times the assets held by a business must match its liabilities (including capital borrowed from its owners). Why is this the case?

First, there exists what accountants call the 'dual aspect' of constructing a balance sheet. Thus, any transaction that is recorded on the balance sheet has two effects that cancel out each other. The following examples highlight this point:

- If a business borrows £575,000 to purchase vehicles, the loan will appear as a liability as it is owed by the business to a bank or other financial institution. However, at the same time the business will have additional assets recorded on its balance sheet (in this case vehicles initially valued at £575,000). Thus this transaction will not cause the balance sheet to become unbalanced.
- Alternatively, the business might sell a non-current asset for cash. In this case the business will have non-current assets of a lower value, but its holdings of cash will rise by the same amount. In these circumstances the value of total assets is unchanged and the balance sheet still balances.

Another feature of the balance sheet that ensures that it continues to balance is reserves. Reserves are simply profit accumulated during previous years' trading and not paid out to the owners of the business. This accumulated profit is not held in the form of cash but is invested into a range of assets that are useful to the business and hopefully generate further profits. If a business is successful, purchases more assets and grows, then its value will increase and so will the value of the assets. It may borrow money to achieve this growth; if it does, liabilities will grow at the same rate. However, if it funds its growth out of profits, then the matching liability will be recorded as reserves indicating that the owners' stake in the business has risen in value. Remember that the owners' funds in the business are a liability as this represents money lent to the organisation.

The structure of a balance sheet

There are two possible formats in which the information on a balance sheet can be presented.

1 **The horizontal format.** This presents a business's assets and its liabilities alongside one another. This style of presentation is now relatively uncommon.

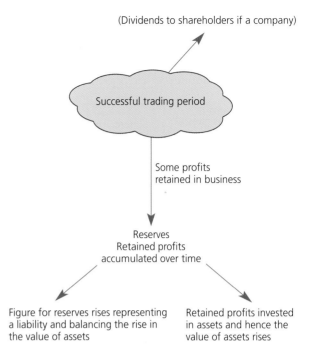

Figure 2.1 Assets, liabilities and reserves

2 **The vertical format.** This is the most common format and all public companies are legally obliged to present their balance sheets in this way. In this chapter we will only consider the vertical format of the balance sheet.

The precise layout of balance sheets can vary a little according to the type of business, and this is more likely following the IFRS-led changes since 2005. However, the structure is similar for all businesses. All balance sheets list assets – non-current first followed by current assets. Next, current liabilities are recorded, allowing a firm to calculate its working capital (simply current assets less current liabilities). Finally, the last section records the sources of finance both borrowed and provided by the owners.

Reading and interpreting balance sheets

Professional managers, potential investors and accountants can gain a great deal of information about a company from reading its balance sheet. In this section we will consider the balance sheet of one of the UK's best-known retailers, Marks & Spencer, to illustrate the uses of this financial statement.

There are a number of features on the balance sheet that are worth examining when assessing the performance of the business in question. It is possible to make some assessment of the short-term financial

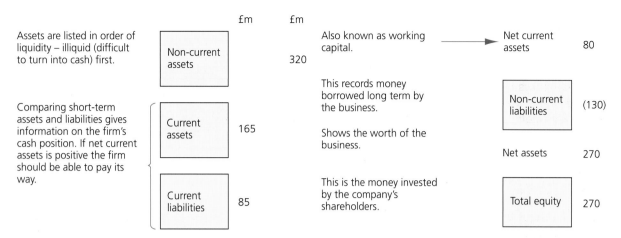

Figure 2.2 The basic structure of a public company's balance sheet in a vertical format

Marks & Spencer's consolidated statement of financial position (balance sheet) as at 2 April 2011 and 3 April 2010 (summarised)		
	2011 £m	2010 £m
Intangible non-current assets	527.7	452.8
Tangible non-current assets	5,174.7	5,180.2
Inventories	685.3	613.2
Receivables and cash	720.5	687.2
Other current assets	235.9	219.8
Total assets	7,344.1	7,153.2
Current liabilities	2,210.2	1,890.5
Net current liabilities	(568.5)	(370.3)
Non-current liabilities	(2,456.5)	(3,076.8)
Total liabilities	(4,666.7)	(4,967.3)
Net assets	**2,677.4**	**2,185.9**
Share capital	655.3	660.3
Reserves and retained earnings	2,022.1	1,525.6
Total equity	**2,677.4**	**2,185.9**

Figure 2.3 Marks & Spencer's consolidated balance sheet (or statement of financial position)

position of the business as well as its longer-term strategy from reading the balance sheet.

The short term

Assessing a business's short-term situation entails examining its ability to pay its bills over the next 12 months. The balance sheet sets out a business's short-term debts (current liabilities) and also the current assets it has available to pay these creditors. The net position of these two factors is recorded as net current assets/liabilities. This is also known as working capital. If a business has more current assets than current liabilities it has a positive figure for working capital and should be able to pay its debts in the short term. However, if current liabilities exceed current assets,

this may cause liquidity or cash problems, depending upon the type of business. Working capital is an issue we shall consider more fully later in this chapter.

The long term

This can be examined in a number of ways.

- Movement of non-current assets: a sudden increase in non-current (fixed) assets may indicate a rapidly growing company, which may mean that the company's financial performance might improve over the medium term.
- Considering how a business has raised its capital may also be valuable. As we shall see in a later chapter, it is risky for a company to borrow too much. Thus a company raising more through

Marks & Spencer plc

Figure 2.3 shows Marks & Spencer's balance sheet. The latest year (2011) is shown in the left-hand column. This method of presenting the latest data on the left is common in company's financial statements. Negative figures are shown in brackets.

We can see from the company's balance sheet that it operates with net current liabilities in both trading years. However, 2011 has a larger negative figure than 2010. This shows us that Marks & Spencer's current liabilities exceeded its current assets by a smaller amount in 2010. Nevertheless, the company did not have sufficient short-term assets to cover

its short-term liabilities. This is not uncommon for retailers. They can rely on customers spending large amounts of cash daily in their shops, thus providing funds to settle short-term liabilities.

Marks & Spencer has reduced the amount of capital that it has borrowed long term. This is shown by the decrease in non-current liabilities. It may have wished to reduce its borrowing during difficult financial times. However, at the same time the company's value has increased substantially. Its balance sheet may be considered stronger in 2011 because its worth has increased significantly, while it has reduced its long-term debt.

---

borrowing (non-current liabilities) than through share capital and reserves might be vulnerable to rises in interest rates.

- Reserves provide an indication of the profits earned by the business. A rapid increase in reserves is likely to reflect a healthy position with regard to profits.

Working capital

What is working capital?

Working capital measures the amount of money available to a business to pay its day-to-day expenses, such as bills for fuel and raw materials, wages and business rates. Much attention is given to the capital firms choose to invest in non-current assets, but of equal importance to the success of a business is the capital set aside to finance regular transactions.

Working capital is what remains of a business's liquid assets once it has settled all its immediate debts.

It is possible to calculate the working capital of a business from its balance sheet by using the following formula:

working capital = current assets − current liabilities

On a balance sheet, working capital may be labelled as net current assets. However, if current liabilities are greater than current assets, then it will be labelled as net current liabilities and the figure will be in brackets. This was the case with Marks & Spencer in Figure 2.3 above.

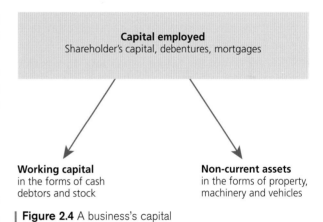

Capital employed
Shareholder's capital, debentures, mortgages

Working capital
in the forms of cash debtors and stock

Non-current assets
in the forms of property, machinery and vehicles

Figure 2.4 A business's capital

Too much working capital?

It is too simple to argue that a business should hold large amounts of working capital to ensure it can always pay its debts in the short term and has spare assets in a liquid form (cash and debtors). Holding excessive amounts of working capital is not wise. The nature of liquid assets, such as cash and trade and other receivables, means that they earn little or no return for the business. Therefore a well-managed business will hold sufficient liquid assets to meet its need for working capital, but will avoid having too many assets in such an unprofitable form.

A number of factors influence the amount of working capital a firm needs to hold.

- The volume of sales – obviously a firm with a high level of sales will need to purchase more raw materials, pay a greater amount of wages and so on. Therefore, its need for working capital will be correspondingly higher.

Figure 2.5 Working capital

The diagram shows:

Working capital — Essential, to pay for day-to-day expenses and keep the business operating

=

Current assets
- Cash in the bank
- Trade and other receivables due to settle their accounts soon
- Inventories – raw materials and components

less

Current liabilities (Debts payable in the short term)
- Debts repayable to the bank, e.g. overdraft
- Trade and other payables who expect to be paid in the near future
- Tax due to HM Revenue and Customs

NB An overdraft only represents a current liability if the bank calls for it to be repaid

- The amount of trade credit offered by the business. If a firm offers customers a lengthy period of time before they are required to pay, this increases the business's requirement for working capital. In effect, companies allowing trade credit offer their customers an interest-free loan.
- Whether or not the firm is expanding. In a period of expansion working capital requirements are likely to rise as the business purchases more fuel and raw materials. If a business expands without arranging the necessary working capital it is described as overtrading.
- The length of the operating cycle (the amount of time that elapses between the firm first paying for raw materials and receiving payment from customers). Some manufacturing industries (for example shipbuilding) have long operating cycles and a correspondingly greater need for working capital.
- The rate of inflation. When prices rise rapidly, firms will require greater amounts of working capital to fund the increased costs of wages, components and raw materials.

As a rough guide, a firm holding current (or liquid) assets of twice the value of current liabilities would normally have sufficient working capital. It is also important for a business to have a significant proportion of its working capital in the form of cash. Cash, the most liquid of assets, is essential to pay the most immediate of bills.

The causes of working capital problems

Difficulties with working capital are a very common cause of business failure, even among firms that have the potential to generate a profit. The fundamental cause of problems in relation to working capital is poor financial management. Managers who plan ahead, forecasting their expected need for working capital against the likely inflow of cash, are less likely to encounter problems with working capital. If periods of potential difficulty can be identified, appropriate action can be taken.

A number of other causes of working capital problems can be identified.

- **External changes.** A number of changes in the economy can place pressure on a business's working capital. A sudden increase in interest rates will increase a firm's interest payments, and thereby drain cash from the business. The economy moving into a recession may restrict demand (especially for income-elastic goods such as foreign holidays and designer clothing), meaning a business's receipts from sales decline dramatically while expenditure is temporarily unchanged.
- **Poor credit control.** In a well-managed business emphasis is given to monitoring debtors to ensure that they settle their accounts and do so punctually. If a business fails to operate an effective system of credit control, then the incidence of bad debts may increase, resulting in a loss of revenue for the business. Furthermore, other customers may delay their payments, resulting in a lengthening of the working capital cycle.
- **Internal problems.** A business can suffer a variety of difficulties resulting in liquidity problems, as working capital proves insufficient to meet the needs of the business. Production problems can lead to a business incurring extra costs while suffering a decline in sales revenue. Similarly, misjudging likely sales can damage a business's working capital position. Production takes place and costs are incurred, including storage, while revenue is not received from sales.

- **Financial mismanagement.** Working capital or liquidity problems may arise simply because managers misread a situation by, for example, underestimating costs of production. Alternatively, they may invest too much in non-current assets as a consequence of overestimating the production capacity the firm requires. A business that borrows too much may not, in fact, improve its working capital position. The high and unavoidable costs of servicing the debts may place a strain on the liquidity position of the organisation.

How important is working capital?

Working capital is important to all businesses. It has been described as the 'lifeblood' of a successful enterprise. If any business is unable to pay its bills promptly, then it may be forced to close down as a consequence of insolvency. However, working capital is of particular importance to certain types of businesses, requiring effective management of this important asset.

- **Small businesses.** This category of business can be especially vulnerable to problems with working capital for a number of reasons. Large firms often deliberately delay payments to small suppliers to improve their own liquidity position. They know that the smaller firm will not complain too much as it cannot afford to lose large orders. Second, small businesses often do not have access to sufficient funds to be able to improve their liquidity position easily. For example, banks may be unwilling to make loans to small businesses with few assets and experiencing liquidity problems.
- **Expanding businesses.** A growing business is likely to find its position with regard to working capital under pressure as it increases its expenditure on raw materials and components before it receives the revenue from its increased output. Even large firms can experience liquidity problems at this time.
- **Businesses with a long working capital cycle.** Many manufacturing businesses have substantial working capital requirements, simply because of the nature of their production. Firms engaged in shipbuilding may incur costs up to three years before they receive complete payment for their products. Clearly a firm that needs to generate large amounts of working capital as a part of its normal trading activity is especially vulnerable to changes such as slumps in demand.

Technique	Advantages	Disadvantages	Suitable for ...
Reduce trade credit	Quick and simple to implement Under the control of the business	May damage firm's image with customers May result in loss of customers	Small firms with few other options
Negotiate extra credit with suppliers	A 'free' source of finance May be able to implement quickly	May lose out on price reductions available for prompt payment	Larger businesses with secure financial reputation
Negotiate additional short-term loans	Can provide immediate inflow of cash Minimal long-term impact	Can be very costly May be difficult to arrange in times of financial crisis.	Firms experiencing short-term liquidity problems
Cut production costs	Can improve profitability as well as liquidity May enhance competitive position	May lead to additional short-term costs (e.g. redundancy payments) May reduce quality if cheaper components used	Businesses with potential to reduce expenditure without harming competitive position
Careful financial planning	Minimal costs Improve business's competitive position	May take time to have any impact Only eliminates problems relating to mismanagement	Firms that do not normally experience liquidity problems
Sale and leaseback	Can provide major injection of cash All assets retained by business	Outflow of cash is necessary to retain use of asset Difficult to obtain the best price for an asset when selling under pressure	Relatively large firms with valuable fixed assets, or those with surplus assets (in which case they may not be leased back)

Table 2.1 Techniques for solving working capital problems

Depreciation

What is depreciation?

Depreciation is the reduction of the value of an asset over a period of time. Thus, a brewery may purchase equipment for the brewing of beer at a cost of £80,000 and reduce its value as shown in Table 2.2.

Year	Value of asset on balance sheet at end of year	Amount depreciated annually
2011	60,000	20,000
2012	40,000	20,000
2013	20,000	20,000
2014	0	20,000

Table 2.2 The Norfolk Ale Company

Table 2.2 illustrates the effects of depreciation on the balance sheet and the income statement of the Norfolk Ale Company. The initial cost of the brewing equipment in 2011 was £80,000. The company expects that this equipment will last for four years and have no resale value. The value of the asset falls by £20,000 each year, reflecting its decline in value. The amount of the decline in value (depreciation) is shown as an expense on the Norfolk Ale Company's income statement.

Why do firms depreciate assets?

Firms have to depreciate their non-current assets for a number of reasons. One of these is to spread the cost of an asset over its useful life. In the case of the Norfolk Ale Company it would have been incorrect to show the value of the brewing equipment as £80,000 throughout its life. Its resale value would decline for a number of reasons:

- the equipment would lose value as a result of wear and tear
- the availability of more modern equipment would mean that the value of this 'older' style equipment would decline

- poor or inadequate maintenance of the equipment may mean expensive repairs are necessary, further reducing the brewing equipment's value.

Thus, reducing the value of an asset in line with these factors ensures that the value of the business recorded on the balance sheet is a relatively accurate indication of the true worth of the business.

Depreciation also allows firms to calculate the true cost of production during any financial year. The Norfolk Brewery would have overstated its costs in 2011 if it had allocated the entire cost of its new brewing equipment to that particular financial year. By depreciating the equipment by £20,000 each year for four years, one-quarter of the cost of the equipment is recorded each year on the Norfolk Ale Company's income statement. This helps to gain an accurate view of the profitability (or otherwise) of the business over the lifetime of the equipment.

Depreciation: a non-cash expense

Depreciation is an expense or a cost to a firm that is recorded on the income statement. However, depreciation is unusual in that it is a non-cash expense. Depreciation does not require a business to make any payment. It is recognition of the cost of providing a particular expense normally made at the time the asset was purchased. Depreciation is not a method of providing the cash necessary to replace the asset at the end of its useful life.

Why does depreciation matter?

Depreciation is an important matter to businesses for a number of reasons.

- Depreciation provides an accurate value of a business's assets throughout the life of those assets. This allows for a 'true and fair' assessment of the overall worth of the business at any time. Having an accurate figure for the overall value of the business is important for stakeholders such as investors.
- The amount of annual depreciation affects the overall value and profits of a business.

Figure 2.6 Depreciation – a link between the balance sheet and the income statement

	Too much depreciation	Too little depreciation
Effects on balance sheet	Fixed assets are valued at less than their true worth – value of business understated	Fixed assets are overvalued giving a false impression of the company's worth
Effects on income statement	Depreciation expenses are overestimated, reducing level of profits	Low rates of depreciation will reduce the expenses incurred by a business. This will result in business's profits being higher than they would otherwise be
Wider effects	Business may look unattractive to prospective investors. Tax liability on profits may be reduced, but HM Revenue and Customs might investigate! Business may record surplus when asset finally sold	This may make the company more attractive to investors but will also increase its tax liability

Table 2.3 The effects of depreciation

How to analyse income statements

What is profit?

At its simplest, profit is what remains from revenue once costs have been deducted. However, in the construction of the income statement there are two main types of profit identified.

1 **Gross profit.** This form of profit is calculated by deducting direct costs (such as materials and shop-floor labour) from a business's sales revenue. This gives a broad indication of the financial performance of the business without taking into account other costs such as overheads.

2 **Net profit.** This is a further refinement of the concept of profit and is revenue less direct costs and indirect costs (or overheads) such as rent and rates, as well as interest payments and depreciation. This gives a better indication of the performance of a business over a period of time as it takes into account all costs incurred by a firm over a trading period.

Net profit can take a number of forms:

- Trading or operating profit. This type of profit takes into account all earnings from regular trading activities and all the costs associated with those activities. However, this form of profit excludes any income received from, or costs incurred by, activities that are unlikely to be repeated in future financial years.

- Net profit before tax is a business's trading or operating profit plus any profits from one-off activities.

- Net profit after tax is the amount left to the business once corporation tax (or income tax in the case of a sole trader or partnership) has been deducted. This is an important form of profit. There are no more charges on this profit and the managers of the business can decide what to do with it.

BUSINESS IN FOCUS

Profit is one of the most commonly used words in business. Clearly it is important for a number of reasons. It acts as a signal to attract new businesses into a market and to encourage an existing business to grow. The pursuit of profit is an important business motive.

However, profit is not always the most important motive. Some businesses (for example charities and mutual organisations) do not aim to make profits. And profits that impose high social costs on others may not be highly valued. Businesses that generate high profits through polluting the environment or hiring sweatshop labour in less developed countries may attract criticism and lose sales in the long run.

Because of increased public awareness of ethical and environmental issues, many businesses are taking a long-term view of profit. They may be prepared to incur higher costs in the short term (through using more expensive materials from sustainable sources, for example) to maintain a positive corporate image and higher profits in the long term.

The quality of profit

It may seem strange, but some profits are better than others. Firms regard profit that is likely to continue into the future as high-quality profit. Thus, if a business introduces a new product onto the market and it immediately begins to generate a surplus and looks to have a promising future, then this will be high-quality profit. On the other hand, for example, Whitbread plc, the UK's largest hotels and restaurant group, sold four of its Premier Inns in 2011 for £58.3 million in a sale and leaseback deal. If sold at a profit, this may have added to the company's overall net profit figure. However, this form of profit will not continue into the future and is therefore low-quality profit.

The amount of trading or operating profit earned by a firm is more likely to represent high-quality profit as it excludes any one-off items. This level of profit might reasonably be expected to continue into the future, depending upon market conditions. Shareholders are interested in profit quality as it gives some indication of the company's potential to pay dividends in the future.

The structure of the income statement

Figure 2.7 provides an initial guide to the structure of the income statement as presented by most companies.

The income statement comprises four main stages:

1 First, 'gross profit' is calculated. This is the difference between the revenue figure (this can be called sales revenue or turnover) and the cost

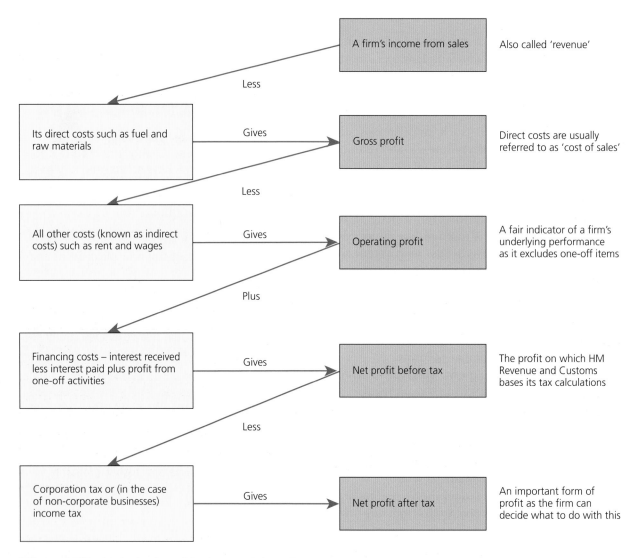

Figure 2.7 The basic structure of the income statement

of the goods that have been sold. The latter is normally expressed simply as 'cost of goods'. This element of the income statement is sometimes called the trading account.

2 Second, 'operating profit' is calculated by deducting the main types of overheads such as distribution costs and administration costs.

3 Next, profit before taxation is calculated, which is arrived at by including interest received by the business and interest paid by it. These are normally shown together as a net figure labelled 'financing costs'.

4 The final stage of the income statement is to calculate profit after taxation. This is arrived at by deducting the amount of tax payable for the year, and shows the net amount that has been earned for the shareholders. At this stage the company may indicate which profits are from continuing operations (those parts of the business that will be trading in the future) and which are from discontinuing operations. These can be seen in the case of Tesco plc in Figure 2.8.

Income statements and public limited companies

Public limited companies are required by law to publish their accounts. This means that they are available for scrutiny not only by the owners (shareholders), potential investors and bankers, but also by competitors.

When a company draws up its income statement for external publication it will include as little information as possible. Public limited companies usually supply no more detail than is required by law. This format is illustrated for Tesco in Figure 2.8.

Public limited companies also provide information on earnings per share on their income statements. Earnings per share are simply the company's profits after tax divided by the number of shares the company has. Diluted earnings per share give a slightly lower figure as it takes into account all possible shares that could be issued by the company at that time, those issued plus those due to be issued as, for example, part of a share option scheme.

Group income statements

During the last 25 years many companies have been taken over by other companies to form groups. Each company within such a group retains its separate legal identity, but the group is also legally obliged to produce a group income statement (and balance sheet). A group income statement simply records the aggregated position of the group as a whole.

Examples of organisations producing such consolidated accounts include The Body Shop International and Tesco (see Figure 2.8 for a summary of Tesco's group income statement). It is quite likely that the accounts of any large organisations you examine will be group accounts.

Income statements and the law

The legal requirements relating to income statements are set out in the Companies Act 2006. This legislation demands the production of financial statements including an income statement. It also specifies the information to be included in these accounts.

The income statement does not have to detail every expense incurred by the firm, but summarises the main items under standard headings. The Act sets out acceptable formats for presentation of the relevant data. A summarised form of one of these is shown for Tesco in Figure 2.8.

The notes to income statements must disclose details of:

- auditor's fees
- depreciation amounts
- the total of directors' emoluments (earnings)
- the average number of employees, together with details of cost of wages and salaries, together with national insurance and pensions.

Companies must disclose the following:

- **Exceptional items** are large (usually one-off) financial transactions arising from ordinary trading activities. However, they are so large as to risk distorting the company's trading account. An example of exceptional is when the high street banks incurred unusually large bad debt charges.
- **Extraordinary items** are large transactions outside the normal trading activities of a company. As a result they are not expected to recur. A typical example is the closure of a factory or division of a business. These items have only been included in the income statement over recent years. In Tesco's case in Figure 2.8 it has made profits from the portfolio of property that it holds, but this profit may not continue into future years. The profit figure is shown in the company's income statement.

Summarised Group Income Statement for Tesco plc (years ended 26 February 2011 and 27 February 2010)		
	2011 (£m)	2010 (£m)
Revenue (sales excluding VAT)	60,931	56,910
Cost of sales	(55,871)	(52,303)
Gross profit	**5,060**	**4,607**
Administrative and other expenses	(1,676)	(1,527)
Profit arising on property-related items	427	377
Operating profit	**3,811**	**3,457**
Profit from joint ventures	57	33
Finance income	150	265
Finance costs	(483)	(579)
Profit before tax	**3,535**	**3,176**
Taxation	(864)	(840)
Profit for the year	**2,671**	**2,336**
Earnings per share		
Basic	33.10p	29.33p
Diluted	32.94p	29.19p

Figure 2.8 Tesco's summarised income statement

Source: Tesco plc

There is no single format for a limited company's income statement. The Companies Act of 2006 sets out the minimum amount of information that must be included, though some modification can be made to ensure a 'true and fair view' of the business's performance.

The accounts of public limited companies also contain notes giving further details of the figures included in the income statement. Thus, in the case of Tesco, there was in the full version of the accounts, a small number 6 next to the row in which the amount paid in taxation was entered. In a detailed explanation, note 6 sets out the precise profit figure on which Tesco had to pay corporation tax and the rate at which it paid the tax (28 per cent). This depth of information is important to allow shareholders and other interested parties to make an accurate assessment of the financial performance of the business.

Interpreting income statements

A number of groups are likely to have an interest in a business's income statement. These stakeholders are illustrated in Figure 2.9.

- **Shareholders** are perhaps the most obvious group with an interest in the income statement. Shareholders will be interested in a business's sales revenue and operating or net profit. This will provide some guidance as to the performance of the enterprise, especially when compared with previous years. They will also be likely to examine the appropriation account closely to see how profits have been utilised. Some shareholders may seek the maximum dividend possible. Others may be interested in a longer-term return and welcome substantial reinvestment in the expectation of future profits.

- **Managers** use the income statement as an important source of information regarding the performance of the business. Managers are, of course, able to see the income statement in much more detail than

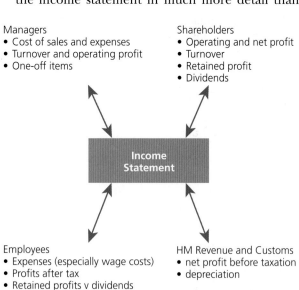

Managers
- Cost of sales and expenses
- Turnover and operating profit
- One-off items

Shareholders
- Operating and net profit
- Turnover
- Retained profit
- Dividends

Income Statement

Employees
- Expenses (especially wage costs)
- Profits after tax
- Retained profits v dividends

HM Revenue and Customs
- net profit before taxation
- depreciation

Figure 2.9 Some groups with an interest in income statements, and the nature of their interests

that provided in the annual report and accounts. Published accounts contain the minimum amount of information required under law to avoid giving competitors any advantage. Managers will monitor sales performance through turnover figures and judge costs against sales revenue. If expenses and cost of sales rise by a greater amount than turnover, action may be necessary. Managers will also consider carefully the effects of one-off items on the account.

● **Employees** may be interested in profits after tax if their pay is related to company performance through a profit-related pay scheme. They may also be interested in the level of dividends if they are shareholders. The level of profits after taxation may also be an indication of the company's ability to fund a pay increase or, alternatively, of the security of their employment.

● **HM Revenue and Customs (HMRC)** is the organisation responsible for collecting corporation tax from companies on the government's behalf. HMRC will therefore scrutinise company accounts and use net profit before tax as the basis for their calculation of tax liability (the amount of tax to be paid). It may also check that the income statement meets all necessary standards (for example, the basis upon which non-current assets have been depreciated).

BUSINESS IN FOCUS

BSkyB's profits rise

BSkyB plc has reported a 33 per cent increase in pre-tax profits to £307 million in the three months to the end of September, as an expected slump in new TV subscribers was balanced by an increase in selling products including broadband and telephone services to existing customers. BSkyB, which was on the brink of being taken over by its largest shareholder, News Corporation, until the phone-hacking scandal at News of the World ended the deal, exceeded most expectations. The company said that operating profit of £327 million, a 32 per cent year-on-year increase, was boosted by a £39 million payout by News Corporation for breaking off the sale and £7 million in costs for advisory fees.

As the economic downturn has hit the UK the company has been aiming to move the focus away from the number of new subscribers it achieves each quarter to how many products it can sell to its existing customer base. BSkyB managed to add 26,000 new pay-TV customers in the quarter, taking the total subscriber base to 10.2 million, well down on the almost 100,000 added in the same quarter last year.

BSkyB added 103,000 customers to its HD service, which makes up 3.9 million of its total subscriber base, while broadband numbers rose 150,000 to 3.5 million. Telephony customers rose 147,000 to 3.2 million, while those taking their line rental through BSkyB rose 212,000 to 2.9 million.

The BSkyB chief executive, Jeremy Darroch, hailed the company's performance and its increase in profits. 'In tough market conditions our move to more broadly based growth and multiple products is serving us well,' he said. 'Looking ahead, the environment is likely to remain challenging as a result of the pressures facing consumers in the UK and Ireland.'

(Source: Mark Sweney in the Guardian, *19 October 2011)*

Question:

To what extent do you agree with Jeremy Darroch's positive view of BSkyB's financial performance, based on the information in this article? *(18 marks)*

Using financial data for comparisons, trend analysis and decision-making

Balance sheets

There are a number of features of a balance sheet that are valuable for comparisons, analysis and for assisting with decision-making.

The business's working capital position

A declining trend here would be shown by a smaller figure for current net assets or a larger negative figure for current net liabilities. A movement from a net assets figure to a negative net liabilities figure may be a cause for concern. It is easier to make a judgement if the trend of figures is compared with those for other businesses operating in similar markets. This can help to make a judgement as to the extent to which the change is due to a declining market situation. This could be due, for instance, to a significant fall in sales. Analysing this trend and conducting comparisons can help a business's managers to decide whether action (such as selling and leasing back non-current assets) is necessary to maintain the financial strength of the business.

The extent of the business's long-term debts

These are shown on the balance sheet under the heading non-current liabilities and represent debts which the business plans to repay in a period of over one year. If the figure for non-current liabilities is rising, especially if the value or worth of the business (as shown by net assets) is not increasing, this may be a cause for concern. A business that borrows too much money may encounter problems in repaying it, especially if interest rates rise unexpectedly.

Income statements

Several key aspects of a business's income statement can be considered as part of the evaluation of a business's performance.

1 **Trends.** A better judgement can be made concerning a business if its performance in one year is measured against that of previous years. As in the case of Tesco, it is normal for businesses to present two years' figures alongside one another. Many companies also offer five-year summaries of financial performance. Using this sort of evidence it is possible to see what has happened to turnover, costs and expenses and profits over a period of time. It is important to look at the trends of sales revenue and profit for the year (that is, after taxation). This gives you an insight into the company's success in selling products, in its markets and also its ability to control its costs and keep them below its revenues.

2 **The period to which the statement relates.** It is normal for an income statement to cover a period of one year. However, the statement can relate to a longer or shorter period. Such changes occur when, for example, the business changes the dates of its financial year. This either prolongs or shortens the year in which the change is made. A 20 per cent increase in profits may not appear so exceptional if the income statement covers a period of 15 months.

3 **Comparing gross and net profit.** The calculation of gross profit only includes direct costs (labelled as 'cost of sales'). Operating profit, on the other hand, takes into account all costs – direct and indirect.

A rise in gross profit but a fall in operating profit may indicate that managers are not controlling indirect costs effectively.

4 **The business(es) to which the income statement relate(s).** Many companies trade as part of a group of businesses. In these circumstances the enterprise will produce an income statement (and a balance sheet) for the individual company and also one for the entire group. These latter accounts are referred to as consolidated accounts. These are an aggregation of the accounts of the individual companies that make up the group.

The strengths and weaknesses of financial data in judging performance

Window dressing balance sheets and income statements

Public limited companies are under considerable pressure to present their financial performance in the most favourable terms possible. There are a number of methods by which a company can improve the look of its balance sheet – these processes are called 'window dressing'.

- Some companies borrow money for a short period of time to improve their cash position just before the date on which the balance sheet is drawn up. This action may enhance the company's apparent ability to pay its short-term debts.
- An alternative method of improving a company's cash or liquidity position is through the use of sale and leaseback. This entails the sale of major non-current assets and then leasing them back. Many retailers have negotiated sale and leaseback deals on their high street properties.
- Businesses may maintain the value of intangible assets on the balance sheet at what might be excessive levels to increase the overall value of the organisation. This tactic is only possible when the assets in question (for example goodwill or brands) have been purchased.
- Capitalising expenditure, which means including as non-current assets items that might otherwise have simply been regarded as an expense and not included on the balance sheet. Thus a firm might spend heavily on computer software and include this as a fixed asset on the basis that it will have a

useful life of several years. This action will increase the value of the business.

- On income statements businesses may bring forward sales to an earlier period and thereby boost revenue for a particular financial year. This does result, however, in a lower figure in the next financial year.

There is a fine line between presenting accounts as favourably as possible and misrepresenting the performance of the firm, which is illegal. The authorities have made several adjustments to accounting procedures in order to restrict the extent of window dressing.

The importance of the balance sheet

The balance sheet is often referred to as the premier financial statement. It is important for a number of reasons.

- The fundamental use of the balance sheet is to provide a measure of the value or worth of a business. If a series of balance sheets over a number of years is examined, a clearer picture of a business's growth may emerge.
- A balance sheet paints a picture of the sources of capital used by a business. This allows stakeholders analysing the statement to assess whether the company has borrowed an excessive amount of capital, making itself vulnerable to rising interest rates.
- It is also possible to see if the business has used expensive sources of short-term finance (for example overdrafts) to purchase non-current assets. A well-managed business would normally use cheaper long-term sources (for example bank loans or mortgages) to finance the purchase of this type of asset.
- The balance sheet illustrates the cash (or liquidity) position of the firm and allows an assessment to be made of its ability to meet its debts or liabilities over the next few months.

However, the balance sheet is not a sound basis for analysing the performance of a business. Any effective analysis would require that other sources of information be used alongside the balance sheet.

- The **income statement** is another very important financial statement. An income statement records a firm's income, expenditure and ultimately profit or loss over a trading period. A much fuller analysis can be made of a business's financial performance by reading the income statement in conjunction with the relevant balance sheet.

- Any **financial statement** is a historical document recording what has happened in the past. This is not necessarily a good indication of what may happen to the same business in the future.
- A balance sheet records financial information. It does not provide any real insight into the quality of the management team, the degree of competition provided by rival firms and any change that may be taking place in the external environment. For example, a sudden alteration in tastes and fashions would not be seen on the balance sheet until after the change has occurred.

The importance of the income statement

Unquestionably, the income statement offers valuable information to a business's stakeholders. This financial statement gives details on a company's revenue, indicating whether or not it has grown. It also provides details about the costs incurred and how successful managers have been in controlling these. Finally, the level of net profit is of value to interested parties, as are the uses to which the profit has been put. This latter information might suggest how successful the venture may be in the future. If large amounts of profit are retained for reinvestment, the company may be expected to grow in the future and generate larger profits.

However, caution has to be exercised when interpreting an income statement. Inflation can distort accounts, exaggerating any increase in turnover that may have taken place. Firms attempt to window dress the income statement by bringing forward sales from the next trading period to increase turnover and profit. Profits can be altered by adjusting depreciation policies or by including one-off items as part of ordinary activities.

As with the balance sheet, an income statement alone is not a good indicator of a business's financial performance. It should be read in conjunction with the balance sheet. However, evaluating the performance of any business requires more than the current year's accounts. Analysts should consider the financial performance of a business over an extended period, perhaps five years. This allows trends in key variables such as turnover and profit to be identified. Furthermore, non-financial factors should be considered. The strength and actions of competitors, the growth (if any) in the market for the firm's

Transport firm's profits fall

In summer 2011, transport operations at haulage firm Eddie Stobart were affected by fluctuating demand over the summer because of the weak economy. The firm's pre-tax profit was down to £14.7 million for the six months to 31 August, compared with £15.4 million for the same period in the previous year. However, revenue increased 15.3 per cent over the same period to £281.1 million.

Stobart said it had increased the efficiency and fleet utilisation of its lorry business, and this had improved profit margins. 'The weak economy, however, has held back our rate of profit growth, particularly in transport and distribution,' said chief executive Andrew Tinkler. 'The road transport operations were affected by fluctuating customer demand during the summer, but we have substantially improved our operational information systems.'

(Source: Adapted from BBC News, 26 October 2011)

Question:

Analyse the possible reasons why it may have been difficult to forecast this fall in profits from examining Stobart Group's financial statements over the previous few years. *(10 marks)*

products and the quality of a business's labour force are also factors that should be taken into account.

The limitations of financial statements

By definition, financial statements such as the balance sheet and the income statement only include financial information. Inevitably they will not provide direct information on important factors such as the following:

- The quality of leadership of the business is not shown by financial data. Do senior managers have the necessary skills and experience to lead the business successfully and do they have the vision to inspire and direct the workforce?
- What is the position of the business in the market? It may have successful products that are selling well and generating acceptable levels of profit. However, the firm may be lagging behind in developing new products or in entering new markets and therefore likely to perform less well in the future. Financial analysis is unlikely to reveal this.

- What about the motivation and performance of the workforce? Balance sheets and income statements do not reveal productivity or levels of labour turnover, or even the rate of absenteeism, which can indicate the level of morale within the business.

One step further: cash-flow statements

A cash-flow statement is a document that is prepared to summarise the cash flows into and out of a business. It records the inflow and outflow of cash over an accounting period. The cash-flow statement is a required part of a public limited company's annual accounts.

The cash-flow statement is different from a cash-flow forecast in that it states what actually happened with regard to cash flow rather than what was forecast. It differs from an income statement because it shows what has happened with regard to cash flow and not to profit. Profit is of little value to a business unless the cash that results from it has actually flowed into the business. The cash-flow statement tells interested stakeholders whether all the business's recorded profit has been realised in the form of cash.

	Financial year ending 2 April 2011 (£m)	Financial year ending 3 April 2010 (£m)
Net cash generated from activities	1,199.9	1,229.0
Net cash used in investing activities	(490.5)	(529.6)
Opening net cash	202.7	298.3
Closing net cash	**263.5**	**202.7**

Table 2.4 Key information from Marks & Spencer's cash-flow statement, 2011

Source: Adapted from Marks & Spencer Annual Report and Accounts 2011

The items in the cash-flow statement (for example the net cash inflow or outflow) can be significantly different from equivalent items on the income statement. This is what makes the cash flow so valuable: it gives an insight into the actual cash the business is receiving and not just the recorded level of sales. The income statement is vulnerable to window dressing in that sales can be brought forward to an earlier trading period to boost revenues. This is not possible with a cash-flow statement.

Examiner's advice

When considering financial statements such as balance sheets and income statements, do think about them from the perspective of a variety of stakeholders. It may be natural to consider them from the standpoint of shareholders and suppliers, but do also think of the conclusions that employees and customers may draw from the same financial information.

Remember that financial information is historical. It relates to previous years and, especially if the business environment is changeable, may not be a good indicator of the future.

Do not worry about constructing balance sheets. AQA A Level Business Studies only requires you to be able to read and interpret them.

In some circumstances current liabilities might be greater than current assets. In this case, working capital will be negative (and called net current liabilities). As a negative figure it is likely to be in brackets.

The quality of profit can be a powerful evaluative theme. It can be very helpful to remember that some types of profit are 'better' than others and to use this in your answers. Considering the quality of profit helps to bring a more strategic element into examination answers.

In the next chapter we consider a technique of financial analysis known as ratio analysis. This will help you to analyse trends in financial data and to make comparisons. You should return to the 'Using financial data for comparisons, trend analysis and decision-making' section when you have completed your study of the following chapter.

1 Merrills Industries manufactures biscuits and other convenience foodstuffs. Identify three stakeholder groups who may have an interest in the company's balance sheet. Outline the likely nature of their interest. *(9 marks)*

2 Explain **two** factors that lead to a business's balance sheet always balancing. *(6 marks)*

3 Outline how the information recorded on a business's balance sheet can be used to assess the cash or liquidity position of the business. *(7 marks)*

4 Explain the difference between the net current assets and the net assets of a public limited company. *(6 marks)*

5 The net assets of Gujarati Products plc is £540 million. The company's non-current liabilities total £339 million. What are the possible implications of this position? *(7 marks)*

6 Smith and Whyte's reserves rose by £54 million last year. Outline the possible causes of this. *(5 marks)*

7 Explain **two** possible consequences of a retailer having too much working capital. *(6 marks)*

8 Explain why a manufacturing business that is expanding rapidly might face problems with its working capital. *(8 marks)*

9 Explain why a road haulage company will have to depreciate its non-current assets each year. *(8 marks)*

10 Outline why it is important to value non-current assets as accurately as possible. *(6 marks)*

11 Explain what is meant by high-quality profit. *(4 marks)*

12 Explain why an extraordinary item should be listed separately in a company's income statement. *(5 marks)*

13 Outline **two** aspects of a supermarket's income statement that might be of particular interest to a shareholder considering buying a large quantity of the company's shares. *(8 marks)*

14 Explain **two** reasons why a balance sheet can be considered a valuable document for stakeholders. *(6 marks)*

15 Outline **three** sources of information, other than its balance sheet and income statement, that might help an investor to assess the future prospects of a computer manufacturer. *(8 marks)*

Analysis question

✕ These questions relate to the case study on page 5.

Kevin Sergeant believes that the company's income statements and balance sheets are the most important evidence in predicting the company's ability to continue to grow in the future. Do you agree with him? Justify your view. *(18 marks)*

Candidate's answer:

The income statements and balance sheets show what has happened in the past but this does not mean that the future will be the same, especially if we are looking a long way into the future or if the markets in which the company trades are volatile and changeable. The company's customers might opt to buy products from a competitor, a recession might occur or a new business might enter the market with a more technologically advanced product, giving it a USP. If this happens suddenly sales can fall sharply, reducing revenue and profits and meaning that the business is less successful financially. In turn this means that it is risky to rely on historical financial documents to predict the future and that these are not the most important evidence – primary market research would be much more valuable.

However, if a business has been trading for a lengthy period of time and if the market in which it trades does not have too many changes then income statements and balance sheets are important items for forecasting the future and whether the company will grow. It is possible to identify trends in sales figures and costs and to project these forward into the future to forecast what is likely to happen in terms of revenue, costs and profits. This allows managers to identify whether growth is likely to occur and to decide what actions may be required.

Overall income statements and balance sheets are important elements of forecasting future growth. Their exact value, however, depends on what is happening in the market – if it is stable and relatively unchanging these financial documents are of greater value in forecasting future growth rates.

Examiner's comments:

This is a disappointing answer in some respects, although it has some strengths. The structure of the answer is logical as it offers arguments for and against Kevin's viewpoint and develops these well, showing knowledge and understanding of financial and other topics. This candidate would score fair marks for

analysis on the basis of the development and focus of these answers. The candidate has also made a clear conclusion and has attempted to justify it.

I hope that you have spotted the obvious weakness – the complete absence of any application. This answer could refer to any business and does not include any data or non-numerical information from the case study. Its absence is perhaps most noticeable and significant when the student tries to justify the judgement in the final paragraph. He or she makes reference to the importance of what is happening in the market, but does not think to use the information provided in the case study to help make this judgement. The lack of application would have a serious impact on the marks awarded for this answer.

Evaluation question

1 To what extent do you think that the strengths of Invicta plc's balance sheets in 2010 and 2011 outweigh their weaknesses? *(18 marks)*

3 Interpreting published accounts

This chapter builds on the material we studied in the previous chapter. It will introduce you to a range of simple mathematical techniques (collectively known as ratio analysis) which can be used to conduct a more in-depth analysis of a business's balance sheets and income statements. The chapter will also explain how to interpret the results of the ratio calculations and to use these as the basis for decision-making.

In this chapter we examine:

- how to conduct ratio analysis, including the selection, calculation and interpretation of ratios
- the value and limitations of ratio analysis in measuring a business's performance.

Ratio analysis

There are a number of groups that are interested in the financial information provided by businesses and especially by public limited companies. Collectively these groups can be referred to as stakeholders and they may take an interest in the published accounts of a business for a variety of reasons. For example, suppliers may want to judge the financial position of a business to evaluate whether they should offer the firm credit. Similarly, individuals contemplating buying shares in the business may try to assess the business's potential to make profits in the future. Figure 3.1 summarises stakeholder groups and their interest in a company's financial performance.

What is a ratio?

Ratio analysis allows stakeholders to evaluate a business's performance through the investigation of key financial statements such as the balance sheet and the income statement. The key feature of ratio analysis is that it compares two pieces of financial information. By comparing two pieces of data in this way it is possible to make more informed judgements about a business's performance.

A comparison of the financial performance of two companies in 2011 can illustrate the advantages of comparing two pieces of data to make more informed judgements. J Sainsbury, one of the UK's largest retailers, announced a net profit of £827 million for the year. In comparison, J D Wetherspoon, a company that operates a nationwide chain of pubs, turned in a net profit of £66.78 million in 2011. A simple judgement would therefore suggest that J Sainsbury had performed more successfully. However, if we took into account the value of sales achieved by the two companies (its revenue), a more meaningful judgement could be made.

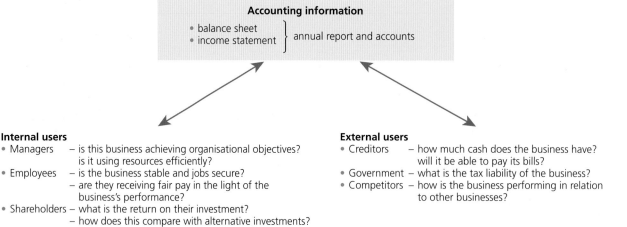

Figure 3.1 Stakeholders and financial information

Table 3.1 shows that when we compare profit for the year with turnover, J D Wetherspoon's performance could be judged superior to that of J Sainsbury. J D Wetherspoon earned over 6 pence of profit from each £1 of sales, while J Sainsbury only made 3.92 pence of profit on each £1 of sales. Using this ratio (which is called the net profit margin) it is possible to make a more accurate judgement than simply comparing levels of profit. We shall consider the net profit margin in more detail later in this unit.

Company	Net profit (£m)	Revenue (£m)	Net profit as a percentage of turnover
J Sainsbury plc	827	21,102	3.92
J D Wetherspoon plc	66.78	1,072	6.23

Table 3.1 Comparing the financial performance of two companies by using a simple ratio

Ratio analysis allows managers, directors, shareholders and other interested parties to place key figures such as profits and turnover in context. Ratio analysis does not guarantee that a manager or shareholder will take a correct decision. The results of ratio analysis do, however, give decision makers more information and make a good-quality decision more likely.

Types of ratio

There are a number of ways of classifying ratios. One approach is to identify five main categories of ratio.

1 **Liquidity ratios**, also known as solvency ratios, measure the ability of the business to settle its debts in the short term.

2 **Efficiency ratios** measure the effectiveness with which an enterprise uses the resources available to it. These are also termed internal control ratios.

3 **Profitability ratios** assess the amount of gross or net profit made by the business in relation to the business's turnover or the assets or capital available to it.

4 **Gearing** examines the relationship between internal sources and external sources of finance. It is therefore concerned with the long-term financial position of the company.

5 **Shareholders' ratios** measure the returns received by the owners of the company, allowing comparison with alternative investments. For obvious reasons they are also called investment ratios.

Type of ratio	Liquidity ratios	Efficiency ratios	Profitability ratios	Gearing	Shareholders' ratios
Ratios used	Current ratio Acid test (or quick) ratio	Asset turnover ratio Stock turnover ratio Debtor days	Net profit margin Gross profit margin Return on capital employed	Gearing – loans: capital employed	Dividend per share Dividend yield Price–earnings ratio
Purpose of ratios	To assess the ability of the business to pay its immediate debts	These provide evidence on how well the managers have controlled the business	Provide a fundamental measure of the success of the business	Assess the extent to which the business is based on borrowed money	Give investors information on the returns on their investment
Interested stakeholders	Creditors Suppliers Managers	Shareholders Managers Employees Competitors	Shareholders Creditors Managers Competitors Employees	Shareholders Managers Creditors	Shareholders Managers

Table 3.2 Types of ratio

Sources of information for ratio analysis

The most obvious sources are the published accounts of the business or businesses concerned. In particular, ratio analysis requires access to a business's balance sheet and income statement. However, although this might be essential information, it is not all that is required to conduct an in-depth ratio analysis of a business. Other possible sources of information include the following:

- **The performance of the business over recent years**. Having an understanding of the trends of ratios over time can assist in making judgements. Thus a profitability ratio might appear fairly low, but if it represents a continuation of a steadily rising trend then the figure may be more acceptable to stakeholders.
- **Norms or benchmarks for the industry**. The results of ratio calculations should be judged against what is normal for the industry. Thus an investor might calculate that a company's receivables ratio is 35 days (the number of days, on average, that customers take to settle their bills). This might be acceptable for a manufacturing business, but not for a fast-food business.
- **The economic environment**. A decline in profit ratios might appear to reflect an unsuccessful business. However, this might be more acceptable in the context of a severe economic recession in which sales and prices have declined.

Expressing ratios

Ratios are normally expressed in one of three forms:

1 as a proper ratio – for example, the current ratio is 1.6:1
2 as a percentage – ROCE expresses operating profit as a percentage of capital employed by the business
3 as a multiple – inventories (stock) are turned over (or sold) five times a year.

Liquidity ratios

These ratios allow managers and other interested parties to monitor a business's cash position. Even profitable businesses can experience problems with liquidity and may be unable to pay their bills as they fall due. Liquidity ratios measure the liquid assets held by a firm (cash and other assets such as debtors that are easily convertible into cash). The value of these assets is then compared with the short-term debts or liabilities the business will incur. In this way stakeholders may evaluate whether the business's performance may be harmed as a result of liquidity problems.

Current ratio

This measures the ability of a business to meet its liabilities or debts over the next year or so. The formula to calculate this ratio is:

$$\text{Current ratio} = \frac{\text{current assets}}{\text{current liabilities}}$$

The current ratio is expressed in the form of a ratio, for example 2:1. This would mean that the firm in question possessed £2 of current assets (cash, debtors and stock) for each £1 of current liability (creditors, taxation and proposed dividends, for example). In these circumstances it is probable that the business would be able to meet its current liabilities without needing to sell fixed assets or raise long-term finance.

Using this ratio

- For years, holding current assets twice the value of current liabilities was recommended. This is no longer accepted, partly due to the use of computers in stock control and the widespread use of just-in-time (JIT) systems of production. A more typical figure might now be 1.6:1.
- In spite of this, the 'normal' figure for this ratio varies according to the type of business and the state of the market. Fast-food outlets and banks typically operate with lower ratios, whereas some manufacturing firms may have higher ratios.
- Firms with high current ratio values (say, 3:1) are not necessarily managing their finances effectively. It may be that they are holding too much cash and not investing in fixed assets to generate income. Alternatively, they may have large holdings of inventories, some of which might be obsolete.
- Firms can improve the current ratio by raising more cash through the sale of fixed assets or the negotiation of long-term loans. (NB: raising more cash through short-term borrowing will increase current liabilities, having little effect on the current ratio.)

Acid test (or quick) ratio

This ratio measures the very short-term liquidity of a business. The acid test ratio compares a business's current liabilities with its liquid assets (current assets less inventories [stock]). This can provide a more accurate indicator of liquidity than the current ratio, as stock can take time to sell. The acid test ratio measures the ability of a firm to pay its bills over a period of two or three months without requiring the sale of inventories.

The formula for the acid test ratio is:

$$\text{Acid test ratio} = \frac{\text{liquid assets}}{\text{current liabilities}}$$

The acid test ratio is also expressed in the form of a ratio (e.g. 2:1).

Using this ratio

- Conventionally, a 'normal' figure for the acid test ratio was thought to be 1:1, giving a balance of liquid assets and current liabilities. However, nowadays many businesses operate successfully with acid test figures nearer to 0.7:1.
- The value of the acid test ratio considered acceptable will vary according to the type of business. Retailers might operate with a figure of 0.4:1, because they trade mainly in cash, and have close relationships with suppliers. A manufacturing business might operate with a ratio nearer to the standard 1:1.
- Firms should not operate over long periods with high acid test ratios, as holding assets in the form of cash is not profitable and does not represent an effective use of resources.
- As with the current ratio, the acid test ratio can be improved by selling fixed assets or agreeing long-term borrowing.

Liquidity ratios are based on figures drawn from the balance sheet relating to a particular moment in time. Because of this some caution should be exercised when drawing conclusions from this type of ratio. The actual figures on the balance sheet may be unrepresentative of the firm's normal position due to factors such as window dressing or a sudden change in trading conditions.

Company	Date of balance sheet	Current assets (£m)	Inventories (stock) (£m)	Current liabilities (£m)	Current ratio	Acid test ratio
J Sainsbury plc	19/03/2011	1,708	812	(2,942)	0.58:1	0.30:1
Rolls-Royce plc	31/12/2010	9,824	2,429	(7,178)	1.37:1	1.03:1
Greene King plc	01/05/2011	173.7	24.7	(324.4)	0.54:1	0.46:1

Table 3.3 The liquidity ratios of three public limited companies

Notes to table: *J Sainsbury, a supermarket which can rely on many customers paying cash or using debit cards is able to operate successfully with lower levels of liquidity than Rolls-Royce, a manufacturer. In contrast, the results for Greene King plc (a brewer) illustrate the trend for some manufacturers to operate with lower liquidity levels. As recently as 2009 Greene King's current ratio was 0.73:1 and its acid test ratio was 0.66:1.*

Gearing

Gearing measures the long-term liquidity of a business. Under some classifications gearing is included as a liquidity ratio. There are a number of methods of measuring gearing; we shall consider the simplest form of the ratio. This ratio analyses how firms have raised their long-term capital. The result of this calculation is expressed as a percentage.

There are two main forms of long-term finance available to businesses.

1 **Non-current liabilities** – this includes preference shares and debentures (all have fixed interest payments). This is long-term borrowing and may be called loan capital.
2 **Total equity** – this arises from selling shares and increases in the value of the business.

The capital employed by a business is simply the total of these two. So this gearing ratio measures the percentage of a firm's capital that is borrowed.

$$\text{Gearing} = \frac{\text{non-current liabilities} \times 100}{\text{total equity} + \text{non-current liabilities}}$$

This measure of a business's performance is important because by raising too high a proportion of capital through fixed interest capital firms become vulnerable to increases in interest rates. Shareholders are also unlikely to be attracted to a business with a high gearing ratio as their returns might be lower because of the high level of interest payments to which the enterprise is already committed.

- A highly geared business has more than 50 per cent of its capital in the form of loans.
- A low-geared business has less long-term borrowing and a gearing figure below 50 per cent.

Much attention tends to be given to businesses that have high gearing and are vulnerable to increases in interest rates. However, this may be considered acceptable in a business that is growing quickly and generating high profits. Furthermore, a low-geared business may be considered too cautious and not expanding as quickly as possible.

Using this ratio

- The key yardstick is whether a business's long-term borrowing is more than 50 per cent of capital employed.
- Companies with secure cash flows may raise more loan capital because they are confident of being able to meet interest payments. Equally, a business with well-known brands may be able to borrow heavily against these brands to increase long-term borrowing.
- Firms can improve their gearing by repaying long-term loans, issuing more ordinary shares or redeeming debentures.

Company	Date of balance sheet	Non-current liabilities (£m)	Total equity + non-current liabilities (£m)	Gearing (%)
Imperial Tobacco plc	31/03/2011	14,435	21,950	65.76
Rolls-Royce Group plc	31/12/2010	5,077	9,056	56.06
Taylor Wimpey plc	31/12/2010	1,374.9	3,196.5	43.01

Table 3.4 Gearing ratios of some leading companies

Notes: *Imperial Tobacco and Rolls-Royce are heavily geared (the former particularly so) as they are in excess of the 50 per cent standard maximum figure. Only Taylor Wimpey has potential to borrow more without being considered highly geared.*

Efficiency ratios

This group of ratios measures the effectiveness with which management controls the internal operation of the business. They consider the following aspects of the management of an enterprise:

- the extent to which assets are used to generate profits
- how well inventories are managed
- the efficiency of creditor control (how long before customers settle their accounts).

There are a large number of ratios that fall under this heading, but we shall concentrate on just four.

Asset turnover ratio

This ratio measures a business's sales in relation to the assets used to generate these sales.

The formula to calculate this ratio is:

$$\text{Asset turnover} = \frac{\text{revenue (turnover)}}{\text{net assets}}$$

Net assets are defined as total assets less current and non-current liabilities.

This formula measures the efficiency with which businesses use their assets. An increasing ratio over time generally indicates that the firm is operating with greater efficiency. Conversely, a fall in the ratio can be caused by a decline in sales or an increase in assets employed.

Using this ratio

- It is difficult to give a standard figure for this ratio as it varies significantly according to the type of business.
- A business with high sales and relatively few assets (a supermarket, for example) might have a high asset turnover ratio and earn low profits on each sale.
- Conversely, other businesses may have a high value of assets but achieve few sales, so having a low asset turnover ratio. A high-class jeweller is an example of this category of business. The compensation for such a firm is that it normally earns a high level of profit on each sale.
- A business can improve its asset turnover ratio by improving its sales performance and/or disposing of any surplus or underutilised assets.

	Data for the financial year ending 31/12/2010			Data for the financial year ending 31/12/2009		
	Revenue (£m)	Net assets (£m)	Result	Turnover (£m)	Net assets (£m)	Result
Rolls-Royce plc	11,085	3,979	2.79 times	10,414	3,782	2.75 times
	Data for the financial year ending 26/02/2011			Data for the financial year ending 27/02/2010		
	Revenue £m	Net assets £m	Result	Turnover £m	Net assets £m	Result
Tesco plc	60,931	16,623	3.67 times	56,910	14,681	3.88 times

Table 3.5 Comparing asset turnover ratios

Notes: *These results highlight the differences in assets turnover ratios between different types of businesses. Rolls-Royce does not achieve particularly high sales in relation to the value of its assets, which is not unexpected for a high technology manufacturer. In comparison, Tesco is a very different company achieving much higher sales from an asset base which is larger. The slight decline from 2010 to 2011 may reflect the increasing competitiveness of the grocery market, or the company's investment in new assets which have not yet generated all the sales its management team expect.*

Inventory (stock) turnover ratio

This ratio measures a company's success in converting inventories into sales. Prior to the introduction of the IFRS rules, inventories were called stocks on financial statements. The ratio compares the value of inventories with sales achieved, valued at cost. This permits an effective comparison with inventories, which is always valued at cost. If the company makes a profit on each sale, then the faster it sells its inventories, the greater the profits it earns. This ratio is only of relevance to manufacturing businesses, as firms providing services do not hold significant quantities of inventories.

$$\text{Inventory or stock turnover ratio} = \frac{\text{cost of goods sold}}{\text{average inventories (or stock) held}}$$

In this form the results of calculating this ratio are expressed as a number of times a year. On 26 February 2011 Tesco held inventories valued at £3,162 million. During the company's financial year, which ended on that day, the company had achieved sales (at cost) of £60,931 million. The company's inventories turnover ratio was therefore 19.27 times.

The inventory turnover formula can be reorganised to express the number of days taken on average to sell the business's inventories.

$$\text{Inventory turnover ratio} = \frac{\text{inventories} \times 365}{\text{cost of sales}}$$

Our Tesco calculation would then become £3,162 million × 365 ÷ £60,931 million, giving an answer of 18.94 days. Thus, if Tesco sells its complete inventories every 19 days, it will sell its inventories approximately 19 times during a year.

Using this ratio

- The standard figure for this ratio varies hugely according to the type of business. A market trader selling fruit and vegetables might expect to sell his or her entire inventories every two or three days – about a hundred times a year. At the other extreme, an antiques shop might only sell its stock every six months – or twice a year.
- A low figure for inventory turnover could be due to obsolete inventories. A high figure can indicate an efficient business, although selling out of inventories results in customer dissatisfaction.
- Improving the inventory or stock turnover ratio requires a business to hold lower levels of inventories or to achieve higher sales without increasing levels of inventories.

Receivables (debtors') days

This ratio (also referred to as receivables or debtors' collection period) calculates the time typically taken by a business to collect the money that it is owed. This is an important ratio, as granting customers lengthy periods of credit may result in a business experiencing liquidity problems. If a company has substantial cash sales these should be excluded from the calculation.

$$\text{Receivables (debtors') days} = \frac{\text{receivables (debtors)} \times 365}{\text{revenue}}$$

Using this ratio

- There is no standard figure for this ratio. In general a lower figure is preferred as the business in question receives the inflow of cash more quickly. However, it can be an important part of a business's marketing strategy to offer customers a period of trade credit of perhaps 30 or 60 days.
- A rise in this ratio may be due to a number of causes. A period of expansion may mean that a business has to offer improved credit terms to attract new customers, or a 'buy now pay later' offer may have been introduced.

This ratio may be improved by reducing the credit period on offer to customers or by insisting on cash payment. A more focused approach is to conduct an aged debtors' analysis. This technique ranks a business's debtors according to the period of credit taken. This allows managers to concentrate on persuading the slowest payers to settle their accounts.

Payables (creditors') days

This ratio (also referred to as payables or creditors' collection period) calculates the time typically taken by a business to pay the money it owes to its suppliers and other creditors. This is an important ratio, as delaying payment for as long as possible can help a business to avoid liquidity problems.

$$\text{Payables (creditors') days} = \frac{\text{payables (creditors)} \times 365}{\text{revenue}}$$

Using this ratio

- Businesses can improve their liquidity position by delaying payment, but this may result in poor relationships with suppliers who may suffer liquidity problems as a result of the delay in payment.
- Businesses may be charged interest on delayed payments, which can add to costs and weaken a business's liquidity position. The 'Business in focus' here outlines legislation in this area.
- By comparing payable days and receivable days a business can assess its liquidity position. If payable days is a lower figure then it is more likely that the business will experience liquidity problems as, on average, it is paying suppliers and other creditors more quickly than it is receiving payment from its customers.

Profitability ratios

These ratios compare the profits earned by a business with other key variables, such as the level of sales achieved or the capital available to the managers of the business.

Gross profit margin

This ratio compares the gross profit achieved by a business with its revenue. Gross profit is earned before direct costs, such as administration expenses, are deducted. The ratio calculates the percentage of the selling price of a product that constitutes gross profit. The answer is expressed as a percentage.

$$\text{Gross profit margin} = \frac{\text{gross profit} \times 100}{\text{revenue}}$$

For example, in 2011 Sainsbury's gross profit was £1,160 million. This was achieved from revenue amounting to £21,102 million. The company's gross profit margin is:

$$\frac{£1,160\,\text{m} \times 100}{£21,102\,\text{m}} = 5.50\%$$

This gross profit margin may appear low, but a judgement should take into account the company's expectations, its performance in previous years and how other similar businesses, such as Asda, are performing. The next 'Business in focus' provides some of the answers to these questions.

Using this ratio

- The figure for gross profit margin varies depending upon the type of industry. Firms that turn over their stock rapidly and then can trade with relatively few assets may operate with low gross profit margins. Greengrocers and bakers may fall into this category. Firms with slower turnover of stock and requiring substantial fixed assets may have a higher figure. House builders may fall into this category.
- The sales mix can have a major influence on this ratio. A farmer selling eggs at a 10 per cent gross profit margin and renting out holiday cottages at a 40 per cent margin could improve the business's overall profit margin (but possibly reduce its turnover) by discontinuing egg production.
- This ratio can be improved by increasing prices, although this may result in lower turnover. Alternatively, reducing direct costs (raw material costs and wages, for example) will also improve the figure.

Net profit margin

This ratio calculates the percentage of a product's selling price that is net profit (after all costs have been deducted). Because this ratio includes all of a business's operating expenses, it may be regarded as a better indication of performance than gross profit margin. Once again the answer to this ratio is written as a percentage.

$$\text{Net profit margin} = \frac{\text{net profit (profit before taxation)}}{\text{revenue}} \times 100$$

Continuing our example of J Sainsbury plc, the company's net profit for the trading year ending in March 2011 was £827 million. The company's net profit margin is:

$$\frac{£827\,\text{m} \times 100}{£21,102\,\text{m}} = 3.92\%$$

Using this ratio

- Results of this ratio can vary according to the type of business, though a higher net profit margin is preferable.
- A comparison of gross and net profit margins can be informative. A business enjoying a stable gross profit margin and a declining net profit margin may be failing to control indirect costs effectively. This may be due to the purchase of new premises, for example.
- Improvements in the net profit margin may be achieved through higher selling prices or tighter control of costs, particularly overheads.

BUSINESS IN FOCUS

Sainsbury's profits rise by nearly 13 per cent

J Sainsbury plc's pre-tax profits in the year to 19 March reached £827 million, up from £733 million in the previous year. Underlying pre-tax profits, which exclude a £108 million gain from one-off items, increased 9 per cent to £665 million. Revenues rose by 7 per cent and like-for-like sales (excluding any new stores that have been opened during the year), grew by 2.3 per cent.

Sainsbury's said its cheaper 'Value where it matters' range had continued to perform well, as customers hit by austerity and record petrol prices tried to cut their spending. The retailer's Nectar loyalty card programme has 17.5 million members, and British Gas and easyJet now offer Sainsbury's customers a different way to spend their Nectar points.

Announcing the financial results, Justin King, chief executive, said: 'Sainsbury's has continued to perform well. Customer numbers are at an all-time high of 21 million transactions every week, which is up one million on last year, a clear indication of our growing universal customer appeal across all channels.'

(Source: Adapted from Andrew Trotman in The Daily Telegraph, *11 May 2011)*

Question:

Analyse the possible reasons why a supermarket in a highly competitive industry might be satisfied with a net profit margin on sales of less than 4 per cent. *(10 marks)*

Return on capital employed

This is an important ratio comparing the operating profit earned with the amount of capital employed by the business. The capital employed by the business is measured by its total equity plus its non-current (long-term) liabilities.

The importance of this ratio is reflected in the fact that it is also termed 'the primary efficiency ratio'. The result of this ratio, which is expressed as a percentage, allows an assessment to be made of the overall financial performance of the business. A fundamental comparison can be made between the prevailing rate of interest and the ROCE generated by a business.

$$\text{Return on capital employed} = \frac{\text{operating profit} \times 100}{\text{total equity} + \text{non-current liabilities (capital employed)}}$$

Using this ratio

- A typical ROCE may be expected to be in the range of 20–30 per cent. It is particularly important to compare the results from calculating this ratio with the business's ROCE in previous years and also those achieved by competitors.
- A business may improve its ROCE by increasing its operating profit without raising further capital or by reducing the amount of capital employed, perhaps by repaying some long-term debt.

Company	Type of business	Date of accounts	Operating profit (loss) (£m)	Total equity + non-current assets (£m)	ROCE
The Burberry Group plc	Clothes manufacturer	31/03/2011	£298.9	£830.1	36.00%
Rolls-Royce plc	Engineering	31/12/2010	£1,130	£9,056	12.48%
Vodafone plc	Telecommunications	31/03/2011	£5,596	£221,772	2.52%
BP Group	Oil extraction, refining and retailing	31/12/2011	(£4,825)	£188,383	–2.56%

Table 3.6 ROCE data for a selection of companies

Notes: *The returns here vary enormously. The most eye-catching figure is that of BP. The company's financial position has been severely effected by the cost of compensation to those affected by the oil spillage in the Gulf of Mexico.*

Shareholders' ratios

The results of this group of ratios are of particular interest to the shareholders of a company or to anyone considering purchasing shares in a particular company. They are also known as investment ratios. Shareholders can receive a return on their purchase of shares in two ways:

1 through dividends paid from the company's profits over the financial year
2 as a result of a rise in the price of the shares – called a capital gain.

Dividends offer a short-term return on an investment and may be of interest to shareholders seeking a quick return. However, other shareholders may seek a long-term return on their investment. They may be prepared to forego high levels of dividends in the short run to allow profits to be invested. They hope that the business will grow, increasing the price of shares and providing a capital gain for shareholders.

There are a number of ratios that may be used by shareholders. However, we shall concentrate on ratios that compare the dividends received against the capital investment made by shareholders when purchasing shares.

Dividend per share

This is an important shareholders' ratio. It is simply the total dividend declared by a company divided by the number of shares the business has issued.

$$\text{Dividend per share} = \frac{\text{total dividends}}{\text{number of issued shares}}$$

Results of this ratio are expressed as a number of pence per share.

In 2011 Marks & Spencer, one of the UK's best-known retailers, announced dividends totalling £250.05 million. The dividend per share for the company was calculated as follows:

$$\frac{£250.05\,m}{1,592.7\,m\,\text{shares}} = 15.7 \text{ pence per share}$$

It is normal for dividends to be paid in two parts: an interim dividend halfway through the financial year and a final dividend at the end of the year.

Using this ratio

- A higher figure is generally preferable to a lower one as this provides the shareholder with a larger return on his or her investment. However, some shareholders are looking for long-term investments and may prefer to have a lower dividend per share (DPS) now in the hope of greater returns in the future and a rising share price.
- It is wise to compare the DPS with that offered by alternative companies. However, it is also important to bear in mind how much has to be invested to buy each share. A low DPS may be perfectly acceptable if the company has a low share price.
- A business can improve this figure by announcing higher dividends (and therefore reducing the amount of profit retained within the business). This may prove attractive to some shareholders, but may not be in the long-term interests of the business, particularly if profits are not rising.

Dividend yield

This ratio is really a development of the previous ratio and provides shareholders with more information. The dividend yield compares the dividend received on a single share with the current market price of that share. This provides shareholders with a better guide to a business's performance, as it compares the return with the amount that would need to be invested to purchase a share. The result of calculating this ratio is given as a percentage.

$$\text{Dividend yield} = \frac{\text{dividend per share} \times 100}{\text{market price of share}}$$

If a shareholder was considering investing in Marks & Spencer and noted that the share price was 315 pence (as it is at the time of writing) and that the dividend per share for the company was 15.07 pence for 2011. He or she could calculate the dividend yield as follows:

$$\frac{15.07 \times 100}{315} = 4.78\%$$

BUSINESS IN FOCUS

Debenhams resumes dividend payments

Debenhams has recorded a 10 per cent increase in its annual profits after it used price cuts to boost its market share. The UK's second biggest department store group beat forecasts to achieve pre-tax profits of £166.1 million for the 53 weeks to 3 September. On average, analysts had predicted profits of £162 million, according to a poll by Debenhams, which has 169 shops in Britain, Ireland and Denmark.

Total sales increased by 2.9 per cent to reach £2.68 billion, as reported last month along with its market share gains, but sales at stores which have been open for more than a year fell by 0.3 per cent.

Debenhams chief executive Michael Sharp said: 'It is right to remain cautious about the strength of consumer confidence over the next 12 months given the uncertain economic outlook.'

Debenhams finished the year with net debts of £383.7 million, down £133.1 million on the figure recorded at the start of the year. It will pay a total dividend of three pence per share (having not paid dividends the previous year) and said it plans to start a share buyback programme in the second half of the financial year of 2012.

(Source: London Loves Business, 20 October 2011 www.londonlovesbusiness.com)

Question

Analyse why some of Debenham's shareholders may have been satisfied by the company's decision not to pay dividends in the previous year. *(10 marks)*

Using this ratio

- A higher return will be regarded as preferable by shareholders seeking a quick return. Longer-term investors might settle for a lower figure, allowing the firm to reinvest profits and offering the possibility of higher profits and dividends in the future.
- Results for this ratio can vary dramatically according to fluctuations in the company's share price.
- This ratio can be improved by increasing the proportion of profits distributed to shareholders in the form of dividends.

The value and limitations of ratio analysis

Ratio analysis provides stakeholders with an insight into the performance of a business. However, to offer the maximum amount of information, the details gained from ratio analysis need to be compared with other data, such as that outlined below.

- **The results for the same business over previous years.** This allows stakeholders to appreciate the trend of the data. Thus, a low but steadily increasing figure for ROCE might be reassuring to investors.
- **The results of ratio analysis for other firms in the same industry.** We have seen that results expected from various ratios vary according to the type of firm under investigation. Thus, the inventory or stock turnover ratio will be much higher for a retailer selling perishable products than for a manufacturer. By comparing like-with-like a more informed judgement may be made.
- **The results of ratios from firms in other industries.** Stakeholders can compare the ratios of a particular business with those from a wide range of firms. This might allow, for example, a comparison between two firms experiencing rapid growth. The Centre for Inter-Firm Comparisons offers anonymous data on the financial ratios of many UK firms.

A significant weakness of ratio analysis is that it only considers the financial aspects of a business's performance. While this is undeniably important, other elements of a business should be taken into account when evaluating performance.

- **The market in which the business is trading.** A business that is operating in a highly competitive market might experience relatively low profits, reducing the results of ratios such as the return on capital employed (ROCE).
- **The position of the firm within the market.** A market leader might be expected to provide better returns than a small firm struggling to establish itself. However, the small struggling firm may be investing heavily in developing new products and establishing a brand identity. The struggling firm may generate large profits in the future.
- **The quality of the workforce and management team.** These are important factors in assessing a business, but not ones that will be revealed directly through ratio analysis. Indeed, a business that invests heavily in its human resources may appear to be performing relatively poorly through the use of ratio analysis.
- **The economic environment.** In general, businesses might be expected to perform better during periods of prosperity and to produce better results from ratio analysis. During the period of low or negative economic growth experienced in the UK in 2008, it is reasonable to expect the financial performance of many (but not all) businesses to decline.

One step further: the operating cash-flow ratio

The AQA specification sets out ten ratios with which you should be familiar. However, there are other ratios that can be of value, and the operating cash-flow ratio is one of these. It relies on the company's cash-flow statement as a principal source of information. We considered cash-flow statements in 'One step further' in the previous chapter (see pages 30–31).

The operating cash-flow ratio measures a company's ability to pay its short-term liabilities. It is measured by using the following formula:

$$\text{Operating cash-flow ratio} = \frac{\text{operating cash flow}}{\text{current liabilities}}$$

If the operating cash-flow ratio is less than 1, it means that the company has generated less cash over the year than it needs to pay off short-term liabilities as at the year end. This may signal a need to raise money to meet liabilities.

So, what is the advantage of using the operating cash-flow ratio, rather than the current or acid test ratios? The current ratio and others based on balance sheet numbers gauge liquidity as at the balance sheet date, whereas the operating cash-flow ratio uses the cash generated over an accounting period.

The operating cash-flow ratio can be used to compare companies across a sector, and to look at changes over time. A higher result from this ratio is preferable, but as with all liquidity ratios, it depends on the type of business and the industry in which it operates.

Key terms

Ratio analysis is a technique for analysing a business's financial performance by comparing one piece of accounting information with another.

A **stakeholder** is any group or individual having an interest in the activities of a business.

Debenture: a long-term loan to a business carrying a fixed rate of interest and a specified repayment date.

Ordinary shares: a financial security representing part ownership of a business that does not entitle

the holder to a fixed payment from profits, but does confer voting rights.

Preference shares: a financial security representing part ownership of a business that entitles the holder to a fixed payment from profits.

Stock: the amount of raw materials, components and finished goods held by a business at a given time.

The AQA specification sets out ten ratios with which you should be familiar. These are: the current and acid test ratios, ROCE, asset turnover, stock or inventory turnover, receivables (debtor) days and payables (creditor) days, gearing, dividend per share and dividend yield.

It is easy to concentrate on how to calculate ratios and to underestimate the importance of interpreting the results. Some examination questions offer the results of ratios as part of the information given to candidates. This type of question places much emphasis on interpreting ratios and students should prepare themselves for this style of question.

It is not necessary to learn the formulae for the ratios that we consider in this chapter. These will be provided for you as part of the examination paper. You should concentrate on carrying out the calculations accurately, and on understanding what the results mean for businesses.

Other aspects of a business's activities can have significant impacts on the results of ratio calculations. For example, if a business uses a JIT system of inventory control it is likely to have a much higher level of inventory or stock turnover.

ROCE is one of three key ratios used to assess the financial performance of businesses. The other two are the acid test ratio and gearing. Using these three ratios enables a company's short- and long-term liquidity positions to be examined, as well as being a fundamental measure of its profitability.

Do think about the ways in which a business may increase its ROCE figure if it is considered to be too low. This may have implications for all the functional areas of the business to increase profits and/or reduce the amount of capital employed in the business.

Do consider the results of any ratios in the light of the type of business that you are considering. Manufacturers may need higher levels of liquidity to enable them to purchase large quantities of inventories; in contrast, retailers may manage with much lower figures because they are paid quickly and usually in cash. Profit margins can vary enormously. Jewellers might make high profit margins as they sell a relatively small number of highly priced products, whereas this may not be true of some other types of retailers.

Progress questions

1. Explain, with the aid of an example, why a ratio might provide more detail on a firm's performance than a single piece of financial information. *(7 marks)*

2. Distinguish between efficiency ratios and profitability ratios. *(6 marks)*

3. Outline **two** sources of information that might be important when conducting ratio analysis. *(6 marks)*

4. Marsham Trading has current liabilities amounting to £2.8 million. Its current assets are: receivables £1.1 million, inventories £2.0 million and cash £0.9 million. Calculate the business's current and acid test ratios. *(8 marks)*

5. Give **two** reasons why the results of liquidity ratios might be treated with caution. *(6 marks)*

6. Pelennor Products is a rapidly growing business providing IT services. The company's receivables (debtors') days ratio has increased from 33.2 days to 41.7 days over the past year. Outline the possible implications of this for the business. *(10 marks)*

7. Fangorn plc has seen an improvement in its gross profit margin over the financial year. At the same time its net profit margin has deteriorated. Explain the implications of this for the business and outline possible actions that the management team might take. *(10 marks)*

8. Explain why the return on capital employed (ROCE) is such an important ratio for stakeholders. *(6 marks)*

9. Why might the dividend yield ratio provide a better indication of a company's performance than the dividend per share ratio? *(5 marks)*

10. Outline two possible external factors that need to be taken into account when conducting ratio analysis. *(6 marks)*

✖ These questions relate to the case study on page 5.

Using ratios to support your answer assess the ways in which the company might finance its expansion plans. *(18 marks)*

Candidate's answer:

Invicta plans to raise £350 million to expand into Europe. One possibility to finance this investment is to raise long-term loans from banks or other investors. At the end of 2011 the company's gearing ratio was 55.44 per cent (up from 51.46 per cent in 2010). If it borrowed the entire £350 million this would result in its non-current liabilities rising to £848.2 million while its capital employed (total equity plus non-current liabilities) would be £1,248.6 million. As a result the company's gearing ratio would increase to 67.93 per cent. This is much too high and far above the recommended 50 per cent maximum figure. Invicta is already above this figure at the end of 2011 and this suggests that loan capital is not really an option to finance this expansion.

In contrast the company's performance as measured by ROCE is much more impressive. In 2010 it achieved a figure of 27.49 per cent and in 2011 this rose to an impressive 29.56 per cent (significantly above Kevin's 25 per cent objective). Although ROCE uses operating profit as its measure we can see from the accounts that the company had nearly £250 million in pre-tax profits in 2011 of which a substantial element could be used towards the sum required for Kevin's proposal.

It is clear that the company cannot borrow more, so loan capital should not be used. A large investment such as this will require more than a single source of finance. We have seen that retained profits can provide a substantial sum, but Invicta should be able to sell shares given its high ROCE figure and the fact that its dividend yield figure has increased from 5.04 per cent to 5.21 per cent at a time when returns from many companies are low. Therefore I recommend that the company should use a mixture of retained profits and share capital to finance its eurozone expansion.

Examiner's comments:

Overall this candidate's answer is excellent. They have demonstrated relevant knowledge and important skills in relation to writing answers using ratios. They have not selected too many ratios – instead they have chosen the most important ones for the particular circumstances. Furthermore, they have interpreted their results in relation to the precise demands of the question and have not simply relied on the calculation to speak for itself. Their decision to calculate gearing and ROCE in this situation was wise, especially as the results contrasted nicely and offered them two sides of the argument. Similarly the use of the dividend yield ratio to support their decision was excellent. There were plenty of evaluative comments in this answer, and not just in the conclusion. A final impressive feature was their clear, focussed and well-supported judgement.

Evaluation question

Do you think that the company's stakeholders will be pleased with the company's performance over the 2010 and 2011 financial years? You should use relevant calculations to justify your views. *(18 marks)*

4 Selecting financial strategies

This chapter links very closely to Chapter 1. It sets out the ways in which a business might seek to achieve its financial objectives and the medium- to long-term plans it might put into place to achieve these targets. It will highlight the implications of using particular financial strategies for other functions within the business.

In this chapter we examine:

● the major financial strategies that may be adopted by large businesses
● how these financial strategies may relate to other functional areas within the business.

Raising finance

A business may need to raise the capital for a number of reasons:

● to purchase non-current assets such as production-line technology
● to pay for research and development
● to buy other companies
● to finance major advertising campaigns.

A business that is opting to raise finance as a financial strategy is likely to be a business that is expanding. Thus a business that has growth as a corporate objective may opt to raise finance as a key financial strategy. In recent years Vodafone has grown rapidly, mainly by purchasing (or taking over) mobile phone operators in other countries and is currently focussing on increasing sales in emerging markets. Much of the company's growth has been financed through borrowing.

However, a business has a number of options when considering the ways in which it may raise its finance for major investments such as those set out above. The method chosen will have significant implications for all areas within the business.

Using retained profits

Using profits retained from previous years' trading is an important internal and long-term source of finance for many businesses. There are distinct advantages for a business in using retained profits to finance its investment spending. First, the funding is available immediately without having to apply for and negotiate loans or organise the selling of shares in the company. Both of these methods of raising finance can take time and may require some considerable administration to complete. However, the major advantage of raising finance by using retained profits is that it avoids interest charges that would be payable on a loan. It also helps to avoid increasing the business's gearing ratio, which is a likely consequence of taking out a large loan. This can be a major advantage for a business that is already heavily indebted. Using retained profits is also preferable in some ways to raising money through selling shares. Raising finance in this way means that a company will be expected to pay dividends to shareholders at some time in the future.

Of course this method of raising finance also has disadvantages. Using profits in this way has an opportunity cost. The money cannot be paid to shareholders as dividends if it is to be retained in the business. This may mean a reduction in the dividend per share and some shareholders may be dissatisfied, especially if they were seeking a short-term gain. One implication could be a fall in the company's share price if the decision is widely unpopular and significant numbers of shareholders sell their shares. It may also make it more difficult for the company to raise finance by selling shares in the near future.

Google Ireland's revenues jump 28 per cent to €10.9 billion

The digital economy is booming, according to results for Google's Irish business, which show a 28 per cent increase in sales. Google Ireland is the Europe, Middle East and Africa (EMEA) headquarters for Google and provides technical, sales and operations support to customers in over 50 countries.

Revenue earned by Google Ireland Limited jumped to €10.9 billion in 2010, from €7.9 billion in 2009, and now accounts for roughly 40 per cent of the search engine giant's global earnings. Google earnings are driven by online advertising revenue.

'Google Ireland continued to reap the rewards of the growth in the digital economy,' said John Herlihy, vice-president of operations at Google and the company's senior executive in Dublin.

Employment at the company rose to 1,513 during the year from 1,397 a year earlier. At the end of last year,

Google staff received an average salary of €78,668, up from €72,207 a year earlier. Continued growth since the end of 2010 has seen employment rise to more than 2,000 people.

The Irish subsidiary spent €29.15 million on research and development last year, a dramatic increase in the €18.8 million spent the previous year.

The accounts show that Google paid taxes of €15.3 million in Ireland in 2010, down from €18.3 million in 2009. The company again decided against paying a dividend and retained profits now stand at €38.87 million.

(Source: Dominic Coyle in The Irish Times, *8 October 2011)*

Question:

Analyse the reasons why Google Ireland might have decided not to pay a dividend and to increase its retained profits instead. *(10 marks)*

However, there is another side to this argument. Not all shareholders will take a short-term view. Institutional investors such as insurance companies and pension funds buy large numbers of shares and many look for long-term returns on their investments. They may support the decision if they believe that the investment will increase the company's long-term profitability and ultimately dividends and the company's share price.

Borrowing

Businesses may choose to raise substantial sums through borrowing from banks or other financial institutions. This borrowing is likely to be long term and will appear on the company's balance sheet as a non-current liability. This type of long-term borrowing also has implications for a company's gearing as we saw in the previous chapter. If the borrowing is sufficient to take the gearing figure in excess of 50 per cent the company is said to be highly geared. This may result in the business having difficulty in repaying the debt and may lead to other functions within the business having less finance available due to the liquidity difficulties.

Banks are lending less, says Bank of England

The amount of money lent by banks to UK businesses shrank in the three months to August 2011, according to new figures from the Bank of England. Official data on lending by all UK banks and building societies shows they lent £2.5 billion less than during the previous period.

According to a report by the Bank, the amount of money available to lend to small and medium-sized enterprises (SMEs) was expected to remain broadly unchanged during the rest of 2011.

Demand for credit, however, was reported to have fallen for smaller businesses in the last three months and was expected to fall for both small and medium-sized businesses until the year end.

Lenders in the survey said that companies were reluctant to hold increased levels of debt given a more uncertain economic outlook and a fall in consumer confidence. Interest rates, particularly those being charged to smaller firms, were also increasing.

(Source: Manchester Evening News, *21 October 2011)*

However, borrowing in this way has the advantage of being relatively quick to arrange, especially if the business has non-current assets (such as property, for example) that can be used as collateral against the loan. Collateral is security for the creditor – it can be sold to repay the loan if the business defaults on its payments. This is more likely to be an attractive option for raising finance if the market rates of interest are low and if finance is readily available.

Selling shares

Another means of raising capital is to sell shares in the business. Clearly this is an option that is only available to companies, and only public limited companies can raise large sums in this way. This is because public limited companies can use the Stock Exchange or other similar markets to sell shares to the general public and to other organisations. The 'Business in focus' box gives information about another market available to UK companies: the AIM.

Selling shares is a slower approach than borrowing and can be a relatively expensive one. It can also be a difficult proposition at certain times if the business's share price is declining. The sale of substantial quantities of shares may dilute the control that a particular group of shareholders holds in the organisation.

However, selling shares does offer significant potential advantages to a business. It does not commit it to regular interest payments, irrespective of the financial position of the business and in this way can help to protect a weak liquidity position. Instead, the managers will be expected to pay a share of the company's profits to the shareholders (this payment is known as dividends). Clearly, if the company is experiencing a period of low profits it always has the option to reduce the amount it pays to shareholders in the form of dividends. In this way the sale of shares is a more flexible form of raising finance, which is adjustable (to some degree) to the circumstances facing the business.

BUSINESS IN FOCUS

The Alternative Investment Market

The Alternative Investment Market (AIM) is a subsidiary market of the London Stock Exchange. It allows smaller companies to sell shares with a more flexible set of rules than is applicable to the London Stock Exchange's main market.

The AIM was launched in 1995 and has raised over £60 billion in capital for the 3,000 companies that have chosen to join it. It is attractive to smaller companies as it has fewer rules and no requirements for the minimum value of the company or number of shares it issues.

Some companies that initially traded on the AIM have since moved on to join the main market, although in the last few years, significantly more companies transferred from the main market to the AIM. This is because the AIM has significant tax advantages for investors, as well as fewer rules for the companies themselves.

Sale of assets

Some businesses may be in the fortunate position of holding surplus non-current assets or have investments in other companies that can be sold to raise finance. This is a good means of raising finance in that it avoids any sort of payments; however, it may result in the loss of assets which could increase in value in the future, or the loss of a source of income as in the case of shares held in other businesses.

A variant of selling assets has become popular in recent years – sale and leaseback. Businesses seeking to raise capital have sold assets that they require for future trading and have leased them back. This allows them to have a large amount of capital available and to retain use of the asset in question. The major disadvantage of this approach to raising capital is that it commits the business to permanent expenditure in the future to pay to lease the assets and retain their use.

Avolon in Ryanair aircraft deal

Irish aircraft leasing group Avolon has announced significant sale and leaseback deals with Ryanair and AirAsia that will see it deliver nine planes to the low-cost airlines by early 2012.

The company, founded last year by Domhnal Slattery, has also raised an additional $600 million to finance these deals.

Avolon has agreed to lease five Boeing 737-800s to Ryanair and four Airbus A320s to AirAsia. These form part of sale and leaseback deals with the airlines. Seven of the planes will be delivered to the airlines this week – including the five to Ryanair – with the other two early next year. Avolon has signed seven-year lease agreements with Ryanair while the AirAsia deals will have a 12-year duration.

The nine aircraft cost $740 million at list price. It is not clear how much Avolon paid to purchase the aircraft but it will have received large discounts on the list prices.

Speaking to *The Irish Times* yesterday, Avolon's chief commercial officer John Higgins said, 'The significance for us is that they are two heavy-hitting global airlines … it's great for Avolon to get over the line with them.'

(Source: Ciarán Hancock in The Irish Times, *26 September 2011)*

Question:

Analyse the reasons why Ryanair may have chosen to use a sale and leaseback deal to raise capital. *(10 marks)*

The implications of a strategy of raising finance

A strategy of raising finance has profound implications for other areas of the business. This financial strategy is likely to accompany a programme of expansion which may mean that the business's human resource department needs to recruit more staff, retrain existing staff or relocate employees. The business's workforce plan will have to be written to support the financial strategy.

The implications of raising finance can be significant for the operations function of a business. It may entail research and development into new products or it could involve investment in new methods of production. In either event the managers responsible for these areas within the business are likely to have to manage programmes of change.

The marketing function of a business will be affected in a variety of ways. The marketing department may be required to research a changing market or to investigate new markets, possibly overseas. The development of new products may accompany a financial strategy of raising finance and the expansion of the business.

Implementing profit centres

What is a profit centre?

A profit centre is an area, department, division or branch of an organisation that is allowed to control itself separately from the larger organisation. It makes its own decisions, following corporate objectives, and may produce its own income statement for amalgamation with the rest of the business. So, a profit centre is some part of an organisation that is allowed to control itself as a separate element from the larger organisation.

- It can be **a factory or department** within a business. For example, BMW builds a new Rolls-Royce model at a factory in Goodwood in Sussex. This factory is a profit centre.
- It can be **a brand**. For example, Cadbury's Dairy Milk is a profit centre for the company.
- Some businesses use **geographical regions** as the basis for profit centres. Ford operates globally and Europe, for example, is a profit centre.
- **Groups of products** can be profit centres. Dairy Crest, the UK manufacturer of cheese and other dairy products, operates all its spreads (Utterly Butterly and Clover, for example) as a single profit centre.
- It is common for businesses, most obviously retailers, to manage each **branch** as a profit centre. French retailer Carrefour has hypermarkets throughout the world and each is a separate profit centre.

HSBC and profit centres

With its headquarters in London, HSBC is one of the largest banking and financial services organisations in the world. Its international network comprises some 7,500 properties in 87 countries and territories in Europe, Hong Kong, Rest of Asia-Pacific (including the Middle East and Africa), North America and Latin America.

HSBC provides a comprehensive range of financial services to more than 125 million customers through four customer groups and global businesses: Personal Financial Services (including consumer finance); Commercial Banking; Global Banking and Markets; and Private Banking.

In 2010 HSBC announced that the company's profits were US$19 billion (£12.67 billion) for the financial year. The company confirmed its commitment to growth and stated that it would target emerging markets such as China and India as it believed rates of growth in these economies would be higher.

HSBC has divided itself into a number of profit centres: Europe, Hong Kong, Rest of Asia-Pacific, Middle East, Latin America and North America. In 2010 HSBC saw Europe contribute $4.30 billion in profits and Hong Kong $5.69 billion, while North America generated a small profit of $0.45 billion. Within these core profit centres other, smaller, profit centres operate. Thus senior managers at HSBC can

Figure 4.1 HSBC is one of the world's largest financial institutions

analyse the performance of the UK market, as this is a separate profit centre within the European profit centre.

(Source: Adapted from HSBC's Annual Report, 2010)

Question:

To what extent do you think that HSBC's use of profit centres offers the company more advantages than disadvantages? *(18 marks)*

The managers of a profit centre can calculate costs and revenues and can make their own decisions in pursuit of corporate objectives. This financial strategy is more appropriate for larger businesses and especially those that sell diverse ranges of products or operate through a large number of outlets. The implementation of profit centres enables the businesses to manage the elements of its operations separately and to make at least some decisions in the context of a distinct part of the business.

This might be an attractive financial strategy for a business for a number of reasons (both financial and non-financial). There are a number of benefits from using profit centres as an integral part of managing a business.

The benefits of using profit centres

- Diseconomies of scale can be avoided. The trend towards globalisation has meant that some businesses have become too large to manage as a single entity. For example, HSBC trades in 83 countries and this is too large to operate as a single entity and to pursue corporate objectives such as expansion. It is important to divide the company in some way to ensure effective management and to prevent problems with coordination and communication. Decentralised decision-making allows areas to make decisions faster and be more responsive to changes in local conditions. In turn this assists the organisation in achieving its financial and corporate objectives.

- Delegating power and authority to centres improves motivation. HSBC is able to give senior managers in each country more authority to run their own affairs, boosting motivation. In turn the bank is able to run branches as separate profit centres, allowing the potential to offer more motivating and challenging work to employees at a fairly junior level within the business. In a service industry such as HSBC it is of great value to be able to motivate staff by use of such techniques and thereby improve their performance. This will help the bank to achieve its growth objective, especially in emerging markets.

- Monitoring of performance is much easier. In 2011 HSBC made global profits amounting to over £12 billion, but this disguised a very poor performance by the North American division of the bank. The North American business made a small profit of £0.45 billion (2.36 per cent of the company's total profits) despite having 20.1 per cent of the company's assets available to it.

The drawbacks of using profit centres

- There is a danger that individual centres can become too narrowly focused. This means that the profit centres may lose sight of overall business objectives. Thus, the UK division of HSBC is focused on cost reduction, especially during the current recession, with the aim of protecting profit margins. However, this may not be entirely in tune with the bank's overall aim of growth.
- Performance of individual areas may be affected by local market conditions. The UK banking market is particularly competitive, especially as a result of mergers activity and the emergence of new financial services providers such as Tesco and Metro Bank. It may not be realistic for HSBC to expect its UK division to match the profitability of some other regions of the world under these conditions.
- Some decisions which result from the use of profit centres may not be in the best interests of the entire business. Managers of profit centres may pursue their own agendas and not those of the business. This may mean that a financial strategy of implementing profit centres may not assist the business in achieving its corporate objectives.
- Costs may rise. The use of a strategy based on profit centres means that a business is likely to have to invest heavily in training to provide staff with the necessary skills to manage more autonomously. In the short term this may damage the business's financial performance and make it more difficult

to achieve certain financial objectives such as profit maximisation.

The implications of a strategy of implementing profit centres

There is a distinction between implementing and operating profit centres. Implementing profit centres means that the business will undergo a period of change as a more centralised system is replaced by a series of profit centres. This will have particularly significant implications for human resources and operations management.

The HR department of a business implementing profit centres is likely to have to take on a series of activities following the development of a new workforce plan. The plan may have to include the following to allow profit centres to be implemented successfully:

- a skills audit across the organisation to uncover relevant skills among the existing workforce which had not been previously acknowledged
- the recruitment of new employees with the necessary skills to take greater control of managing financial and non-financial resources within separate branches or regions
- the redeployment of existing employees to new positions, often in different geographic locations
- the redundancies of some employees who may not have roles in the new organisation. These may include some relatively senior employees whose roles have in effect been delegated to more junior employees.

In addition, communication may become more important and possibly more difficult as more decisions are made at a lower level and greater amounts of information have to be disseminated throughout the organisation.

The operational implications of implementing profit centres are also significant. The operation of strategies of lean production may become more complex within an organisation that is likely to have become more decentralised. For example, the organisation of JIT production methods may be much more difficult. In addition, that business may not be able to benefit as fully from economies of scale if decision-making power is delegated to individual profit centres. For example, economies of scale which arise from purchasing in bulk may be dissipated if budgets are managed by different sections of the business and each makes individual purchasing decisions.

Cost minimisation

A business operates a strategy of cost minimisation where it reduces its level of expenditure as far as is possible to allow it to provide goods or services of acceptable quality to its customers. This strategy has received much publicity as a result of its use by budget airlines such as Ryanair and easyJet. Cost minimisation is likely to be an effective financial strategy in markets where demand for products is price elastic. That is, demand is sensitive to price reductions, and firms that can cut costs and pass on the benefits to customers can reap large increases in sales. Cost minimisation may also be an effective way of 'opening up' a market to consumers with lower incomes and thereby increasing sales.

Cost minimisation can be classified as a financial strategy as well as a financial objective. Businesses will seek to implement a cost minimisation strategy by implementing one or more of a number of policies.

Minimising labour costs

This may be important for firms supplying services, as many of them are likely to face wage and salary expenses which are a high proportion of total costs. Therefore cutting labour costs can have a substantial impact on overall costs of production. The implementation of this particular financial strategy may have a number of differing effects on the workforce as managers attempt to reduce expenditure.

- **Reductions in staffing levels**. This is the most obvious move and can have a significant impact on total costs, especially if the number of full-time employees is reduced significantly. However, it may lead to short-term increases in expenditure if redundancy payments have to be made. In addition, it may leave the organisation short of skilled and knowledgeable employees and therefore impair its performance.
- **Using more flexible workforces**. This type of workforce makes greater use of temporary and part-time staff, as well as zero-hours contracts, in order to match staffing levels more accurately to the needs of the organisation. The use of flexible workforces has the potential to cut labour costs by avoiding a situation where staff are paid when there is no work to be done.
- **Outsourcing**. This means that a business hires an outside organisation to carry out part of its work. It is common for businesses to use outside firms to maintain IT systems and to provide catering and cleaning services. Outsourcing cuts labour costs because the business only pays for such staff when they are required and is not responsible for certain fixed costs of employing people, such as paid holidays and pension contributions.

It is apparent that a financial strategy of cost minimisation that relies heavily on reducing labour costs will have huge implications for the business's HR department. HR managers will be responsible for drawing up a new workforce plan to reduce costs and then implementing it.

Relocating

Many UK businesses have taken the decision to relocate to areas of the world where production costs are lower. Dyson, the innovative vacuum cleaner manufacturer, moved its production facilities from Wiltshire to Malaysia, and Cadbury (now owned by the American food company Kraft) relocated some of its factories to Poland. The motive behind these decisions has been to lower the costs of production.

Producing in Eastern Europe or Asia will assist in reducing labour costs too as wage rates are much lower. In Poland in 2011 unemployment was over 11.8 per cent and the average weekly wage was a little over £180. The equivalent figure for the UK at the time of writing is £466. Thus, for labour-intensive industries where employees require relatively few skills, relocating to a low-cost country can be an attractive proposition. Other cost savings which may be achieved through relocation are cheaper land and property, as well as fewer laws which can be expensive to adhere to.

Some businesses have partly relocated through a process known as offshoring. Using this approach businesses transfer part of their operations to a lower-cost location. The offshoring 'Business in focus' box here considers how expenditure on wages for IT staff in the UK has been affected by this process.

However, in the case of manufacturing the cost advantages may be offset to some extent by increased transport costs. There are other costs that businesses might incur as a consequence of relocating. There are the short-term costs of carrying out the relocation and ongoing costs associated with coordinating a business that may operate from different sites. Communication becomes more difficult as does the coordination of the business. Many of the costs may be hidden, for example lower productivity because of language barriers. Some financial services providers have reversed their policies of offshoring customer services operations to India as a consequence of increased levels of customer complaints about the quality of service received.

Relocating may have considerable implications for managers responsible for operations, as they are required to manage a production process spread across more than one country. There will be obvious transportation issues with the possibilities of delays in supplies of raw materials and final products. For managers of service operations there may be incompatibility of technical equipment, and production in different time zones may make the coordination of the production process even more complicated than normal.

Using technology

Technology can replace expensive staff for businesses located in high-labour-cost countries such as the UK. For example, low-cost airlines such as easyJet rely heavily on the internet to capture and process bookings by passengers for flights. It is also used to facilitate a speedy and inexpensive check-in procedure for passengers. This allows the company to employ fewer workers and to reduce its operating costs.

Technology may also be used on the production line to reduce production costs. This is a common practice in manufacturing. For example, most car manufacturers use robots to some extent on their production lines.

Allocating capital expenditure

Capital expenditure is spending on new non-current assets such as property, machinery or vehicles. The way in which a business decides to spend its capital can have a significant effect on the operation of its finance department, and can also impact upon the other functions within the business. Businesses only have access to a limited amount of capital and any expenditure decisions normally have significant opportunity costs.

Investing in technology

Businesses may opt to do this to reduce the amount of labour deployed within the organisation and the associated costs. This approach will involve heavy initial expenditure on technology but may lead to a reduction in expenditure at a later stage. It also offers the potential advantage of increasing the productivity of the business. Nissan's car manufacturing plant in Sunderland has one the highest levels of labour productivity in Europe. In part this is due to the extensive use of technology on the production line. There are drawbacks, however. The initial costs are high and workers may need retraining in order to operate the technology efficiently.

BUSINESS IN FOCUS

Abercrombie & Fitch to open Spanish store

American casualwear retailer Abercrombie & Fitch is to open its first store in Spain this month.

The 12,379 sq ft store situated in the Palacio de Aguas in Madrid, is spread over four floors and is Abercombie's seventh wholly-owned store outside of its US home market.

The young fashion label launched its first European flagship near London's Savile Row four years ago, and last May opened a flagship store in France on Paris's Champs-Elysées. The retailer has also opened stores in Milan, Copenhagen, Brussels and Tokyo.

According to reports, Abercrombie & Fitch is soon to start work on a second Spanish store in Barcelona's Paseo de Gràcia.

(Source: Ruth Faulkner in Drapers, *1 November 2011)*

Question:

Analyse why a fashionable clothing brand might decide to allocate its capital in this way. *(10 marks)*

Investing in other assets such as property

Some businesses invest heavily in property to enable them to trade effectively or possibly to support their corporate image. Thus supermarkets in the UK hold a portfolio of property in high street and out-of-town locations, which is essential to enable them to conduct their business effectively. Some also hold considerable amounts of land for possible development as sites, but also to prevent competitors from acquiring it. Hotels and restaurants may purchase desirable property in prosperous locations to support an upmarket corporate image. In both cases allocating capital expenditure in this way can help the business to achieve its overall corporate objectives.

Key terms

A **financial strategy** is a medium- to long-term plan designed to achieve the objectives of the finance function or department of a business.

A **financial objective** is a goal or target pursued by the finance department (or function) within an organisation.

Retained profit is the profit that remains on the income statement once all additions to and deductions from revenue have been allowed for.

Investment has several meanings, but in the context of this chapter it refers to undertaking major programmes of expenditure, often over the long term, on which a return is expected. →

Gearing examines the relationship between internal sources and external sources of finance.

Sale and leaseback is an agreement to raise finance by selling an asset, such as property, and immediately retaining its use on a long-term lease.

A **profit centre** is an area, department, division or branch of an organisation that is allowed to control itself separately from the larger organisation.

A **cost centre** is an area, department, division or branch of an organisation for which it is possible to calculate costs (but not revenues). A marketing department might be an example of a cost centre.

Economies of scale are the factors that lead to unit or average costs *reducing* as an organisation increases its output.

Diseconomies of scale are the factors that lead to unit or average costs *increasing* as an organisation increases its output and becomes less efficient.

Cost minimisation occurs when a business reduces its level of expenditure as far as is possible to allow it to provide goods or services of acceptable quality to its customers.

Offshoring describes the relocation by a company of a business process to another (lower cost) country. This may include manufacturing, or supporting processes such as customer service.

Capital expenditure is spending on new non-current assets such as property, machinery or vehicles.

Examiner's advice

Opportunity cost is a very useful concept in business studies. It is useful for you to think in this way about many of the strategic decisions that a business takes. Thinking about the alternative that was foregone as the result of the decision may help you to assess the correctness of that action.

Capital is a word with several meanings in business and you should use it precisely in examinations. In the way we are using it here it refers to the finance that is invested in the company, either as a result of selling shares, or by borrowing. It can also mean accumulated wealth that has built up in a business as a result of years of successful trading. Finally, it may refer to the machinery that is used within a business, such as production-line technology.

Do consider the value of profit centres in relation to the type of business concerned. They may be attractive to a business that operates a large number of discrete sections or branches.

Do think about the value of a strategy of cost minimisation in the context of the market in which

the business is trading. How important is price to the typical customer? If products are generally undifferentiated, a low price may act as an effective USP.

The value of relocation as a means of cost minimisation depends on the nature of the product and the market in which it is sold. The supply of some services, such as customer service for financial products, is not particularly dependent on location. Hence it can be relocated without creating too many difficulties or incurring large additional costs. Similarly, manufacturers that sell their products globally may not be so dependent on a specific location as transport costs do not play such a large part in a move to Eastern Europe or Asia.

Do not think that a business will always operate a single financial strategy. It is perfectly possible to use strategies in combination. For example, strategies of raising finance and allocating capital expenditure may be operated alongside one another.

Progress questions

1. Outline **two** reasons why a car manufacturer may need to raise large sums of finance. *(6 marks)*
2. Explain the benefits a business may receive from using retained profits to finance a major investment programme. *(6 marks)*
3. Explain why raising finance might be an appropriate financial strategy for a business aiming to sell in a global market. *(8 marks)*

→

4 Why might a business with a corporate objective of growth seek to raise finance through a mixture of selling shares and negotiating bank loans? *(8 marks)*

5 Why have many retailers with large numbers of stores chosen to raise finance through sale and leaseback? *(8 marks)*

6 Explain why implementing profit centres is a common financial strategy for large businesses with diverse product ranges. *(8 marks)*

7 Why might the implementation of profit centres as a financial strategy have significant implications for a business's HR department? *(7 marks)*

8 In what ways might a large business manufacturing non-branded T-shirts implement a financial strategy of cost minimisation? *(8 marks)*

9 Why might a UK manufacturer choose to allocate finance to investing in technology? *(5 marks)*

10 Which types of business might opt to allocate large sums of capital expenditure to the purchase of property? Explain your answer. *(6 marks)*

Analysis question

These questions relate to the case study on page 5.

Analyse the possible reasons why the company's managers decided upon a financial strategy of implementing profit centres. *(10 marks)*

Candidate's answer:

A profit centre is part of a business (in this case a retail outlet) for which it is possible to draw up a separate income statement.

The company was possibly in need of a system to motivate its employees. This was an issue for Invicta as its wages had barely increased in 2011 (only by 0.2 per cent) and this was at a time of inflation reducing spending power. If Taylor is correct and money motivates this might explain why the company's labour turnover shot up to 17 per cent. Using profit centres could overcome this as it allows the company to delegate more authority to employees in the retail outlets giving them greater control over their working lives and more self-esteem as identified by Maslow. Meeting these needs in this way could improve employees' motivation and performance – which is important in a service industry.

The company plans to open 65 new outlets in various city locations across Europe. Using profit centres will assist its senior managers in identifying the most successful outlets and possibly the reasons for their success. It may be possible to copy the successful outlets' approaches in other locations and this will help the company to increase its profit margins and thus improve its ROCE figure to help to meet Kevin's 25 per cent target.

Examiner's comments:

This student has planned and written a high-quality response to this question. He or she offers a clear definition at the outset to demonstrate his or her understanding and then develops a strong and relevant argument for the choice of profit centres as a financial strategy. This is applied well using data from the case study and he draws on (AS) motivational theory to develop his or her arguments.

The second argument is also good and again draws on the case study very effectively to apply the argument. Overall this answer would receive a high mark.

Evaluation question

Analyse the possible implications for the company of its decision to implement profit centres as a financial strategy. *(10 marks)*

5 Making investment decisions

This chapter looks at the techniques that businesses can use to make major investment decisions. It considers the reasons why businesses undertake programmes of investment and will look at financial and non-financial methods of assessing the worth of alternative investment projects. This topic was not studied at AS level. However, obvious links exist with the financial strategies chosen by businesses – especially allocating capital expenditure, which we considered in the previous chapter.

In this chapter we examine:

- the financial techniques for making investment decisions
- the criteria against which businesses judge investment decisions
- the qualitative influences on investment decisions.

Introduction

Investment is an important term within business studies and often entails managers taking major decisions. Investment can mean a decision to purchase part or all of another business, perhaps as a result of a takeover bid. However, it is perhaps more common to use the term in relation to the purchase of a fixed asset or some other major expenditure. What is common is that all such actions involve a degree of risk. This must be judged against the likely return. The final decision will depend upon managers' assessment of these two factors.

Businesses take decisions regarding investment in a variety of circumstances.

- When contemplating introducing new products a business may assess the likely costs of and returns from investing in one or more new products.
- Expansion may entail evaluating whether or not to invest in new fixed assets as part of a planned programme of growth. Tottenham Hotspur Football Club is considering investing an estimated £400 million in developing a new stadium, built in part on its existing ground, White Hart Lane. The club hopes to increase its sales revenue by attracting larger crowds into the new stadium, which will have a capacity of 60,000 spectators.
- Investing in new technology is often undertaken to reduce costs and improve productivity. For example one of the world's largest mining companies, Rio Tinto, is to start using driverless trucks in its iron ore mines in Western Australia. Using this latest technology means that the company can shift enormous quantities of materials quickly and safely, thereby increasing productivity.

- Businesses may also use techniques of investment appraisal before spending heavily on promotional campaigns, developing new brands or products or retraining the workforce.
- In each circumstance, however, the business must adopt an appropriate appraisal technique to decide whether the returns received from an investment are sufficient to justify the initial capital expenditure.

Financial techniques for making investment decisions

A number of techniques are available to managers to assist them in taking decisions on whether to go ahead with investments, or to help in making a judgement between two or more possible investment opportunities. This section will look at three of the most important of these techniques: payback, the average rate of return and discounted cash flow.

These financial techniques are valuable but do depend upon a number of assumptions:

- that all costs and revenues can be forecast easily and accurately for some years into the future
- that key variables (for example, interest rates) will not change
- that the business in question is seeking maximum profits.

There are two major considerations for managers when deciding whether or not to invest in a fixed asset or another business:

1 the total profits earned by the investment over the foreseeable future

Hewlett-Packard cuts forecasts as consumers curb PC buying

Hewlett-Packard, the biggest personal-computer maker, cut its sales forecast for 2011 by a billion dollars as consumers moved away from buying PCs. Full-year sales were expected to be $129 billion to $130 billion, the US firm said in a statement in May.

The change in forecasts came a day after Bloomberg News reported that Hewlett-Packard's chief executive officer (CEO) Leo Apotheker had written a memo warning of 'another tough quarter' in the July period. The disappointing forecasts reflected rivalry from tablets such as Apple's iPad and lower margins in services. Apotheker's predecessor, Mark Hurd, eliminated more than 48,000 jobs, so it was unlikely that there were more savings to be made.

Purchases of smartphones and tablets were reducing demand for PCs, Brent Bracelin, an analyst from Portland, Oregon, told Bloomberg. Shipments of PCs for sale declined by 3.2 per cent between January and March 2011. Tablet computer sales, in contrast, were expected to nearly triple during 2011.

Hewlett-Packard would also need to adapt its technology services business as its customers made the transition to cloud computing, the delivery of applications and data through the Internet, Bracelin pointed out.

(Source: Adapted from Aaron Ricadela and Dina Bass in Bloomberg Businessweek, 17 May 2011)

Question:

Analyse why, despite having huge resources to conduct primary market research, Hewlett-Packard appears unable to forecast its sales accurately. *(10 marks)*

---

2 how quickly the investment will recover its cost. This occurs when the earnings from the investment exceed the cost of the investment.

The process of assessing these factors is called investment appraisal and refers to the process of assessing one or more potential investments. Forecasting future costs and revenues can be a very difficult, and at times expensive, exercise to undertake. Forecasts about future revenues could prove to be inaccurate for a number of reasons.

- Competitors may introduce new products or reduce their prices, reducing forecast sales and revenues.
- Tastes and fashions may change, resulting in an unexpected slump in demand. The popularity of flying (as a result of low-cost airlines) has led to large falls in demand for cross-channel ferries and has led Eurotunnel to overestimate its sales.
- The economy may move into recession or slump (or, alternatively, into an upswing) resulting in sales figures radically different from those forecast.

Costs can be equally tricky to forecast. Unexpected periods of inflation, or rising import prices might result in inaccurate forecasts of expenditures. This can lead to a significant reduction in actual profits when compared with forecasts.

Companies that operate in a stable economic environment are much more easily able to forecast into the future as they have confidence that their predictions on the rate of inflation, likely rate of interest, level of unemployment and hence demand are as accurate as they can make them. A stable economic environment should lead to more accurate forecasts of both costs and revenues associated with investment projects.

Investment appraisal and the other functions within a business

It is easy to regard investment appraisal as simply a technique to be used when a business is contemplating purchasing fixed assets. However, investment appraisal can be used in relation to a number of a business's activities across each of its functional areas, all of which involve significant investment expenditure. These might include:

- investing in a major new advertising campaign
- expanding into new markets, perhaps overseas
- attempting to adjust management styles and corporate cultures, possibly entailing reorganisation and retraining
- adopting new techniques of production, including JIT and kaizen
- researching and developing new products.

Investment appraisal is an important element of most aspects of business activity. It can help to quantify proposed actions by managers and provide important information, assisting managers in taking good-quality decisions.

Payback

Payback is a simple technique that measures the time period required for the earnings from an investment to recoup its original cost. Quite simply, it finds out the number of years it takes to recover the cost of an investment from its earnings. In spite of the obvious simplicity of the payback technique, it remains the most common method of investment appraisal in the UK.

Here is an example of payback:

Year	Cash outflow (£)	Cash inflow (£)
1	500,000	100,000
2		200,000
3		200,000
4		150,000

In this case the calculation is simple: payback is achieved at the end of year three, when the initial investment of £500,000 is recovered from earnings – £100,000 in year 1 plus £200,000 in each of years 2 and 3.

Calculations can be a little more complex, however, as shown in the following example:

Year	Cash outflow (£)	Cash inflow (£)
1	500,000	100,000
2		100,000
3		200,000
4		300,000

In this case payback is achieved during the fourth year. The formula used to calculate the point during the year at which payback is achieved is as follows:

$$\text{number of full years} + \frac{\text{amount of investment not recovered}}{\text{revenue generated in next year}} \times 12$$

In the second example the investment has recovered £400,000 after three years. Therefore £100,000 remains to be recovered in year 4 before payback

point is reached. During year 4 the investment will generate £300,000. Thus:

$$\text{payback} = 3 \text{ years} + \frac{100,000}{300,000} \times 12 = \begin{array}{l} 3 \text{ years and} \\ 4 \text{ months} \end{array}$$

Figure 5.1 illustrates the concept of payback in the form of a graph.

Payback has the advantage of being quick and simple and this probably explains its popularity, especially with small businesses. However, it does have disadvantages. It ignores the level of profits that may be ultimately generated by the investment. For profit-maximising businesses this may represent an important omission. Furthermore, payback ignores the timing of any receipts. The following example highlights this weakness.

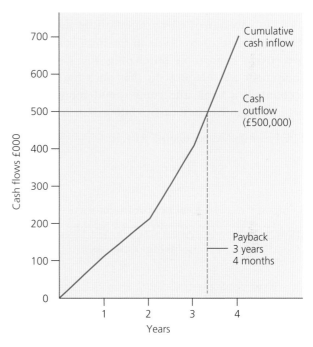

Figure 5.1 Payback on a graph

Two investment projects, A and B, each require an investment of £1 million. Their expected earnings are as follows:

Year	Project A cash inflow (£)	Project B cash inflow (£)
1	500,000	100,000
2	300,000	200,000
3	200,000	300,000
4	100,000	500,000

Both investment projects achieve payback at the end of year 4. However, A is obviously more attractive because it yields greater returns in the early years. Payback does not take into account the timing of any income received.

Average rate of return

The average rate of return (ARR) is a more complex and meaningful method of investment appraisal. This technique calculates the percentage rate of return on each possible investment. The resulting percentage figure allows a simple comparison with other investment opportunities, including investing in banks and building societies. It is important to remember, however, that a commercial investment (such as purchasing CAD/CAM equipment for a production line) involves a degree of risk. The returns may not be as forecast. Therefore it is important that such an investment earns significantly more than the rate of interest available in the local bank. If the percentage return on purchasing the CAD/CAM equipment was identical to that on a high-interest account in a bank, the latter would represent the better investment, as it carries little risk.

The formula for calculating ARR is:

$$\frac{\text{average profit}}{\text{asset's initial cost}} \times 100\%$$

$$\text{average profit} = \frac{\text{total net profit before tax over the asset's lifetime}}{\text{useful life of the asset}}$$

The ARR is considered to be more useful than payback because it considers the level of profits earned from an investment rather than simply the time taken to recover costs. It also offers easier comparison with returns on other investments, notably financial investments in banks and building societies. However, this technique also fails to differentiate between investments that generate high returns in the early years and those that offer greater rewards later on.

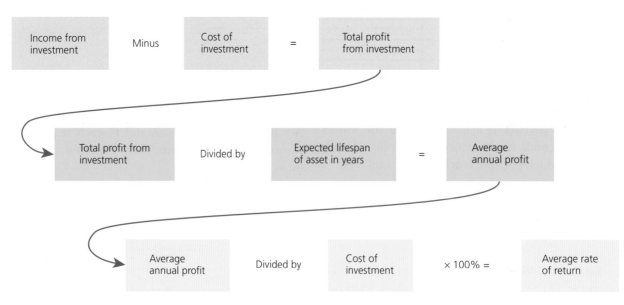

Figure 5.2 How to calculate average rate of return

Discounted cash flow

The technique of discounted cash flow takes into account what is termed the 'time value' of money. The time value of money is based on the principle that money at the present time is worth more than money at some point in the future. Thus, according to this principle, £1,000 today is of greater value than £1,000 in one or two years' time. There are two major reasons why this time value principle exists.

1 **Risk** – having £1,000 now is a certainty; receiving the same amount at some point in the future may not occur. The full £1,000 payment may not be made; indeed no payment at all may be made. An investment project may fail to provide the expected returns because of a competitor's actions, because of a change in tastes and fashions or as a consequence of technological change.

2 **Opportunity cost** is the foregone alternative. Even if no risk existed, the time value of money would still exist. This is because the money could be placed into an interest-bearing account generating a return. Thus, if we assume that a rate of 5 per cent is available on an interest-bearing account, £1,000 in one year's time is worth the same as £953 today. The reason for this is that by investing £953 at an interest rate of 5 per cent, we would have £1,000 after one year.

This time–value principle means that the longer the delay before money is received, the lower its value in present-day terms. This is called 'present value'. Table 5.1 shows two investments requiring identical outlays. Both projects also receive the same cash inflow over a four-year period and would generate the same average rate of return (10 per cent). However, the majority of the cash inflow for project A occurs in year 1, while in

project B this is delayed until year 3. The time–value principle would suggest that project A is preferable to project B. To show the effect of the time principle we need to calculate the present value of cash inflows and outflows through the use of discounting.

Year	Investment project A £000s	Investment project B £000s
0 (now)	(500)	(500)
1	400	100
2	100	100
3	100	100
4	100	400

Table 5.1 Two similar investment projects with different time patterns for cash inflows

Discounting

Discounting is the process of adjusting the value of money received at some future date to its present value (its worth today). Discounting is, in effect, the reverse of adding interest. Discounting tables are available to illustrate the effect of converting future streams of income to their present values. The rate of interest plays a central role in discounting – in the same way as it does in predicting the future value of savings. Table 5.2 shows the discounting figures and the value in present-day terms of £1,000 over a period of five years into the future. If the business anticipates relatively high interest rates over the period of the investment then future earnings are discounted heavily to provide present values for the investment. Lower rates result in discounting having a lesser effect in converting future earnings into present values.

Year	Discounting factor used to convert to present value assuming 10% rate of interest	Present value of £1,000 at a discount rate of 10% (£)	Discounting factor used to convert to present value assuming 5% rate of interest	Present value of £1,000 at a discount rate of 5% (£)
0 (now)	1	1,000	1	1,000
1	0.909	909	0.952	952
2	0.826	826	0.907	907
3	0.751	751	0.864	864
4	0.683	683	0.822	822

Table 5.2 The process of discounting

The basic calculation is that the appropriate discounting factor is multiplied by the amount of money to be received in the future to convert it to its present value. Thus, at a rate of interest of 10 per cent, the present value of £1,000 in two years' time is £826 (£1,000 x 0.826). The present value of £1,000 received in four years' time is £683. This figure is lower because the time interval is greater and the effect of the time–value principle more pronounced.

From this example we can see that the rate of interest has a significant effect on the present value of future earnings. The higher the rate of interest, the greater the discount. Thus, the present value of £1,000 in three years' time is £751 if the rate of interest is assumed to be 10 per cent. However, if the rate of interest is estimated to be 5 per cent the present value is greater: £863.

The choice of interest rate to be used as the basis for discounting is an important decision by a business undertaking investment appraisal. The discounting rate selected normally reflects the interest rates that are expected for the duration of the project. However, as we shall see later, another approach is to choose the rate the firm would like to earn on the project and to use this as the basis of the calculation.

Net present value

Discounting expected future cash flows is the basis of calculating net present value. This method of investment appraisal forecasts expected outflows and inflows of cash and discounts the inflows and outflows. To calculate net present value we need to know:

- the initial cost of the investment
- the chosen rate of discount
- any expected inflows and outflows of cash
- the duration of the investment project
- any remaining or residual value of the project at the end of the investment (if the investment is to purchase production equipment this may have scrap value once it is obsolete, for example).

The outflows of cash are subtracted from the discounted inflows to provide a net figure: the net present value. This figure is important for two reasons.

1 If the net present value figure is negative, the investment is not worth undertaking. This is because the present value of the stream of earnings is less than the cost of the investment. A more profitable approach would be to invest the capital in an interest-bearing account earning at least the rate of interest that was used for discounting.

2 When an enterprise is considering a number of possible investment projects it can use the net present value figure to rank them. The project generating the highest net present value figure is the most worthwhile in financial terms. In these circumstances a business may select the project – or projects – with the highest net present values.

Here is an example of calculating net present value. *Do it yourself* is one of the UK's most popular DIY magazines. The owners of the magazine, Bure Publishing, are investigating the production of an online edition especially designed for tablet computers. The company has conducted negotiations with two software houses regarding the development of a website for its new product, e-DIY. The two software houses offered very different ideas: one (proposal A) suggesting a basic product allowing Bure Publishing to offer access to the magazine at a bargain price; the other (proposal B) proposing a more sophisticated product, to a higher technical standard, offering the opportunity for premium pricing.

The cash flows associated with these proposals over a five-year period are set out in Table 5.3. These show the cost of developing the website and the expected revenues, less operating costs for the site each year. Bure Publishing estimates that a 10 per cent discount rate would reflect likely market rates of interest.

Bure Publishing would opt for proposal A on the basis of this financial information, as the net present value for proposal A (the cheaper option) is higher than that for proposal B. The net cash flow for proposal A is also positive as cash inflows exceed outflows. Therefore the investment is viable. However, non-financial information may affect this investment decision.

Year	Proposal A			Proposal B		
	Annual cash flows (£s)	Discounting factors at 10%	Present value (£s)	Annual cash flows (£s)	Discounting factors at 10%	Present value (£s)
0	(212,000)	1	(212,000)	(451,000)	1	(451,000)
1	46,000	0.909	41,814	89,400	0.909	81,265
2	57,500	0.826	47,495	115,000	0.826	94,990
3	63,250	0.751	47,501	122,500	0.751	91,998
4	69,000	0.683	47,127	144,275	0.683	98,540
5	71,000	0.621	44,091	140,000	0.621	86,940
Net present value			16,028	Net present value		2,733

Table 5.3 Comparing Bure Publishing's investment projects using discounted cash flow

A comparison of investment appraisal methods

The method of investment appraisal chosen will depend upon the type of firm, the market in which it is trading and its corporate objectives. A small firm may be more likely to use payback because managers may be unfamiliar with more complex methods of investment appraisal. Small businesses also often focus on survival, and an important aspect of any investment will be how long it takes to cover the cost of the investment from additional revenues. Payback is therefore valuable for firms who wish to minimise risk.

Larger firms that have access to more sophisticated financial techniques may use the average rate of return or discounted cash flow methods. These methods highlight the overall profitability of investment projects and may be more appropriate for businesses where profit maximisation is important.

Method of investment appraisal	Advantages	Disadvantages
Payback	Easy to calculate Simple to understand Relevant to firms with limited funds who want a quick return	Ignores timing of payments before payback Excludes income received after payback Does not calculate profit
Average rate of return	Measures the profit achieved on projects Allows easy comparison with returns on financial investments (bank accounts, for example)	Ignores the timing of the payments Calculates average profits – they may fluctuate wildly during the project
Discounted cash flow	Makes an allowance for the opportunity cost of investing Takes into account cash inflows and outflows for the duration of the investment	Choosing the discount rate is difficult – especially for long-term projects A complex method to calculate and easily misunderstood

Table 5.4 A comparison of techniques of investment appraisal

Investment criteria

Once the investment appraisal process has produced an answer, this needs to be compared with something in order to make a decision. There are a number of criteria that a business may use to make an investment decision.

The rate of interest

Average rate of return and net present value (NPV) methods produce figures that can be compared with the rate of interest. Any interest rate chosen for this process will be based on the interest rate set by the Bank of England. In essence, the managers of the business will seek a return that will be greater than the current and forecast interest rates if the average rate of return is used or, if they are using NPV, the interest rate that is current should produce a positive net present value.

Using the interest rate as a criterion does involve a number of problems, however. First, many investment projects are long term and expenditure and returns may take place over many years. It is highly unlikely that interest rates will remain unchanged for this period of time. Therefore managers have to decide on a rate or range of rates to use in their calculations.

Second, investments involve risks – we consider this more fully in the section below. When choosing a minimum rate of return the management team has to build in an allowance for risk.

The level of profit

We saw in the chapter on interpreting company accounts that a series of ratios can be used to assess the profitability of a business. One of these (return on capital employed or ROCE) provides a figure which measures profits generated against the value of resources available to the business. It is not unusual for a business to set itself targets in terms of ROCE. Managers may insist that any new investment project should generate returns which will at least match (and hopefully exceed) the business's overall target for ROCE.

Alternative investments

It would be unusual for a business to consider only a single investment project. Most managers contemplating a major investment will have other options. These could be very different investments or simple variants on the first proposal. The business may simply select the project or projects which perform the best subject to some minimum criteria in terms of profits or percentage returns. In such circumstances opportunity cost is an important concept for managers to bear in mind.

Assessing the risks and uncertainties of investment decisions

It is not a simple matter to assess the degree of risk involved in an investment decision. Risk is the chance of something adverse or bad happening. In the context of investment decisions there are two broad

BUSINESS IN FOCUS

IAG bid for bmi looks set to go ahead

The International Airlines Group (formed through the merger of British Airways and Spain's Iberia) has pledged to target booming Asian destinations from Heathrow airport if it is successful in its takeover bid for rival airline bmi.

Willie Walsh, IAG chief executive, rejected concerns that the deal will put a fares squeeze on consumers as he promised to use bmi's take-off and landing slots as bridgeheads to cities in China, Korea, Vietnam and Indonesia. The Asia-Pacific region has become the financial powerhouse of the aviation industry but Walsh and Heathrow owner BAA have long complained that the airport's growth constraints are preventing the development of new routes.

'We don't fly to places like Korea, Indonesia, Vietnam. There are a lot of destinations in Asia that are booming,' he said, adding that building links with Asian cities was 'absolutely critical' for the UK economy and IAG's long-haul business. 'The potential growth in Asia is way in excess of anything we will see around Europe.'

(Source: Dan Milmo in The Guardian, *4 November 2011)*

Question:

Analyse the criterion (or criteria) that IAG might have used to judge the value of its proposed investment in buying bmi. *(10 marks)*

possibilities: costs may be higher than forecast or sales lower than expected.

Forecasting future sales can be a very difficult, and often expensive, exercise. Market research can be used, but it is costly and not always reliable. The difficulties in forecasting sales arise from a number of factors.

- **Timescales**. It is much harder to forecast sales accurately many years into the future. Over a longer timescale it is more likely that tastes and fashions may change or that new competitors or new products may enter the market.
- **New markets**. If an investment project is based on a business entering a new market (either in geographical or product terms) then the business has less experience and no financial records to use as a guide in forecasting sales. In 2011 Tesco

announced that it was pulling out of Japan having failed to break into one of the world's toughest retail markets. Operating costs proved to be high and sales figures did not reach expectations. Apparently even one of Britain's largest companies does not find it easy to forecast its sales accurately.

- **Competitors' reactions**. Deciding on a particular programme of investment may bring a business into competition with rivals in news ways. Entering a new market (as in the case of Tesco above), producing new products or developing new methods of production may all provoke a response from competitors. This may take the form of increased advertising, cutting prices or bringing out new products. Each of these actions will impact on the sales associated with the investment project. However, not knowing the type or extent of reaction in advance makes it very difficult to estimate its effect on future sales.

Equally, costs may rise above the forecast level, reducing the returns from the investment, as we saw earlier with Tesco's unsuccessful expansion into Japan. In 2011 the price of oil rose to over $125 per barrel, reducing the profit margins of many companies including airlines such as Virgin. Since this high point in spring 2011 the price of oil has dropped markedly. Its lowest point in the year has been a little over $80 a barrel. At the time of writing, in November 2011, its price is around $110 per barrel. The volatility of prices for such a fundamentally important product highlights the difficulties that firms face when attempting to forecast future costs of production.

Managers may seek to identify and manage the risk in investment decisions by taking a range of actions, including the following.

- **Purchasing raw materials on forward markets.** This means that the firm concerned negotiates a price at the present time for a product to be delivered at some agreed date in the future. For example, many airlines have agreed future prices for the delivery of aviation fuel and therefore know for certain this element of their future costs. Although it removes the risk of a sudden increase in costs, it may be judged a mistake if prices fall between agreeing the deal and the delivery of the product.

- **Building in allowances for fluctuations in sales revenue and costs.** Prudent managers may opt to forecast a range of sales figures and costs of production which are based on their market research, but which allow for the market to change in some way that may be either adverse or favourable. Building in this flexibility in forecasting, and thinking about how wide the ranges for sales revenue and costs should be, will help managers to judge the degree of risk as well as the value of an investment project.

- **Ensuring the business has sufficient financial assets available.** If a business is trading in a volatile or rapidly changing market it would be sensible to make certain the business has sufficient resources to deal with any adverse circumstances. Tesco plans to quadruple its sales in China to £4 billion by 2014. The company is likely to have sufficient finance to support its ambitious plans even if sales do prove to be below forecasts for an extended period of time.

BUSINESS IN FOCUS

Southwest Airlines' hedging strategy

Southwest Airlines is an American low-cost airline based in Dallas, Texas. It is the largest airline in the United States by number of passengers carried domestically per year (as of 31 December 31 2007). In 2011 Southwest operated approximately 3,400 flights each day. The company buys enormous quantities of aviation fuel (it amounts to about 30 per cent of the airline's total costs) and for many years has operated a very successful strategy of hedging against oil price rises.

What is hedging? Hedging is a financial strategy that lets airlines or other investors protect themselves against rising prices for commodities such as oil by locking in a price for fuel. It has been described as everything from gambling to buying insurance.

In 2008, Southwest Airlines paid $1.98 per gallon for fuel. American Airlines paid $2.73, and United paid $2.83 per gallon in the same period. For many years hedging its expenditure on fuel has saved Southwest billions of dollars. It has sometimes meant the difference between profit and loss. However, the company's fuel strategy can also go wrong. ➡

Question:

Discuss the case for and against Southwest Airlines continuing its fuel hedging strategy. *(18 marks)*

Is it worth using techniques of investment appraisal?

The results of investment appraisal calculations are only as good as the data on which they are based. Firms experience difficulty in accurately forecasting the cost of many major projects. It is even more difficult to estimate the likely revenues from investment projects, particularly long-term ones. It is perhaps possible to make an allowance to represent risk (for example, the possibility of a competitor taking actions that result in sales being lower than forecast) by perhaps reducing cash inflows or increasing costs. More sophisticated techniques use the theory of probability to attempt to arrive at more accurate predictions.

Risk should be distinguished from uncertainty. Uncertainty is not measurable and cannot be included in numerical techniques of investment appraisal. An investment project which appears to have a high degree of uncertainty attached to it may not be undertaken because the firm in question may be unable to assess its likely costs and benefits. Uncertainty may make any investment appraisal worthless.

In assessing the value of numerical techniques of investment appraisal, some thought has to be given to the alternative. Without the use of payback and the like, managers would operate on the basis of hunches and guesswork. Some managers may have a good instinct for these matters, whereas others may not. As markets become more complex and global, the need for some technique to appraise investments becomes greater. It is more difficult for an individual or a group to have an accurate overview of a large international market comprising many competitors and millions of diverse individuals. Detailed market research to forecast possible revenues and the use of appropriate techniques of investment appraisal may become even more important in the future.

Qualitative influences on investment appraisal

The financial aspects of any proposed investment will clearly have an important influence upon whether a business goes ahead with the plan. However, a number of other issues may affect the decision.

- **Corporate image.** A firm may reject a potentially profitable investment project, or choose a less profitable alternative, because to do otherwise might reflect badly on the business. Having a positive corporate image is important in terms of long-term sales and profits and may be considered more important than gaining short-term advantage from profitable investments. In the UK the National Westminster Bank has invested heavily in internet banking and had planned to close many high-street branches as part of this investment programme. However, the bad publicity given to branch closures by all banks led the National Westminster to reverse the closure decision. The firm's investment in internet banking may prove less profitable as a consequence.
- **Corporate objectives.** Most businesses will only undertake an investment if they consider that it will assist in the achievement of corporate objectives. For example, Rolls-Royce Engineering, a company that publicly states its aim to produce high-quality products, may invest heavily in training for its staff and in research and development. This will assist in the manufacture of world-class aero engines and vehicles.
- **Environmental and ethical issues.** These can be important influences on investment decisions. Some firms have a genuine commitment to trading ethically and to inflicting minimal damage on the environment. This is a core part of the business philosophy of some firms. As a consequence they would not exploit cheap Third World labour or use non-sustainable resources. Other firms may have a less deep commitment to ethical and environmental trading but may avoid some investments for fear of damaging publicity.

- **Industrial relations.** Some potentially profitable investments may be turned down because they would result in a substantial loss of jobs. Taking decisions that lead to large-scale redundancies can be costly in terms of decreased morale, redundancy payments and harm to the business's corporate image.

BUSINESS IN FOCUS

Tesco aims to be carbon neutral by 2050

Tesco, Britain's largest retailer and one of the world's largest supermarket chains, has a fleet of vehicles appropriate to its size. In the UK, it operates 1,600 tractor units and 2,800 home delivery vans. Tesco says its British secondary distribution alone covers the same mileage every year as 377 round trips to the moon. On a daily basis, the fleet's mileage would circle the earth 20 times, the company boasts.

But Tesco – like most other big companies in all sectors – is aiming for superlatives of another kind, as it seeks to cut costs and to reduce the environmental footprint of its fleet.

The company says that its carbon reduction initiatives have saved 83 million miles worth of trips. As part of its corporate social responsibility goals, Tesco aims to be carbon-neutral by 2050, and to cut its carbon emissions on its deliveries 50 per cent by the 2012–13 financial year, compared with 2006–7.

Alex Laffey, Tesco's network development director, says the company's focus on stringent environmental goals is no gimmick – although he is also clear in stating that cutting CO_2 also helps the bottom line. 'Reducing carbon reduces cost', he says.

(Source: John Reed in the Financial Times, 20 October 2011)

Question:

Do you think that qualitative or quantitative factors would have influenced Tesco more strongly when reaching this decision? Justify your decision. *(10 marks)*

Key terms

Investment appraisal is a series of techniques designed to assist businesses in judging the desirability of investing in particular projects.

Profit is the surplus of revenues over total costs at the end of a trading period.

Cash flow is the movement of cash into and out of a business over a period of time.

Return on capital employed (ROCE) is the net profits of a business expressed as a percentage of the value of the capital employed in the business.

Discounting is the reducing of the value of future earnings to reflect the opportunity cost of an investment.

Present value is the value of a future stream of income from an investment, converted into its current worth.

Examiner's advice

Do not spend too long on investment appraisal calculations and do not carry out the same calculation repeatedly. If your answer is incorrect and you use it to support an argument in a later answer the examiner will credit it (in the later answer) as if it was accurate.

Investment criteria can be useful to you when responding to examination questions on investment appraisal. When judging whether or not a business should go ahead with a particular investment, it is important to think what criteria the business would expect the investment to meet. The case study may directly state these or they may be implied. In either case, by relating your answer to the criterion or criteria you have a basis for making a judgement that you are able to justify. ➡

It is essential to think about quantitative and qualitative factors when making decisions on investment projects. Most case studies will include some qualitative issues for you to weigh up, and a top-quality answer will take these into account as well as any quantitative information.

Progress questions

1 Outline **three** business decisions that may require the application of investment appraisal techniques. *(9 marks)*

2 Explain why forecasts of sales revenues arising from an investment may prove to be inaccurate. *(7 marks)*

3 Why might investment appraisal be easier to conduct in a stable economic environment? *(7 marks)*

4 Thames Radio is contemplating investing in new broadcasting equipment. The cost of the investment is forecast to be £150,000. The expected additional revenue from being able to broadcast to a larger area is £40,000 per annum. What is the payback period of this investment? *(5 marks)*

5 Explain one disadvantage of using payback in the circumstances in question 4. *(4 marks)*

6 Outline the stages that have to be completed to carry out an average rate of return calculation. *(6 marks)*

7 Wessex Leisure is considering the purchase of a pleasure cruiser for use on the Solent. The *Meriden* is available at a cost of £900,000 and would cost £100,000 each year to operate. Over its ten-year life the cruiser would generate £280,000 in revenue each year. Calculate the average rate of return on this investment. *(7 marks)*

8 Explain what is meant by the 'present value' of a stream of earnings from an investment. *(5 marks)*

9 Chedgrave Printers Ltd is appraising the costs of and benefits from a new piece of machinery. The equipment costs £300,000 and has a working life of four years. The company expects to generate revenue of £120,000 each year if it purchases the machine. Calculate the net present value of this project assuming an interest rate of 10 per cent. *(7 marks)*

10 Outline **two** qualitative factors that an oil company may consider as part of the appraisal of a proposed investment to extract oil from the seabed under the English Channel. *(6 marks)*

Evaluation question

✗ These questions relate to the case study on page 5.

Do you agree that the returns on the company's proposed investment are 'excellent'? You should use relevant calculations to support your decision. *(18 marks)*

Candidate's answer:

The key measures to appraise an investment are average rate of return and net present value.

The ARR of this investment:

Its profit over five years is £279.9 million and so its yearly average figure is £55.98 million. This means that the ARR is £55.98 million ÷ £350 million = 15.99 per cent.

This is a good return when judged against the interest the company might receive if it held the money in a bank account at the moment, so in this regard Kevin is correct. But the company achieved a ROCE figure of 29.56 per cent on its trading in 2011 and, when compared with this, Kevin's judgement that these figures are 'excellent' seems very wrong.

The table below shows that the investment does produce a positive net present value result after five years. However, this is a relatively low figure for such a large investment and also does not seem to support Kevin's view.

Year	Annual cash flow (£m)	Discounting factor	Present value (£m)
0	(350)	1	(350)
1	36.6	0.909	33.27
2	72.3	0.826	59.72
3	99.1	0.751	74.42
4	142.0	0.683	96.99
5	179.9	0.621	111.72
Present value			26.12

I do not think that Kevin was correct in his judgement. These figures do not appear to be excellent and I think he was wrong.

Examiner's comments:

This answer has a lot of good elements, although it ends rather abruptly. There is an elementary error in calculating the average rate of return (an extra £100 million has been added to total profits) but the candidate has interpreted the answer thoughtfully and made an excellent comparison with the ROCE figure achieved by the business's existing operations. This is the highlight of this response as they have used other data within the case study to justify a decision.

They have also calculated the net present value accurately and have made a clear judgement about it in relation to Kevin's opinion. However, a shortcoming is that the candidate did not offer clear support for their overall judgement. This was a pity as there was clear evidence elsewhere which could have been drawn together.

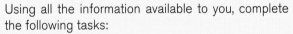

Analysis question

Using all the information available to you, complete the following tasks:

- analyse the arguments **in favour of** the proposed strategy

- analyse the arguments **against** the proposed strategy

- make a justified recommendation on whether this strategy should be adopted. *(34 marks)*

Marketing at A2

When you studied marketing at AS level the focus was on how medium-sized businesses changed their marketing activities to make the business more successful. For example, you may have considered changing the price to boost revenue or switching from one form of promotional activity to another. At A2 we are interested in 'the bigger picture'. We want to know more about why a business decides to compete in one market rather than another or why it chooses to offer one product line rather than another. We are also interested in the strategy businesses choose to use to compete against their rivals. For example, do they decide to compete with a low price strategy or by offering a premium product or service? How should managers position their business relative to the competition? Of course issues such as whether to spend money on advertising or your sales team matter but a fundamental question is should you be in that market to begin with and do you have the right strategy?

The study of marketing at A2 therefore includes:

- understanding the fundamentals of a market such as its growth and the trends of particular segments
- marketing strategy – how a business competes and positions itself relative to the competition
- marketing plans – detailed breakdowns stating the marketing objectives, strategy and budget and also showing how a strategy will be implemented and the objectives achieved.

Case study for Section 2: Aspire plc

Mark Frantini had recently been appointed as Chief Executive of Aspire plc, a UK coffee shop business. The company had been experiencing disappointing financial results and so Mark had been appointed to transform the business.

Mark commissioned a full analysis of market conditions by an external consultancy as well as an internal review of the business's strengths and weaknesses. Following this audit he and the directors analysed the strengths and weaknesses of the business

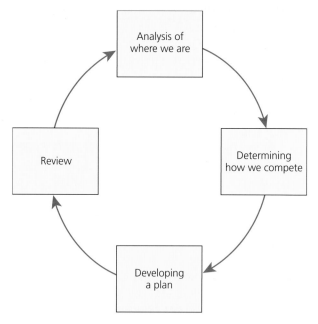

Figure 6.0 Analysis of where we are

in relation to the potential opportunities and threats. Mark believed the future lay in expansion overseas – in particular China. Obviously the population there was much bigger than in the UK and the economic growth was attractive relative to the UK. 'Starbucks and Costa have proved it can be done and are opening more than one store a week there – there is plenty of room for us as well. Coffee consumption per person is extremely low at present but is growing by over 20 per cent a year.' said Mark. Some of the other directors were not so convinced and felt there was still room for growth in the UK; they had built the business up cautiously and worried about major changes. 'I accept it is risky,' said Mark 'but we need to take more risks if we are to return to a strong financial position. We are faced with a highly competitive domestic market where several other coffee chains have gone out of business recently and we are getting squeezed by the fast food outlets such as Pret A Manger and McDonald's. Add to this high inflation in the UK and rising coffee bean prices worldwide and something has to change.'

The level of expansion Mark wanted would require an investment of £200 million in the first five years but he felt the long-term rewards would be worth it.

Susan, the company's marketing director, was clearly concerned by Mark's strategy. Although excited by the idea of a very new venture she had no experience at all of overseas markets and so would be relying heavily on outside advice; with 15 years' experience of marketing the business in the UK a move to China was well out of her comfort zone. She also knew that several other business such as Walmart and Marks & Spencer had struggled with their overseas operations in the past. 'We have a well-established brand in the UK with a 15 per cent market share. Why not build on that?' she said at the last directors' meeting. Mark seemed very confident. Perhaps too confident she thought; after all, his international experience was limited to a couple of years working in France fairly early in his retail career, and with a young family would he really want to spend lots of time abroad?

'I am not worried about our apparent inexperience,' he said. 'I intend to find a local partner so we can work with them to build the business rather than going in blind. My marketing objective is to open 1,000 outlets in the next five years.' Susan thought it was wrong to set such a specific target when there was so much uncertainty about the markets and so many of their competitors were clearly thinking along the same lines in terms of targeting China; and Aspire had no brand awareness there at all. However, she could tell already that Mark was a determined character and could be very persuasive. 'You've brought me in to do a job so let me get on with it,' he said recently to the directors. 'It's clear this business lacks coordination and leadership so that's what I am here to change.'

Appendices

Appendix A: Market size and forecast

	Total (£m)	Index (base = 100 in 2010)	% annual change	£m	Index	% annual change
2005	665	55	n/a	778	64	n/a
2006	834	68	25.4	950	78	22.2
2007	1,035	85	24.1	1,142	94	20.2
2008	1,155	95	11.6	1,223	100	7.1
2009	1,195	98	3.5	1,232	101	0.7
2010 (est.)	1,218	100	1.9	1,218	100	-1.1
2011 (forecast)	1,269	104	4.2	1,231	101	1.0
2012 (forecast)	1,315	108	3.6	1,238	102	0.6
2013 (forecast)	1,376	113	4.7	1,257	103	1.6
2014 (forecast)	1,437	118	4.4	1,273	105	1.3
2015 (forecast)	1,505	124	4.8	1,294	106	1.7

Table 1 Market size and forecast (2005–15) of coffee shops

(Source: Mintel 2011)

Appendix B: GDP forecasts

	UK	China
2013	1.1%	9%
2014	2.3%	9.5%
2015	2.4%	9.6%
2016	2.5%	9.9%
2017	2.7%	10.1%

Table 2 Forecasts of GDP (value of output of economy) growth for UK and China

Appendix C: Index of prices

	Index (base = 100 in 2008)
2008	100
2009	89
2010	103
2011	161
2012	188

Table 3 Index of prices of coffee beans, 2008–12

Appendix D: Comparative populations in 2010

Population of China: 1,338 million.
Population of UK: 62.2 million.

Appendix E: coffee consumption

	2005 (kg)	2009 (kg)	% change 2005–09
Germany	6.3	6.5	+3.0
Canada	5.2	5.9	+14.5
Italy	5.7	5.9	+3.0
France	4.7	5.4	+13.8
Spain	4.2	4.5	+6.9
US	4.2	4.1	−1.7
Japan	3.4	3.4	+0.0
Netherlands	7.1	3.3	−54.1
United Kingdom	2.7	3.1	+17.6

Table 4 Per person consumption of coffee in selected countries, 2005 and 2009

Appendix F: Current sources of long-term finance

- Borrowing via loans: £250 million
- Share capital: £100 million
- Retained profits: £150 million

6 Understanding marketing objectives

Marketing activities need a focus. To market anything effectively you need to know what it is you are trying to achieve (the marketing objective). Are you trying to increase demand? If so by how much and when? Which products in particular are you trying to push? On which markets are you focusing? By defining exactly what you want to achieve it is easier to plan.

In this chapter we consider:

- the meaning of marketing
- the meaning and significance of marketing objectives
- the internal and external influences on marketing objectives.

What is marketing?

Marketing is the process by which a firm tries to identify, anticipate and satisfy customers' needs and wants and at the same time meet its own objectives. A firm will aim to provide goods and services that customers want and in return it will usually seek to generate a profit. Marketing therefore involves an exchange process in which both sides hope to benefit.

Effective marketing requires a good understanding of customers' requirements. This is usually achieved through primary or secondary market research, although in some cases managers may rely on their experience and intuition; for example if a decision has to be made quickly or markets are changing so rapidly that past data is of limited use.

Marketing activities help organisations understand their customers. They also influence the customers' decisions to buy the product.

According to the American Marketing Association (2004), 'Marketing is an organizational function and set of processes for creating, communicating and delivering value to customers and for managing customer relationships in a way that benefits both the organization and the stakeholder.'

As you can see from this:

- Marketing is a function of the business, that is, it is an element or part of the business. Whether or not it is a separate department all organisations however small will engage in marketing activities – after all they have a product, they need to make people aware of it, they need a price for it and they need to make it available. Other business functions include finance, human resource management and operations. These functions must interact effectively for the overall corporate plan to be successful.
- Marketing is a process. This means that it is a series of stages rather than a one-off action. For example, managers will analyse the market to identify the market segments that exist. They will then target segments of interest and decide how to position the business relative to the competition. This is a process of segmentation, targeting and positioning (STP).
- Marketing can involve many different individuals and groups (known as stakeholders); when you are selling toys for example you are affecting the children who want the toys and the parents who may have to buy them and both these groups need to be considered in the process. The government will also be involved because it has introduced regulations on how you can promote these products as well as safety and labelling laws.
- Marketing involves a relationship between the buyer and seller. In the past we have tended to see marketing as a one-off transaction. For example, when you sold someone a car the aim was to find the right car for the buyer so the customer would feel he or she received value for money.

However, businesses are increasingly realising the high level of costs and additional difficulties of finding new customers compared with keeping existing ones. For example, a car dealership would aim to provide customers with all the cars they wanted during their lives; the dealership would understand the needs of customer, provide a high-quality service and keep the customer informed of relevant new models and provide incentives to try and encourage them to come back. The idea would be to lock someone in to being a 'Lexus customer' or a 'Ford woman'. It is much better to get your existing customers to keep coming back

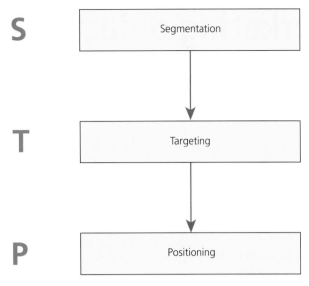

Figure 6.1 STP

to you than to have to rely on constantly finding new ones. Marketing managers are increasingly trying to build relationships with customers: frequent flier plans, customer loyalty cards, newsletters and updates for customers are all ways of building a relationship. For instance, once you have searched for books on Amazon you will find suggestions for similar books that you might like; the company is trying to provide you with additional services to build the relationship, so you trust its advice and want to come back and buy more from it.

Marketing can refer to a business, a person, a place, an idea … in fact anything at all! In politics these days great use is made of focus groups to understand what electors want, and this often influences the policy of a political party. Marketing was needed to secure London's bid for the 2012 Olympics. This highlighted the importance of stakeholders – those bidding for London had to understand the needs of the Olympic Committee which awards the bid, the local communities in London, the athletes, the UK government, the spectators and also future generations as it involved a major investment in facilities for the future. Anything and everything involves marketing, not just cans of cola or bars of chocolate.

Responsibility for marketing activities

Who is responsible for marketing and what does it involve? This depends. An entrepreneur who has just started up may have to do everything: marketing, finance and operations. In a bigger business there is likely to be a specialist department; there may even be several different sections to the marketing department. There may be people responsible for the various products the business offers, or different divisions or regions; there may be a sales team making contacts with potential clients, a research department gathering and analysing data and a brand manager controlling brand positioning and image. The precise jobs and priorities within the marketing function will depend on the nature of the business. In the soft drinks industry, for example, marketing may involve heavy expenditure on mainstream advertising to generate demand. In the industrial equipment market a sales team may be the central element of the marketing team; advertising may be less significant. In some industries exhibitions and launch events are vitally important (think of the opening of a new film or a new Apple product), other sectors rely a great deal on sponsorship (such as sports events and Formula 1) because this reinforces the brand, others try to generate a great deal of press coverage (think of Ryanair and Virgin), some use viral marketing (such as the famous Cadbury ads with the gorilla drumming); the communication mix is enormously varied.

Key issues

Advances in technology make it easier to find suppliers of products online. Advances in transportation make it easier to move products around the world. Trade agreements are making it easier to enter markets. These factors all combine to make markets more competitive. This makes it even more important for firms to understand their customers properly and meet their needs effectively if they want to survive and prosper and remain competitive. Technology also enables a business to track their customers more effectively and target their communications more effectively. For instance, using Google ads you can target someone using a specific search term from a specific city.

The way that businesses communicate varies enormously between industries and between organisations. Mass-market consumer products such as bottled water products may rely on heavy levels of mainstream advertising whereas service industries such as accountants, cosmetic surgeons and dentists may rely more on word of mouth.

Brand	Advertiser	2010	Total 2008–10	Market share
		£000	£000	%
Volvic	Danone	1,410	3,962	15
Buxton	Nestlé	1,464	3,537	13
Evian	Danone	1,065	3,203	12
Drench	Britvic	841	2,888	11
Isklar	Isklar	775	2,687	10
Highland Spring	Highland Spring	819	2,627	10
Robinsons Fruit Shoot H2O	Britvic	–	2,263	9
Glacéau vitamin water	Coca-Cola GB	661	1,746	7
Total of all producers		8,242	26,206	100

Table 6.1 Mainstream advertising spend in the bottled water market, by brands, 2008–10

Questions:

1 Analyse why producers in the bottled water market use high levels of advertising. *(10 marks)*

2 To what extent does this act as a barrier for other businesses wanting to enter this market? *(14 marks)*

Market-oriented businesses

A market-oriented business is one where the customer is placed at the heart of everything the organisation does. Everyone in the business thinks about decisions from the perspective of the customer. This approach can be seen in the highly successful Zara fashion retailer. Zara store managers monitor their local market and twice a week they contact their manufacturing base directly to order items for the store based on the information they have gathered. The business holds relatively little stock because it orders so frequently. As a result it rarely reduces prices to get rid of slow selling items.

Figure 6.2 Zara

Questions:

1 Discuss the possible reasons why some organisations, such as Zara, are more market oriented than others. *(14 marks)*

2 Analyse two ways in which a business can try to ensure it is market oriented. *(6 marks)*

What are marketing objectives?

A marketing objective is the target or targets set for the marketing function. As with all targets, these should not be imposed on individuals but discussed and negotiated with them so that they believe the objectives are feasible, understand the logic behind them and are committed to achieving them.

Typically, marketing objectives might include the following:

- **Sales targets** – for example, managers may have to boost overall sales by 15 per cent in a year, or achieve specific sales targets for particular products or particular customer groups. For example, a business may be eager to push sales of some services more than others perhaps because they provide a bigger profit margin or it may be trying to grow sales in some areas more than others. For instance, in 2011 Mothercare's performance in the UK was disappointing and it announced a shift in focus and set ambitious sales growth targets in markets such as China and India where the potential market was much bigger.
- **Market share** – sales targets will often be set in terms of market share. For example, when a product is first launched it might have a target of achieving a 10 per cent market share within two years. An absolute sales figure may not be effective enough because it does not take account of overall market conditions. Imagine your sales increase from £200,000 to £220,000 but meanwhile the market has increased by 200 per cent – your performance would seem poor. If, however, your sales increased from £200,000 to £220,000 while the market shrank then you have done well. By measuring your market share you get an idea of how you are performing relative to others.
- **Brand awareness** – a company may feel that it is not recognised enough and not included on customers' 'shopping lists' when they are thinking of possible suppliers. They might therefore develop a promotional campaign to raise awareness (also called 'share of the mind'). This might be the first stage of a campaign to increase market share in the future. For instance, Skoda has been trying to reposition itself as a brand for many years to build a stronger reputation as a high quality producer of cars.

Any objective should be:

- specific – it should be clear exactly what the business is trying to achieve
- measurable – it should be clear how much the specific item is expected to change
- time specific – it should be clear by when a target should be achieved.

For example a marketing objective might be to increase market share by 5 per cent in the next five years.

BUSINESS IN FOCUS

Philip Kotler

Philip Kotler (born 1931) is Professor of Marketing at the Kellogg School of Management. His book *Marketing Management*, published in 1967, is a classic marketing textbook and bestseller; by 2006 there were 12 different editions. In this book he developed a systematic approach to marketing in a way that had never been done before. According to Kotler, 'Marketing is not the art of finding clever ways to dispose of what you make. Marketing is the art of creating genuine customer value. It is the art of helping your customers become better off.'

Kotler has argued that the process of marketing develops over time, as does our understanding of what it does or should involve. At first Kotler focused on marketing as a transaction. Now he pays much more attention to relationship marketing – the idea that firms need to build customer loyalty and engage in a series of transactions with them during their relationship.

(*Sources:* Marketing Management: Analysis, Planning, Implementation and Control, *Prentice Hall, 1967; 12th edn, 2006; material adapted from Economist.com, 12 September 2008*)

Question:

Analyse two examples of relationship marketing. (8 marks)

Influences on marketing objectives

The marketing objective must be derived directly from the corporate objective. Does the business want to grow? How much? In what areas? In which markets? Is it trying to spread risk by building a broader portfolio or is it trying to specialise?

Imagine a restaurant that is booked up months in advance and without any space to fit in more customers. The corporate objective in this case might aim to sustain the existing scale of the business but not actually increase it because the managers do not want to take the risk of increasing capacity. If, on the other hand, the directors were pursuing a growth strategy and opening up several new restaurants per month (for example, in the way that Costa Coffee has grown rapidly in recent years), the marketing function would be working hard to identify new areas of demand to fulfil this growth strategy and the sales target would be higher than last year. The precise nature of the marketing objective will therefore depend on the culture of the business. Are managers ambitious and will they set high targets that stretch individuals? Or are they more conservative and likely to consolidate before expanding further? Are they innovative and constantly looking to launch new products and develop new markets, or do they prefer to focus on the core established business?

The setting of the corporate and therefore the marketing objective will be influenced by internal and external factors.

Internal factors

- **Operations** – the capacity of the business will limit how much can be produced. For instance, Wembley Stadium has a capacity of around 90,000 so there is no point trying to sell more tickets than this. The Boeing A380 has seats for around 550 passengers so again this sets a limit to how many tickets can be sold. The operations process will also affect the quality of the product and the flexibility that can be offered (for example, the variety that can be provided). Particular strengths in operations (for example, the speed of delivery or excellent design) are likely to feed in to the marketing strategy, and therefore the marketing objectives. Of course, the relationship is two-way; a sudden boost in bookings for your gig may mean you put on another performance – so marketing can affect operations.
- **Human resources** – what a business is capable of producing will depend on the skills, attitudes and motivation of its staff. A business with a high level of diversity in its workforce, for example, may be in a relatively strong position to expand overseas because it may understand the cultures and needs of those markets better than its competitors. A highly skilled workforce may enable a business to offer high quality service whereas a business with unskilled labour may focus more on lower costs to affect its likely volume of sales.
- **Finance** – the finance function will determine what is affordable and what will generate an acceptable return on investment. A lack of finance may prevent the marketing manager from undertaking many of the activities he or she would like to. The finance function will influence the amount that can be spent on marketing, which is included in the marketing budget. When sales are falling, for example, you may want to set an objective of increasing them again, but this may require heavy investment at a time when funds are not easily available.

External factors

What is realistic as an objective will be affected by the external macro- and micro-environments. The macro-environment relates to factors well beyond the control of any one firm, such as political, economic, social, technological, environmental and legal factors (PESTEL). These changes may make sales more difficult to achieve. An ageing population might limit the sales of children's computer games. Technological advances might make certain consumer electronic products obsolete. Legal changes may limit sales opportunities; the banning of smoking in public places hit cigarette sales, for example. Equally, PESTEL changes may create more sales possibilities. The expansion of the European Union (a political change) may make it easier to sell in more countries abroad. A booming economy may make sales easier.

The effect of any given change in the macro-environment on the likely sales of a business will depend on the nature of the change and the nature of the business. A fall in UK national income will hit demand for income-elastic products such as city centre apartments, health clubs and cruise holidays more than income-inelastic products such as shampoo, toothpaste and socks. Greater interest in environmental issues may have a greater impact on the demand for flights and cars than on the demand for ties and bread.

The micro-environment refers to factors in the immediate environment of a business, such as its suppliers, customers, substitutes and competitors. A substitute product is different from yours but performs the same function; a big promotional campaign by flower growers may hit sales of boxed chocolates, for example, as both are gift products.

Actions by competitors may also make sales more difficult. The lower prices approach of Aldi and Costco started to hit sales of higher priced supermarkets in the UK in 2008, for example, as the country moved into an economic downturn. A marketing objective may have to be adjusted as competitors change their approaches and make you rethink what is feasible in the altered competitive landscape.

Figure 6.3 Factors affecting marketing objectives

Key issues

All planning should involve assessing the external environment and comparing this with internal resources in order to work out what to do next. The marketing objective will depend on the opportunities and threats of the external environment and the strengths and weaknesses of the internal environment.

Of course at any moment there are likely to be many different marketing objectives in different parts of the business and for different products and markets. You may be trying to consolidate the position of one product while entering a new market with another. Remember, large organisations are very complex, usually having many different divisions and departments in several countries around the world. This means there are many different marketing decisions being made consecutively.

Summary

The marketing function is the interface between the business and its customers. Without customers there is no revenue. The marketing function will set objectives on what it is trying to achieve; for example, a certain level of sales or a given market share in a given time period. These marketing objectives will be linked to the corporate objectives, that is, the marketing function will aim to help the business fulfil its overall targets.

One step further: relationship marketing

One of the main areas of interest in marketing in recent years has been the growth of customer relationship management. Businesses are looking to build long-term relationships with their customers. For example, a bank wants you to bank with it and wants to understand the various stages of your life so it can offer you:

- money for university
- money to buy your first flat
- money for your first house
- money for your holidays

and then to understand when to offer:

- pension advice
- investment advice
- insurance advice.

Amazon wants to understand what you like to read so it can offer you news of books you might like. So, marketing is no longer seen as a 'one-off' transaction – it is a series of ongoing experiences.

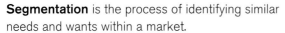

Key terms

Segmentation is the process of identifying similar needs and wants within a market.

Targeting is the process of selecting which segments to compete in.

Positioning is the process of deciding how a product is perceived relative to the competition.

A **marketing objective** is a target set for the marketing function.

Market share measures the sales of one product as a percentage of the total market sales. Market share = (your sales/total market sales) × 100 = per cent.

Sales growth occurs when the value (or volume) of sales increases.

A **marketing budget** consists of forward financial targets set for revenue and the amount to be spent

on marketing activities. The marketing expenditure budget will be broken down into spending on different activities such as online advertising, sponsorship deals, sales teams and direct mailings.

The **income elasticity of demand** measures the percentage change in the quantity demanded given a percentage change in income.

Income elastic means that the percentage change in quantity demanded is greater than the percentage change in income.

Income inelastic means that the percentage change in quantity demanded is less than the percentage change in income.

Examiner's advice

Remember that marketing is not just about 'making customers happy' – the business has to meet its objectives as well (for example, to make a profit). There are likely to be trade-offs between what customers want and what the organisation can offer with the resources it has. Remember also that marketing is not just about promoting something – it involves understanding what the business should be offering in the first place. It is a two-way, not a one-way process.

Also remember that decisions regarding the marketing mix can only be taken once you are clear what segment you are aiming for and how you intend to position your business. Don't rush to develop your communication message until you know who you are aiming it at and what you are trying to say, don't develop the offering until you know where it wants to sit next to competitors, don't set the price until you are sure what benefits you are offering and how much these are valued.

Marketing at A2 involves much more than just thinking about the marketing mix. You have to consider the

whole approach of the business – is it competing in the right markets? Does it have the right product portfolio? And how is it positioning itself relative to its competitors? If the marketing strategy is wrong then no matter how good the marketing mix is you will struggle. Imagine you were trying to run a video rental business from the high street – this market has all but disappeared and so no matter what you charge or how you promote it you are going to struggle.

Be aware that setting a marketing objective does not necessarily mean you will achieve it. This depends on how it was set (Is it realistic? Did the different groups involved agree to it?), and the strategy and resources behind it.

However, if there is no objective it is difficult to know where you are headed, whether you are on track and whether or not you need to take action. The objective enables you to think of the scale of the task, the resources needed to fulfil it and the best way of achieving it. It enables you to plan and coordinate your activities.

1 Define marketing. *(3 marks)*

2 Explain what is meant by a marketing objective. *(3 marks)*

3 Give an example of a marketing objective. *(3 marks)*

4 Explain **two** benefits of setting a marketing objective. *(5 marks)*

5 What is meant by 'the external environment'? *(3 marks)*

6 State four functions within a business. *(4 marks)*

7 Explain two internal influences on a firm's marketing objectives. *(6 marks)*

8 Explain two external influences on a firm's marketing objectives. *(6 marks)*

9 Explain what is meant by market share. *(3 marks)*

10 Explain what is meant by sales growth. *(3 marks)*

Analysis question

✄ These questions relate to the case study on page 72.

Analyse the benefits to Aspire plc of setting a clear marketing objective. *(12 marks)*

Candidate's answer:

A marketing objective is a target for the marketing department. It should be specific, measurable, agreed, realistic and time specific. For example, a marketing objective might be 'to increase sales by 20 per cent over three years'. Having an objective is a good idea because it sets out where the business wants to go and this means that everyone knows where they are and what they need to do. The marketing targets affect all aspects of the business. For example, your target sales affect the likely sales and therefore revenue and cash flow. The sales targets also affect the likely production required and therefore this might affect operations decisions affecting capacity and scheduling. The marketing objective therefore coordinates much of what happens with a business and enables other managers to plan.

Examiner's comments:

This is a very general answer and so would score relatively low marks. Although the student clearly knows a lot about marketing objectives this knowledge is not applied to the given situation. A good answer would relate to the specific target that Mark had set and how this might help in the context of entering a new market that was unfamiliar. The student has learnt what a marketing objective means (in some detail) and there is some attempt to analyse its value in general but it is a weak response because it shows no relation to what is happening in this business.

Evaluation question

Discuss the factors that might have influenced Mark to set a marketing objective of opening 1,000 outlets in the next five years. *(12 marks)*

7 Analysing markets and marketing

Before setting a marketing objective and before deciding how best to achieve it managers will want some understanding of market conditions. This means they will want to examine the market to find out more about it and decide what to do next. This is known as market analysis.

In this chapter we examine:

- the reasons for and value of market analysis
- methods of analysing market trends
- the use of information technology in analysing markets
- difficulties in analysing data.

What is market analysis?

Market analysis occurs when a firm undertakes a detailed examination of the characteristics of a market. This is an essential part of marketing planning. Only by knowing the features of a market will a firm be able to plan effectively what to do next. A good understanding of markets should help the business to target the right segments and to market its products effectively in a targeted way. A lack of analysis may mean the wrong markets are selected and/or the marketing is wasteful because it is not targeted effectively.

Analysing a market involves gaining an understanding of the following:

- **The market size.** This may be measured in terms of the volume or value of sales. For example, in the soft drinks market a firm may measure the number of cans or bottles sold (volume) or the monetary value of the total sales (value). A firm must ensure that the market is big enough to generate sufficient returns to make it worth competing in. If a market is only worth £2 million a year in revenue but would cost, say, £10 million to enter then it is unlikely to be worthwhile. Furthermore, a firm will be reluctant to enter a declining market. When measuring the change in the size of the market, the firm will want to examine what is happening to the value of sales as well as the volume. If it finds the volume of sales has been going up but the value has been falling, for example, this means the average price has been falling. Will it be able to make a profit if this continues? Markets can vary significantly from one region to another and from one country to another. Consumption of coffee in the UK has risen by about 20 per cent in the last

few years; in the US it has fallen slightly and in The Netherlands it has halved.

- **The market share of firms within the market.** This measures the sales of a firm relative to the total market size. In some markets, such as banking, airlines, petrol stations, sugar refining and pharmaceuticals, a few firms dominate. These are called oligopoly markets. In other markets there are no dominant firms – there are many smaller firms competing; for example, the hairdressing, advertising and taxi markets tend to have a large number of relatively small firms. The structure of a market can be measured by a concentration ratio. For example, a five-firm concentration ratio measures the market share of the largest five firms in a market.

Highly concentrated markets (those dominated by a few firms) include tobacco, soft drinks, sugar, pharmaceuticals and banking. Markets with low levels of concentration (those with many small firms) include farming, hairdressing and advertising.

A business will be measuring its own market share over time but also the changing shares of competitors – what are they doing to change their competitive position? It is important to consider share as well as the overall size of the market to assess relative performance. Imagine your sales have increased 5 per cent but the market is growing at 20 per cent – you are actually losing market share.

- **The likely costs and difficulties involved in entering the market.** What is the typical spending on marketing in the industry, for example? What are the main channels to market and how easy is it likely to be to access these? How brand loyal are customers? Entering the soft drinks market for example is difficult because the awareness and power of existing brands such as Coca-Cola is so strong.

- **Patterns and trends of sales.** For example, is the overall trend of sales upwards? At what rate is the market growing? The growth in demand for takeaway foods has been rapid in recent years, whereas the growth in demand for high-fat foods has been slower; this may affect new product development. Managers will also look for patterns within the overall trends. Are sales seasonal, for example? This could have implications for cash flow and production. (Think of sun cream, fireworks, school clothes, textbooks, garden furniture and holidays.) Are some segments growing faster than others (for example, the demand for mints has grown faster than the demand for chocolate within the overall confectionery market)? This could have implications for new product development.

You may also find, for example, trends in the where, how and why customers are buying products, which might create new possibilities. In recent years there has been growth in the sales of hot cereals (such as porridge) being eaten at breakfast, there has been a growth of alcohol consumed at home rather than in the pub and there has been decline in CD sales.

- **Substitute products.** Managers will be interested not only in the firm's core product, but also in substitute products and how likely customers are to switch. For example, if customers decide not to buy cereal then what else are they buying? Fruit? Toast? Yoghurt? Developments in these markets, such as new forms of yoghurt and a concerted push to increase their sales may for instance damage sales of cereal.

BUSINESS IN FOCUS

The UK smoothie market

After the recent economic downturn, consumers proved reluctant to increase their spending on items such as smoothies. Producers have tried to promote demand with new product development, such as the family pack 1.25 litre carton and the extended children's range launched by Innocent, but this has not been easy given the economic climate.

However, producers may gain from increasing health concerns and a perception that smoothies are healthier than other soft drinks like fruit juices.

Demographic changes may also help this market, with the growth of 25–34 year olds; this age group has a higher than average consumption of smoothies. Producers are also beginning to target the older buyer by including more fibre in the product. As a result sales of smoothies are predicted to grow steadily after a dip in the recession.

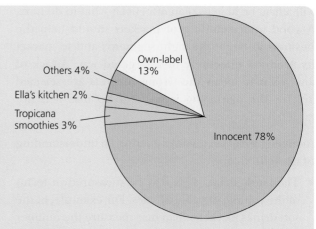

Figure 7.1 The smoothie market

Questions:

1 Analyse two factors affecting the demand for smoothies. *(10 marks)*
2 Discuss the possible problems there might be entering the smoothie market. *(14 marks)*

In marketing planning, as in all forms of planning, information is a vital resource. Getting good quality products on time, at a reasonable cost and to the right people can make a difference to the competitiveness of a business. Amazon understands what its customers have looked at in the past, so it can recommend suitable books that might interest them in the future. Google can display adverts that link only to the search term you used in the language you searched in. Banks can send you a chequebook before you run out of cheques. A hotel database can show that you prefer a ground floor room whenever you stay in these hotels. Tracking what customers do can help ensure marketing activities are tailor-made to individual requirements. Looking for ways of gathering, maintaining and using good information is a key issue.

Question:

Analyse two ways in which analysing markets more effectively might help a business. *(10 marks)*

Why analyse markets?

It may be possible to set a marketing objective and develop a plan to achieve this target without gathering or analysing any data. You could simply rely on a hunch or your 'gut feeling'. Akio Morita, for example, is said to have launched the hugely successful Sony Walkman with very little reference to market research. Steve Jobs at Apple said that market research was of little value because customers did not know what they wanted.

However, while this can obviously work it is likely to be a high-risk decision equivalent to trying to find your way around a house in the dark – you may get lucky but the chances are you will cause some damage. Gather valuable data and interpret it correctly and this is the equivalent of having the lights turned on – navigating your way around should be that much easier. You know where you are, you can see where you want to go and how to get there. The marketing spending by businesses can run into millions of pounds in some cases. Analysing markets should help to reduce risks and ensure marketing is focused and relevant and does not involve wasteful activities.

It is useful, therefore, to analyse the markets you are in or want to be in before you set an objective or develop a plan. Only when you know where you are and what is going on around you can you really set a target to say where you hope to end up in the future. Analysis is also important to determine where you are and what you might do next (i.e. it helps you assess the alternatives), and it helps you to assess the effectiveness of any action you take. If you are going to put resources into a particular marketing activity (advertising or promotion, for example) you need to know whether this will be a good use of funds.

By undertaking a market analysis a firm should be able to identify existing market conditions. However, analysis will also be used to predict where the market is going in the future. Analysis should help identify possible opportunities and threats for the future. An opportunity is a future possible event that could benefit a business. A threat is a future possible event that could harm the business. Opportunities may include particular segments that are likely to grow fast; threats may be markets that are about to decline.

Market analysis is important because markets differ so much and you need to understand the key issues in each one. Take the market for coach holidays, for example. This market has actually done quite well in recent years in terms of sales because when people had less spending money they chose a relatively cheap UK coach holiday compared to a more expensive holiday overseas. The market has also benefited from an ageing population because people who go on coach holidays tend to be older. On the other hand the market for tourist attractions (which includes museums, stately homes, zoos and theme parks) has suffered due to lower incomes – people have cut back on 'days out'. The ageing population and the decline in 15–24 year olds has shifted demand to stately homes from theme parks. Each market is unique and to do well in it you need to understand all kinds of issues, such as what influences demand, where people buy and what their attitudes to different aspects of the product are.

Deciding how to analyse a market will involve:

- deciding exactly what you need to know (and what you do not need to know)
- considering how much time and cost is involved
- considering the level of accuracy and detail required; this will affect factors such as the sample size and the amount spent on undertaking the research
- thinking about the risk if you get it wrong.

Methods of analysing trends

Managers are naturally interested in how markets will develop in the future as well as their present situation. It is important, therefore, for firms to look ahead when undertaking marketing. Marketing managers will be eager to forecast what sales in the market are going to be in the future. From this they can estimate the likely sales of their own products and produce their sales forecasts.

A firm's sales forecast sets out targets for overall sales and for particular products and services. It is a key element of a marketing plan and influences decisions throughout the organisation.

To understand market trends managers might use one or more of the following methods of analysing trends.

Moving averages

If you look at the following sales data and plot the figures on a chart, you will see that the sales are quite erratic during the year. In June, for example, sales are relatively high, whereas in July they are lower.

However, although the sales clearly change from month to month, the overall trend is clearly upwards.

One way of plotting the underlying trend is to calculate the moving average. This looks at several periods at a time and averages out the data; by doing this, the effect of particularly high or low figures is reduced because an average has been taken.

For example, for a three-month moving average we average out the figures for January, February and March. Then we average out February, March and April; then March, April and May, and so on.

The three-month moving average highlights the underlying trend of the sales figures, as shown in Figure 7.3.

	Sales £000		Three-month moving average £000
January	9		
February	12	(9 + 12 + 15)/3	12
March	15	(12 + 15 + 15)/3	14
April	15	(15 + 15 + 18)/3	16
May	18	(15 + 18 + 21)/3	18
June	21	(18 + 21 + 9)/3	16
July	9	(21 + 9 + 18)/3	16
August	18	(9 + 18 + 21)/3	16
September	21	(18 + 21 + 24)/3	21
October	24	(21 + 24 + 12)/3	19
November	12	(24 + 12 + 24)/3	20
December	24		

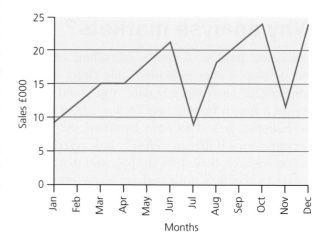

Figure 7.2 Sales

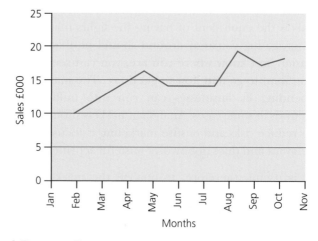

Figure 7.3 Three-month moving average

By using the moving average you get a better understanding of the underlying movement in a market.

Extrapolation

To estimate the future sales in a market, managers may look back to identify trends that have occurred (using, for example, moving averages) and then, based on these, predict forwards. This is known as extrapolation. When extrapolating you will, of course, take account of any underlying patterns in the data – for example, if sales tend to be higher in the December period because of Christmas sales you will build that in to any future projection.

This technique is useful, provided the trends identified in the past continue into the future. If, in fact, there has been a major shift in buying patterns (for example, the timing of buying has changed or the economy has unexpectedly entered a recession) extrapolation could provide a poor estimate of future sales.

The problem is that many markets are very dynamic and change rapidly. The market for cameras, for example, has seen rapid change in the last 20 years with the arrival of digital cameras; in this situation extrapolation may be very misleading – examining the past may provide little indication of what is going to happen in the future. Sales can drop suddenly regardless of what has happened in the past, perhaps due to a recession, competitors launching a new product or a problem with production. In the 1990s farmers could hardly have predicted the collapse in the sales of beef due to the BSE crisis. In 2001 they could not have foreseen foot-and-mouth disease. Similarly, Coca-Cola could not have predicted the short-term drop in sales in 2000 when it had to take some of its products off the shelves temporarily due to a health scare or Toyota when its cars experienced quality problems in 2011.

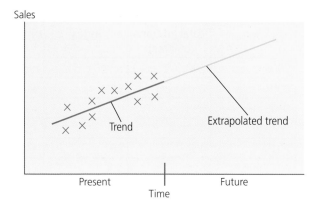

Figure 7.4 An extrapolated trend

Extrapolated figures must therefore be treated with caution – their reliability depends entirely on the extent to which the future will imitate the past. Obviously firms can learn from past trends – retail sales are likely to increase in the run-up to Christmas, holidays in Spain are more likely to be popular in the summer, central heating is likely to be used more when the weather is colder, and so on – but they must also look out for future changes in the market conditions. Rapid developments in technology, for example, can lead to major changes in terms of what we produce and how business is conducted, and this may make extrapolation more risky. Sales of netbook computers looked to be soaring upwards until tablets such as the Ipad were launched. In 2011 Mervyn King, the Governor of the Bank of England was reporting on the state of the economy and highlighted how difficult it was to predict what was going to happen tomorrow let alone next year, given the economic crisis with European currencies at the time – this would make extrapolation very dangerous.

BUSINESS IN FOCUS

Energy drinks

An index number shows a percentage change. In Table 7.1 the base (or starting point) is given as 100 and the percentage changes are worked out from this base point. Between 2011 and 2012, for example, the volume of sales is expected to increase from 528 million litres to 597 million litres. We could work

this out as a percentage ourselves but the index number does it for us: it goes from 100 to 113 showing there is a 13 per cent increase. Similarly, between 2010 and 2013 the index number goes from 100 to 129 showing a 29 per cent increase. The index for 2006 was 55 showing that sales then were 45 per cent less than 2010.

	Total (millions of litres)	Index	% annual change	Total (£m)	Index	% annual change
2006	293	55	n/a	625	54	n/a
2007	351	66	+19.8	750	65	+20.0
2008	380	72	+8.3	800	70	+6.7
2009	400	76	+5.3	850	74	+6.3
2010	467	88	+16.8	990	86	+16.5
2011 (est.)	528	100	+13.1	1,150	100	+16.2
2012 (forecast)	597	113	+13.1	1,314	114	+14.3
2013 (forecast)	683	129	+14.4	1,516	132	+15.4
2014 (forecast)	774	147	+13.3	1,730	150	+14.1
2015 (forecast)	864	164	+11.7	1,943	169	+12.3
2016 (forecast)	975	185	+12.8	2,208	192	+13.7

Table 7.1 Market forecasts for total energy/sports drinks in volume and value sales, 2006–16

Questions:

1 How much is the volume of sales of energy drinks expected to increase from 2010 to 2016?
(2 marks)

2 How much is the value of sales of energy drinks expected to increase from 2010 to 2016?
(2 marks)

3 Why can the changes in volume and value differ?
(3 marks)

Correlation

Rather than using extrapolation, future market sales may be estimated using correlation. This process attempts to identify whether there is any correlation between different variables and the level of sales. Correlation occurs when there appears to be a link between two factors. For example, a firm might discover a correlation between its sales and the level of income in an economy – with higher income consumer sales might increase. In the energy drinks market (see above) the key factors influencing consumption are levels of consumer expenditure and the number of men aged 15 to 24. In the market for hotels from overseas visitors key factors are UK inflation and the value of the UK currency in terms of foreign currencies.

Correlation analysis examines data to see if any relationship appears to exist between different variables. This is important for marketing managers because, if they can identify the key factors which determine demand for their goods, and they can estimate what is happening to these factors (e.g. estimate income growth), they can estimate total market sales and then their likely sales.

In Figures 7.5 and 7.6 you can see examples of different types of correlation.

- 'Positive correlation' means that there is a direct link between the variables. An increase in advertising, for example, might lead to an increase in sales and vice versa. The sales of a product might be positively correlated with income levels and the number of customers in the market.
- A 'negative correlation' means that the two factors are inversely related; an increase in price, for example, is likely to lead to a fall in sales, so price and demand have a negative correlation.

It is important to note that correlation analysis simply identifies an apparent link between the two factors; it does not show cause and effect. For example, there is often a strong link between coffee drinkers and smokers; people who smoke often drink a lot of coffee as well. There is a link between the two but this does not mean that drinking coffee actually makes you smoke or vice versa. It is important, therefore, to treat correlation figures with some caution. Just because sales figures and the amount of money spent on advertising expenditure are both increasing does not necessarily mean that the advertising is boosting

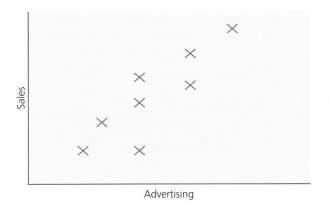

Figure 7.5 Positive correlation between advertising and sales

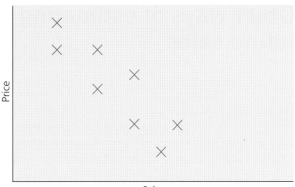

Figure 7.6 Negative correlation between price and sales

sales. In many cases firms feel that high sales mean they can spend more on advertising (that is, sales may determine advertising spending rather than vice versa). Alternatively, the increase in sales could be coincidental – it could be caused by factors other than advertising.

However, the more times a correlation appears to exist (for example, if a firm has regularly advertised and at the same time sales have regularly increased), the more likely it is that managers will believe that a link does exist.

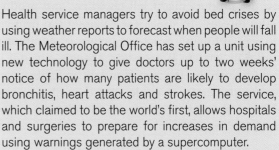

BUSINESS IN FOCUS

Tracking online activity

Market researchers are increasingly using online media as a means of gathering information. Studying the pattern of tweets on Twitter can you give an insight into the national mood, for example. (Not surprisingly, more people say they are feeling happy on national holidays!) By tracking moods researchers can estimate general spending and investment patterns. For example, there does seem to be some link between happiness, share purchases and share prices. Some firms are also looking at search engine data to estimate changes in sales for particular products or product categories. For example, when a new film comes out the number of people who start searching for information about it may give an early indication of its likely success.

Question:

To what extent do you think it might be useful to track online searches to predict sales? *(14 marks)*

BUSINESS IN FOCUS

Influences on health services

Health service managers try to avoid bed crises by using weather reports to forecast when people will fall ill. The Meteorological Office has set up a unit using new technology to give doctors up to two weeks' notice of how many patients are likely to develop bronchitis, heart attacks and strokes. The service, which claimed to be the world's first, allows hospitals and surgeries to prepare for increases in demand using warnings generated by a supercomputer.

In the past the National Health Service has been caught out by sudden changes in the number of patients suffering respiratory and cardiovascular diseases. Meteorological Office experts say the timing of these changes was due almost entirely to changes in temperature and climatic conditions. According to a spokesperson, 'there is a very close link between weather conditions and illness. We can predict almost the day when large numbers of patients will seek treatment.'

More patients die in Britain from weather-related illnesses than almost any other country in western Europe. For every one degree fall in temperature, 1.37 per cent more people die; this is much higher than in other countries because the British are less well prepared; they do not dress warmly against the cold, their houses are less well heated or insulated and they take less exercise.

(Source: The Sunday Times)

Question:

Discuss the factors that are likely to influence demand for healthcare services. *(14 marks)*

Other ways of estimating future sales

Using market research

Market research can be used to try to identify likely future trends rather than assuming they will be similar to the past. The value of this research depends on whether it is primary or secondary and the quality of the information received. If a small sample is used, for example, the forecast is less likely to be accurate than if a larger sample had been used. Types of research might include test marketing (trying the product out in a given area) or surveys. A test market is a representative selection of consumers which the firm uses to try out a new product. Having seen the results in the test market the firm can estimate how the product might sell elsewhere and produce a sales forecast. By using a test market the firm can also see customers' reactions before committing to a full-scale launch. If necessary, changes can still be made before the product is widely available. Many film companies, for example, show their films to a test audience before they go on general release, to assess the public's reaction.

The disadvantage of using test marketing is that competitors have an opportunity to see what you are planning to launch. This gives them time to develop a similar product and race you to launch first on a wide scale.

A test market may also give misleading results. This might be because the test market chosen is not representative or because competitors' actions lead to misleading results. For example, rivals might increase their promotional activities in the test market to reduce a firm's sales and lead it to believe that the new product will not do well.

Using your best guess

Managers could use their own experience or hire industry experts for their opinion of what is most likely to happen. This approach to forecasting is common if the rate of change in the market is great or if the firm is facing a new scenario and does not have past data to build on. In the Delphi technique, managers assemble a group of experts who are all asked individually for their views. These views are analysed and key areas extracted. These findings are circulated again to the experts for feedback.

BUSINESS IN FOCUS

The flawed market research of New Coke

In 1985 the chairman of Coca-Cola announced, 'the best has been made even better'. After 99 years the Coca-Cola company decided to abandon its original formula and replace it with a sweeter version named 'New Coke'. Just three months later the company admitted it had made a mistake and brought back the old version under the name 'Coca-Cola Classic'!

Despite $4 million of research the company had clearly made a huge mistake. The background to Coca-Cola's decision to launch a new product was that there was much slower growth in its sales in the 1970s, especially compared with Pepsi. Pepsi was also outperforming Coca-Cola in taste tests. The relatively poor performance was even more disappointing given that Coca-Cola was spending over $100 million more than Pepsi on advertising. The taste testing of the new recipe for Coca-Cola involved 191,000 people in more than 13 cities. Fifty-five per cent of people favoured New Coke over the old formula.

However, once the launch was announced the company was amazed by the negative response; at one point calls were coming in at a rate of 5,000 a day. People were most annoyed by the fact that Coca-Cola dared to change the formula of one of the USA's greatest assets.

What went wrong? Possibly one problem was that when undertaking the testing, customers did not know that choosing one cola would mean the other was removed (that is, if they chose a new flavour the old one would be withdrawn). Also, the symbolic value of Coca-Cola may have been overlooked.

Question:

Coca-Cola did extensive (and expensive) market research and yet still made a mistake. To what extent does this mean that market research is a waste of time? *(14 marks)*

Forecasting

The method of forecasting used by a firm will depend on the nature of the product and the market situation. When the National Lottery (now called Lotto) was launched in the UK, for example, Camelot (the organiser of the lottery) could have forecasted sales by looking at existing national lottery systems in other countries and tried to adjust this data to take account of the differences in culture and the precise nature of the system in the UK.

Camelot might also have used secondary research to identify gambling trends within the UK and primary research to identify customers' likely reaction to the lottery scheme. However, although the company probably used very sophisticated research techniques it is likely there was also an element of hunch in there too. After all, it was a completely new product within the UK and so there were no past data within this country to build on. Obviously once the lottery had been up and running for a few months the organisers were able to make better predictions of expected weekly sales because they were accumulating backdata and gaining a better insight into the market.

The benefits of forecasting

Inevitably, a firm's external and internal conditions are likely to change and this can make it extremely difficult to estimate future sales. It depends in part how much good-quality data it has gathered and the rate of change in the environment. However, the fact that there are difficulties in forecasting does not necessarily make this a useless management tool. The simple process of forecasting makes managers think ahead and plan for different scenarios. This may help to ensure they are much better prepared for change than if they did not forecast at all.

Also, even though a forecast may not be exactly accurate it may give an indication of the direction in which sales are moving and some sense of the magnitude of future sales, which can help a firm's planning. Ultimately it may not matter much whether sales are 2,000,002 units or 2,000,020 units, but it makes a big difference whether they are 2 million or 4 million in terms of staffing, finance and production levels (so, provided the forecast is approximately right it can still be very useful even if it is not exactly correct).

It is also important to remember that sales forecasts can be updated. A firm does not have to make a forecast and leave it there. As conditions change and new information feeds in, the managers can update the forecast and adjust accordingly.

Gathering data

Many organisations are likely to have a great deal of data available to them. They may, for example, have details of customers' locations, their orders and the frequency of purchase. Part of developing a management information system is considering exactly what information needs gathering, how to collect it, how to analyse it and how to make the findings available to those who need it.

Gathering and analysing data has become a lot easier, faster and cheaper with developments in information technology. Store cards, such as Tesco Clubcard, enable the business to collect huge quantities of data on shoppers and their habits and to link this to the address of the card holder. Businesses can then build up a map of the UK and see how customers respond to different incentives and external changes, such as changes in the weather. This provides a detailed insight into shoppers' behaviour which is invaluable to marketing decisions.

Managers can also use secondary sources of data, such as industry surveys produced by the media such as the *Financial Times* and *The Economist*. Secondary research is also available – for a fee – from businesses such as Mintel (Market Intelligence – a market research company).

This does not mean that every business has all the information it needs at any moment, but there is a lot of data available at any time and managers need to be careful not to just gather more instead of thinking carefully about what they need. Think of applying to university – rushing to visit every university and getting every prospectus is quite an inefficient and time-consuming way of going about things; much better to plan what you need and target key information.

The reliability of forecasts

Forecasts are most likely to be correct when:

- a trend has been extrapolated and the market conditions have continued as before
- a test market is used and is truly representative of the target population

- the forecast is made by experts (such as your own sales forces) and they have good insight into the market and future trends
- the firm is forecasting for the near future – it is usually easier to estimate what sales will be next week rather than estimating sales in five years' time. In its report Mintel distinguished an estimate from a forecast. An estimate is when you are part way through a year and estimating what the year as a whole will be like. A forecast looks at the next few years and a projects the longer term. This distinction can highlight how the level of confidence in future levels of sales declines the further ahead you look.

The importance of a sales forecast

A sales forecast acts as a goal against which a firm can measure its progress. It also drives many other decisions within the firm. For example:

- The production schedule will have to be closely linked to the sales forecasts to ensure the firm has the appropriate mix and number of products at the right time. Operations managers will need to know the likely pattern of demand to ensure there is sufficient capacity. As demand changes it may be that some products or services are withdrawn and resources can be switched into other areas.
- The sales forecast will also influence the cash-flow forecast; only by knowing what sales are expected to be can the finance department estimate cash inflows. Having compared the expected inflows with expected cash outflows, the finance function can then decide if particular steps need to be taken, such as arranging overdraft or loan facilities. The expected level of sales will also need to be known to estimate expected revenues and likely levels of profits. Break-even analysis highlights the likely profits at different levels of sales; the key piece of information that is needed is what sales will actually be – this is what a sales forecast should tell you.
- Human resource decisions will also depend on the expected level of sales. Decisions about staffing levels and the allocation of staff to particular duties will inevitably be determined by the expected sales levels. Strong sales growth may require more recruitment, for example, whereas a drop in sales may require transfers or redundancies.

The relationships between the sales forecast and the other functions are two way. A capacity constraint will limit total possible sales. A financial constraint may

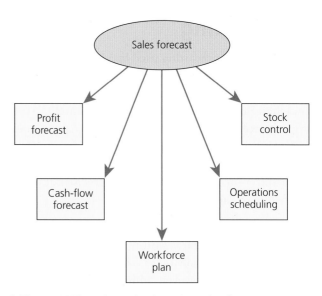

Figure 7.7 The relationship between sales forecasts and other functions

limit the amount of promotional activity that can be undertaken and limit potential sales.

Why might forecasts be wrong?

Forecasts can only be predictions of the future. A variety of factors may make them wrong.

- **Customer buying behaviour changes suddenly.** For example, customers may suddenly decide that a product is unsafe or unfashionable following a problem, such as a fault emerging with the product or ethical issues emerging regarding the way the product was produced. Changes in the weather might also change sales levels, along with other external factors such as economic change or new entrants into the market. Sales forecasts may also be wrong because of internal factors (e.g. poor quality control). In 2011, for example, Blackberry had a problem with its systems which meant users had no connection for a number of days – this may well have damaged the brand and potential sales.
- **The original market research was poor.** This may be because the sample was too small or was unrepresentative. It is always important to think about the data that was gathered. Alternatively, there are sometimes problems in the way results are interpreted; this could be because the firm is in a rush to launch the product or managers think the idea is right and so ignore data that seems to contradict this. In some cases the research may actually have been ignored – managers may have been certain that they knew best and gone ahead

with the decision regardless of the findings of market research.

- **The experts were wrong.** Even the best-informed people can misread a situation and make mistakes – just look at the predictions of so-called experts before any horse race or football match, or the many different and often conflicting forecasts of growth in the economy that are often published in the papers. Weather forecasters generally estimate that there is only an 80 per cent chance of them getting it right and this is only predicting the weather for the next day or two!
- **You are looking too far ahead.** It may be possible to estimate sales with some degree of accuracy in the short run but the further ahead you look the less likely you are to get it right. The numbers for a sales forecast are really very tentative when you are looking, say, seven years ahead.
- **You are trying to be too precise.** Sales forecasts will be presented with a degree of confidence based on the way they are produced and the range given. For example, if you are asked to predict exactly what sales will be in three years' time you cannot be very confident of getting it right. If you can predict sales will be between £3 million and £8 million the range is so wide that you can be more confident of getting it right. The confidence level you can give depends on your research methodology and how precise you are trying to be.

BUSINESS IN FOCUS

Forecast of UK console sales

You can see from the chart below that the broader the possible outcomes given the more confident the company is of its forecasts; the more precise the future sales forecasts are, the less confident it is. To produce these forecasts Mintel used the correlation between sales of consoles and consumer expenditure as well as the number of men aged 16–34 (as consumer research shows that this is the group most likely to play console games regularly), and the number of over-55s, as this is an increasingly important age group for the industry.

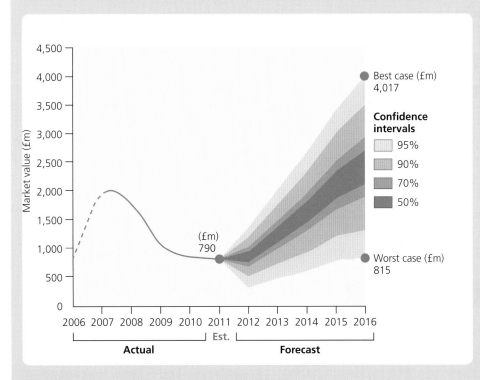

Figure 7.8 Forecast UK sales of consoles

(*Source: Mintel 2011*)

Question:

Analyse how this data might be useful to producers of computer consoles. *(10 marks)*

Problems with analysing markets

There are always likely to be difficulties when analysing a market. For example:

- Data is likely to relate to the past; what you really want to know is what will happen next, but this is not as easy to do as analysing what has already happened.
- Data may not be in exactly the form you want; you want to know about the spending habits of 18–22 year olds but the secondary data focuses on 19–25 year olds, for example.
- It can take time to gather and analyse the data and then decide what action to take; by this time market conditions may have changed.
- You have to make sense of the data. If sales are falling does this mean that this market is not worth bothering with or simply that action should be taken to reverse this? If most businesses distribute via supermarket chains do you need to do the same or are you better focusing on a different form of distribution? Ultimately managers have to analyse the data to make the decisions – this is risky, but it is exactly what they are paid to do! However, different managers can make different decisions from the same data.

The use of information technology in analysing markets

Information technology (IT) refers to systems used to store, analyse, manipulate and exchange data. IT is increasingly becoming cheaper but more powerful, allowing organisations to analyse huge amounts of data relatively cheaply and relatively quickly. IT can enable data to be gathered, analysed and passed on more efficiently and more effectively than in the past.

This should enable better overall decision-making, better marketing decisions and less waste.

For example:

- A business can analyse its till receipts to see the trends within their overall sales. For instance, how are sales of men's clothes at Marks & Spencer doing compared with women's clothing compared with food?
- Loyalty cards can be used to link personal information about customers to their actual purchases; businesses can track exactly what different income groups, genders, postcodes and regions are buying.
- Software can be used to help analyse data. For example, statistical packages can be used to identify correlations and then, based on future estimates of these factors, forecast sales. Databases can be used to store customer data, organise mailings and identify major clients more easily. Businesses can now track the visits to their websites in great detail, including information about what search engines were used, what search terms were entered and in what city the search was made. They can also track the response to online advertising very effectively by measuring the click-throughs for different advertising campaigns.

However, more use of IT can just mean there is more data to wade through and therefore slow up decision making even more. As ever, data has to be turned into information (useful data) and what matters has to be pulled out of what does not matter. For example, what is the key information you need about your customers? Average spend? Age? Income group? Shoe size? Place of birth? Favourite band? Favourite colour? You could carry on trying to gather huge amounts of data and waste lots of resources doing so, but you need to think about the opportunity, the cost and the extent to which it is likely to help you.

BUSINESS IN FOCUS

Marketing 'paralysed by facts'

Marketers used to struggle to get all the information they wanted about their customers. With the growth of the internet and other technological developments, the opposite is true: many marketing managers have so much data that 'analysis paralysis' has set in, according to Tim Calkins, a professor at the Kellogg School of Management in the US.

Other commentators have coined a profusion of phrases to describe the problems of too much information: 'data asphyxiation' (William van Winkle), 'data smog' (David Shenk), 'information fatigue syndrome' (David Lewis), 'cognitive overload' (Eric Schmidt) and 'time famine' (Leslie Perlow). Calkins says that marketing managers need to become less preoccupied with gathering information and more focused on turning analysis into action. 'If all you do is know your customer really well, that doesn't help you.' For example, bad marketing plans can run for hundreds of pages without delivering a clear call to arms. They confuse strategy with tactics and overwhelm their audience with too much detailed information. Good plans realise they are tools for winning over colleagues to a desired course of action and have three or four memorable objectives linked closely to the company's profit goals.

(*Source: Adapted from A Jones in* Financial Times, *13 October 2008*)

Question:

To what extent can a marketing manager have too much information? *(14 marks)*

BUSINESS IN FOCUS

Customer relationships

Good customer relationships are not easy to create and maintain; they rely on an effective communications strategy and that must be based on accurate data. Unfortunately, the data kept on customers is often out of date and can make a business appear out of touch with its customers, as well as leading to waste.

Organisations that invest in the quality of their data can send out targeted communications that are relevant, make customers feel valued, and build a sense of loyalty to a brand.

Recent research conducted by Experian QAS revealed that 75 per cent of businesses across the globe believed they were losing business opportunities and revenue by not profiling their databases. Despite recognising the value of good customer data, many firms did not have any structures in place to improve the quality of their data. Thirty-four per cent of organisations did not validate any of the information they collected on customers and prospective customers, such as name and address, contact number, email address or bank account information.

The effects of poor data may not be immediately obvious. It is only when other activities that rely on the accuracy of data (such as customer profiling) go wrong that a business starts to take note. Then damage has already been done. Other 'hidden costs' include reduced staff productivity and wasted marketing and communications spend, which may in turn hamper good customer relationships. Businesses may even find themselves breaking the law.

Under the Consumer Protection from Unfair Trading Regulations 2008, direct marketing companies that continue to 'make persistent and unwanted solicitations' could face a maximum fine of £5,000 or, in some cases, up to two years in prison.

Direct marketing (direct contact with customers via mailings) to both existing and prospective customers has traditionally received a bad press because of a perception that consumers are bombarded by 'junk mail' in untargeted, badly managed marketing campaigns. As a result, marketers increasingly have to take the 'customer experience' and customer wishes into account. As people register with preference services and more data becomes available (for example, when individuals pass away or move house), keeping customer data up to date becomes even harder. This is supported by data from the Office of National Statistics, which claims that the average consumer database loses accuracy by 14 per cent each year. With such a high level of 'database decay', it is crucial that marketers take more of a hands-on approach to the management of their contact data. Contact data management needs to be part of a long-term strategy for the capture, 'cleaning' and control of data. It's not possible to check and update data once, occasionally or just before a specific marketing campaign. Data quality needs ongoing management.

(*Source: Adapted from Stuart Johnston in* Financial Times, *28 October 2008*)

Question:

Discuss the ways in which the use of information technology to manage customer relationships can benefit a business. *(14 marks)*

Summary

To make decisions about what marketing strategy to adopt, marketing managers should analyse their markets. This means identifying the state of the markets at the current time, changes that have happened and future possible changes. This is important in order to identify where and how to compete and to set targets. Market analysis is therefore an important aspect of developing a relevant and evidence-based marketing strategy and plan.

Key terms

The **value of sales** measures the amount of money spent on products in a market.

The **volume of sales** measures the number of units sold in a market.

Extrapolation involves identifying the underlying trend in past data and projecting this trend forwards.

Correlation occurs when there are apparent links between variables (e.g. promotional spending and sales).

Market research is the process of gathering, analysing and presenting data relevant to the marketing process.

Primary research uses data gathered for the first time.

Secondary research uses data that has been gathered previously (it uses the data for the second time).

A **sales forecast** is an estimate of the volume or value of a firm's sales in the future.

A **confidence level** shows how certain the market researcher is of the results given. A 95 per cent confidence level means that the researchers are confident that 95 per cent of the time (19 times out of 20) if they repeated this research you would get the same results.

Examiner's advice

There are many sources of information which may help with a market analysis, such as internal, external, primary and secondary data. Although the temptation may be to gather as much data as possible this can lead to too much data and actually delay action. A challenge to all businesses is getting good-quality information – the right amount at the right time telling you the right things. Also, in an exam look at how the data is gathered – the value of market analysis depends on the quality of the information used. If information was gathered using a small sample or leading questions were asked then it may be very misleading.

In many of the cases you are likely to face, a business will be making a major decision. In this type of situation large sums of money may be at stake and the future of the business may be at risk. It is possible, but very unlikely, that in this situation a decision will be made without some market analysis. You may question the way the analysis has been undertaken, but some information is likely to be better than none. How likely is it that a marketing manager will spend millions of pounds without analysing the market or putting a plan together? What you might want to think about is how reliable the analysis is likely to be. How was it conducted? By whom? When?

Remember how important a sales forecast is. If you do not have any sense of the scale of the possible sales, how can you plan how much to spend, how much to produce, how many people to employ? The sales forecast drives much of the planning in an organisation, such as the production schedule, the cash-flow forecast, the projected income statement and the workforce plan.

When looking at market data in an exam question think about how it was gathered and who by – is it likely to be biased? Is the sample size big enough? If there is a sales forecast what is it based on? Has this product been selling before and, if so, are market conditions similar enough now to use extrapolation? Try to identify the key issues and how they affect marketing decision-making. For example, the size of the market will affect the likely returns and the likely budget, and changes within different segments may affect your desired product portfolio.

1 What is meant by market analysis? *(3 marks)*

2 Give **two** reasons why a business might want to analyse a market, and explain them. *(6 marks)*

3 Explain **two** ways of measuring the size of a market. *(4 marks)*

4 Explain why producing a sales forecast is important to a business. *(5 marks)*

5 What is extrapolation? *(3 marks)*

6 Explain one way of producing a sales forecast, apart from extrapolation. *(4 marks)*

7 Explain how information technology can help a firm analyse a market. *(3 marks)*

8 Explain **two** difficulties of forecasting sales. *(6 marks)*

9 What is a moving average? *(2 marks)*

10 Explain how developments in information technology have helped organisations undertake more effective marketing. *(6 marks)*

Analysis and evaluation questions

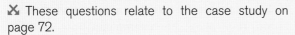 These questions relate to the case study on page 72.

What do you think would be the best way for Aspire to forecast sales in China? Justify your answer. *(16 marks)*

Candidate's answer:

Sales forecasts set out the expected level of sales in the future. Businesses need this because it affects the planning of all the other functions of the business such as cash-flow forecasts, workforce planning and production scheduling. There are many ways to forecast sales but this is a very unique situation because the business is entering a new market. It cannot extrapolate from its own sales because it has not been in China before and countries are so different in terms of populations, buying habits and competition that it would be very dangerous to base Chinese sales on the UK. (Just think of the population of China being over 1 billion compared to the UK's just over 60 million.) The business could however look at what has happened to Starbucks and Costa in terms of the sales per store (it would probably have to estimate this as these companies would not want to give this information away) and then estimate its sales given the number of stores it will have. However, it will have to take into account where its stores are and whether these are in similar locations. If they are opening in the same places as the other businesses it may mean they end up sharing customers which will distort their figures even more. However, they should be able to get a rough idea of likely sales per store even if they have to sit and watch who buys what in competitors' stores for a while. They could also try to buy in expert advice from local analysts.

However, the business must recognise that its forecasts will need large margins of error because it is such an unfamiliar market. They will probably want to have a range of forecasts with different degrees of confidence.

Examiner's comments:

This is an excellent answer. The candidate clearly understands what is meant by sales forecasting and looks at different ways of doing this. What is good about the answer is that it does actually try to answer the question and think about how to forecast sales in this case rather than just repeating textbook information. The candidate is trying to decide on the best way to forecast sales in the given situation. Notice how he or she evaluates the option – he or she outlines possible ways of forecasting but questions the value of these. This is good in terms of gaining evaluation marks. Then there is a final conclusion – again good for evaluation because there is a clear final judgement that it can be done but is likely to have a wide margin of error.

Evaluation question

To what extent do you think a market analysis is essential to Aspire before entering the Chinese market? *(16 marks)*

8 Selecting marketing strategies

A market analysis should enable a marketing manager to understand where the market is and where it might be going. This should feed into developing a marketing plan.

In this chapter we examine:

- the meaning of marketing strategies
- the difference between low-cost and differentiation strategies
- the meaning and significance of market penetration strategies
- the meaning and significance of product development and market development strategies
- the meaning and significance of diversification.

Introduction to marketing strategies

Once a firm has undertaken market analysis it should have a good insight into the nature of its market and how it might develop in the future. Market analysis should provide information on the size of the market, the major firms competing within it and expected trends. Armed with this information, the firm can think about it in relation to its own sales patterns, its own strengths and its corporate objectives. It can decide its marketing objectives and determine the required marketing strategy to achieve them.

Marketing objectives are quantifiable marketing targets; they may focus on the:

- desired level of sales
- composition of sales (for example, the sales of one brand compared with another)
- timing of sales (for example, in an attempt to smooth sales out over the year and remove seasonal patterns)
- brand image (for example, positioning relative to competitors)
- nature of the buyers (for example, you may be trying to focus on larger corporate clients rather than smaller ones).

The marketing objective determines exactly what the firm is aiming to achieve in marketing terms. This will contribute to and be derived from the overall corporate objective. The marketing strategy is the plan a firm adopts to achieve its marketing objectives. This will involve deciding:

- which segments of the market you want to target
- how to position yourself.

The requirements of each segment differ and so effective marketing requires managers to understand these needs, decide on which segments are likely to be profitable for the business and then develop appropriate plans. For example, a hotel chain may aim at the business traveller, the family holiday group or couples on a romantic break – each of these segments will want different types of hotel and the business must decide which segment it wants to target. This depends on its own strengths relative to the competition. Then it must decide where to position itself; does it want to be at the budget end of the market or the premium end?

This process of Segmentation – Targeting – Positioning (STP) is an important part of strategic planning.

Imagine we want to increase sales by 50 per cent over the next five years. What marketing strategies can we use to do this?

1 We may decide to boost sales of our existing products. If we do this we could try to:
   - increase the amount existing customers buy when they purchase (for example, by encouraging people to spend more every time they visit our shops)
   - increase the number of customers (for example, by encouraging people to switch to our shop)
   - increase the number of times they buy (for example, by encouraging more visits to the shop)
   - increase the amount they spend (for example, by encouraging them to trade up to premium items).

Unilever's corporate objective is to double its sales. To achieve this its marketing objectives focus on increasing users of their products, increasing usage of their products and persuading users to trade up.

2 Or we may decide to develop new products.

3 Or we may decide to target new segments. For example, we might expand overseas or target a different age group.

For each of these options we then have to consider how to position ourselves; for example are we a premium brand or the low price value option?

As you can see, there are different ways of achieving a marketing objective, and each marketing strategy will have different implications in terms of the precise marketing activities being carried out.

BUSINESS IN FOCUS

Barbie

In recent years Barbie has faced robust competition from Bratz dolls. To boost sales of Barbie, managers could target:

- those who buy Barbie already and try to get them to buy more
- those who used to buy Barbies but are older now, to try and get them to return to buying the dolls (for example, adult collectors)
- those who do not buy Barbies but buy Bratz dolls, to try to win over these customers
- those who do not buy dolls at all.

Each of these options would require a different strategy in order to achieve the same objective – that of increasing sales.

Question:

Which of the above strategies would you recommend? Why? *(14 marks)*

Deciding on a marketing strategy

When deciding on a marketing strategy there are many issues to consider, such as:

- Where should the business compete and which segments should it target? For example, should the firm compete in a niche or try to compete head-on with the major players in a mass market? Should it compete in particular regions, in the UK as a whole or globally? This will depend on its own strengths relative to the competition.
- What should it offer? For example, what product lines should it offer? How many different types of products should it offer? How similar should these be?

- How should it compete and position itself against competitors? For example, should the firm try to match competitors' offerings but sell them more cheaply (a low-cost strategy), or should it aim to differentiate itself and charge more (a differentiation strategy)?

Managers will make different decisions in answer to these questions.

- Lobbs, for example, is an exclusive shoemaker producing expensive made-to-measure shoes – this is a niche, differentiation strategy. Clarks competes much more in the mass market.
- Primark aims at the mass market via low prices; Karen Millen aims more for the expensive fashion market.
- The Ford Ka is aimed at the younger driver (perhaps their first car); the Aston Martin DB7 is aimed at the highly successful executive.
- Asda offers a range of foods aimed at the 'average' customer and seeks to maintain a lower price than competitors; this is a low-cost, mass-market strategy. Waitrose offers a more exclusive range of goods at a higher price, which is a differentiation strategy.
- The soft drink, Irn Bru, competes mainly in the UK; Coca-Cola is a global product. Sainsbury's focuses on the UK; Tesco is going global.

A firm's marketing strategy should aim to exploit its market opportunities and defend itself against threats. It should naturally build on the firm's strengths and avoid entering market segments or offering products where its weaknesses will be exposed.

Figure 8.1 Forming a marketing strategy

BUSINESS IN FOCUS

Unilever

Unilever is a large multinational business. Its mission is 'to add vitality to life'. 'We meet everyday needs for nutrition, hygiene, and personal care with brands that help people feel good, look good and get more out of life.'

Its marketing strategy is now focused on what it calls 'power brands' – key brands such as Dove and OMO that it wants to develop globally. These brand names will be extended to a wider range of products, and lesser-known brands have been or are being sold off. To achieve growth in the future Unilever is targeting emerging markets; these are markets in countries such as China and India where the average income per person is low but growing relatively fast.

In these markets Unilever has two strategies:

* to persuade customers to buy products for the first time
* to persuade customers to trade up.

Question:

Discuss the factors that might determine the success of Unilever's marketing strategy. *(14 marks)*

What determines a firm's marketing strategy?

When considering a marketing strategy a firm's managers should consider the following:

* What is the firm trying to achieve – what are its marketing objectives? There is no point in cutting prices, for example, if the firm is trying to build an exclusive brand image. Similarly, there is little point diversifying if the firm's objective is to focus on its core products.
* What are the market opportunities? What market segments appear to be growing? Businesses will be unlikely to target declining markets or segments that are small relative to the investment needed to enter them and compete in them.
* What are the firm's strengths and key capabilities? What is it good at? What are its competences (the areas where it has expertise)? Does it have any unique selling points (USPs)? Some businesses are good at innovating (such as W L Gore); others are good at extending the brand onto other products (in 2011 Virgin, for example, moved into high street banking when it took over Northern Rock);

some are good at service (such as Disney), others are excellent at changing the price to match demand conditions (such as easyJet) – these key capabilities should influence the chosen strategy if a firm is to play to its strengths.

* What resources does the firm have? For example, what is its financial position? Will it be able to finance any plans for expansion, for example? Some firms have a good liquidity position and can finance growth internally. Others may be heavily in debt (this is known as highly geared) and therefore cannot easily borrow more, which might limit the marketing strategy.

The marketing strategy should therefore be firmly based on an effective SWOT analysis, which examines the **s**trengths, **w**eaknesses, **o**pportunities and **t**hreats facing a firm.

Figure 8.2 SWOT analysis as part of strategic planning

Analysing marketing strategies

There are several different ways of analysing the various marketing strategies. In this section we examine the Ansoff matrix, which looks at strategies in terms of the products offered and the markets a business competes in, and Porter's model, which distinguishes between a low-cost and a differentiated strategy.

The Ansoff matrix and marketing strategies

Market penetration

This strategy occurs when a firm tries to sell more of its existing products to its existing customers; the aim

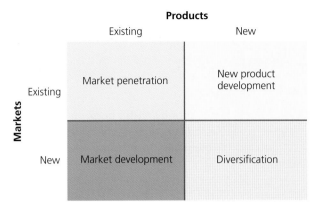

Figure 8.3 The Ansoff matrix

is to increase market share. To achieve more sales the firm may adjust elements of its marketing mix. For example, it may increase its spending on promoting its products or it may cut its price. Market penetration is a relatively low-risk strategy because you are dealing with a market and products you know well; this can be implemented in the short term.

New product development

This strategy focuses on developing new products and offering these to existing clients. Firms operating in the soap, shampoo and laundry detergent markets, for example, are continually developing new brands for their customers. This strategy is risky in the sense that many new products often fail. The majority of products never get through the development phase. Typically only about 5 per cent of research products ever get to the commercialisation stage. Once launched, only about one in ten new products survives the first two years so all the investment in developing the product can be lost.

On the other hand, managers should have a relatively good understanding of the market and their customers' buying processes, and so they may feel confident that their offering will be successful despite the high failure rate of others. This belief that you can 'beat the odds' often drives product development decisions and can prove extremely costly.

Market development

This strategy occurs when a firm offers its existing products to a new market. For example, it may try and sell its products overseas or it may try and target new segments of its existing market. Many sportswear companies have successfully marketed their products as fashion items, for example. Chewing-gum

companies have offered their product as an aid to giving up smoking, as something which helps prevent tooth decay and as a breath freshener; the product, therefore, has been offered to many new segments. Again, there are real risks involved with this strategy because you may not fully understand the needs of the market. What shoppers in Beijing are looking for and how they want their food prepared and presented may be very different from shoppers in Hanoi, Berlin or Paris. Understanding the factors that buyers consider and the buying process in different markets is no easy task. When Innocent smoothies entered the French market for instance, it found its humorous approach to communications was not very effective and had to switch to more serious messages about the healthiness of the product.

Diversification

This strategy involves offering new products to new markets. For example, a chocolate company may decide to diversify into the soft drinks market. This is a high-risk strategy because the firm may have only a very limited understanding of the production and marketing requirements of the new sector. If it is successful, however, it actually reduces the firm's risk because it is operating in two different markets. If sales decline in one market, demand may be sustained or even increase in another one.

Diversification is risky in the sense that managers are operating in an unfamiliar zone. Imagine that your senior managers at school decided to move the organisation into clothes retailing as well. Of course, it is possible they could run a business like this very well, but it would be completely different from running a school and they are likely to have real problems adjusting to the different circumstances. On the other hand, by operating in different markets managers are spreading the risks of demand falling; if demand falls in one market, sales in the other market may continue to sustain the business. Market penetration, by comparison, is safe in that managers are operating within their comfort zones; your school managers are still running the school but trying to make it bigger. The managers know the suppliers they want to work with, the competitors and market conditions. The danger is that the business is dependent on one market alone, which can make it vulnerable.

Igor Ansoff

Igor Ansoff (1918–2002) is well known as a leading writer about business strategy. He lived in Russia until he was 18, then moved to America where he studied mechanical engineering and physics. He went on to work on strategic problem solving for NATO, developing approaches he later applied to business when he worked for Lockheed, an aerospace company.

He went on to be the founding dean of the Graduate School of Management at Vanderbilt University in Nashville, Tennessee.

Ansoff is most famous for his 1965 book on strategy highlighting various processes and checklists he felt were required for managers to produce an effective strategy.

Mars corporate fact sheet

In 1911, Frank C. Mars made the first Mars candies in his Tacoma, Washington kitchen and established Mars' first roots as a confectionery company. In the 1920s, Forrest E. Mars, Sr. joined his father in business and together they launched the Milky Way® bar. In 1932, Forrest, Sr. moved to the United Kingdom with a dream of building a business based on the philosophy of a 'mutuality of benefits' for all stakeholders – this vision serves as the foundation of the Mars, Incorporated we are today.

Based in McLean, Virginia, Mars has net sales of more than $30 billion and six business segments including Petcare, Chocolate, Wrigley, Food, Drinks and Symbioscience.

Mars business units

Chocolate

Headquartered in Mount Olive, New Jersey, US, Mars Chocolate is one of the world's leading chocolate manufacturers and employs more than 13,000 people across 110 sites worldwide.

It has:

- 28 manufacturing sites
- four billion-dollar global brands – M&M's®, Snickers®, Dove®/Galaxy® and Mars®/Milky Way®
- 36 brands in total, and four – Mars®, Milky Way®, Snickers® and M&M's® – are more than 50 years old

Petcare

With headquarters in Brussels, Belgium, and more than 33,000 Associates in 199 locations around the world, Mars Petcare has been in operation for more than 75 years and is one of the world's leading pet care providers.

Brands include Pedigree®, Royal Canin®, Whiskas®, Kitekat®, Banfield® Pet Hospital, Cesar®, Nutro®, Sheba®, Chappi®, Greenies® and The Waltham® Centre for Pet Nutrition.

Food

Mars Food is headquartered in Rancho Dominguez, California, US. We employ more than 1,600 Associates in 11 manufacturing facilities on five continents. Mars Food is a growing company with a passion for making great-tasting food that gives consumers easy, healthy options. Our brands include: Uncle Ben's®, Dolmio®, Masterfoods®, Seeds Of Change®, Ebly®, Royco®, Kan Tong®, Suzi Wan® and Raris®.

Uncle Ben's® is a billion-dollar global brand and more than 50 years old.

Drinks

Mars Drinks provides more than a billion drinks to more than 35,000 businesses each year. With US headquarters in West Chester, Pennsylvania, and UK headquarters in Basingstoke, we employ 670 Associates in 10 locations. Our business categories are Klix® drinks vending systems and Mars Drinks single-serve technology.

We have:

- more than 650 Associates
- two manufacturing sites
- five brands in total: Klix®, Flavia®, Alterra™, The Bright Tea Co.™ and Dove®/Galaxy® hot chocolate drinks.

Mars Symbioscience

Mars Symbioscience (MSS) was established in 2005 as a technology-based health and life sciences business with a focus on delivering evidence-based science.

We have three business units: Mars Plantcare, Mars Veterinary and Mars Botanical. With sustained funding from Mars, Incorporated, MSS acts as an incubator for business ideas generated throughout our segments. For example, we are currently testing MyCocoaPaper products. This project turns the waste from cocoa plants into paper, providing an additional income stream to cocoa farmers. Our ability to bring to market a range of cocoa paper products also creates a real business opportunity for MSS.

We have:

- 200 Associates
- two manufacturing sites
- five brands in total, including CocoaVia™, Wisdom Panel™ and Seramis®.

Wrigley

Headquartered in Chicago, Illinois, US, Wrigley operates 102 sites worldwide. We have more than 16,000 Associates in 40 nations who together are dedicated to bringing simple pleasures to consumers in 180 countries around the world.

We have:

- more than 16,000 Associates
- 23 manufacturing sites
- two billion-dollar global brands – Extra® and Orbit®
- 41 brands in total, and three – Altoids®, Juicy Fruit® and Spearmint® – are more than 100 years old.

(*Source: Mars*)

Question:

Do you think the Mars strategy of operating in several different regional and product markets is a good one? (*14 marks*)

Low cost v differentiation strategies

Another way of analysing marketing strategies was developed by Michael Porter in 1985. Porter distinguished between a low-cost and a differentiated strategy. A low-cost strategy focuses on providing similar benefits to competitors, but doing so at a lower price. This is the strategy adopted by companies such as Ryanair and Ikea. Managers of such organisations consistently look for ways of reducing costs to make their businesses leaner. They strip away costs to enable low prices. At Ikea, for example, you select your own furniture purchases, take them off the shelves on your own and take them to the tills. You then take them to your car – once again without help. You then assemble the furniture yourself at home. All of this means the labour costs of the business are reduced significantly. The stores themselves are out of town (reducing rents) and fairly basic in terms of design and layout (reducing decoration and maintenance costs).

To be successful with a low-cost strategy a firm must be able to deliver its products more cheaply than the competition. This may be achieved through economies of scale, special relations with suppliers or by removing some elements of the marketing mix. For example, a firm may try to make distribution more direct and so be able to avoid the middleman's profit margins; alternatively it may provide fewer additional services – some supermarkets, for example, compete on price by keeping overheads low and offering a more basic service and a more limited range of goods in the store itself.

The alternative approach is to differentiate your offering, for example by offering more benefits than your competitors – provided the benefits are ones that customers want (for instance, a better product range, a strong brand or high levels of customer service). This should enable you to charge a higher price. For example, Bang and Olufsen produces top of the range music systems for which it charges high prices because of the quality and design; Jo Malone produces expensive but distinctive fragrances; Creed aftershave is expensive but was first made for Napoleon III! If a business is pursuing a differentiation strategy, the distribution of the product or service is often exclusive; the firm is likely to want to keep a tight control over distribution to maintain an exclusive image. The products are often innovative and the firm may invest heavily in research and development. The promotional strategy is likely to emphasise the difference between this product and rivals' products.

Inevitably firms which do differentiate their offerings successfully may be imitated over time – just look at the way in which Coca-Cola, Dyson, Apple and Pringles have been copied. At this point the firm will only be able to justify a higher price if it can continue to stress its role as the market leader or position itself effectively as the 'first of its kind' or the best. Dyson, for example, ran an advertising campaign emphasising that, 'if you want a Dyson you have to buy a Dyson', to highlight its uniqueness; Coca-Cola often stresses that it is the 'original'.

The worst of all worlds, according to Porter, is to get 'stuck in the middle', for example, offering a product with similar benefits to competitors at a higher price – this is a no win situation.

BUSINESS IN FOCUS

Michael Porter

The concept of 'competitive advantage' was outlined by Michael Porter in 1985.

Porter argued that competitive advantage is a function of either providing comparable buyer value more efficiently than competitors (low cost), or performing activities at comparable cost but in unique ways that create more buyer value than competitors and, hence, command a premium price (differentiation).

You win either by being cheaper or by being different (which means being perceived by the customer as better or more relevant). There are no other ways. Behind Porter's idea was the value chain. This highlighted the different interrelated activities within a business and that lower costs or added value came from the activities within these elements and the way they link together.

In a book called *Competitive Strategy*, Porter identified five factors that affect a company's profitability: buyer power, supplier power, rivalry, entry threat and substitute threat.

In a later book, *The Competitive Advantage of Nations*, Porter highlighted how the choice of location by an internationalising business might be a source of competitive advantage. He found that businesses from a particular industry often cluster together and this creates national advantages.

Further reading

Porter, M., 'How Competitive Forces Shape Strategy', *Harvard Business Review*, March–April 1979
Porter, M., *Competitive Strategy: Techniques for Analysing Industries and Competitors*, 2nd edn, Free Press, 1998
Porter, M., *Competitive Advantage: Creating and Sustaining Superior Performance*, 2nd edn, Free Press, 1998
Porter, M., *The Competitive Advantage of Nations*, 2nd edn, Macmillan Business, 1998

BUSINESS IN FOCUS

Amazon

Amazon entered the tablet market in 2011 with a low-price offering that matched its brand and overall competitive strategy. On 28 September Jeff Bezos, Amazon's founder and CEO, introduced the Kindle Fire to compete with products such as Apple's iPad. Like Apple, Amazon boasts a huge collection of online content, including e-books, films and music. And like Apple, it lets people store their content in a computing 'cloud' and retrieve it from almost anywhere. However when it comes to pricing their approaches differ considerably: The Kindle Fire was launched at only $199. The cheapest iPad cost $499. Amazon also announced a new range of Kindle e-readers, the cheapest of which costs just $79. 'We are building premium products and offering them at non-premium prices', said Mr Bezos.

Amazon's decision to undercut its rivals is partly a tactic designed to disrupt the tablet market, which is

Figure 8.4 The tablet market is growing

still dominated by the iPad. Amazon's pricing strategy also reflects one of the firm's core beliefs, which is that low prices make customers happy. Its ability to drive down the prices of everything from cameras to cloud computing gives it a major competitive advantage.

One factor that enables Amazon to compete in this way is that as an online business Amazon does not pay sales tax in American states where it has no physical presence. However, the main reason for its low prices is the firm's huge scale. Even so, its profit margin is a very small 3–4 per cent, partly because it has invested so heavily in cloud computing. Now it is going head-to-head with Apple, which made a $7.3 billion net profit on revenues of $28.6 billion in the latest quarter. Apple may not want to provoke a price war in the tablet market, where it sees plenty of growth to come. But if it does respond, Amazon might struggle to compete with it.

Question:

Do you think Apple would be wise to cut the price of its products? Why? *(14 marks)*

The comparison of a low-cost strategy to one of differentiation can be more fully explored using the concept of value. This considers the benefits a business offers relative to its competitors and the price it charges.

If a business offers more benefits than its competitors it may be able to charge the same, less (if this is possible financially) or even more and still be competitive. Mont Blanc pens are very expensive but still regarded as good value because of the prestige of the brand. Bose music equipment has a high price but people are willing to pay for the design and sound quality.

If a business matches the competition in terms of the benefits offered it will have to charge the same or less to offer better value and be more competitive. In the latter case the challenge is to find a way of being able to offer lower prices. This is often an issue for operations.

If a business offers fewer benefits than the competition it must charge a lot less to be competitive. Again the challenge is to find ways of doing this that cannot easily be imitated by competitors.

From this we can see the importance of understanding customers to know what they would regard as a benefit; we can also see the importance of clearly positioning yourself. It is perfectly possible to charge more than competitors and be regarded as good value provided you offer more benefits.

Why change a marketing strategy?

It may be necessary for a firm to change its marketing strategy for a number of reasons, such as:

- **It may have changed its marketing objectives** – rather than wanting more sales from a given product range managers may now seek to diversify (for example to spread risk) or there may be more pressure from investors to boost profits.

- **Market conditions may have changed** – the slowing down of the rate of growth in the PC market has led firms like Microsoft to look for new markets to enter, such as computer games. The decline of the traditional film camera market has led the camera shop Jessops to reconsider what it offers. Concerns over diet have made McDonald's think about how to make its offering healthier.

- **Competitors' actions** – a head-on attack from other firms may force an organisation to move into a new segment or to focus on particular areas of its business where it has a competitive advantage. The threat of supermarkets such as Walmart attacking its core business led Boots to move into segments such as optical and dental care.

- **Changes in the firm's own strengths** – as a firm develops its staff, technology and product range it may find that its strengths create new opportunities and this brings about a change in strategy.

- **Poor performance** – if your strategy is working well you are likely to keep on with it. If your strategy is failing you need to rethink. In 2008 Woolworth's went into administration. It had no clear positioning in the market. Was it a sweets store? A music business? A children's clothes shop? It was not clear to a buyer why you would go there, and in each of its areas it faced attacks. In this situation (or hopefully before it happened) a business would reconsider its corporate and its marketing strategy.

A change in marketing strategy may be prompted by the possibility of exploiting an opportunity and/or to protect itself against threats or poor performance.

Changing your marketing strategy can be a difficult process. For example:

- If you keep the same brand name and try to move upmarket it can be difficult to win customers over. For many years Skoda has been trying to reposition itself as a relatively low-priced but reliable, well-designed brand; for older buyers who remember quality problems in the past and the very basic design this is quite a shift in its positioning and those buyers may take time to be convinced. Equally, changes to the strategy can damage the brand and hurt the long-term success of the business. At one point Burberry was growing so fast and using its brand on so many products that it started to devalue its image and the company had to be more selective to maintain a premium image.

- It will involve changes in the other functions. For example, the operations process may need to change, perhaps to achieve higher volumes, fewer defects or faster service; equally, responsibilities and duties of staff will change which can be disruptive and may be resisted.
- More funds may be needed to enable the strategic change. This may be to research the options, develop new products or launch them in the market. This can be difficult if, for example, the reason for the change was that the business had financial difficulties.

BUSINESS IN FOCUS

Kellogg's

Kellogg's, the US breakfast cereal and snack maker, has said it will not change its marketing strategy to children despite concerns about obesity. Its managers said that the obesity issue was about calorie intake and exercise, not 'bad food'. Kellogg's plans to launch its Kashi brand of wholegrain cereals in the UK and will soon introduce a new version of All-Bran to Japan.

The development illustrates how US food companies are responding to increased concern about the contribution of some processed foods to obesity, and marketing to children by highlighting efforts to develop healthier products.

The company's chief financial officer said: 'The whole issue with obesity is really calories in, calories out. There aren't any bad foods, it's all about balance.'

Concern about the role of food companies in contributing to obesity increased with a landmark lawsuit against McDonald's by New York teenagers who claimed the fast-food company played down the health effects of eating Chicken McNuggets. Kraft Foods has focused attention on the issue by voluntarily pledging to stop marketing in schools, advertising to children under six and shifting food promotions to the 6- to 11-year-old towards healthier items.

Asked whether Kellogg's would be changing its promotional strategy in the wake of Kraft's move, the company's chief executive said: 'We don't move based on what the competition does.'

Both Kellogg's and its main rival in the breakfast cereals market, General Mills, have in the past year stepped up the introduction of cereals containing whole grains, including those aimed at children.

The chief executive said: 'Kids have been eating our products for decades. Offering options for what kids may want and what their mothers may want them to eat is certainly a thing we're interested in doing.' The vice-president in charge of marketing said: 'We think advertising cereal to kids is a very good thing to do and we'd like to do it more. Twenty-five per cent of kids walk out of the door in the morning having eaten nothing. We think that those kinds of problems are really much more significant and if we can put a dent in that, that would be very positive.'

(*Source: Adapted from* Financial Times *2008*)

Questions:

1 Should Kellogg's stop all advertising to children? *(14 marks)*
2 'We don't move based on the competition'. Is this a sensible marketing strategy to pursue? *(14 marks)*

Overseas marketing strategy

One issue facing a firm when determining its marketing strategy is whether to focus purely on the domestic market or whether to expand overseas. Overseas expansion may be appealing for several reasons.

- **The domestic market is saturated.** Many markets in the UK are mature (such as the demand for microwaves, fridges and televisions). This means that companies can only generate replacement sales rather than many first-time sales. In emerging economies such as Brazil, Russia, India and China the economies are growing much faster, creating opportunities for a rapid growth in sales. If investors are pushing for fast growth it may be that this is more likely to come from abroad.
- **The domestic market is subject to increasing competition or regulation.** Tesco cannot expand much more in the UK for fear of being blocked by

the Competition Commission for having too big a market share. It has therefore expanded overseas in countries such as South Korea, Thailand, the US and India to enable faster growth.

- **The benefits of particular market opportunities overseas**, for example China has a population of over 1 billion that could be targeted.
- **Reducing the risk of being dependent on one market;** by operating overseas a business may protect itself from changes in one market.

Entering an overseas market does, of course, bring various problems. Perhaps most importantly the firm is unlikely to know the market as well as its domestic market. It will need to ensure it fully understands market conditions, including consumer buying behaviour, legal and economic factors and the possible response of the competition. Given that the market is not known as well, entering an overseas market can be seen as risky. This is why many firms entering overseas markets find a local partner to help them understand the market.

BUSINESS IN FOCUS

Disneyland Paris

In 1992 Disney opened its holiday and recreation park 20 miles from the centre of Paris. It features two theme parks, an entertainment district and several Disney-owned hotels. By 2008 it had over 15 million visitors a year; however, at the start it had encountered many problems.

These included:

- the very American menus on offer, which did not meet local tastes
- a ban on alcohol – not popular with the French who expected wine and beer on sale
- resistance from local politicians who felt that France was being invaded by American culture
- a policy by the American managers of demanding everyone spoke English at all meetings
- Disney's long list of regulations and limitations on the use of make-up, on whether facial hair, tattoos and jewellery were allowed; these policies were very unusual in France
- the name of the park; it began as Euro Disney Resort but is now Disneyland Paris.

Question:

Essentially, Disney encountered problems because it did not think enough about the local culture and customers. Why do you think these mistakes were made? *(14 marks)*

BUSINESS IN FOCUS

Minute Maid Pulpy

Minute Maid Pulpy was launched nationally in China in 2005, and is now among the premier juice drink brands in 18 countries across three continents including Indonesia, Taiwan, Philippines, Thailand and India. The drink was supported by a marketing campaign that highlighted the content of orange pulp within the beverage. Coca-Cola claim people of the region enjoy chewing on the orange pulp as they consume the drink, and so developed the Minute Maid Pulpy to meet local tastes.

In 2010, Pulpy was introduced in Algeria, Malaysia, Singapore and Vietnam. In addition, Pulpy was introduced in Mexico as Valle Pulpy under the del Valle trademark. In Kazakhstan, Pulpy is sold as Piko Pulpy. The brand is poised for further global expansion in 2011.

Minute Maid Pulpy is a significant global innovation, and reached $1 billion sales in only five years.

Western food and drinks businesses that target the Chinese and Asian markets typically have to adapt their products. McDonald's, Starbucks and KFC all offer products in Asia which are specific to the area. For instance, McDonald's menus include Corn Cups, and Starbucks sells green tea Frappuccinos in their Chinese franchises.

Question:

Discuss the effects on other functions of the business of changing products for different markets. *(14 marks)*

China

China is the world's fastest-growing major retail market and is likely to become the biggest. Not surprisingly, overseas chains such as Carrefour, Walmart and Tesco are all developing their presence there. However, none of them are anywhere near to dominating the market in the way that Walmart dominates the US supermarket sector. Even the largest local chain in China, Shanghai Bailian, has only 11 per cent of the market in its region.

Entrants into this market adapt their produce to local tastes. For instance, they sell live fish and sea turtles that clients can kill at home or have slaughtered there and then. Other delicacies offered in China that would not sell as well in the UK or US include birds' nests and pigs' feet.

Walmart, the huge American supermarket entered China in 1996, but despite a relatively early entrance their progress in the market has been slow. Today, Walmart has 338 shops in 124 Chinese cities, with 90,000 employees and annual sales of some $7 billion – although this sounds high, it is less than 3 per cent of its sales in America.

The market looks very attractive in terms of numbers and willingness to spend, although purchasing power is still relatively low. China's 1.4 billion people are rapidly urbanising and eager for all the goods their parents were unable to have. Their government is eager to promote domestic consumption, but only 1.4 per cent of urban households have an income of more than $15,000 a year, and only 11 per cent earn $5,000–$15,000. Also, the Chinese all have to save a high proportion of their earnings because unless they work for the government they are unlikely to receive a significant pension. Even so, the potential is there and western retailers have their eyes on the future.

Question:

Do you think Western retailers should invest now or later in China? Why? *(14 marks)*

Stages of entering an overseas market

Typically, firms will begin to sell abroad by exporting. This means they will continue to focus on the domestic market but accept orders from abroad. This is a low-risk strategy – it simply involves a firm sending its products to other countries. It may at this stage do some marketing abroad, for example advertising its products or attending promotional events. If sales from abroad continue to grow the firm might look for an agent or representative overseas. This means it has someone based abroad who knows its business well and understands local conditions. The agent or representative will try and generate business for the firm and may be paid on commission. Again, the risk of this approach is relatively low.

A bigger commitment would be made when the firm finds a partner and forms some type of joint venture or alliance. For example, it might collaborate on projects and share the profits. At this stage the partner is not just someone representing the firm, but someone who the firm is working with locally to generate more sales. For example, a drinks company might have an alliance with a local drinks company to share distribution costs or to gain access to some outlets. It might also franchise, if that was appropriate. This would mean that it was working with local partners who would better understand the political, legal, economic, social and technological issues in the chosen overseas market.

If the chosen market looks as if it will prosper long term, a business might take over a foreign partner or invest to set up its own operations there. These two options show real commitment to the market and are

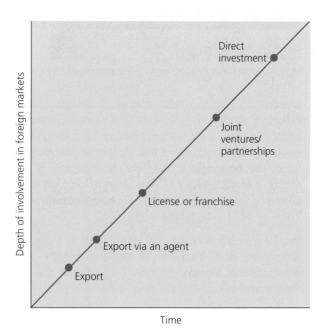

Figure 8.5 Stages of entering an overseas market

major strategic decisions; this involves a high degree of risk and expenditure. Several UK businesses have found it difficult to succeed abroad because of the real differences in approach between regions.

Globalisation or localisation?

Once the decision has been made to enter an overseas market a firm must consider the extent to which it will adapt its offerings to local conditions. Is it possible to market the product in almost the same way in every country (as Gillette does with its razors), or will the marketing have to be adjusted for each market? If a firm pursues a global strategy this means it is adopting essentially the same marketing mix wherever it competes. A global marketing strategy has been adopted by firms in several markets such as jeans, soft drinks, cigarettes and luxury goods. A Rolex watch, for example, is positioned and marketed in a very similar way across the world.

One advantage of a global approach is that it offers marketing economies of scale, for example, the firm can develop one advertising campaign and one approach to packaging worldwide. However, this type of strategy does not respond to the requirements of different national markets and so the firm may lose sales to competitors who focus more on local needs. In markets such as food and drink and the media a firm may need to adapt significantly to local requirements. On the other hand, a more local approach may meet customer needs more precisely but may be more expensive and more complex to manage.

In reality, most companies will choose a balance between the global and local approach. Unilever, for example, has built several superbrands (such as Dove). These are global brands which sell in many different markets. They have the same name and logo everywhere. However, some adjustments are made in the way they are promoted to reflect local conditions. Unilever calls itself a 'multi-local multinational'. This is reflected in its structure – it has brand managers who look after a brand globally and local country managers who look after all related issues in their areas. This approach is also called a 'think global, act local' strategy. Companies try to find economies of scale where they can be doing things the same but, where necessary, they adjust to the local market. McDonald's has the same basic brand image and approach everywhere, but sells wine in France, does not sell pork in Muslim countries and adjusts their menu in different areas. Coca-Cola sells its main brands globally but has over 200 local brands that only sell in limited areas.

BUSINESS IN FOCUS

Diageo marketing overseas

Drinkers of whisky have tended to associate the drink with success. This is why the Johnnie Walker brand has used its image of a confident, successful striding man on its packaging for several years. However, people celebrate success in different ways and therefore Diageo, the group that owns the Johnnie Walker brand, has started to adjust its marketing. In China, for example, a recent advertising campaign has featured an extreme game of golf played by two young men culminating in shots taken from a golf cart, up a tree and even beneath the chin of a crocodile!

Johnnie Walker has 34 per cent of the Chinese whisky market, making it the second most popular brand behind Chivas Regal, which has a 50 per cent share. The market is certainly worth fighting for. According to the Scotch Whisky Association, whisky exports to China rose from £1.5 million in 2001 to £46 million in 2005. China's rapidly growing ranks of high earners are attracted to upmarket international brands; the country's membership of the World Trade Organisation has also made scotch more widely available and affordable. Between 2001 and 2005, China reduced import tariffs on spirits from 65 per cent to 10 per cent, making the market even more appealing.

Diageo introduced its strategy for expanding in China in 2004, but understanding the complexities of a different regional market is not easy.

Chinese consumers drink whisky in a more diverse range of venues than western consumers, from traditional restaurants to trendy bars and nightclubs. Tastes and spending power vary greatly among Chinese consumers, depending on where they live. One popular mixer with scotch is iced green tea.

Diageo has identified four consumer groups. 'The Chinese people are not monolithic,' said the managing director of Diageo China. 'The size of the market and the complex demographic composition leads to totally different consumption habits and patterns in different parts of China.'

➡

The first, and most strategically important consumers are 'guanxi men' – status-driven 35- to 45-year-olds often entertaining business contacts.

The second are 'strong independent women' aged 35 to 45.

The third group is 'upwardly mobiles' – 25- to 35-year-old men and women who want to be on trend.

The final group, the 'choice generation', is early twenty-somethings who are eager for new tastes and experiences.

Diageo developed a seasonal promotional calendar focusing on important dates such as Chinese New Year and National Day.

Another promotional tool is event sponsorship. Diageo sponsors the McLaren Formula 1 team,

and this led to an opportunity to work with different local authorities on initiatives to promote responsible drinking, culminating in the 2006 Chinese Grand Prix in Shanghai.

Diageo launched a digital marketing campaign to take advantage of its raised profile, and that resulted in 11 million Chinese people viewing its ad online in the week before the Grand Prix.

(*Source: Adapted from Meg Carter in* Financial Times, *14 November 2006*)

Question:

To what extent should companies like Diageo change their marketing strategies for different markets? *(14 marks)*

Assessing a marketing strategy

To assess a marketing strategy you should consider the following questions:

- Does it help the business to fulfil its marketing objectives (and therefore its corporate objectives) within the given time frame?
- Does it do this using the set resources and in a way which reflects the values of the brand and organisation?
- Is it sustainable (can you protect what you have achieved) or is it easy for others to imitate, forcing you to move on before you can fully reap the gains of the strategy?

Summary

The marketing strategy is the long-term plan to fulfil the marketing objectives and ultimately the corporate objectives. This may be analysed using Ansoff's matrix, considering which products to offer and which markets to compete in. It may also be analysed using Porter's low-cost and differentiation strategies or using the concept of value. The selection of the marketing strategy will depend on factors such as the external environment, the strengths of the business and competitors' actions.

Key terms

Globalisation occurs when a business treats the world as one market and offers the same products to every country.

Localisation occurs when a firm adapts what it offers to local market conditions.

Examiner's advice

When assessing a marketing strategy, make sure you are clear about:

- the characteristics of the target market, via market analysis
- the positioning of the business relative to its competitors
- the nature of the marketing strategy (is it aiming to justify a premium price or is it offering a low price?)
- the link between the marketing strategy and the other functions
- the marketing objectives (how will success be judged?)
- the risk involved in any strategy relative to the likely returns
- whether it fits with the business strengths – could Primark suddenly move into the premium market, for example? What about Gucci chewing gum? Ryanair luxury hotels? Virgin old people's homes?

Choosing where to compete (markets), what to compete with (products) and how to compete (positioning) are the key strategic decisions. Once these decisions are made the tactical decisions (that is, the marketing mix) are more straightforward – if you know what to offer, whom to offer it to and what you are trying to achieve, the mix should follow logically. You start with the marketing strategy and the marketing mix follows from this.

Remember that it is not just a question of choosing a marketing strategy – the business must be able to deliver it. If you choose a low-price strategy, can the business actually get its costs down? Does it have a more efficient way of providing the product or service than others? Does it have better relations with suppliers? Can it avoid some costs by missing out some stages (such as direct selling)? You cannot sustain low prices unless you somehow have lower costs to make sure this is feasible for the business. Similarly, if you offer a differentiated product, how is it differentiated? What value have you actually added? Is this sustainable or can it be imitated easily?

Changing a marketing strategy is a common scenario in case studies. Just think carefully about whether it fits with the business strengths and the many implications it will have for all the other functions. Imagine Primark decided to become a leading, exclusive design business – what would have to happen to bring this about? What if British Airways decided to target the low-price airline segment – what would need to happen for them to do this? Is it a wise strategy or not? How long is it likely to take and how much is it likely to cost?

When considering entering an overseas market, think about:

- the likely costs
- the likely risk
- the likely competition
- the understanding of the market
- the time frame
- the link with the firm's strengths and experience.

Progress questions

1. What is a marketing strategy? *(2 marks)*

2. Outline the key features of the Ansoff matrix. *(4 marks)*

3. What is meant by market penetration? Give an example. *(3 marks)*

4. What is meant by market development? Give an example. *(3 marks)*

5. What is meant by new product development? Give an example. *(3 marks)*

6. What is meant by diversification? Give an example. *(3 marks)*

7. What is meant by a low-cost strategy (Porter)? Give an example. *(3 marks)*

8. What is meant by a differentiation strategy (Porter)? Give an example. *(3 marks)*

9. Explain two factors likely to influence a marketing strategy. *(6 marks)*

Analysis question

This question relates to the case study on page 72.

To what extent might a market penetration strategy be a better option than Mark's plan to enter China? *(16 marks)*

Candidate's answer:

Market penetration is a strategy set out as part of the Ansoff matrix. It involves selling more existing products in existing markets. This is meant to be a relatively low-risk strategy because managers know the market and the product already. In this case neither Susan nor Mark have any international experience and yet clearly have UK experience (Susan has been working in this market for 15 years). This means they have significant experience domestically and this should help them make better decisions. By comparison they know very little of the Chinese market and will have to buy in advice which could be expensive and they still might not know if it is reliable. This means staying in the UK may be the best option. →

However, the UK market may be saturated as growth seems to be slowing. Others have gone abroad and seem to have been successful so they might be successful as well. The costs of coffee are rising and the prices in the UK falling, so this is reducing margins. Other businesses in the UK have closed and so this is clearly a competitive market and so going abroad may be the best option.

The right option may depend on how much pressure there is for growth and profits and the risks that the business is likely to take. It says the directors are generally quite cautious in their approach. It may be that China is too unfamiliar and may be it should look for more similar markets where they have some understanding (for example, Mark worked in France for a while). In the short term staying in the UK and exploiting the brand more is probably the safest option but if you are looking at the long term, a move to target China may be desirable if risky. Sometimes you need to take risks.

Examiner's comments:

This is a very strong answer because it is clearly rooted in the case study and because it provides a clear answer to the question. According to this candidate the domestic market is safer in many ways but actually over time it may not be. Other firms have closed and market conditions are not especially favourable in the UK, whereas China offers more opportunities (and also more dangers). Of course it depends on the decision makers and what their priorities are, as the student has recognised; however the case for and against is made well and there is a conclusion summing up the issues to be considered.

Evaluation question

To what extent would a differentiation strategy be a better option than a low cost option for Aspire when entering China? *(16 marks)*

9 Developing and implementing marketing plans

Once a business has a marketing objective it needs to implement the marketing strategy to achieve it. This requires careful planning. A marketing plan sets out what a business wants to achieve and how and provides the detail required to monitor and review its progress.

In this chapter we examine:
- the meaning of a marketing plan
- the components of a marketing plan
- the internal and external influences on a marketing plan
- issues in implementing a marketing plan.

Introduction to marketing plans

A marketing plan sets out in detail:
- the marketing objectives
- the marketing strategy
- the marketing budget
- the marketing activities.

A marketing plan should set out exactly what needs to be achieved, how it is to be achieved, how much will be spent on it and what is going to be done when, who is responsible for each activity and what resources are needed for the activity. For example, imagine the strategy to launch a new product; the marketing plan would set out information such as:
- when the launch is
- what promotional activities will accompany the launch
- what activities need to be undertaken pre-launch
- how much can be spent on each activity
- who is responsible for the successful completion of each part of the plan.

So the marketing plan is almost a checklist for managers to make sure they have thought through what needs to be done and to monitor progress as activities are completed. The plan also helps to integrate all the different elements of the business. It shows the human resources department when different staff will be needed. It shows finance what expenditure is going to happen when and when inflows might be expected. It shows operations when production is going to be required.

The benefits of a marketing plan

Marketing planning is useful for several reasons:
- By setting out in detail what it wants to achieve the firm should be in a better position to coordinate its activities.
- Managers can review the firm's progress by comparing the actual outcomes with the planned outcomes. If these are not the same it can analyse why these variances occurred and learn from this; this should then improve planning in the future.
- The process of planning is useful in itself because it forces managers to think ahead and consider what might happen and what they need to do to succeed. This should make success more likely.
- The plan should provide a sense of direction for all of those involved and help them to assess whether what they are doing is the right thing.

Many marketing decisions will involve significant amounts of money and other resources. Managers will not want to commit such resources without a clear idea of how they are to be used and what is to be done at each stage. A plan of some form is therefore very desirable – without it there is likely to be a lack of coordination and direction. Remember the old saying, 'Planning prevents poor performance'.

However, getting the right plan means making sure that you have the right set of activities, that the strategy itself is right and that everyone delivers at each stage. The process of planning may itself have flaws and disadvantages.

The possible drawbacks of marketing planning include the following:

- It is possible for the plan to become out of date because of changes in market conditions. In this case, sticking to the plan can do more harm than good. Managers must be flexible and be prepared to review the plan regularly to check that it remains appropriate.
- It may take up valuable time and delay decision-making. The firm could spend so long planning that it actually misses out on opportunities.

To evaluate a marketing plan, managers must consider several issues:

- Is it realistic? Can the firm actually achieve the goals that have been set?
- Does it help ensure that the strategy is achieved? To be successful a plan must obviously help the firm to achieve its overall goals.
- Is it affordable? Does the firm have the finance necessary for it to work?
- Does it fit with the firm's strengths? If it is based on differentiating its offering can the business actually do this? If it is based on matching competitors' offerings at a lower price is this actually possible? How can lower costs be achieved?

The ultimate test of any plan is, of course, whether it actually works! To some extent this is in the hands of the firm, but it also depends on external factors. Even the most successful businessperson is usually willing to accept that luck played some part in his or her success. Succeeding when market conditions are against you is obviously more difficult than succeeding when the business climate is very favourable.

The marketing budget

A marketing budget is a quantifiable financial target which is set by a firm and which relates to its future marketing activities. It may involve a target level of sales for a particular product (a sales budget), or set out the amount a firm intends to spend to achieve its marketing objectives (a marketing expenditure budget). The sales budgets may include targets for the absolute level of sales a firm would like to achieve, or for a desired level of market share; they may also include targets for particular regions or for particular types of customers or distribution channels. Marketing expenditure budgets, by comparison, set out the desired amount of spending on activities such as advertising, sales promotions, paying the sales force, direct mailings and market research.

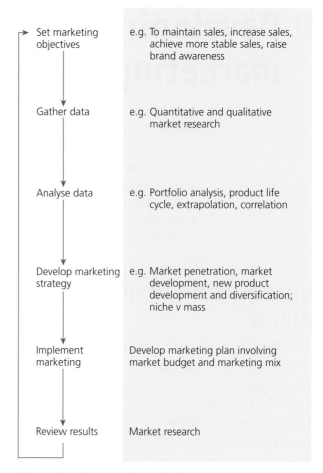

Figure 9.1 The scientific marketing model

The size of the marketing expenditure budget will depend on:

- **The firm's overall financial position** – the amount of money allocated to a particular function such as marketing will inevitably depend on what it has available to spend in total. In a successful year it may be easier to have a bigger budget than in an unsuccessful year. On this basis the marketing budget is likely to be lower when sales are lower and bigger when they are higher. This is often what actually happens within organisations, although in many ways this is not a particularly sensible way to budget. In unsuccessful years the budget should arguably be higher (not lower) in order to improve the firm's sales, assuming of course that the firm can raise the funds needed to finance this. Unfortunately, though, the size of the budget does not just depend on what the firm would like it to be – it must depend on what the firm actually has available or what funds it can raise; as a result the budget may be lower at precisely the time when managers would like to increase it.

- **The firm's marketing objectives and strategy** – the amount of money allocated for marketing activities should clearly depend on what the firm is trying to achieve and the returns it expects to gain from its plans. When first launching a product, for example, the promotional budget is likely to be higher than it is for a more established product. Similarly, when first entering a new segment, spending on market research may be higher than in a 'normal' year.
- **The amount the firm expects to receive back** is also of critical importance: a firm is likely to be prepared to spend more on marketing a project with a high rate of return than on one which has a low expected rate of return.
- **Competitors** – a firm's budget is very likely to be affected by the amount its competitors are spending. If its competitors increase their spending on product development or promotion, for example, a firm may feel it necessary to increase its own expenditure to maintain its competitive position.

Of course, just because a firm has a large marketing budget does not mean that its marketing is necessarily more effective; the effectiveness of marketing activities will depend in part on the funds available, but it will also depend on whether the right activities have been chosen in the first place and how effectively they are being managed and implemented.

How to set the marketing budget

The marketing budget should be set in consultation with those who will be responsible for undertaking the activities it involves. The amount of money to be spent on marketing overall, for example, should be agreed with the marketing manager. Given that the marketing manager is the person who will be held accountable if the budget is not hit, he or she should obviously be involved in deciding what the figure should be.

By involving the people who will actually have to achieve these financial targets the firm is more likely to gain their commitment. If, instead, people are simply told that they have to achieve certain targets without any prior discussion they are unlikely to feel much ownership of the budgets and as a result are unlikely to be committed to them. They may resent the fact they have not been involved in the process of setting the targets and consequently they may not be motivated to achieve them.

Furthermore, the process of discussing the targets may well highlight important issues which their superiors need to be aware of; the people who implement the policies are the ones who are most likely to know what is and what is not feasible and it therefore makes sense to make use of their expertise.

However, it is important not to get involved with prolonged negotiations over the size of a budget if this delays decision-making for too long. The process of budget setting can at times be quite slow and it is important to make sure it does not prevent managers from getting on with the job in hand.

Also, superiors must be aware that subordinates may well try to set targets which suit themselves rather than the organisation. It is perfectly understandable, for example, if people exaggerate the likely costs of a project to make sure that they will be able to stay within their expenditure budgets. Similarly, employees may set relatively low sales targets to make sure they are easy to hit.

It is also important for managers to consider the size of the marketing budget in the context of the overall spending and income of the firm. Resources diverted towards marketing are clearly not available for use elsewhere and so there is an opportunity cost, which should be taken into account. As well as the overall size of the budget, managers must also consider the timing of the payments and earnings in relation to the firm's overall cash-flow position. A major marketing campaign, for example, may involve very heavy expenditure and managers must ensure this does not lead to liquidity problems.

Marketing planning and other functions

The marketing plan will have a direct effect on other functions within the firm. A reduction in price to increase sales, for example, may require investment in production equipment and greater recruitment or training. A decision to cease production of a particular brand may leave the firm with excess capacity, less revenue and the need to make redundancies.

At the same time, the marketing plan will also depend on these functions. For example, if a firm has a highly skilled workforce it may be able to build this into its promotional activities (think of football clubs and the way they promote their star players). The talents of the staff may also affect the design of the product – just think of the importance of designers in the software business. A firm's financial position is also important: a business with a strong financial position is more likely to be able to finance new product development than one with limited funds, for example. The production system can also make a difference: the capacity, the flexibility and the quality of the production will inevitably influence the nature of the marketing plan.

Implementing the marketing plan

Developing a marketing plan is one thing. Implementing it effectively is another. The implementation involves making sure you complete the activities as planned, on time, to budget and to the standards set. This means you must have set realistic targets and have had appropriate time set aside for activities. It also means you should regularly review progress at various stages throughout the process. This means that at set times managers should consider whether they are on course relative to the plan. Have the right activities been completed on budget? If not, what is the impact of this on the remaining activities? If the plan has not been fulfilled managers must take corrective action to get it back on track.

Of course it may be that the environment has changed and that the plan itself is no longer viable. In this case it needs to be reviewed and adjusted. All decisions should be dynamic and should be constantly assessed. This is the feedback loop. The feedback loop enables managers to decide what to do next.

Problems of implementing a marketing plan therefore include:

- The external environment or marketing conditions may change, meaning the plan needs to be revised.
- Delays may occur, meaning some elements of the plan have to be reconsidered and amended or delayed as well. The launch of a website might be late due to technical problems or design conflicts, for example.

The fact that marketing plans do not always turn out as expected does not mean that planning itself is not useful. The fact you have a plan means you can see where you are relative to where you want to be and you can calculate how bad any unexpected changes are; without a plan you are operating in the dark.

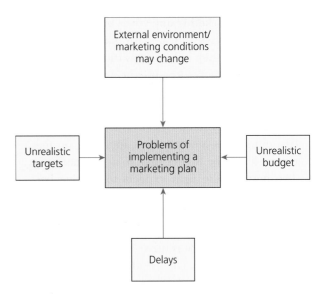

Figure 9.2 Problems of implementing a marketing plan

Marketing mix

The marketing mix is the combination of factors that influence a customer's decision about whether or not to buy a particular product or service. There are many different factors which make up the mix (think of all the things that influence your decision to buy the latest music release or computer game), but they are often categorised under the headings of:

- **price**: the amount the customer has to pay for the product, the payment terms and conditions (for example. the length of time to pay)
- **promotion**: the way in which the firm communicates about the product (for instance, advertising, sales promotion, mailshots and via its sales force)
- **place**: the way in which the product is distributed
- **product**: the actual product or service itself – its features, specifications, reliability and durability.

When considering services we would add:

- **People**: the people involved in customer service become very important in retailing for example; how well trained they are can affect the quality of service and the customers' buying experience
- The **physical environment**: for example, a store's fixtures and fittings can affect your impression of a business and whether you are likely to go back. You may choose a restaurant, pub or coffee shop on the 'feel' of the place and whether it's the kind of place you want to be seen in as well as the actual food and drink

- The **process**: is it easy to get served? Are you served quickly and efficiently? Do you have to fill in lots of forms? Can you pay by credit card? All these factors will also influence your impression of a brand and the benefits it provides.

The role of the marketing mix is to implement the firm's marketing strategy. The strategy determines what goods and services are to be offered and in what markets. The mix determines how these goods are presented to the customer.

The marketing mix should be linked directly to the strategy. If the strategy is to position the product at the upper end of the market this will influence the price charged, where the product is distributed, how the firm promotes the brand and the actual design of the product itself. A premium product, for example, is likely to have some form of USP, to be relatively highly priced and to be distributed through well-selected distribution channels. If, on the other hand, the firm repositions the product towards the lower end of the market the product is likely to be sold at a lower price, to have a more basic design and to be more widely distributed.

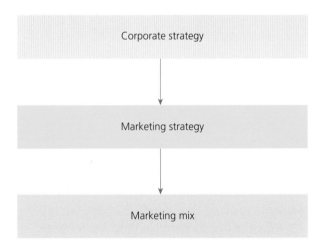

Figure 9.3 Relationship between company strategy and the marketing mix

The marketing mix will also be related to the particular stage a product is at in the product life cycle. In the introduction stage, for example, there is likely to be a great emphasis on promotion to launch the product; the promotion will tend to be informative at this stage to let customers know that the product exists.

Later on, the promotional budget may be reduced and the emphasis is more likely to be persuasive.

To be successful, all of the elements of the marketing mix must be well integrated. This means that the price, promotion, place and product should complement each other. Imagine that when you go shopping you find a well-known brand selling at a very low price in a cheap discount store – you may be suspicious that it is a fake because the price does not fit with the brand image. Similarly, a high-priced bottle of perfume will be unlikely to sell in a discount store because the elements do not fit together – the place is not complementing the price.

Summary

The marketing plan sets out in detail the marketing activities of the business. It will include the marketing objectives, strategy, tactics and budget. Producing a marketing plan is a useful exercise because it sets out in some detail what has to be done, when, by whom and involves a given budget. This should clarify for everyone within the marketing function and in other functions what they have to achieve at any moment and who is responsible for what.

Key terms

A **marketing budget** is a quantifiable financial target which is set by a firm and which relates to its future marketing activities.

The **marketing mix** is the combination of factors that influences a customer's decision about whether or not to buy a particular product or service.

Examiner's advice

Make sure that you are clear what is actually in a marketing plan; it is much more than the marketing mix. It sets out the objectives, the strategy and the budget and then organises the various activities in terms of who has to do what by when and involving what resources. It organises all the marketing activities and is referred to by the other functions as well, to determine what they have to have ready at any given moment.

Implementing the marketing plan links with topics in the study of other functions. To get ready for a new product launch a manager may use critical path analysis in order to be as efficient as possible (Chapter 14). The need for more staff may →

involve workforce planning (Chapter 16). The impact of a change in spending may affect cash-flow forecasts.

You will have studied the marketing mix at AS level. The focus there tended to be on individual elements of the mix and how these might be used to solve marketing problems. At A2 the focus is on the overall strategy; the strategy is supported by the marketing mix, for instance a decision to enter an overseas market may need a different product, price and promotion. You need to think of the mix in the context of the overall strategy.

Progress questions

1. What is a marketing plan? *(2 marks)*

2. State **two** items you might expect to be in a marketing plan. *(2 marks)*

3. What is meant by a marketing budget? *(2 marks)*

4. Explain **two** factors likely to influence the size of a marketing budget. *(4 marks)*

5. What is meant by the marketing mix? *(3 marks)*

6. Explain **two** factors that would influence a firm's marketing mix. *(6 marks)*

7. Explain **two** benefits to a business of producing a marketing plan. *(6 marks)*

8. Explain how the marketing plan is linked to the other functions of the business. *(5 marks)*

9. Explain **two** possible problems of implementing a marketing plan. *(6 marks)*

10. Explain **two** reasons why a business might change its marketing plan. *(6 marks)*

Analysis question

This question relates to the case study on page 72.

To what extent would a marketing plan guarantee the success of Aspire's entry into China? *(18 marks)*

Candidate's answer:

A marketing plan includes the marketing objectives, the strategy, the budget and the details of how the objectives will be achieved. In this case Mark wants to open 1,000 stores in the next five years and intends to do this by targeting China, which is his strategy. When starting a new venture such as this there will be many different people involved such as operations, human resources and finance. They need to know what is happening so they can make their own plans – for example, to open these stores will require major recruitment of staff so the HR team need to know where and when they are going to open them. The marketing budget is likely to be high when starting a new venture especially because there is such a rapid programme of expansion and no brand awareness at present. Launching the stores and the brand and competing with Starbucks and Costa could be expensive especially in the first years when money is needed to keep opening new stores. Finance will have to plan carefully how to raise the money and manage cash flows so timings of what is to be spent when, which will come from the marketing budget, will be very important.

Having a plan will also ensure the activities are organised so that, for example, the press releases come at the right time and the promotional messages are targeted and cost effective. This helps ensure efficient and effective marketing. This will be essential to success. No one would enter a new market spending millions of pounds without a plan so it is vital.

Examiner's comments:

This has plenty of potential as an answer. The student clearly understands what a marketing plan is and why it is useful. There are several references relevant to the case study which shows that he or she is thinking about how a marketing plan would be helpful in this particular situation. The student also makes a judgement that a marketing plan is essential. The problem with the answer is that it is one sided. It does not question the value of a plan or the problems it might have. It does not directly address the question of whether it guarantees success – for example, it could discuss how good the plan is likely to be and how well implemented it might be. The student needs to focus more on two sides of the argument and consider whether success is guaranteed by having a plan.

Evaluation questions

How big do you think the marketing budget should be if the business decides to enter the Chinese market? Justify your answer. *(18 marks)*

Overall question for Section 2:

Do you think the directors of Aspire should accept Mark's strategy of targeting China or not?

Your answer should:
- analyse the arguments in favour of the strategy
- analyse the arguments against the strategy
- provide a justified recommendation on whether to adopt Mark's strategy or not. *(34 marks)*

Operations management focuses on managing the transformation process; it takes inputs and transforms them into goods and services. Everything you use is the result of operations processes from the books you read, the food you eat, the clothes you wear and the music you listen to. At AS we focused on how managers solve operations problems or exploit operations opportunities. The emphasis was on short-term tactical decisions and involved topics such as:

- choosing suppliers
- managing quality.

At A2 the emphasis is more on long-term strategic issues such as:

- deciding where to locate the business
- deciding on the scale of the business (how large the business should be)
- how to increase the efficiency of the business through leaner operations methods.

We are particularly interested in how these operational decisions fit within the overall strategy of the business and how they help the business to be more competitive. While this is new material you will still be able to bring in your AS understanding. Successfully meeting quality targets, for example, is an important element of any strategy, and the effectiveness of an operation's plan will be measured in terms of unit costs, productivity and waste – indicators of performance that you studied at AS.

Case study for Section 3: Pramus Pharmaceuticals plc

All change at Pramus

'The situation in front of us at the moment is extraordinarily bleak and we need to act quickly.' So said Sarah Freemantle, the new chief executive of Pramus Pharmaceuticals plc. 'The economic downturn has hit sales of our energy drinks, vitamins and medicines sold through retailers such as Boots. Consumers are making do whenever they can and the recovery is so fragile that we cannot afford to put prices up at the moment. Meanwhile, several of our medical products aimed at conditions such as high blood pressure and heart conditions are nearing the expiry of their patents. Some of the new products we had expected to be blockbuster drugs, such as Xandol for cancer, have performed badly in their trials and will not be ready for some time … if at all. The corporate objective is to restore much higher levels of profitability and that is what I have been brought in to do.'

Sarah looked around the room at her senior managers. 'The challenges we face add up to the greatest crisis this company has ever been in and we all need to look at our areas of the business and find ways to improve. I have a number of proposals. First, I want every department to look for significant cost savings – if it is not essential and it is not adding value I want you to cut it. There must be waste around from when we were doing better and probably did not pay enough attention to costs. We need to cut 20 per cent of existing costs from every department by next year. It is time to introduce a much leaner approach to everything we do. I know it will hurt but with losses of £125 million this year it is time to act.'

Peter the HR director looked up, 'what worries me about this is how staff will react. It is bound to involve job losses and much greater scrutiny of every item of spending and I worry we will end up in a lot of disputes. We have already frozen everyone's pay for a year and yet we all know the costs of essentials such as food and petrol are rising rapidly. We are not popular now with most of the staff so this new proposal comes at a very bad time. We might be better to wait if we can. When we as a business are struggling wouldn't we be better trying to work with staff rather than making life more difficult for them. This is a people business and focusing on costs is dangerous', he said.

'There is no good time for changes such as these Peter', said Sarah, 'but I think it has got to be done. I want you all to draw up a plan of cost cuts with each of your teams and work out when you can all meet with your specific proposals of when the cuts will happen. Use critical path analysis to calculate everything. There is a lot to do, some of which will be new to you; for example, you are going to need to analyse the existing position, come up with some ideas, discuss with staff and finalise your proposals. So, we need to get on with this as efficiently and as fast as possible – we need these cuts to be taking shape as soon as we can. Please get back to me with realistic plans and timeframes. Meanwhile, we have lost our edge in new product development and I want to know what we can do about that. Mary, what are your thoughts?'

Mary was the director responsible for research and development. 'Changes in legislation involve more testing are making it more difficult to get a product to market. We have also had a few setbacks where things have taken longer than expected. We have not come up with the ideas we need to overcome difficulties when they arise – when we hit a wall we are not able to get around it. We seem to have lost some of our innovative spirit and may need to think about who we have in our teams. However, what we really need is more finance to get our projects up and moving.'

Sarah had been getting feedback from the managers under Mary. Mary had joined the company about two years before and they felt she was not very tolerant of failure. They had told Sarah, 'To be honest it is not worth trying to think of new ways of doing things because you do not get any credit; in fact, if it goes wrong you get an awful lot of blame. One of the problems is that Mary does not like any other ideas apart from her own, so we often go round and round trying to solve the problem her way when we know it will not work. Not only that, our track record in recent years means we are struggling to get the best people to apply to us – winners want to work for winners.'

Sarah listened to Mary's points at the meeting and then announced: 'From now on I want 15 per cent of our revenue in any given year coming from products launched in the previous five years. I also want us to think about reducing the scale of our operation. We are producing now in six different countries at 11 different bases. We have grown quickly in recent years and now have over 100,000 employees, and I fear we are just too big. Staff regularly feedback that they do not know who runs the business, what the business is trying to do and where they fit in the organisation. We know that with a complex operation such as ours we seem to be juggling many different balls at the same time. So we need to think about restructuring, removing layers of management and reorganising to get more focus on the products rather than the regions and we should look at outsourcing. I am convinced we could subcontract a lot of the production and reduce costs, and even some of the research could be done by others. Our research bases are close to some of the best universities and in attractive locations around the world to try get the best talent we can – do we really need to do all this research ourselves these days? Can we re-locate? It is true that in the past as we grew we experienced falling unit costs for many reasons – not least that we could share our costs over more sales and we benefited from mass production techniques as sales of products took off. However I worry we have gone too far and that we need to rethink our approach now.'

Sarah looked around the room again and saw that many of her managers were shaking their heads in disagreement. 'I know this is going to hurt but the alternative would be the failure of the business – we have become too big, too complacent and too inefficient. We need to get nimble, innovative and efficient once again. I want it to be clear to everyone that this is what I want and I want it done quickly.' As she said this she knew she would need to win over the directors and her managers. She had been brought in to make changes, but many thought she was being too dramatic and that, coming from an electronics industry, she did not fully understand the pharmaceuticals industry. 'She needs to take her time to make sure she gets it right and understands the real issues. Things take longer to do in this industry and it relies heavily on investment. I am not sure that short-term cost cutting is the best way forward. She has got to remember the customers, and that we need much more investment in and focus on marketing', said Shauna the marketing director. 'Our side of things has been neglected in the focus on costs. We may end up leaner but with no sales.'

Appendices

Appendix A: Research and development spending

	Pramus	Industry average
2009	13.5	13.1
2010	12.9	13.2
2011	12.7	13.3
2012	12.2	13.5

Table 1 Pramus' research and development spending as a percentage of turnover

Appendix B:

	Number of levels of hierarchy	Average span of control
2009	7	7
2010	9	8
2011	11	8
2012	12	10

Table 2

Appendix C:

	Profit margin	% sales from products launched in last five years	Sales (£m)
2009	23%	18%	1,500
2010	22%	17%	1,300
2011	18%	14%	1,200
2012	16%	12%	1,100

Table 3

Appendix D: Index of marketing spending

2009	100
2010	98
2011	95
2012	94

Table 4 Index of marketing spending (base = 100 in 2009)

10 Understanding operational objectives

Operations is one of the functions of a business – some say (usually operations managers!) that it is the key function because it is responsible for delivering the product or service. Marketing may identify customer needs but operations has to fulfil the promises made. Operations managers will need to agree on the targets that need to be achieved and plan how to do this. For example, what level of quality is required? When you buy a new microwave how long do you expect it to last? Five years? Ten years? Operations will need to deliver the lifespan that marketing identifies as required by customers, and even exceed these targets to some extent (but this does not mean, for example, that it wants to build an 'everlasting' microwave as this is likely to be too expensive and not what customers actually want).

In this chapter we consider:
- the meaning of operations management
- typical operations objectives and their link with the corporate objectives
- the internal and external influences on operations objectives.

Introduction to operations management

Operations management is the planning, organising and coordination of activities involved in the production of a firm's product or service. According to Nigel Slack, an expert on operations, 'Operations management is the activity of managing the resources which are devoted to the production and delivery of products and services.' It is the management of the whole process that transforms inputs into outputs and adds value. It considers factors such as the quality of the goods and services produced, the cost of the process and the speed of delivery. The nature of the operations of a business will depend on the overall corporate strategy. If the business aims to differentiate itself with more benefits than its competitors (such as a wider range of products or faster delivery) then operations will have to provide this. If the business aims to achieve lower costs then again operations must find ways of being more efficient.

Operations management will include decisions regarding the following:

- **Where to produce.** What is the best location for the business? In the case of manufacturing this may be primarily driven by costs; in the case of retail it may be influenced more heavily by where customers are based. Should the business operate several small outlets or stores or would it be better to operate from one large location? Would the business be better shifting operations overseas or can it control the process more effectively in the UK? Given that location affects so many factors such as costs, speed of delivery, ease of recruitment and likely demand levels it is a key operational decision.

- **What scale of facilities are needed.** What is the best scale of production? For example, how many rooms should our hotels have? How many planes will our airline need? How many airports will it need to operate from? What capacity will our database need for our insurance business? How large should our production plant be? How many packages are we going to need to move today? These are all issues regarding the scale of the operations of the business and the nature of facilities the organisation will require. The difficulty is knowing not just what capacity is needed now, but also in the future – overcommit now and you could have unnecessarily high overheads; underinvest and you may hit capacity problems early on.

- **What production methods should be adopted.** What is the best method of delivering the goods or services and meeting the required targets? What is the best way of combining the firm's resources? Should the business adopt a capital-intensive or labour-intensive process? How should the production be organised? How should the store or production plant be laid out? If we are a restaurant chain, will we have a standardised menu in every store or make each meal to customers' requirements? Will we have food pre-prepared?

- **How much of the transformation process to undertake yourself and how much should be outsourced to other businesses.** If we are a school, for example, should we take responsibility for the security of the school? The canteen facilities? The sports provision? In some cases, we may decide to buy these services in rather than provide them ourselves, but there will be some parts of the process that are key to our competitiveness and that we want to control ourselves.

- **Where to purchase supplies from.** Should we always try to have two suppliers for everything we buy, just in case one fails? How much stock do we need to hold to meet production and sales demands? Should we buy from local supplies wherever we can? Should we take into account the way in which our supplies produce (for example, their environmental record)? How much should we care about the way suppliers treat their staff? The way in which a business deals with its suppliers is known as supply chain management. This has become increasingly important as customers have become more concerned not just with what they are buying, but all stages of the operations process. Are the eggs in our supermarket free range? Have we checked? Is the paper used by our business recycled? Is the wood used in the construction process from a sustainable source?

Types of operations systems

There are, of course, many different types of production process – everything from an artist producing a few paintings a year to a bottling company turning out many thousands of bottles every day. Operations managers can face many different challenges and have very different priorities. The differences in operations systems can be categorised using Slack's 4Vs model:

- **Volume**: examples of high-volume production include bars of chocolate and soft drinks; examples of low-volume production include the outputs of an architect and landscape gardener. High-volume production usually involves:
  - capital-intensive production (for example, production lines) which usually requires heavy investment initially
  - large outputs of similar products with limited flexibility
  - low unit costs as fixed costs can be spread over many units.

- **Variety**: high-variety operations include a hairdresser and a personal financial adviser, who are capable of producing a wide range of products; low-variety operations include fast-food restaurants, which turn out a relatively limited variety of products. Processes that have high variety usually involve very flexible production and a complex process to meet many different needs; this generally results in high costs. Many fast food restaurants have relatively little flexibility but this enables them to quickly process orders by using standardised processes.

- **Variation in demand**: products such as bakeries have relatively low fluctuations in demand; by comparison, the emergency services, such as the ambulance service, have a big variation in demand. Processes that have a high variation in demand usually involve:
  - the need to be flexible in production
  - high costs per unit
  - the need to anticipate what demand may be. (The AA, for example, cannot easily anticipate the demand for its emergency assistance services on any given day; it must have the capacity to cope with high levels of demand and reach breakdown customers within its promised time. This business needs to be able to call on equipment and staff at short notice.)

- **Visibility**: this refers to the extent to which a business deals directly with its final customers. A manufacturing business has low visibility – it produces and sells to intermediaries who sell to the final customer; a hairdresser and an accountant have high visibility – they deal directly with their customers. A business with high visibility:
  - needs good customer service skills
  - will involve a great deal of variety to meet individual customer needs.

Slack's 4V model highlights the considerable variation in operations management – there are many different processes and many different priorities. In a continuous 24-hour chemical production process, for example, the focus will be on keeping the process going at all times; stopping or starting the process is hugely expensive. In the case of constructing a new stadium the challenge is to coordinate a set of activities unique to this project. This can prove very difficult especially when new technologies are involved.

Boeing's Dreamliner

In 2011 Boeing's Dreamliner aircraft finally completed its first commercial flight (from Tokyo to London) as part of the All Nippon Airways fleet. The plane, which can travel up to 15,200 km, is a unique design and uses carbon fibre rather than aluminium; this significantly reduce its weight, and as a consequence fuel consumption is 20 per cent less than similar-sized planes. However, the delivery of this first plane was three years overdue because of difficulties with the technology. Boeing now aims to produce 480 Dreamliners a year. Interestingly Airbus, Boeing's competitor, is due to launch a similarly designed plane within two years, highlighting the extent to which innovation leads to imitation.

Questions:

1 Use Slack's model to categorise the production process of the Dreamliner. *(4 marks)*
2 Analyse the possible reasons why the production of the first plane was three years late. *(10 marks)*
3 Discuss the possible consequences of this delay for the business. *(16 marks)*

Types of operations processes

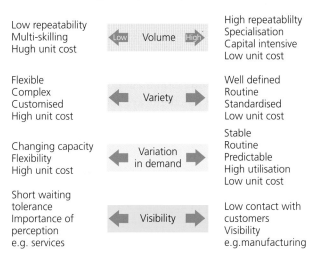

Figure 10.1 The 4Vs of operations

Operational objectives

All managers need to know what they are aiming for. This means they need objectives. An operations objective is a target related to the delivery of the product or service. These objectives should be specific and measurable and state when they must be achieved by. Operations objectives might include:

- **Volume targets**: ensuring that the firm can produce the quantities demanded by customers at the time they want them without running out or having extensive queues. At certain times of the year a business may overproduce in anticipation of higher levels of demand later in the year. There may also be periods when firms are stockpiling because demand has fallen, but managers want to wait and see if the fall is long term before reducing production levels. Equally, there may be times when the volume produced is too small, leading to queues and waiting lists; over time the business will hope to expand capacity if higher levels of demand are likely to continue. The link between operations and sales forecasting is clear here.

- **Quality targets**: achieving an appropriate level of service and quality. For example, serving you within a given time in a restaurant, ensuring you are not waiting for more than a certain number of minutes in a queue, ensuring that products are delivered to you within a given period. Remember that quality does not always entail producing the world's biggest, fastest, quickest or lightest – it involves meeting the set standards consistently.

- **Efficiency targets**: for example, producing products within a given timeframe and ensuring the production is carried out as cost effectively as possible. Remember, the aim is to be efficient while meeting desired quality and volume targets rather than cutting costs and watching standards fall below acceptable levels.

- **Environmental targets**: ensuring that operations are not excessively harmful to the environment. Targets might include reducing waste and pollution levels or ensuring the production process is sustainable. Customers are increasingly interested in whether the production process is using up natural resources. (Velvet toilet paper ran a successful marketing campaign recently highlighting that for every pack purchased three trees are planted.)

- **Innovation targets**: ensuring the products are as up to date as they need to be, for instance by providing new benefits or delivering in an innovative way (for example, films online, making your own calendar online, online greetings cards). Businesses such as 3M and W L Gore compete by being innovative and set targets for a percentage of revenue to be from relatively new products.

- **Dependability targets**: ensuring you do what you say and do not let customers down. Companies such as Dyson test their products extensively to make sure they deliver what is promised.
- **Flexibility targets**: for example, using production processes that can cater for the range of products that need to be provided. However, this does not mean that you must have the most flexible process possible – simply that you meet customer needs. For instance, at university you are likely to be able to choose different modules, but this does not mean each student has an individually tailored course as this would be too expensive to organise and provide.
- **Ethical targets**: for example, ensuring that suppliers do not use child labour and that their employees are paid fairly. Companies such as Nike and Gap have been criticised for allegedly using suppliers that may exploit labour; both companies have taken action to improve conditions at their suppliers.

The effectiveness of operations management may therefore be measured using indicators such as:

- **Productivity**: for example, the output per person, per factory or per machine. In a retail environment this may be measured by sales per employee or sales per square foot.
- **Unit costs**: the cost to produce one unit. The more efficient the process is the lower the unit cost will be.

Figure 10.2 Typical operations objectives

- **The number of defects**: for example, what percentage of the units produced or services completed is faulty? How many goods are returned? How many bills to clients are inaccurate? What is the level of customer satisfaction or dissatisfaction?
- **The speed of production**: for example, are items delivered on time? How fast is delivery relative to our rivals'?
- **The flexibility of production**: for example, how many different pack sizes of cereal can we produce? How many different A-level subjects can our school offer?
- **The amount of waste generated**. Organisations will be trying to reduce the amount of products thrown away.
- **The amount of energy used**. To be more environmentally friendly and save costs, businesses will try to reduce energy usage.

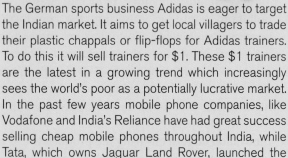

BUSINESS IN FOCUS

Adidas

The German sports business Adidas is eager to target the Indian market. It aims to get local villagers to trade their plastic chappals or flip-flops for Adidas trainers. To do this it will sell trainers for $1. These $1 trainers are the latest in a growing trend which increasingly sees the world's poor as a potentially lucrative market. In the past few years mobile phone companies, like Vodafone and India's Reliance have had great success selling cheap mobile phones throughout India, while Tata, which owns Jaguar Land Rover, launched the world's cheapest car. The Tata Nano was launched as the world's cheapest car for 'One Lakh' rupees or around £1,200, and aimed to persuade families travelling five to a motorbike to trade up. The company followed the model with India's cheapest water purifier and the country's lowest cost apartments.

Adidas had originally planned to launch its venture in Bangladesh but switched to India after a pilot project lost money. The company's boss, Herbert Hainer, blamed high import taxes and the firm's lack of presence in the country for the failure. He is banking on the foothold Adidas's subsidiary Reebok has in India to keep production and distribution costs low. He believes in India, the firm can sell its trainers for $1 and still make a profit.

Question:

Adidas has set a target price of $1 for a pair of trainers. Analyse the possible operational implications of this target for the business. *(10 marks)*

Changing operational needs

Operations aims to deliver appropriate quantities of what customers need at a suitable level of quality and a suitable cost. As customers' needs and expectations change so must operations. In recent years there has been increasing interest in issues such as how and where a product is produced, the environmental impact of the operations process and the impact of the process on stakeholders. This has implications for the operations function; operations managers need to consider:

- who they are working with; their relationships with their suppliers and their suppliers' behaviour may be closely scrutinised
- what resources they use and how they use them; for example what is the environmental impact of their actions? How sustainable are the resources used?

- the impact of their activities on various groups such as the local community and employees
- customer demands; for example demands from customers for more flexibility in terms of the range of options they want, the quality they expect, and increased pressure for quicker delivery.

The last few years have been a buyer's market. With the economy still growing sluggishly demand for many products is low and therefore customers can demand better products and better deals. The bargaining power is more with buyers than suppliers. These changes in terms of customer expectations of what is produced, how it is produced and where it is produced can have significant implications for operations management and require continuous improvements in the processes.

BUSINESS IN FOCUS

Starbucks: responsibly grown coffee

We have always worked to buy our coffee in a way that respects the people and places that produce it. It is simply what we believe to be right.

Over the last decade, Conservation International has helped us develop buying guidelines that address our principles for ethical sourcing. Called Coffee and Farmer Equity (C.A.F.E.) Practices, these guidelines help our farmers grow coffee in a way that is better for both people and the planet. C.A.F.E. Practices is a comprehensive set of measurable standards focused on the following four areas:

Product quality (requirement):

All coffee must meet Starbucks' standards of high quality.

Economic accountability (requirement):

Transparency is required. Suppliers must submit evidence of payments made throughout the coffee supply chain to demonstrate how much of the price Starbucks pays for green (unroasted) coffee gets to the farmer.

Social responsibility (evaluated by third-party verifiers):

Measures in place that concern safe, fair and humane working conditions. These include protecting the rights of workers and providing adequate living conditions. Compliance with the indicators for minimum-wage requirements and addressing child labour/forced labour and discrimination is mandatory.

Environmental leadership (evaluated by third-party verifiers):

Measures in place to manage waste, protect water quality, conserve water and energy, preserve biodiversity and reduce agrochemical use.

Our goal

By 2015 we aim to have 100 per cent of our coffee certified or verified by an independent third party.

(Source: Starbucks, www.starbucks.co.uk)

Questions:

1 Analyse the possible operational implications of the decision to use C.A.F.E. coffee. *(10 marks)*
2 Discuss the possible benefits to Starbucks of buying C.A.F.E. coffee. *(16 marks)*

Achieving the different operational objectives simultaneously may be difficult – for example, if you raise the quality criteria this may lead to an increase in costs. Similarly adopting flow production techniques may lead to lower unit costs but may reduce the amount of flexibility the business has in terms of variety of products produced. Alternatively in an effort to boost productivity, a firm may demand much greater effort from workers, possibly resulting in lower-quality products as work is rushed. The impact of any given operations target on other targets must be considered. Therefore, for example, an effort to reduce waiting times in doctors' surgeries may lead to patients being seen very quickly but the quality of advice may suffer. This means that operations managers must decide on the key aspects of the process in relation to overall strategy of the business. Operations managers often try to identify 'order qualifiers' – these are things that are needed in order to be considered by potential buyers and 'order winners' – the aspects of operations that are the ones that close the deal. The order qualifiers and order winners determine the areas of operations that the managers need to focus on.

Operations and competitiveness

The competitiveness of a business depends on whether it can provide better value than its competitors. This in turn depends on the price it charges in relation to the benefits it offers. The operations function is critical when it comes to determining the competitiveness of a business because it influences:

- Costs: the efficiency of production will have a major influence on its price; if the business can get costs down it may be able to reduce price and maintain profit margins.
- Quality: one important benefit a business can provide is a product that clearly meets the needs of its customers. If it can do this effectively customers may well be prepared to spend more and still regard it as good value.
- Speed: the speed of production or delivery may be an important benefit for example, if you need machines fixed quickly then customers may be willing to pay more for faster service. Think of a school and the importance of the photocopying machines working properly; it may be worth paying more for a provider that guarantees fast repair service if problems arise.

- Reliability: one of the main USPs of McDonald's is its reliability – you know what you are going to get each time. This removes any uncertainty and if you are short of time it is an important benefit. The ability to deliver benefits consistently is an important element of some key brands.
- Flexibility: the ability to amend the product to meet different customer demands may be important and worth paying for. Investment in research and development and new product development may enable a business to meet a variety of different and changing needs.

Operations management can therefore increase the benefits a business offers via its products and/or reduce the costs of delivering these. If as a result of operations management a business can provide more benefits at a lower price this increases its competitiveness. The relative focus on benefits versus costs will depend on the overall strategy of the business. Primark may focus more on costs, Mercedes more on benefits.

BUSINESS IN FOCUS

Shell

The multinational energy business, Shell, measures its performance using a number of different indicators. As well as measuring its financial position, such as its profits, it also considers its impact on stakeholders such as employees and society in general. Indicators of its operational performance include:

- carbon dioxide emissions
- sulphur dioxide, nitrogen oxide and methane emissions
- oil spills
- fresh water use
- waste
- fatal accidents
- occupational illness
- percentage of staff with access to staff forums (where their views can be represented)
- gender diversity.

(*Source: www.shell.com*)

Question:

Discuss the possible reasons why Shell is interested in measuring these operational indicators as well as profit. (*16 marks*)

The most appropriate measures of operational effectiveness depend on the nature of the business. An airline might measure the proportion of flights that take off and land on time. A call centre might measure how many calls are taken per day and how long it takes to answer them. A school might measure its absolute exam results or the value it has added to students' performance. A hospital might measure the cleanliness of wards, the number of patients recovering, the time spent in hospital and the success of operations.

BUSINESS IN FOCUS

Marks & Spencer

In 2007 Marks & Spencer announced that it was to spend £200 million over five years on a wide-ranging 'eco-plan'. Marks & Spencer calls its approach 'Plan A – because there is no Plan B'. It aims to reduce its environmental impact in all areas of the business, for example to:

- reduce the effect of its stores and delivery vehicles
- reduce the amount of packaging
- reduce the amount of energy, water and waste
- reduce ozone depleting HCFC gases with less harmful HFCs in their refrigerators
- source supplies from sustainable sources.

In 2011 it said in its annual report:

'We've set-up a range of programmes with our food suppliers, growers, farmers and clothing factories to develop sustainability frameworks for measuring progress on energy, waste, water and employment standards.

'On climate change, we've improved energy efficiency in our stores by 23 per cent (after weather adjustment) and warehouses by 24 per cent against 2006/07. We've also met our target to improve the fuel efficiency of our delivery fleets by 20 per cent. Our total carbon emissions have been reduced by 13 per cent, down by over 90,000 tonnes CO_2e from 2006/07 whilst our sales floor footage has continued to grow. We're now recycling 94 per cent of all the waste we generate from our stores, offices and warehouses. Total waste is down by over a third and we're taking further action to reduce food waste. We've also met our 25 per cent target to reduce non-glass packaging per item sold against 2006/07, a year ahead of plan. On natural resources, 90 per cent of wild fish (last year 62 per cent) and 76 per cent of wood (last year 72 per cent) now meet our sustainable sourcing standards.

'We've continued the extension of our Ethical Model Factory programme into India and provided training to 37,000 workers in our supply chains. We've also continued to increase our range of Fairtrade food. Plan A is a journey, so we still need to maintain progress across the board. However, there are also a few areas where our progress has not been as good as we'd have liked. We've had to evolve our plans to become carbon neutral in response to changes in government policy on renewable energy. We've also struggled to identify steps to meet our water efficiency targets, but we now have a robust plan to achieve our 20 per cent reduction target by 2012.'

(Source: Marks and Spencer)

Questions:

1. Analyse the possible operational problems that might occur when Marks & Spencer adopts the approach outlined above. *(10 marks)*
2. Should other retailers follow the Marks & Spencer approach? Justify your answer. *(18 marks)*

Operations decisions, like all business decisions, will need to be regularly reviewed as conditions change. This may lead to changes in targets and approach. In the last decade, for example, many manufacturers have switched production to China because it is cheaper. However, as China's standard of living increases wages have begun to rise, and manufacturers have started to look elsewhere such as Vietnam for production bases. Between 2000 and 2010, for example, *The Economist* calculates that productivity in China grew by about 13 per cent per person, but wages grew by about 16 per cent. This led to an increase in the labour cost per unit over this period. Location decisions may change. Over time new production possibilities may also become possible. With ongoing improvements in technology, for example, much greater flexibility is now available even when mass-production techniques are being used; car factories can now produce in huge volumes but adapt each car for the requirements of the buyer.

Operations management and corporate objectives

The precise nature and priorities of operations management activities will depend on the overall corporate objectives and strategy. If the corporate objective is to double the size of the business then operations may have to increase capacity. If the corporate objective is to diversify then operations managers must be prepared to increase the flexibility of the business's production capabilities. If the focus is on profitability then operations may look to deliver efficiency gains; this may be through adopting different production methods or relocating production.

The operations objectives will therefore be directly related to and derived from the corporate objectives and strategy. Think about IKEA, for example. According to its website this business 'is based on offering a wide range of well-designed, functional home furnishing products at prices so low that as many people as possible will be able to afford them. The IKEA Concept guides the way IKEA products are designed, manufactured, transported, sold and assembled. All of these factors contribute to transforming the IKEA Concept into a reality.' In practice this means:

- choosing relatively cheap out-of-town stores
- flat packing furniture so households assemble it themselves, saving IKEA assembly costs; it also means the business can hold more stock more cheaply
- having relatively few staff around the store; customers find what they want and pick it off the warehouse shelves
- having a warehouse approach, so saving on expensive décor.

These operational approaches help the business fulfil its corporate strategy.

The corporate objective of Costco, for example, is to position itself as a low-cost retailer. To achieve this, the operations managers must:

- choose retail locations out of the city centre which are cheaper than central locations
- invest minimal amounts on display (large stacks of goods are displayed in huge quantities)
- buy in bulk to get better deals
- have a relatively low number of sales and administrative staff.

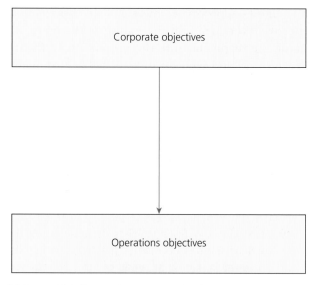

Figure 10.3 Corporate objectives lead to operations objectives

Figure 10.4 Costco

The food store, Pret A Manger, by comparison, stresses the freshness and quality of its foods and service. This requires:

- good-quality suppliers of fresh foods
- regular orders from suppliers so that the business is not left with high stocks at the end of each day (therefore, frequent small deliveries)
- well-trained staff who can produce good-quality sandwiches quickly.

Operations management and other functions

To achieve their goals, operations managers must work closely with the other functions of the business. For example, the marketing function must specify exactly what customers want and what they are willing to pay; marketing will also help determine what needs to be produced and when. Meanwhile, the finance function will specify what equipment and processes can be afforded and the level of costs that the operations function must achieve. The human resources function will also need to work with operations to know what numbers of employees are required, what skills they must have and what training requirements there are.

The relationships between operations and the other functions are two way. For example, the marketing department may set out what customers want but the operations function must specify what it can actually produce. Similarly, the desired level of operations might determine human resource requirements but equally the numbers and skills of staff available at any moment also determine what it is feasible to produce.

Influences on operational objectives

As we have seen, the nature of the operational objectives that are set will depend on the corporate mission and the other functions of the business.

The corporate mission

This is the corporate values, objectives and strategy. Innocent Drinks will insist on production without preservatives. Lego prides itself on high quality, so Lego bricks must be made within 0.006 mm of each other in terms of their length, width or depth. Marks & Spencer has set several environmental targets and so operations must fulfil these by reducing waste and saving energy. American Apparel believes it is important to produce within the US rather than shift production to a lower wage economy overseas. Decisions by senior managers about the positioning of the product and how it will compete therefore have implications for operations managers and their objectives. They determine the relative importance of factors such as quality and cost.

BUSINESS IN FOCUS

Differing corporate values in the clothing market

Uniqlo has grown quickly in Japan by focusing on basic clothes products as T-shirts, socks and jeans. It is now expanding overseas. Its clothes are regarded as stylish but are low price and Uniqlo is now one of Japan's top ten brands.

Fast Retailing has a distinctive business model, selling only around 1,000 product lines (far fewer than its rivals). Unlike companies such as Zara, it does not change these rapidly and is not attempting to compete via fast changing fashions. This enables the business to win high-volume low-priced deals with suppliers and makes managing stock more straightforward. However, although the number of product lines is quite limited it does sell the same product in many colours! There are 50 different colours of socks at its flagship store in Tokyo.

Question:

Analyse the advantages of Uniqlo's operational approach. *(10 marks)*

The other functions of the business

The targets for the volume, variety and quality of a product or service will depend on what marketing identifies as the key requirements to being competitive, and what marketing has promised customers. Finance may set required profit margins, which will influence the cost per unit operations must achieve. At any moment, the existing resources of the business including the skills and experience of its staff determine what is feasible in terms of production and what is likely to be competitive.

The operations objectives of a business will also be influenced by:

- **Demand** – the volume targets (how many to make) will obviously depend on the demand for the product. Demand will also influence the type of products produced in terms of their features, durability and reliability and the price you are likely to be able to sell them at.
- **Competitors' actions** – if competitors are increasing the quality of their service you may have to do the same to match or surpass their offering. If your rivals can cut prices because of

greater efficiencies you may have to look for ways of doing the same. Can you deliver as quickly and reliably as your competitors? Can you respond to individual customer requirements as easily? As competitors improve their offering you may have to improve yours as well; just look at the rapid growth of the netbook, followed by the increase in the tablet market in computing as an example of businesses chasing the innovations of rivals. Similarly, if competitors are driving down prices this will put pressure on you to drive costs down to be competitive.

- **Customer expectations** – customers are increasingly interested in where the materials used in the operations process are from. Are they sourced locally, supporting the local community? Are they ethically sourced (for example, is it a Fairtrade product)? Is the production process environmentally friendly? Are the resources being used in sustainable way (for example, are fish stocks being replenished or forests replanted)? Organisations need to respond to such pressures, for example through using recycled paper, less packaging or more energy-efficient processes.

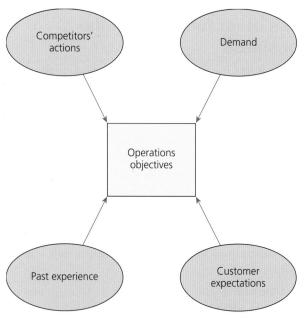

Figure 10.5 Influences on operations objectives

Increasing efficiency

A key operations objective is to be more efficient. Productive efficiency will involve a number of factors, such as employees' productivity, the nature of the production process, the degree of innovation, the scale of production and the capacity utilisation.

Productive efficiency is a measure of the success with which a firm turns its inputs into outputs. The more efficient a firm is the more output it generates with its inputs, or the less inputs it uses to achieve a given level of output.

The efficiency of a firm is measured by the cost per unit. The more efficient a business is the lower the cost per unit; the less efficient it is the higher the cost per unit.

By improving its productive efficiency a firm can reduce its cost per unit. This means that it can then reduce the price per unit and still maintain the same amount of profit per unit. This should lead to an increase in sales. By lowering its price the firm can offer better value for money and may achieve a competitive advantage over its competitors.

Alternatively, it can maintain the same price and benefit from a higher profit per unit. This profit can be invested into the firm or paid out to the owners.

BUSINESS IN FOCUS

Carpetright

In 2011 Carpetright, the carpet retailer, announced that its sales had fallen 5.2 per cent in the second quarter of the year. Lord Harris of Peckham, the firm's chief executive, said, 'Looking forward, I see no respite from the challenging environment over the next year.' He added that the group had plans to reduce its cost base by £4 million. The company had already closed 11 shops during the year, leaving it with 643 stores.

Question:

Analyse the possible human resource problems that are created by the operational efficiency measures taken by Carpetright. *(10 marks)*

Greater efficiency is a key element of operations management. Organisations should constantly be trying to reduce inefficiency and reduce the cost per unit for any given level of service or quality.

To become more efficient in production a firm will consider the following.

- **Labour productivity.** This measures the output per employee. Firms will usually try to increase the output per employee (provided that quality is maintained). An increase in productivity may be achieved through training, better capital equipment, better working practices (for example, team working) or a change in management style or human resource procedures to improve motivation and commitment.
- **The nature of the production process.** Firms must consider the nature of their market and their customer requirements and decide on the most efficient process available. For example, should the business tailor-make each item to individual customers' requirements (this is called job production), or use flow production to continuously produce high volumes of similar products? Flow production, for example, is likely to require more investment in equipment than job production and is only likely to be efficient if there are high levels of demand for a relatively standardised product.
- **Capacity utilisation** (the extent to which a firm is making full use of its resources). A firm's capacity measures the maximum output it can produce given its existing resources. Capacity utilisation measures a firm's actual output in relation to its capacity. The lower the capacity utilisation the fewer resources are being utilised, and the higher the unit cost is likely to be because resources are not being used efficiently. To ensure a high level of capacity utilisation a business must estimate likely long-term levels of demand through market research and ensure it has an appropriate capacity for this. During the economic downturn of 2008 and 2009 many UK businesses found that they had excess capacity (that is, capacity utilisation was low); this led to several of them shutting down production, or in some cases such as Honda, reducing the number of days worked a week.

- **The scale of production.** A firm must decide on the most appropriate scale of production. Up to some level of output a firm may experience economies of scale; by expanding, the unit costs may fall due to, for example, purchasing or technical economies. However, if a firm grows too big it may suffer from diseconomies of scale and unit costs may increase; this may be due to problems with communication, coordination and control as the firm gets too big.
- **Investment in innovation.** For example, increasing investment to develop new ways of providing a product or service can lead to cost savings. Online bookings rather than paper ones, car park payment via mobile phones rather than requiring machines to be maintained and emptied, and swipe cards to enter a building rather than a security firm can all save costs. More about innovation can be found in Chapter 12.
- **Lean approaches to operations.** Lean production is a set of techniques designed to reduce waste in the operations process. For example, if you can reduce the number of times you have to redo an operation because it is faulty you can save money. If you can avoid overproducing and throwing items away again you can save money. Key elements of lean production are outlined in Chapter 14.

BUSINESS IN FOCUS

Tesco

Tesco is able to offer low prices as it enjoys greater bargaining power than its competitors. As part of its drive to lower prices for customers, Tesco also:

- tries to cut out the middlemen and source products from manufacturers or developers
- is building on the strength of its online channel. It now has 12,500 products online, a non-food catalogue and 240 in-store desks for access to the online store, boosting Tesco's range in a number of non-food categories and helping it to compensate for lack of a full non-food offer in some of its locations.

To further increase efficiency, Tesco has focused on investments in information technology (IT). The company has invested heavily in IT over the years, and this has played a very important role in improving its sales, the supply chain, and its efficiency. For example, greater use of IT has enabled it to significantly improve its stock management. ➡

Tesco has implemented more efficient ordering systems and introduced better in-store monitoring processes, which has helped to increase availability of products in stores and reduce warehouse stocking costs. Customer service has also improved through the increased investment in self-service checkouts. These increase cost efficiency and lead to fewer and shorter waiting lines for customers.

Question:

Analyse the ways in which Tesco has tried to increase its efficiency. *(10 marks)*

Being efficient is important to all businesses but especially those that compete via low price. Think of Aldi, Ryanair, Poundland, Primark and Travelodge. All these businesses operate in very price-sensitive segments, and finding ways of keeping costs low is crucial for them. For example, they might choose out-of-town stores, offer a narrower range of products (that they can buy in bulk), have lower staff to customer ratios and spend less on fixtures and fittings.

BUSINESS IN FOCUS

Tata: The Nano

A team of 500 people worked on developing the Nano car. This car is 3 metres long, seats four people comfortably, can reach 65 m.p.h. and aims to revolutionise travel for millions. The 'People's Car' is the cheapest in the world at 100,000 rupees (£1,300); this is the same price as the DVD player in a Lexus! The Nano is produced by Tata, the Indian conglomerate. The company's chairman said at its launch, 'I hope this changes the way people travel in rural India. We are a country of a billion and most are denied connectivity. This is a car that is affordable and provides all-weather transport for the family'.

The aluminium shell contains a rear-mounted 33bhp two-cylinder petrol engine and weighs about half a tonne. The standard version comes with brakes, a four-gear manual transmission, seatbelts, windows and a steering wheel. It lacks a passenger-side mirror and has only one windscreen wiper. The deluxe version will have air-conditioning, while extras such as a radio and an airbag could be added.

The car is the culmination of five years' research and input from across the world, including Italy and Germany. But it was designed and made in India. Tata cut costs by minimising components, particularly steel, and taking advantage of India's low production costs. Because of its size, it uses less sheet metal, has a smaller and lighter engine than other cars, smaller tubeless tyres and a no-frills interior. The company has applied for 34 patents to cover its innovations. 'We shrunk it, made the engine smaller and used fewer materials but we haven't taken any shortcuts in terms of safety or emissions,' Mr Tata, the chairman, said.

Figure 10.6 The Nano

The most basic Nano model is roughly half the price of the cheapest car available today. China's QQ3Y Chery and India's Maruti 800 are both about £2,550. The idea of millions of Nanos on the road alarms environmentalists. The chief UN climate scientist said that he was 'having nightmares' about it. Green campaigners point to India's terrible road system and rising pollution levels. 'Even if they claim it will be fuel efficient, the sheer numbers will undermine this.'

(Source: Adapted from The Times, *11 January 2008)*

Questions:

1 Analyse the operational objectives that might be set for the operations function of the Nano division of Tata. *(10 marks)*
2 Discuss the ways in which Tata might be able to produce a car at this low cost. *(12 marks)*
3 To what extent does low-cost production guarantee that this new car from Tata will be a success? *(16 marks)*

Summary

Operation objectives set out measurable, time specific targets for the operations function such as reducing unit costs by 10 per cent. The targets set will be influenced by many factors such as the strategy of the business. If a business competes on its low prices it needs to reduce costs to be able to do this. The operations targets must be closely linked to the targets in other functional areas – if the overall corporate aim is to grow fast then the operations function must be able to deliver more services.

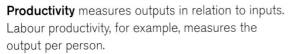

Key terms

Productivity measures outputs in relation to inputs. Labour productivity, for example, measures the output per person.

Unit cost measures the cost of producing one unit; it is also called average cost. This is linked to productivity in that a higher output per employee should reduce the average variable costs per unit.

Operations objectives are targets set for the operations function, such as output levels or unit costs.

Job production involves producing one-off items such as building bridges.

Batch production involves producing groups of items that move together from one stage of the process to another for example, baking bread.

Flow production occurs when items move continuously from one stage of the production process to another (for example, a float glass process which operates continuously 24 hours a day).

Examiner's advice

Operations is one function of a business. The operations activities will be determined by the overall strategy of the business and by the other functions. When considering what operations should or could do, do not forget the constraints of the other functions as well the corporate objectives. If the business wants to position itself as offering better quality than competitors it has to be able to deliver on this; this may require more training, better technology or reliable suppliers. This in turn may require different human resource policies and more funds for investment.

In any case study you need to think what the key operational issues are for a business to be competitive. Is it to be able to meet high standards or is the speed of response the most important thing? How important is it to be flexible and offer a wide range of services or is offering a low price essential? All of these things will affect how a business competes. The ability of the business to provide specific operational features will depend on its resources and internal strengths.

A successful business is a combination of effective, efficient, interrelated activities. The operations function is crucial because it delivers the actual service or product. However, marketing has to assess and determine how to fulfil demand. Finance is needed to enable the business to undertake the activities, and human resource management is there to maximise the human input into the process. Corporate success comes through the combined actions of the different functions.

Remember that simply getting costs down is not necessarily an objective in itself. If you cut costs in the wrong way quality may suffer and the customer will no longer want your products. The objective should be to meet the desired quality criteria in the most efficient way possible (that is, to reduce costs while also achieving certain standards). Also remember that efficiency and effectiveness are not the same things. Efficiency refers to how operations are carried out whereas effectiveness refers to what is being done. You can be very efficient but be doing the wrong thing!

1 State **two** possible operational objectives, with examples. *(2 marks)*

2 What is meant by efficiency? *(2 marks)*

3 What is meant by productivity? *(2 marks)*

4 How can a business increase its efficiency? *(3 marks)*

5 How can an increase in efficiency help a business? *(3 marks)*

6 Explain the link between corporate objectives and operations objectives, with examples. *(4 marks)*

7 Explain how an operations decision can influence other functions. *(5 marks)*

8 Explain how other functions can influence operations objectives. *(5 marks)*

9 Explain what is meant by capacity utilisation. *(3 marks)*

10 Explain the disadvantages to a business of low capacity utilisation. *(4 marks)*

Analysis question

The questions relate to the case study on page 120.

Analyse the possible factors influencing the operations objectives set by Sarah. *(10 marks)*

Candidate's answer:

An operations objective is a target for the operations function. It will be derived from the corporate objective. In this case Sarah has been brought in to increase profitability and the focus in operations is to reduce costs. Sarah will be keen to make her mark and show what she can do so she is being fairly drastic in her changes and pushing a lot through quickly. She wants to cut costs in all departments as this, if achieved, will help increase the profit margin, which has fallen to 16 per cent (showing there is a problem within the business). At the same time, she wants new products to stimulate customer interest because sales have been falling quite dramatically (from £1.5 billion to £1.1 billion) – she wants to take action to boost sales, and in these markets new products may be the key. That is why Sarah has set a target of a certain percentage of sales coming from newish products to emphasise to her team that innovation is important.

The key influences on the operations are therefore ultimately from the need to improve the financial position of the business and increase margins through lower costs and more sales through innovation.

Examiner's comments:

This is an excellent answer. It is in context, addresses the question directly and provides a relevant answer to the question. It identifies the pressures on the business and appreciates how operations objectives are derived from the corporate objective.

Evaluation question

Analyse the possible consequences of Sarah's operations objective of cutting costs by 20 per cent. *(10 marks)*

11 Scale and resource mix

Choosing the right scale of production can have a big influence on the efficiency of a business and on how easy it is to manage. The efficiency, flexibility, quality and effectiveness of operations management will also be affected by the mix of resources used in a business.

In this chapter we examine:
- issues involved in choosing the right scale of production
- economies and diseconomies of scale
- capacity and capacity utilisation
- choosing the right combination of resources.

Introduction to scale

When we talk about the scale of production, we are referring to a firm's output level; this will depend on its capacity. The capacity is the maximum output that an organisation can produce at any moment, given its resources.

The capacity of a firm at any moment will depend on:
- its capital, such as office space, store space, level of machinery and equipment
- the existing level of technology
- the number and skills of its employees.

If a business increases its capacity it is increasing the scale of its production. Deciding on the correct scale for an organisation is a critical decision for its managers. If the capacity is too low compared with demand, they will have to turn away orders, possibly losing customers. If the level is too high compared with demand, they will have idle resources such as equipment and machinery.

The 'right' scale for a business will depend on:
- **The expected levels of sales**. The higher the level of demand, the greater the desired scale, assuming the demand can be sustained.
- **The costs involved in growing.** Can the business afford to expand? Expansion often involves investing in the short run and may take months or even years to gain a return. The organisation may not be able to produce on the scale it wants because it does not have the money to buy all the resources it needs.
- **The resources available.** For example, firms may not be able to recruit sufficient numbers of staff if the skills they want are in short supply.

A firm can increase its scale by:
- investing in new capital such as IT systems, equipment and technology
- investing in its labour, for example training the workforce to increase its productivity; hiring more employees to provide more 'people input'
- taking over another business or merging with another organisation (for more on mergers and takeovers see Chapter 25).

As a business grows and changes its scale it tends to experience efficiency gains (called economies of scale) up to a certain scale and then inefficiencies (called diseconomies of scale) after that.

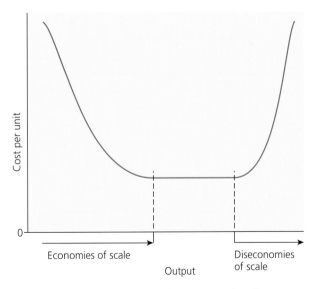

Figure 11.1 Economies and diseconomies of scale

Economies of scale

Economies of scale occur when the cost of producing a unit (the unit cost) falls as the firm increases its scale of production (its capacity level). There are several types of economy of scale.

Technical economies of scale

As a firm expands, it may be able to adopt different production techniques to reduce the unit cost of production. For example, a business may be able to introduce a production line. This is expensive in itself, but if it can be used to produce on a large scale the costs can be spread over many units, reducing the unit cost. At Mars' Slough factory, 3 million Mars bars are produced each day.

Specialisation

As firms grow bigger, they are able to employ people to specialise in different areas of the organisation. Instead of having managers trying to do several jobs at once or having to pay specialist companies to do the work, they can employ their own staff to concentrate on particular areas of the business. For example, they might employ their own accountants or market researchers. By using specialists rather than buying in these services from outside firms, the business can make better decisions and save money. For example, a specialist finance director may be able to find ways of reducing the tax burden or organising cheaper sources of finance. Specialisation also occurs when, as a business grows it splits its process into a series of separate routine tasks. Each individual then completes their task and because they are focusing on a relatively small task and repeating it they become faster at it and more efficient.

Purchasing economies

As firms get bigger, they need to buy more resources. As a result, they should be able to negotiate better deals with suppliers and reduce the price of their components and raw materials. Large firms are also more likely to get discounts when buying advertising space or dealing with distributors. If a firm can become a big customer, the supplier will be eager to keep that deal and so is likely to offer better terms and conditions. The bargaining power of firms may mean lower unit costs and also better cash flow. This approach is what enables a business such as Walmart to compete so effectively.

Businesses that grow also tend to benefit from 'learning by doing'. More experience of what to do, how to do it, what not to do and who to use to do it can make the whole process more efficient. This efficiency gain should not be underestimated. If you are trying to start a business, for example, there is a tremendous amount you simply do not know how to do; a more experienced business will have made the errors in the past and will now be getting it right and operating more efficiently.

Why do economies of scale matter?

Economies of scale can be important because the cost of producing a unit can have a significant impact on a firm's competitiveness. If an organisation can reduce its unit costs, it can either keep its price the same and benefit from higher profit margins, or it can pass the cost saving on to the customer by cutting the price. If it chooses the first option, this may mean higher rewards for the owners or more funds for investment. If, on the other hand, it cuts the price, it may be able to offer better value for money than its competitors. The ability to lower price and still make a profit may be very important in a market with falling demand; this means such firms may be in a better position to survive a recession.

Firms with economies of scale may be able to price competitors out of the market if they wish; this can act as a threat to potential entrants who know they would be less efficient than the established business at first because they would be operating on a smaller scale and therefore may not want to take the risk of a price war. This means that economies of scale can act as a barrier to entry.

The extent to which economies of scale exist will vary between industries. In industries such as energy or telecommunications there is very heavy investment required to start operations and these costs can be spread over large outputs meaning economies of scale are important. It is difficult for small businesses to survive in these industries because they are very inefficient relative to the bigger firms. In other industries such as hairdressing the costs are mainly labour costs, and growth requires more people; this means economies of scale do not exist to the same extent and as a result many small businesses exist in this industry.

Diseconomies of scale

Diseconomies of scale occur when a firm expands its capacity and the cost per unit increases. Diseconomies of scale are often linked to the problems of managing more businesses. As organisations grow they have more products, operate in more regions, have more staff and simply keeping everyone focused and working together can be difficult. Diseconomies of scale can therefore occur for several reasons.

Communication problems

With more people involved in the business, it can be difficult to ensure that messages get to the right people at the right time. Although developments in information technology, such as emails and intranets, have helped, it can still be quite difficult to make sure everyone in a large business knows exactly what they are supposed to know when they are supposed to know it. When businesses are in different parts of the world there can be differences in time zones but even if people are based in the same building, if there are hundreds of them it can be difficult meeting up. With increased numbers there is greater reliance on email rather than face-to-face discussions and this reduces the quality of communication. There may be more messages in your inbox, but this does not mean communication within your company is actually effective.

Coordination and control problems

Just as communicating properly gets more difficult in a large organisation, so does controlling all the different activities and making sure everyone is working towards the same overall goals. As the firm expands and sets up new parts of the business, it is easy for different people to be working in different ways and setting different objectives. It becomes increasingly difficult to monitor what is going on and to make sure everyone is working together. Culture differences are likely to emerge as differences in the values of different parts of the business emerge. The UK division will do things differently from the French division, the operations team see themselves as different from the marketing team. These differences in approach, management styles and values can lead to difficulties in terms of how the different parts of the business work together, causing inefficiency. These differences can get worse and lead to resentment due to the communication problem outlined above.

Motivation

As a firm gets bigger, it can become much harder to make sure everyone feels a part of the organisation (again highlighting the importance of communication). Senior managers are less likely to be able to stay in day-to-day contact with all the employees and so some people may feel less involved. In a small business there is often a good team environment; everyone tends to see everyone else every day and it is easier to feel they are working towards the same goal. Any problems can be sorted out quickly, face-to-face. As the organisation grows, its employees can feel isolated and have less sense of belonging. As a result, they can become demotivated. Think of Maslow's hierarchy of needs and you can appreciate that social needs and ego (esteem) needs may be neglected due to less personal contact.

Diseconomies of scale often occur when mergers and takeovers take place. Managers often anticipate economies of scale from sharing resources, synergy and the power of a large scale. In reality the difficulties of agreeing on standard policies, cultural clashes, different priorities and strategies can lead to significant diseconomies which lead to cost disadvantages overall. In practice, most takeovers and mergers lead to worse financial performance for the combined companies than they achieved individually.

To avoid diseconomies of scale, managers use practices such as:

- having a mission statement to unify the business and outline the central purpose
- managing by objectives – an approach in which all employees are set targets tying them to the overall corporate objective
- using appraisals to review individuals' progress and ensure that they feel involved and as if they acting in line with the overall aims of the business
- communicating regularly in a variety of ways to ensure people feel informed. This could be via newsletters, corporate videos, emails or staff meetings.

Getting the 'right' size of firm is a crucial issue for managers. Firms want to be big enough to have market power and benefit from economies of scale, but not be so big that they suffer from diseconomies of scale. In industries such as brewing and pharmaceuticals many firms have joined together to benefit from economies of scale. At the same time, other firms such as Cadbury, Hanson and ICI have split up into smaller units because of the problems of large size. There is, it seems, no ideal size. It depends on the particular nature of the business, its own culture and communication and the nature of the industry.

Capacity utilisation

The scale of an organisation is determined by the level of capacity it chooses. The bigger the scale, the greater the level of capacity. As mentioned earlier, not having enough capacity can mean the business cannot meet demand. Having too much capacity can mean resources are being wasted. The extent to which capacity is being used is measured by the capacity utilisation. The capacity utilisation of a firm measures the amount it is producing compared with the amount it could produce given its existing resources.

$$\text{Capacity utilisation} = \frac{\text{present output}}{\text{maximum output}} \times 100$$

To increase its capacity utilisation, a firm could increase the amount it is producing. However, there is no point producing more if it will not be able to sell the goods. A firm may need to boost demand, therefore, so that it can be sure to sell the extra output. It may try to do this in a number of ways, including:

- adjusting the marketing mix – changing elements of the marketing mix, such as promotion, the price or the distribution, can stimulate sales
- agreeing to produce products for other firms – sometimes producers of well-known brands also produce items for the supermarkets, which are sold with the supermarket's name on them (these are called own-label items). Although this may seem strange, because it is helping the competition, the manufacturers may actually benefit because they are using their machinery at full capacity and this reduces the cost of each unit produced. When one firm gets another to produce for it, this is known as sub-contracting.
- If a firm is operating below capacity and does not believe that demand will increase again, it may decide to close part of its production process and reduce its capacity. This is known as rationalisation. The banking industry has recently undergone massive changes as firms join together to rationalise their production.

BUSINESS IN FOCUS

International trade has benefited a great deal from the growth in containerisation. Using standard-sized containers has enabled much faster, much cheaper movement of goods and services. Container ships are designed so that no space is wasted. Capacity is measured in the 20-foot equivalent unit (TEU), the number of standard 20-foot containers measuring 20 × 8.0 × 8.5 feet (6.1 × 2.4 × 2.6 metres) a vessel can carry (although in fact, most containers used today measure 40 feet (12 metres) in length). The loading and unloading is usually done by specialised cranes at the ports. Container ships now carry up to 15,000 TEUs on a voyage. The world's largest container ship, the MV Emma Mærsk has a capacity of 15,200 containers.

Emma Mærsk is a container ship owned by the A. P. Moller-Mærsk Group. The number of crew on board is usually 13!

In recent years customers of the Emma Mærsk have been concerned about the pollution it generates; as a result of this the owners of the ship now cross the

Figure 11.2 MV Emma Mærsk

seas at a lower speed. This reduces the environmental impact of the crossing but means deliveries take longer, highlighting one of the many trade-offs in operations management.

Question:

To what extent is transportation important in the operations process? *(16 marks)*

Choosing the right resource mix

As we have seen, operations involves managing resources. It includes:

- deciding the best way of producing
- deciding the best resources to use and the combination of resources required (the resource mix)
- deciding where to get resources from (for example, which suppliers)
- deciding how many resources to hold in stock.

When deciding how to produce a product or service, operations managers will consider the mix of resources to be used. Should more resources in schools be put into teachers, teaching assistants, learning support, computers, sports facilities or the canteen? The answer to this question is likely to depend on who you ask – a case could probably be made for all of these resources and many others. Some would argue that with more teachers the class sizes could be smaller and this would make a dramatic difference to the learning. Others might say that the money would be better used developing a virtual learning environment. Others might argue that diet has a big impact on how we learn. Given that finances are likely to be limited we cannot have all these different resources even though they might be useful; the question then is which are the best ones to focus on and which mix of resources would deliver the best outcomes? The same sorts of decisions face managers in all businesses. Would it be better to have more staff in our supermarkets or introduce self-scanning equipment at the tills? Would it be better to spend more money to have stores in the centre of town or is out of town acceptable?

Businesses will, of course, have differing views on what is the best resource mix and this will affect the nature of the product provided. Dell put money into technology for many years and avoided much direct face-to-face contact with customers. Interestingly, in recent years Dell has felt that customers want advice and therefore more customer assistants and selling via retailers is desirable. In the area of customer enquiries many firms have switched towards computerised systems to direct the caller rather than having operators take the calls. This is reducing the human element of the process. However, some banks and insurance companies have started to reverse this trend and reintroduce 'people' on the end of the phone.

When analysing the resources mix, the combination of resources chosen will depend on factors such as:

- **the type of operations process and the operations strategy**. If volume is the key (for example, in a bottling plant) then a business may adopt a capital-intensive process. If adapting to individual needs is essential (for example, in management consultancy) then the process is likely to be more people focused, A restaurant that wants to produce different meals for each customer will want highly skilled chefs; a fast food chain wanting large batches of products with a limited range of choice will develop a production system in which each person's role is quite specialised and narrowly defined.

- **The relative price of the resources.** In some developing economies where employees are relatively cheap many processes are very labour intensive. This means they use a high proportion of labour relative to capital (machines). The same processes in the UK may be more automated, using more machines because labour is relatively expensive. This difference in labour costs explains why so much UK manufacturing has been outsourced to countries such as China and Vietnam.

- **The availability of resources.** In some sectors there may be a shortage of land or land may be very expensive, which might reduce the size of the offices or production facilities (or mean that the firm has to shift production elsewhere). Machinery or technology might not be available to do the job of a person – we have yet to come up with a computer program to design adverts or slogans, for example. However, in some cases we have tried to pool the knowledge of people into a program to reduce the number of people needed (for example, NHS direct online is a series of yes/no questions which is linked to the knowledge gained from many doctors on illnesses to try and build a program to diagnose you automatically).

- **The nature of the product and process.** Cars could be produced by hand, for example, but for mass production the efficiency gains are so great that production lines are much more likely – mass-market products are likely to be produced by capital-intensive production methods.

- **The state of technology.** The flexibility of technology and the ability to use technology to complete tasks will affect the resource mix used. Cheaper, more effective technology has made farming far more capital intensive than it used to be, for example.
- **Ethics.** The way in which people are used in the production process and the amount they are paid will depend on the ethical stance of the business. Managers may decide not to produce in low-wage economies for example, but invest more in technology and produce domestically if they are concerned about the treatment of staff.

Becoming more capital intensive

A business may become more capital intensive by investing in more information technology, machinery, equipment or transport. This may involve:

- **Raising finance** – the business may try to finance this internally if it has the funds available. However, this can sometimes delay much-needed investment. Alternatively it may seek outside sources such as a loan (but this incurs interest charges) or investors (but this involves a loss of control).
- **Employee resistance** – some employees may resist the move towards greater capital intensity because they fear losing their jobs, they fear they will not have the necessary skills required to use it and/or they do not want to retrain.
- **Changeover** – introducing new equipment often involves disruption to the existing process. This can mean delays for customers if it is not planned properly and people are not kept well informed. There are often initial problems setting up processes, which can also cause delays. Effective project management is therefore very important.

BUSINESS IN FOCUS

Biofuels

As the west demands more biofuels to replace oil as a source of energy, there is increasing pressure on Brazil's booming sugar cane industry to change the way it produces. Western firms now want more socially acceptable working practices.

Sugar cane cutters have been working Brazil's land since 1525, when Portuguese colonialists started growing the crop; they are now being replaced by machines because western firms have decided the way that employees are treated is unacceptable.

The Brazilian Sugar Cane Industry Association (UNICA) has said 80 per cent of the 500,000 jobs would be gone within three years and admitted that moving to a tractor-based system would adversely affect its migrant workforce.

The conditions of sugar workers was rarely noticed when the commodity was exported for sugar, but the position has changed now that Brazil is the world's second-largest exporter of sugar-based ethanol to use as a biofuel in petrol.

Behind the move to phase out sugar cane cutters are stories of exploitation that have damaged the image of Brazilian biofuels in big importing countries such as Sweden and potentially in Britain, where the government has stated that 2.5 per cent of all petrol comes from biofuels. Critics have accused Brazil's sugar cane industry of allowing child labour, high accident rates and workers earning as little as $1.35 (67p) an hour. Manual labour is also blamed for poor environmental practices such as crop wastage and the burning of stubble.

Question:

Should businesses be concerned about the ethics of their actions when making operational decisions? Justify your answer. *(18 marks)*

BUSINESS IN FOCUS

Ford Model T

The Ford Model T car was produced by the Ford Motor Company between 1908 and 1927. It was the first mass-market car produced at a price low enough for millions of people to be able to afford it. Ford was able to offer it at a relatively low price by developing assembly-line production. The first production Model T was built on 27 September 1908, at the Piquette Plant in Detroit, Michigan.

Henry Ford said: 'I will build a car for the great multitude. It will be large enough for the family, but small enough for the individual to run and care for. It will be constructed of the best materials, by the best men to be hired, after the simplest designs that modern engineering can devise. But it will be low in price that no man making a good salary will be unable to own one – and enjoy with his family the blessing of hours of pleasure in God's great open spaces.' The Model T was the first automobile mass produced on assembly lines with completely interchangeable parts.

At the beginning the Model T was produced using assembly methods typical at the time; it was assembled by hand, and production was small. Ford's Piquette plant could not keep up with demand for the Model T, and only 11 cars were built there during the first full month of production. In 1910, after assembling nearly 12,000 Model Ts, Henry Ford moved the company to the new Highland Park complex. Ford developed the assembly line there and eventually cars were coming off the production line in three-minute intervals. By 1914, the assembly process for the Model T had been so streamlined it took only 93 minutes to assemble a car. That year Ford produced more cars than all other carmakers combined. The Model T was a huge commercial success, and by the time Henry made his

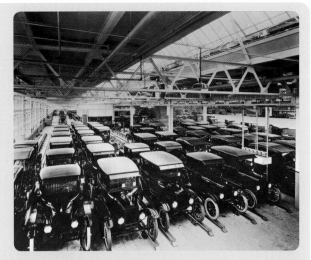

Figure 11.3 Model T Fords

10 millionth car, 9 out of 10 of all cars in the entire world were Fords. In fact, it was so successful that Ford did not even purchase any advertising between 1917 and 1923; in total, more than 15 million Model Ts were manufactured, more than any other model of its day. (Model T production was finally surpassed by the Volkswagen Beetle on 17 February, 1972.) However, for many years Ford refused to make any changes to the Model T. As other companies started to offer more comfort and better styling the Model T lost market share. Production ceased in 1927. The price of a Model T started at around $850 but by the 1920s had fallen to $300.

Questions:

1 Analyse the possible factors that influenced the design of the Model T. *(10 marks)*
2 Discuss the advantages and disadvantages of introducing capital-intensive production techniques in a business such as Ford. *(12 marks)*
3 Evaluate the possible reasons for the success of the Model T Ford. *(16 marks)*

The importance of people

Although some processes, particularly in manufacturing, have become very capital intensive (just think of bottling plants, glass factories, car assembly plants and chemicals plants), the importance of people should not be underestimated. After all, it is people who think of the product idea, research the market, design the products, develop the operations process and manage the business.

Many businesses are focused on what we now call the knowledge economy: designers, consultants, advisers, trainers, architects, film producers, authors, investors, brokers, doctors and surgeons. These are all roles in labour-intensive organisations and the people play a vital part in adding value. Their knowledge is the key resource. Even though manufacturing in the UK has declined significantly over time British firms do still compete in the higher end of markets where design and quality is key rather than trying to fight with lower prices.

The importance of 'knowledge' and 'skills' in the operations process has major implications for human resource management in terms of:

- **Attracting the right people** to work for the business – think of how important people are to organisations such as Google, the Dreamworks film company, Goldman Sachs investment bank, Saatchi the advertising agency and Oxford University.
- **Keeping the right people** – if businesses want to keep good people they need to look at issues such as how they reward them, how they manage them and how their jobs are designed. In the case of highly able individuals who are employed for their knowledge, a more democratic style in which they are given freedom to develop their ideas may be important.
- **Managing people's knowledge** – having knowledge within an organisation is one thing, but making sure it is stored and shared effectively is another. If a business can get people to compare and discuss ideas, brainstorm and problem solve together, it may well end up with better decisions.

BUSINESS IN FOCUS

Zappos

In 1999 Nic Swinmurn could not find the right pair of shoes in any store in San Francisco so decided to set up his own online business which is exactly what he did. The business is called Zappos and the founder had a clear vision, which is:

- One day, 30 per cent of all retail transactions in the US will be online.
- People will buy from the company with the best service and the best selection.
- Zappos.com will be that online store.

At Zappos employees 'believe that the speed at which a customer receives an online purchase plays a very important role in how that customer thinks about shopping online again in the future, so at Zappos.com, we have put a lot of focus on making sure the items get delivered to our customers as quickly as possible. In order to do that, we warehouse everything that we sell, and unlike most other online retailers, we do not make an item available for sale unless it is physically present in our warehouse.'

The business also believes that the happiness of employees is a vital ingredient of business success: 'One of the things that makes Zappos different from a lot of other companies is that we value being fun and being a little weird. We do not want to become one of those big companies that feels corporate and boring. We want to be able to laugh at ourselves. We look for both fun and humour in our daily work.'

'This means that many things we do might be a little unconventional – or else it wouldn't be a little weird. We're not looking for crazy or extreme weirdness though. We want just a touch of weirdness to make life more interesting and fun for everyone. We want the company to have a unique and memorable personality.'

Question:

Analyse the ways in which Zappos's approach highlights the links between operations and human resource management. *(10 marks)*

Summary

Businesses transform their resources into outputs. Decisions have to be made in conjunction with marketing about what to produce and where to position the business; operations then has to try and deliver this. This will involve combining resources to create value for the business and for customers. The way these resources are combined will depend on a number of factors such as the technology available, the price of factors of production and key competitive issues in operations (for example, volume versus flexibility).

One step further: productivity and operations management

A business's level of output is the total amount it produces. The success of operations management depends not just on the total output but also on the value and quantity of inputs used up in the production process. The aim of operations managers is to use as few resources as possible to produce a given output. At the same time, managers seek to maintain a given level of quality.

A business's productivity measures the output produced in relation to the inputs it has used.

There are actually many different measures of productivity, such as:

- output per worker per hour or day or year (labour productivity)
- output per machine per time period (capital productivity).

The most commonly used measure is output per worker.

Labour productivity measures the output of the firm in relation to the number of employees. For example, if 10 people produce 50 units in total each week, their productivity is 5 units each. The higher the productivity, the more is produced per person per time period.

Productivity is a crucial concept in operations management because it can have a significant effect on the costs of producing a unit. The higher the productivity, the more units each worker is making and, if wages are unchanged, the labour cost per unit should be cheaper. As a result, managers are constantly seeking ways to improve labour productivity because this means the firm will either make more profit per unit or can reduce the price to become more competitive.

Productivity may be increased by using a variety of techniques.

- **Increasing the number of hours worked** – If employees work more hours or more days each week, this could increase their output. However, this is not a long-term means of increasing employees' productivity because they are likely to get tired and stressed, and may therefore become less productive in the long term. Also, there is a limit to how many extra hours can be worked.
- **Training** – This is a very important way of increasing productivity. Training can increase employees' output by helping them to gain more skills and to learn new and better ways of doing things.
- **Investment in equipment and technology** – If employees have modern and more efficient machinery, they should be able to make more output. As a government business adviser said when commenting on UK productivity compared with that of other countries: 'A worker can be 100 per cent efficient with a shovel but it won't count if his international counterpart is equipped with a JCB!'
- **Changing the way the work is done** – If the way in which a product is made is changed this can affect the speed and the effectiveness of the production process. Many firms have implemented teamworking in recent years, resulting in improved productivity levels.
- **Motivating employees** – If employees can be motivated (perhaps by offering more rewards or by giving people more responsibility) effort and productivity may increase.

While managers might be eager to increase productivity, employees may resist such efforts because:

- they do not want to work longer or harder
- they do not want to learn new skills
- they fear that higher productivity levels may lead to job losses
- they feel it is unfair that they are producing more unless they receive higher rewards.

Key terms

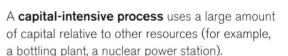

Economies of scale occur when the unit costs fall as the scale of production increases.

Diseconomies of scale occur when unit costs increase as the scale of production increases.

Capacity measures the maximum a firm can produce given its existing resources at any given moment.

Capacity utilisation measures the amount a firm produces relative to its maximum output at any given moment.

A **labour-intensive process** uses a high labour input relative to other resources (for example, teaching, hairdressing, accountancy).

A **capital-intensive process** uses a large amount of capital relative to other resources (for example, a bottling plant, a nuclear power station).

The **knowledge economy** refers to those businesses that compete with the knowledge of their employees rather than with any physical products (for example, management consultants, public relations advisers, advertising agencies).

Progress questions

1. What is meant by capacity? *(2 marks)*

2. State two factors that determine the capacity of a business. *(2 marks)*

3. What is meant by economies of scale? *(2 marks)*

4. Explain two economies of scale. *(4 marks)*

5. Explain two benefits to a business of achieving greater economies of scale. *(4 marks)*

6. What is meant by diseconomies of scale? *(2 marks)*

7. Explain two diseconomies of scale. *(4 marks)*

8. What is meant by 'a labour-intensive process'? Give an example. *(3 marks)*

9. Explain one advantage of adopting a more capital-intensive process. *(4 marks)*

10. What is meant by 'the knowledge economy'? *(2 marks)*

Analysis question

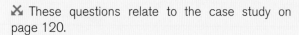 These questions relate to the case study on page 120.

Analyse the possible economies of scale that Pramus might have benefited from. *(10 marks)*

Candidate's answer:

Economies of scale occur when a business expands and the cost per unit falls. There are several types of economy of scale that the business could have experienced:

a) Technical. These occur when firms use production lines and spread these costs over more units. In the case of Pramus it is producing products such as medicines and energy drinks. If it can sell a lot of these then the cost of the investment in capital can be spread over lots of cans and packets and this makes them cheaper per unit.

b) Research and development. This is likely to be the key in this market as research is so important and so expensive. Its sales are over £1 billion and over 12 per cent of this is spent on research and development so we are talking about large sums of money. For this to be viable the business needs products to be launched and succeed and then it can share these costs over lots of units making each one absorb less of the overall costs.

c) Management. As businesses get bigger they can use specialists who can focus on particular tasks rather than do everything. Pramus is clearly a huge business and so is likely to have specialist lawyers, researchers, marketing people, HR people and so on. We know some of these positions such as Mary and Peter from the meeting. Having people specifically trained for a job with a clear area of responsibility can lead to better and more efficient decision-making with fewer mistakes.

Examiner's comments:

An excellent answer which takes theory and applies it well to the case study. The candidate relates their understanding to the given industry. They use the context of the pharmaceutical industry well, thinking about the significance of research and development. They make use of the numerical data to give some idea of scale. A very good response. They analyse the points and do not waste time evaluating as this is not required.

Evaluation question

Evaluate the actions Sarah could take to reduce the diseconomies of scale at Pramus plc. *(18 marks)*

12 Innovation

The business environment is constantly changing and firms need to prepare for and adapt to these changes, or even to create change themselves. If they do not they may get left behind, as Nokia found in the smartphone market even though early on it had been a pioneer. To achieve and to maintain competitiveness may require investment in innovation to develop new products and processes. Innovation can affect the costs and quality of a business's products.

In this chapter we consider:

- the meaning and significance of innovation and research and development
- the purpose and benefits of innovation
- the risks of innovation.

What is innovation?

The process of turning an idea into a saleable product or service is known as innovation. Innovation is defined as 'the successful exploitation of new ideas'.

Innovation allows businesses to develop new products and new processes. Apple may innovate by creating a new iPad (a product) and/or internally improving its communication systems (a process). Innovation can help you create new markets, such as Nintendo shaping the family gaming market with its Wii games (having started out many years ago as a producer of playing cards) or Apple creating the tablet market. It can help to create new ways of doing business, such as online booking of parking spaces or printing books to order.

However, innovation can also bring new competitors into your market. For example, Wrigley was threatened by Trident's entry into the chewing gum market, Kodak was attacked by Sony's entrance into the camera market, Gillette was challenged by King of Shaves' move into the razor market. It can also make markets obsolete (think of typewriters, VHS cassettes and CDs) if substitutes provide better value.

Given that customers are likely to be demanding more each year, innovation can be essential to help a business remain competitive by increasing the benefits it provides and/or reducing the costs of providing the product. Innovation may be essential just to keep pace with what competitors are doing (think of how many 'new improved washing powders' and new cereals you have seen). A failure to innovate may see a business lose market share.

The extent to which innovation occurs in some markets is clear. For instance, looking at the razor market you can see enormous innovations on a regular basis: more razorblades, better razorblades, faster, smaller electric shavers and shavers for women. The same is true in the toothbrush market: electric toothbrushes, tongue brushes, battery-operated toothbrushes. Other markets may seem to have less innovation (for example, socks and pencils), but even here some progress is continually being made in terms of the way things are produced or the nature of the final product. Marks & Spencer, for example, is very innovative in the clothes it offers: suits you can put in the washing machine, non-iron shirts and fabrics that resist stains.

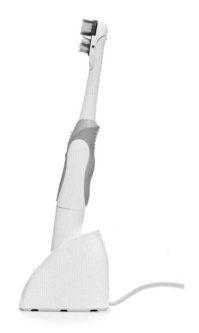

Figure 12.1 One type of toothbrush

The aims of innovation may include:

- developing products which have a unique selling point, allowing a business to differentiate itself from the competition and earn higher profit margins
- developing better-quality products which meet customer needs more successfully
- developing more efficient ways of producing to reduce the cost per unit
- developing better ways of doing things (for example, making it more original or more distinctive).

Innovation helps businesses to compete by creating more value. This means they can offer more for less (more benefits for the same price) or they can offer the same benefits at a lower price (due to greater efficiency).

BUSINESS IN FOCUS

Dyson

James Dyson has always pulled things to pieces. He has always been interested in how they work, asking, 'why does it do that?'. 'Just because it does' has never satisfied him as an answer. While he was at London's Royal College of Art, James Dyson developed the Sea Truck – a high-speed landing craft. Then came the Ballbarrow; its large red pneumatic ball stopped it sinking into soft ground. The Trolleyball boat launcher and the amphibious Wheelboat followed. Then one day he had an idea for a new type of vacuum cleaner. Five years and 5,127 prototypes later, he had developed a machine that had no bag and no loss of suction. Uninterested in new technology and wedded to vacuum bags (worth £250 million every year), major manufacturers turned James and his invention away.

James licensed his design in Japan. The Japanese loved the pink G-Force and, in 1993, the royalties allowed James to manufacture a machine under his own name, the DC01. He patented his invention (which meant he kept the rights to it). In 1999, after a lengthy court battle, Hoover was found guilty of infringing James' patent. Other manufacturers, unable or unwilling to develop their own vacuum cleaners, still try to copy Dyson technology and are taken to court. James and his engineers not only develop inventions, but also improve existing Dyson technology. For example:

- Dyson machines now have smaller multiple cyclones, which create greater centrifugal forces, capturing more microscopic dust.
- A Dyson Ball™ machine rides on a ball, pivoting on a single point, allowing it to go in any direction, unlike traditional vacuum cleaners that only move in straight lines.
- Developing the Dyson digital motor, which is controlled by microchip and spins at 98,000 rpm

Figure 12.2 James Dyson

– five times faster than a Formula 1 car engine. Because of its speed, the digital motor is half the size and half the weight of conventional motors. With no brushes or fixed magnets, it doesn't emit carbon either.

One recent product was developed by a Dyson engineer who discovered that a high-speed sheet of air can act as an invisible wiper blade, literally scraping water from hands. With a 400 mph airflow, the Dyson Airblade™ hand dryer takes just ten seconds and uses less energy than warm air hand dryers – but it is only possible because of the Dyson digital motor.

The latest Dyson product is a fan without blades.

(Source: www.dyson.co.uk)

Questions:

1 Discuss the ways in which Dyson can try and ensure it continues to come up with new products. *(16 marks)*
2 Evaluate the factors likely to determine the long-term success of the Dyson Airblade™. *(16 marks)*

Successful innovation allows firms to keep ahead of their competitors and to keep finding better ways of doing things. This is often the key to long-term success in a market.

Innovation is often linked to research and development (R&D).

Research and development

Research and development (R&D) is part of the innovation process. It refers to the generation and application of scientific knowledge to create a product or develop a new production process. For example, it may involve a team of employees at a confectionery company researching into a new flavour or a new variety of sweet and then trying out different versions until they have one they (and the customers) are happy with. Or it may involve another team in the business focusing on new ways of producing the confectionery.

In some sectors, such as the car industry, pharmaceuticals and energy, research and development can take many years and be very expensive. Glaxo calculates that on average a new pharmaceutical takes 10 to 15 years and costs £500 million on average to develop. However, research and development is often very risky. This is because you may never end up with an idea that is actually viable. Even if you do manage to launch a product, you may find that you do not have very long to recover the costs of development. In the software industry, for example, new products are being developed very rapidly indeed; a successful film may only be showing for a few weeks. In Formula 1, innovation is so fast that the car that is the fastest at the start of the season would finish last by the end of the season if it failed to develop its technology in line with competitors.

Innovation in the shaving market

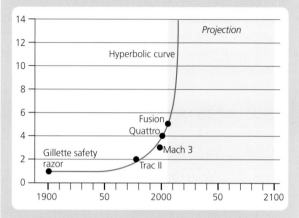

Figure 12.3 Number of blades per razor system

In the diagram shown here, from *The Economist*, it forecasts that given the rate of development in the number of razorblades being offered in recent years, if this rate continues a razor with 14 blades would be available by about 2020! Even in a market as established as this companies are continually finding new ways of delivering a shave.

The King of Shaves launched the Azor in 2010. According to the company 'The unique flexible hinge incorporates our "Bendology Technology", which allows the Endurium coated super long-lasting blades to shave at optimum pressure against the skin whilst the large soft rubber "bumper" helps reduce risk of unwanted nicks and lifts stubble for a smoother more comfortable shave. The ergonomically designed, lightweight handle allows for a superbly comfortable shave which effortlessly follows every contour and curve of your face.'

The leading investors in R&D in Europe

Rank	Company	Sector	R&D investment 2010 (€m)	Net sales 2010 (€m)	R&D/Net sales ratio 2010 (%)	Operating profit 2010 (% of net sales)
1	Volkswagen	Automobiles & parts	6,258.00	126,875	4.9	7.1
2	Nokia	Telecommunications equipment	4,938.00	42,446	11.6	4.5
3	Daimler	Automobiles & parts	4,852.00	97,761	5.0	7.1
4	Sanofi-Aventis	Pharmaceuticals	4,390.00	32,367	13.6	23.0
5	GlaxoSmithKline	Pharmaceuticals	4,378.96	33,136	13.2	13.5

Question:

Discuss the possible factors that determine the amount that a company invests in R&D. *(16 marks)*

Akio Morita

Akio Morita was the founder of Sony. After serving in the Japanese navy he set up a small electronics company, Tokyo Telecommunications Engineering, with his friend Masaru Ibuka. Ibuka was an engineering genius who created many of the technical advances behind the brand Morita created.

The company became very successful in the 1950s when it produced a small transistor radio. The transistor was invented in America, but Morita bought a licence from Bell Laboratories to produce it in Japan. By the end of the decade Morita was exporting from Japan to the US and Europe. In 1958 he changed the company's name. After weeks of searching he found the name Sonus, which is Latin for 'sound'. He changed this to Sony because the phrase 'sony boys' is the Japanese for 'whizz kids'. In 1961 Sony became the first Japanese company to be listed on the New York Stock Exchange.

After further successes with televisions and videotape recorders Morita developed the Sony Walkman. This product (which changed the way we listened to music) was launched with almost no market research and against the views of many within the business.

'The public does not know what is possible. We do,' said Morita. Interestingly, Steve Jobs had the same message many years later. The visionaries have the ability to look beyond where we are now to develop what customers want whether or not they know it.

In 1998 the Sony Walkman was declared the number one consumer brand in America. Morita's famous view of globalisation was 'think globally, act locally'. In America Sony was seen as American; in Japan it was seen as Japanese.

(Source: Adapted from Tim Hindle, The Economist Guide to Management Ideas and Gurus, *Profile Books)*

Question:

Do you think it is right to develop products without market research? Justify your answer. *(16 marks)*

Innovation and swimming

Speedo's LZR swimsuit was introduced in February 2008. Thirty-eight of the 42 world swimming records that were broken in the following six months went to swimmers wearing LZRs.

To make the LZR, four innovations came together.

1 The fabric. The new suit is made from a densely woven nylon-elastane material that compresses the wearer's body into a hydrodynamic shape but is extremely light. There are no sewn seams: the suit is bonded by ultrasonic welding. This removes 6 per cent of the drag that would otherwise occur. Compared with Speedo's previous suit, which was worn by several gold medallists in the 2004 Olympic Games, the new swimsuit weighs only half as much but has triple the power to compress the body.

2 The suit has what Speedo calls an 'internal core stabiliser' – this is like a corset that holds the swimmer's form. As swimmers tire, their hips hang lower in the water, creating drag. By compressing their torsos, the LZR not only lets them go faster, because it maintains a tubular shape, it also allows them to swim longer with less effort. In tests, swimmers wearing the LZR consumed 5 per cent less oxygen for a given level of performance than those wearing normal swimsuits.

3 Polyurethane panels are placed in spots on the suit. This reduces drag by another 24 per cent compared with the previous Speedo model.

4 The LZR was designed using a three-dimensional pattern rather than a two-dimensional one. It hugs a swimmer's body like a second skin; when it is not being worn, it does not lie flat but has a shape to it.

The results are a suit that costs $600 and takes 20 minutes to squeeze into! Some think the LZR improves performance by as much as 2 per cent – the difference between fourth and first place.

(Source: Adapted from The Economist, *12 June 2008)*

Question:

Do you think innovation in sport such as the Speedo LZR is a good thing? *(16 marks)*

Protecting successful innovation

If a firm manages to develop new products and new processes successfully it will naturally want to protect these from being copied or imitated by competitors. If an innovation is genuinely new a firm may protect it by taking out a patent. Under the 1988 Copyright, Designs and Patents Act the holder of a patent has the right to be the sole user of a process or manufacturer of a product for 20 years after it is registered.

The owner of a patent may sell the right to produce the product or use a process to others. This can be a valuable source of income to some organisations. If one firm suspects another of illegally producing a patented product or using its patented technology it can sue the offender. However, this can be costly and time consuming. To protect a product or process worldwide a firm must register the patent in different countries; this can also be an expensive and slow process.

By comparison, the work of artists, writers and musicians is automatically protected by copyright; copyrights do not have to be registered, although once again it is up to the copyright holder to sue offenders. Designs and logos can be protected by registering a trademark.

Mobile handsets and operating systems

In 2011 Google bought Motorola, thus entering the handset market. Google's operating system (Android) had already been extremely successful but now this meant it would be producing the hardware as well as the software. Google's competitors have tried to limit the success of the Android operating system (which Google gives away free) by suing users of it for various infringements of patents. In early 2010 HTC, a leading vendor of Android devices, agreed to pay royalties to Microsoft for the use of its patents.

And in July 2011 Apple won a legal victory against HTC which could lead to even higher payments. By gaining control of Motorola, Google was ensuring an outlet for its software and enables the software and hardware to be better integrated.

Analyse the importance of innovation in the mobile phone market. *(10 marks)*

L'Oréal Group mission

For more than a century L'Oréal has been pushing back the boundaries of science to invent beauty and meet the aspirations of millions of women and men. Its vocation is universal: to offer everyone, all over the world, the best of cosmetics in terms of quality, efficacy and safety, to give everyone access to beauty by offering products in harmony with their needs, culture and expectations.

With the opening up of the emerging markets, L'Oréal's mission is broadening in response to the vast diversity of populations. The whole company is focused on this new horizon: teams enriched by their cultural diversity, a portfolio of international brands present in the different distribution channels, and research that is capable of grasping the world's complexity.

The exploration of new scientific and technological territories is being enriched by this global dimension. Knowledge of different cultures and rituals worldwide enables the laboratories to anticipate and invent the products of the future.

L'Oréal's group profile:

- has 23 global brands
- operates in 130 countries
- has over 66,000 employees
- has over 600 patents filed in 2010 alone.

(*Source: extracts from www.loreal.com*)

Question:

To what extent is innovation crucial to the success of L'Oreal? Justify your answer. *(16 marks)*

Sources of ideas

Firms may generate the ideas for innovation internally or externally. Internally, ideas may simply come through discussion, employees' suggestion schemes, brainstorming activities or the firm's own research department, if it has one. However, to generate good ideas regularly requires a culture in which innovation is valued. This means people will be encouraged to question, to challenge and to improve the existing way of doing things (rather than adopting an attitude of 'it has always been done like that'). This means the business will want to build an innovative culture (see below).

Externally, many new ideas are registered at the Intellectual Property Office; firms may search the patent office records and if they find a product or process they would like to use they can pay a fee to the owner of the patent for the right to use their technology. Alternatively, a firm might buy a franchise to produce under another firm's name; in return for this right a firm pays a fee and/or a percentage of its turnover.

A firm's customers can also be a valuable external source of new ideas. You will notice that many companies have a customer phone line or a comments book to gain feedback from their consumers on their service and to discover more about what customers really want. Innocent drinks, for example, has a 'banana phone' which customers can ring with their ideas.

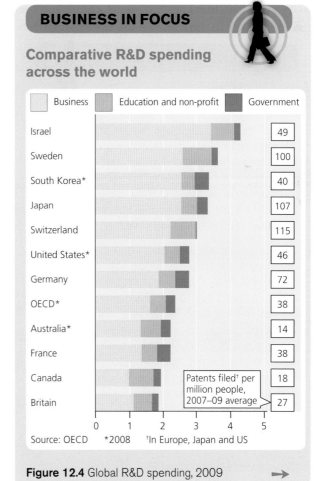

Comparative R&D spending across the world

Figure 12.4 Global R&D spending, 2009

Innovation, culture and structure

To encourage innovation internally a business will want a culture that encourages people to try out new ideas. If the standard way of doing things is to do as you are told and if the people who keep their heads down and just follow instructions are the ones that get promoted then this will not encourage new ideas and new ways of doing things. Innovation therefore requires a culture that encourages people to try new ideas, that does not punish failure and that rewards those who do come up with new approaches.

The commitment to innovation can be shown by the leaders of the business: what do they value, what do they recognise and praise? If you really want innovation to occur you need the senior managers to set an example. This will include making the funds available to those who need them to experiment and try ideas out. Apple, Hewlett-Packard, Intel and W L Gore, for example, are organisations that are said to have particularly innovative cultures.

The culture of a business is important because it supports all other actions and highlights the priorities for the business. The culture is supported by and directly related to the structure of the organisation. Innovation requires the sharing of ideas and approaches. This is more likely in a structure that puts people together from different departments than one where individuals stay very much within their own area. By using cross-functional teams that cut across functional boundaries (for example, bringing together marketing, operations, finance and human resources), a project can be seen from different perspectives and this can help create new solutions to problems. Using Handy's models of culture, innovation is more likely to be a task culture than a role culture (see page 356).

How much should a firm spend on innovation?

Innovation can be an important means of gaining a competitive advantage. Washing powder tablets, pyramid tea bags, combined shampoo and conditioners and razors with four blades are all examples of how firms have gained market share through innovative products. To compete and remain ahead of the market a firm may decide to invest relatively heavily in research and development. To do this it may milk its cash cows and use these to finance question marks and stars. For example Tyrrell's has used the funds from its crisps to move into the vodka market and, more recently, the popcorn market.

However, investing in R&D does involve risk and may waste funds which could have been used elsewhere. There is therefore an opportunity cost, which should be taken into account. To avoid the risk of investing in R&D a firm may pursue a 'me-too strategy', whereby it imitates other firms rather than tries to break into new areas itself. Zara, for example, does not try to lead fashion but is very good at following it quickly. Its designers are great at imitating rather than creating from scratch.

The amount a firm spends on R&D will therefore depend on its strategy. It will also depend on the nature of its market. In fast-changing markets such as consumer electronics the need to bring out new products is very strong – if you do not the chances are that your competitors will. Perhaps not surprisingly, one of the biggest sectors for R&D spending is the pharmaceutical industry; to succeed in this market firms are continually striving to develop medicines which they can patent and which will bring them a stream of future income. The firm that develops a cure for the common cold, for AIDS or for Alzheimer's will make a fortune. There may be less pressure to invest in a more protected market – where the need to innovate is less intense or where the rate of change is slower.

However, simply pumping more money into R&D does not guarantee success. Money may be wasted, ideas may not be forthcoming, the desired breakthrough may not come, the testing may reveal faults with the process, competitors may launch their own products or consumers may not adopt the new products in the desired numbers. The actual number of products that are actually successful is very low, highlighting the problems of undertaking successful R&D.

Innovation as a strategy

While all businesses will be seeking to improve, some organisations put innovation at the heart of their strategy. These are companies in industries such as electronics, pharmaceuticals and computers (for example, 3M, Intel, Google, Microsoft and GlaxoSmithKline). A failure to innovate in these industries means you will fall behind. Similarly, in the music and film industry businesses need to keep moving forward.

If innovation drives your strategy:

- You must be prepared to invest for the long term. There may be big projects that will only pay back over 15 years, if at all.
- You must be prepared for failure; not every new idea will work. The culture will have to encourage people to try. This means your human resource management team must recruit people with ideas, people willing to challenge, and people looking to move things forward. You must provide a reward strategy and management style that fosters such creativity.
- Your marketing strategy may well be one of differentiation as you 'sell' the benefits of your new products and systems. The product may cost more money but the benefits are much greater for the customer. Alternatively, if the innovation is about finding cheaper ways of delivering the service then a low-cost strategy may be appropriate.

A strategy of innovation therefore has an impact on all the other functions of the business.

GlaxoSmithKline

'Headquartered in the UK and with operations based in the US, we are one of the industry leaders, with an estimated 7 per cent of the world's pharmaceutical market … we care about the impact that we have on the people and places touched by our mission to improve health around the world … we have a flair for research and a track record of turning that research into powerful, marketable drugs. Every hour we spend more than £300,000 (US$562,000) to find new medicines.

'We produce medicines that treat six major disease areas – asthma, virus control, infections, mental health, diabetes and digestive conditions.

'We also market other consumer products, many of which are among the market leaders:

- over-the-counter (OTC) medicines including Gaviscon and Panadol
- dental products such as Aquafresh and Sensodyne
- smoking control products Nicorette/Niquitin
- nutritional healthcare drinks such as Lucozade, Ribena and Horlicks.

'Our scientists work hard to discover new ways of treating illness and disease. In addition to their wide-ranging talents, we use the resources of a company devoted to the application of science to improve the quality of life. It takes about 12–15 years and costs over £500 million to discover and develop a new medicine, so we need to be determined and innovative to develop our molecules into medicines as fast as possible …

'We maintain a healthy product pipeline which ensures a flow of new products to people around the world.

'Like all innovative pharmaceutical companies, we carry out a series of clinical trials to test each investigational drug for the potential to become a new medicine. The effect of the potential drug will often be compared to that of an inactive substance, a placebo, which is prepared to look like the drug so as to prevent bias during the trial. The investigational drug may also be compared against marketed medicines.'

Phase I drug trials typically involve healthy volunteers. These trials study the safety of the drug and its interaction with the body, for example, its concentration and duration in the blood following various doses.

Phase II studies enrol patients with the illness an investigational drug is designed to treat. These trials evaluate whether the drug shows favourable effects in treating an illness and seek to determine the proper dose. Phase III trials are designed to provide the substantial evidence of efficacy and safety required … before regulatory agencies will approve the investigational drug as a medicine and allow it to be marketed.

Therefore, a pharmaceutical company performs a comprehensive analysis of its studies for submission to regulatory agencies.

(Source: GlaxoSmithKline, www.gsk.com)

Questions:

1 Analyse why the launch of a new drug by GlaxoSmithKline can take several years. *(10 marks)*
2 Discuss the factors that might influence the research and development budget of GlaxoSmithKline. *(14 marks)*
3 To what extent does the success of a business such as GlaxoSmithKline depend on its research and development? *(16 marks)*

Google

'We're building a company around the idea that work should be challenging and the challenge should be fun. Having a few lava lamps, exercise balls, dogs and pool tables on hand doesn't hurt either.

'Additionally, we've become known for providing free gourmet breakfasts and lunches, kitchens on every floor, a gym allowance (with on-site showers in our office building), lockers, bicycle racks and on-site massage. Recently, we've added a travel allowance to help you save transportation costs. We're green, too: recycling receptacles abound.

'Google is dedicated to your career growth as well. We offer regular conferences, formal and informal training/learning opportunities, subsidised language classes and education-leave programmes.

'Our culture allows you to invent technologies and solutions we haven't even imagined yet. After all, Googlers are our greatest asset!'

(Source: Google)

Question:

How important do you think things like lava lamps, exercise balls and pool tables really are for Google? Justify your answer. *(16 marks)*

Why might firms not invest in innovation?

There are many reasons why firms may fail to invest heavily enough in innovation:

- They may not be able to raise the necessary funds. Innovation involves investment now in the hope of future returns. Firms that lack enough internal funds may struggle to borrow the money from banks. This may be because the banks are concerned that the R&D will not be successful and are not willing to take the risk.
- Alternatively, the bank may be willing to lend but the rates of interest charged may be perceived as too high. Even if a firm does have the necessary finance itself, some of the managers may be reluctant to use it in this area, preferring to use it elsewhere within the firm. For example, training or marketing may be seen as more of a priority than investing in R&D.
- The pressure from investors for short-term rewards may prevent managers from putting money into long-term projects. Investors may not be willing to wait for their rewards.
- The relatively low success rate may deter some firms from investing; even if firms manage to get a product to the launch stage, for example, it still has a very low chance of success. Firms are naturally reluctant to put money into projects which have a high failure rate, and may prefer to modify existing products instead.

- The business strategy may be to imitate what others do rather than take risks and try and be the pioneer.

Progress questions

1. What is meant by innovation? *(2 marks)*

2. Why do many new ideas fail to be launched? *(5 marks)*

3. What is meant by research and development? *(2 marks)*

4. What is a patent? *(2 marks)*

5. Explain why the culture of a business can influence how innovative it is. *(6 marks)*

6. Identify **two** industries where research and development spending is likely to be high. Explain why. *(6 marks)*

7. Explain the factors that might determine how much a firm spends on research and development. *(6 marks)*

8 Explain two reasons why firms might be reluctant to invest in research and development. *(6 marks)*

9 How might greater innovation increase the profits of a consumer electronics business? *(6 marks)*

10 Explain **two** possible sources of ideas for innovation. *(6 marks)*

Analysis question

✖ These questions relate to the case study on page 120.

To what extent would increasing the budget for research and development be a good idea for Pramus Pharmaceuticals? *(18 marks)*

Candidate's answer:

Research and development is an investment for the future, You are spending money to try and develop new products and processes. This can help with efficiency by doing things better; this might help reduce costs and improve the falling profit margin. It can also lead to more products (question marks hopefully turning into stars) which if successful can help generate more sales and therefore reverse the decline in turnover.

Spending more money may make it easier to get projects going and to move ahead with them. Without funds you cannot invest and there would be no R&D. It is clear from the appendix that we are dealing with large sums of money and so money does matter because of the complex technical development of products and the heavy testing period. Cash flow could be a significant issue because of the long time to develop and get a product to market and so more money might help overcome liquidity problems.

However, just increasing funding does not guarantee success in this sector. Money may be invested and the desired breakthrough not occur. In this case there are clearly issues between Mary and her team and so however much money there is she may misdirect it so it is not used effectively. The business is having trouble attracting the best people and so more money in the wrong hands may be wasted.

It is important therefore to track how money is used, who uses it and what it is used for. Increasing the budget may be a good idea but only if done properly. Also the problem is that the business is struggling and so whether or not it is a good idea, it may not even be feasible.

Examiner's comments:

A great answer. The candidate puts both sides well. They explain their points and they are always related back to the case study. They think about the particular issues in this industry but also the issues in this business − without the right people and the right use of funds simply spending more may not be a good idea.

Evaluation question

What would be the best way for Pramus plc to become more innovative? Justify your answer. *(18 marks)*

13 Location

The location of a business can affect its costs, its demand, its image and its ability to attract employees to work for it. The location decision is therefore a strategic decision that can affect the ability of the business to compete. The decision of where to locate can also reflect the values of the business, for example if it wants to help employment in a particular area. So, location choices should not be taken lightly and will involve decisions at the most senior level.

In this chapter we examine:

- what influences a location decision
- how location decisions are made
- the benefits of an optimal location
- the advantages and disadvantages of optimal location
- the advantages and disadvantages of multi-site location
- issues relating to international locations.

Choosing a location

An important strategic operational issue facing businesses is where to locate their operations. A location decision can involve high levels of investment and have a major impact on competitiveness. The right location(s) may affect:

- the costs of production and of running the business
- the tax rates paid
- the availability of employees and the skills available
- demand for the products
- the ease of accessing markets.

Given the impact on costs and revenues a location decision will involve an assessment of the payback period, the average rate of return and the net present value (for more on these investment appraisal techniques see Chapter 5).

Location decisions may involve several different elements: first which country, then which region and finally which specific plot of land.

The benefits of the optimal location

It may not always be possible to get the best (or optimal) location. You may find that a particular site is already taken or is too expensive. However, getting the best or nearly the best location can have several advantages:

- Lower costs may make the break-even output and the payback period lower and reduce the risk of

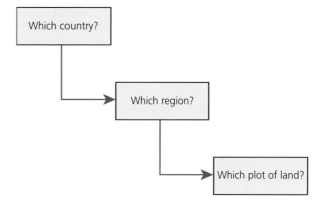

Figure 13.1 Levels of decision

losses if sales are lower than expected. Lower costs may increase the return on investment and make a project worthwhile.
- Being closer to the customer (and therefore possibly getting more customers as a result) may boost sales and profits. Stores based in the city centre have a higher footfall than those a few streets away.
- Overcoming trade barriers (for example, it is difficult to export to some countries because of barriers to trade) may increase sales. By basing itself inside a customs union such as the European Union a firm may be able to sell in a particular country.
- It may add to the brand image. For example, having your flagship store on Fifth Avenue in New York or Convent Garden in London may be important for the status of your business.

Deciding where to locate

The decision on where to locate a business will be based on a combination of quantitative and qualitative factors. This means that it is a combination of factors that can be measured, such as the expected impact on costs and revenues (these are quantitative), as well as other factors that are less easy to quantify, such as the attraction of the surroundings and the quality of life in the area (these are qualitative).

BUSINESS IN FOCUS

Dov Charney

Dov Charney is the founder and chief executive of American Apparel, the largest T-shirt manufacturer in America. He is widely admired for almost single-handedly creating one of America's most successful fashion retailers, for devising his company's provocative approach to advertising and for treating employees better than his rivals.

Mr Charney opened his first shop in 2003. He now has over 240 stores in 20 countries selling casual clothes for men, women and children. Sales are over $500 million and in 2007 the company had an 80 per cent gross profit margin, which was well above the industry average of 60 per cent. Its unbranded, brightly coloured and moderately priced T-shirts, sweatshirts, underwear and jeans have become extremely popular among young, cosmopolitan consumers from what Mr Charney calls the 'world-metropolitan culture'.

From the beginning Mr Charney has put great emphasis on making his employees happy. Pay is performance-related, and amounts to $12 an hour on average, far above California's minimum wage of $6.75. American Apparel staff can buy subsidised health insurance and there is a medical clinic at the factory. They are entitled to free English lessons, subsidised meals and free parking. Their workspace is properly lit and ventilated. When the company went public in late 2007, employees were given shares (approximately 250 shares, then worth about $3,600, for each year they had worked at the firm).

Anti-sweatshop activists praise Mr Charney as a pioneer of the fair treatment of garment workers. The employee benefits are not cheap: subsidising health insurance costs his firm $4m–5m a year; subsidising meals costs another $500,000. He considers contented workers to be important for the business. Treating them well means they are less likely to leave, which saves money. 'American Apparel is not an altruistic company,' says Mr Charney. 'I believe in capitalism and self-interest. Self-interest can involve being generous with others.'

Gap, another American fashion business, outsources 83 per cent of its production to factories in Asia, but all of the 5,000 or so workers involved in American Apparel's manufacturing process work in the same factory in downtown Los Angeles. But this is not because Mr Charney is opposed to offshoring or globalisation. His motive, once again, is self-interest; he keeps control over every stage of production, and the arrangement allows him to monitor the fashion market and respond quickly to new trends. In any case, he cannot outsource anything, he says, because he lacks the necessary infrastructure – and he has no plans to set it up.

American Apparel now plans to open more shops across the world. It also has an online retail operation. Retail analysts also doubt that American Apparel will be able to expand without resorting to outsourcing. Mr Charney continues to insist that China is too far away for his T-shirt production, even though moving textiles by ship from Hong Kong to Los Angeles takes just 11 days.

(*Source:* American Apparel; The Economist, *4 January 2007*)

Question:

Is American Apparel right to base its production in the USA? *(16 marks)*

Factors affecting a firm's location

- **The costs of a particular location relative to other options.** For example, the cost of land itself will vary from area to area; so will the cost of labour and services such as electricity. Taxation rates can also vary significantly from country to country. The decision to locate can therefore have a significant impact on a firm's profits.

- **The availability of lower-cost locations abroad** has been a major factor for UK firms considering relocating to the Far East or Eastern Europe. Low-wage employees and a much lower cost of living often make it very financially attractive for UK firms to be based overseas.

- **The availability of government grants and incentives.** If, for example, a government offers low rents or lower taxes to attract firms, this can obviously act as an incentive to locate there. In the last 20 years, for example, the development agencies in regions of the UK, such as Wales and Scotland, were very effective at attracting overseas investment not just because of financial aid but also because of the general level of local and national government cooperation in areas such as planning permission. Governments often use a combination of push and pull techniques to encourage firms to locate in particular regions. Incentives such as grants help to pull firms to an area; refusing permission to build in other areas helps to push firms to locate where the government wants them to be.

- **The infrastructure of the region.** The availability of energy sources and transport facilities will affect the ease, speed and cost of production. The importance of such factors will vary between industries, for example transport facilities are crucial to a wholesaler but less significant for an online insurance business.
- **The nature of the business itself.** The extent to which a firm has freedom over the location decision depends in part on what it actually does. A self-employed website designer, for example, may be able to work from home. A fast-food restaurant, by comparison, must be located somewhere near its customers, while a mining company must base its production facilities where the actual minerals are.
- **The location of the market.** In some cases, such as retailing, it will often be important to be close to the market. A central high-street location is more likely to attract businesses than a site located several miles away from the main shopping areas. In other industries, such as telephone banking, it is not so important to be close to the customer.
- **Market access.** The location of a firm may affect its ability to trade in particular markets. Firms based outside the European Union, for example, must pay a tax (a tariff) to sell their goods within the EU. Firms located within the EU do not have to pay this tax. This is one reason why many Japanese firms have set up in the UK in the last 20 years – if they have UK production facilities using a proportion of UK components they can export to other EU states and not pay a tariff; this obviously makes their goods more competitive compared with exporting from Japan.
- **Exchange rates.** If the pound is strong it is expensive for UK-based producers to export. On the other hand, it means UK firms have strong purchasing power overseas, which may lead some firms to relocate overseas when the pound is strong in value in terms of other currencies.

- **Political stability.** The political climate can have an impact on the appeal of a certain area. For example, terrorist threats in countries post-11 September 2001 have created instability in certain regions, and the UK's reluctance to commit to the single currency has meant some overseas investors have been wary of locating in the UK because they have been worried about the possible impact of being outside the 'eurozone'.
- **Resources.** A firm may locate in a particular area because of the resources it offers. Microsoft located near Cambridge in the UK because it wanted easy access to top graduates and research facilities.
- **Image.** A perfume company, for example, may benefit from being based in Paris or Milan, but may not gain the same prestige from being located in Scunthorpe.
- **Quality of life.** For example, how attractive is the area in itself? What are the facilities like? What is the standard of living like?
- **Ethical issues.** Some firms have avoided locating in low-wage areas for fear of being criticised for 'exploiting' local staff or of taking jobs away from the UK. In many cases firms expand in areas where they already have established links (and therefore feel some responsibility to the community) rather than take jobs elsewhere. The Body Shop set up one of its manufacturing operations at Easterhouse in Scotland specifically to bring jobs to a deprived area.

BUSINESS IN FOCUS

Marks & Spencer

In the 1990s the French seemed to love British food as sold by Marks & Spencer. In particular the ready-made sandwiches and ready meals seemed especially profitable. However in 2001 Marks & Spencer closed the Paris store along with the other 38 stores in continental Europe that it had. Now Marks & Spencer is considering a return to Paris. The company remains very British with 90 per cent of its sales revenue generated at home, but it is now planning to invest £850–950million a year in the company's online sales channels and its international operations.

Question:

Analyse the operational problems a retailer such as Marks & Spencer might face when opening stores abroad. *(10 marks)*

The risks of operating in different countries

'Risk Briefing' rates operational risk in 150 markets on a scale of 0–100. The overall scores are an aggregate of underlying scores for ten categories of risk: security; political stability; government effectiveness; legal and regulatory; macroeconomic; foreign trade and payments; financial; tax policy; labour market; and infrastructure. The model is run when events require it, and at least once a quarter for each country.

Least risky			Most risky		
Rank	**Country**	**Score**	**Rank**	**Country**	**Score**
1	Switzerland	8 (7)	150	Iraq	84 (88)
2	Denmark	10 (8)	149	Guinea	80 (79)
	Singapore	10	148	Myanmar	79 (78)
	Sweden	10	147	Zimbabwe	78 (77)
5	Finland	12 (10)	146	Turkmenistan	77
6	Austria	14		Uzbekistan	77
	Luxembourg	14	144	Venezuela	75 (74)
	Norway	14	143	Tajikistan	71 (70)
9	Netherlands	15 (13)	142	Eritrea	70 (69)
	Britain	15 (12)	141	Chad	68
11	Canada	16 (15)		Ecuador	68
	Hong Kong	16	139	Kenya	66
13	France	17 (16)	138	Cote d'Ivoire	65
	Germany	17 (16)		Nigeria	65 (67)
15	Australia	18 (16)		Sudan	65
	Belgium	18			
	Malta	18 (19)			

Table 13.1 Rankings of operational risk, September 2008 (September 2007 score, if different)

(Source: Economist Intelligence Unit)

Note: Out of 100, with higher numbers indicating more risk

Question:

To what extent do you think the table above should influence a firm's decision where to locate? *(14 marks)*

Reasons for locating abroad	
Supply-side issues	**Demand-side issues**
Overcome trade barriers (e.g. locate within a customs union)	Access global markets (e.g. the fast growth BRIC economies of Brazil, Russia, India and China)
Benefit from lower costs abroad (e.g. in China)	Expand out of a mature market

Table 13.2 Reasons for locating abroad

Disney

In the early 1980s the heads of Disney were looking for a location in Europe to open a new theme park. The first one outside the US was Japan and now Disney was looking for another base.

They initially came up with over 1,000 possible locations in Europe. By March 1985, the number of possible locations for the park had been reduced to four; two in France and two in Spain. Both of these countries saw the potential economic advantages of a Disney theme park and were offering financial deals to Disney. A strong possibility was a site near Toulon in southern France, not far from Marseille. The pleasing landscape of that region, as well as its climate, made the location a likely winner for the European Disney.

However, thick layers of bedrock were discovered beneath the site, which meant construction would be too difficult. Finally, a site in the rural town of Marne-la-Vallée was chosen because it was close to Paris and its location was estimated to be no more than a four-hour drive for 68 million people and no more than a two-hour flight for a further 300 million. The agreement to build was signed in 1986.

Questions:

1 Analyse the main operational issues involved in running a theme park. *(10 marks)*
2 Analyse the ways in which the operational issues involved in operating a theme park relate to other functions of the business. *(10 marks)*

Methods of making location decisions

A location decision is likely to be a combination of quantitative and qualitative analysis. This means that managers will consider what the numbers say (for example, what is the likely rate of return in a particular location?) but also qualitative factors such as the effect on the quality of working life or the impact on the environment.

Quantitative analysis

The location decision can be absolutely critical to a firm because of its impact on costs and revenues and therefore profit. It can also be a difficult and expensive decision to change once it is made, which makes it even more important to get it right first time. To help ensure that the most financially attractive decision is made firms may use quantitative decision-making techniques. These are tools used to measure the value of a decision and may include the following:

- **Break-even analysis.** A firm will want to know how many units must be sold in order to break even (for the revenue generated to cover the costs). It will also want to calculate the margin of safety (the extent to which sales could fall from the forecast figure before the firm starts to make a loss [see Figure 13.2]). If the fixed costs of a particular location are lower than another (perhaps because of lower rents), this will reduce the break-even level of output – fewer units will need to be sold to cover

costs. Similarly, if the variable cost per unit is lower (for example, due to lower wage rates) this will also reduce the break-even output (see Figure 13.3).

Figure 13.2 Margin of safety

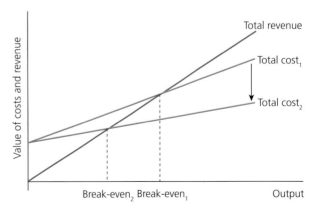

Figure 13.3 Lower variable costs reduce the number of units that need to be sold to break even

- **Investment appraisal.** The decision to be based in a particular location is often a large-scale investment and as such firms are likely to undertake a detailed financial analysis of the expected payback period, the average rate of return and net present value. Given a choice a firm will usually choose the option with the quickest payback, the highest average rate of return and the highest net present value. In reality the decision may not be that straightforward, for example, one option may have a quicker payback but a lower average rate of return.

Qualitative factors

Although firms are likely to examine the potential impact on revenues and costs of selecting a particular site, the decision may also be affected by less measurable factors such as whether the location itself appeals to the managers, and the quality of life in the area. For example, many Japanese firms have been attracted to the UK because of the importance of the English language in business. It is also because English is learnt in Japanese schools – this makes it easier for these firms to set up here than in France, for example. The culture of the country and the extent to which you think you understand its traditions, its ways of working and its customers are all very important. According to Rugman (2000), the probability of an American multinational opening its first operations outside the US in Canada or the UK is 70 per cent; these are similar countries and therefore appear familiar territories. The probability of an American multinational opening its first operations outside the US in Germany or Japan is 2 per cent; these seem less appealing as the cultures are more different.

Once a few firms have set up in a location this can also act as an incentive for others to locate there, as they may think this proves it is safe and that networking (using the expertise and experience of others) will be easier. The growth of Hollywood as a film centre and Silicon Valley as a centre for computing are in part because the success of some firms has drawn in others.

Other possible qualitative factors which could attract managers to particular areas include the fact that they like the region or because they have particular attachments to the place. William Morris, for example, set up a car factory based in Oxford simply because he lived there. Managers might also choose a location because the name of the place enhances the product's image; a fashion house in New York sounds more exclusive than a fashion house in Grimsby; an advertising agency in London may have more appeal than one in Dundee. The reasons a particular location is chosen are, of course, varied: in the case of call centres, some firms have located in the north east or north west of the UK because callers like the accent of people from these areas more than the accents of people from the south east. Although this factor may well impact on a firm's profits it is difficult to place an absolute value on an accent and so this also counts as a qualitative factor. Interestingly, other firms have located to India to cut costs.

Types of location decision

There are in fact many types of location decision which managers may have to consider. There is the initial decision of where to set up the business. In many ways this is the easiest decision in that the managers have no commitments to existing facilities. On the other hand, it usually occurs at a time when money is tight and the firm will be heavily constrained by what it can afford. A key decision at this time is the desired capacity level – how big must the factory be? Or how much office space is needed? Managers may want to be optimistic about the possible growth of the business; at the same time they do not want to commit to large facilities and then find these are under utilised.

Once a firm is established it may have to consider relocating at some point in its development. This occurs when a firm wants to move its facilities. This may be necessary because the initial reasons for choosing a place have now gone (for example, government grants have been withdrawn or tax rates have been increased), or perhaps because the firm has outgrown its premises.

When relocating, a firm may have more experience of the type of facilities it needs than it did when it first chose its location; it may also have greater financial resources than when it started up. However, relocation brings with it all sorts of new problems, including:

- staff who do not want to move (or the firm does not want to pay to relocate) – these people may need compensation
- there could be a period of lost production time during the move
- the costs of notifying customers and suppliers and administrative costs such as changing the firm's literature to include the new addresses.

A new location may also be part of an expansion process: a firm could be building new production facilities or opening up a new outlet, for example. The acquisition of new premises inevitably brings with it issues of management structure and control. A new facility will need controlling and the senior managers will need to decide on the best way of structuring the business, such as deciding what new jobs are created, what the reporting relationships will be and how to ensure effective communication.

BUSINESS IN FOCUS

Heathrow Terminal 5

Terminal 5 at Heathrow opened in 2008. This enabled the airport to serve another 30 million passengers a year. However, the decision to locate an additional terminal at Heathrow met huge resistance from various pressure groups. Environmentalists said it would mean more pollution. Defenders of the terminal said it was essential to improve the service for passengers and would create more jobs in the area. Work started in 2002 after a record-breaking public inquiry. The project cost £4.3 billion.

The main building measures 400 metres by 180 metres and contains 105 lifts, 65 escalators and consists of 80,000 tonnes of steel. You can fit 52 full-sized football pitches in its floor space and it is the largest free-standing building in the UK.

It is 40 metres high, 396 metres long and 176 metres wide. It has 30,000 square metres of reinforced glass and 5,500 glass panels have been used to glaze the terminal building and roof, giving the whole terminal a light and airy feel. The Terminal is located between Heathrow's two runways on land previously occupied by a sludge works. The project has successfully moved 9 million cubic metres of earth and two rivers have been diverted to create space for the new building.

Water from Terminal 5's rainwater harvesting and groundwater boreholes is being used for non-potable uses, reducing the demand on the mains water by 70 per cent. The harvesting scheme reuses up to 85 per cent of the rain that falls on Terminal 5's campus.

Question:

Discuss the factors that might have been considered before deciding to add an extra terminal at Heathrow rather than another airport. *(16 marks)*

Offshoring

Offshoring occurs when a business shifts production overseas ('off shore'). This has been common in recent years as many businesses have moved some of their operations to countries such as India, China, Turkey and Vietnam where production costs are so much lower. Printing, toy manufacturing, call centres, clothes production, shoe manufacturing and a great deal of manufacturing has moved abroad. Dyson, Burberry and MG are just a few examples of where production has gone abroad. Many support activities such as computing and accounting have also gone overseas.

The aim of offshoring is to reduce costs. In India, for example, there are many highly skilled computing and engineering graduates who are much cheaper and much easier to recruit than their UK counterparts. Moving to countries such as China may mean:

- lower wages
- less regulation
- less concern over methods of production and the impact on the environment

- lower or fewer taxes.

This all enables cheaper and more flexible production which may be difficult to match in more developed economies.

The difficulty can be maintaining quality because you are not so close to the production. There may also be difficult ethical issues involved, for example, is it right to lose UK jobs by closing production here and moving it to another country? Is it right to pay much lower wages abroad than in the UK? Gap, Next, Primark and Nike have all faced criticism at some time over the way people working for their suppliers have been treated.

The choice of where to shift production is affected by cultural issues as well as costs (for instance, moving to where you feel you know something about the culture). Japanese companies are starting to outsource to China, where large numbers of Japanese speakers can be found. German companies tend to outsource to Poland and Romania, where proficiency in German is common. French companies outsource to North Africa where France has many connections.

Although offshoring has increased in recent years as it has become easier for UK companies to base themselves in countries such as China, this does not mean that all production has gone from the UK. What tends to be left is higher value-added production activities such as design, research and development or the production of premium craft products.

BUSINESS IN FOCUS

Outsourcing

When Ford's River Rouge Plant was completed in 1928 it included everything it needed to turn raw materials into finished cars: 100,000 workers, 16 million square feet of factory floor, 100 miles of railway track and its own docks and furnaces. Today it remains Ford's largest production plant, even though it is nowhere near as big as it was. Most of the parts it uses are now made by sub-contractors and simply assembled by the plant's 6,000 workers.

Outsourcing such as this has transformed global business as companies have bought in more and more services. However, this does create dangers of poor quality and late delivery (as Boeing found with its Dreamliner aircraft which ended up being three years late).

Question:

To what extent is outsourcing a good idea for a business such as Ford? Justify your answer. *(16 marks)*

BUSINESS IN FOCUS

Offshoring

Many companies have moved their call centres abroad, particularly to India. However, some UK clients have complained that the people they are talking to do not know enough about Britain. In an effort to change this, some firms such as Infovision, which runs a call centre for the AA, has been training its Indian employees in the subtleties of British accents and culture. A month-long crash course in UK culture and pronunciation included television programmes such as *EastEnders* and *Coronation Street*, as well as information on festivals such as Christmas and Guy Fawkes' Night. Indian staff were introduced to British food, pubs, British education and shops, political parties and how to say the names of places and famous people. The thinking is that call-centre staff in India are more likely to be successful if they not only sound like the John Smiths and Karen Joneses they are helping, but also understand the kind of lives the British lead.

A report on the Indian economy from investment bank Goldman Sachs estimated that about 7 per cent of India's population speaks English, making the sub-continent the second-largest pool of English speakers in the world.

The number of workers suitable for outsourcing in the service and IT industries grew from 6,800 in 1986 to 650,000 in 2004, the report said. HSBC paid Indian call-centre workers around £2,500 a year, compared with £18,750 in the UK. The average salary for a highly qualified Indian business graduate was just £7,000, a fraction of the cost of an MBA graduate in the West.

The Indian call-centre agents' salaries are lucrative by local standards, and they also receive free meals and transport to and from work. Being a call-centre worker is felt to be good work. The occupation carries kudos – a far cry from its image in the UK.

Accounting, financial services and health and pharmaceutical jobs are increasingly outsourced. Goldman Sachs estimated that the pharmaceutical sector alone could double the value of goods and services provided in this way to $50 billion (£28 billion) in three years. India, in particular, is well placed to carry out research and development and the manufacturing of drugs because it has a highly trained workforce and good infrastructure.

Information and news businesses such as Thomson Financial and Reuters have outsourced some of their IT operations to India and also employ Indian journalists to report company results and other announcements.

Unions in Britain have lobbied against offshoring, and politicians have not been slow to address the issue. In the US, the issue is far more sensitive, as American companies are the largest users of offshore services in the world. The government has recently imposed restrictions on the outsourcing of US federal contracts.

(Source: Adapted from The Independent, 2 May 2004*)*

Question:

Discuss the possible reasons why India may be such a popular location for offshore operations. *(16 marks)*

BUSINESS IN FOCUS

Made in Britain

Many products are now produced abroad because it is cheaper. Even famous 'British brands' are often made overseas, such as most of Hackett's products or Burberry clothes.

A spokeswoman for Marks & Spencer said: 'You can still be a British brand but sell products that are sourced globally – like Marks & Spencer. The British manufacturing base has shrunk drastically over the years, but even if you do not manufacture here, it doesn't mean you are not a British brand.'

But if you do want to buy British, what is still made in the UK?

Clothes: the luxury brand Barbour, whose products are worn by the Queen, still has all its factories in the UK. All of its classic wax jackets are still made in South Shields, Tyne and Wear, where 180 skilled machinists are based.

Shoes: Charles Tyrwhitt makes its shoes here (but makes its shirts abroad). Its website says: 'We still manufacture all our shoes in the UK and this is because the UK still makes the best shoes in the world. Unfortunately, investment in infrastructure and training has not been maintained sufficiently in other areas of UK manufacturing. We wish it had.' The town of Northampton has been manufacturing footwear since the seventeenth century. Even its football team rejoices in the nickname of 'the Cobblers'. There are still about eight factories there, including John Lobb, Tricker's, Crockett & Jones, Edward Green and Church's Footwear (owned by Prada). Church's employs more than 500 people in its manufacturing group in the area. Spokeswoman Jenny Mead says: 'Shoe-making has always traditionally been in Northampton, because of the oak woods for tanning material. We've built up a niche product here, and shoe-making skills have been passed down through generations of families. If we were to move elsewhere, we'd lose our tradition.'

Ceramics and homeware: Waterford Wedgwood (which owns the Royal Doulton, Waterford Crystal and Wedgwood brands) is based at plants in Stoke-on-Trent, along with Emma Bridgewater, Portmeirion Potteries, Royal Stafford and Moorland Pottery.

Furniture: DFS makes its sofas in Britain and has three factories in Yorkshire, Nottinghamshire and Derbyshire, while Marks & Spencer's made-to-order upholstered furniture is largely produced at its own 'eco-factory' in Wales.

Electrical products: While many electrical products are now made overseas, some are still produced here. Dualit has been making all its Vario toasters in Britain for 60 years and has its own factory in Crawley.

Bicycles: Brompton Bicycles, famous for its folding bikes, is one of the few companies to keep all its manufacturing in England – it has had a factory in Middlesex for the past 30 years. A spokesman for Brompton says: 'Most companies make their bikes in Asia, but we would never consider making them abroad because we want to stay British and we feel the quality is better here.'

Chocolate: Cadbury, one of the best-known British brands, has been making chocolate in Bournville, Birmingham, since 1879. But in 2007 it announced that it would close one of its factories, near Bristol, and shift some operations to Poland. A Cadbury spokesman said: 'It makes better business sense to transfer some production to Poland, but Bournville is Cadbury's spiritual home.' Most chocolates will still be made in Bournville but individual bars will be made in Poland.

Prestat has been making and selling chocolate since 1902, and the company still uses its original recipes at its North London factory, which employs 30 people. The company has invested £250,000 on a bar-wrapping machine so that it can keep production in the UK.

Bill Keeling, managing director of Prestat, says: 'We consider ourselves to be a very English company and believe wholeheartedly in English production as being at the core of the company. Too many bars sold to UK consumers by iconic brands are being made abroad – it is utterly unnecessary. We aren't in the business of cutting costs to the bone at the expense of quality.'

(Source: Huma Qureshi, The Observer, *30 November 2008)*

Question:

What do you think is the main reason why relatively few manufacturing operations are based in the UK? Justify your answer. *(16 marks)*

Multi-site locations

Many business will operate from many sites. In the case of retail operations this may be because there are different stores in different places. In the case of manufacturing it may involve different production bases in different locations.

By operating in different sites a business may benefit from:

- the gains of different resources in different locations (for example, cheap labour in some countries, lower taxes in other regions)

- being closer to customers in different regions, enabling a better understanding of market needs and faster response times to local needs
- providing a safety net by splitting production to different sites so that if there are problems with production on one site it can continue elsewhere.

The disadvantages of multi-site location include:

- the problems of managing and coordinating operations that are geographically separate; simply from a management perspective this is difficult
- if some decisions are now taken separately rather than for the business as a whole there may be a loss of some economies of scale.

Toyota

In over 50 years since Toyota first began exports, Toyota vehicles have found their way to over 170 countries and regions throughout the world. As their exports have continued to develop, so has the localisation of their production bases, in line with the Toyota policy of 'producing vehicles where the demand exists'. Currently there are 51 bases in 26 different countries and regions. In addition, there are design and R&D bases in nine locations, showing that, from development and design to production, sales and service, Toyota has now achieved consistent globalisation as well as localisation.

There are a number of hurdles that this globalisation of production has to overcome. The most important is 'quality assurance', which requires that 'no matter where Toyota vehicles are made, they have the same quality'. To put it another way, the firm does not put a label on the vehicles which says 'Made in such and such a country'; it puts the same label on all vehicles which reads 'Made by TOYOTA'. This means spreading Toyota's manufacturing philosophy – the 'Toyota Way' – to all of the overseas bases. And on top of this it is important to minimise the necessary support that comes from Japan and let each of the overseas bases become self-reliant.

For example, the Toyota plant that recently commenced production in Texas made maximum use of the know-how which has been cultivated over the past 20 years by the Toyota plant in Kentucky. This is just the latest example of how the localised 'Toyota Way' is being passed on overseas.

Toyota believes that the way to achieve 'quality assurance' and to 'spread the Toyota Way' is by educating people: 'Making things is about developing people'. So, in 2003, it established the Global Production Center (GPC) within the Motomachi Plant in Toyota City. Furthermore, in 2006, it established regional GPCs in the United States, the United Kingdom and Thailand to carry out corresponding activities in the North American, European and Asia-Pacific regions respectively.

(Source: www.toyota-global.com)

Question:

Discuss the advantages and disadvantages of Toyota's approach to locating its factories. *(16 marks)*

Multinationals and overseas locations

A multinational business is one that has bases in more than one country. Examples of multinationals are Shell, Ford, Coca-Cola and Walmart. Locating overseas naturally adds another dimension to any location decision. Many individuals in the UK, for example, have acquired properties in France or Italy, either as a second home or to go and live there, only to find it brings with it all sorts of problems they had not originally imagined. For example, acquiring properties abroad will involve an understanding of different legal requirements and processes. Overseas specialists will usually be necessary to make sense of the different requirements and to oversee the process of acquisition. Communicating and controlling facilities abroad may also prove more difficult simply due to the geographic distance between sites.

Why become multinational?

There are many reasons why firms might want to become multinational. These include:

- To benefit from lower costs overseas.
- To benefit from less regulation (for example, fewer health and safety restrictions).
- To benefit from a greater pool of labour (for example, locating overseas may enable the firm to recruit more cheaply or to benefit from particular skills). The labour market may also be more flexible, meaning that a firm can hire and fire staff more easily. The rights of employees in the UK, for example, have tended to be relatively low compared with those in other countries in the EU in terms of redundancy and dismissal rights and protection at work. This is one reason why the UK has been so attractive to overseas investors wanting to operate within the EU.
- To benefit from particular resources such as minerals.
- To benefit from market opportunities overseas. Firms may decide to expand overseas because the domestic market is saturated and there seems to be relatively slow growth compared with opportunities abroad, or simply because a firm identifies attractive possibilities in foreign markets. Opening up new stores or new factories abroad therefore provides an opportunity for growth. This then creates the possibility of economies of scale. By operating on a larger scale worldwide a firm may benefit from purchasing economies reducing the cost per unit.
- To be closer to their overseas customers; it may be easier to understand customer requirements and to provide a faster more efficient service by being based in that country.
- To overcome protectionist trade barriers. Trading in China, for example, is very difficult unless a firm actually sets up there or at least has a form of partnership with a local firm. The Chinese government is eager to prevent what it regards as exploitation of the Chinese market unless western firms are actually investing into China at the same time.
- To weaken trade union power. If a firm produces only in one country it is vulnerable to industrial action within that country. If, for example, there is a dispute with a trade union this could halt production completely; by having production facilities in several countries it is less likely production will ever be halted fully. Also it is more

difficult for trade unions to organise themselves if they are in different countries so if a firm has their factories in, say, three different countries it reduces the union power compared with having all three factories in one country.

- To overcome exchange rate problems; by producing in the market where it sells, a firm will not face the difficulty of fluctuating exchange rates which can suddenly make exports from its home country seem uncompetitive.

BUSINESS IN FOCUS

Entering India

In 2007 Walmart entered the India market. It did this by signing an agreement to start a wholesale operation in equal partnership with Bharti Enterprises, an Indian conglomerate. Under the name Bharti Walmart, the new company plans to open around 12 cash-and-carry stores by 2015.

Walmart would like to grow at a faster rate than this in India. After all, it has huge potential. At current growth rates India will be the world's fifth-biggest consumer market by 2025, according to McKinsey, a management consultancy. However, around 97 per cent of Indian retailing is in the form of small, often family-run stores rather than chains of supermarkets, mostly of less than 500 square feet (46 square metres). This creates an opportunity for large retailers such as Walmart, except for one thing: foreign firms are only permitted to own up to 51 per cent of shops selling single-brand products or to sell to others on a wholesale basis. They cannot open supermarkets directly. This limits what foreign retailers can achieve in the India market.

In 2008 Tesco also announced it would enter the India market by investing £60 million to open a wholesale cash-and-carry business based in Mumbai. The group has also signed a deal to help the retail arm of India's Tata group, Trent, develop its hypermarket business, for a fee. Chief executive Sir Terry Leahy added that the move would give the group 'access to another of the most important economies in the world'. At the time Tesco operated 3,729 stores employing more than 440,000 people in 13 countries across the globe, including Hungary, Slovakia, Malaysia and Thailand.

Question:

Discuss the factors Walmart or Tesco should consider when choosing a new market to enter. *(16 marks)*

Is a low-cost location the best?

Although firms will often be seeking to increase efficiency and reduce their costs, this does not necessarily mean they will always seek the lowest-cost location. First, they may be influenced by qualitative factors – they may prefer to move to a location where they are familiar with the culture or language, for example. Second, they must consider the possible impact on quality. A cheaper location may not have the same access to high-quality resources. Third, a firm's location may impact on its revenue; a high-street location may be an expensive option for a retailer but attract far more customers and so prove more profitable.

The location decision must therefore involve an overview of many different factors, including qualitative issues and overall profitability as well as costs.

BUSINESS IN FOCUS

Steiff

The world's most famous teddy bear is turning its back on China as Steiff moves to take production of its plush animals back to Germany.

Steiff is rejecting globalisation to keep the fur gleaming on the world's poshest bears. Fed up with poor workmanship, high staff turnover, delays and rising shipping costs, it is moving bear production back to its birthplace in Giengen an der Brenz.

Steiff's managing director said China was not capable of making a product to the level of sophistication it requires. It takes 18 months to train a worker to make a Steiff animal.

'If one of the glass eyes is a millimetre off, it means the adorable devoted look on the teddy bear's face ends up more like a stupid stare,' he said.

Steiff invented the teddy bear in 1902, branding its creations with a button in the bear's ear. In an effort to reduce the high cost of production, the company began outsourcing four years ago when it sent hundreds of staff to China to train the workforce.

Mr Frechen said: 'What we expect, they cannot produce.' The rapid turnover of the Chinese workforce has been a problem as staff chase higher wages.

'At one of our competitors, one morning a third of the employees didn't turn up to work.' Steiff makes an expensive product and the firm has no desire to compete with mass-market toymakers. However, the rising cost of manufacturing and shipping products from China is eroding the advantage of outsourcing a premium product. Delays have caused difficulties for a firm that has to respond quickly to fast-moving toy fashions.

The company suffered months of delays in the delivery of toys modelled on Knut, the famous polar bear cub in Berlin zoo. 'What we have learnt from the experience is that the things we do much better we do ourselves and that is how we keep our competitive advantage.'

Steiff was founded in 1880 by Margarete Steiff who, despite being disabled and wheelchair-bound from childhood, created a toy business sewing and stuffing felt animals. In 1903 the first Steiff bear was shown at a Leipzig trade fair where an American department store buyer ordered 3,000 and it became an immediate success.

(*Source:* The Times, *3 July 2008*)

Questions:

1 Analyse the possible reasons why Steiff originally chose to locate production in China. *(10 marks)*
2 Discuss the main factors that should determine the resource mix used when producing Steiff bears. *(16 marks)*
3 To what extent can the location of production influence the success of Steiff? *(18 marks)*

Summary

Location can influence a firm's costs and revenues. It is a strategic decision in that once a decision is made it may be expensive and time consuming to move. Decisions may include which countries to operate in and whether to operate on several sites.

Key terms

A **customs union** occurs when there are free-trade agreements between member countries but these members have a common tax on products from non-member countries. The European Union is a customs union.

Offshoring refers to the relocation by a company of a business process from one country to another.

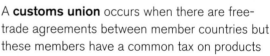

Business ethics refer to what is regarded as right and wrong and what is acceptable behaviour.

Localisation refers to the extent to which a business adjusts to local market conditions.

Quality assurance refers to a process by which organisations aim to prevent errors occurring.

Examiner's advice

Make sure you are able to interpret data derived from investment appraisal in relation to location – is a higher net present value better than a lower one? Why?

Progress questions

1. Explain how a location decision can affect a firm's competitiveness. *(5 marks)*
2. What is the difference between quantitative and qualitative factors affecting a location decision? Give examples. *(5 marks)*
3. Outline **two** factors that might influence the location of a clothes retailer. *(6 marks)*
4. Outline **two** factors that might influence the location of a health club. *(6 marks)*
5. Explain how the labour market might influence a location decision. *(3 marks)*
6. Outline how investment appraisal is useful in a location decision. *(6 marks)*
7. Explain how location can affect break-even output. *(4 marks)*
8. What is meant by a multinational business? *(2 marks)*
9. Explain **one** advantage of having multi-site locations. *(3 marks)*
10. Explain **one** disadvantage of a multi-site location. *(3 marks)*

Analysis question

✂ These questions relate to the case study on page 120.

Analyse the possible factors that might have influenced the choice of Pramus' research and development bases. *(10 marks)*

Candidate's answer:

Research and development involves developing new products and process. Locating your research base means deciding where to put them. This could be for various reasons:
- The costs of land
- The costs of labour and the availability of the right staff
- The laws of the land
- Whether there are government incentives to locate there
- The travel and transport costs to get to the market
- The location of competitors; some businesses such as restaurants and fast-food shops like to locate near each other.

Overall a combination of factors affect the location of a business.

Examiner's comments:

This is a very basic and general answer. It identifies possible points but these are not in context. Which of the factors mentioned are likely to be important to Pramus? These are the ones that need to be selected and analysed. There needs to be a development of the arguments presented and they need to be applied to the context. There is no application and very limited analysis here. Weak.

Evaluation question

Is outsourcing likely to be a good idea for Pramus? Justify your answer. *(18 marks)*

14 Lean production

> Lean production aims to reduce wastage and thereby make a business more efficient. This may be crucial in an age of growing competition.

In this chapter we consider:

- the meaning and significance of lean production
- the effective management of time
- the meaning and value of critical path analysis.

Introduction to lean production

With greater globalisation and competition from all over the world the pressure is on organisations to become more efficient. They are often facing demands for increased pay and higher input costs, but cannot easily pass these on to their customers so, to maintain profits, there is a pressing need for greater efficiencies. Managers are constantly looking for ways of reducing the cost per unit. This does not necessarily mean producing cheaply – a Ferrari car, a Chanel dress and Jimmy Choo shoes are always likely to be expensive to make. However, many managers will want to find the cheapest way of producing at a given quality level. As we saw earlier, this may be achieved by innovation. It can also be helped by trying to become leaner in the way a product is produced.

Lean production aims to reduce all forms of waste in the production process. It is an approach that was developed most fully in Japan. Waste is called 'muda' in Japan and lean production aims to drive out all forms of muda. This includes the waste of materials, of time, of energy and of human effort. Lean production streamlines operations so that costs are reduced and efficiency increased. To achieve this, a number of techniques have been developed (mainly in Japan) aimed at getting things right first time and reducing wastage levels.

According to Taichi Ohno (from Toyota) the seven types of waste include:

1 Defects; these only have to be put right later on and cost money or the product has to be thrown away or reworked.

2 Overproduction of goods not demanded by actual customers; if they are not needed why produce them? They only have to be reworked or thrown away.

3 Inventories awaiting further processing or consumption; this represents idle money.

4 Unnecessary processing; why add features or extra work if it is not needed?

5 Unnecessary motion of employees; this wastes time and energy.

6 Unnecessary transport and handling of goods; again, a waste of resources.

7 Waiting for an earlier stage of the process to deliver; waiting time is idle time.

Lean production therefore aims for:

- Zero delays
- Zero stocks
- Zero mistakes
- Zero waiting
- Zero accidents.

The techniques involved in lean production include:

- time-based management
- critical path analysis
- cell production
- benchmarking
- kaizen
- just-in-time (JIT) production.

Lean production involves focusing on problem areas and finding the most efficient ways of doing these. Once the 'right' method has been found staff then need to be trained and shown how to do this and then follow this approach. The aim is to develop clear and reliable ways of doing things. At Toyota, for example, every activity is completely specified, then applied routinely and repetitively. This is because:

- All variation from best practice leads to poorer quality, lower productivity and higher costs.
- Variations hinder learning and improvement because they hide the link between the process and the results.

The lean approach includes the five Ss:

- Sieketsu: the aim is to standardise the approach in every area so there is a right way of doing things and this is applied consistently.
- Seiso: employees are expected to keep their work area clean.
- Seiton: employees are expected to organise their tools, materials and documents and so they can find them easily and quickly.
- Seiri employees need to have only key equipment and remove unnecessary tools from their work area.
- Shitsuke: employees are expected to follow the ways set out to complete a task.

Time-based management

With the levels of competition in most markets increasing rapidly, businesses are always looking for new ways of out-competing their rivals. Many firms have tried to use time as a competitive weapon. If an organisation is able to produce an item in a shorter period of time than its competitors, or deliver it more rapidly to customers, more sales may result. Sony keeps producing new models of its products, for example, so that by the time the competition has copied the features of the last one, it has already moved on to a new version. Domino's Pizza has competed aggressively in the fast-food market by trying to achieve pizza delivery within 30 minutes. Similarly, Dell can produce a computer to a customer's specifications within weeks. Photo developers now promise a one-hour service. Opticians can produce glasses in hours. Amazon can deliver within 24 hours. At Yo Sushi you can help yourself rather than wait for a waiter or waitress to come to you.

As customers become eager for 'instant' service, the ability to supply items as and when they are wanted may be crucial to a business's success. The growth of internet shopping, 24-hour telephone banking and home delivery by supermarkets all reflect a desire for quick, easy access to products. Firms must try to react by reducing the time it takes to develop products. Also, with new products being launched more frequently and with rapidly changing customer tastes, products do not tend to survive for as long as they used to in the past. Over 80 per cent of new products are likely to fail in the first few years. It may be important, therefore, to develop products very quickly to keep competitive in the market.

To speed up the development of products, businesses have adopted simultaneous engineering methods. These involve getting all the engineers and designers who are concerned with a project to work on it at the same time. Instead of having one person look at a product idea, develop it and then pass it on to the next person or department, time can be saved if everyone is looking at and discussing the work simultaneously. This process has become easier due to the increasing use of information technology. This enables employees to communicate and share information more easily.

Time-based management also involves building a flexible production system able to respond quickly and effectively to customer demand. This requires employees and equipment that can produce 'just in time' so that production reacts to orders. If production can be made to follow demand, firms should be able to gain a time advantage over their competitors.

An important element of time-based management is scheduling activities effectively so that they are undertaken as efficiently as possible. There are various ways to do this, including using critical path (or network) analysis. This is particularly important in project based industries such as construction where every project may be slightly different and need very careful coordination.

Critical path or network analysis

To achieve productive efficiency managers will want to plan projects as effectively as possible to ensure that time and resources are not wasted. They do not want to have people and machines sitting idle unnecessarily or materials delivered well before they are required. To help them in the planning process managers may use network analysis, also called critical path analysis.

Network analysis is a method of organising the different activities involved in a particular process in order to find the most efficient means of completing the task. The aim is to complete the project in as short a time as possible. To do this a firm will determine the exact order in which activities have to be undertaken and identify which ones can be undertaken simultaneously to save time. Network analysis can be used in any type of project that involves several activities – anything from opening a new store to planning a new advertising campaign to organising the relocation of the firm. The technique was developed for DuPont in 1957 to speed up the building of a new plant.

To undertake network analysis managers must:

- identify all the different tasks involved in the process
- estimate the expected length of time each task will take
- determine the order in which tasks must be completed. For example, in some cases particular tasks cannot be completed until another one has taken place first (these are known as 'dependent' activities). In other cases activities can be undertaken simultaneously (these are known as 'parallel' activities because they can be undertaken at the same time as each other – 'in parallel').

The next step is to construct a network chart. This is a diagrammatic representation of all the activities involved in the project, the order in which they must be undertaken and the times each one will take.

When drawing a network diagram the following features are used:

- a circle (called a 'node') represents the start and end of an activity
- a straight line represents the activity itself.

A line showing an activity is labelled in the following way: above the line the name of the activity is given; below the line the length of time the activity is expected to take is shown – this is known as the expected duration of the activity. In Figure 14.1 activity B is expected to last ten days; activity A is expected to last four days; activity B can only be started when activity A is completed (that is why it only begins once A is complete).

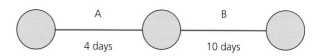

Figure 14.1

In Figure 14.2 activities C and D can only be started after activity B has been completed. Activity E can only start when C and D are finished.

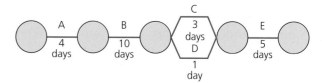

Figure 14.2

In Figure 14.3 we have added in some more activities. You can see that:

- activity F can start immediately
- G can start once F is completed
- H can start once E and G are completed.

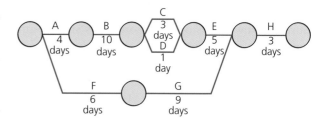

Figure 14.3

All this information can also be shown as it is in Table 14.1.

Activity	Preceded by	Duration (days)
A	–	4
B	A	10
C	B	3
D	B	1
E	C and D	5
F	–	6
G	F	9
H	E and G	3

Table 14.1

We now have a whole network diagram. Remember the following rules when constructing a chart:

- The lines showing different activities must never cross.
- The lines showing activities should always begin and end at the mid-point of the nodes.
- The diagram must begin and end with one node.
- When drawing the activities and nodes, do not put the end node on any activity until you are sure what comes next and whether anything else must also be completed before the following activity takes place.

Adding earliest start times and latest finish times

The next stage in producing a network chart is to show various information that can be calculated from the duration of each activity. This information is shown inside the node and to do this we now draw nodes in the following way:

- The left-hand side shows the number of the node; this is used simply for reference and is done by numbering the nodes left to right.
- The right-hand side of the node is used to show two other pieces of information known as the 'earliest start time' (EST) of the next activity and the 'latest finish time' (LFT) of the activity before.

Earliest start times

The earliest start time (EST) is exactly what it says: it is the earliest time a particular activity can begin. This piece of information is shown in the top right of the node at the beginning of an activity.

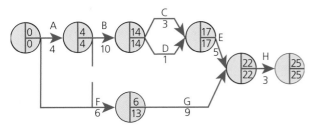

Figure 14.4

As you can see in Figure 14.4, the earliest times have now been added. To calculate these figures you take the earliest start time of the activity before and add on the duration of that activity.

The earliest time A can start is day 0 (this is the first activity in the project); this activity takes four days so the earliest time that B can start is day 4. B takes ten days so the earliest C and D can start is day 14.

E can only start when C and D are both finished. C takes longer than D so the project must wait for this activity to be completed before moving on; the earliest that E can start is therefore day 17.

If you have a choice of numbers to add on to calculate the earliest start time, choose the bigger number; the projects cannot continue until all previous dependent activities are finished, so you must wait for the longest one to be completed. Before H can start, for example, it must wait for both E and G to be completed, which means it cannot start until day 22.

By identifying the earliest start times a firm can see when materials are likely to be needed. This means that components and supplies can be ordered to arrive just in time to be used rather than arriving too early and sit around taking up space and costing money, or arriving late and delaying the whole project. Materials and resources for activity E, for example, do not need to be ready until day 17.

Calculating the earliest start time is therefore an important part of developing a lean approach to a project and ensuring people and materials are coordinated and ready at exactly the right moment.

Latest finish times

The bottom-right space of a node is used to show the latest finish time (LFT) of an activity. Again this shows exactly what it says – the latest an activity can be finished without holding up the whole project.

Activity H must finish on day 25 – the day the whole project can be completed; since H takes three days it means the activities before must be finished by day 22 if the project is to be completed on time. Activity E must therefore be completed at the latest by day 22. Since E takes five days this means the activities before (C and D) must be finished by day 17. Given that C takes three days (which is the longer activity out of C and D), if this stage is to be completed by day 17 the stage before must be finished by day 14.

To work out the latest finish times, therefore, you work right to left deducting the duration of a particular activity from its latest finish time to get the latest finish time of the one before. If there are two or more activities involved (such as C and D), choose the longer duration.

Rules when calculating ESTs and LFTs

- To calculate the earliest start time of an activity, work left to right and add on the duration of the next activity to the previous earliest start time; if there is a choice, choose the biggest number to add on.

- To calculate the latest finish time of an activity, work right to left and deduct its duration from the previous latest finish time; if there is a choice of numbers, choose the largest number to deduct.

Total float time

Using the earliest start times and the latest finish times it is possible to calculate the total float time of an activity. The total float time shows how long an activity can overrun without holding up the whole project.

To calculate total float use the equation:

$$\text{Total float time} =$$
$$\text{latest finish time} - \text{duration} - \text{earliest start time.}$$

For example, if activity D has to be finished by day 17, can start on day 14 and lasts one day then the total float is 2 days ($17 - 1 - 14 = 2$). This activity has two days' slack – it could overrun by two days and the project would still finish on time. By comparison, if activity B has to be finished by day 14, can start on day 4 and lasts ten days, its float is 0 days ($14 - 10 - 4 = 0$). There is no float – it must be completed on time or the whole project will be delayed. B is therefore known as a 'critical' activity because it has no total float. By identifying all of the critical activities the firm can see which activities must be finished on time; this is known as the critical path.

The critical path for the project in Table 14.2 is ABCEH because these activities have no total float time. If they are delayed at all the whole project will be late and will not be finished in 25 days.

By identifying the activities on the critical path managers can see exactly which activities are the priority in terms of making sure they stay on time; the critical path also shows the shortest time in which a project can be completed.

Benefits of critical path analysis

When undertaking a critical path analysis:

- Managers must consider exactly what activities are involved in a project. This is a useful exercise in itself because it helps to make sure that nothing is forgotten. It also means that managers are likely to consult all the different departments and functions

Activity	Preceded by	Duration (days)
A	–	4
B	A	10
C	B	3
D	B	1
E	C and D	5
F	–	6
G	F	9
H	E and G	3

Table 14.2

involved and this can help to improve everyone's understanding of the issues and challenges involved in getting the project completed.

- Managers can calculate the earliest time by which the project should be completed. This can be important information for customers (for example, the firm can announce a release date) and is important to help plan the launch arrangements. It can also help the managers decide whether or not a deadline can be hit.

- Managers can identify the 'critical' activities that must be completed in time to get the whole project finished as quickly as possible. This means that they can focus on these specific activities and make sure they do not overrun. At the same time the amount of float time on non-critical activities can be calculated. While managers cannot ignore these activities entirely it may not matter so much if they overrun (provided they do not use up all their float time); it may even be possible to transfer labour and other resources from non-critical activities to critical ones to ensure the latter are completed promptly.

- Managers may be able to produce items or develop products more quickly than the competition, providing the business with a possible competitive advantage. By seeking to reduce the time taken for a project, network analysis is an important element of time-based management.

- Managers can implement just-in-time ordering. Network analysis shows the earliest start times for each activity. Using this the firm can order materials and supplies to arrive exactly when they are needed and not before. This saves storage costs and also the opportunity cost of having money tied up in stocks. This can improve the firm's liquidity and free up cash which can be used elsewhere in the organisation.

- Managers can use network analysis as a control mechanism to review progress and assess whether the project is on target. If there have been delays the effects of the earliest start times and latest finish times can be reworked to see the effect on the completion of the project.

Although some of the estimates of the likely durations may prove to be wrong, and although external factors may cause delays, this does not mean that critical path analysis is unnecessary. On the contrary, by having a network diagram the effects of any delays can be relatively easily calculated in terms of the impact on the final completion date. Critical path analysis enables managers to understand the significance and likely dangers of any delay. Projects may still overrun, but managers should be able to predict if this is going to happen as soon as a problem emerges (rather than being taken by surprise) and if possible take action to get the project back on track.

Limitations of critical path analysis

Although critical path analysis can help business decision-making, it can have a number of drawbacks and limitations.

- It relies on the estimates for the expected duration. If these prove to be inaccurate the calculations for earliest start times and latest finish times, and so the critical path analysis, may be wrongly identified. The estimates may be incorrect because some managers may exaggerate how long an activity takes to make it easier for them to complete within the agreed time. On the other hand some managers may be too optimistic, particularly if these activities have not been carried out before. A more complex version of critical path analysis, called programme evaluation and review technique (PERT), includes a range of estimates for the durations of different activities; PERT produces a number of network diagrams based on optimistic, pessimistic and most likely durations of activities to take account of the fact that estimates cannot be completely relied on.
- If JIT is used for the delivery of materials, the ability to complete the project on time will depend on the reliability of suppliers. If they are late this will prevent the next activity starting on time.
- Critical path analysis simply shows the quickest way to complete a project; it does not guarantee that this is the right project to be undertaking in the

first place. It may be that the firm's resources could be used more effectively elsewhere.
- All projects must be managed properly if they are to be completed on time. Drawing up a network diagram is only the starting point. Managers must agree on who is responsible for each stage of the project. They must be given the resources and budget to complete in the time agreed. There must be an effective review system to make sure the project is on schedule and to agree what action to take if it is not. A network diagram can provide a valuable focal point for the management system, but it is up to the managers to make sure that everything is implemented correctly and that each activity is completed on schedule.

Other issues in critical path analysis

Before a project is started managers must agree on a definition of success. They must set out exactly what they want to achieve otherwise subordinates may cut corners to get the project done on time. The result may be that the project is completed quickly but that the quality is poor.

Managers must also agree on what resources and spending they are willing to commit to the project. Obviously the quickest way of completing a project will depend on what facilities and resources are available and how much the firm is willing to invest into getting it completed. With more people, more money and more machines the project could probably be speeded up. Whether particular activities can be conducted simultaneously will often depend on whether the firm has or is willing to invest in the necessary resources.

Managers will also be interested in the utilisation of resources throughout the project. It may be that certain activities could be undertaken simultaneously, but that as a result some weeks would require very high levels of personnel whereas in other weeks very few people would be needed. If it adopted such an approach a firm may have to bring in extra staff for the busy week and pay its existing staff to do little in the other weeks. Rather than have such fluctuations in staffing levels managers may want to shift activities around; this may mean that the project takes a bit longer but it may nevertheless be more desirable if it means that its full-time staff are fully employed each week.

Cell production

Cell production is a method of organising production around teams. Organising work in this way rather than a traditional production line can lead to less wastage. Instead of producing items on a production line, the process is divided into a series of different stages undertaken by teams or 'cells'. Each team is given the responsibility for a stage in the process.

An advantage of this approach is that teams are responsible for a complete unit of work. Instead of each individual working on one simple task and having no real involvement with the final product, working in cells can give employees a sense of team spirit. It can also improve quality because teams have work for which they have overall responsibility and they can clearly see the results of their efforts.

Cell production can be very motivating for employees because they feel they have more control over their own work. The team members can organise among themselves when and how items are produced. They can also share their skills and expertise.

Team members are also likely to feel much greater responsibility for their work because the next cell has the right to refuse their work if it is poor quality. Cell production involves self-checking by team members.

Hackman and Oldham (1976) developed a model of job design which highlighted the key elements of a motivating job. This model stressed the importance of designing jobs in which individuals have:

- skill variety: they use a range of skills
- task significance: they are working on something that has some significance in terms of the overall business rather than just working on a small section and thereby not appreciating why what they do matters
- task identity: the work they do has a sense of competition (for example, handing over a complete unit of work to the next stage of the process)
- autonomy: individuals have some independence to make decisions on how they do the work
- feedback: employees receive information on the quality of their work.

Cell production helps in most of the areas above and should therefore create more motivating work. Teams have control over what they do; together they produce a complete unit of work, they hand it over to the next cell, which will give feedback and each member of the cell may undertake a range of tasks. This should be more motivating than simply undertaking the same task again and again on a production line – in that system you probably have no idea why your part of the process matters, there is almost no skill variety or sense of task significance.

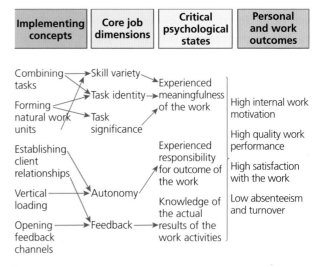

Figure 14.5 The Hackman and Oldham model of job design

Benchmarking

Benchmarking occurs when one business measures its performance against other organisations. Firms benchmark against other organisations that are strong in particular areas. The aim of benchmarking is to learn from the best firms in the world and discover ways of improving operations. If you want to know how to manage large numbers of visitors, talk to Disney; if you want to know how to come up with great design, ask Apple; if you want to move things around reliably, talk to UPS.

Looking for the ways to improve corporate performance internally assumes that a business's staff know the best way of doing something, or how to improve it. Analysing the actions of other organisations, especially experts in the relevant business area, means a business is more likely to find the best solution. This is particularly true if firms benchmark against the best in the world. Benchmarking may be against other firms in the same industry or even against organisations in a completely different sector. It highlights the importance of being a learning organisation and not being complacent.

Firms may use benchmarking to help them improve in areas such as:

- the reliability of their products
- their ability to send out the correct bills (also called invoices)
- their ability to deliver items on time
- the time it takes to produce a product.

Organisations undertaking benchmarking are those most eager to learn and improve and those that are unafraid to seek outside help.

The benchmarking process

1 The firm must plan what it wants to benchmark, which firms it wants to benchmark with, how it is going to collect the data, what resources to allocate to the project and who is responsible for the project.
2 The firm must collect data from the other firm or firms. This may be through visits to their factories or offices.
3 The firm must analyse its findings to identify how it could improve its own process.
4 The firm must adapt its findings so it can implement the new methods in its own firm given its own circumstances.

The benefits of benchmarking

By undertaking benchmarking a firm should be able to:

- develop a better understanding of customers and competitors
- have fewer complaints and more satisfied customers
- reduce waste and improve quality.

Benchmarking can be difficult because some firms will naturally be unwilling to share their information. They may want to keep their methods and processes secret and might be reluctant to provide rival

businesses with ideas on how to improve. One way of avoiding this problem is to benchmark against firms in different industries.

Firms must also be careful about trying to copy another organisation's methods exactly. Every organisation has its own way of doing things, its own skills and its own circumstances. They may have to adapt the other firm's methods for their own use.

Kaizen

The belief that firms can always do better is known as 'kaizen'. Kaizen is a Japanese word meaning continuous improvement. The kaizen approach tries to get employees to improve what they do in some small way every day of every week of every year. If workers improve the quality of their work by 1 per cent every single day, the effect over just one year would be enormous. Too often, businesses seek dramatic changes instead of small, regular changes. If you want to improve your grades in your exams, it is unlikely that there is any one thing you can do which will lead to a sudden improvement in your marks. However, if you begin to change many things over time, your grade is likely to improve gradually.

The idea of continuously improving can be seen in the work of Edward Deming. Deming was an American who actually achieved great fame in Japan for his work on quality. Deming advised managers to focus in on a specific problem and find the best way of doing this and set appropriate quality targets. Managers would plan what needs to be done, then do it, then check to see the results and then take action. If the targets were consistently being met managers could then increase the level of quality they were trying to achieve and focus on how to do this. If the existing targets were not being met managers should find out any problems and fix them before raising the bar.

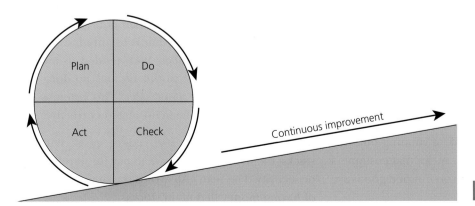

Figure 14.6 The Deming cycle

Just-in-time production

Stocks are goods which have been produced or are in the process of being produced but which have not been sold yet.

All firms hold different types of stocks. Stocks can take a variety of forms:

- **Raw materials and components** are stocks waiting to be used in the production process.
- **Works in progress or unfinished goods** are stocks of goods in the process of being manufactured.
- **Finished goods**, as the name suggests, are goods produced and ready to be sold. In the case of the manufacturer, these are goods waiting to be sold or delivered to the shops, or the final customer. Retailers hold finished goods on their shelves ready to be sold.

The way in which stocks are managed is an important element of operations management.

Holding stocks is important to firms because they are often needed to maintain production and to meet customers' demand. With stocks available, a business can produce at any time and has goods available for customers.

However, the problem is that holding stocks can be expensive and risky. For example, the more stocks a business has:

- the greater the warehousing space needed
- the more money there is tied up in stocks, which means the firm incurs a high opportunity cost because the money that is invested in stocks could be used in other ways
- the higher the security costs to protect the stocks
- the greater the risk; inevitably if a firm holds stocks there is the danger that they will perish or become obsolete.

The decision on how many stocks to hold is, therefore, a trade-off between the costs of holding the stocks and the problems which might occur if stocks are not held.

The minimum amount of stock that a firm wants to hold at any time is known as the buffer stock (or the safety stock). If the level of stocks falls below the buffer level, there may be a risk of running out; this could either halt production or mean that customers have to be turned away because no finished goods are available.

Several factors influence the level of buffer stocks a business holds:

- The rate at which stocks are generally used up – the faster stocks are used up, the more the firm will have to hold at any moment.
- The warehousing space available – the smaller the space the firm has for storage, the lower the level of stocks.
- The nature of the product – if the product is fragile or likely to depreciate, the firm will not want too much stock in case it breaks or loses value rapidly.
- The reliability of suppliers – the more reliable suppliers are, the fewer buffer stocks the firm needs to hold because it knows it can get more as and when required.
- The suppliers' lead time – the lead time is the time it takes for products to arrive from when they are ordered. If the lead time is two days, for example, this means that it takes two days for supplies to arrive once you have ordered them. The shorter the lead time, the smaller the amount of stocks a firm needs to hold. If, however, the lead time is long, the firm will need to hold more stocks to last while it waits for a delivery.

One particular approach to stock control is known as just-in-time (JIT) operations.

Just-in-time production occurs when firms produce products to order. Instead of producing as much as they can and building up stocks, firms only produce when they know they can actually sell the items. Similarly, components and supplies are only bought in by a firm as and when they are needed.

The aim of just-in-time production is to reduce a firm's stock levels by as much as possible; in an ideal world there would be no stocks at all. Supplies would arrive and be used to produce items that are sold immediately to the final customer. A just-in-time approach should provide a firm with tremendous flexibility; firms produce what is required, when it is required. In the past, firms have tended to try and estimate what demand would be and produce this amount in advance of actual sales. This system works provided demand has been estimated correctly.

JIT production should also reduce costs. With no stocks, the firm does not have to pay for warehousing or security. The firm also avoids the opportunity cost of having money tied up in stocks.

Just-in-time production should help minimise wastage. If goods are produced and left to accumulate as stocks, they are likely to get damaged, to depreciate, to go out of fashion or be stolen. JIT avoids these issues.

However, introducing a just-in-time system is complex and places many demands on a business, as explained below.

Excellent relationships with suppliers

Businesses need to be able to rely on suppliers to deliver goods at precisely the right time. They cannot afford delays as this halts production. Also, the goods must be perfect quality; the manufacturer has no stocks to replace faulty supplies. A firm must be able to trust its suppliers completely.

Reliable employees

Because the business does not have many (if any) stocks at any stage of the process, the firm cannot cope with stoppages. If strikes occur, for example, the whole production process stops. A business cannot supply customers using stocks as none exist. JIT relies upon maintaining a good relationship between employers and employees.

A flexible workforce

To ensure that production can respond to demand, a firm needs a flexible labour force. This means that if someone is ill, another employee must be able to cover for them, or that if demand is high in one area of the business, people can be moved to that area to help out. Firms using JIT expect employees to be ready to work anywhere, anytime. People must change to meet the demand for different products because JIT is focused entirely on matching supply to customer orders.

Introducing just-in-time production involves:

- investment in machinery which is flexible and can be changed from producing one type of item to another without much delay
- training employees so that they have several skills and can do a variety of jobs (multi-skilling)
- negotiation with employees so that their contracts are flexible and allow them to move from one job to another
- building relationships with suppliers who can produce just-in-time as well.

BUSINESS IN FOCUS

Zara

Zara, the clothes retailer, offers 'disposable fashion', with prices ranging from $33 for a red tank top to a black blazer for $145. Employing an army of 200-plus designers, Zara produces 12,000 different items a year. The fabric is cut in Zara's factory, then subcontracted out to local workshops for stitching. The company offsets the higher costs of European labour by avoiding markdowns, keeping stocks to a minimum, and spending very little on marketing.

Tight control over design and production allows Zara to take a trend from catwalk to store shelf in as little as two weeks. Rival Gap Inc. takes about a year, albeit on a much larger scale, and the company is trying hard to get that process down to six months.

The chain's greatest advantage may be its salespeople, who act as grassroots market researchers. Each carries a wireless organiser that is used to punch in trends, customer comments and orders to headquarters. If an item does not sell, it can be off shelves in weeks. If it is successful, Zara designers know immediately and can churn out new versions in myriad colours. This year, Zara sold a pink men's dress shirt. Customers suggested they would prefer purple. Zara's in-house manufacturing sped into action and was able to get a new shirt into the store within days.

The company has a no-advertising policy. It depends mainly on its stores' elegant front windows to sell its merchandise. In New York, Zara has four outlets, including one on Fifth Avenue and one in SoHo. At the store on 34th Street, the company tore out the entire interior, added marble-like floors and high-tech lights to create a stunning 10,000-square-foot emporium. The crowd, mostly in their 20s, also includes more mature businesswomen.

Overseeing all these details is Zara's secretive founder, Armancio Ortega, who, with the rest of his family, owns 100 per cent of Inditex's shares.

(Source: W. Echison, 'The mark of Zara', Business Week, Issue 3683, 2000)

Problems of JIT

Although the just-in-time process has many advantages, there are several potential problems or disadvantages as well.

First, the system relies on suppliers providing parts and components at exactly the time they are needed. If this type of flexible and reliable supplier cannot be found, the system breaks down. If the suppliers fail to deliver on time the manufacturer has no buffer stock and so cannot produce.

The JIT system also means that the firm is vulnerable to action taken by employees. Any stoppage can be extremely expensive because production is halted completely.

The earthquake in Japan in 2011 was a disaster for those directly affected by it. It also caused enormous problems for businesses operating a JIT process and reliant on supplies from Japan. With a delay in supplies they struggled to produce.

Switching to JIT can also lead to an increase in costs because of the extra reordering. Because parts are ordered much more frequently, the firm may lose bulk discounts and will also have more administration costs.

BUSINESS IN FOCUS

Toyota

In April 2011 the Japanese car maker, Toyota, had to temporarily halt production at its engine manufacturing plant on Deeside, Flintshire and five other of its factories across Europe.

The company said the stoppage was due to a shortage of supplies from Japan, caused by the earthquake and tsunami.

Dr Paul Nieuwenhuis from the Centre for Automotive Industry Research at Cardiff Business School, Cardiff University, said: 'The problem is they rely on parts coming in from Japan.'

'They have not been affected by the earthquake for the last few weeks but now that this "pipeline" [of parts] has come to an end, suddenly they are hit by this problem,' he said.

He pointed out that Toyota uses a 'just in time system' of supply which operates without a lot of slack in the system. Once the supply of parts stops, it does not take much time for plants around the world to be affected.

(*Source: Adapted from BBC News, 13 April 2011*)

Question:

Does the halt in production suggest that Toyota should stop using lean production techniques? Justify your answer. *(16 marks)*

Summary

Lean production is an approach to operations that seeks to minimise waste in all areas while achieving other targets such as volume and quality. It aims to find ways of continuously improving and reducing excess effort and resources. By being more efficient this enables a business to be more competitive.

Key terms

Simultaneous engineering occurs when as many activities as possible involved in developing new products are undertaken at the same time, as opposed to in sequence, to save time.

Float time is the length of time an activity can overrun without delaying the completion of the whole project.

The **critical path** refers to activities that have no float time; if they overrun at all the whole project is delayed.

Cell production occurs when the production process is divided into stages undertaken by teams.

Benchmarking occurs when one business decides to measure its performance against the leaders in the field.

1 What is meant by lean production? *(2 marks)*

2 What is time-based management? *(2 marks)*

3 What is critical path analysis? *(2 marks)*

4 What is float time? *(2 marks)*

5 What is just-in-time production? *(2 marks)*

6 Explain why firms hold stocks. *(4 marks)*

7 Explain **two** factors necessary for the successful introduction of just-in-time production. *(6 marks)*

8 What is meant by kaizen? *(2 marks)*

9 What is benchmarking? *(2 marks)*

10 Explain **two** possible benefits of cell production. *(6 marks)*

Analysis question

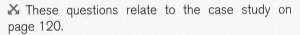 These questions relate to the case study on page 120.

'Getting leaner might bring more problems than it is worth for Pramus.' To what extent do you agree with this view? *(16 marks)*

Candidate's answer:

Lean production involves ways of reducing all forms of waste – wasted time, wasted resources, wasted staff. By being lean you become more efficient. This is important to Sarah because she wants to get the profit margin back up again. All other things being equal a lower cost increases profits relative to sales. In this case lean production would not be a waste of time.

However, it depends on how it is done and what costs are cut. The case study seems to imply the business has become complacent and therefore there are unnecessary costs around; for example, there may be overstaffing, excess expense accounts, money being spent in unnecessary projects, and so on. Cutting costs here may not be a problem and simply boost profits. However if costs are cut on key research projects it might lead to even fewer sales in the future and may make it impossible to meet Sarah's target of having a significant percentage of sales from products

launched within five years. Lean production may also involve redundancies and these may be resisted by staff; bad relations with staff may make it harder generally to recruit staff (perhaps in the future) in an industry where getting the best talent is important. Lean can also be dangerous – for example if you use just-in-time you do not have stocks. If there is a problem with a supplier this means you cannot produce. Given the difficulties the business has had launching new products it will not want more problems with a lack of supplies ever holding up production.

Examiner's comments:

A good answer in many ways in that it analyses the issues and also applies it to the case study. There is an argument for and against and the candidate relates the answer to the situation of Pramus. This is all good. The analysis and application is good.

However, the candidate does not directly answer the question – is lean more trouble than it's worth? Yes or no? To what extent do they agree with this view? The candidate argues that lean production can be good and that it can be bad but does not pull these arguments together to consider directly whether it is more trouble than it's worth. The evaluation is therefore very limited.

Evaluation question

To what extent might using critical path analysis help bring about cost reductions more quickly? *(18 marks)*

The subject matter that makes up the management of human resources within A Level Business Studies is divided between the AS and A2 elements of the specification. The major parts of your AS programme will have included the following topics:

- introductory issues in employing people
- organisational structures
- measuring the effectiveness of the workforce
- motivation – in theory and practice
- recruitment, selection and training.

The A2 specification for business studies builds upon the subject knowledge and skills acquired during the AS programme. It is worthwhile looking back over your AS materials before starting to study this section. More specific advice is given on any prior knowledge required at the outset of each chapter.

As part of Unit 3 of your A2 programme you will study the following:

- human resource objectives
- human resource strategies
- developing and implementing workforce plans
- developing competitive organisational structures
- managing employer–employee relationships effectively.

In addition, there are two topics within Unit 4 of the A2 specification that are also closely linked to the management of human resources within an organisation. These are:

- leadership
- organisational culture.

Unit 4 considers the importance of these topics in the context of managing change.

Case study for Section 4: Kevar Travel plc

Established in 1966 by Kevin Morris and Anne Robins, Kevar Travel sells holidays to UK consumers headed for southern European destinations. The company has developed a reputation for price-competitive products in a market that has become increasingly dominated by larger rivals, many of whom have merged to create huge organisations with considerable market power.

Changes in the competitive power of rivals and also in consumers' tastes and fashions regarding holidays over recent years has meant that Kevar Travel has faced fluctuating demand for its products. It has had to constantly seek new destinations in Spain, Greece and Portugal to allow it to continue to offer low-cost holidays. It has struggled to maintain its market share and its profits have declined steadily.

The company values skilled staff – a vital asset in a highly competitive service industry. It uses specialists in functional areas such as operations, marketing and finance and benefits from their skills. However, this view has not always been reflected in the way it has treated its more junior staff. Operating in a price-elastic market it has sought to minimise wage costs, has relied on bonuses as the principal means of motivation and has made extensive use of short-term and temporary contracts. Despite this, five out of seven of the company's current directors have 'risen through the ranks'. The use of two-way communication remains limited within the company's relatively tall hierarchical organisational structure. Since 1998 the company's principal HR objective has been to match its workforce to the needs of the business.

Kevar Travel's 2010 cost-cutting strategy

Eighteen months ago the company revised its corporate strategy for 2010 onwards in an attempt to address its weak and declining financial position. The company started to offer a range of budget-priced holidays in Eastern European countries such as Slovakia and Bulgaria. An important element of the new strategy was to reduce the company's operating costs to enhance its price competitiveness. The strategy included the closure of the company's main offices in London and relocation to Stoke, where costs are significantly lower. This decision was opposed by the trade union (ATPU) that represents many of the company's employees as it involved some job losses as well as relocation for many staff.

The associated workforce plan was designed to improve the efficiency of its workforce by making it more flexible and to assist it in meeting the changing needs of its consumers. Despite being cost conscious, the company has invested heavily in primary market research to allow it to produce detailed sales forecasts. HR director Alexandra Bagley argued that the nature of the contemporary holiday market means that sales forecasts are the most important influence on Kevar Travel's workforce plan. She stressed that the company has to be able to operate flexibly in a fluctuating market while maintaining tight control over labour costs.

As a consequence of the changing corporate strategy and the new workforce plan, the company's expenditure on training rose substantially during 2010–11 and 2011–12 as it equipped its employees with the knowledge and skills to sell a wide range of new holidays. By late 2011 industrial relations had improved and a single union deal was negotiated bringing benefits to both parties and the promise of improved two-way communications.

A further change of approach

In January 2012 Charlie Johnson become Kevar Travel's CEO. He had previously held a senior role with a larger competitor. His arrival led to a major review of the company's strategy and to a number of new proposals being placed before the board of directors.

Charlie Johnson planned a new strategy which would have significant implications for all the business's functions, but HR most of all. Its key elements were as follows.

- To sell higher priced holidays to more exotic destinations offering greater profit margins.
- To target different and higher income market segments, but especially those aged over 60.
- To employ more full-time permanent staff with excellent skills, increasing spending on training as necessary.
- To organise the company's workforce into empowered teams as part of a policy of decentralisation.
- To reduce the number of people employed at head office in Stoke by 15 per cent within one year. A number of temporary jobs will also be lost.

Several of the directors were strongly opposed to this major change in strategy, believing the company required a period of stability and that the trade union should be involved in discussions. The finance director estimated the strategy would require an investment of £2.1 million in its first year and £0.8 million in the second year.

Appendices

Appendix A: HR data

HR data	2011–12	2010–11	2009–10
Average span of control	8	8	7
Sales per employee (£)	73,410	76,765	77,011
Labour turnover (%)	21.1	21.6	28.8
Percentage of employees on temporary contracts	29.7	20.1	9.2
Average span of control	6.5	6.9	7.3
Percentage of employees in a trade union	38.6	41.1	22.7
Percentage of employees located in London	3.7	4.1	15.8
Days lost due to industrial action	42	0	576

Table 1 Kevar Travel plc's HR data

Note: *Kevar Travel's average hourly pay rates:*
London = £17.89; Stoke = £13.17.

Appendix B: Marketing data

- Number of UK citizens aged over 60: 2012 = 14.47 million; 2030 (est.) = 19.86 million.
- Percentage of sales to new customers: 51.4 per cent (three-year average).

Appendix C: Other data

- The company's ROCE has fallen steadily from 23.3 per cent in 2008–09 to 16.6 per cent in 2009–10 and 13.1 per cent in 2011–12.

- Net cash flow: (£9.86 million) in 2011–12; (£3.3 million) in 2010–11.
- Percentage of company profits paid as a bonus: 2011–12 = 9.25 per cent; 2010–12 = 10.12 per cent.
- Change in expenditure on primary market research from 2009–10 to 2010–11: +336 per cent.
- Labour costs were 68.4 per cent of the company's total costs in 2011–12; 69.9 per cent in 2010–11.

15 Understanding human resource objectives and strategies

A human resource (HR) function or department is responsible for the use of labour within the organisation. You will have already encountered some HR-related topics and responsibilities as part of your AS course: employing people; how organisations structure themselves; recruiting, selecting, training and motivating staff. In this section we will build on your AS knowledge and consider strategies that a business may adopt to achieve its human resource objectives.

In this chapter we examine:

- the HR objectives that businesses may pursue
- the internal and external influences on HR objectives
- the types of HR strategies that businesses may adopt.

Introduction to human resources

A business's human resource (HR) function or department is responsible for the use of labour within the organisation. Human resource management (HRM) views activities relating to the workforce as integrated and vital in helping the organisation to achieve its corporate objectives. People are viewed as an important resource to be developed through training. Thus, policies relating to recruitment, pay and appraisal, for example, should be formulated as part of a coordinated human resource strategy. HRM is an all-embracing integrated approach that aims to make the best use of human resources in relation to the business's overall goals. Human resource management involves the strategic planning of the management of employees.

The nature of human resource objectives

Human resource objectives are the targets pursued by the HR function or department of the business. The achievement of these goals should assist the business in attaining its overall corporate objectives. Tesco, the UK's largest retailer, has a number of corporate objectives, including: 'Developing the talents of its people through sound management and training practices, while rewarding them fairly with equal opportunities for all.' The company's human resource function will set itself a number of objectives to allow the business to achieve its objective. For example,

it would set objectives relating to the provision of training to all of its 472,000 employees.

There are a number of HR objectives, the importance of which will vary according to the type of business, its products and the market in which it is trading.

Matching the workforce to the needs of the business

It is normal for the labour needs of a business to change over time. A business might grow, move overseas, replace employees with technology or take a decision to produce new products. Each of these actions will mean that the business will require a different workforce. Our earlier example of Tesco can apply here too. Tesco has grown rapidly recently, and has opened stores in Asia and the US. It has expanded its product range to incorporate financial services and personal services such as eyesight tests. This has required the company's HR department to recruit new employees, redeploy employees to a new location or to train employees to provide the necessary skills.

Meeting this objective is essential as it allows the firm to be as competitive as possible because the business needs to have sufficient employees to ensure that it can meet the needs of its customers and to provide the best-quality goods or services possible. Having a workforce of the correct size also assists the business in providing high-quality customer service. Ensuring that the business has the right number of employees to meet its customers' needs can be challenging for businesses that face seasonal demand, and is an important HR objective.

Heavy job losses at BAE

Around 1,900 jobs are expected to go at BAE Systems as managers are due to tell workers of heavy cuts to the workforce. The bulk of the jobs will go at the company's factory at Samlesbury, near Preston and the neighbouring Warton site. Parts for the Typhoon jet are built by workers at the company's factory at Samlesbury, with final assembly and testing work at the Warton site, which employ around 11,500 people across both sites.

The company confirmed the Government is to buy aircraft over a longer period of time, slowing production. Fylde MP Mark Menzies told the Lancashire Evening Post on Monday that the scale of cuts would be 'devastating' for Lancashire's defence industry. He said he knows many of the workers 'and I know how passionately they care about the jobs they do'. The Unite union said it needed immediate clarification of which sites will be hit and pledged to press for redundancies to be voluntary.

The cuts come on top of more than 1,300 job cuts announced over the last 12 months on the back of the Government's decision to scrap the Harrier and Nimrod projects, which employed thousands of staff across BAE. The company employs 40,000 staff in the UK and just under 100,000 globally.

(*Source: Helen Carter on* The Guardian *website, 26 September 2011*)

Question:

The company is set to reduce its workforce by 1,900 people. To what extent do you think that this decision will help BAE Systems to achieve its HR objectives? *(18 marks)*

For example, the Royal Mail requires additional employees at certain times of the year, such as Christmas when demand for postal services is much higher. In 2011 the company advertised 18,000 temporary Christmas jobs. Thus the company's HR objectives will include the need to have a flexible workforce that can meet the varying demands of its customers. Fulfilling this objective requires ongoing action on the part of the HR function.

Making full use of the workforce's potential

HR managers may select this as an objective if they feel that the business is not making the most effective use of its existing employees. Making more use of employees can result in an increase in output without necessarily incurring further costs. A workforce's potential can exist in a number of forms.

- **Skills**. It is possible that employees have some skills which they do not use as part of their working lives. This is entirely possible in a large business where managers may not be familiar with all of their employees. It is possible that employees have recognisable skills, such as speaking a second language or skills relating to information technology. Businesses can use a skills audit to identify such skills and then make use of them as and when appropriate.
- **Underutilised employees**. Some employees may find that their jobs are not really challenging. Their current roles may not stretch them or utilise their talents to anything like their full extent. This means that the employees are not contributing as fully to the business as is possible. On the other hand, some employees may not have sufficient work to occupy them fully; this would result in lower levels of productivity than might be expected. Identifying and responding effectively to this underutilisation of staff will improve the performance of the workforce.
- **Overworked or stressed employees**. The opposite circumstance to the above can occur, especially if a business is seeking to improve its profitability by reducing its operating costs. This can result in employees having excessive workloads or being asked to take positions within the organisation for which they are not properly trained or qualified.

Maintaining good employer–employee relations

Maintaining good relations with employees is an important HR objective for all businesses. Good employer–employee relations give businesses a range of benefits.

- It makes strikes and other forms of labour disputes less likely. This avoids the business suffering from periods when it is unable to function normally due to a partial or complete loss of output. Such a scenario can reduce the business's revenue as well its profitability. It may also result in the long-term loss of customers who are dissatisfied with the lack of supplies.

- Research has shown that businesses with good industrial relations attract higher-calibre and better-qualified applicants for positions. This can assist a business in improving its performance. High-quality employees may be more creative, take better-quality decisions and provide a higher level of service for customers.
- Good employer–employee relations assist a business to maintain a positive corporate image which may have a positive effect on sales. A business that suffers from regular occurrences of industrial action may receive a lot of adverse publicity. This may result in a loss of customers who shun the business in the belief that employees are not treated well.
- With good relations, employer–employee communications may be highly effective, helping to resolve problems before they develop into a dispute. Efficient channels of communication between employer and employee may also improve the operation of the business in many ways by, for example, encouraging suggestions for improving production from employees.

The internal and external influences on HR objectives

Human resource managers are subject to influences from inside the business as well as external factors when deciding on the objectives for their department.

Internal influences on HR objectives

There are a number of internal factors that may influence a business's decision regarding which HR objectives to adopt and pursue.

- **Corporate objectives**. As with all functional objectives, those set by the HR department must assist the organisation in achieving its overall objectives. Thus, if the business has a corporate objective of maximising long-term profits, the HR objective might set itself objectives concerned with reducing labour costs or making the most effective use of the workforce. The low-cost airline easyJet has the corporate objective of operating at minimum cost and thereby remaining highly competitive in its particular market niche. The

company therefore closely monitors its need for employees to keep wage costs at a minimum to maintain its competitiveness.

- **The attitudes and beliefs of the senior managers.** The senior managers of a business can have an important influence on HR objectives. If they consider the workforce to be a valuable asset, they may want a long-term relationship with employees and may set objectives such as developing the skills of the workforce to their fullest extent. Alternatively, they may see employees as an expendable asset to be hired when necessary and paid the minimum rate possible. This can have considerable implications for the HR strategy operated by a business. We consider HR strategies more fully below.
- **The type of product.** If the product requires the commitment of a highly skilled labour force then objectives such as making full use of the workforce's potential may be most important. However, a key HR objective for a business selling products which are mainly produced by machinery and require little in the way of skilled labour may be to minimise labour costs through having the smallest possible number of employees at all times. Some retailers may focus on matching the workforce to the needs of the business as a prime objective because a number of their staff may be relatively low skilled and relatively easy to replace as necessary.

BUSINESS IN FOCUS

Tesco in the US

In 2007 Tesco started its expansion into the US by opening 55 stores in southern California and Nevada. These stores have not been trading under the Tesco brand, but as 'Fresh & Easy' convenience stores. The American stores have not yet earned a profit for the company. However, in 2011 Tesco announced that it intends to open a further 12 stores in northern California, including in San Francisco. Ultimately the company intends to build 1,000 stores along the entire western coast of the US.

Question:

Analyse the possible ways in which the introduction of the Fresh & Easy stores in the US might affect the objectives set by the company's HR department. *(10 marks)*

External influences on HR objectives

External factors will have a significant impact on the HR objectives that are set by businesses.

- **The state of the market**. A growing market will have a significant impact on the HR objectives pursued by a business. Sales of many products have fallen in the UK in recent times due to the recent recession, and fears of a second one. The media have carried a series of stories about how businesses are adjusting their workforces to reflect these changed times. The recession and subsequent fears will have encouraged many businesses to think about matching the workforce to the needs of the business. The McDonald's story in the 'Business in focus' here highlights that a rise in demand for the product requires increased staffing levels.

- **Price elasticity of demand for the product.** When demand for a product is strongly price elastic (demand is very sensitive to price changes) it is more likely that a business will opt for HR objectives that allow it to reduce labour costs. This can be seen in the case of budget airlines. If demand is price elastic, a reduction in price is likely to lead to a substantial increase in sales. Setting suitable HR objectives to match the need to minimise costs of production will be vital in these circumstances.

- **Corporate image.** Most businesses will set HR objectives that include maintaining good relations with employees. To become embroiled in an industrial dispute can be damaging to the image of a business and may lead to a loss in sales. This might be particularly important for large and potentially dominant businesses which may be vulnerable to accusations of abusing their power.

- **Employment legislation**. The UK government and EU authorities have passed a series of laws designed to protect labour in the workplace. The existence of such laws may encourage businesses to set HR objectives to develop the potential of their workforces as the law may make it difficult to hire and fire employees at will. In particular, a change in the law will have an impact on the objectives that a HR department pursues.

Human resource strategies

A human resource strategy is the medium- to long-term plan that is implemented to achieve the

business's HR objectives. It is a central element of a business's approach to HRM.

A number of factors have persuaded UK businesses to implement human resource strategies.

- A principal argument is that the Japanese have had apparent success in managing people using this approach. The Japanese have been seen to gain significant competitive advantage from managing a human resource that produces high-quality products at minimum cost. It is human resource management that is credited with achieving this match between employee behaviour and organisational objectives.

- Changes in organisational structure have led to many managers taking on responsibility for managing people within the organisation. Techniques such as delayering and the development of empowered teams have been an integral part of the implementation of human resource strategies. Acquiring, developing, motivating and rewarding employees are, it is argued, best done by managers and colleagues close to the employees in question. Under HRM, managers can carry out many of the more routine tasks of traditional personnel management.

- The increasing popularity of psychological approaches to motivation has encouraged the adoption of HR strategies. Human resource strategies demand styles of working that meet the social and psychological needs of employees. The adoption of flatter organisational structures and psychological techniques of motivation are essential elements of HR strategies – organisations that adopt these techniques and structures would naturally move towards adopting some type of HR strategy.

However, the adoption of HR strategies by UK businesses is not as sweeping and as clear-cut as some might suggest. Surveys have indicated that many companies have opted to select only the elements of the human resource management package that fit in with their philosophies, management style and corporate objectives. For example, a firm might choose to implement rigorous selection and appraisal methods but ignore other aspects, particularly developing employees through training.

This means that there is not a single HR strategy or approach to HRM. Different firms have interpreted the HR philosophy in different ways.

- **'Hard' HR strategies.** Some firms operate 'hard' HR policies, treating employees as a resource to be used optimally. Such firms regard employees as yet another resource to be deployed as efficiently as possible in pursuit of strategic targets. Employees are obtained as cheaply as possible, controlled and disposed of when necessary.
- **'Soft' HR strategies.** Other firms use an HR system that can be regarded as 'soft'. This approach is based on the notion that employees are perhaps the most valuable asset a business has and they should be developed to maximise their value to the organisation. This makes a long-term approach essential. Employees are seen as a resource to be valued and developed over time and in response to changing market conditions.

	'Hard' HRM	'Soft' HRM
Philosophy	Sees employees as a resource like any other available to the business.	Sees employees as different from, and more important than, any other resource available to managers.
Time scale	HRM seen as a short-term policy: employees hired and fired as necessary.	Takes a long-term view of using the workforce as efficiently as possible to achieve long-term corporate objectives.
Key features	<ul><li>Employees paid as little as possible.</li><li>Employees only have limited control over working life.</li><li>Communication mainly downward in direction.</li><li>Leaders tend towards Theory X view of workforce.</li><li>Employees recruited externally to fulfil human needs – giving short-term solution.</li><li>Judgemental appraisal.</li></ul>	<ul><li>Managers consult with employees.</li><li>Managers give control over working lives to employees through delayering and empowerment.</li><li>Leaders tend towards Theory Y view of workforce.</li><li>Emphasis on training and developing employees.</li><li>Employees promoted from within, reflecting long-term desire to develop workforce.</li><li>Developmental appraisal.</li></ul>
Associated leadership style	Leaders operating this style of HRM are more likely to be at the autocratic end of the spectrum of leadership.	Leaders implementing 'soft' HRM are more likely to be democratic in nature.
Motivational techniques used	Probably mainly motivated by pay, with limited use of techniques such as delegation and teamworking.	Motivate through delegation and empowerment. Heavy use of techniques designed to give employees more authority.

Table 15.1 Approaches to human resource management

The strengths and weaknesses of hard and soft HR strategies

Hard HR strategies

A hard HR strategy offers a number of advantages to a business.

- It makes it easier for businesses to adapt the size and composition of their workforces to match the needs of their customers. Thus, a business using this type of strategy will be prepared to hire and dismiss workers as necessary without the need to maintain the size of its workforce during a downturn in sales. This allows a business to cope more effectively when trading in markets that suffer from regular fluctuations in levels of demand.

- It can result in lower costs, especially in the short-term. Adopting a 'hard' approach to employees may mean that a business only uses employees with minimal skill levels and relies on the use of technology and a small number of highly skilled core employees to meet the needs of its customers. This means that the business may be able to reduce expenditure on its workforce by paying low wage rates (perhaps minimum wage) and to avoid heavy and regular expenditure on employee training. Such a strategy, if successful, may boost profits to the satisfaction of shareholders.

- A 'hard' approach to HR allows managers to retain control over the workforce and to direct operations as they wish. Under such an approach employees will be told what their duties are, with relatively little opportunity for discussion on how to complete a job and limited input in terms of suggestions on how to improve the production process. This approach can assist a business in maintaining its focus on its corporate objectives.

However, the 'hard' approach to HR can also bring about a number of disadvantages.

- The level of labour turnover might be very high. This can impose a number of costs on the business. First, it has to recruit replacement employees. This can be costly in terms of advertising and using managers to select the new staff from the applicants. Second, even if the jobs are relatively unskilled some training is likely to be required which may involve further expenditure. Finally, new employees are likely to be less productive during the initial period of their employment, which will detract from the overall levels of productivity achieved within the business.

- Employees may be demotivated by this approach to employment. The failure of managers to develop a long-term relationship with employees will mean that it is unlikely that what Herzberg identified as motivators will be present in the job to any great extent. For example, the chance to take responsibility for projects and opportunities for promotion will be limited. This approach relies heavily on pay as a motivator and ignores the potential of social and psychological factors to motivate employees and improve their performance at work.

BUSINESS IN FOCUS

Tesco's Leahy tells HR directors the 'soft' side matters

The former chief executive of Tesco, Sir Terry Leahy, has reminded HR directors: 'The soft side of management matters much more than the hard stuff.' Addressing delegates at the CIPD Conference and Exhibition in Manchester, Leahy, who left Tesco in March this year said: 'The key ingredients [to good management] are trust and confidence. We can have collective intelligence, but this will only work if we trust each other.'

(Source: David Woods in HR Magazine, 9 November 2011)

Soft HR strategies

A soft HR strategy offers a number of advantages to a business, in many cases these are the opposite of those discussed above.

- A soft HR strategy can help a business to build a reputation for being a 'good' employer. Good employers seek to offer their employees diverse and interesting jobs and the opportunity to develop their skills. The pay and conditions on offer are attractive and the employer ensures that employees receive regular training to improve their skills and enhance promotion prospects. Being regarded as a good employer allows businesses to attract higher-quality candidates, which in turn improve the quality of the workforce and the overall performance of the business. A recent survey showed that working for a respected employer was one of the most important factors to job seekers when applying for employment.

- A soft HR strategy can improve knowledge management within a business. This means that the business is more likely to possess a workforce with the knowledge and skills essential for the business to continue trading effectively. This comes about because this approach usually results in a lower level of labour turnover and therefore employees develop long-term working relationships with businesses, allowing them to bring experience to bear in decision-making.

- A soft HR strategy may also develop a more creative workforce. Employees will be given more opportunities to contribute to decision-making and to provide suggestions and ideas on improving the operation of the business. This can motivate the employees (by meeting what Maslow identified as an individual's higher needs) and also provide an organisation with some excellent ideas without incurring the costs of hiring consultants. Because these ideas are generated from people with a different perspective on the organisation they can be different and creative.

Of course, this type of human resource strategy does have its drawbacks.

- It can be very expensive, especially in the short term. The costs of training employees can be significant, particularly if they are given off-the-job training. These costs could be wasted to some degree if the employee leaves soon after completing the training, possibly as a consequence of being 'poached' by an unscrupulous rival. Higher rates of pay and good working conditions can also add to an employer's costs.
- It can be difficult and expensive to alter the workforce in response to a change in market conditions. The soft HR strategy is likely to rely heavily on full-time and permanent employees and thus the business might have surplus capacity

Figure 15.1 A soft HR strategy encourages long-term employment, keeping knowledge and skills in the business

if demand falls, and little potential to increase output if demand rises.

The approach to HR strategy used will obviously depend upon the type of business. It may be that businesses employing less-skilled employees may opt to use a harder approach as the costs of losing employees may be less and the potential from increasing responsibility within the organisation is less obvious. On the other hand, a more skilled workforce might be more suited to a softer approach to make the most effective use of their talents and to minimise the risk of highly trained, skilled and productive employees leaving the organisation.

HR strategies and competitive advantage

Adopting and implementing the right HR strategy has the potential to provide businesses with a significant competitive advantage over rivals. Using the right strategy should make the organisation more competitive, and to some extent this is borne out by the performance of Japanese companies.

Soft human resource management recognises the individual rather than producing personnel policies for the whole workforce. Reward systems, training and development, appraisal and communication are all geared to fulfilling the needs of the individual as well as those of the organisation. The key principle of HRM (or at least 'soft' HRM) is that each employee should be nurtured and developed in pursuit of the organisation's objectives. All aspects of the HRM 'package' should be coordinated to ensure coherence and to assist in the attainment of strategic targets.

If an organisation is successful in operating its HR strategy, the outcome should be motivated and creative employees who are committed to the firm and who do not seek to leave. Such employees should be aware of the goals of the organisation and understand how they can contribute towards the attainment of organisational targets.

Under this scenario a business should incur fewer recruitment costs, enjoy higher levels of productivity and a reduction in faulty products. It may attract top-class applicants to vacancies because of its reputation as a caring and enlightened employer. All of these factors should make the organisation more competitive and better able to cope with the rigours of operating in international markets.

However, in the real world there are differing views on the best HR strategy. Many businesses in the UK differ in their interpretation. Some take a 'hard' attitude, viewing employees as simply another resource to be used as effectively as possible. This approach has a much more short-term focus.

There are, however, theoretical arguments suggesting that whichever HR strategy is adopted, it may not enhance a business's competitiveness. Trade union recognition is a problem under the HR approach to managing employees. The strategy requires people to be treated as individuals and as such to contribute to the attainment of corporate objectives. Yet, in spite of a decline in their importance during the 1980s and 1990s, unions have a long-established role in businesses in the UK. But there is an obvious tension in an organisation that attempts to deal with its employees on an individual basis within a framework of collective bargaining. This tension may manifest itself in employee dissatisfaction or, in extreme cases, in industrial action. Both scenarios could prove extremely damaging to a business's competitive performance.

Further problems may exist if the culture of the organisation is not suited to an HR approach to managing people. Even a 'hard' HR strategy implies some degree of delegation and at least a limited commitment to training. This can involve a degree of expenditure and some managers may oppose the lessening of control that this entails. Furthermore, the adoption of any HR strategy may involve additional costs in the short term as managers and employees adjust to the new strategy and to revised roles within the organisation. The elevation of human resources to a strategic role may incite some opposition from those with responsibility for, say, marketing or finance. All of these factors can detract from the competitive performance of the organisation, especially in the short term.

One step further: Guest's model of human resource management

David Guest has developed a model of managing human resources within businesses that stresses the importance of integrating the various elements of the human resource strategy, which can result in better outcomes in terms of business performance. The integrated nature of this model supports the use of human resource strategies as part of human resource management rather than the use of personnel management.

Guest's model emphasises the close relationship between the business's corporate strategies and its HR strategies. However, the key point of this model is that HR strategy should lead to human resource outcomes that are strongly beneficial to the business. These are:

- commitment by employees to the business and its goals, involving higher levels of effort and cooperation
- the supply of quality goods and services (as a result of having a well-trained and motivated workforce)
- flexibility of employees in responding to innovation in the process of production and, more generally, to respond flexibly to changing circumstances.

HRM strategy	HRM practice	HRM outcomes	Behaviour outcomes	Performance outcomes	Financial outcomes
Differentiation (innovation) Focus (quality) Cost (cost-reduction)	Selection Training Appraisal Rewards Job design Involvement Status and security	Commitment Quality Flexibility	Effort/ motivation Cooperation Involvement Organisational citizenship	**High:** Productivity Quality Innovation **Low:** Absence Labour turnover Conflict Customer complaints	Profits Return on investment

Table 15.2

Source: Guest, 1997

Guest presented the HR outcomes as a package and argued that only if all three of the HRM outcomes were achieved could the organisation expect to see a change in the behaviour of its workforce and a consequent improvement in its workforce. This would result in improvement in the financial outcomes shown in the right-hand column of Table 15.2.

Key terms

Human resource objectives are the targets pursued by the HR function or department of the business.

A **skills audit** is a procedure used to identify the talents and abilities that employees have which may not be fully used by the business.

Labour turnover is the percentage of a business's employees who leave the business over some period of time (normally a year).

Examiner's advice

Remember that HR objectives that are decided by a business's HR managers have to support the business in the achievement of its corporate objectives. Thus, HR objectives can often be understood and their relevance judged in the light of the business's corporate objectives.

It is essential, when dealing with questions on the advantages and disadvantages of the two types of HR strategy, to consider the nature of the business and its workforce. This may enable you to justify the use of a particular approach, either hard or soft.

1 Of what is the following a definition: 'it views activities relating to the workforce as integrated and vital in helping the organisation to achieve its corporate objectives'? *(1 mark)*

2 Which **two** of the following are HR objectives?
   a increasing market share
   b maintaining good employer–employee relations
   c matching the workforce to the needs of the organisation
   d maximising capacity utilisation. *(2 marks)*

3 Explain why a fruit farm might select 'matching the workforce to the needs of the business' as a HR objective. *(5 marks)*

4 Outline **two** external factors that might influence a large retailer's HR objectives. *(6 marks)*

5 Which of the following is *not* an external influence on HR objectives?
   a the state of the market
   b price elasticity of demand
   c corporate objectives
   d corporate image. *(1 mark)*

6 Explain why the type of product that the business produces might affect its HR objectives. *(5 marks)*

7 Explain the difference between 'hard' and 'soft' HR strategies. *(5 marks)*

8 What is likely to be the major motivational technique used within a 'hard' HR strategy? Why? *(6 marks)*

9 Outline **two** possible disadvantages of using a 'soft' HR strategy. *(6 marks)*

10 Explain why a university might opt to use a 'soft' HR strategy. *(5 marks)*

✎ These questions relate to the case study on page 184.

Analyse the possible reasons why Kevar Travel plc chose to 'match its workforce to the needs of the business' as a key HR objective for many years. *(10 marks)*

Candidate's answer:

A company's HR objective is a target or goal that is pursued by the HR department of the business. Examples of HR objectives are using the workforce to its full potential and making sure that the company keeps good industrial relations with its workers.

This is a good objective for this company because of its financial position. Kevar Travel has a negative cash flow and this figure is increasing quickly from (£3.3 million) in 2010–11 to (£9.86 million) in 2011–12. This means that the company must take steps to reduce its cash outflows and, as it is a service industry, wages are its biggest cost. Therefore, ensuring that it has the right number of workers at all times is a vital objective for this company.

Kevar Travel sells its holidays in a market that is changing rapidly and one that must be seasonal.

So the company will need different numbers of staff at different times of the year. Creating a flexible workforce by using temporary employees will help with this and avoid paying employees who are not busy.

Examiner's comments:

The first brief paragraph is of mixed quality. It is a good idea to start with a relevant definition as it earns marks and helps to focus your answer. However, this is too lengthy. The second sentence (stating example HR objectives) was not necessary.

In contrast the quality of writing in the second paragraph is excellent. This paragraph illustrates the importance of linking Unit 3 subject matter. Although this is a HR question, the candidate has developed a really good line of argument based on cash flow. It has also been applied well to the case study using data and the reference to the 'service industry' as part of the argument. Finally, the argument has been developed fully ending up back at the question – why the company may have chosen this particular HR objective.

The final paragraph is sound and overall this is a good quality answer.

Analysis question

Analyse the problems that Kevar Travel plc might have suffered from operating a 'hard' HR strategy. *(10 marks)*

16 Developing and implementing workforce plans

A workforce (or human resource) plan assesses the current and future capacity of a business's workforce, and sets out actions necessary to meet the business's future workforce needs. You will have already encountered some of the actions necessary to carry out workforce planning as part of your AS course. In order to turn a plan into reality the business may need to recruit employees and provide training. In this chapter we will develop these aspects of your AS studies and see how they fit into the strategic process of planning an organisation's future labour needs and changing the workforce to meet its requirements.

In this chapter we examine:

- the components of workforce plans
- the internal and external influences on workforce plans and how to judge their importance
- issues that may be encountered by managers when implementing workforce plans
- the value to businesses of using workforce plans.

The components of workforce plans

Workforce planning is one of the core activities of human resource management, whatever style is operated. Workforce planning entails a number of stages.

1 The starting point of workforce planning is to consider the overall or corporate objectives of the business. The workforce plan must contribute to the achievement of the business's overall or corporate objectives.

2 The next stage is to take a strategic view of employees, and to consider how human resources can be managed to assist in achieving the business's corporate objectives. This may entail considering factors such as the use of technology and how this might complement or replace some human input into the production process.

3 At this stage, those responsible for workforce planning will have to make a judgement about the size and type of workforce the organisation will require over future years.

4 This desired future workforce is compared with that available to the business at the time of planning.

5 Once this comparison is complete the firm can decide upon policies (for example, recruitment, training, redeployment and redundancy) necessary to convert the existing workforce into the desired one. This process is shown in Figure 16.1.

The workforce plan will specify the business's desired workforce and how the business will implement its human resource policies. An important element of the plan is a skills audit to identify the abilities and qualities of the existing workforce. This may highlight skills and experience of which managers were unaware. For example, some employees could possess language skills which could prove invaluable to a business that trades overseas.

A business's workforce plan will contain at least the following information.

- Information on the business's current workforce. This will set out:

  the number of employees the business currently has

  the skills and qualifications possessed by its current employees

  where its employees are currently employed (for multinational companies this could be in many different countries)

  the age profile of its employees, which will help to forecast likely future changes (for example, due to retirement).

- An analysis of likely changes in the demand for the business's products. In turn this will affect the business's need for labour in the forthcoming period. Clearly changes in demand will have a significant effect on the number of employees that are needed, especially if the business is heavily dependent upon employees as a central part of

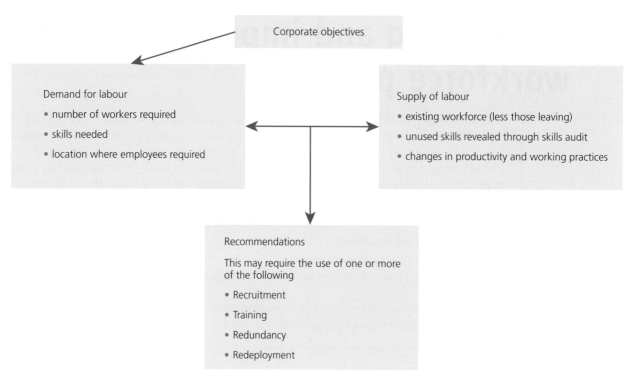

Figure 16.1 Workforce planning

the production process. This is the case for many businesses providing services, such as banks and hospitals.

- An analysis of the likely factors affecting the supply of labour. This could include a wide range of factors, including forecast rates of labour turnover for the business; factors affecting the local labour markets, such as the entry of a new business in the local area, which may recruit heavily; or the arrival of large numbers of migrants into the local labour market.

- Recommendations on actions needed to acquire the desired workforce. These actions are likely to set out changes in recruitment, training, redeployment and redundancy. The workforce plan will set these out in detail and will also explain the impact on each element of the business and also the timescale over which the changes will be implemented.

A workforce plan assists a business in using its human resources effectively and at minimum cost in pursuit of its corporate objectives.

Human resource managers require specific information when developing workforce plans.

- They need to carry out research to provide sales forecasts for the next year or two. This will help identify the quantity and type of labour required. Clearly, rising levels of sales will have an impact on the number of employees required. Such a situation may mean that more employees are required to directly provide the goods or services for customers, but also more employees in roles such as managers and administrators.

- Data will be needed to show the number of employees likely to be leaving the labour force in general (and the firm in particular). Information will be required on potential entrants to the labour force. Sources of this type of information could include the government or local authorities.

- Information regarding future wage rates for the types of employees that it hires. If wages are expected to rise, businesses may reduce their demand for labour and seek to make greater use of technology. Alternatively, a multinational business may transfer production to areas or countries where wage rates are lower.

- Information on the numbers of people entering specific training or education courses that may result in employment within the industry in question.

- The plan will reflect any anticipated changes in the output of the workforce due to changes in productivity or the length of the working week.

- Technological developments will impact on planning the workforce. Developments in this field may reduce the need for unskilled employees while creating employment for those with technical skills.

Full-time employees in the UK work the longest hours in Europe. The average for full timers in the UK is 43.5. In France it is 38.2 and in Germany 39.9, yet both countries have higher levels of productivity than the UK.

At issue: The working time directive

The Conservative leadership yesterday warned it might demand Britain's exemption from European Union employment protection laws. The Education Secretary, Michael Gove, said he would like to see regulations governing 'whom we can hire, how we can hire and how long they work' taken away from Brussels.

The Working Time Directive guarantees workers in the European Union a minimum number of holidays each year, paid breaks and rest of at least 11 hours in any 24 hours, and makes a default right to work no more than 48 hours per week.

The Tories – who refused to sign up to the directive in Government – have always been hostile to it, arguing that it is anti-competitive and has had a damaging effect on the National Health Service, where junior doctors traditionally worked long hours 'on call'.

(Source: Oliver Wright in The Independent, *26 October 2011)*

Question:

Analyse the ways in which the HR managers of a multinational company such as Nestlé might make use of this information when drawing up a workforce plan. *(10 marks)*

The process of HR planning can be assisted by a business creating an HR planning group which brings together senior human resource managers and also key managers from the other functions (marketing, operations and finance, for example) within the business. This can speed up the process of HR planning and help to ensure that it truly meets the needs of all parts of the business. The process is also dependent upon the availability of accurate and up-to-date records on all employees. These can assist managers in analysing likely future trends of labour turnover and also identifying employees with particular skills. This analysis is easier if the records are available in electronic format.

Internal and external influences on workforce plans

HR managers have to take a number of factors into account when drawing up workforce plans. Some of these factors are external to the business and others are internal.

External factors

Sales forecasts

Estimating sales for the next year or two can be a prime influence on workforce plans. This helps the business to identify the quantity and type of labour the firm will require to meet the expected demand for its products. Businesses experiencing rising sales will expect to recruit more employees. At the time of writing the UK is experiencing a period of economic uncertainty and low growth in which demand for goods and services will rise slowly, if at all. As a consequence businesses from many sectors of the economy are announcing redundancies. Examples of such businesses include BAE Systems (aerospace manufacturer), Lloyds Banking Group, British Gas and HMV (the music and book retailer).

In some circumstances businesses may not immediately adjust their workforce plans in the light of changes in sales forecasts. If a period of slow sales is expected to be short term it may be worth maintaining employment levels, especially if the workers concerned are highly skilled. In 2011 Shropshire County Council negotiated with representatives of its 7,000 employees to reduce working hours in an attempt to maintain employment (and the range of skills available to it). Reducing working hours would help the Council to save 400 jobs at a time of budget cuts.

Demographic trends

Workforce planners need information on potential entrants to the labour force, which depends on demographic factors such as migration and birth rates. This can be a major influence on their decision-making.

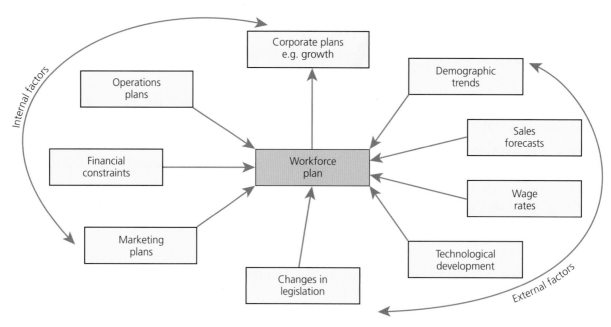

Figure 16.2 Factors influencing workforce plans

Wage rates

If wages are expected to rise, then businesses may reduce their demand for labour and seek to make greater use of technology. This may entail a large investment by businesses in technology and also in training the remaining employees to operate the technology efficiently. The inward migration into the UK has helped to keep wage rates down, and this trend has been strengthened by rising unemployment rates. A greater supply of labour tends to depress wage rates and many immigrants (especially those from Eastern Europe) have been prepared to work for relatively low wages by UK standards.

Technological developments

Changes in technology will impact on planning the workforce, as they may reduce the need for unskilled or even skilled employees, while creating employment for those with technical skills. Workforce planners liaise with operations managers to investigate the impact of introducing technology into the production process. For example, businesses manufacturing pottery have introduced technology onto their production lines for cups, saucers and other types of crockery and this has led to a reduced need for employees.

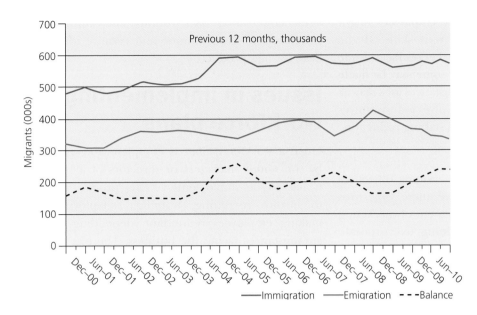

Previous 12 months, thousands

Figure 16.3 UK migration 2000–10

(Source: National Statistics website www.statistics.gov.uk)

―――Immigration ―――Emigration ‒ ‒ ‒Balance

Changes in legislation

Employment laws may limit the number of hours employees can work each week or may require businesses to offer employees benefits such as paternity leave. Such changes may mean that a business requires greater amounts of labour or persuade it to replace labour with capital equipment. For example, the Equality Act became law in October 2010. It replaces previous legislation (such as the Race Relations Act 1976 and the Disability Discrimination Act 1995) and ensures consistency in making the workplace a fair environment. This has considerable implications for HR managers, not least in relation to recruitment.

Internal factors

Corporate plans

These set out the goals of the entire organisation. Corporate plans relate to the business's mission statement. The goals included in corporate plans may include:

● growth
● increased market share
● competing in new markets (perhaps overseas)
● earning the highest possible profits.

A corporate plan suggesting expanding into a new market could, for example, have significant

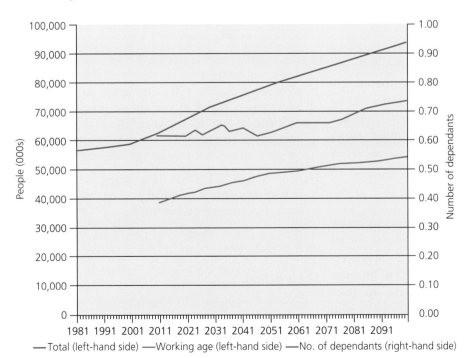

— Total (left-hand side) — Working age (left-hand side) — No. of dependants (right-hand side)

Figure 16.4 Actual and projected changes in the UK population 1981–2091

(Source: National Statistics website www.statistics.gov.uk)

implications for employees. More employees might be required, possibly with different skills. If the expansion involves entering a market overseas, some employees may be redeployed, or some may be made redundant. Finally, in some circumstances jobs may be lost as part of expansion if this involves joint ventures allowing some rationalisation and staffing reduction.

Marketing plans

Marketing plans detail a firm's marketing objectives and how they intend to achieve these objectives (marketing strategy). The achievement of marketing objectives assists a firm in attaining its corporate objectives. If a firm plans to increase market share it may introduce new products. This might require the workforce plan to create a labour force with different skills through recruitment, training and redeployment.

Operations plans

This type of plan details a business's objectives in relation to operations management. As with marketing plans, the objectives in operations plans are a central part of a firm's corporate strategy. Plans for production inform a business's workforce plan. Operations may become capital intensive, requiring fewer employees with greater skills. Alternatively, a business might wish to give employees more responsibility for operations as it adopts total quality management. This may require the workforce plan to prepare for delayering and empowerment.

Financial constraints

Workforce planning operates within tight financial guidelines. Training, recruitment, redeployment and even redundancy are expensive. Firms operating a 'soft' approach to HRM may be prepared to grant a larger budget for workforce planning as they seek to develop their employees. On the other hand, advocates of 'hard' HRM would wish to effect workforce planning with minimal costs.

The type of business

The type of workforce required by a business is highly likely to be influenced by the type of business and its circumstances. In turn this will impact on the process of workforce planning. For example, a business committed to global growth may have to have redeployment of experienced employees as a central feature of its workforce plan. In contrast, innovative businesses may require diverse workforces (different ages, educational backgrounds and cultures) to generate and assess unique and creative ideas as a basis for new products.

Issues in implementing workforce plans

Once a workforce plan is complete and approved by the senior managers or directors of a business, it has to be implemented. This process is likely to involve recruiting, training, redeploying and making employees redundant, depending on the circumstances facing the business. There is a range

BUSINESS IN FOCUS

Bectu fights job cuts as STV confirms news restructure

The media and entertainment trade union, Bectu, has called for a guarantee from Scottish broadcaster STV that there will be no compulsory redundancies as it announces a restructure of news teams and studio operations across the country. STV confirmed that its news programme for Edinburgh and the east of Scotland will continue after a successful trial of new technology.

The trial also includes the rolling out of new technology to support these services, which has been trialled since May. However, this decision means around 20 jobs are now at risk within technical areas. Bectu said in a report on its website that this includes those working in camera, sound and craft editing positions.

The broadcaster has also said it will be introducing seven new posts within its news and current affairs programme Scotland Tonight, which launches on 24 October. Within its restructure announcement STV added that its audience share at 6pm had gone 'from strength to strength', increasing by 11 per cent year-on-year across Scotland.

According to STV, news 'is a hugely popular area of our website, with over half a million unique users visiting stv.tv/news each month'.

(Source: Rachel McAthey at Journalism.co.uk, 7 October 2011)

Question:

Do you think that internal or external influences are more likely to influence STV's final workforce plan? Justify your decision. *(18 marks)*

of factors or issues that can affect the process of implementing a workforce plan.

Employer–employee relations

If a workforce plan entails a significant reduction in a business's workforce through redundancies or the redeployment of employees to other areas of the UK or to other countries, its implementation may damage the working relationship between the business and its employees. If the changes to the size and location of the workforce are implemented compulsorily, the workforce may resist its implementation and may take industrial action such as strikes in an attempt to prevent its implementation. Such a series of events may damage the business's financial position due to a loss of sales and revenue.

Conversely, good employer–employee relations can assist the process of implementing workforce plans. One major advantage can arise from the involvement of trade unions or other employee representatives in the planning process. The involvement of such groups can bring greater knowledge and different perspectives to the process. For example, a trade union might have conducted research into labour market issues, such as migration, and be able to advise HR managers of likely trends in specific sectors of particular labour markets. Good relations between employers and employees can also be useful in providing an effective channel of communication with employees, reducing the chances of rumours and misunderstanding causing problems at any stage of the implementation of the plan. If new employees are required or if redundancies are necessary, a trade union or other group representative of employees may assist in the relevant selection procedures and reduce the possibility of conflict or disputes.

The cost of implementing workforce plans

All workforce plans are subject to some financial constraints. The implementation of the workforce plan will have to be carried out within a certain budget. This limits the extent of spending of the HR managers in putting their plans into action. Implementing workforce plans can entail a number of different forms of expenditure.

- **The cost of recruiting and selecting new employees**. To increase a labour force in this way can entail advertising (sometimes nationally or even internationally), screening applications and

BUSINESS IN FOCUS

Organisations boost training spend

UK businesses are increasing the amount of money they spend on training to make sure they can cope with the changing business environment, it has been claimed.

A recent survey found that 77 per cent of companies believe that using learning technologies in training will enable them to deal with any changes to the world of business. The survey found that 64 per cent of businesses that responded are allocating a greater proportion of their training spend to learning technologies for the next two years.

The research revealed that HR professionals are looking at learning technologies to increase access to training, improve quality of training and reduce training costs.

Craig McCoy, HR director of Bupa Health and Wellbeing who participated in the survey, said: 'Investment in innovative learning approaches facilitates business agility and can support business generation, improve customer service and increase organisational efficiency.'

(Source: Adapted from Helen Mayson, The Institute of Leadership & Management, 11 November 2011 www.i-l-m.com)

Question:

Analyse the possible reasons why businesses might increase spending on training at a time when the economy is performing poorly. *(10 marks)*

operating a selection procedure using interviews and/or other methods such as psychometric testing. These activities are expensive in terms of direct costs as well as the cost of using HR employees in these ways. The Chartered Institute of Personnel and Development estimates that the average cost of recruiting a single new employee exceeds £4,500.

- **Training costs** can be substantial. Most new employees will require some training, if only induction training. However, other forms of training may be required to improve the skills and performance of employees to match those set out in the workforce plan.
- **Making redundancy payments to staff**. This can be expensive, with the law requiring that a payment of up to £400 for each year of employment is made.

The cost of making a single person redundant can run to many thousands of pounds.

- **Redeployment** can also be a costly exercise. This may involve paying the costs that the employee incurs in moving to another part of the UK, or even overseas. These may include the legal and professional costs of selling and buying houses, other costs such as fitting out new houses and transport costs.

However, operating within a financial constraint does also offer some benefits. Human resource managers may look carefully, for example, at the skills that are available to the business internally before opting for an expensive external recruitment programme. Equally, it can provide a line of argument to use when negotiating with trade unions or other employee representatives and a reason for not paying higher sums of redundancy pay, for example.

Corporate image

A corporate image is the public's perception of a business. Increasingly businesses wish to present themselves in the most favourable light possible. They recognise that they might gain a competitive advantage from being held in high esteem by their stakeholders, and especially their customers. Being seen to offer significant training schemes can assist in this regard. On the other hand, making large numbers of employees redundant can damage a business's reputation and may harm its commercial performance. In 2011 British Aerospace (BAE) revealed that it planned to make over 1,000 employees redundant and emphasised that there would be no compulsory redundancies in an attempt to minimise the harm to its corporate image.

Implementing workforce plans can also have a positive impact on a firm's corporate image. The creation of new jobs or the implementation of a major scheme of training can help to improve the image of a wide range of businesses. Many businesses issue press releases to announce positive HR actions that may have been taken as part of the implementation of their workforce plans. For example, in January 2012 McDonald's announced the creation of 2,500 new jobs in the UK and received favourable media coverage. The creation of the new jobs will have been built into the business's workforce plan. Coordination with the company's marketing department will ensure that a positive news story is reported.

The value of using workforce plans

The process of planning can be highly beneficial to businesses. Workforce planning is no exception. It offers management the opportunity to coordinate and integrate the business's entire human resource management activities and hence to avoid any inconsistencies or waste of resources through duplication of activities.

Workforce planning offers businesses other benefits as well.

- The in-depth investigation of likely future events will encourage HR managers to think of the most effective (and cost efficient) ways of responding to these events. Managers have time to reflect on and discuss their responses and to consider the full implications of proposed actions. In this way all the data relating to any HR decisions can be collected and considered at length. This avoids crisis decision-making and reduces the likelihood of errors.
- HR managers are afforded the opportunity to consult with other managers with responsibility for other functions within the business, such as marketing or finance. This allows HR decisions to be taken in an integrated fashion and to have the greatest possibility of assisting the business in achieving its corporate objectives.
- Workforce planning gives HR managers the opportunity to assess whether the business's HR objectives are feasible given the constraints (for example, finance) under which the function operates. It should also afford the opportunity to change the HR objectives.

However, workforce planning can go wrong and be of limited value to a business. The value of workforce plans depends, to a great extent, on the accuracy of the company's forecasting of its future labour needs. In particular it will depend upon the company's ability to forecast the level of demand for its goods and services with some degree of accuracy. If the company underestimates demand it may have insufficient labour available and the result may be dissatisfied customers. On the other hand, employing too many staff leads to unnecessary costs and reduced profit margins. There are many reasons why forecasts of future sales (and therefore the required labour force) may be inaccurate. There may be a sudden and unexpected change in customer tastes. For example, recently firms selling products associated with keeping chickens have experienced a surprising increase in demand for their products due to the increasing popularity of this hobby. By 2011 nearly 1 million chickens were kept in back gardens. Alternatively, the economy may perform differently from what was expected. Few economists predicted the crisis surrounding some countries that use the euro and its enormous impact on other economies. Finally, competitors may alter their behaviour by bringing out new products, or new competitors may emerge. So, forecasting labour demand can be a tricky business, especially if the forecast extends several years into the future.

The exact value of workforce planning will depend on the circumstances in which it is being conducted. The experience of the managers engaged in the process will play a part, as will the volatility of demand for the products that the business sells. The time and resources devoted to the planning process will also affect the quality and accuracy of the outcomes and therefore its value. Finally, the timescale to which the plan relates is also important: the further into the future the plan extends, the less value it is likely to provide to the organisation.

One step further: employer branding

Brett Minchington is sometimes credited with 'discovering' the concept of employer branding. Employer branding is defined as creating the image of the organisation as a 'great place to work' in the minds of current employees and other key stakeholders such as potential employees, customers and suppliers.

A company brand is used to gain customer loyalty and therefore increased profits through differentiation. An employer brand can be used to similar effect by HR and organisations, to compete effectively in the labour market and drive employee loyalty through effective recruitment, engagement and retention policies. A business's employer brand will inevitably be linked to the way in which the organisation is perceived by the general public and key stakeholder groups.

Employer branding is how an organisation presents and sells what it has to offer to both potential and existing employees. A strong employer brand should connect an organisation's values, HR strategy and HR policies and be inseparable from the business's corporate brand. It will make the business an attractive employer in terms of pay and conditions, but also job satisfaction, training and the possibilities of promotion. The successful development of an employer brand should lead to a business being regarded as 'a good employer'.

There are a number of reasons why a business would want to engage in employer branding. Figure 16.5 illustrates the most important ones.

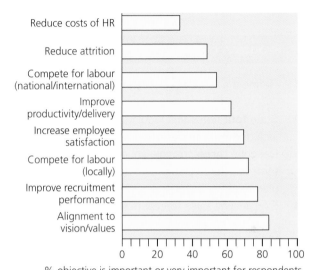

Figure 16.5 Employer branding objectives (in order of importance)

Source: CIPD www.cipd.co.uk

Key terms

Human resource management (HRM) is the process of making the most efficient use of an organisation's employees.

A workforce (or human resource) plan assesses the current and future capacity of a business's workforce, and sets out actions necessary to meet the business's future workforce needs.

Labour turnover is the proportion of a business's staff that leave their employment over some period of time, normally one year.

Labour productivity is the volume of output produced per worker over a given time period.

A trade union is an organisation formed with the objective of protecting and enhancing the working conditions and economic positions of its members.

Induction training is the provision of job-related skills and knowledge given to a new employee within a business.

When responding to questions on issues relating to the implementation of workforce plans, it is important to appreciate that the impact of these factors can be both positive and negative. It is also important to recognise that workforce plans do not always reduce the size of a business's workforce; they are also used to expand it.

Do consider the pros and cons of workforce planning and do assess its value in the context of the business. Any evaluation of its value is bound to draw on the circumstances in which it is being used.

Progress questions

1   Define the term 'workforce plan'. *(2 marks)*

2   State **four** items that would be likely to be included in a workforce plan. *(4 marks)*

3   Describe **three** possible sources of information for a workforce plan drawn up by a food manufacturer based in Devon. *(6 marks)*

4   Explain why sales forecasts are such an important influence on workforce plans for all businesses, but especially those supplying services. *(6 marks)*

5   Outline **two** other external factors that might influence the workforce plan drawn up by a large supermarket such as J Sainsbury. *(6 marks)*

6   Explain **two** internal factors that might influence the workforce plan of the low-cost airline easyJet. *(6 marks)*

7   A manufacturing business has taken a decision to switch to capital-intensive production. How might the business's workforce plan assist in effecting this change successfully? *(8 marks)*

8   How might a trade union assist HR managers in implementing a workforce plan? *(6 marks)*

9   Explain why a pharmaceutical company implementing a workforce plan during a period of rapid growth might allocate a large budget to its HR department. *(8 marks)*

10 Explain **two** possible benefits that workforce planning might provide to a UK restaurant chain considering its first overseas expansion into Europe. *(8 marks)*

Evaluation question

✘ These questions relate to the case study on page 184.

To what extent do you agree with Alexandra Bagley's view that the company's sales forecasts were the most important influence on its workforce plan? *(18 marks)*

Candidate's answer:

A workforce plan considers the workforce a business will need in the future, and details the actions necessary to meet the business's future workforce needs.

The company thinks that sales forecasts are important and it has invested heavily in primary market research to identify likely future trends in figures. The company has increased expenditure in this area by 336 per cent at a time when it

is suffering from worsening negative cash flow position. The market in which it operates is subject to large fluctuations for two reasons (the merger of existing companies creating new large competitors and, more importantly, changes in consumers' tastes and fashions). The impact of these changes means that the level and types of sales have altered hugely meaning that more or fewer employees are required, although the skills required are unlikely to change.

However, a more important influence after 2010 was the company's idea of reducing its operating costs to reduce its losses. The company's profits have been steadily declining and its ROCE figure has fallen to 13 per cent. This is a public limited company and its shareholders will not be happy with this trend. As Kevar Travel supplies services its labour costs are a high proportion of its expenditure (at nearly 70 per cent) and so if it is to satisfy its shareholders by increasing profits then cutting labour costs is essential and its workforce plan will detail how this is to be achieved. One example of this is a large increase in temporary contracts which should cut wage costs.

Examiner's comments:

This answer started well with a clear definition. The second paragraph is of mixed quality. The first argument is tangential to the question as it explains the company's response to the nature of its market rather than considering an influence on the workforce plan. The answer then develops into a better argument on why the variable market might have influenced the shape of the company's workforce plan. This emphasises the importance of planning an answer before commencing writing.

The third paragraph is good and focuses precisely on the question. It makes effective use of the case study to support those arguments and develops its point fully. The major omission of this answer is a final paragraph which makes and supports a clear judgement. Although there is some judgement (or evaluation) scattered throughout this answer, an overall conclusion is required.

Analysis question

Do you think that the benefits of drawing up a new workforce plan in 2010 outweighed the costs involved? Justify your answer. *(18 marks)*

17 Competitive organisational structures

An organisational structure is the way in which a business is arranged to carry out its activities. In this chapter we will build on the material you covered in Unit 2 of your AS business studies course, and especially issues such as levels of hierarchy, spans of control, delegation and workforce roles. This chapter will consider the particular issues facing larger businesses when deciding on the organisational structure to adopt and how they organise their employees to give themselves the greatest possible competitive advantage.

In this chapter we consider:

- the types of organisational structure that firms might use
- the factors that influence a business in its choice of organisational structure
- how organisations adapt their structures to improve their competitiveness.

Introduction to organisational structure

An organisational structure, which may be shown in an organisation chart, sets out:

- the routes by which communication passes through the business
- who has authority (and power) and responsibility within the organisation
- the roles and titles of individuals within the organisation
- the people to whom individual employees are accountable and those for whom they are responsible.

Businesses change the structure of their organisation rapidly and regularly; some managers believe that they should be continually reorganising their firms to meet the demands of a dynamic marketplace. By improving the organisational structure on a regular basis a business is better able to meet the needs of its customers.

Types of organisational structure

Businesses can adopt a number of organisational structures according to a number of factors, such as the size of the organisation, the environment in which it operates and the personal preferences of the owners and senior managers. We will discuss the factors influencing the choice of organisational structure in detail in the next section of this chapter.

Formal or traditional hierarchies

This structure shares decision-making throughout the business and gives all employees a clearly defined role, as well as establishing their relationship with other employees in the business. It is common for this type of organisational structure to be based upon departments and, because of the dependence upon agreed procedures, it can be bureaucratic.

This type of structure normally has a number of other features.

- It is a relatively 'tall' hierarchy with the associated narrow spans of control.
- The organisation will be centralised, with the most important decisions taken by senior managers.
- Hierarchy is important and senior managers expect to be treated with respect.
- Tradition is important and change is often implemented slowly.

Communication in formal organisations is principally downwards and uses established routes moving down from senior to junior employees. This structure allows specialists to operate (for example in marketing and finance) within their area of expertise. They can generate new and very innovative ideas, but other areas of the business may be unaware of such developments. Employees are aware of lines of command and communication and the position of their department or unit within the organisation. All employees appreciate the possibilities for promotion that exist in the business.

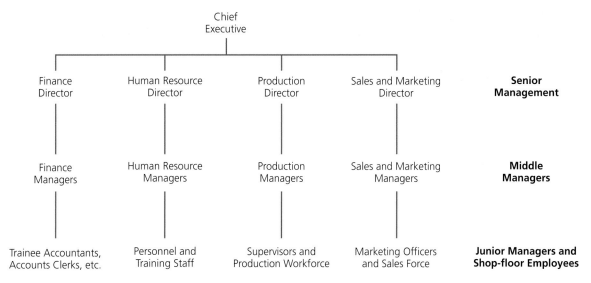

Figure 17.1 A traditional hierarchy

The organisational structure of the BBC

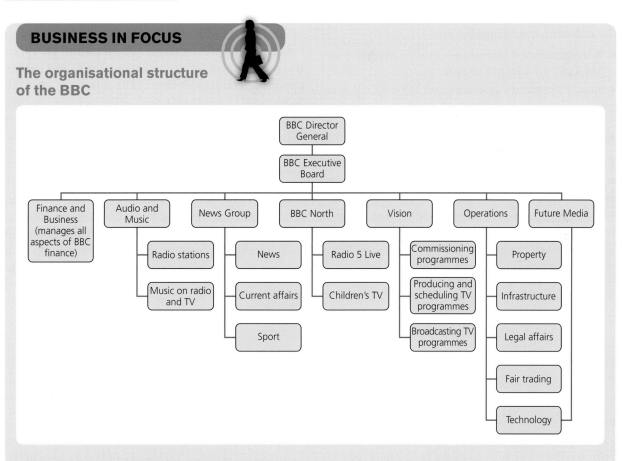

Figure 17.2 The organisational structure of the BBC

The British Broadcasting Corporation (BBC) is the largest television and radio broadcaster in the world with, in 2011, about 23,000 employees. Its headquarters is at Broadcasting House in London, but it has moved some of its operations to Salford. Its structure is based around seven divisions which cover all aspects of the organisation's work.

(Source: Adapted from BBC website www.bbc.co.uk)

The disadvantages of this structure can become more apparent as the organisation grows in size. Departments may bid for resources in an attempt to increase their size and prestige within the business, rather than because this will benefit the organisation. Furthermore, as the business becomes larger, decision-making can become slower as communication has to pass through many layers within the organisation. Simultaneously, coordinating the business's attempts to achieve its objectives becomes difficult. Senior managers become more remote and may take decisions that are not appropriate to local situations or to the needs of particular groups of customers.

Advantages	Disadvantages
• Authority and responsibility are clearly established. • Specialist managers can be used effectively. • Promotion path is clearly signposted. • Employees are often very loyal to their department within the business.	• The organisation can be slow to respond to customer needs. • Communication, and especially horizontal communication, can be poor. • Inter-department rivalry may occur at the expense of the performance of business as a whole.

Table 17.1 The advantages and disadvantages of traditional hierarchies

Traditional organisational structures can be found in the following types of businesses:

- long-established businesses such as merchant banks in the City of London
- family businesses operating on a relatively small scale.

Matrix structures

This type of organisational structure is task orientated and is intended to overcome many of the problems associated with the traditional or hierarchical structure. It is a combination of a vertical chain of command operated through departments or units and horizontal projects of product teams. A typical matrix structure is illustrated in Figure 17.3.

Businesses using matrix structures put together teams of individuals with the specialist skills necessary to complete a particular project. Each individual within the project team brings a particular skill and carries appropriate responsibilities. The aim is to allow all individuals to use their talents effectively irrespective of their position within the organisation. So a project manager looking to develop a new product may be able to call on IT and design skills from relatively junior employees elsewhere in the organisation.

Matrix structures focus on the task in hand – launching a new product, opening new retail outlets, closing down factories or entering overseas markets for the first time. Project groups often have strong senses of identity in spite of being drawn from various areas

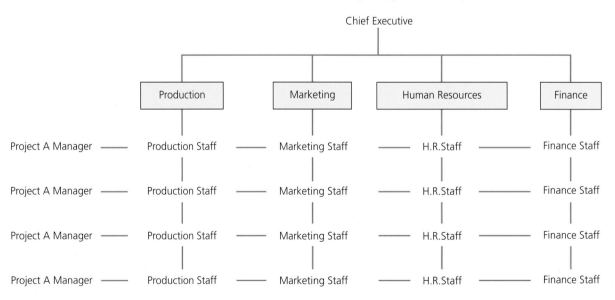

Figure 17.3 A typical matrix structure

in the business. This is because they are pursuing a clearly defined objective providing team members with a sense of purpose and responsibility.

Matrix structures bring problems with them. Employees can find it difficult having two managers (project managers and departmental managers) because of divided loyalties. They can be uncertain about which parts of their work to prioritise and conflict can result. Matrix structures have a reputation for being expensive to operate: administrative and secretarial staff can be costly when used in support of a number of projects.

Advantages	Disadvantages
<ul><li>Focuses on tasks necessary for business success.</li><li>Encourages organisations to be flexible and responsive to customers' needs.</li><li>Motivates and develops employees by providing varied and challenging tasks.</li></ul>	<ul><li>Employees can have divided responsibilities.</li><li>Conflict can occur between project and departmental managers, reducing performance of organisation.</li><li>Heavy expenditure on support staff may be required.</li></ul>

Table 17.2 The advantages and disadvantages of matrix structures

Entrepreneurial structures

These are frequently found in businesses operating in competitive markets and particularly in those where rapid decisions are essential. Television and radio news organisations, for example Sky News, often operate with an entrepreneurial structure. A few key workers at the core of the organisation – frequently the owners in the case of small businesses – make all the major decisions. The business is heavily dependent upon the knowledge and skills of these key workers. Power radiates from the centre under this structure, as illustrated in Figure 17.4.

Entrepreneurial structures are suited to markets where rapid decisions are essential and where organisations are small enough to be controlled effectively by a few trusted employees. It is a structure frequently used by charismatic and dynamic leaders: Alan Sugar used this approach in managing his electronics company Amstrad during the early years of the business. Because all-important decisions are taken at the centre, little use is made of hierarchies and the organisation is relatively 'flat'.

However, there are distinct drawbacks to the entrepreneurial structure. Its effectiveness depends upon two factors:

1 The quality of management and decision-making by the 'core' employees. If decisions are delayed or if the workers lose touch with the market the business is unlikely to perform effectively.
2 As the business grows, the 'core' employees experience increasing difficulty in managing the business. The volume of work may overwhelm them and the quality (and speed) of decisions

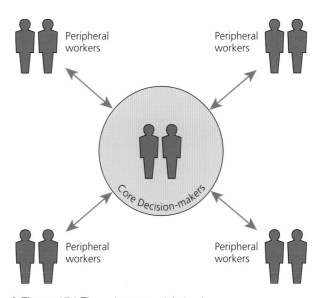

Figure 17.4 The entrepreneurial structure

may suffer. At this point the business may adopt another structure.

Informal structures

This type of structure exists where the organisation does not have an obvious structure. This is common is the case of professionals (doctors and lawyers, for example) where they operate as a team. The professionals normally receive administrative support from others within the organisation.

This form of organisational structure allows highly trained and motivated employees to organise their working lives and to take decisions with a high degree of independence. However, it is less appropriate for many businesses as it lacks coordination and control by senior managers.

The choice of organisational structure

When deciding upon an organisational structure a business will take into account a number of factors.

The size of the business

This is arguably the key factor. As the scale of the business increases an entrepreneurial structure, for example, becomes unsuitable. As the business grows further the chain of command is likely to be lengthened, encouraging the removal of some layers of hierarchy and broader spans of control as a consequence.

In Figure 17.2 we saw the organisational structure for the BBC. It is a very large organisation, generating revenues of nearly £4,741 million in 2010 from its broadcasting activities and from selling programmes, books and music worldwide. With over 23,000 employees it is necessary to break it into smaller units in order to manage it. The BBC organises itself into seven divisions covering its broadcasting activities and managing its physical assets and finances. The sheer size of the organisation makes (a complex) hierarchical structure inevitable.

The nature of the product supplied by the firm

If the firm supplies a diverse range of products it may organise itself traditionally – perhaps in the form of divisions reporting to the board of directors. Hard Rock Café operates in this way. It was originally started as a restaurant business, by Peter Morton and Isaac Tigrett, but later expanded into hotels and casinos. Its current CEO is Hamish Dodds. Key areas of the business, such as casinos, have some degree of independence. Such circumstances may allow a more entrepreneurial structure, at least to some extent, if a large business is subdivided into a number of much smaller entities.

BUSINESS IN FOCUS

Nokia Siemens abandons matrix structure

Nokia Siemens Networks is abandoning its matrix organisational structure and drastically cutting its workforce as part of its strategy to streamline operations and cut costs. The company announced plans to reduce its global workforce of 74,000 by approximately 17,000 by the end of 2013.

It is not alone in the industry in announcing large-scale job cuts. French rival Alcatel Lucent cut 12,500 jobs in 2007 while Ericsson cut 5,000 jobs in 2009 and a further 1,500 in 2010. Nokia Siemens has made financial losses for most of 2010 and 2011. However, in the three months to September 2011, the company reported an operating profit of £5.4 million, as sales rose 16 per cent.

The job losses and the change of structure have been driven by the company's new corporate strategy requiring it to develop an associated workforce plan. The company plans to slim down its range of operations and to cut its operating costs by £835 million by the end of 2013 (compared with December 2011). The changes are expected to result in the closure of a number of the company's sites and the sale of a number of business areas which do not fit in with the new strategy.

'We believe that the future of our industry is in mobile broadband and services – and we aim to be an undisputed leader in these areas,' said Rajeev Suri, CEO of Nokia Siemens Networks. 'At the same time, we need to take the necessary steps to maintain long-term competitiveness and improve profitability in a challenging telecommunications market.'

'Our goal is to provide the world's most efficient mobile networks, the intelligence to maximise the value of those networks, and the services capability to make it all work seamlessly,' Suri said. 'Despite the need to restructure parts of our company, our commitment to research and development remains unchanged, with investment in mobile broadband expected to increase over the coming years.'

(Source: Adapted from Nathan Eddy in E-Week Europe, 23 November 2011 www.eweekeurope.co.uk)

Question:

To what extent do you think the Nokia Siemen's decision to abandon its matrix structure might prove to be a handicap in the long term? *(18 marks)*

The skills of the workforce

The higher the level of skill the typical employee has, the more likely it is that businesses will organise along matrix or informal lines. Groups of professionals, such as management consultants or surgeons, may simply carry out their professional duties with administrative support from the organisation. This may mean that the business is more likely to operate with an informal structure or a matrix structure, depending on the type of business and the products it supplies.

However, in the case of less-skilled employees a hierarchical structure may be preferred. It could be argued that a large organisation employing relatively unskilled workers will perform better with a more formal structure and more authority retained further up the hierarchy.

The culture of the organisation

This can be a major influence on the structure a business adopts. If it has a highly innovative culture whereby it wishes to be a market leader selling advanced products, then it may adopt a matrix structure to minimise bureaucracy and to allow teams to carry out the necessary research and development and market research. On the other hand, an organisation which places importance on tradition (and derives its commercial success from appearing conventional) may be best suited to a formal hierarchical structure. This structure places emphasis on positions rather than people and this factor encourages the continuance of existing policies and practices. Some high-class hotels may fall into this category.

The business's strategic objectives

An innovative and highly competitive organisation may opt for a matrix structure in order to complete tasks effectively. The matrix structure is task orientated and set goals and can permit employees to be rewarded for achieving such goals. This can increase the performance of the business's workforce and the competitiveness of the whole organisation. On the other hand, a business focusing on quality of design and production (as opposed to growth) may suit an entrepreneurial structure. This could operate with the intention of encouraging creativity and innovation.

The environment in which the business is operating

Fierce competitive pressures may encourage delayering in an effort to reduce costs. The process of delayering, if successful, will allow reductions in costs and increased price competitiveness. This can be an attractive strategy for a business supplying services where labour costs are frequently a high proportion of total costs. Firms that operate in markets subject to rapid change (such as technology) may opt for a matrix structure (in at least a division of the business) to ensure that the organisation can complete the necessary tasks to ensure it remains competitive in terms of product development. The matrix structure would also help to eliminate the possibility of inflexible hierarchies getting in the way of rapid decision-making.

Adapting structure to improve competitiveness

Organisational structures are subject to constant change. Changes in technology, changes in competitors' behaviour, changes in government policies and changes in tastes and fashions can all act as a catalyst for a change in an organisation's structure. For example, a new competitor entering a market might result in an increase in price competitiveness, necessitating existing firms to cut costs. Reducing the size of the workforce and adapting its structure may be one way to achieve this.

There is a range of methods a business may use to alter its organisational structure as it attempts to achieve its corporate objectives.

Delayering

As already mentioned, delayering is the reduction of the number of layers of hierarchy within an organisation's structure. A number of businesses have implemented large-scale delayering programmes over recent years. Many such businesses have opted to remove middle managers from their organisational structures.

The increasing level of competition in international markets, and particularly from businesses in the Far East, has forced UK firms to reduce their costs. This trend of cost reduction has been given further impetus by slow rates of economic growth in many western economies creating a greater need to reduce costs to survive a period in which sales are likely to stagnate at best. The need to delayer has not been limited to organisations entirely in the private sector. In 2011, the Lloyds Banking Group, which is 65 per cent publicly owned, announced plans to shed 15,000 jobs, a number of which would be as a result of delayering.

Delayering has been encouraged further by the widespread acceptance of management theories emphasising the benefits that may result from fewer layers of hierarchy. Modern writers on business have identified significant competitive benefits to be gained from giving relatively junior employees greater authority and control over their working lives. This combination of the need to reduce costs and the move to enhance the role of shop-floor employees has put the jobs of middle managers at risk. Delayering is credited with creating 'flatter' organisations, which some describe as 'leaner and more responsive'.

Advantages	Disadvantages
• It reduces costs by removing a number of expensive middle managers. • It can improve responsiveness by bringing senior managers and customers closer together, speeding up decision-making. • It can motivate employees lower down in the organisation by giving them greater authority and control over their working lives. • Communication may improve as there are fewer levels of hierarchy for a message to pass through. • It can produce good ideas from a new perspective as shop-floor employees take some decisions.	• It can lessen organisational performance as valuable knowledge and experience may be lost. • Morale and motivation may suffer because employees feel insecure. • Some businesses may merely use the excuse of delayering for making a large number of employees redundant. • Because delayering means employees have to take on new roles within the organisation, extensive (and expensive) retraining may be required. • It can lead to intolerable workloads and high levels of stress among employees.

Table 17.3 The advantages and disadvantages of delayering

Delayering on its own is unlikely to achieve very much. Components of HRM strategy that typically accompany the process of delayering include:

- a greater emphasis upon teamworking
- cross-functional working, possibly through the use of a matrix structure
- increased employee involvement in decision-making through a process of empowerment.

It is essential that managers implementing a policy of delayering incorporate one or more of the above factors to achieve an effective outcome. These factors will function as replacements for the coordination and controlling role of the organisation's missing levels of hierarchy.

Centralisation and decentralisation

Centralisation and decentralisation are opposites. A centralised organisation is one in which the majority of decisions are taken by senior managers at the top (or centre) of the business. Centralisation can provide rapid decision-making as few people are likely to be consulted. It should also ensure that the business pursues the objectives set by senior managers.

Decentralisation gives greater authority to employees lower down the organisational structure. In recent years many businesses decentralised for a number of reasons.

- Decentralisation provides subordinates with the opportunity to fulfil needs such as achievement and recognition through working. This should improve motivation and reduce the business's costs by, for example, reducing the rate of labour turnover.
- Decentralisation is doubly beneficial to management. It reduces the workload on senior managers, allowing them to focus on strategic (rather than operational) issues. At the same time it offers junior managers an opportunity to develop their skills in preparation for a more senior position.
- Many junior employees in the organisation may have better understanding of operational matters and delegation may allow them to use their skills and understanding to good effect.

However, some businesses remain centralised. This might be because the senior managers like to remain in control of the business and to take the major decisions. The decision to centralise may reflect the preferred style of management of the business's senior managers and their desire to retain authority. This may occur when employees are relatively low skilled and the organisation is likely to perform more effectively if power remains at the centre of the organisation.

Flexible workforces

In recent years a number of trends have emerged in the UK's workforce.

- **Rising numbers of temporary workers.** The number (and proportion) of workers on temporary contracts (for a fixed time period) within the UK rose steadily from the early 1980s until 2000, since when it does appear to have levelled out. However, since the recent recession the proportion of temporary workers in the UK workforce has started to rise once again. In September 2011 1.51 million employees were recorded as being on temporary contracts.

- **Part-time working**. The number of employees within the UK who work part time rose for many years, but appears to have shown a slight decline recently. This may be explained by some large organisations hiring workers on a self-employed basis. In 2011 about 7.8 million people in the UK worked part-time.

- **Self-employment**. This form of employment has generally been increasing over recent years, and particularly since 2000. The Labour Force Survey in 2011 showed that approximately 4.1 million people in the UK can be classified as self-employed.

- **Contractors and consultants.** Many businesses have replaced full-time employees with consultants or have contracted out duties to other organisations. For example, it is common for firms to employ contract staff to design and manage IT systems rather than use permanent full-time employees in these roles.

- **Full-time permanent employees**. Firms use fewer full-time employees than was the case in the 1990s. Such employees are relatively expensive as the firm incurs all the costs of employment, such as making pension contributions and providing training. Using consultants and contractors avoids these costs and ensures employees are only hired when needed. Full-time employees tend to be highly skilled and perform central roles within an organisation.

Royal Mail receives 110,000 applications for 18,000 Christmas jobs

Figure 17.5 Royal Mail seasonal jobs

The Royal Mail has received a record 110,000 applications across the UK for 18,000 seasonal workers, it was announced today. Last year, the total number of applications for the seasonal jobs was 70,000.

The temporary employees have already started working in Royal Mail locations across the country to help the 130,000 permanent postmen and postwomen deal with an expected 2 billion Christmas items.

More than six people have so far applied for every Christmas job since the recruitment campaign was launched in September.

Royal Mail's managing director of operations and modernisation, Mark Higson, said: 'We are delighted at the response from people keen to help us sort the Christmas mailbag. More seasonal recruits are required in Bristol, Peterborough, Portsmouth and Northampton. We look forward to receiving applications from people who want to work in those areas and earn some extra money over the festive season.'

The seasonal staff will work in mail and distribution centres across the UK, helping to sort Christmas cards and packets before they go to around 1,400 delivery offices for postmen and postwomen to take out on their rounds.

(*Source:* Daily Telegraph, *16 November 2011*)

	Total employment (millions)	Full-time employees (% of total)	Part-time employees (% of total)	Temporary employees (% of total)	Self-employed (% of total)
1995	26.25	64.56	24.43	7.1	10.38
2000	27.98	65.75	25.05	7.0	8.8
2004	28.38	63.91	26.00	5.25	9.8
2008	29.41	64.47	24.99	5.4	12.90
2011	29.07	62.85	22.42	6.11	14.05

Table 17.4 Trends in employment in the UK 1995–2011

Source: National Statistics website www.statistics.gov.uk

UK businesses have opted for workforces containing increasing numbers of part-time and temporary employees. Labour forces with high proportions of these types of employees are called flexible workforces.

Core and peripheral workers

One way in which a flexible workforce can be organised is part of a 'flexible firm'. This idea was developed by John Atkinson and the Institute of Manpower Studies. They explained that flexible workforces comprise a core workforce and a peripheral workforce, as illustrated in Figure 17.6.

The business's core workers would be highly qualified and trained, would be motivated and would be in permanent full-time employment with security of employment. In contrast the peripheral workers would only be hired when necessary. They may be low skilled or have highly specialised skills that are not required all the time. An example of the latter category could be experts on environmental pollution. This would allow the business to respond to fluctuations in demand without incurring the ongoing costs of employing all its workers on a permanent basis. The peripheral workers could be employed part time or by using temporary contracts.

Figure 17.6 The organisation of a firm with a flexible workforce

Other methods of flexible working

Businesses can also employ people flexibly using:

- **annualised hours contracts** – employees working in this way are expected to work, say, an average of 38 hours each week, but can be employed to work longer hours during busy weeks, with an equivalent reduction in working hours during quieter periods
- **zero-hour contracts** – these are given to people who are employed by the business but only work and receive pay when both the business and employee agree to do so.

BUSINESS IN FOCUS

Park Cakes workers may strike over 'zero-hour' contracts

Workers at Oldham-based bakery manufacturer Park Cakes Bakeries Ltd will walk out on strike for four days this month, following a branch meeting with union members. Ian Hodson, national president of the Bakers Food and Allied Workers Union (BFAWU), confirmed that around 70 staff voted in favour of a strike.

Workers at the meeting claimed that changes to employment contracts could result in them losing up to £4,000 a year in pay. The changes mean that workers that previously earned wages above minimum rates will have new 'zero-hour' contracts where no fixed hours are guaranteed.

In September, BFAWU claimed that Park Cake Bakeries was attempting to bypass new legislation covering agency workers. It also claimed that the firm was planning to introduce new contracts without consultation and without agreement.

A spokesperson for Park Cakes said that the company had introduced the new contracts for new employees in order to control costs and remain competitive following the effects of the recession, and in order to safeguard existing jobs at its Bolton and Oldham sites.

(*Source: Adapted from* British Baker Magazine, *September 2011, www.bakeryinfo.co.uk*)

Question:

Analyse the disadvantages to Park Cake Bakeries Ltd of employing a flexible workforce. *(10 marks)*

Homeworking

Homeworking refers to anyone who works from home for a significant part of their working week. Homeworking is also sometimes referred to as teleworking. Homeworking is an increasingly important feature of the operation of many businesses in the UK and throughout the world. Over 25 per cent of the UK workforce 'sometimes' works at home. The number of people working 'mainly' at home is 2.5 per cent of the workforce (727,000) people, and this is more than twice the number who did so in 1981 (346,000). British Telecom advocates homeworking and it alone has 11,000 people working from home.

The Labour Force Survey shows that between the two census years of 2001 and 2011, the number of self-employed homeworkers in the UK rose by 24 per cent to over 2.3 million. In total the number of people working from home in 2011 was nearly 3.75 million.

This group is the fastest growing part of the workforce. In comparison the number of commuting employees rose by only 1.9 per cent in the same period. Why have businesses advocated homeworking?

- Many managers have argued that homeworking has a positive effect on the motivation of employees. Homeworking naturally allows employees greater responsibility for their own work. Interestingly, some studies suggest that homeworking can reduce stress levels, especially those associated with commuting.
- Employment costs incurred by businesses can be substantially reduced as a consequence of homeworking. Firms can reduce their capacity, avoiding the need to pay expensive office rents in city centres. Other savings to businesses can take the form of reducing travelling expenses and the need for social facilities at work. A survey by the Henley Centre has suggested that for each employee converted to homeworking a business saves £6,000 per year.

- Employees can actually spend more time working as travelling time is eliminated and time spent talking informally with colleagues is reduced. Thus, there is the potential for increasing productivity and employee performance.

The UK government has expressed support for homeworking on environmental grounds, as any significant reduction in commuting offers society substantial benefits in terms of reduced pollution. In view of the apparent benefits of homeworking and governmental approval, it seems surprising that homeworking has not been adopted on a larger scale. However, a number of factors have influenced firms, as well as individual employees, in their decisions not to adopt homeworking.

At times during the 1990s office rents were relatively low and this eliminated a major incentive for businesses to encourage homeworking. The same is true now as the economy slowly recovers from a deep recession. At the same time many companies have 'downsized', creating vacant space within their offices which is almost impossible to sell or lease. Once the main financial inducements have been removed the attractiveness of homeworking to businesses is sharply diminished.

Many companies have operated trials into the costs and benefits of homeworking. Inevitably, these have attracted much media attention. However, the outcomes of such experiments have often been to retain the status quo and keep the majority of employees at the office. Many businesses, especially those in the financial sector, have drawn back from the move to have significant numbers of employees working at home.

As long ago as the 1930s, Elton Mayo wrote that the social dimension was an important aspect of employment. Homeworking eliminates much contact with fellow workers and certainly removes the opportunity to indulge in workplace gossip and banter. Failing to fulfil the social needs of employees at work could damage motivation and performance. Furthermore, there is some evidence that it is the social isolation inherent in homeworking that has resulted in numerous employees opting to return to more traditional patterns of employment.

Some employers are reluctant to encourage homeworking as they feel that employees may not work as hard if they were not closely supervised. It may be that a more democratic style of leadership is likely to promote and encourage homeworking among employees.

Many forms of employment are not suited to homeworking. If a job involves significant communication with colleagues on a regular basis, or if it requires the skills of a number of people simultaneously, homeworking is unlikely to be an effective method of organising the workforce.

Outsourcing

Outsourcing means finding a person or business outside the organisation to complete part of the production process. Businesses may decide to outsource to reduce their labour costs and this can be an attractive option if the type of employee required is highly skilled and/or the business does not require their services all of the time. Sometimes work may be outsourced because the business does not have employees with the skills necessary to complete the work. Examples of the type of work that is outsourced can include cleaning, the provision of IT services and management consultancy services.

Outsourcing brings obvious advantages in terms of reducing labour costs. The business does not have to contribute to pension funds or the government's national insurance scheme on behalf of the employee, provide training or paid holidays. However, communication between outsourced workers and permanent employees can be more difficult and the level of motivation of such workers can be low.

The case for …	… and the case against
Flexible employees are cheaper because firms avoid many of the costs of full-time employment (such as pension contributions). Wages are also generally lower. This makes the firm more price competitive, which may be important in an increasingly global market.	Communication is tricky with flexible workforces. More employees, unfamiliar with one another and with different patterns of attendance, make it difficult to pass on information. Formal and informal communication is poorer, causing lower-quality customer service and damaging the firm's image.
Flexible workforces assist businesses in dealing with fluctuations in demand. Being able to call on part-time or self-employed workers at a busy time avoids the problems associated with unfulfilled orders. At quiet times firms do not have expensive workers with little to do, and do not have to pay to make employees redundant.	The turnover of staff is higher with flexible workforces. Lack of job security leads people to move to permanent employment when possible. High rates of labour turnover mean workers are unfamiliar with their duties and firms incur greater recruitment costs.
Firms can reduce training costs by subcontracting work to other organisations or by hiring self-employed workers. Businesses acquire staff with up-to-date skills without having to pay for their training. This is particularly useful in industries subject to rapid change, such as the microelectronics industry.	Morale can be lower with flexible workforces. Security needs may not be met through these forms of employment and employee performance may be hampered by this factor. The failure to form groups at work – or the regular breaking up of these groups – may mean that social needs also remain unfulfilled, leading to lower levels of motivation.
Flexible patterns of employment allow businesses to have access to highly specialised skills without bearing the costs of permanently employing what can be hugely expensive workers. Thus, even relatively small businesses may hire self-employed systems analysts to carry out highly technical work with their computer systems.	

Table 17.5 The case for and against flexible workforces

The balance between advantages and disadvantages of employing flexible workforces depends upon the circumstances. Flexible workforces arguably offer the greatest potential to businesses when the employees in question are either highly skilled or have few skills. Highly skilled employees are expensive to hire and may require constant retraining to ensure their skills remain up to date. Employing such people through temporary contracts, or as self-employed workers, may provide benefits without incurring heavy long-term expenditure.

Equally, employees with few skills may be hired on a part-time, flexible-hours or temporary basis. This allows firms to have the appropriate amount of labour available to meet varying levels of demand. High levels of turnover of staff may not be a problem in such circumstances, as training is likely to be minimal.

One step further: global delayering

The Boston Consulting Group (perhaps best known for developing the Boston Matrix) has spent some time researching delayering and has produced a number of articles on this topic. A recent article considers a more complex type of delayering: global delayering. The group argues that advantages of delayering (lower costs, quicker decision-making and improved communication) can be achieved in a global context. It argues that the benefits of global delayering may be greater than can be achieved through the domestic variety. The authors of the article argue that it is easier to ignore inefficiency at a global level and therefore easier to do nothing about it. The implementation of a strategy of global delayering will have to stretch across several, and perhaps many, countries. However, the group believes that delayering forces senior managers to look closely at and address many other issues in an organisation that may reduce its international competitiveness.

For example, the concept of global delayering may be very necessary in global businesses that have grown through takeovers. Takeovers can result in the bringing together of businesses with different organisational structures and may result in too many layers of hierarchy. The buying business may be more interested in thinking about the new customers and products this purchase may give. Thoughts as to rationalising functions such as finance may not be at the front of executives' minds, although it offers potential for significant cost savings. You can find out more about global delayering by reading the Boston Consulting Group's article at the web address given below.

Source: Boston Consulting Group, adapted from www.bcg.com

Key terms

An **organisational structure** is the way in which a business is arranged to carry out its activities.

Levels of hierarchy refer to the number of layers of authority that exist within an organisation.

A **span of control** is the number of subordinates directly responsible to a manager.

The **culture** of a business refers to the attitudes, ideas and beliefs that are shared by the employees in a particular business.

Delayering is the reduction of the number of layers of hierarchy within an organisation's structure.

Delegation is the passing of authority (but not responsibility) down the organisation structure.

Centralisation exists when the majority of decisions are taken by senior managers at the top (or centre) of the business.

Decentralisation is the passing of authority from those working at the centre of the organisation to those working elsewhere in it.

Flexible workforces exist when businesses place less reliance upon permanent full-time employees and make greater use of part-time and temporary workers.

Temporary workers have contracts of employment that only exist for a specific period of time – perhaps six months.

Annualised hours operate when an employer states the number of hours employees must work over a year. Weekly working hours can be varied to suit their circumstances.

Homeworking refers to anyone who works from home for a significant part of their working week.

Teleworking has a similar meaning to homeworking, but implies that this style of employment is dependent upon technological forms of communication.

Outsourcing means finding people or a business outside the organisation to complete part of the production process.

The A2 specification looks at large businesses and so the size of the business is an important influence. This makes entrepreneurial structures and informal structures less relevant to the types of businesses on which examination questions may be asked. However, these two structures should not be ignored.

You should be aware of the advantages and disadvantages of each of the methods that businesses may use to adapt their organisational structures to become more competitive. You should also judge these against the specific circumstances of the particular business.

Delayering is a 'live' topic at the moment. Many firms are using this approach as a means of improving their performance, principally through cutting costs. However, delayering has important links with motivation through providing junior employees with enhanced roles. However, an important evaluative line is to consider why firms delayer: is it simply to cut labour costs or because of a genuine belief in the benefits of employees having greater control over their working lives?

You must think about the advantages and disadvantages of flexible workforces in relation to the type of business under consideration. Factors such as the stability of patterns of demand and the degree of price elasticity may shape your opinion on its value.

Progress questions

1 Explain the key distinctions between a hierarchical organisational structure and a matrix structure. *(6 marks)*

2 Outline **two** factors that may determine the effectiveness of an entrepreneurial organisational structure. *(6 marks)*

3 Explain why a large, multinational business might be expected to choose a hierarchical organisational structure. *(8 marks)*

4 Outline the ways in which the skills levels of its workforce might affect the choice of organisational structure chosen by a design company. *(6 marks)*

5 Explain why the drawbacks of delayering might be felt in the short term, whereas the benefits might only arise in the long run. *(8 marks)*

6 Explain possible reasons why a policy of delayering on its own may be unlikely to achieve much in terms of improving the performance of the workforce. *(6 marks)*

7 Explain, with the aid of examples, the term 'flexible workforce'. *(3 marks)*

8 Outline **two** ways in which a major ice cream manufacturer might increase the flexibility of its workforce. *(8 marks)*

9 Outline **two** reasons why some firms make little attempt to make more use of homeworking to increase the flexibility of their workforces. *(6 marks)*

10 Explain the possible ways in which a UK high-street bank might make use of outsourcing. *(8 marks)*

✖ These questions relate to the case study on page 184.

Analyse the possible reasons why Kevar Travel plc operates a hierarchical organisational structure. *(10 marks)*

Candidate's answer:

A hierarchical structure is formal, relatively tall and is organised into functions with decision-making shared and employees having roles which they understand.

This structure often has a large number of levels of hierarchy and therefore offers all junior and senior employees a clear line of promotion to more senior positions. This provides motivation for employees as promotion offers the chance to meet one of Maslow's higher needs (self-esteem) and this may result in an improvement in productivity and overall performance.

Kevar Travel's relatively tall hierarchical structure with many levels of hierarchy means that it can maintain a narrow span of control and that

its managers and supervisors do not have to manage excessive numbers of junior employees. This has permitted the company to employ a large number of workers on temporary contracts without damaging the operation of the business. Managers and supervisors have the capacity to support relatively inexperienced workers. It has also helped the company to cope with a high labour turnover and deal with large numbers of new employees who have relatively little knowledge about the business and its customers.

Examiner's comments:

The best part of this answer is in the final paragraph, suggesting that it may not have been planned before writing. The second paragraph lacks application as there is no reference to Kevar Travel or its circumstances. It is a fair theoretical argument but not one to attract high marks. The final paragraph is much better. It applies knowledge to the case study by combining data on temporary employees and labour turnover and develops a strong argument. It is often easier to write fluently in context.

Analysis question

Analyse the possible reasons why Kevar Travel plc wished to make its workforce more flexible. *(10 marks)*

18 Effective employer–employee relations

This chapter looks at the relationship between employers (usually represented by managers) and employees in the workplace. A good relationship can be of great value in improving the competitive performance of the business. Although this chapter builds on your general understanding of the management of people within businesses, it does not build on any specific aspect of your study of AS Business Studies.

In this chapter we examine:

- the nature and importance of communication
- how employers manage communications with employees
- the methods of employee representation
- the methods of avoiding and resolving industrial disputes.

The nature and importance of communication

The theory of communication

Communication is the transfer of information between people. A transmission mechanism is simply the means by which one person communicates with another (for example, by letter or email).

Communication involves a number of elements as shown in Figure 18.1.

Advertising is an example of business communication, as shown by the example from Marks & Spencer in Figure 18.2. The company is linking together its different methods of advertising communication.

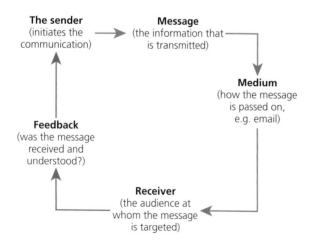

The sender (initiates the communication) → **Message** (the information that is transmitted) → **Medium** (how the message is passed on, e.g. email) → **Receiver** (the audience at whom the message is targeted) → **Feedback** (was the message received and understood?) →

Figure 18.1 The process of communication

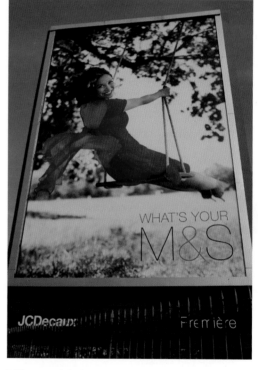

Figure 18.2 An advert by Marks & Spencer plc

- The **sender** is the company who commences the process of communication.
- The **message** is the information that the business wishes to send to its audience. In the case of Marks & Spencer it wishes to convey information concerning clothes for sale.
- The **medium** is the way in which the message is communicated. Marks & Spencer used a billboard to communicate the message in Figure 18.2, but it could also have been an advert in a magazine.

- The **audience** is the target group at whom Marks & Spencer aimed this message – adult men and women, but those who are still relatively young.
- **Feedback** could take the form of a company analysing the number of people who respond to their website and place online orders while a television advert is running alongside the internet version.

Businesses engage in communication for a variety of purposes, as illustrated in Figure 18.3. This communication can be **internal** (with other individuals or groups within the business). Thus, a memo sent from the director of human resources to team leaders concerning overtime rates would be an example of internal communication. **External** communication takes place between a business and other organisations or individuals. For example, a business providing details of job vacancies as part of the process of external recruitment would be communicating externally.

Communication can also be classified in other ways.

- **Formal communication** is the exchange of information and ideas within and outside a business using official channels. Examples of formal communication include board meetings or team briefings, and communication through email, memos and letters.
- **Informal communication** takes place outside the official channels of an organisation – gossip is an obvious example.

Effective communication

Effective communication is an essential element of business success. A survey by the Institute of Management and UMIST stressed the importance of good-quality communications within businesses. The survey reported that good communication could assist employees of all types within a business.

- Good communication makes it easier to implement change – an important issue in a business environment subject to rapid and continual change.
- Good communication encourages and develops commitment to the business from employees at all levels within the organisation.
- Effective communication helps to ensure that the business is coordinated and that all employees pursue the same corporate objectives.

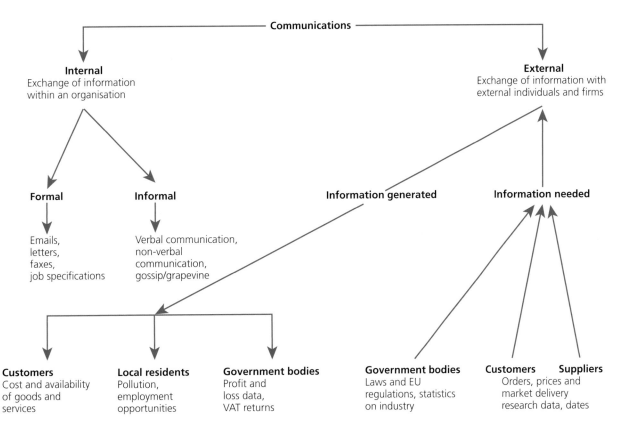

Figure 18.3 Internal and external communication

The role of a manager in a modern organisation is to communicate with everyone – shareholders, the media, superiors, customers and suppliers. The measure of today's managers is more about how well they communicate than what they communicate. Good-quality communication by managers with the business's stakeholders offers many benefits.

Successful decision-making requires that managers have access to as much relevant information as possible. The key management roles of planning, prioritising, coordinating and controlling depend upon access to information. This emphasises the importance of good communication to businesses.

A business that has not set up good systems of communication with other stakeholders such as customers and suppliers is unlikely to have effective systems in place with which to communicate with employees. It is to this aspect of communication that we now turn our attention.

Managing communication with employees

Communication is the cornerstone of the coordination of employees. In large businesses it is easy for different departments or parts of the organisation to pursue different objectives. Regular and effective communication can help to ensure that all employees remain closely focused on agreed corporate objectives.

The communication medium

There are a number of techniques or media through which managers at all levels in the organisation might choose to communicate with their subordinates; equally, these techniques may be used for upwards communication.

- Meetings can occur in a variety of forms, including formal meetings between trade unions or other groups representing employees, or less formal discussions between individual representatives of the two sides. Social events may also provide forums for the exchange of information.
- Presentations are frequently used in businesses to explain policies and procedures to large groups of employees. Many presentations use Microsoft PowerPoint. Detailed information (especially relating to employment and working practices) can be exchanged using this software.

Technology can be used by larger businesses to communicate with their employees, and this can be of particular value to businesses that operate in several locations, especially if these locations are in different countries.

- **Electronic mail (email)** allows people throughout the world to communicate with each other via their computers for the cost of a local telephone call. Messages are stored on servers and can be accessed by the recipient through the use of a password. This is particularly useful for quick international communication between employers and employees groups across different time zones, as messages can be stored until the recipient is available.
- **Intranets** are electronic, computer-based communication networks, similar in nature to the internet but used internally by individual businesses. They are ideally suited to large companies, especially those with a number of locations. They provide an email service as well as access to information of interest to large numbers of employees.
- **Video conferencing** allows people to communicate face-to-face while in different locations, nationally or internationally. It saves time and avoids the need for employers and employees to travel to meetings.

The precise method or methods that a business elects to use to communicate with its employees will vary according to the circumstances and the nature of the business. A business that is large, with employees in a number of locations, possibly in different countries, may rely more on electronic communication, though other means of communication will also be used.

Issues in communicating with employees

The effective management of communication with employees is not simply about choosing the right medium through which to exchange information. Other factors make up an effective employer–employee communication package.

Appreciating the nature of effective communication

Good-quality communication is normally two-way communication. This means that information will flow in both directions between employers and employees or their representatives. Two-way communication allows for feedback to establish that the message has been received and understood. However, it has much more potential than this. It affords the opportunity for employees to offer ideas and suggestions which may result in some excellent ideas for improving the way in which the business operates. The opportunity alone to offer suggestions may improve employees' motivation, and thereby their performance, by providing a sense of recognition and an opportunity for achievement if ideas and suggestions are effective. Finally, two-way communication can alert managers to potential problems which may result in confrontation and conflict if not resolved at the earliest opportunity.

Using the appropriate style of management

The writings of Elton Mayo, and especially the Hawthorne experiment, offer evidence that employees respond positively to receiving attention from managers. Later research has strengthened this link. Abraham Maslow developed his hierarchy of needs, and argued that good communication underpins some of the higher-level needs identified in his theory. The need for recognition, for example, relies heavily upon managers communicating with subordinates. Similarly, Frederick Herzberg wrote that direct communication (rather than through unnecessary layers of hierarchy) was an important means of improving employee motivation. Electing to manage in a style that offers employees the chance to participate in decision-making does more than provide a forum for communication – it encourages it as well.

Adapting the organisational structure to encourage effective communication

We saw in the previous chapter that businesses can organise themselves in different ways. By opting for a structure which allows employees to have greater authority and control over their working lives, employers can encourage communication at all levels within the organisation. Using techniques such as delegation and empowerment has costs in terms of loss of power for managers and in terms of training relatively junior employees to take on more demanding roles. However, alongside the benefit of improved communication, the performance of employees should also improve as levels of motivation increase.

Good communication can have a positive impact upon employee motivation and performance. Praise

and recognition are widely seen as motivators, but rely upon communication. Effective communication can also give employees important feedback about their performance and help to improve it in the future.

It has become more difficult in some ways to manage communication effectively between employers and employees over recent years. Mergers and takeovers continue to create larger and more complex business. It is not uncommon for businesses in different countries to merge, or for one to buy another in a takeover deal. As a consequence, the need for effective communication between employers and employees can increase. At such a time job losses may be expected and effective communication will be essential to quell rumours and to negotiate mutually acceptable deals. However, the scale of the new business and the possible absence of effective mechanisms for communicating can make this process very difficult.

BUSINESS IN FOCUS

Creating a large airline

The merger between British Airways and Iberia was completed on 21 January 2011, finally creating the International Airlines Group (IAG). The Group employs over 56,000 employees and operates 420 aircraft. It serves around 200 destinations and carries over 62 million passengers per year. IAG has its operational headquarters, which controls the management of both its Spanish and British subsidiaries, at London's Heathrow Airport. The company is incorporated according to Spanish law with the board's meetings occurring in Madrid. Between them the two airlines operate seven subsidiaries including Sun-Air, Vueling and Iberia Express.

In 2011 the group announced that it had increased its profits by increasing capacity without operating additional aircraft or hiring extra employees.

(*Source: Adapted from* BBC News, *6 May 2011*)

Question:

Analyse the possible reasons why IAG might experience problems with its internal communications. *(10 marks)*

Collective and individual bargaining

When communicating with employees about issues such as pay and conditions, there are two broad approaches that managers can take in negotiations.

Collective bargaining

Collective bargaining is a tradition for which businesses in the UK are noted. Collective bargaining entails negotiations between management and employees' representatives, usually trade unions, over pay and other conditions of employment. Collective bargaining can only occur if the employer recognises the right of a trade union or other representative group to act on behalf of the workforce. Under a collective agreement the terms negotiated by the employees' representatives are binding upon the entire workforce – this is the 'collective' aspect of this form of negotiation.

In spite of the tradition of collective bargaining in the UK, for many years it became less common. Simultaneously, the proportion of firms recognising trade unions for the purposes of collective bargaining declined. However, the situation was reversed to some degree by the passing of the Employment Relations Act, which came into force in 2000. Under this Act a trade union with a membership exceeding 50 per cent of the employees in any particular business (or part of a business where negotiations take place) can demand union recognition and thereby the right to reintroduce collective bargaining. If a union has more than 10 per cent of the workforce as members it can call for a ballot and needs the support of 40 per cent of the employees to be successful. The newly formed Central Arbitration Committee may settle disputes about union recognition.

The European Union may help the reintroduction of collective bargaining into the workplace. In 2000 the EU announced that it was planning to make consultation with employees on a range of items compulsory for companies with over 50 employees.

The use of collective bargaining as a means of communication between employers and employees in the UK declined for a number of reasons.

- Since the early 1980s trade union membership in the UK has declined. In 1979 union membership reached 13 million but by 2010 the number had fallen to 6.54 million. As a consequence the influence of unions has waned, allowing businesses to move away from collective bargaining more easily. At the same time that trade union membership has declined, the number of trade unions has fallen due to a series of mergers.
- Governments have passed legislation designed to restrict the power of trade unions and to allow labour markets to operate more freely, thereby discouraging collective agreements.
- Employers have introduced strategies that emphasise and reward individuals and teams. This represents a change of approach from collective employer–employee relationships conducted through trade union officials.

Individual bargaining

The move away from collective bargaining has been driven by a change in philosophy within many modern businesses. The adoption of the principles of human resource management has resulted in many enterprises seeking to make the most effective use of each and every member of the workforce. This has had two main consequences.

1 Instead of paying a standard wage or salary to every worker carrying out a particular role (as would have been likely under collective bargaining), individual bargaining means that workers may be paid according to their contribution. This may reduce the labour costs of a business and has the potential to provide financial motivation for employees.

2 The other side to individual bargaining is that some businesses seek to develop their employees to encourage them to make the maximum possible contribution to the performance of the business.

Other firms have simply chosen not to recognise trade unions in the hope of being able to keep wage increases and costs to a minimum without the upward pressure of collective bargaining.

In spite of the move away from collective bargaining in the early years of the new millennium, individual bargaining is most commonly used when employees have substantial skill levels and the ability to negotiate their own packages of pay and conditions. Nevertheless, it has led to a different pattern of communication between employers and employees.

Many employees in the UK have their pay determined by one of two systems, as follows.

1 Pay reviews are frequently used in the public sector to settle the pay levels for groups such as teachers

and nurses. A committee of 'experts' considers all the relevant information before arriving at a decision.

2 Management determines pay unilaterally. It is used in some workplaces, often as part of a decentralised arrangement. Management decisions commonly reflect the current rate of inflation. This is common in some schools, for example 'Free schools'.

These methods of settling pay and working conditions may involve minimal communication.

Methods of employee representation

Employees are not only represented by trade unions in their negotiations with employers. In fact, in the UK only a minority of workers are members of a trade union. In this section we will consider the various ways in which employees can be represented in negotiations with employers.

Trade unions

A trade union is an organisation of workers established to protect and improve economic position and working conditions of its members. A number of different types of trade union exist, although a series of amalgamations over recent years has resulted in the distinctions between them becoming less clear.

BUSINESS IN FOCUS

Unite

Created through the merger in 2007 of Amicus and the Transport and General Workers Union (T&G), Unite has 1.5 million members in 2011, in diverse workplaces. The new union represents workers in the public and private sectors and in almost every industry and profession; it is the dominant union in manufacturing, energy, transport, finance, food and agriculture. It also represents members working in the National Health Service, education, local authorities, government departments and the voluntary sector.

With a network of more than 500 salaried officers and thousands of trained workplace representatives, Unite is instrumental in improving working practices and training and development initiatives for thousands of UK workers.

Trade unions are normally organised on a regional basis. For example, Unite operates in ten regions throughout the UK and Eire. Each region has a regional office staffed by full-time union employees (called organisers or officers). The region is made up of a number of branches and each branch has an elected shop steward. The shop steward communicates with employers on behalf of the union's members and reports back to members regarding management decisions. The head office has an administrative, statistical and legal staff and the senior officials of the union. Other trade unions operate similar structures.

Most trade unions in the UK have similar objectives. These focus on improving the economic position of their members by fulfilling the following objectives:

- **Maximising pay** – unions engage in collective bargaining to provide their members with the highest possible rates of pay.
- **Achieving safe and secure working conditions**. For unions representing workers in the public sector protecting pensions rights is an important issue currently.
- **Attaining job security** – arguably this is the most important objective of a modern trade union and one that is difficult to fulfil in the light of pressures resulting from globalisation and the increasing use of technology in the workplace.
- **Participating in and influencing decisions in the workplace** – trade unions may achieve this through collective bargaining or through having representatives on works councils and other employer–employee committees.

In addition, many unions have social objectives, such as lobbying for higher social security benefits, improved employment legislation and improved quality of provision by the National Health Service.

Trade unions achieve their objectives by carrying out a range of functions to the benefit of their members.

- Their most important and time-consuming function is protecting members' interests over issues such as discrimination, unfair dismissal and health and safety matters.
- They negotiate pay and conditions for their members through collective bargaining.
- Trade unions provide their members with a range of personal services, including legal advice, insurance, education, training and financial advice.

Employers can also benefit from the existence of trade unions for the following reasons:

- They act as a communications link between management and employees.
- Professional negotiation on behalf of a large number of employees can save time and lessen the likelihood of disputes occurring.

Trade unions are responsible for collective bargaining in the workplace. They negotiate with employers on behalf of their members on matters such as pay, conditions and fringe benefits. Unions are in a better position to negotiate than individuals in that they have more negotiating skills and power.

Works councils

A works council is a forum within a business where workers and management meet to discuss issues such as working conditions, pay and training. Employee representatives on a works council are normally elected. It is common for works councils to be used in workplaces where no trade union representation exists. However, in businesses where works councils and trade unions co-exist, the former is normally excluded from discussing pay and working conditions.

Employees like to know what their employers are planning, and since 2008 all UK employers with 50 or more staff have been obliged to keep employees regularly informed. Under the new European Union regulations, companies will be required to establish formal works councils on demand.

Before 2008, the obligation only applied to organisations with 100 or more employees. But this has now been extended, and a significant number of UK employers will have to get acquainted with the new legal regulations. The EU takes works councils seriously: non-compliant employers may face fines of up to £75,000 and could have a works council imposed on them that is ill-suited to their business.

BUSINESS IN FOCUS

Union identifies legal loophole

USDAW, the shop workers union called for a legal loophole to be closed after 1,200 former employees from Ethel Austin (the fashion store chain that collapsed in 2010) were denied compensation. USDAW took the matter to an employment tribunal on behalf of its members after administrators MCR, who were appointed to close the business, failed to consult the union before making 1,700 staff redundant.

The tribunal found that MCR had failed in their legal obligations to consult with USDAW and awarded about 500 union members compensation of eight weeks' pay, capped at £380 a week – the maximum payable in the circumstances.

However, the compensation was limited to employees from the retailer's former head office and distribution centre. In a judgment that the union may appeal, the tribunal stated that MCR was not obliged to consult about workplaces where less than 20 redundancies were being made, thus ruling out all but one of the 186 individual shops that were closed.

John Gorle, USDAW National Officer said: 'While the award can never fully compensate for staff losing their jobs, I'm sure our members will welcome the money and appreciate the effort USDAW has made to secure this compensation for them. Cases like these really demonstrate the value of belonging to a trade union.'

(Source: Adapted from Andy Richardson in The Northern Echo, 23 November 2011)

Question:

Analyse why fewer employees are joining trade unions such as USDAW, when it offers possible benefits such as those outlined above. *(10 marks)*

European works councils bring together employee representatives in a multinational companies from across Europe, to inform and consult them on the group's performance and prospects. They can help trade unionists and employee representatives to respond to the decisions that employers increasingly take on a European and global basis. European works councils affect any business with at least 1,000 employees and at least 150 employees located in two or more member states of the European Union.

A European works council is made up of at least one elected employee from each country in which the multinational is based and representatives from senior management. They normally meet annually and discuss issues affecting employees throughout the organisation. These include health and safety, merger proposals, the closure of plants and the implementation of new working practices such as teamworking.

Although European works councils have been operating for several years, it is only since January 2000, when new regulations came into force, that multinational firms in the UK have been obliged legally to have this type of works council. These regulations mean that more UK companies have to implement European works councils and UK employees have gained new rights.

Other types of employee representation

Employee representation can take other forms. Employers may allow the development of any arrangement which allows communication to take place. For example, a factory or office committee may be established. These committees can have members/employees elected by the workforce as well as the employer's representatives. They discuss such matters as working conditions, employment and production changes, safety and welfare matters. To be effective committees should meet regularly. If disillusionment is to be avoided, such committees should be seen to have a real effect on how matters are determined. This requires that the workforce be regularly informed about the committee's work.

Alternatively, a staff association may be formed to provide employee representation. Staff associations usually operate on behalf of a single company or even a part of a larger business. Staff associations are often independent from external influences and this can be a reason for them to be popular with both employees and employers. However, it can also limit their effectiveness in the long term, which often depends on the input and commitment of a small number of individuals. As a result it is not uncommon for staff associations to eventually merge with a larger trade union. This is especially likely when employees seek to negotiate collectively their terms and conditions.

Methods of avoiding and resolving industrial disputes

Industrial disputes and industrial action

An industrial dispute is a disagreement between an employer and its employees, usually represented by a trade union, over some aspect of the terms or conditions of employment. Trade unions or other employee groups can take a number of actions as part of an industrial dispute. Such actions are called industrial action. Industrial action refers to any measure taken by trade unions or other employee groups meant to reduce productivity in a workplace.

Trade unions or other employee groups can take a number of different types of industrial action.

- **Strikes.** Workers can withdraw their labour, as long as this course of action is agreed through a secret ballot of employees. Strikes may be continuous or a succession of one-day actions.
- **Picketing.** This occurs when strikers stand at entrances to a place with an industrial dispute, to attempt to persuade others not to cross the picket line and go into work, thereby breaking the strike action. Legislation restricts the number of people able to picket at any one time.
- **Work to rule.** Under this action unions dictate procedures to be followed by members in the course of working. This leads to employees being less productive and output declining.

Figure 18.4 The June 2011 protest over pensions in public sector

- **Sit in.** A sit in takes place when employees occupy a workplace for a specific period of time, thus causing production to be stopped.
- **Go slow.** Similar to a work to rule, this is a measure designed to slow production and reduce workers' productivity with adverse effects on the firm's profits.
- **Overtime bans.** Under this sanction employees are not prepared to work beyond their normal hours, reducing the flexibility of the labour force. Overtime bans may mean employers have to recruit more employees, incurring additional costs.

Methods of avoiding industrial disputes

No-strike and single-union agreements

The field of industrial relations has seen a number of developments that have limited the power and influence of trade unions within the workplace.

A 'no-strike deal' is an agreement between employers and unions whereby in return for a pay and conditions package a union agrees to refrain from strike action for an agreed period. Often such agreements are accompanied by a commitment by both parties to go to binding arbitration in the event of a dispute. This reassures the union that it is not making itself too vulnerable by agreeing not to take industrial action. A no-strike agreement can benefit a trade union in a number of ways.

- By presenting itself as non-confrontational the union may attract a greater number of members from within the workforce, increasing its income and strength.

- A less confrontational stance might allow the union to appoint worker directors, increasing the union's influence and role in decision-making.
- Such agreements can improve the public perception of trade unions. This will assist the union in its activities in other businesses and industries and may persuade employers to recognise it.

A further advantage of no-strike deals is that they may lead to a single-union agreement, strengthening the position of the union within the business.

Single-union agreements have become more common over the last 20 years. Under this type of deal employees agree to be represented by one union. This makes negotiation simpler for the employers (as there are only two parties to the discussions) while reducing the possibility of disputes between rival unions. Single-union deals also assist in maintaining good communications between employers and employees, lessening the possibility of industrial action.

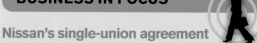

BUSINESS IN FOCUS

Nissan's single-union agreement

In February 1984, Nissan and the British government signed an agreement to build a car plant in the UK, and the following month a site in Washington (with the City of Sunderland), Tyne and Wear was chosen. At the time Sunderland qualified for financial assistance from the government, Nissan receiving in total about £100 million in grants.

One of Nissan's more controversial demands during the talks was that the plant be single-union. This was unprecedented in UK industry, at a time when industrial disputes were more common than they are today. An agreement was reached with the Amalgamated Engineering Union (AEU).

Critics argued this meant the plant workforce was weakly represented. But the company disagrees. Productivity levels are high and the factory is going from strength to strength. It has been selected to produce the all-electric Nissan Leaf as well as the next generation Qashqai. After 25 years of production, the factory's future looks assured.

(Source: Adapted from Michael Kelly in The Journal, 1 August 2011, www.journallive.co.uk)

Question:

Analyse the benefits to a company establishing a new factory of operating a single-union agreement. *(10 marks)*

Advisory, Conciliation and Arbitration Service (ACAS)

ACAS is an independent and impartial organisation established to prevent and resolve industrial disputes. ACAS's mission is to improve the performance and effectiveness of organisations by providing an independent and impartial service to prevent and resolve disputes and to build harmonious relationships at work. ACAS offers a number of services to employers and employees:

- preventing and resolving industrial disputes, particularly through the use of arbitration and conciliation
- resolving individual disputes over employment rights, including individual cases of discrimination and unfair dismissal
- providing impartial information and advice on employment matters such as reducing absenteeism, employee sickness and payment systems
- improving the understanding of industrial relations.

ACAS was established in 1975 by the government, during a period of industrial conflict, to provide advice on industrial relations matters. Initially ACAS's role was mainly the resolution of industrial disputes. More recently the organisation has focused on improving business practices to reduce the possibility of industrial disputes. In the new millennium, demand for ACAS's services is greater than ever: the number of cases in which it is involved has almost tripled since 1979. Much of ACAS's work nowadays is conciliating in disputes between an individual employee and his or her employer. This trend reflects the decreased influence of trade unions in modern businesses. In 2010–11 ACAS dealt with 1,054 disputes, a 15 per cent increase on the previous year.

Methods of resolving industrial disputes

It is normal for industrial disputes to be resolved without unions taking any form of industrial action. The decline in industrial disputes in the UK over recent years has, in part, been a consequence of the effective use of the measures outlined below.

Arbitration

Arbitration is a procedure for the settlement of disputes, under which the parties agree to be bound by the decision of an arbitrator whose decision is in some circumstances legally binding on both parties. The process of arbitration is governed by Arbitration Acts 1950–96. There are three main types of arbitration.

1 **Non-binding arbitration** involves a neutral third party making an award to settle a dispute that the parties concerned can accept or not.
2 **Binding arbitration** means that the parties to the dispute have to take the award of the arbitrator.
3 **Pendulum arbitration** is a binding form of arbitration in which the arbitrator has to decide entirely for one side or the other. It is not an option to reach a compromise and select some middle ground. This system avoids excessive claims by unions or miserly offers by employers.

BUSINESS IN FOCUS

Unite calls for ACAS to resolve dispute

Unite, the UK's largest trade union, has called on ACAS to help resolve a dispute with Thomas Cook Group plc that could result in cabin crew walking out over the travel operator's plan to shed about 500 jobs.

Thomas Cook Airlines' managing director Frank Pullman said the company is committed to continuing with meaningful consultation and seeking the best possible outcome for those potentially affected. 'We are now arranging a further meeting for Unite and the company,' he said.

Thomas Cook plans to reduce its airline fleet to 35 aircraft from 41 planes, and has embarked on a £200 million asset disposal plan. Restructuring efforts come after Thomas Cook issued its third profit warning this year, which led to the resignation of its chief executive Manny Fontenla-Novoa in early August.

Unite has called for a minimum of three weeks' pay per year of service, plus a lump sum payment of £5,000. The average cabin crew individual is paid £15,000 a year. Thomas Cook is offering two weeks' pay for every year worked.

The company has recently agreed a deal with its banks that gave it greater flexibility ahead of December when cash is typically at a low point. It also signed a new £100 million loan. The new terms also mean that Thomas Cook won't be able to buy anything or pay dividends until it has repaid an existing £150 million loan.

(Source: Adapted from The Wall Street Journal, *10 November 2011)*

Question:

Do you think that the Thomas Cook Group plc should call on ACAS's services? Justify your decision. *(18 marks)*

Conciliation

This is a method of resolving individual or collective disputes in which a neutral third party encourages the continuation of negotiations and the postponement (at least) of any form of industrial action. Conciliation is sometimes called mediation. The conciliator's role does not involve making any judgement on the validity of the position of either party. The conciliator encourages the continued discussions in the hope that a compromise can be reached.

Employment tribunals

Employment tribunals are an informal courtroom where legal disputes over unfair dismissal or discrimination can be settled. Employment tribunals were established in 1964 (when they were called Industrial Tribunals) and are to be found in most major towns and cities in the UK. Each tribunal comprises three members: a legally trained chairperson, one employer representative and an employee representative. Most employee complaints are still settled by Employment tribunals. In 2010–11 over 218,000 cases went before Employment tribunals.

One step further: Does conciliation work?

New research, led by Dr Paola Manzini of the Department of Economics at Queen Mary College, University of London is critical of the contributions made by mediators (or conciliators) in helping to resolve industrial disputes. The potential ability of third parties (such as the government) to make contributions to settle strikes may lead to severe inefficiency.

The research, funded by the Economic and Social Research Council (ESRC), examined the effect on negotiations of the presence of third parties not directly involved in industrial action but able to provide additional resources to help reach agreement. Collaborating with Clara Ponsati of Universitat Autonoma de Barcelona, the researchers observed that since the third party, or 'active mediator', had no direct claim to the dispute, the only threat against the other parties was to withhold the additional resources, thus stalling any agreement.

Dr Manzini said: 'We found that the mere possibility that the mediator may intervene in negotiations creates the potential for delays, in the hope of pressurising them into conceding extra resources. On the other hand, so long as the amount of resources that the mediator can make available is sufficiently small, the bargainers' incentive for stalemate is reduced.'

The study highlights the motivation for governments to decentralise negotiations and to avoid becoming directly involved. The report says its findings suggest that the Government should use legislation to limit its involvement as far as possible by introducing tougher requirements for firms to consult their workforce before taking decisions which may gave a great impact on jobs.

Source: Queen Mary College, University of London www.qmul.ac.uk

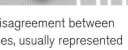

Communication is the transfer of information between people.

Delegation is the passing of authority down the organisational structure.

Empowerment is giving employees greater control over their working lives.

Trade unions are organisations of workers established to protect and improve the economic position and working conditions of their members.

A **works council** is a forum within a business where workers and management meet to discuss issues such as working conditions, pay and training.

An **industrial dispute** is a disagreement between an employer and its employees, usually represented by a trade union, over some aspect of the terms or conditions of employment.

Industrial action refers to any measure taken by trade unions or other employee groups meant to reduce productivity in a workplace.

Arbitration is a procedure for the settlement of disputes, under which the parties agree to be bound by the decision of a third party.

Conciliation is a method of resolving individual or collective disputes in which a neutral third party encourages the continuation of negotiations and the postponement of industrial action.

Examiner's advice

Do not just think about trade unions in a negative sense. They offer many benefits to employers such as acting as a channel of communication, offering advice on issues such as health and safety and may be proactive in preventing disputes.

Remember, industrial action does not just refer to strikes. Strikes are normally the final resort. Do also remember that the threat of industrial action may be used by trade unions or employee groups to persuade employers to negotiate or to give ground in negotiations.

Progress questions

1 Describe the process of communication. *(4 marks)*

2 Explain the benefits a rapidly expanding business might receive from having effective communication links with its employees. *(8 marks)*

3 Explain **two** ways in which a major UK retailer with 80 stores might improve communication with its employees. *(8 marks)*

4 Outline the difference between collective and individual bargaining. *(4 marks)*

5 Explain the benefits a large multi-site business may receive from having a highly unionised workforce. *(8 marks)*

6 Outline the benefits an employer might receive from negotiating a single-union agreement. *(6 marks)*

7 Outline **two** benefits a trade union might receive from negotiating a 'no-strike' agreement. *(6 marks)*

8 Outline why staff associations might not be particularly effective in the longer term. *(4 marks)*

9 Explain the difference between conciliation and arbitration. *(4 marks)*

10 Explain the benefits that might result from the use of binding arbitration to resolve an industrial dispute. *(6 marks)*

✖ These questions relate to the case study on page 184.

To what extent might Kevar Travel plc benefit from having about 40 per cent of its employees represented by a trade union? *(18 marks)*

Candidate's answer:

A trade union is a group of workers who join together to protect and improve their working conditions and pay.

The company will probably benefit from improved communications as many of its employees are in a trade union. This may be a key factor for Kevar Travel as it has a tall organisational structure and there is limited two-way communication so this means that any factors which improve it could be important. It is especially true that effective two-way communication between the company's employees and managers could be particularly valuable for a business that is operating in a changeable market environment. Having a single trade union will aid this process and reduce the chance of misunderstanding occurring as well as providing important upward communication which may assist in improving productivity and performance.

On the other hand, the trade union's skilled negotiators and the power of a single union representing 40 per cent of the workforce may pressure the company's managers into conceding costly improvements in working conditions or pay rises that the company cannot afford, given

that its sales per employees have fallen by more than 4.5 per cent over the last three years. The company operates in a price-elastic market and therefore controlling wages tightly (especially when they will be a high proportion of total costs) is essential. Working with a potentially powerful trade union will make this objective difficult to achieve.

Overall it is likely that the benefits in terms of communication, motivation and productivity will be outweighed by the probable impact of rising wage costs. Therefore I do not believe that the company will benefit.

Examiner's comments:

There is much to admire in this answer. Following a clear opening definition the candidate has prepared strong arguments in favour of working with a trade union and also opposing that view. They have combined arguments and have made especially good use of the numerical and non-numerical information in the case study. Another positive feature is that there is a tight focus on the question throughout this answer and these paragraphs do contain some evaluation.

There is one significant weakness. The final paragraph contains a clear judgement but relatively little support for this opinion. This may be because the student spent too long developing the analytical elements of the answer. How might you have developed the evaluation further?

Using all the information available to you, complete the following tasks:

- analyse the arguments **in favour** of Charlie's proposed strategy
- analyse the arguments **against** Charlie's proposed strategy
- make a justified recommendation on whether this strategy should be implemented. *(34 marks)*

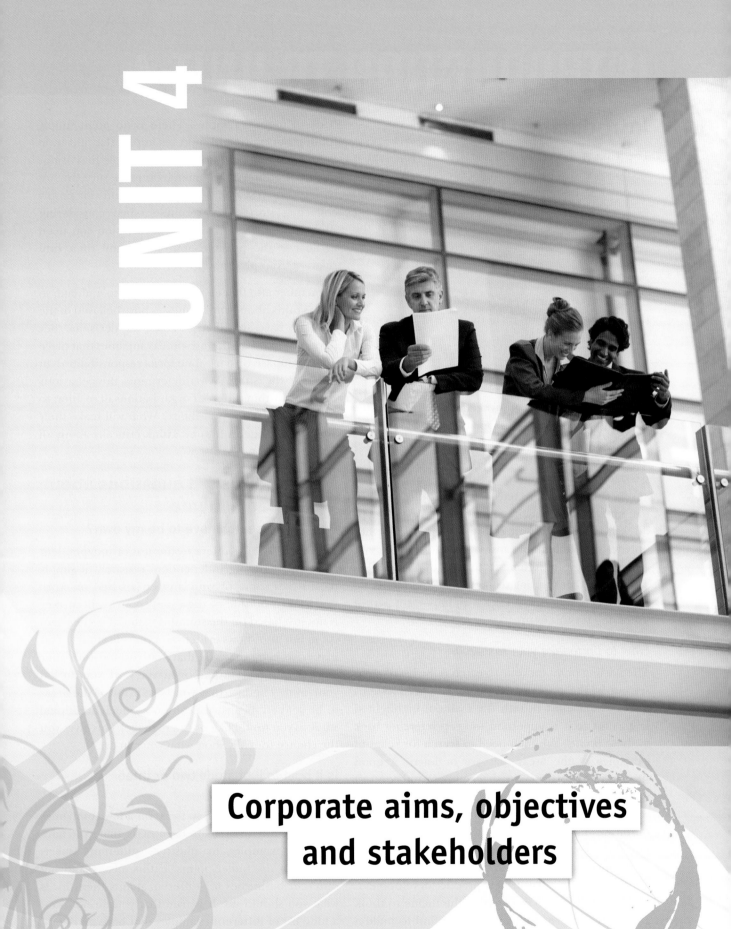

UNIT 4

Corporate aims, objectives and stakeholders

INTRODUCTION TO UNIT 4

Introducing Unit 4

The Unit 4 exam has two parts to it. The first is Section A and is based around a pre-released theme; candidates choose one essay from two. The second part is Section B and involves a choice of one essay from three. These are drawn from any area of the Unit 4 specification.

Section A

At the end of January each year AQA will release a theme. This theme will form the basis of the Section A exam questions for the following January and June exams. In previous years themes have included emerging markets, the recession and corporate social responsibility. Candidates are given a list of areas within this theme that they need to study. The idea of this list is to define the scope of the research – the questions in the exam will be drawn from the areas on this list. In the exam itself candidates are given a short passage about a business or industry and in their answers they are expected to draw on this stimulus material and combine it with their own research. To do well in this exam, therefore, it is important not only to be able to apply answers to the stimulus but also to apply your arguments to your own examples. This means that studying real businesses and building up a collection of case studies is an important part of preparing for this exam.

How to undertake your research

The starting point for your research is the list of areas set out in the pre-released material. The questions in the exam must fit with the material highlighted in this list so it is important to keep referring back to these points. You then need to search for relevant examples of the areas that are outlined. A good strategy is to find examples that compare and contrast with each other. For example in the recession theme you were asked to research different strategies that businesses might adopt, so it was useful to consider one that expanded and one that reduced the scale of its operations, or one that tried to cut costs and another that invested in new product development. It is important when researching the theme to think about what information you need to find to build a

bank of useful examples. There is no point simply finding out more and more examples that illustrate the same point; better to find an example that brings out another line of argument. Do make sure you are basing your research around theory and not simply collecting stories. For example, when considering suitable strategies to adopt in a recession you need to analyse the possible approaches and then find relevant examples to support these.

Remember also that essays require you to evaluate, so always think about why businesses have behaved in the ways you have identified or taken the decisions they have. You may have found some companies that place more emphasis on corporate social responsibility than others – why is this? What determines the behaviour of people within different organisations in relation to corporate social responsibility? What will make their attitudes change in future? Think critically about all the information you discover.

Frequently asked questions about the research theme

Does the research have to be my own?

The mark scheme refers to the use of independent research. By 'using independent research' it simply means that some of your answer is based on work undertaken outside of the exam room (your answer is not just based on the stimulus material in the exam room but also shows evidence of outside study). This may have been material that you covered with your teacher in the classroom or maybe work you did on your own. The fact that you have a list of the areas to be studied means you can do as much additional study as you would like or can manage! This gives you the chance to really show what you can do.

Is it best to just study two or three companies?

It might be a good idea to focus on a few companies in depth, but what matters most is that you have business examples to illustrate different aspects of each of the bullet points. If this means studying different businesses for different points then this is what you should do. It is true that you do not want a long list of different examples that have no depth;

much better to focus on a few examples that can be used effectively to support an argument but it may be that several different businesses are needed to cover all the points. Make sure there is some depth to your research – for example you are not simply trying to describe what a business did in a recession or what a business did that was socially responsible, you need to consider why they behaved in this way and why others did not.

Where should I research the information?

This may depend a bit on the nature of the theme but, if you can, try and find some articles by good newspapers or magazines, or reports published by organisations such as governments, associations or banks. For example, a good article on how the recession affected businesses in the UK by a bank is likely to contain a great deal of data and detailed analysis. Similarly, when studying corporate social responsibility an organisation called 'Business in the Community' provides some good case studies on one side of the debate. Do spend some time looking at the sources you find and deciding which ones are most useful. If you start cutting and pasting every search result you get on Google you will end up with files and files of notes but this may simply be a great deal of the same type of examples rather than a key detailed set of well selected cases.

How do I avoid being descriptive?

Try to work out your arguments based around the bullet points so that you can analyse the issues. For example, you can analyse the potential benefits and costs of corporate social responsibility. The business examples should be used to illustrate the arguments being made. Don't just collect stories. Make sure you are evaluating by comparing one reaction with another and thinking what are the differences and why there are differences.

Should I just use my research in my answers?

The questions in the exam in Section A ask you to use the stimulus material and your own research. It is likely that you will have more evidence and insight from your own studies so this may form the bulk of your essay but make sure you refer to some extent to the stimulus material.

Can I use my research in Section B?

Obviously the questions in Section B should not overlap with the questions in Section A but in your research you may have come across many different aspects of the businesses you have looked at. If relevant it is perfectly acceptable to use these insights in Section B.

Section B

In Section B there are three essays and you have to choose one of them. Think very carefully before you choose which one you want to answer. Once you start writing it is very difficult to start again – you have committed yourself and given the time available in the exam it will be difficult to change your mind and switch to another question. This means it is critically important to start answering the right question. Many candidates seem to want to select the question they feel they know most about rather than the one they can discuss and debate most successfully. The planning stage is there for you to think about what you might write – you do not need to plan every word but you want some idea of the basic structure and how you will be able to make judgements. A good essay is not one with lots of content – it is one which uses the content effectively to argue its points and answer the question.

When reading the question make sure you 'unpick' it fully. There are likely to be lots of areas that create opportunities to apply and evaluate. For example you may be able to relate your answer:

- to the specific business/es mentioned in the title
- to the sector involved (for example, computing is quite fast-changing, the pharmaceutical industry involves long-term investment, construction is very vulnerable to the state of the economy)
- the state of the business (for example, is it a multinational? Is it growing? Is it innovative?).

Given that 16 marks out of 40 are for evaluation it is important to make judgements on what you are arguing. Make sure these judgements relate directly to the question. Are you trying to decide on the extent of something? Whether something is desirable? Whether is it advisable?

Remember also that in Section B essays you can bring in your own examples if you wish. This is not required (you can gain full marks without doing this) but this does enable you to show your depth of reading and understanding and it can be useful to support an argument or contrast with the points being made in relation to the business in the question.

How to write great essays

Read the question, then read it again. And again

When reading candidate answers it is always surprising how often they wander off from the question set. Time and time again examiners read an answer and think 'if only they had answered the question that was actually asked'. So, never underestimate the importance of reading the question very carefully indeed before starting writing, and in fact throughout the writing of your essay – at the end of each paragraph check back and make sure you are still focused on the question set. Try to use the precise wording of the question in your answer – if it is asking what is 'right' make sure you make judgements about how right it is; if it is asking how a change affects the profits then relate everything to profits.

When reading the question also make sure:

- you read the adjectives carefully – is it a 'big' business? A 'growing' business? A retailer or a manufacturer? You can pick up on these issues in your application and evaluation.
- you think about the context. By understanding the context you will make better judgements. The options open to a business with a strong financial position is different than the options available to a highly geared business with liquidity problems.

Structure your answer

First, you will need an introduction. Often candidates' introductions are rather vague and do not say a lot. They tend to repeat the title. The better ones tend to show evidence of planning. A candidate will have thought through what they want to say and this shows through in an introduction that provides an overview of the essay.

After the introduction most essays tend to be based around arguments for and against the question; typically this means the structure might consist of two arguments for and two against but you may want to have more on one side than the other. Think carefully about the end of each paragraph – you may want to highlight how the paragraph has argued for or against the question; alternatively you may want to evaluate the argument made in the paragraph and highlight that it depends on certain factors.

The conclusion of the essay is crucial in that it should bring together your arguments and make a supported judgement. Again, the precise wording of the question is very important: is it asking you whether something is 'always' likely? 'Inevitable'? 'Desirable'? A good answer will provide a clear answer to the question asked and explain its findings.

Evaluation may argue:

- why one side of the argument is greater than the other
- why one argument is stronger in some circumstances rather than others
- why one argument may be more appropriate for one type of business rather than another.

Practise

Essay writing is a skill. You do not just wake up one day and start writing fantastic essays. You need to practise how to structure your ideas, how to analyse your arguments, how to support your ideas with evidence and how to pull your arguments together in a coherent conclusion. One method you might use early on is to word-process your answers; this gives you the opportunity to review your work and improve it. You can move paragraphs around, add greater depth and edit it to make it more concise. If your teacher is happy to mark it word-processed you can then improve it easily and resubmit. Obviously you will need to practise writing by hand under timed conditions for the exam but using word-processing to help you develop the necessary skills can be useful.

How do I approach studying Unit 4?

Unit 4 is very different from the other units because of the way it is assessed. As you know you will end up writing one essay on the pre-released theme and one essay drawn from all the other areas of the Unit 4 specification. This means the essay titles set have to cover a considerable amount of material and are likely, therefore, to be fairly broad. It is unlikely, for example, to have a question based on income tax because this is quite a specific aspect of the economic environment. It will be more likely to have a question on a broader theme such as the economy itself or a broad area of the economic environment such as government economic policy. (Do look at past papers to get an insight into the type of questions asked. You can do this via the GCE Business Studies section of the AQA website www.aqa.org.uk.) The fact that the essay titles are likely to be relatively broad means you have some freedom to bring in relevant areas within the overall topic. This means, for example, that you want to focus on understanding the key issues within the broader sections of the specification and have relevant evidence to support your understanding more than focusing in on every single specific item at the expense of the 'big picture'. A lot of Unit 4, for example, focuses on the opportunities and threats created by external change; you need to have studied change in the key areas such as the political, economic, social, technological and legal environments and have relevant insights within each one to construct relevant arguments. You should also have studied real businesses and how they have responded to and been affected by change.

The second half of the syllabus for Unit 4 is mainly about factors that influence how a business is affected or how it reacts to change, such as its culture, its leadership, the information it has, the strategy it adopts and how it manages change. Again, it is useful to study real businesses and consider how these influence their success of failure. You should also think about links between topics. How does leadership affect culture and vice versa? How does change link with culture? How does information management link with change, and so on.

In the exam you can respond purely using the context provided in some of the Section B questions but it is also useful to have your own examples to help illustrate different arguments. So to study Unit 4 you do want to keep watching the business news and reading business analysis whenever you can to keep up to date and build a portfolio of cases. It is quite a good idea to start a business diary tracking stories each week, collecting them as they highlight relevant issues. Unit 4 therefore gives you an opportunity to really apply your studies to the real world and to learn from actual business to help deepen your understanding and write better essays. So the key is to read, watch and listen to what is happening in the business environment, think critically about it (debate and discuss in class and with friends) and practise, practise, practise how to write essays.

19 Corporate aims and objectives

This chapter examines what a business is trying to achieve, which is set out in its mission statement, which in turn helps to shape a business's aims and objectives, and the corporate strategies that it adopts. We have considered the concepts of functional objectives and functional strategies in Unit 3, but in Unit 4 we consider these topics at a whole business or corporate level. This chapter also considers the different views that stakeholders may have on strategic decisions and the extent to which such differences may have the potential to cause conflict.

In this chapter we examine:

- the nature and purpose of mission statements
- the corporate aims and objectives that a business may pursue
- the corporate strategies a business may adopt to achieve its aims and objectives
- the different perspectives of different stakeholders on business decisions.

Mission statements

A mission statement sets out what a firm is trying to achieve (that is, the reason it exists). For example, a firm may set out to be 'the lowest-cost producer in the industry' or to 'maximise the returns for our shareholders'. The mission may include a statement of what the firm believes it is, what it values, which markets it wants to compete in and how it intends to compete.

Mission statements commonly focus on:

- what the business wants to be
- the values of the business
- the scope of the firm's activities
- the importance of different groups, such as employees, customers and investors.

The mission of a business will be influenced by:

- the values of the founders – many companies such as Johnson & Johnson and Hewlett-Packard still talk with reverence of their founders and what they believed in
- the values of staff working there today – although they may have been employed because they shared the values of the founders and so these views may overlap, with new staff inevitably some changes occur
- the industry – in some cases the nature of the industry has an impact on what the values need to be to do well. In the music industry a business must value creativity and original thinking for example. A research-based company is likely to think long term and value innovation. WPP is the world's largest marketing business. Its mission is to develop the talents of its employees because it believes that if it does this its profits will increase. In such a knowledge-based industry looking after your people is key.
- society – what is acceptable and desirable and appealing depends on what society is thinking. The growing concern for the environment has put environmental issues into the mission statements of many organisations.
- the ownership of the business. A government-run organisation may have more social values; an employee cooperative will value staff; a business run by private venture capitalists may put more emphasis on short-term profits.

By setting out a mission everyone within the firm knows what they should ultimately be trying to do and what managers regard as important. Employee actions should be directed towards the same thing. This should make decision-making easier: when faced with a series of options managers can compare them in relation to the overall objective, purpose and values of the business. Mission statements can also motivate people – they know exactly why they are there and what the business is trying to achieve, and this can give them a sense of belonging and direction.

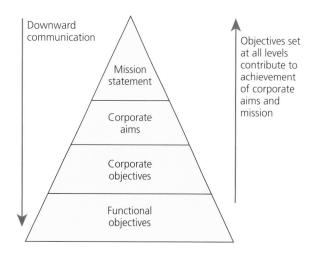

BUSINESS IN FOCUS

The mission has a huge impact on what happens within an organisation.

The BBC mission is to inform, educate and entertain. Note that entertaining is third on the list – and it can do this because it is financed by the taxpayer and so viewer figures do not determine whether a programme is made or not. It has an agenda for information and education as well.

Oxford University Press is part of Oxford University and assesses projects on the basis of how they advance knowledge rather than simply whether they are profitable. Some universities define their mission as to increase human knowledge through research and to teach; teaching comes second to research in terms of priorities. Looking at the mission of a business gives you an insight into what the business truly values.

Question:

What is the mission of your school or college?

However, some mission statements are so unrealistic, or clearly just public relations exercises, that employees pay little attention to them. In some organisations managers clearly ignore the mission statement and so other employees lose faith in it as well. Imagine that the mission of your organisation was supposed to be 'to delight all of our customers', but every time you had an idea to improve customer service it was ruled out on the grounds of cost; you would soon realise that what the managers said they wanted to do was not the same as what they actually wanted to do. A mission statement will only have value, therefore, if the behaviour of everyone within the firm supports it. In these circumstances it can be a powerful way of uniting people and developing a corporate spirit.

At their best mission statements are a clear and concise expression of the purpose of the business and impart a sense of purpose and direction.

'To create value for customers to earn their lifetime loyalty … ' (Tesco).

'To enable people and businesses throughout the world to realize their full potential' (Microsoft).

'To enrich people's lives with programmes and services that inform, educate and entertain' (BBC).

The mission of the business will ultimately depend on the owners and what they want or allow the business to be. However, feeding into the personality and values of the business will be all the other stakeholders. The desire of more businesses to be environmentally friendly for example may be externally influenced as much as internally driven.

Corporate aims and objectives

Corporate aims

The corporate aim is usually part of the mission statement and sets out what a business wants to achieve. An aim gives some sense of the direction in which the business wants to move. Company objectives, which are more specific targets, are derived from this aim. Businesses do not normally state aims as numerical targets, but rather in qualitative terms. For example, the Dutch airline KLM states that its corporate aim is 'to achieve profitable and sustainable growth'. In contrast, Tesco's aims are growth and diversification.

Corporate aims are set by the directors of the business and are intended to provide guidance for setting corporate and functional objectives and also to guide and assist more junior managers in their decision-making. Thus, for example, managers throughout Tesco will take decisions intended to achieve the corporate aims of growth and diversification. In this context opting to open supermarkets in China and to sell electrical products and clothing are all strategic decisions which the company has taken with the intention of meeting its corporate aims.

Downward communication

Objectives set at all levels contribute to achievement of corporate aims and mission

Mission statement

Corporate aims

Corporate objectives

Functional objectives

Figure 19.1 The hierarchy of objectives

From its corporate aims a company can set quantifiable objectives, such as gaining a 35 per cent share of a particular market in Europe within three years.

Corporate objectives

The corporate objectives turn the mission statement into something which is more quantifiable. Rather than simply being a statement of intent, an objective sets out clearly what has to be achieved.

Corporate objectives are medium- to long-term goals established to coordinate the business.

To be effective objectives should be SMART. SMART objectives must be:

Specific – they must define exactly what the firm is measuring, such as sales or profits.

Measurable – they must include a quantifiable target, for example a 10 per cent increase.

Agreed – if targets are simply imposed on people they are likely to resent them; if, however, the targets are discussed and mutually agreed, people are more likely to be committed to them.

Realistic – if the objectives are unrealistic (for example, they are too ambitious) people may not even bother to try and achieve them. To motivate people the targets must be seen as attainable.

Time specific – Employees need to know how long they have to achieve the target – is it three or five years?

An example of a good objective might be: 'to increase profits by 25 per cent over the next four years'. By comparison, a bad objective would be 'to do much better' – it is not clear what 'doing better' actually means, how it will be measured or how long you have to achieve it.

Businesses may have a number of objectives, and some of these are considered below.

Survival

This objective is for the company to continue to trade over a defined period of time, rather than to submit to some form of commercial pressure and be forced to cease trading. This is an important objective, even for the largest of businesses at certain times – for example, Kodak was fighting for survival in 2012. Times when survival becomes a key objective include:

- periods of recession or intense competition
- times of crisis, such as during a hostile takeover bid.

BUSINESS IN FOCUS

Whitbread

In 2011 the new boss of Whitbread announced an aggressive five-year expansion plan for its Premier Inn and Costa Coffee chains, increasing the group's budget for new site openings by 75 per cent to £350 million. Andy Harrison set out a plan to exceed 65,000 hotel rooms in Britain and 3,500 coffee bars worldwide in the next five years. This expansion is equivalent to an almost 50 per cent increase in capacity at Premier Inn, which currently has 43,219 rooms, and nearly doubles the size of the Costa chain.

Costa is competing head to head with Starbucks in a number of fast-growing markets, including China, Russia, Central Europe, the Middle East and India. 'This is an exciting and profitable plan to build on Whitbread's success and to create substantial value for our shareholders,' said Harrison.

Whitbread also plans to open 2,000 more Costa Express self-service kiosks after it bought the vending machine business Coffee Nation for £59.5 million recently. This deal put Costa in the lead in the fast-growing 'self-service' coffee market, which is aimed at consumers who are too busy to queue.

(*Source: Adapted from Zoe Wood and Simon Bowers in* The Guardian, *28 April 2011*)

Question:

Analyse why Whitbread has set such major growth targets. *(10 marks)*

Profit maximisation

Profits are maximised when the difference between sales revenue and total costs is at its greatest. Some firms seek to earn the greatest possible profits to satisfy their shareholders' desire for high dividends. This might be a shorter-term objective. Others may pursue the longer-term objective of providing acceptable levels of dividends, but also growth in the value of the company and therefore in the share price. This can provide shareholders with long-term financial benefits.

Growth

Many businesses pursue growth because their managers believe that the organisation will not survive otherwise. If a firm grows, it should be able to exploit its market position and earn higher profits in the long run, but, due to the cost of expansion, profits may fall in the short term. We saw earlier that Tesco has set itself the aim of growth and this will have been transferred into quantified objectives, possibly relating to sales figures or grocery market share in other countries.

Diversification

Adopting this objective allows a business to spread its risk by selling a range of products (rather than one) or through trading in different markets. Thus, if one product becomes obsolete or a market becomes significantly more competitive, then the alternative products or markets will provide a secure source of revenue for the business while it seeks new projects. Diversification avoids a business having 'all its eggs in one basket' and has been the principle behind the creation of conglomerate businesses such as the Tata group (see page 245).

Improving corporate image

This has become a more important objective for many companies recently. Companies fear that consumers who have a negative view of them will not purchase their products. This applies to any action that damages the company image. Some airlines have pursued this corporate objective for fear of losing customers who believe that they are damaging the environment through their commercial activities.

The objectives pursued by a business vary according to its size, ownership and legal structure. Thus, for example, survival might be important to a newly established firm, and profits to a large public limited company, whereas government-owned organisations may have social objectives such as increasing the number of council houses.

Corporate strategies

A corporate strategy is a long-term plan to achieve the business's corporate objectives. For example, if a firm's target was to increase profits, it might try and do this by reducing costs or by increasing revenue; these would be two strategies to achieve the same goal. Similarly, if a firm was trying to boost overall sales the managers might take a strategic decision to do this by trying to sell more of its existing products or by increasing sales of new products; again these would be two different ways of achieving the same end goal.

Strategies tend to involve a major commitment of resources and are difficult to reverse. For example, the decision to invest in new product development is likely to involve a high level of finance and take several years. Strategic decisions also tend to involve a high level of uncertainty. Over time market conditions often change significantly and so firms must change their strategies to cope with unfamiliar conditions.

The value of producing a clear strategy is that it sets out the firm's overall plan; this helps employees develop their own plans to implement the strategy. If employees know that the firm wants to diversify, for example, they know that it is realistic to consider market opportunities in new segments of the market. In contrast, if they are aware that the strategy is to boost the firm's market presence in a particular region, they are likely to focus on putting more resources into this area.

The decisions made about how to implement the strategy are called 'tactical decisions'. Compared to strategic decisions, tactical decisions tend to:

- be shorter term
- involve fewer resources
- be made more regularly and involve less uncertainty.

BUSINESS IN FOCUS

Sportswear

In recent years JJB Sports plc has struggled to maintain its market share. Its main competitors are JD Sports and Sports Direct. Part of the problem for JJB is that it has lost a clear positioning in the market. JD Sports focuses on fashion – people buying in their stores want sportswear to wear out socially rather than to actually play in. Sports Direct has competed by being a discounter. It has extended the brands it offers and continually has price reductions and sale items. JJB Sports has traditionally positioned itself as 'serious about sport' targeting people who want to use sportswear to actually participate in sports. In recent years, however, the business has lost this clear focus and has engaged in discounting and different stock policies, thereby confusing customers and staff in terms of what it wants to be.

Question:

Think of the clothing market and the stores where students might shop. Analyse how these businesses position themselves differently. (10 marks)

Strategic planning

The strategy for a business usually comes from an internal analysis of the strengths and weaknesses of the position of the business and an analysis of the external business environment and the opportunities and threats that exist. This is known as SWOT analysis. Managers consider the corporate objectives and try to determine the best strategy to adopt given the strengths, weaknesses, opportunities and threats facing the business. This will then be implemented and reviewed.

For more on strategic planning see page 356.

Models of business strategy

There are many models and theories of business strategy. We will consider two in the following section and a further one in 'One step further' on page 249.

Ansoff's matrix

Igor Ansoff developed his matrix in 1957. His matrix measures the degree of risk associated with various growth strategies. The model gives an organisation four strategic options for growth.

1 **Market penetration**: This involves increasing sales of an existing product and thereby penetrating the market further by either promoting the product heavily or reducing prices to increase sales. This may mean increasing revenue by, for example, selling to existing customers.

2 **Product development:** The organisation develops new products to aim within their existing market, in the hope that they will gain more custom and market share. In order to be successful the company will develop and innovate new products in place of existing ones. The new products are sold to existing customers in existing markets. Companies such as Microsoft have adopted this strategy with products such as Xbox Kinect.

3 **Market development:** The organisation here adopts a strategy of selling existing products to new markets. Basically the product remains the same, but it is marketed to a new group of potential buyers. Kellogg's did this when it placed its breakfast cereals into the 'eat healthily anytime' market.

4 **Diversification:** This is the most risky strategy for growth. By diversifying, businesses seek to sell new products to new customers or markets. As the business is unfamiliar with both the products and its customers, the chance of failure is increased. Some organisations diversify quite successfully; Virgin is a well-known example of a business that uses this strategy.

Figure 19.3 Ansoff's matrix

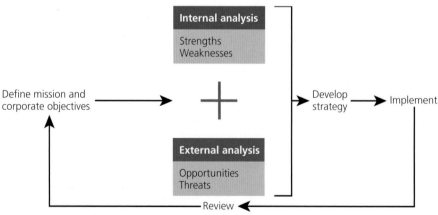

Figure 19.2 Developing a strategy

Mothercare

In 2011, the baby goods retailer Mothercare announced that it would close 110 stores and renegotiate rents on 40 more, in order to focus on its international operations, where sales increased by over 16 per cent last year to £571 million.

Ben Gordon, the chief executive of Mothercare said the 'acceleration' of this strategy was caused by the expiry of 120 shop leases over the next two years. Some 80 per cent of the closures are Early Learning Centre shops – the toy retailer Mothercare bought for £85 million in 2007.

The company said that, given the growth of out-of-town and internet shopping, high-street rents were now too high.

Mr Gordon said Mothercare would focus on developing franchises abroad, where the retailer now has 894 stores in 54 countries, including joint ventures in Australia, China and India. He expected to open 150 shops during 2011, including its first stores in Latin America, in Colombia and Panama.

'In India 24 million babies are born each year and 19 million in China against 700,000 in the UK,' Mr Gordon said. 'If you get a small percentage of that, it's quite a big business.'

Profits in the 'challenging' UK part of the business fell from £36.1 million to £11.1 million in 2011; international profits rose by 18.5 per cent to £27.5 million.

(*Source:* Adapted from *Alistair Osborne in* The Telegraph, *18 May 2011*)

Question:

Discuss the possible reasons why Mothercare might have chosen the strategy outlined above. *(14 marks)*

Tata

Ratan Tata is chairman of the Tata group. This is a conglomerate, meaning it owns a collection of different businesses whose products include cars, consulting, software, steel, tea, coffee, chemicals and hotels. Tata Consultancy Services (TCS) is Asia's largest software company. Tata Steel is India's largest steelmaker and number ten in the world. Taj Hotels Resorts and Palaces is India's biggest luxury hotel group by far. Tata Power is the country's largest private electricity company. Tata Global Beverages is the world's second-largest maker of branded tea. Under Ratan Tata the company became more efficient and centralised. It also expanded abroad aggressively. For example it owns Tetley Tea, Jaguar and Land Rover in the UK.

In all Tata has spent around $20 billion on foreign companies in recent years. It now earns about three-fifths of its revenue abroad and employs more British workers than any other manufacturer.

Question:

Discuss the advantages and disadvantages of a business strategy that focuses on being a conglomerate. *(14 marks)*

Porter's generic strategies

Michael Porter first wrote about his generic strategies in 1985 in *Competitive Advantage: Creating and Sustaining Superior Performance*. Porter's generic strategies are ways of gaining competitive advantage by giving a firm, brand or product an 'edge' that rival products do not have. Porter's generic strategies are shown in Figure 19.4.

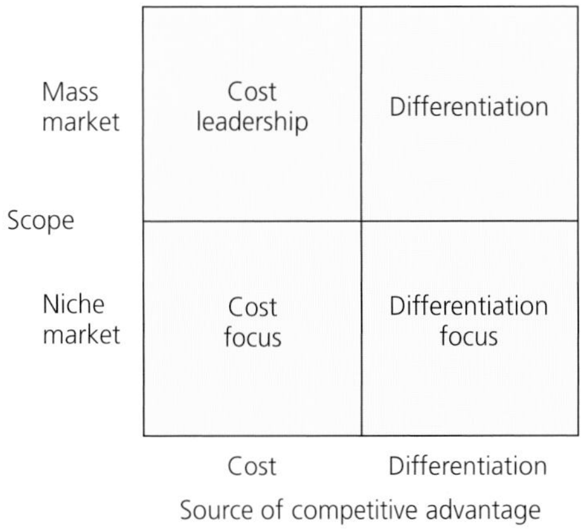

Figure 19.4 Porter's generic strategies

Porter set out three generic strategies.

1 **Cost leadership** through providing basic products at minimum cost. A cost leadership strategy means that a business seeks to produce its products at the *lowest* possible cost. This gives it flexibility in pricing: it can increase market share by selling at prices below those of its rivals and still generate profits; alternatively it can set its prices at the general industry level and reap higher profit margins on each sale. A business adopting this strategy needs to be confident that it can achieve the lowest costs in the industry, perhaps through its scale or by efficient techniques of production or by use of kaizen groups. It is important that competitors will not have access to these same sources of low-cost production or the competitive 'edge' will be lost.

2 **Differentiation** by creating products that are unique. This means that the products might have different features, designs, functions, after-sales support or durability from those offered by rivals. For example, Apple stresses the fact that its latest iPod Nano is thinner than any rival MP3 player. Depending on the type of industry it is in, a business may only be able to sustain a differentiation strategy if it has one or more of the following: an effective research and development department, a highly skilled and efficient workforce able to supply top-quality goods or services, and a good marketing department able to bring the unique features of the product to the attention of the right group of consumers.

3 **Focus** on offering a specialised service in a niche market. Within this strategy Porter identified two elements: focus on cost or focus on differentiation. Businesses using focus strategies target niche markets. SAGA targets its products at consumers who are aged over 50. These products include holidays, insurance and other financial services. This strategy is more likely to succeed when the businesses concerned have a good and clear understanding of the particular consumers they are targeting. A focus strategy has to be in terms of either cost leadership or differentiation. In addition, the focus has to offer something extra that competitors do not provide. SAGA's products are tailored to meet the specific needs of the over 50s, and the company promotes its many years of experience in the market.

Michael Porter was adamant that companies have to choose a particular strategy and not attempt to follow some 'middle course' with elements of more than one strategy. He pointed out that a cost leadership strategy requires a business to look inwards and to examine its internal functions to minimise costs. In contrast, a differentiation strategy calls for a business to look outwards at its customers to meet particular aspects of their needs.

International corporate strategies

A global strategy

A global market is one that is worldwide in scope. There is an increasing number of examples of products which are sold in global markets. Soft drinks such as those produced by Coca-Cola and Pepsi, and sports clothing supplied by Nike or Adidas, are both examples of products sold in global markets. A global market requires firms to compete in all its component markets to be competitive.

To succeed in global markets businesses need to adopt strategies that reflect the particular needs and demands of these markets. Key elements of a global strategy may include the following.

- Being competitive in all markets across the world.
- Producing a standardised product for all markets to benefit from economies of scale.
- Organising and controlling the business from the centre.
- Coordinating activities in different countries and markets to maximise efficiency.
- Seeking to minimise costs in all possible ways, including locating production capacity in low-cost countries.
- Bringing new products to the market ahead of competitors.

A global strategy is most appropriate when global patterns of demand are not dissimilar and a single product (possibly with slight variants) is likely to meet the needs of the global consumer.

A well-designed global strategy can help a business to gain a competitive advantage in some potentially very large markets. The competitive advantage can arise from a number of sources.

- **Efficiency**. This can arise from economies of scale as the business operates in more markets and sells to greater numbers of customers. A global strategy may also derive its efficiency from using cheap resources, such as raw materials or labour, from other nations.
- **Risk**. A global strategy may allow the business to spread operational risks by producing in several

locations, reducing the chance of adverse weather or political unrest disrupting production. The global strategy can also permit a business to operate in numerous economies meaning the chance of an economic downturn in all its markets simultaneously is most unlikely.

- **Reputation**. Businesses operating global strategies may be able to develop a strong brand identity in global markets, encouraging global brand loyalty.

This type of strategy does have drawbacks. It can arouse opposition in some local markets due to a perceived imposition of foreign cultures and loss of differentiated products. The fast-food retailer McDonald's has been criticised on these grounds in a number of countries, notably India and France. Many people regret the development of global and standardised products.

Multi-domestic strategy

Businesses operating a multi-domestic strategy produce different products for different countries and markets. Decisions are taken at a local level wherever possible to allow the business to meet the needs of different customers. This strategy can encourage an entrepreneurial spirit at relatively junior levels in the organisation and high levels of innovation. Activities such as research and development may be conducted in local markets and supplies may be sourced locally.

Japanese car manufacturers have operated highly effective multi-domestic strategies, especially in the lucrative American market. They have customised car designs to meet the tastes of American consumers. For example, Toyota released the Tundra with V8 engines, which look like a heavy-duty pickup truck with a powerful engine. Nissan gave its American employees responsibility for the design and development of most of its vehicles sold in North America.

This strategy is attractive in many ways, in particular as it allows for differentiated products in global markets. However, the most obvious and fundamental drawback is that it increases costs in comparison with a global strategy, as economies of scale are lost.

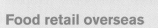

BUSINESS IN FOCUS

Food retail overseas

In 2010 Carrefour decided to close its operations in much of South-East Asia. Its 44 stores in Thailand, 23 in Malaysia and 2 in Singapore were put up for sale.

Carrefour was one of the first overseas food retailers to open stores in the South-East Asia in the 1990s. However, Tesco, although it arrived later, was better at finding out what customers actually wanted. When Tesco discovered that Thai shoppers travelled for miles by bus to its big stores, it opened smaller stores in rural towns. Carrefour focused on the big spenders in the capital Bangkok and kept its hypermarket approach.

Tesco also used local partners, linking with Thai businesses to give it an insight to the market. It has done the same in other markets such as Malaysia. Carrefour, on the other hand, decided to do it all alone and paid the price for this.

Carrefour's chief executive has said he wants to leave markets where Carrefour is not one of the top two retailers because he needs to scale in order to keep prices low. With operations in over 30 countries (nearly twice as many as Tesco) Carrefour may simply have got too big to manage easily.

Question:

Discuss the possible reasons why Tesco may have done better than Carrefour in overseas markets. *(14 marks)*

Different stakeholder perspectives

Whenever a business makes a decision it affects various groups. These are called stakeholders. Any business has a number of stakeholder groups with interest in its affairs. Table 19.1 identifies some of the major groups and some of the interests that they might be expected to have.

Stakeholder group	Possible nature of stakeholders' interest
1 Shareholders	Expectation of regular dividends Rising share prices Preferential treatment as customers – for example through lower prices
2 Employees	Steady and regular income Healthy and safe working conditions Job security Promotion and higher incomes
3 Customers	Certain and reliable supply of goods Stable prices Safe products After-sales service and technical support
4 Suppliers	Frequent and regular orders A sole-supplier agreement Fair prices
5 Creditors	Repayment of money owed at agreed date High returns on investments Minimal risk of failure to repay money owed
6 The local community	Steady employment Minimal pollution and noise Provision of facilities (e.g. scholarships, arts centres or reclaimed areas) for local community

Table 19.1 Stakeholders and their interests

Over recent years businesses have become much more aware of the differing expectations of their stakeholder groups. Previously managers operated businesses largely in the interests of the shareholders. A growing awareness of business activities among the general public has complicated the task of the management team of a business. Today's managers have to attempt to meet the conflicting demands of a number of stakeholder groups. Table 19.1 highlights the different demands stakeholders might place on a business.

The terms 'stakeholders' and 'social responsibility' are interrelated and thus difficult to distinguish. Social responsibility is a business philosophy proposing that firms should behave as good citizens. Socially responsible businesses should not only operate within the law, but should avoid pollution, the reckless use of limited resources or the mistreatment of employees or consumers. Some businesses willingly accept these responsibilities, possibly because their managers want to do so, possibly because they fear a negative public image.

BUSINESS IN FOCUS

Barclays

In 2011 Bob Diamond, Chief Executive of Barclays Bank warned of 'social unrest' unless the UK generated more growth and jobs. He said that banks could play a key role to help but must also apologise for mistakes they had made. Many criticise banks for taking too many risks and causing the recent banking crisis. Diamond said that banks need to show they can contribute to society. They must reconnect with customers and re-build trust.

However, Diamond also said that a lot of the demonisation of banks had been wrong, citing criticism of financial risk-taking. Risk-taking had an important social purpose, he said. When banks put capital at risk, they were providing a market for buyers and sellers in all sections of society. 'Providing this kind of support to clients requires banks to take risk, but this is not speculative trading, so it bothers me when these activities are caricatured as gambling,' he said. 'These activities serve a social purpose and meet a real client need whether they are carried out on behalf of governments, pension funds businesses or individuals.'

The result was that banks played a critical role in supporting businesses and generating jobs and growth. Mr Diamond, whose total pay packet last year was worth £9 million, also said banks should never again have to be bailed out by the taxpayer. 'No taxpayer money should ever again be put at risk to rescue a failed or failing bank,' Mr Diamond said.

(*Source: Adapted from BBC Radio 4, 4 November 2011*)

Question:

Do you think banks are good or bad? Justify your answer.

Every decision will involve different stakeholders and businesses will consider each of their objectives and their relative power. Do they want to listen to them? Do they need to listen to them? What will happen if they ignore them? This means they need to think about their relative power. A well-organised workforce that is unionised, for example, may be able to negotiate for more consultation and participation in decision-making than individual employees could on their own. Businesses may want to pay more attention to an investor who owns 65 per cent of the company compared with one who has 1 per cent. A key supplier of a major component will have more influence than the supplier of a component which can be bought in thousands of stores. So the more a business needs a particular stakeholder, the more it likes or agrees with them and their objectives, the more likely the stakeholder is to influence its decisions.

The ways in which different stakeholders may be treated by managers can be shown using a stakeholder map (Figure 19.5).

Stakeholder groups in quadrant D are likely to influence decisions a lot. They are interested in what is going on in the business and are very powerful (for example, a major investor); you will need to keep this group happy.

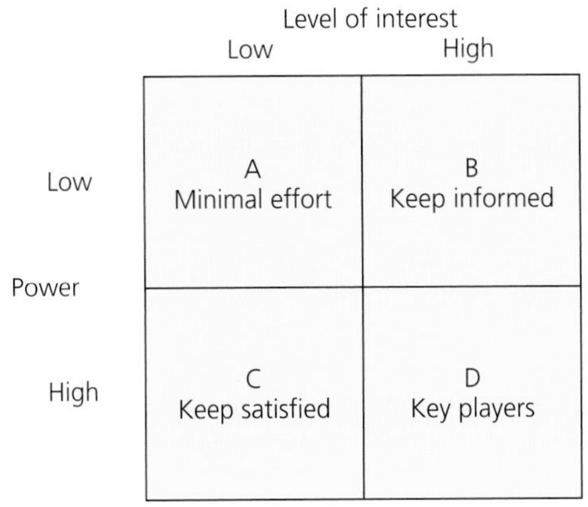
Level of interest
Low
High
Low
Power
High
A
Minimal effort
B
Keep informed
C
Keep satisfied
D
Key players

Figure 19.5 A stakeholder map

By comparison, stakeholders in quadrant A are not very interested and are not powerful (for example, your milk delivery service or local newsagent); you do not need to worry much about this group. Obviously over time the relative interest of different groups may change – you may not be bothered about a new building project until it ends up being planned next to your house. The power of different groups can also change – for example legislation might limit trade union action, reducing employee power, or by grouping together individuals may gain more bargaining power.

There are many ways in which the strategies adopted by businesses may cause conflict between stakeholder groups. For example, a business pursuing what Porter would identify as cost leadership would aim to generate high returns for its shareholders through increasing profitability. However, this may entail paying minimal wages to employees and also seeking to minimise other costs related to employment, such as expenditure on training and pensions.

Equally, a strategy of differentiation may entail a business investing heavily in research and development to create innovative goods or in training staff to provide the highest-quality services. In either case such strategies may result in reductions in short-term profitability. Thus, employees may be satisfied with such a strategy but shareholders seeking a quick return on their investment may be dissatisfied.

Summary

The mission of a business sets out what it wants to be. The business must turn this general aim into specific targets and then develop the strategy to achieve this. The possible strategic approaches can be examined using the Ansoff matrix or Porter's strategies. Decisions about strategies may depend on the impact on different stakeholders, the ability of stakeholders to influence decisions and the underlying objectives and values of the business.

One step further: the balanced scorecard

The balanced scorecard was developed by R S Kaplan and D P Norton and first published in the *Harvard Business Review* in 1992.

A balanced scorecard can be defined as 'a strategic planning and management system used to align business activities to the mission statement of an organisation'. A balanced scorecard attempts to help to manage the business better at all levels in pursuit of the company's mission statement.

The scorecard looks at the financial and non-financial elements of a business's operations from a variety of perspectives. To use the balanced scorecard path a management team first must know (and understand) the company's mission statement (its purpose or vision).

The four perspectives that the balanced scorecard considers are:

- the financial perspective
- the internal business perspective: how its internal processes are operating
- the employee perspective (are employees learning new skills? Is communication effective so they can solve problems quickly? Are they being innovative?)
- the customer perspective.

Taking this approach allows managers to look at the business from four important perspectives and gives a 'balanced' picture of its overall performance. This highlights the aspects of the business's activities that need to be improved. The balanced scorecard includes both quantitative and qualitative measures and links the assessment of the business's performance to the strategy that it has adopted.

The scorecard produces a balance between the four key business perspectives and how the organisation views itself and how others see it. In some senses it brings together the notion of strategy and the different perspectives of stakeholders.

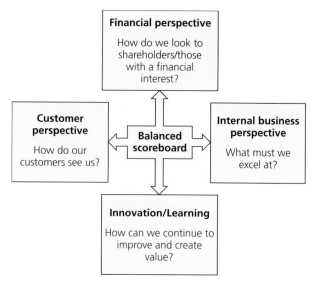

Figure 19.6 The balanced scorecard

Examiner's advice

You should look to master a number of theories and models relating to all aspects of Unit 4. The style of question here will not be to ask you to write about a specific theory or model, so having a range of theories and models such as Porter and Ansoff at your fingertips will be a distinct advantage in developing arguments and making judgements.

Table 19.1 shows the primary stakeholders for most businesses, but a number of others exist. When writing about stakeholders it is important to develop answers fully. This is impossible if you attempt to cover too many stakeholder groups – just concentrate on a small number of the ones that are most relevant to the circumstances.

1 Distinguish between a mission statement and a corporate aim. *(5 marks)*
2 What benefits might a large multinational company gain from having a mission statement? *(7 marks)*
3 Explain **two** criticisms of mission statements. *(6 marks)*
4 Explain the relationship between corporate aims and corporate strategies. *(6 marks)*
5 Why might oil companies such as BP pursue a corporate objective of improving their corporate images? *(8 marks)*

6 How might Ansoff's matrix assist managers in assessing the risk of a particular strategy? *(7 marks)*
7 Outline Michael Porter's generic strategy of cost leadership. *(6 marks)*
8 Why did Porter argue that a business should not try to mix strategies of cost leadership and differentiation? *(6 marks)*
9 In what ways might the objectives of Marks & Spencer plc's shareholders and employees differ? *(6 marks)*
10 How might a strategy of cost leadership lead to conflict between stakeholders? *(8 marks)*

Essay questions

1 Some businesses, such as Marks & Spencer plc, seem to believe that it is important to take account of stakeholders when making decisions. To what extent should stakeholders matter to a business? Justify your answer with reference to Marks & Spencer plc and/or other organisations you know. *(40 marks)*
2 Businesses such as Mont Blanc pens and BMW focus on differentiating their offering from their competitors. To what extent do you think this is the best strategy for a business to pursue? *(40 marks)*
3 The mission of British Airways is 'to fly and to serve'. To what extent does the mission statement of a business influence its success? Justify your answer with reference to British Airways and/or other organisations you know. *(40 marks)*

Candidate's answer:

A mission statement sets out the purpose of an organisation and why it exists. It may include something on the values of the business and what the business believes in. A mission statement can send messages to employees and other stakeholders about what the business thinks is important and therefore how they should behave. BA could easily focus on being an airline and just flying planes; it could invest in equipment to make the planes faster or more fuel efficient or just fun to fly. However, the mission makes it

clear to everyone that the aim is not just about flying but about service. This means the business will think about what customers want, not just what the airlines wants. Customers may be more concerned about check-in time than saving a few minutes flight time. Customers may want comfort even if it makes the plane a bit heavier and slower. Customers meet cabin crew not the pilots and so the vital role of cabin crew must be recognised by the company; if they give all the rewards to the pilots and fail to recognise the cabin crew they will not fulfil their mission.

This mission statement will therefore influence the functional objectives of the business. Marketing will be looking at customer services, HR will be thinking about training for customer service, and operations will think about which aspects of the flying process matter most to customers. Making sure the baggage ends up in good order at the right place may be crucial whereas fitting a new engine may not in itself be of interest to customers.

The mission statement can therefore affect success because it affects behaviour and can set out in broad terms what the business sets out to be and how it wants to do it. However, it is not just having a mission statement, it is making sure it has an impact – you can write as many mission statements as you wish but ultimately the key thing is whether these bed in and are believed ➞

and pursued by people with the business. How you reward people, what you reward people for, what you praise, what you punish, what you give resources to will all reinforce or conflict with the mission. So we need to see if BA does actually reward good customer service and if this issue features in decision-making within the business.

However, the mission does not guarantee success. However good it is and however much it is pursued success is relative and therefore you must think about how you are doing relative to others. This will depend on your strategy – if BA focuses on long haul flights while customers want short haul it has a problem (although you might argue this means it is not serving customers so its mission would have helped avoid this situation occurring). If Ryanair undercuts or opens more routes this is also a problem and the mission of BA in itself may do little to protect it against such action. So the macro- and micro-environments matter and a successful business will navigate its way through such change. Focusing on the customer as well as operations sounds a good start but it has to be implemented and linked with other factors such as the marketing and management of the finances.

Examiner's comments:

A great essay. It is linked throughout to BA and deals with the value of a mission statement but also its limitations very well. The candidate is well informed and develops arguments in the context of the airline industry effectively. A very strong response.

20 Businesses and the economic environment

This chapter introduces you to a range of economic factors and considers the possible effects of changes in these factors on different types of large businesses. The chapter encourages you to think about the positive as well as the negative consequences of changes in these external factors and to reflect on the ways in which different businesses will be affected. Throughout this chapter we will consider the strategies that large businesses may deploy in response to changes in the economic environment.

In this chapter we examine:

- recent trends in key economic variables
- the impact of economic variables on different types of businesses
- the effects of globalisation and developments in emerging markets
- the strategic responses of businesses to changes in the economic environment.

The economic environment and business strategy

A business's strategy is simply the long-term plans through which it seeks to attain its corporate objectives – i.e. the objectives of the whole business. For example, a business may have growth as a major corporate objective and will develop plans to achieve the desired rate of growth. These plans may include increasing innovation as part of the development of new products, entering new markets or pursuing a policy of takeovers and mergers. Figure 20.1 summarises the major economic variables that might impact upon strategic planning and decision-making. The diagram also emphasises the interrelationships that exist between the elements that make up the economic environment for businesses.

Factors such as interest and exchange rates, the business cycle, inflation and unemployment combine to shape one aspect of the environment within which businesses operate. Thus, as the economy moves through the various stages of the trade cycle rates of inflation and unemployment may change.

Equally, interest rates may be adjusted to dampen the effects of the business cycle creating further implications for firms. Finally, the strategic decisions taken by businesses in response to opportunities and constraints that appear in the economic environment also determine that environment. Thus a decision to rationalise because the economy is moving into recession may contribute to the economic downturn.

The business cycle

All countries suffer fluctuations in the level of activity within their economies. At times spending, output and employment all rise; during other periods the opposite is true. The value of a country's output over a period of time is measured by a nation's gross domestic product (GDP) – this figure is dependent upon the level of economic activity. A rising level of economic activity will be reflected in a higher level of GDP.

The business cycle describes the regular fluctuations in economic activity (and GDP) occurring over time in economies. Figure 20.2 illustrates a typical business cycle.

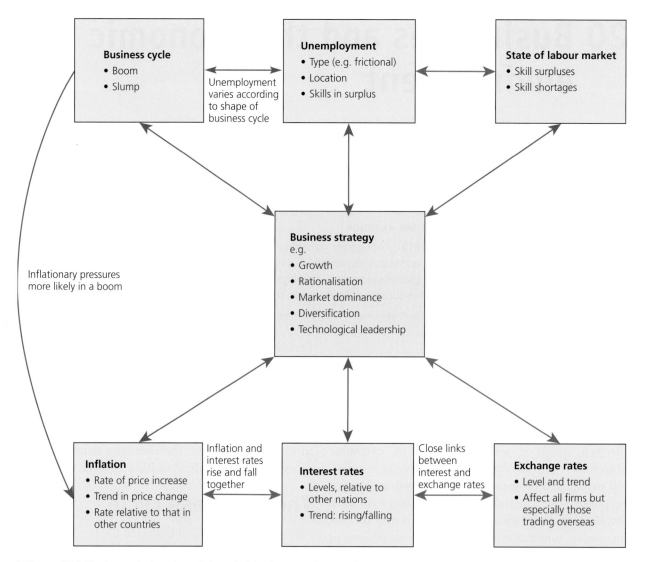

Figure 20.1 Business strategy in an integrated business environment

Trade cycles generally have four stages:

- **Recovery or upswing** as the economy recovers from a slump production and employment both begin to increase. Consumers will generally spend more in these circumstances as they are more confident in the security of their employment. Initially businesses may respond cautiously to signs of increasing consumer confidence. No major decisions are required to meet rising demand while spare capacity exists: firms simply begin to utilise idle factories, offices and other assets. As business confidence increases firms may take the decision to invest in further non-current assets (factories, machinery and vehicles, for example). Employees experience less difficulty in finding jobs and wages may begin to rise.

- **A boom** follows with high levels of production and expenditure by firms, consumers and the government. Booms are normally characterised by prosperity and confidence in the business community. Investment in fixed assets is likely to increase at such times. However, many sectors of the economy will experience pressure during booms. Skilled workers may become scarce and firms competing for workers may offer higher wages. Simultaneously, as the economy approaches maximum production, shortages and bottlenecks will occur as insufficient raw materials and components exist to meet demand. Inevitably this will result in their prices rising. The combination of rising wages and rising prices of raw materials and components will create inflation. It is the existence of inflation that usually leads to the end of a boom.

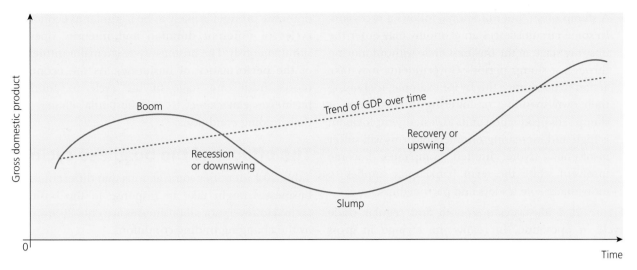

Figure 20.2 The stages of the business cycle

- **A recession** occurs when incomes and output start to fall. Rising prices of labour and materials mean that businesses face increased costs of production. This will begin to eat into their profits. In circumstances such as this the UK government has tended to raise interest rates in an attempt to avoid inflation. Falling profits and rising interest rates are likely to lead to plans to invest in new factories and offices being delayed or abandoned. The level of production in the economy as a whole may stagnate or even fall. The amount of spare capacity within the economy will rise. Some businesses will fail and the level of bankruptcies is likely to rise.

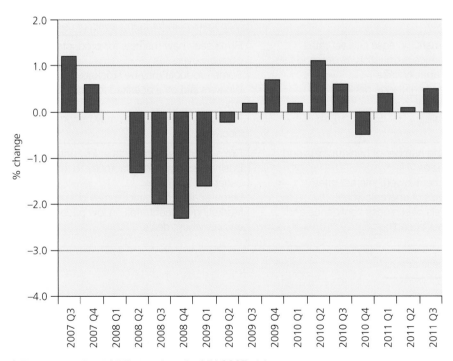

Figure 20.3 Real GDP growth in the UK 2007–11

(Source: National Statistics Online)

Note: *This quarterly data has been adjusted to remove the effects of rising prices so that the underlying trend is revealed. This is why the data is described as 'real'. Gross domestic product fell by 0.5 per cent in the fourth quarter of 2010, compared to 0.6 per cent growth in the previous quarter.*

- A **slump** often, but not always, follows a recession. In some circumstances an economy may enter the upswing stage of the business cycle without moving through a slump period. Governments may take action to encourage this by for example, increasing their own spending or lowering interest rates. A slump sees production at its lowest, unemployment is high and increasing numbers of firms will suffer insolvency. (Note: limited companies become insolvent while the term bankruptcy applies to individuals, sole traders and partnerships.)

Figure 20.2 illustrates a smooth and regular trade cycle in operation. In reality the change in gross domestic product is likely to be irregular as economic cycles of different duration and intensity operate simultaneously. The business cycle is a major influence of the performance of businesses. As the economy moves from one stage of the cycle to another, businesses can expect to see substantial changes in their trading conditions.

The effects of the business cycle

Table 20.1 identifies some actions that different large businesses might take in response to the business cycle. However, not all businesses are equally affected by the changing trading conditions.

Stage of business cycle	Key features	Likely reactions by businesses
Recovery or upswing	Increasing consumer expenditure Existing spare capacity used Production rises Business confidence strengthens Investment increases	Opportunity to charge higher prices Rising numbers of business start-ups Businesses take decisions to invest in fixed assets Business operate nearer to (or at) full capacity
Boom	Rate of inflation increases Bottlenecks in supply of materials and components Some firms unable to satisfy demand Profits probably high – but hit by rising costs	Firms face increasing pressure to increase prices Businesses seek alternative methods to increase output Wage rises offered to retain or attract skilled labour Managers plan for falling levels of demand
Recession	Government increase interest rates Firms reduce production as demand falls Spare capacity rises Business confidence declines and investment is cut Profits fall	Firms seek new markets for products – possibly overseas Some products may be stockpiled Workers laid off – or asked to work short-time Financially insecure firms may become insolvent
Slump	Increasing number of bankruptcies and insolvencies Government lowers interest rates High levels of unemployment Low levels of business confidence and consumer spending	Firms offer basic products at low prices. Businesses may close factories to reduce capacity Large-scale redundancies may occur Marketing concentrates on low prices and easy payment deals

Table 20.1 The trade cycle and business actions

A number of businesses may find that demand for their products are relatively unaffected as the business cycle moves through its stages. Producers and retailers of basic foodstuffs, public transport and water services may notice little change in demand for their products. This is because these are essential items consumers continue to purchase even when their incomes are falling – demand for them is not sensitive to changes in income.

Demand for other categories of products is more sensitive to changes in income levels and therefore the stages of the business cycle. Examples include foreign holidays, electrical products such as televisions and MP3 players and construction materials such as bricks and windows.

Thus, firms selling basic foodstuffs might have to take little or no action to survive a recession; in fact demand for their products might increase as consumers switch from more expensive alternatives. At the other extreme businesses supplying materials to the construction industry could be hard hit as firms delay or abandon plans to extend factories and build new offices. Their position might be made worse by a fall in demand for new houses as hard-up consumers abandon schemes to move home.

Government policy and the business cycle

Governments attempt to offset the most extreme effects of the business cycle. The UK government is no exception in this respect and it took a number of high profile actions in an attempt to lessen the effects of the recession that occurred in 2008–2009. The government implements counter-cyclical policies to limit the fluctuations in gross domestic product and hence the consequences of these fluctuations for businesses. These counter-cyclical policies have implications for businesses in the same way that the business cycle does.

In a slump the government seeks to lessen the impact of falling confidence amongst businesses and declining expenditure by individuals and businesses. By reducing interest rates and possibly cutting the level of taxes paid by individuals and businesses the level of economic activity may remain relatively stable. Recent governments have favoured reducing interest rates in the expectation that they will encourage firms to undertake investment programmes as borrowing money becomes cheaper. Similarly consumers may spend more if credit is less expensive. In March 2009

the Bank of England reduced its base rate (which influences most other interest rates in the economy) to 0.5 per cent. This was its lowest rate ever.

At the other extreme a boom may result in governments raising interest rates in an attempt to lower the level of economic activity. Higher interest rates are likely to discourage investment by businesses and spending by consumers. Reducing expenditure in this way can assist in avoiding resources becoming too scarce as firms attempt to produce more than available resources will allow.

Businesses need to take into account the likely effects of counter-cyclical policies when considering their responses to changing trading conditions brought about by the business cycle. Such counter-cyclical policies can be beneficial as they avoid the need for firms to prepare for the worst excesses of boom and slump.

Business strategy and the business cycle

The business cycle is a permanent feature of the economic environment for firms, and one that is receiving a great deal of publicity at the time of writing (December 2011). Many economists fear that the UK may be facing a prolonged recovery or upswing stage or that it may slip back into recession. The effects of changes in the business cycle vary from industry to industry. Firms selling goods whose demand is sensitive to changes in income (known as income-elastic goods) such as designer clothes and foreign holidays may find that sales rise in a boom and fall

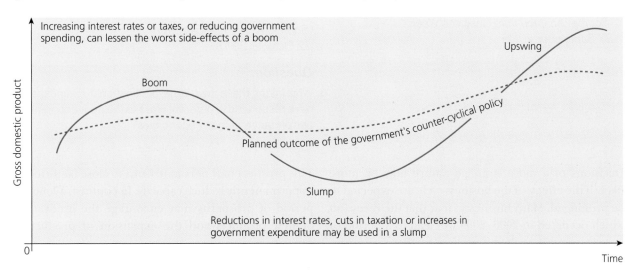

Figure 20.4 Counter-cyclical policies and the business cycle

during recession. Conversely, businesses selling staple products such as foodstuffs where demand is not income-elastic, may be relatively unaffected by the business cycle.

The business cycle may only provoke short-term responses in many firms, because its effects are relatively short-lived, though this may not be the case over the next few years. Booms and slumps do not last for ever and businesses can take actions to see them through difficult trading periods. During boom periods managers may increase prices to restrict demand and increase profitability; they may subcontract work to other firms or seek supplies from overseas. Equally, in conditions of recession or slump, lay-offs may occur or short-time working may take place while overseas markets are targeted to increase sales. Well-managed firms will predict the onset of a boom or slump and take appropriate action in advance. Short-term responses may be all that are required if governments are successful in eradicating the more extreme effects of the business cycle.

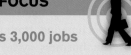

BUSINESS IN FOCUS

BAE Systems cuts 3,000 jobs in the UK

BAE Systems plc has announced 3,000 job losses in the UK to end a century of aircraft manufacturing at a site in Lancashire as it slows fighter-jet production. About 900 jobs will go at Brough and BAE is also cutting more than 1,400 positions at two other facilities in northern England.

'These job losses are the unintended consequence of government austerity measures,' said Jason Adams, an analyst at Nomura International. 'The defence industry is in a state of excess capacity, and I'd expect further consolidation and restructuring.'

BAE has cut about 2,500 jobs in each of the last two years as it scales back production to adapt to falling defence budgets. The company's customers (mainly governments) are under 'huge pressure' to reduce their spending, and BAE has had to 'significantly' change some of its plans, chief executive officer Ian King said.

(*Source: Adapted from* Business Week, *27 September 2011*)

Seat unveils temporary layoff for 700 Spanish workers

Seat, the ailing Spanish subsidiary of German auto giant Volkswagen, unveiled a new temporary layoff plan on Friday that would affect 700 workers from its 7,500-strong plant at Martorell near Barcelona. Workers over the age of 53 and those who do not qualify for unemployment benefits will be excluded from the temporary layoffs, which will last for up to seven months.

This is the fifth temporary layoff plan at Seat's plant at Martorell since the company announced in 2008 that it would reduce production at the plant due to the downturn in demand for new cars due to the global economic downturn.

Seat has been hit hard by a fall in demand in Spain since the country was plunged into its worst recession in decades during the second half of 2008 due to the collapse of a property bubble.

New car sales in Spain plunged 26.9 per cent in 2010.

(*Source:* AFP, *Expatica.com, 22 October 2010*)

Question:

Why might these two large multinational businesses have responded in different ways to the poor economic performance in many economies?

Decisions of a more strategic nature may be more likely if the effects of the business cycle are expected to be prolonged. Many businesses fear that the recession which occurred in 2008–2009 will lead to a period of low economic growth and perhaps further recessions. This prospect may persuade firms to close factories or to permanently reduce capacity. In contrast, a lengthy period of prosperity may encourage the innovation of new products and the expansion of productive capacity as consumers' income rises.

Interest rates

The rate of interest can best be described as the price of borrowed money. Most textbooks and newspapers refer to the interest rate as if there is only a single rate. In fact there are a range of interest rates operating in the UK economy at any time. However, the base rate of interest is set officially and all other interest rates relate to this.

In May 1997 the government gave the Bank of England responsibility for setting interest rates. The Bank of England's Monetary Policy Committee (MPC) meets each month and takes decisions on whether to alter the base rate of interest.

Rates of interest normally vary according to the period of time over which the money is borrowed and the degree of risk attached to the loan. Changes in interest rates have significant effects on businesses and the environment in which they operate. For many years UK governments relied heavily upon interest rates to control the level of economic activity in the economy and to avoid the worst effects of the business cycle. However, rates have been set at 0.5 per cent since March 2009, offering little scope for further reductions and forcing governments to consider other options.

Interest rates and consumer spending

Interest rates affect the level of spending by UK citizens. The level of their spending is dependent upon interest rates for a number of reasons.

- Consumers are more likely to take a decision to save during a period in which interest rates are rising. The return on their saving is greater and will persuade some consumers to postpone spending decisions. Conversely when rates are falling consumers might save less and spend more.
- Changes in interest rates alter the cost of borrowing. Many goods are purchased on credit – electrical goods, cars and caravans and satellite TV systems. If rates fall then the cost of purchasing these goods on credit will decline persuading more people to buy the product. Demand for consumer durables are sensitive to interest rate rises and sales of these products decline significantly following an upward movement in the base rate.
- An increasing number of UK consumers have mortgages. A rise in interest rates will increase the amount paid each month by householders. This reduces the income available for expenditure on other products. Demand for a range of products will fall in these circumstances. A fall in rates will have the opposite effect.

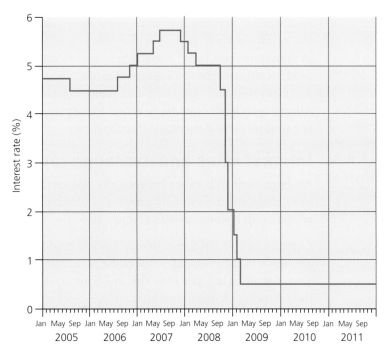

Figure 20.5 The base rate in the UK, January 2005 to December 2011

- Britain's population is steadily ageing, meaning that more people are dependent upon pensions and savings. This means that their income is highly dependent upon the rate of interest and this makes consumer expenditure highly sensitive to rate changes.

Businesses and changes in interest rates

Interest rates affect businesses in a number of ways. It is not simply a case of whether they rise or fall: businesses also take into account the overall level of rates. Thus a small increase in interest rates may have little impact if rates are low. This is unlikely to be the case when rates are high before the change is introduced.

- A change in interest rates will affect a firm's decisions on investment and expansion. Thus rising rates may cause the postponement or cancellation of investment plans. Businesses may decide to invest in other countries if they feel that interest rates may be volatile or high relative to other countries.
- Changing interest rates affect consumers' spending decisions. As a result of increasing interest rates consumers may decide to save more (attracted by high rates) or to delay spending decisions requiring borrowing. Purchases of products such as cars, white goods (fridges and cookers, for example) and televisions are sensitive to changes in interest rates. Consumers may demand more of these products when interest rates fall.
- Interest rates also affect the value of the pound in terms of other currencies. Increases in interest rates tend to exert upward pressure on exchange rates; similarly falling rates encourage the value of the pound to decline. Thus rising interest rates may make it more difficult for exporters to sell their products overseas. We will consider the effects of exchange rates on business strategy more fully later in this unit. Figure 20.6 illustrates the relationship between interest rates and exchange rates.

Businesses tend to take a long-term view of interest rates. Rates can be altered each month, and strategic decisions are rarely taken on the basis of factors that may alter again within a month or two. However, a country with a reputation for having persistently high rates, or for interest rate volatility, may be unattractive to businesses. Volatile rates make long-term planning more difficult. Unpredictable changes in interest rates may have significant effects on domestic demand and the exchange rate (in turn affecting overseas consumers). In these circumstances firms may seek to relocate overseas and diversify into products for which demand is less dependent upon interest rates.

Not all businesses are equally affected. A number of types of businesses are particularly susceptible to changes in interest rates. These include the following.

- Businesses supplying luxury products such as sports cars, jewellery and expensive hotel accommodation. These sorts of products will be amongst the first to be cut from consumers' budgets following a rise in interest rates and become attractive to consumers following a fall in rates.
- Businesses who are heavily involved in overseas trade. Interest rate changes influence exchange rates and this, as we shall see later, directly determines the prices of exports and imports.
- Businesses whose products are frequently purchased on credit. Prices on goods purchased in this way fluctuate directly with the rate of interest. Thus a rise in rates may lead to a significant fall in sales of fitted kitchens as the increased interest charges mean consumers have to pay more.

Clearly any business's response to rising rates will depend to some degree on the extent to which its sales are sensitive to changes in interest rates. Suppliers of fuels and basic foodstuffs may take little or no action to maintain sales revenue. Those offering products on credit or luxuries are more likely to respond by use of tactics such as interest-free periods of credit or 'buy now, pay later' deals. These techniques are used extensively by businesses manufacturing and supplying personal computers and domestic furniture. Alternatively businesses might accept lower prices and reduced profits – if they can afford to do so.

Interest rates and exchange rates

An important link exists between the domestic rate of interest and the value of a nation's currency. This relationship is summarised in Figure 20.6.

Changes in the UK's rate of interest will lead to an alteration in the exchange value of the pound sterling. Thus following a 1 per cent rise in UK interest rates the following changes could occur:

- the value of one pound rises against the US dollar, e.g. from $1.54 to $1.65 and
- the pound is worth more in terms of the euro, e.g. rising from €1.20 to €1.30.

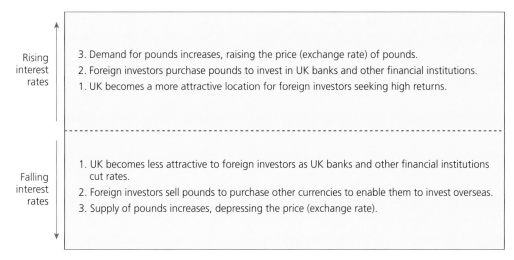

| Rising interest rates | 3. Demand for pounds increases, raising the price (exchange rate) of pounds.
2. Foreign investors purchase pounds to invest in UK banks and other financial institutions.
1. UK becomes a more attractive location for foreign investors seeking high returns. |
| Falling interest rates | 1. UK becomes less attractive to foreign investors as UK banks and other financial institutions cut rates.
2. Foreign investors sell pounds to purchase other currencies to enable them to invest overseas.
3. Supply of pounds increases, depressing the price (exchange rate). |

Figure 20.6 The relationship between interest rates and the exchange value of the pound

When interest rates rise the pound will increase in value against most foreign currencies. Similarly a reduction in interest rates causes a fall in the exchange value of the pound.

As interest rates fall in relation to the rates available in other countries, the UK will become a less attractive target for international investment. Foreigners with money to invest will be tempted by the high returns available from banks in other countries. To take advantage of the relatively higher rates overseas, investors will withdraw funds from UK banks to invest abroad. To do this they will have to exchange their sterling for the currency of the country in which they wish to invest. This will mean that an increased supply of sterling will be put onto the world's currency markets. As with most products an increase in the supply of pounds will tend to lower its price – in this case the exchange rate.

Exchange rates

An exchange rate is simply the price of one currency expressed in terms of another. Thus, at a particular time, £1 may be worth US$1.45 or 2,900 Japanese Yen.

London is one of the premier international centres for buying and selling foreign currencies: each day transactions total billions of pounds. Exchange rates between most currencies vary regularly according to the balance of supply and demand for each individual currency.

Why do firms buy foreign currencies?

The main reason businesses purchase foreign currencies is to pay for goods and services bought from overseas. Firms purchasing products from abroad are normally expected to pay using the currency of the exporting country. For example, Sainsbury's purchases wine from Chile. Chilean wine producers would expect to be paid in their local currency – Chilean pesos (Ch$). Thus traders acting on behalf of Sainsbury's would sell pounds sterling in order to buy pesos on the foreign exchange market. This process is illustrated in Figure 20.7.

Demand for foreign currencies may also arise because individuals and businesses wish to invest in enterprises overseas. Thus a UK citizen wishing to invest in a South African business will require South African rands to complete the transaction.

The effects of exchange rate changes

Exchange rates can change significantly over time. A rise in the value of a currency is termed appreciation; a decline in its value is called depreciation.

In May 2011 £1 exchanged for ¥10.9 (Chinese yuan). Just six months later, in November 2011 the exchange rate was £1 = ¥9.8. This meant that the value of the pound had depreciated by just over 10 per cent over the period. Alternatively, the value of the Chinese yuan had increased (or appreciated) by the same amount.

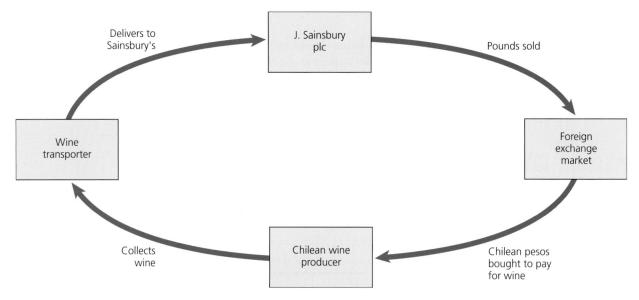

Figure 20.7 The operation of the foreign exchange market

The exchange rate of pounds	Prices of UK exports overseas (in foreign currencies)	Prices of imported goods in the UK (in pounds)
Appreciates (rises)	Increase	Fall
Depreciates (falls)	Fall	Increase

Table 20.2 The effects of changes in the value of sterling

Changes in the value of currencies affect the prices of exports and imports as shown in Table 20.2.

Using the information in Table 20.2 we can see that the fall in the value of the pound against the Chinese yuan during 2011 could have had the following effects.

- Prices of UK exports to China (for example Scotch whisky) would have fallen by approximately 10 per cent.
- Chinese imports to the UK would have been up to 10 per cent more expensive. However, the price the Chinese received in yuan would not have changed. It is likely, however, that because prices were lower in the UK they would sell greater quantities of their products.

Small changes in the UK's exchange rate occur all the time as demand for the currency and supplies of it alter. A series of slight rises and falls over a period of time is not necessarily a major problem for industry. Of more concern is a sustained rise or fall in the exchange rate – or a sudden and substantial change in the exchange rate.

Exchange rate changes can create uncertainty for a number of reasons.

- If firms agree deals priced in foreign currencies, they may receive more or less revenue from a particular transaction than expected if the exchange rate alters in the intervening period. Thus, a deal to sell whisky to China, may give Scottish distillers less revenue than anticipated if the contract is agreed in terms of yuan and the pound then rises in value against the Chinese yuan. In these circumstances the amount of yuan stated in the contract will convert into a smaller number of pounds, causing a shortfall for the exporter.
- Changing exchange rates can affect prices and sales in overseas markets, even if the exporter avoids direct exchange risk by insisting on payment in domestic currency. For example, a London-based clothes designer may sell clothes overseas, but stipulate that they are paid in pounds sterling. A rise in the value of the pound may mean that foreign retailers are forced to increase the prices of the clothes to maintain profit margins. As a consequence sales may be lower than expected

giving the London-based design company less revenue than forecast.

- Competitors may respond in unexpected ways to exchange rate changes. Foreign firms may reduce prices to offset the effects of an exchange rate change, putting rivals under pressure to do the same or lose market share.

Price elasticity can be an important part of a discussion on the possible effects of exchange rate changes. If overseas demand for a product is price-inelastic, then an increase in the exchange rate may not be too harmful. It might be that the Chinese will continue to buy Scotch whisky when the price rises. In this case demand may alter little. If demand is price-elastic exporters might be badly affected by a rise in the exchange rate, but benefit greatly from a fall.

Business strategy and exchange rates

Fluctuations in exchange rates create a great deal of uncertainty for businesses trading internationally. When exchange rates are volatile, businesses become uncertain about earnings from overseas trade. This adds to the risk businesses incur as part of their trading activities.

Firms like to operate in a relatively risk-free environment and to reduce uncertainty. The undesirable consequences of exchange rate changes can be reduced through the use of techniques such as forward foreign currency markets. This sets a guaranteed exchange rate at some future date (when transactions are completed) meaning that the amount received from overseas trading is more certain. However, fixing an exchange rate in this way does not guarantee a particular level of sales. Furthermore, the bank arranging this service may require a fee.

How might UK firms respond to a rising value of the pound?	How might UK firms respond to a falling value of the pound?
EXPORTERS	**EXPORTERS**
Allow price to rise in foreign markets reducing probable sales. Remember exporters receive the same price in pounds for each overseas sale, but will sell less in this situation.	Exporters could allow prices to fall in overseas markets as a result of the exchange rate change. They will receive the same amount in pounds from each sale but should achieve higher sales.
Leave prices unchanged in overseas markets. Sales should be unchanged but the exporter will receive fewer pounds from each sale.	Increase their prices to maintain price levels in terms of the foreign currency. Sales should remain constant (depending on competitors' actions) and revenue should rise in pounds as a result.
(Neither of these options is attractive to exporters – rising exchange rates are bad news.)	
DOMESTIC PRODUCERS	**DOMESTIC PRODUCERS**
Reduce prices to compete with cheaper imports. Enjoy the benefits of cheaper imports of materials and components.	Enjoy increased sales as a result of rising prices of competitors' imported products, assuming foreign businesses do not hold prices down.
Emphasise other elements in the marketing mix, for example, the quality of the product.	Increase prices (to some extent) to enjoy increased revenues from each sale.
	Beware the increased cost of imported raw materials and components.

Table 20.3 Changes in exchange rates

Exchange rate changes are more of a problem in markets where fierce price competition occurs. In these circumstances demand is more likely to be price elastic and businesses are under pressure to respond quickly to any change in exchange rates.

UK manufacturers gloomy

UK manufacturers are gloomy about the future with expectations of a significant fall in activity over the next three months. Ian McCafferty, the Confederation of British Industry's (CBI's) chief adviser commented that manufacturers' expectations are at their lowest since the height of the recession in 2008.

The CBI said manufacturing orders and output are expected to fall over the next quarter, following modest rises in domestic demand and production over the past three months. Expectations about both the general business situation and export prospects fell for the second consecutive quarter, with significant majorities of firms reporting that they were less optimistic than three months ago. 'Confidence among manufacturers is no doubt also being sapped by uncertainty over developments in the eurozone, leading to broader concerns over global growth,' said McCafferty.

The CBI said that of the 446 manufacturers responding to the latest Quarterly Industrial Trends Survey, 30 per cent said that domestic orders rose in the three months to October 2011 and 25 per cent said that they fell. Over the same period, export orders were flat (a balance of +1 per cent), in line with expectations. This has taken place at a time when the value of the pound has weakened against those of major trading partners such as the US and China.

(*Source: Adapted from Moneymarket.com, 27 October 2011*)

Question:

What actions might exporters take when, despite the pound falling against some major currencies, sales continue to fall?

Businesses may respond to the pressures of exchange rate changes by seeking to create productive capacity in overseas markets to avoid the effects of changing currency values. A number of foreign motor manufacturers located in the UK have revealed that they are considering relocating in Europe to avoid the difficulties imposed by fluctuations in the value of the pound against the euro.

An alternative approach, currently used by Toyota, is to require suppliers to price their products in a different currency. The company, which sells cars throughout Europe, has announced that it intends to pay UK suppliers in euros. As a result, fluctuations in the exchange rate will have less impact on the company as it pays suppliers in the same currency that it receives from European customers.

Inflation

What is inflation?

Inflation can be defined as a persistent rise in the price level and the associated fall in the value of money. For many businesses a low rate of inflation is not a problem. So long as wages are rising at about the same rate or higher, a low constant rate of price increase simply serves to help maintain demand. Inflation only becomes a major problem for businesses when it is high, rising rapidly or (worst of all) is doing both together.

Inflation in the UK, and in many industrialised nations throughout the world, has been at historically low rates over the last 15 years or so. Despite a rise in UK inflation rates to over 5 per cent (as measured by the CPI) in 2011, inflation in the UK is forecast to fall back to around 2–2.5 per cent by early 2013.

How is inflation measured?

The UK government measures the rate of inflation by use of the Retail Price Index (RPI) as well as the Consumer Price Index (CPI). The CPI was introduced in December 2003 and will operate alongside the RPI. The CPI measures the average monthly change in the prices of goods and services purchased by households in the UK and the government will use this to set targets for inflation in the future.

The main difference between the CPI and the RPI is that the CPI excludes housing and Council Tax costs. The use of the CPI as the official measure of inflation brings the UK into line with most other European countries. CPI gives a lower rate of inflation. Figure 20.8 illustrates that this is normally the case.

Expectations and inflation

Expectations are an important part of the process of creating inflation. If managers and businesses anticipate rising inflation they might take actions which, in fact, further fuel the inflationary process. If firms expect their suppliers to increase the prices

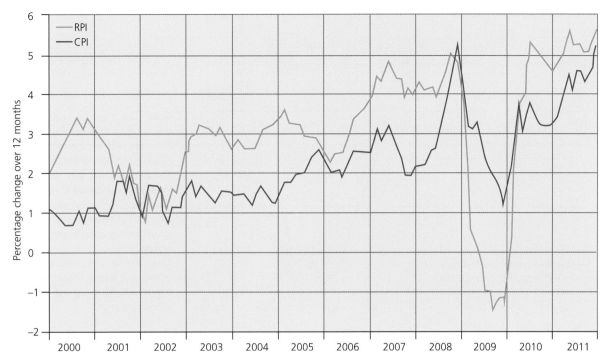

Figure 20.8 Inflation in the UK 2000–2011

(Source: National Statistics website: www.statistics.gov.uk)

of raw materials and components they may raise their selling prices in anticipation of this. This avoids any possibilities of lower profits if costs rise before prices can be increased. The action also provides a windfall profit in that for a while firms sell at higher prices while their costs have not risen.

Trade unions build their expectations of inflation into their wage demands for the coming year. If, as in 2013, inflation is forecast to be around 2.5 per cent this is likely to be the base figure for a wage rise. In such circumstances, unions will demand a 4 or 5 per cent increase in wages to give their members an increase in their standard of living. Unless productivity rises, paying workers wage rises in excess of the rate of inflation may result in businesses having to increase their prices.

Consumers, by their actions, can also add to inflation. If they expect prices to rise in the near future they may make major purchases immediately to avoid the price increases. If the economy is near to full capacity (it is in a boom) this can add to demand-pull inflation. A large number of consumers deciding to purchase consumer durables may result in price rises as producers are unable to respond to the orders and shortages take place.

Thus, the expectation of inflation can sometimes contribute to its existence. Governments wishing to control inflation have to be seen to be acting against it in order to reduce the expectations of future price rises.

The impact of inflation on business

Inflation can have a number of effects on businesses.

- Many businesses may suffer falling sales in a period of inflation. Consumers might be expected to spend more during inflationary periods as they would not wish to hold an asset that is falling in value. However, research shows that people save more (perhaps due to uncertainty) and sales for many businesses fall.
- It can be difficult to maintain competitiveness (and especially international competitiveness) during bouts of inflation. Rising wages and raw material costs may force firms to raise prices or accept lower profit margins. Firms operating in countries with lower rates of inflation may gain the edge in terms of price competitiveness under such circumstances.

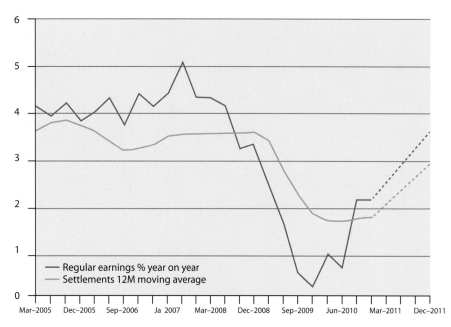

Note: *The graph compares annual growth in regular earnings with a 12-month moving average of settlements. The difference is 'pay drift' – the additional boost to earnings from progression up payscales, interim adjustments and restructuring outside the annual review.*
(Pay drift also reflects changes in average weekly hours, which fell during the recession but recovered in 2010.)

Figure 20.9 Regular earnings and pay settlements in the UK private sector

(Source: Henderson Global Investors)

Look at Figure 20.9. Do you think the trends revealed by this graph suggest that UK businesses will inevitably lose international competitiveness over the coming months?

The impact of government anti-inflationary policies

At the time of writing, the UK is experiencing a period of rising inflation, as illustrated in Figure 20.8. This is pushing up the costs paid by businesses and squeezing profit margins. The UK government or the Bank of England can control the worst effects of inflation in a number of ways.

- Rises in interest rates have been the government's main weapon. Increasing the base rate reduces the possibility of demand-pull inflation occurring. Consumers are discouraged from spending their money by higher rates on savings accounts and they are less likely to buy on credit as it is more expensive. Businesses reduce investment as borrowing becomes more expensive. Output and sales decline and the inflationary pressure is reduced. However, at the time of writing (December 2011) the Bank of England is reluctant to take this step for fear of pushing the UK economy back into recession.

- Successive governments have introduced legislation designed to restrict the power of trade unions. Acts controlling picketing and making ballots compulsory before unions can take industrial action have served to reduce trade union power. This legislation has lessened the chance of cost-push inflation as a result of rising wages while reducing the number days lost to strikes and other industrial action.

- Over time the government has reduced the expectation of inflation. In 2009 inflation in the UK reached its lowest rate for over 30 years. This helped businesses to be confident in setting prices and avoided unions putting in excessive (and inflationary) pay claims. The low rate of inflation enjoyed by the UK has also been one of a number of factors persuading foreign firms to move to Britain.

We will consider government policies to control the economy in more detail in the next chapter.

Inflation can offer some benefits to businesses, however. Some analysts suggest that low and stable rates of inflation may be beneficial. A steady rise in profits can create favourable expectations and encourage investment by businesses. Inflation can also encourage long-term borrowing and investment by businesses as the value of their repayments (in real terms) declines over time.

Business profitability hit as inflation soars to 4.5 per cent

Business leaders in the West Midlands are urging the government to maintain low interest rates following yesterday's announcement that inflation has reached 4.5 per cent. Birmingham Chamber of Commerce Group (BCCG) said the rise in Consumer Prices Index (CPI) inflation had underlined the concern businesses had for the severe damage it was causing to their profitability.

In the second quarter of this year, 24 per cent of service companies and 20 per cent of manufacturers cited inflation as the external factor most affecting their business. Christine Braddock, president of Birmingham Chamber, said: 'Inflation hurts businesses in many ways. It drives up the cost of raw materials adding pressure on businesses to increase prices.'

'However, it also puts pressure on people's wages, decreasing household disposable income and putting pressure on businesses to increase wages. Inflation is also beginning to negatively impact on exporters as it is rapidly negating any gain seen by the devaluation of the pound after the recession.'

(*Source: Midlands Business News,*
14 September 2011)

Question:

In what ways might government policies intended to curb inflation impact negatively on UK businesses?

If the government is successful in reducing inflation as expected by 2013 this will offer UK businesses a number of advantages.

- Costs are much easier to control in periods when prices are rising slowly.
- Pricing strategies are easier to establish (and simpler for consumers to understand) when inflation is low.
- If UK inflation is lower than that experienced by other nations, businesses based in the UK may receive a competitive advantage. Rival firms located in other countries may face increased costs and face pressure to increase their prices in an attempt to maintain profit margins.

- Sales forecasts are more likely to prove accurate during periods of relatively low inflation. During bouts of severe inflation consumers may switch to cheaper overseas products or decide to save against an uncertain future.

However, government policies to reduce inflation may have adverse effects on businesses, reducing the levels of expenditure on the business's products.

In an environment of relatively stable prices businesses may be willing to expand capacity through investment and to develop new products. Price stability removes an element of risk from business planning, engenders confidence amongst senior managers and may result in more positive business strategies.

However, businesses' responses to a period of inflation will depend upon the perceived cause of inflation, the level of inflation and the confidence they have in the government's ability to control price rises. Inflation caused by high levels of demand (so-called demand-pull inflation) may encourage firms to expand to meet the high and potentially profitable levels of demand. Even cost-push inflation (fuelled, for example, by high wage claims) may not be regarded as too damaging, if the resulting inflation is at a low level and the government appears capable of preventing price increases from accelerating.

Unemployment

Unemployment remains an important issue in most countries. It is important because it represents a waste of resources if labour is unused – if all available workers were used the country concerned would be able to produce more and its citizens would enjoy a higher standard of living. The social effects of high and prolonged rates of unemployment can be devastating: poor health and crime are just two factors associated with unemployment and poverty.

At the time of writing (in December 2011) unemployment is a major concern for the UK Government. In November 2011 the rate of unemployment in the UK was 8.3 per cent of the working population, which represents 2.62 million people without a job. A particular concern is the high rate of youth unemployment: 1.02 million people aged 16–24 are unemployed.

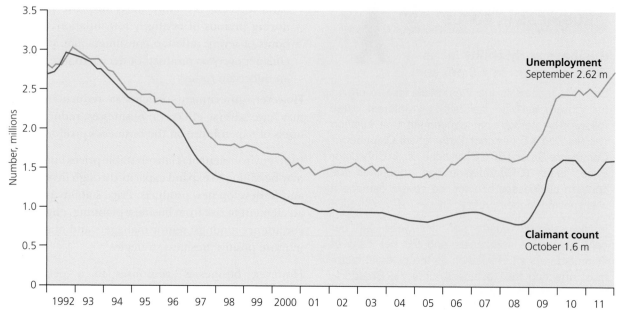

Figure 20.10 UK unemployment 1992–2011

(Source: National Statistics website: www.statistics.gov.uk)

Types of unemployment

People can be unemployed for a number of reasons. Governments find it useful to distinguish between the various types of unemployment, as each type requires a different remedy. Equally the type of unemployment has consequences for businesses when responding to it. Although many different types of unemployment exist, we shall focus on three main types.

Structural unemployment

Economies continually change: some industries die and others emerge to replace them. Structural unemployment occurs due to fundamental changes in the economy whereby some industries reach the end of their lives. Structural unemployment occurs for a number of reasons.

- the adoption of new methods of production
- increasing competition from overseas
- rising income levels meaning demand for some products declines.

But structural change in the economy also offers opportunities to businesses. Rising incomes and technological developments have, for instance, lead to the development of a market for electronic book readers such as Amazon's Kindle. This industry employs a large number of people in manufacturing and supplying the product.

Structural unemployment is a difficult problem for governments to solve. Because large numbers of employees may no longer have the skills that employers require training is an important part of any solution. Other approaches include encouraging foreign producers to establish themselves in the UK to provide employment for those with skills not needed by domestic businesses. The UK has been particularly successful in attracting motor vehicle producers from throughout the world.

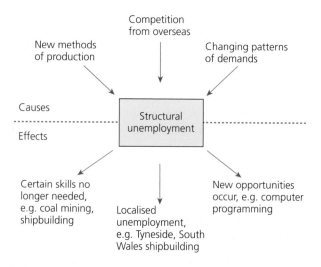

Figure 20.11 Causes and effects of structural unemployment

Cyclical unemployment

This type of unemployment arises from the operation of the business or trade cycle – a topic we considered in detail earlier in this chapter. The boom stage of a business cycle will see this type of unemployment minimised as firms increase their production levels. At this stage of the business cycle those who have been unemployed for some time (and with relatively few skills) may find work.

At the other extreme much of the unemployment experienced during a slump will be cyclical. Some firms have moved to protect themselves against cyclical unemployment by the introduction of profit-related pay. Such schemes allow pay to fall during a recession along with profits, reducing the need to make workers redundant. We saw earlier in this chapter that the car manufacturer Seat has temporarily laid off some of its employees for a fifth time as a response to the poor economic performance of many European economies.

Frictional unemployment

People moving between jobs cause frictional unemployment. If a person leaves one job they may not be able to move into a new position immediately.

While they are searching for new employment they are classified as frictionally unemployed. The government providing improved information on job vacancies available may reduce the level of frictional unemployment. A healthy economy will have some amount of frictional unemployment as people move between jobs.

Business and changing unemployment levels

Rises in unemployment can have serious implications for businesses, though the precise impact and likely responses of firms will depend upon their circumstances and the type of unemployment.

Cyclical unemployment might result in businesses suffering from falling sales. In the short term firms may be able to add any surplus production to stocks. Alternatively businesses may seek new markets, perhaps by selling overseas. Not all businesses will be equally affected by changes in unemployment levels. Businesses selling essential products may be relatively unaffected by cyclical unemployment, while suppliers of luxury products could suffer substantial reductions in sales.

BUSINESS IN FOCUS

Lloyds Banking Group announces 15,000 job cuts

António Horta-Osório, CEO of Lloyds Banking Group has announced that the company is cutting 15,000 jobs. On a bleak day for employment in the banking industry, HSBC also cut 700 jobs at its UK arm to save £9 million – a sum officials at Unite noted was the same as the bonus of chief executive Stuart Gulliver.

While unions were furious about the scale of the job losses at Lloyds – which are now expected to reach 45,000 – the City applauded the actions of Horta-Osório, who was presenting the outcome of a strategic review he conducted after taking over as CEO of the company. He insisted the cuts were essential. 'We have to do this. This bank has lost money, it's losing money this year on an after-tax basis. We have to get this bank back on to its feet to support the UK economy and we have to pay taxpayers' money back', he said.

The deep cuts to the workforce, to take place by 2014, added more than £1 billion to the value of the company.

Trade unions took a very different view. 'Astonishingly one in eight roles will be lost over the next three years', said David Fleming, national officer of the Unite union. Lloyds hires 10,000 staff a year and Horta-Osório stressed that he hoped that 'natural attrition and internal deployment' would help achieve the cuts, which are expected to target middle managers and back-office staff.

The job cuts should help Lloyds achieve £1.5 billion of annual savings in 2014, on top of £2 billion of savings achieved through other means.

(*Source: Jill Treanor in* The Guardian, *30 June 2011*)

Questions:

1 Why should investors and those in the City of London have such a positive view of the effects of making large numbers of people unemployed?
2 Why might the company be disadvantaged by these actions?

Structural unemployment can have a significant effect on businesses because it is frequently highly localised and often very persistent. Thus high levels of unemployment suffered by former coal mining communities had considerable implications for most businesses in the locality. Unemployment brought about by the decline of an industry also has an impact upon associated industries. For example, falling production in the UK's shipbuilding industry contributed to the decline in the country's steel industry.

BUSINESS IN FOCUS

Net migration to UK in 2010 at record high

Annual net migration to the UK in 2010 was 252,000 – the highest for any calendar year on record. Data from the Office for National Statistics showed that immigration had remained steady at 591,000, but the number of people leaving the UK had fallen.

Provisional data from the ONS for the 12 months to the end of March 2011 suggests that net migration has since fallen slightly to 245,000.

The Government has pledged to cut net migration to just tens of thousands by 2015.

Overall, emigration was at its lowest for ten years, with just 339,000 people leaving the UK. Emigration for work fell to its lowest level since 2006, reflecting the difficult economic environment around the world.

The previous record high for net migration was 245,000 in 2004.

Net migration of people from central and eastern European EU nations increased.

Education remains the most common reason for people to come to the UK from all parts of the world. Some 238,000 people arrived to study in the UK during 2010, the highest calendar year figure on record, although provisional figures for March 2011 suggest the number of students arriving may now have begun to fall.

Net migration – which the Government aims to reduce – is the balance between the number of people who come to live in the UK for the long term and the number who leave.

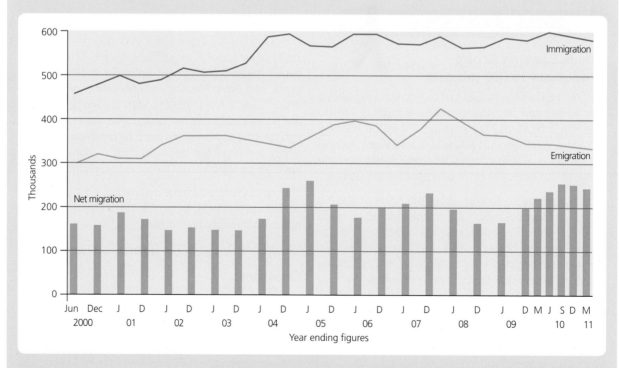

Figure 20.12 Long-term international migration, UK 2000–2011

(*Source: National Statistics website: www.statistics.gov.uk*)

If there is a need to reduce output then rationalisation and redundancy might follow and factories and offices may be closed. Research and development plans may be abandoned or postponed as firms seek to reduce their costs to match their (reduced) revenues. The predicted fall in the level of demand may encourage the firm to diversify, possibly into foreign markets. Businesses may consider mergers with other firms to help reduce costs or to broaden product ranges.

Periods of low unemployment cause different problems for businesses and provoke different responses. Falling unemployment and accompanying skill shortages create problems that take time to solve. Businesses look to the government to assist through the provision of state training schemes and the development of relevant vocational courses in schools and colleges. Recent UK governments have attempted to support industry in these ways.

However, businesses can take action.

- Skill shortages encourage the development of capital-intensive methods of production in manufacturing and service industries. Using technology to replace labour can boost productivity thereby enhancing international competitiveness.
- Businesses may relocate to take advantage of more plentiful and cheaper sources of skilled labour. However, this may require location outside Europe as most of the EU is experiencing similar skill shortages.
- Businesses may invest in training schemes to develop the required skills in their employees.
- This may entail giving relatively junior or unskilled employees additional skills to enable them to carry out a wider range of activities. This can be a risky approach, however, as unscrupulous competitors may entice away skilled employees once training is completed.

The skills shortage creates difficulties for many businesses, but opportunities for others. Recruitment agencies and firms providing training for other businesses may enjoy increasing demands for their services during a period of skill shortages.

Economic growth

Economic growth is an increase in the value of goods and services produced by a nation's economy. This links closely with the business cycle which we considered in an earlier section. If the rate of economic growth is negative (if the economy is getting smaller) for a successive six months, then it is said to be in recession.

Economic growth is normally measured by an increase in gross domestic product (GDP). In 2010 the GDP of the UK was £1,458,452 million. The population of the UK is approximately 61 million giving a GDP per head, or per capita, equal to £23,909. Governments seek to increase this figure over time as it represents a rise in the country's standard of living.

Most countries' economies experience economic growth over a period of time, though in the short term, economies may stagnate or even decline in size. Figure 20.13 illustrates the economic growth rates for the UK from 2007 until 2011.

Governments aim to maintain steady and sustained economic growth over a period of time. However, this is a difficult target to achieve, as the operation of the business cycle tends to create the fluctuations apparent in Figure 20.13. Governments use counter-cyclical policies (including control via interest rates and taxation levels) to attempt to eliminate the more extreme fluctuations. High rates of economic growth

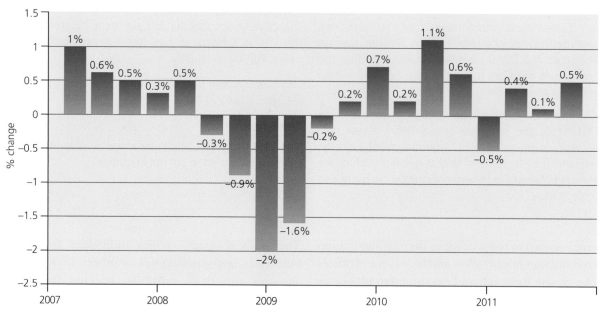

Figure 20.13 Quarterly changes in UK real GDP 2007–2011 (third quarter)

(Source: Trading Economics)

are not desirable, as they tend to result in slumps whereby economic growth may become negative.

Governments can stimulate growth as a consequence of their economic policies. Short-term growth can be encouraged by cuts in interest rates and taxation which fuel borrowing and spending, prompting greater output and hence economic growth. The danger is, however, that firms and individuals purchase products from overseas, promoting growth in foreign economies. Supply-side policies may be implemented to achieve sustained economic growth. This type of policy entails increasing the productive capability of the economy by improving the skills of the workforce, encouraging more people into employment and promoting competition within markets to increase output and GDP.

The case for economic growth is not clear-cut. Growth brings disadvantages as well as advantages. These arguments are summarised in Table 20.4.

The benefits	The drawbacks
High rates of economic growth provide the government with increased tax revenues permitting greater expenditure on health, education and transport benefiting all businesses in the UK and encouraging further growth.	Not all regions within an economy benefit equally during periods of economic growth. Firms selling in the south of England are likely to enjoy increased sales while those in less prosperous regions such as Wales and the north of England may only see a marginal increase in revenues.
Growth provides opportunities to all in society. Individuals benefit from greater chances of promotion; high levels of consumer spending encourage enterprise. Businesses small and large may thrive in a growing environment.	Growth may result in shortages of labour and other materials. This may result in higher wages and prices fuelling inflation and creating uncertainty amongst the business community.
Businesses generally enjoy higher sales and increased profits. Expansion is likely for firms selling income elastic products such as cars and foreign holidays. Growth creates new markets for products.	Growth places individuals and businesses under pressure. Workloads increase and decisions may be rushed. In these circumstances it may prove impossible to maintain the quality of management and businesses may lose coordination and a clear sense of direction.

Table 20.4 The benefits and drawbacks of economic growth for businesses

Globalisation and growth

The fact that economic growth is not always an advantage has been highlighted in the well-publicised opposition to further economic development and especially to globalisation. Opponents of uncontrolled economic growth argue that other factors such as a clean environment, the protection of plants and wildlife and adequate leisure time contribute to the standard of living as much (and maybe more than) consumer products. As societies become richer this argument may become even more persuasive. We will consider the effects of globalisation fully on pages 273–77.

The economic environment as a single entity

In this chapter we have looked at the major economic factors individually and considered how they might affect the decisions taken by businesses. However, in reality managers and directors do not consider a single economic factor when assessing the behaviour of an economy and constructing their responses to changes in the economic environment. Instead they assess the state of the economy by taking into account all the factors that can be used to judge its performance. It is important to judge the state of the economy by considering all the relevant key variables such as unemployment and bearing in mind their interrelationships.

In 2012 the UK economy is struggling to recover from recession and the banking crisis. Its problems are compounded by the difficulties experienced by many economies in the eurozone. This will attract the headlines, but any detailed analysis of the economy will also consider the effects of changes in other economic variables.

First, the exchange rate of the pound has fallen against the currencies of some of the UK's major trading partners such as the US and China. This has the potential to offer increased export sales to businesses that sell in the US and China. The increase in sales will be more likely if the product that is sold is price-elastic and so foreign consumers respond positively to price reductions in their own currencies. However, the decline in the international value of the pound could increase costs for businesses that import large amounts of raw materials and components from overseas adding to the UK's inflationary pressures.

The UK is struggling to reduce its rate of inflation, although many economists expect it to fall by the start of 2013. This may help to boost sales as consumers feel less need to save, and especially if real wages begin to rise again enhancing consumers' sense of well-being.

Finally, strongly rising unemployment can have a number of effects. It can result in falling levels of sales as consumers have less money to spend as a result of an increasing number becoming jobless. However, rising unemployment tends to depress wage levels and this may help a business to maintain its price competitiveness. This may be a particularly important factor for businesses that employ large numbers of employees and where labour costs represent a high proportion of total costs.

Globalisation

What is globalisation?

The world's economies have developed ever-closer links since 1950, in trade, investment and production. This process has resulted in globalisation, and is not new. However, its pace and scope have accelerated in recent years, to include more industries and more countries.

At its simplest globalisation refers to the trend for many markets to become worldwide in scope. Because of globalisation many businesses trade throughout the world, whereas in the past they may have focused on one country, or possibly a single continent such as Europe. Improvements in global transport systems and communications, notably the internet, have encouraged this trend.

However, globalisation is not a beneficial trend in the views of many people. The term globalisation brings to mind visions of large numbers of protestors confronting police forces in towns and cities across the world. We will consider the aspects of globalisation that have caused such responses later in this section.

Why is there a trend towards globalisation?

Many governments and businesses believe that increased and freer trade between nations will offer prosperity and growth for all countries and businesses. Globalisation, they argue, has already brought many benefits: global food production has risen steadily over the last 20 years and malnutrition rates have fallen accordingly. Citizens in less developed countries have access to health care, often supplied by foreign businesses.

For its supporters globalisation offers an opportunity rather than posing a threat. The leaders of the world's major economies and big businesses are committed to protecting and promoting global commerce and trade and emphasise the benefits it can bring. Globalisation has been encouraged by falling transport and communication costs and greater international flows of investments as illustrated in Figures 20.14 and 20.15.

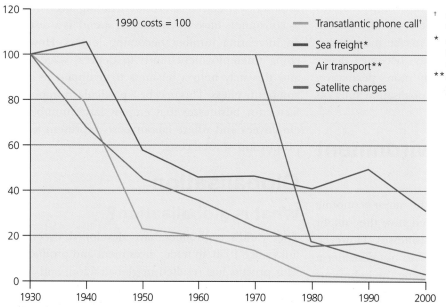

† Cost of three minute telephone call from New York to London
* Average ocean freight and port charges per short ton of import and export cargo
** Average air transport revenue per passenger mile

Figure 20.14 Falling transport and communication costs

(Source: HM Treasury)

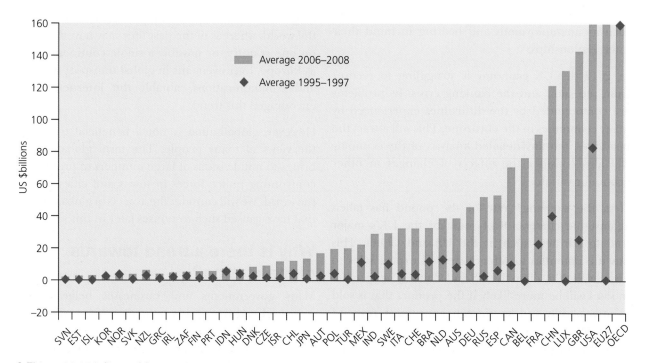

Figure 20.15 Inflows of foreign direct investment

(Source: OECD)

BUSINESS IN FOCUS

Open the skies

Given that flying people around the world is the ultimate globalised industry, there is oddly little competition in the airlines business. Passengers who are prepared to change planes once or twice to get to their destinations have lots of choice, but on transatlantic routes between hubs there are often only one or two carriers to choose from.

This lack of competition is partly the result of collusion sanctioned by regulators. On transatlantic routes members within each of the world's three big alliances of airlines – Star, oneworld and SkyTeam – share costs and agree on prices. They are spreading their tentacles around the world. The expected purchase by BA (a oneworld member) of a smaller rival, bmi, from Lufthansa (a Star member), may boost oneworld's position by adding bmi's Heathrow slots to oneworld's already dominant position in transatlantic flights.

America's Department of Transportation (DoT), which has some anti-monopoly powers, has not only given its blessing to the rise of alliances, but actually requires airlines to collude fully within each of their groupings, and to share costs and agree on prices.

The 2007 'open skies' agreement between Europe and America has done some good: for instance, it has allowed BA to go head-to-head with Air France, flying from Paris to New York and Washington, DC (although it recently suspended the Washington route), and Aer Lingus to compete with Iberia between Madrid and Washington. But the blessing America has given the three cartels has more than undone this good work. BA's struggle to establish itself in Paris shows that it is hard for a

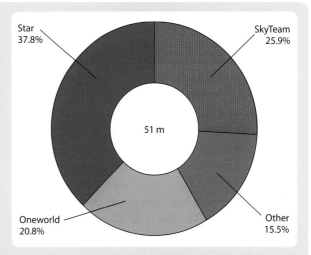

Figure 20.16 Airline seat capacity, April–October 2011

competitor, even a powerful one, to achieve sufficient sales in a hub airport dominated by a rival alliance. And the remaining independents flying across the Atlantic – such as Virgin and Aer Lingus – are looking vulnerable.

Sit back, relax and enjoy the competition

Blessing the cartels across the Atlantic was a mistake, and should be reversed. Letting the airlines join together in global alliances brings a number of benefits to passengers: frequent-flyer points, smoother transfers and so on. But travellers should be asking themselves: at what cost?

(*Source:* The Economist, *12 November 2011*)

Question:

Do you think that businesses have benefited from globalisation at the expense of consumers?

Globalisation and businesses

Globalisation offers a number of opportunities to businesses from any country and not just the UK.

- **Increased sales, revenues and profits.** Being able to trade freely in international markets offers the chance to increase sales substantially and to enjoy higher revenues and profits – if the business is sufficiently competitive. It has become possible to sell similar products to billions of global consumers and this has offered unrivalled opportunities for growth. Companies such as McDonald's and Toyota have derived enormous benefits from this increased access in terms of rising revenues.

- **Cheaper resources.** Increased volumes of trade also make more resources available to businesses

and allow them to source raw materials and, of course labour, significantly more cheaply than in the past. For example, many UK manufacturers including the train-maker Hornby and cosmetic manufacturer Avon have moved production facilities to China and Poland respectively to take advantage of cheaper labour. This has only been possible as a result of reduced costs of transportation and political and economic changes that have made it possible for UK businesses to locate in these countries.

- **Economies of scale.** The increased scale of production gives greater potential to benefit from economies of scale. This is especially true if it is possible to implement a global strategy whereby a similar product can be sold to consumers across the world. This means that fixed costs such as research and development can be spread across larger volumes of production lowering unit costs. At the same time the company is likely to benefit from marketing and purchasing economies.

- **Developing different products for different markets**. The increased scale of production and access to large overseas markets such as China and India means that foreign companies can produce cars that meet the needs of local consumers. Thus, for example, increasing awareness of environmental issues and limited incomes mean that most Asian car consumers will wish to purchase small cars. The product that will be required will be different to that purchased in North America.

But globalisation brings drawbacks for all businesses too.

- **Downward pressure on prices.** All businesses have access to cheaper sources of raw materials and labour enabling them to reduce costs and selling prices. This has led to a sharpening of price competition. Prices of clothing, footwear and electronic products have fallen in the UK over recent years once inflation is taken into account. This means that for businesses to remain competitive in markets such as these it is imperative that they are able to reduce prices to match the general market trend. Some businesses have, however, recognised that they cannot compete in terms of price with producers based in countries with lower costs. As a result they have adopted strategies to differentiate their products by for example, developing a USP based on quality or advanced technology.

- **New producers.** Established businesses in markets in Europe and North America have found themselves facing new competition from businesses in developing countries. For example, Petro China is China's largest company and was only founded in 1999. However, by 2010 it had generated annual revenues of more than £140 billion and profits of nearly £14 billion. Clearly this company has become a fierce global competitor in drilling and refining oil. Established producers have found that many markets have been subject to increased levels of imports from producers in countries such as Russia and India.

- **Increased need for investment**. Globalisation, by sharpening competitive pressures, has increased the pressure for businesses to invest to compete with firms from around the globe. Investment is required to produce new products which are

differentiated from those currently available or to increase the skills and productivity of the businesses' workforces. These competitive strategies require investment in research and development or in training employees.

- **The threat of takeover**. Globalisation has seen the development of larger businesses more able to face the full force of global competition. Many businesses have taken over smaller competitors to give them greater economies of scale and, in some cases, a brand name that is familiar in other parts of the world. Smaller successful businesses might be particularly vulnerable to takeover because of the globalisation of markets.

Why is globalisation controversial?

One of the reasons that globalisation is so controversial is because different groups can interpret it in many different ways. For some groups globalisation is a uniquely threatening word. It prompts visions of large multinationals dominating the world, selling Coca-Cola and Big Macs to consumers in pursuit of ever-higher profits. Many pressure groups fear that globalisation threatens the environment as well as national cultures and predict that it will make the rich nations richer while impoverishing developing countries.

The World Trade Organisation

The World Trade Organisation (WTO) was created in January 1995 as a forum for trade negotiations and with the brief to resolve trade disputes. It cooperates with other international organisations in pursuing its aim of ensuring that trade flows as freely and smoothly as possible. It administers and polices existing and new free trade agreements, settles trade disputes between governments and organises trade negotiations. In February 2011 the WTO had a membership of 153 countries. China joined in 2001 and Russia is expected to become a member in 2012. The WTO role in promoting world trade has attracted ferocious opposition from anti-globalisation protesters resulting in violent scenes at WTO meetings, most notably in Seattle in 2000.

Citizens in rich and poor countries alike see the threat posed by globalisation to their local cultures and have acted to protect them. In India consumers wrecked McDonald's restaurants for violating Hindu dietary laws. At the same time Canadian communities are fighting to keep out the giant Walmart chain for fear it will destroy neighbourhood shopping centres. Some people fear that the development of larger and more powerful global businesses offer threats to their jobs (lost to countries where wages are lower) and their way of life – being sold products that are unfamiliar to their cultures.

Strategies in response to globalisation

Globalisation is likely to remain a hot potato for governments and big businesses alike for the foreseeable future. Some consumers from developed and developing countries can be expected to continue to voice their opposition to the actions of businesses that damage their local cultures and their local environments. Multinationals need to achieve a tricky balance in their strategic planning between achieving their ambitions to operate in a global market while ensuring they do not alienate large numbers of the consumers who make up that market.

Unfortunately for big businesses they operate in an environment in which information on their activities is increasingly available and consumers are better informed than ever before. Some companies have already recognised that there are significant commercial advantages in being seen to react to at least some of the demands of the anti-globalisation campaigners. International furniture retailer IKEA has announced that it will protect the world's ancient forests by only using timber from sustainable sources. Other multinationals may be more reluctant to respond until and unless the protesters' actions begin to have substantial financial consequences.

Some multinationals may opt for strategic alliances with businesses from other parts of the world to respond the changes in the world economy that have been created by globalisation. This has been apparent in the car manufacturing and supermarket industries. For example, Tesco sought a deal with a Chinese supermarket group (Ting Hsin) as a first step to operating in what is a very different market for a food retailer. In 2010 it set itself the ambitious expansion target of quadrupling sales in China to £4 billion by 2015.

Others will seek to establish production capacity through the world and to sell differentiated products targeted to meet the needs of consumers in local markets. Toyota has adopted this strategy, producing different cars for the American and Asian markets.

Developments in emerging markets

The rise of emerging markets is inextricably tied up with globalisation. Globalisation is the result of the freeing up of trade by reducing political and legal barriers to it and of the improvement in international communications and transport links. These developments have allowed economies such as China and India to thrive. Freer trade and political systems have allowed businesses to thrive in emerging markets and have encouraged established producers to locate in these countries. At the same time domestic businesses have grown rapidly. These changes, in total, have helped the emerging economies to achieve very high rates of economic growth.

Emerging economies: key players of the future?

China has received much attention in the media as a rapidly growing economy and an economic powerhouse of the future. The economy has achieved rapid rates of growth (around 10 per cent per annum over the last seven years) and has produced enormous quantities of manufactured goods. In 1980 the Chinese economy was about 25 per cent of the size of the UK's; by 2011 it was more than twice as large. However, it is a mistake to think of China as the only emerging economy. There are a number of other economies with enormous potential. India's population is nearly as large as China's and the country has specialised in providing services. We saw earlier that Ittiam Systems is an example of an Indian company that is able to compete successfully in global markets and an example of India's growing economic power. Other key emerging market countries are Brazil and Russia. These countries benefit from sizeable populations as well as other resources such as oil and gas. Together these four emerging markets are referred to as the BRIC countries.

Other emerging economies include Mexico, South Korea, Turkey, Poland, Indonesia, Saudi Arabia, Taiwan, Iran, Argentina and Thailand, which together had a collective GDP of £5.71 trillion in 2009.

The growth rates achieved by the emerging economies is much higher than that achieved by developed economies such as France and the UK, as is shown in Figure 20.17.

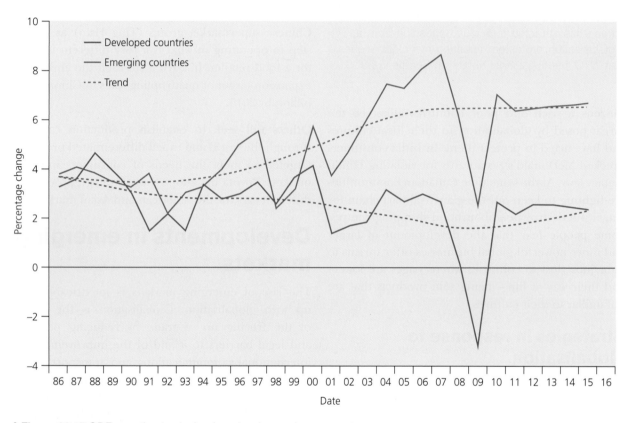

Figure 20.17 GDP growth rates in developed and emerging economies

(Source: Financial Times)

BUSINESS IN FOCUS

Coca-Cola reports £1.4 billion profit and 45 per cent revenue jump

Coca-Cola, the world's largest drinks manufacturer, has reported a third-quarter profit of £1.4 billion. This was a 9 per cent rise on the same period last year. Its revenues rose 45 per cent to £7.99 billion.

Coca-Cola's revenues were helped by price rises. Rising costs have eaten into profit margins at the company, and in the US it raised prices by about 2 per cent to offset these higher costs.

Its volume sales rose 5 per cent globally and by the same level in North America. Sales in Europe were up

2 per cent, and by 7 per cent in China. Coca-Cola is increasingly focusing on emerging markets such as Latin America, India and China to drive growth. Sales in these regions outperformed Europe and North America. In India volumes increased by 17 per cent and in Argentina they rose by 11 per cent.

(*Source:* BBC News, *18 October 2011*)

Question:

What other benefits might emerging markets offer to Coca-Cola, apart from rising sales?

The strengths of emerging economies

Emerging economies have numerous strengths and this allows them to offer real benefits to businesses.

- **Enormous labour resources**. China and India are the world's two most populous nations with 1.3 billion and 1.1 billion inhabitants respectively. As a consequence the two economies have workforces each in excess of 500 million people. In China this allows wages to be very low and has permitted the production of manufactured goods at very low costs. India's workforce is nearly as large as China's and many Indians speak fluent English. An increasing proportion is highly educated allowing the country to provide large numbers of employees for the global IT industry.
- **Large markets**. The large number of citizens in emerging economies also means that Russia, Mexico, China and India are important markets for many companies because of the number of consumers and the fact that their incomes are rising rapidly. Companies such as McDonald's and Coca-Cola have targeted increasing sales in these countries as their incomes rise. For some companies, such as those supplying tobacco, these markets can be exceptionally attractive as levels of health education are lower than in developed economies.
- **Rapid growth rates**. Many of the emerging markets are achieving rapid rates of growth. The Chinese economy is growing at around 9–10 per cent each year and India is achieving growth rates approaching 8 per cent. In 2011 Indonesia's economy grew at 6.5 per cent and Argentina's at 8.5 per cent. This growth means that many consumers have increasing disposable incomes to spend on consumer goods such as cars, clothes and electrical goods. Emerging economies are increasingly attractive markets for many multinational businesses because of the number of consumers and their rising incomes.

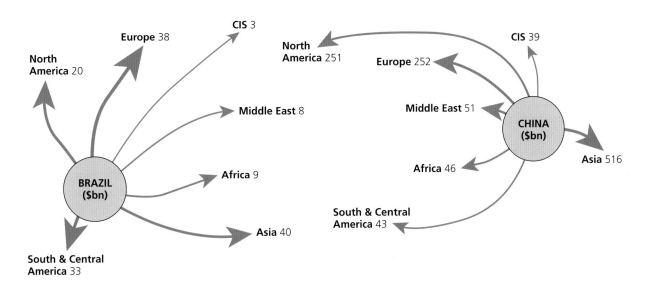

Figure 20.18 Exports from Brazil and China, 2009

(*Source: World Trade Organisation*)

- **Natural resources**. Some of the emerging economies, notably Brazil benefit from extensive natural resources. Brazil has huge amounts of timber, agricultural land and mineral resources. This has been reflected in the value of its exports, as shown in Figure 20.18.

Weaknesses of emerging economies

- **Poor transport infrastructures**. India has a congested and fragmented road structure and this limits the locations that are feasible and cost-effective for multinational companies; the Government has agreed to make improving this a priority. China has invested heavily in developing its transport and communications, yet problems remain, especially in areas away from its east coast.
- **Inflation**. This is a pressing problem for several of the emerging economies. China's rate of inflation was 5.7 per cent in 2011, India's 8.3 per cent, Argentina's 9.6 per cent, Brazil's 6.7 per cent and Russia's 8.5 per cent. This poses a number of problems for businesses that opt to locate in these countries. Interest rates may increase as governments attempt to reduce rates of inflation and the companies might find the cost differentials that attracted them to locate there in the first place are slowly eroded.
- **Import restrictions**. It can be difficult to export to countries such as India, China and Russia. The governments may impose taxes or other restrictions on imports or limit the ability of foreign businesses to operate there. Foreign supermarket chains have experienced problems in breaking into the Indian market because of the reluctance of the Indian Government to admit them. The Indian Government also imposes high import taxes on some products. In 2011, for example, it came under pressure from Scottish whisky distillers to reduce its 150 per cent tariff on imports of spirits.
- **Lack of appropriate skills**. Some decisions to locate production capacity in emerging economies have not been successful as employees have not had the necessary skills. For example, Lloyds TSB removed its call centres from India following complaints from customers who said staff did not have the necessary local knowledge to carry out their duties effectively.
- **Vulnerability to recession**. Although they have achieved spectacular rates of economic growth in recent years, countries such as India and China are poor in international terms. For example, India is home to 40 per cent of the world's malnourished children. Because of this a downturn in spending across the world can lead to companies closing production facilities in the emerging economies resulting in large increases in unemployment. Multinational companies may also find it more acceptable to close down some of their overseas facilities first when sales fall. Some observers fear social unrest, especially in China if rates of growth slow significantly and large numbers of people become unemployed suddenly. Equally, continued and dramatic falls in the prices of resources such as oil can have severe adverse effects on economies such as Russia and Brazil.

Strategic responses to changes in the economic environment

The economic environment is an important factor for many businesses and changes are likely to provoke a range of responses as outlined below.

- **Relocation**. If the economic position in a particular economy deteriorates then it may be that a business will relocate to a different country where the economic conditions are more favourable. This may be an appropriate response to an economic downturn if an economy is moving towards recession or suffering higher rates of inflation than other countries, damaging price competitiveness. This strategy has been made easier by the relaxing of barriers to trade and improving global transport links. However, the global economy is increasingly integrated and an economic downturn in one economy is likely to be experienced by others, though not necessarily to the same degree.
- **Selling new products or entering new markets**. These are strategies that Ansoff would recognise and are included in his matrix. Businesses may opt to enter markets in countries whose economies are buoyant or to sell products that are 'recession-proof'. Globalisation and the emergence of economies such as India and China may encourage such strategic responses amongst firms whose products are in demand across the globe.
- **Retrenchment or cost cutting**. Retrenchment essentially means that a business downsizes and operates with a smaller productive capacity.

Managers will identify less profitable (or major loss-making) areas of the business and eliminate these in the expectation of making the entire enterprise more efficient. Cost cutting may be a less dramatic strategy, but can help a business to maintain an acceptable level of profitability during a period of adverse economic conditions.

- **Mergers and takeovers**. By increasing its scale a business may be better equipped to deal with the rigours of global markets. It may enable a business to benefit from economies of scale and to control costs more effectively and be price competitive. Mergers and takeovers may enable a business to extend its product range and to compete in other markets. In this way the strategy may help to protect the business against an adverse economic environment by providing new products whose sales are not as vulnerable to falling incomes or rising costs.
- **Joint ventures and alliances**. This strategy falls short of a full merger or takeover but offers similar benefits. It can be an effective way of gaining access to a new market or a means of reducing costs, not least through the achievement of substantial economies of scale.

The precise strategic response taken by any business will depend upon a range of factors including the nature of the product that the business sells, the financial position of the business and the extent of the change in the economic environment. However, a key influence on any decision about strategic responses to changes in the economic environment will be the extent of any change and the period over which it is expected to last. Thus the emergence of economies such as India, Brazil and China or the globalisation of markets may provoke a range of responses, many of which are outlined above. In contrast an economic downturn, or a period of inflation, which are expected to be of limited duration may only lead to tactical responses such as changing prices or other elements of the marketing mix.

Key terms

Economic activity relates to the level of spending, production and employment in the economy at any given time.

Gross domestic product (GDP) measures the value of a country's total output of goods and services over a period of time, normally one year.

Economic growth is the rate of increase in the size of an economy over time.

A recession is characterised by falling levels of demand and declining levels of output and employment over at least a six-month period.

A slump takes place when production is at its lowest, unemployment is high and there are many business failures.

Interest rates are the price paid for borrowed money.

A currency **appreciates** when its value rises against another currency or currencies.

An **exchange rate** is the price of one currency expressed in terms of another. For example, £1 might be worth €1.1.

Depreciation occurs when the value of a currency declines against another currency or currencies.

Cost-push inflation happens when firms face increasing costs due to rising wages or increasing costs of raw materials and components.

Demand-pull inflation occurs when the demand for the country's goods and services exceeds its ability to supply these products.

Inflation is a persistent rise in the general price level and an associated fall in the value of money.

The Retail Prices Index (RPI) measures the rate of inflation based on the changes in prices of a basket of goods and services.

Unemployment exists when people who are seeking work are unable to find any employment.

Counter-cyclical policy is operated by the government with the intention of reducing the worst effects of booms and slumps.

Cyclical unemployment is caused by the operation of the business cycle rising in slumps and falling in booms.

Frictional unemployment exists because people may be temporarily out of work between leaving one job and starting another. →

Structural unemployment occurs due to fundamental changes in the economy whereby some industries reach the end of their lives.

Globalisation is the trend for many markets to become worldwide in scope.

A global strategy exists when a business produces a single product (possibly with slight variants) to meet the needs of consumers across the global market.

An emerging market (or economy) describes a country with low incomes per head but one which is enjoying high rates of economic growth.

The **BRIC countries** are Brazil, Russia, India and China and are often referred to as prime examples of emerging markets.

Economic growth is the rate of increase in the size of an economy over time.

A multinational business is one that has production capacity in more than one country.

Examiner's advice

Remember that products are not sold on the basis of price alone. When considering the likely consequences of a change in exchange rates it is important to note that factors such as quality, reputation, after-sales service and meeting delivery dates are important influences on buyers' decisions.

It is important to relate the impact of unemployment – or changes in other economic factors – to the precise type of business under consideration. Some businesses rely heavily on labour as a key element of production – this is more likely to be true of businesses that supply services. Hence a change in the level of unemployment will have a greater impact on this type of business.

The effects of changes in the economic environment and the consequent change in business strategy will depend upon the type of business, the markets in which it changes and the extent of the changes. This chapter provides you with general guidance but you must think about the precise effects and consequences in the light of the situation you are faced with.

Remember globalisation offers advantages and disadvantages to most businesses. You should be prepared to analyse these and to assess the overall impact on the business in question.

The emerging economies are very different and businesses become involved with them for different reasons. Some produce there, others buy resources from emerging economies, while a third group of companies sell their products in emerging markets. You should consider these differences when responding to any questions on this area.

The list of strategic responses to changes in the economic environment in this chapter is not exhaustive – there are others that a business may adopt. It is important that you consider the possible responses in the context of the scenario with which you are presented. This will assist you in selecting and justifying the most appropriate response in any circumstances.

Progress questions

1 An economy is in the upswing stage of the business cycle. What are the most common features of this stage of the cycle? *(4 marks)*

2 Outline **two** ways in which a company manufacturing digital televisions might be affected by a recession. *(6 marks)*

3 Examine **two** factors that might determine a business's response to a rise in interest rates. *(6 marks)*

4 Explain **two** ways in which a UK-based manufacturing business, trading across the EU, might be affected by a fall in UK interest rates. *(7 marks)*

5 Archer & Sons, based in Norwich, purchases raw materials from overseas and sells half its output in foreign markets. Consider the probable effects of a rise in the exchange value of the pound on the company. *(8 marks)*

6. Explain why price elasticity of demand may partly determine the responses of a business to a substantial change in exchange rates. *(7 marks)*

7. Consider the responses of a large insurance company to a steady fall in the rate of unemployment. *(8 marks)*

8. Examine the ways in which an international airline might respond to a large and unexpected rise in the rate of inflation in its home market. *(8 marks)*

9. Outline why a business would be more likely to monitor long-term interest rates. *(6 marks)*

10. In what ways might a hotel chain in the UK respond to a high rate of UK economic growth? *(8 marks)*

11. Explain **two** advantages of globalisation for a major UK supermarket such as Tesco. *(6 marks)*

12. What disadvantages might McDonald's face as a result of globalisation? *(6 marks)*

13. Why might a car manufacturer opt for a multi-domestic strategy in the face of globalisation? *(8 marks)*

14. Why might emerging economies such as India and China offer opportunities to multinational businesses such as Vodafone? *(7 marks)*

15. Explain **two** risks for a clothes manufacturer of locating in an emerging economy. *(7 marks)*

Essay questions

1. The UK economy is forecast to grow slowly over the next few years. Tesco has set itself an objective of quadrupling its sales in China over a period of five years and fashion clothing manufacturer Burberry is targeting a range of overseas markets including China, Turkey and India. Do you think that seeking to expand into overseas markets is the only way for businesses to respond to a forecast period of slow growth in their domestic markets? Justify your answer with reference to Tesco, Burberry and/or any other business with which you are familiar. *(40 marks)*

Candidate's answer:

China is an attractive market for many UK businesses, apart from Tesco and Burberry, because it is growing at around 10 per cent per year at a time when many western economies such as the UK are showing little if any growth. Tesco has an aim of 'sustainable growth' and seeking markets where consumers are enjoying rising incomes offers the opportunity to the company to sell more products, generating more revenue. China is particularly attractive to this company because of the scale of this market (it has 1,300 million people) and that the rising incomes are currently concentrated in a relatively small area of eastern China. This means that Tesco can focus its efforts on this part of China where incomes are probably rising at more than 10 per cent each year and this may result in rapid rises in sales and increasing profitability. Tesco's sales target is very optimistic and would be the result of extensive market research.

But this is not Tesco's only plan for growth. In the UK it continues to expand its food retailing business by opening more small shops (its Express stores) as well as building large supermarkets in areas where it has none. Because much expenditure on food is a necessity, rather than a luxury good, it is not affected as much by the forecast lack of growth in the UK. As a consequence the company will simply adjust its product range to include more basic and value products and fewer expensive products. In this way it may be able to achieve some growth in UK sales over the next few years. The company is also expanding its online business in an attempt to reach more UK consumers. At the same time Tesco is seeking to extend its product range by entering new product markets in the UK. It is about to start providing legal services by, for example, helping people to buy houses. Sales in this market may be low at the moment in the UK, but Tesco would probably take a long-term view of this move.

Sales of Burberry's products are more dependent on income levels. At a time when incomes are barely rising for many people in the UK, the company is sensible to look overseas to increase its sales. In countries where incomes are rising quickly many consumers are now able to afford to buy fashion products and well-known brands such as Burberry are very attractive to many people. However, although some people in the UK are experiencing little increase in their incomes, this is an average figure and it is still perfectly possible for Burberry to target high income earners, perhaps in the more prosperous parts of the UK.

Clearly, looking to enter overseas markets is not the only response to low income growth in the UK. Although Tesco is targeting China (and many other countries) this is not its only strategy. It is seeking to enter new product markets as well as to increase its penetration into the UK grocery market. Moving overseas is risky and, although this has been responsible for much of Tesco's increases in profits recently, sales in the UK remain hugely important to the company. Moving into China and other overseas markets is a long-term strategy for both Tesco and Burberry and these markets are attractive because of their size and potential for future growth. These decisions have not been taken just because of a forecast of low growth in the UK for a few years. The UK economy is expected to grow by about 2 per cent in two years' time and so other factors will have prompted this move.

To conclude, moving into overseas markets can be risky as cultures are different and international rivals will probably be there. This is one response, albeit a long-term one, to low forecast rates of growth. However, the real attraction of these markets is that they are expected to generate high profits in the future and moving there would be part of a sensible growth strategy for many companies, not just those from the UK when its economy is going through a period of slow growth.

Examiner's comments:

There is much to admire in this answer. First the focus was good throughout the answer. The candidate does not drift at any point from directly answering the question. Each paragraph plays a role in responding to this precise question and it is likely that the candidate planned this carefully to ensure relevance at all times. The candidate has also shown that they have the ability to apply their knowledge to relevant companies. They have written particularly well on Tesco's moves into overseas markets and balanced this with some account of other activities in the UK market. They were perhaps less fluent on Burberry, but did recognise the nature of the products it sells. They did not have to write about these two businesses, any other relevant examples would have been equally acceptable.

The candidate has provided good evidence of other examination skills in this answer. They have developed effective arguments which directly address the question and used theory to structure their thoughts at times. For example, they used Ansoff's matrix to underpin their consideration of the options available to Tesco and this helped them to make and support their judgement. There was plenty of evaluation throughout this answer and overall the quality was good.

Question:

2 Some major UK companies such as Cadbury have been bought by foreign rivals while Nokia has struggled to compete with rivals from overseas. Is globalisation more of a threat than an opportunity for most businesses? Justify your answer with reference to Cadbury, Nokia and/or any other business with which you are familiar. *(40 marks)*

21 Businesses and the political and legal environment

This chapter builds on the previous one and does not relate directly to any materials you covered as part of your AS course. It considers the actions that the government takes in an attempt to provide a more supportive economic environment for businesses and the effects of these actions on businesses – these effects are not always as intended. It also examines the legal framework that the UK and EU authorities have created for businesses. As we cover these topics we will consider how a variety of businesses have reacted to changes in their political and legal environments.

In this chapter we will examine:

- the government's economic policies
- the effects of the government's intervention in the economy
- political decisions affecting trade and access to markets
- the impact of legislation relating to businesses
- the different responses of businesses to changes in the political and legal environment.

Introduction

The operation of the UK's economy affects everyone and every business in the country. Changes in the level of production, employment or prices can have significant consequences for managers, for employees and for consumers. However, we cannot consider the UK economy in isolation. The UK is a part of the wider EU economy and is an important component of the global economy that is assuming ever greater importance. Not surprisingly the government has a number of objectives for the economy and all of its policies are intended to fulfil these objectives.

As early as 1945 the government had established economic objectives that still broadly apply today. These objectives are as follows.

- Price stability. This means controlling the rate of inflation as measured by the retail price index. In the 1980s the UK suffered high rates of inflation, but they have declined steadily since that time, and although it is around 5 per cent at the time of writing (December 2011) it is expected to fall back to around 2–2.5 per cent by 2013. Having an inflation rate below that of other nations offers firms a potential price advantage.
- Steady and sustained growth in the economy, allowing greater levels of production. Economic growth offers firms and individuals the potential for increased incomes and greater prosperity. Most western economies (including the UK) aim for a

growth rate of around 3 per cent, although some developing economies such as China have achieved annual rates of 10 per cent.

- A low rate of unemployment. It is impossible to have everyone in the economy employed. Unemployment in 2011 is hovering around the 2.6 million mark, a worryingly high figure and twice what it was as recently as 2004. Unemployment represents a major waste of resources by an economy.
- A balanced balance of payments, avoiding long-term deficits and surpluses. Governments usually aim to avoid deficits on the current account of the balance of payments. This means the value of goods and services sold overseas should at least be equal to the value of imports of goods and services. On occasions governments seek to avoid the exchange rate rising which can contribute to a balance of payments deficit on the current account.

The Bank of England has responsibility for operating some of the government's economic policies, which we shall consider in more detail later in this chapter. The Bank recently restated the Government's economic objectives.

The Government's central economic policy objective is to achieve high and stable levels of growth and employment. Price stability is a precondition for these high and stable levels of employment and growth. In the past inflation has contributed to the UK's poor economic performance, not least by holding back the long-term investment that is the foundation for a successful economy.

Most governments would be satisfied if they could manage the economy to achieve the following targets in relation to the economy:

- the rate of inflation below the Government's target of 2 per cent annually
- less than 5 per cent of the workforce unemployed
- steady economic growth at rates of 2–3 per cent each year
- avoiding large deficits on the current account of the balance of payments as a result of the value of imports of goods and services exceeding exports of the same.

However, managing the economy to achieve these objectives simultaneously is not an easy task. Many governments over recent years have failed to achieve these objectives. In part this is because in introducing policies to attain one objective, others become less achievable. There is a trade-off, as illustrated in Figure 21.1. Government economic policies designed to achieve objectives such as higher rates of economic growth and reductions in unemployment can have undesirable consequences. A consequence of higher growth and lower unemployment might be increasing inflation as shortages of raw materials, factories and offices as well as skilled labour force up prices. Another result might be increasing imports as individuals and consumers spend increasing sums of money on imports causing a balance of payments problem.

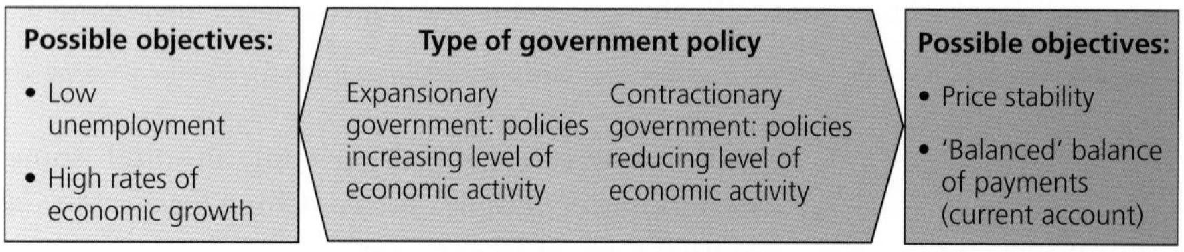

Possible objectives:	Type of government policy		Possible objectives:
• Low unemployment • High rates of economic growth	Expansionary government: policies increasing level of economic activity	Contractionary government: policies reducing level of economic activity	• Price stability • 'Balanced' balance of payments (current account)

Figure 21.1 Government policies and economic objectives

The government's economic policies

The government operates a number of different policies with the aim of providing the best possible economic environment for UK businesses. This entails adjusting the level of activity in the economy to avoid the excesses of booms and slumps. The government's economic policies can be divided into three categories.

1 **Monetary policy**. Using this policy the government (or the Bank of England acting on its behalf) manipulates the amount of money and/or interest rates within the economy in order to achieve the desired level of economic activity.
2 **Fiscal policy**. This refers to the government's use of taxation and public expenditure to manage the economy. By adjusting the levels of taxation and government expenditure, the government can alter the level of activity within the economy.
3 **Supply-side policies**. These are designed to improve the free operation of markets and therefore the total amount that is produced (or supplied) by the economy. Privatisation is one type of supply-side policy along with limiting trade union power and providing training for unemployed workers.

Monetary policy

This type of economic policy involves adjusting the amount of money in circulation and hence the level of spending and economic activity. Monetary policy can make use of one or more of the following:

- altering interest rates
- controlling the money supply
- manipulating the exchange rate.

Although at times all three techniques have been used, more recently governments have tended to rely upon altering interest rates to manage the economy. Since 1997 the Monetary Policy Committee of the Bank of England has had responsibility for setting interest rates. The Monetary Policy Committee sets interest rates monthly with the aim of achieving the government's target for inflation while attaining long-term growth in the economy. Table 21.1 highlights the aims that may lie behind the authorities altering interest rates and, importantly, the implications for individuals and businesses.

Rising interest rates	Falling interest rates
The likely *objectives* of increasing interest rates include the following:	Reductions in interest rates may be introduced with the following *objectives* in mind.
Reducing the level of consumer spending Limiting inflationary pressure in the economy Slowing the level of economic growth (as measured by GDP) Avoiding increasing imports creating a deficit on the balance of payments (In general higher interest rates will assist in dampening down an economic boom.)	Reducing levels of unemployment Stimulating the level of production in the economy Promoting exports sales by reducing the exchange value of the pound Increasing rates of economic growth in the economy (Reducing interest rates can assist an economy in recovering from a slump.)
The likely *consequences* of increasing interest rates include the following:	The *consequences* for businesses and individuals of falling interest rates include the following:
Many businesses may experience falling sales as consumers increase savings Demand for products purchased on credit may decline significantly Businesses cancelling or deferring investment plans Firms reduce borrowing by, for example cutting levels of stocks Increased value of sterling increasing the prices of exports while reducing import prices (In general higher interest rates will assist in dampening down an economic boom.)	Demand and sales are likely to increase especially for products bought on credit Production is likely to be stimulated increasing employment Export sales of price sensitive products may increase while imports become less competitive Businesses may undertake increased investment promoting growth in industries such as construction

Table 21.1 Changes in interest rates – objectives and implications

Broadly speaking, rises in interest rates depress the level of economic activity and reductions promote an expansion of economic activity.

Interest rates are the price of borrowed money. Although the Bank of England sets the base rate, many other interest rates operate in the UK. The precise rate of interest charged on a loan depends on several factors, including the time period of the loan and the degree of risk attached to it.

In the UK, expenditure is sensitive to changes in interest rates. One prime reason for this is mortgage interest payments. Millions of UK consumers have mortgages. A rise in interest rates increases the payments made on mortgages, leaving less money available for other types of expenditure. Similarly, a cut in rates reduces mortgage payments freeing money for other forms of expenditure.

Effects of changes in interest rates

The impact of rising interest rates will depend upon the size of the change as well as the initial rate. A small increase at a relatively high level of rates will have little impact, while a larger increase from a low base rate will have a significant impact.

Not all businesses are affected equally. We can identify several categories of businesses that are particularly susceptible to changes in interest rates.

- Small firms are often affected greatly by changes in interest rates as they have smaller financial reserves and a relatively greater need for borrowing. The Bank of England estimates that every 1 per cent rise in interest rates costs the UK's 1.5 million small firms an extra £200 million in interest rate payments. Significant rises in interest rates can lead to substantial increases in bankruptcies among small firms.

- Even larger firms with high levels of borrowing (and therefore high levels of gearing) can be affected by alterations in interest rates. For example, a rise in rates can lead to a hefty increase in interest payments forcing firms to reduce costs elsewhere or to pass on the extra expenses in the form of higher prices – if this is possible. Alternatively a cut in interest rates offers a substantial reduction in expenses to such firms improving their competitiveness.

- Firms trading overseas are affected by alterations in interest rates. Rising interest rates tend to lead to an increase in the exchange rates as individuals and businesses overseas purchase sterling to invest in UK financial institutions to benefit from higher rates. A fall in interest rates would have the opposite effect.

However, it is not only the direct effects of altering interest rates that affect businesses. The use of interest rate policy by the authorities can have a profound impact upon the general economic environment in which businesses operate. The Bank of England's Monetary Policy Committee changes interest rates to assist the government in achieving its economic objectives. This means that altering rates affects the level of unemployment, inflation and growth existing in the economy. They also change managers' expectations of these key economic variables affecting their day-to-day and strategic decisions.

Table 21.2 illustrates the relationship that exists between the level of interest rates and key economic variables such as economic growth and unemployment.

Other economic variables	Rising interest rates	Falling interest rates
Unemployment	Unemployment increases as levels of production decline	Unemployment declines as the level of economic activity rises
Inflation	Falling demand and output reduces inflationary pressure	Increasing output and spending causes prices to rise fuelling inflation
Economic growth	Will slow as business cut output and investment	Is stimulated by cheaper loans and rising business investment
Exchange rates	Value of the pound is likely to rise	Exchange value of the pound generally falls
Balance of payments (current account)	Less imports purchased improving the current account balance	Increased spending will 'suck in' imports worsening current account balance

Table 21.2 Interest rates and other economic variables

Quantitative easing (QE)

Since March 2009 interest rates in the UK have been held at 0.5 per cent by the Bank of England, the lowest figure ever. This removed the possibility of lowering rates further to expand production and to help the economy achieve higher rates of economic growth and recover from the 2008–09 recession. But when interest rates can go no lower, a central bank's only monetary policy option is to pump money into the economy directly. That is quantitative easing (QE).

The way the central bank does this is by buying assets – usually financial assets such as government and corporate bonds – using money it has simply created. The institutions selling those assets (either commercial banks or other financial businesses such as insurance companies) will then have 'new' money in their accounts, which then boosts the money supply. The hope is that this money is subsequently used to purchase goods and services and to boost output and growth. The UK government has injected £275 billion into the UK economy through QE since 2009.

Fiscal policy

Fiscal policy is the use of government expenditure and taxation as a means of controlling the level of activity within the economy. In particular a government's fiscal policy is the relationship between the level of government expenditure and the amount raised in taxation in any given year. The fiscal year runs from 6 April to 5 April the following year.

The balance between taxation and government expenditure is determined annually when the Chancellor of the Exchequer announces the annual budget. The government can operate two broad types of fiscal policy.

1 Expansionary fiscal policy. This entails cutting taxation and/or increasing government expenditure on items such as health, education, social services, defence and transport. The effect will be to increase the amount the government borrows to fund its expenditure (known as the public sector net cash requirement or PSNCR) or to reduce the surplus held in the government's coffers at the end of the fiscal year.

2 Contractionary fiscal policy. This is brought about by reducing government expenditure or increasing taxation, or by both policies simultaneously. The effect is to increase the government's PSNCR or to reduce its surplus on its budget for the fiscal year.

Figure 21.3 summarises the operation of fiscal policy. Fiscal policy can help to stabilise the economy (avoiding the worst effects of the business cycle) through the operation of the 'automatic stabilisers'. For example, lower unemployment when the level of economic activity is high means temporarily lower social security spending, higher income tax receipts and higher National Insurance contributions. Higher company profits generate higher corporation tax receipts, and higher spending by consumers yields higher VAT receipts and excise duties. These factors together will have a contractionary effect, dampening an economic boom.

The Government's fiscal worries

Since the recession of 2008–09 the UK Government has sought to reduce its spending as well as increasing its revenue through tax rises such as the increase in VAT in January 2011. In March 2011 the Government estimated that the current budget deficit would be £99 billion in 2011–12, of which £49 billion could be expected to continue and needed action to eliminate it by the target date of 2015. Eliminating such a large deficit over a relatively short time period has resulted in the Government introducing a spending review which set out severe cuts in its expenditure over the next five years. One effect that this is expected to result in is the loss of between 400,000 and 600,000 jobs in the public sector.

Inevitably such large cuts in government expenditure will have a contractionary effect on the UK's economy, at least in the short term, although politicians have differing views on the likely effects.

BUSINESS IN FOCUS

Public sector job losses 'worse than forecast'

The current rate of public sector job losses is far greater than official projections and suggests total job cuts in the sector will be 50 per cent higher than forecast, researchers said in October 2011.

Since April, the public sector had lost jobs at five times the rate predicted by the Office for Budget Responsibility (OBR), the Chartered Institute of Personnel and Development (CIPD) said.

The CIPD called on the government to halt public sector job cuts.

The government responded that the cuts were needed. A spokesman said: 'Risks in the global economy make it even more essential to stick to the government's essential deficit reduction plan, which is supported by the International Monetary Fund, the OECD and the CBI. This plan is essential for sustainable growth and has helped deliver record low interest rates for families.'

However, the CIPD research suggested that the public sector job cuts could be far greater than the OBR's latest projections. In June 2010, the OBR had forecast that the government's spending cuts, designed to reduce the UK's budget deficit, would lead to 610,000 public sector job losses between 2010–11 and 2015–16. However, in November 2010 it reduced this projection to 410,000.

The CIPD said that, based on the current rate of job cuts, the actual number of jobs lost in the public sector would probably be 610,000 – 'exactly the same as the initial OBR projection'.

As a result, it called for the government to 'call a halt to public sector job cuts while the economy and labour market remain in the current fragile condition'.

Several economists and opposition politicians also called on the government to rethink its planned spending cuts given the weak performance of the UK economy.

(*Source: Adapted from BBC News, 10 October 2011*)

Question:

What might be the advantages and disadvantages to businesses of job losses in the public sector on this scale?

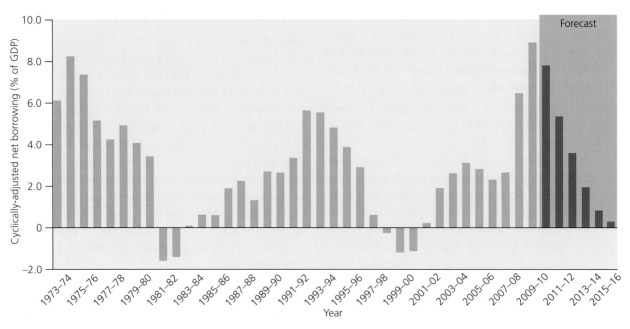

Figure 21.2 The Government's budget deficit. This shows the extent to which government spending has exceeded its revenue or income and the impact of the Government's spending review in reducing the deficit by 2015–16.

(Source: HM Treasury)

The effects of tax and expenditure policies

Tax and expenditure policies can have immediate effects on the level of economic activity, although the precise effects will depend upon the types of tax altered and the nature of government expenditure.

- Direct taxes. These are taxes on income and profits and include income tax and corporation tax (levied on company profits). Direct taxes take a larger amount from individuals earning high salaries and companies announcing handsome

profits. The government can forecast with some accuracy the effects arising from an increase (or reduction) in income tax. Although the overall effect may be predicted, the implications for individual businesses will vary according to the type of product supplied. Firms supplying luxury goods (long-haul foreign holidays, for example) might be significantly affected by a change in income tax rates, especially for those earning higher incomes, while those selling basic foodstuffs may be relatively unaffected.

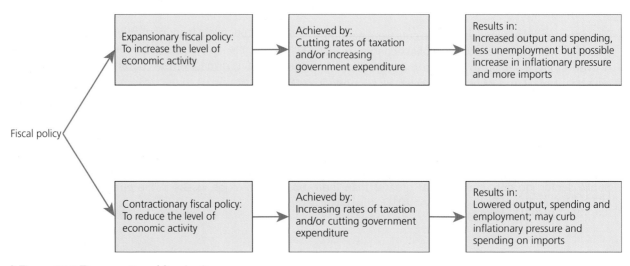

Figure 21.3 The operation of fiscal policy

- Indirect taxes. VAT (value added tax) and other taxes on spending are classified as indirect. Changes in this type of taxation can have a rapid effect on the level of economic activity, although its effects are difficult to predict. An increase in VAT (as in January 2011, when it rose from 17.5 per cent to 20 per cent) will cut consumer spending, reducing demand for goods and services and eventually lower the level of economic activity. However, the extent of the fall in demand will depend upon the price elasticity of demand for the goods in question. Consumers will continue to purchase essentials such as fuel and food, although demand for products associated with DIY, for example, may decline. An important side effect of increasing indirect taxes is that it is inflationary.

BUSINESS IN FOCUS

Focus DIY stores to close

The administrators of collapsed DIY chain Focus have confirmed that about 3,000 jobs will go after they failed to find a buyer for the loss-making chain. A massive everything-must-go sale will start. Focus, which had debts of about £230 million, collapsed earlier this month and buyers have been found for only 55 out of its 178 shops. The DIY chain employed 3,920 people and the sale of clusters of stores to rivals B&Q and Wickes, as well as discount chain B&M Retail, has saved just 900 jobs.

The scale of the closure programme is another grim milestone for the beleaguered UK retail sector, which continues to suffer as a result of weak consumer spending more than a year after the end of the recession. The jobs blow follows last week's announcement by Mothercare that it planned to close 110 of its high street shops, as trade shifted online and to out-of-town retail parks where the operating costs were lower.

Focus's problems were compounded by weak consumer confidence, caused in part by the rise in VAT in January. The DIY sector has been among the hardest hit as the housing market, one of the most important forces behind spending on home improvements, seized up. 'UK retailers are facing one of the most challenging retail environments in recent times and the DIY sector has become highly competitive, with only the strongest players being able to thrive and survive,' said Simon Allport (one of the administrators). He said the administrators were still in talks about a number of stores but the plans to liquidate the stock would see stores close and remaining employees going through a 'redundancy process'.

(*Source: Zoe Wood and Julia Kollewe in* The Guardian, *25 May 2011 www.guardian.co.uk*)

Question:

What actions might retailers such as Mothercare take to survive in 'one of the most challenging retail environments in recent times'?

Government expenditure is the other half of fiscal policy. Governments may spend more in two broad categories.

1 Transfer payments. This is expenditure on unemployment benefit, pensions and other social security payments. Changes in expenditure on these items will have a rapid impact as they are received by relatively poor members of society who will most likely spend the increase or cut back if necessary almost immediately. An increase in transfer payments often results in substantial increases in demand for basic goods such as food, public transport and gas.

2 The infrastructure. Governments improve the infrastructure through their spending on housing, roads and flood protection. Investment in these areas can increase the level of economic activity by boosting demand for the services of construction firms while reducing costs for other firms. A new road, for example, might cut a business's transport costs. This, however, is a much slower method of altering the level of economic activity. In 2011 the Government has announced that it is planning to bring forward much planned expenditure on infrastructure projects to boost the UK economy.

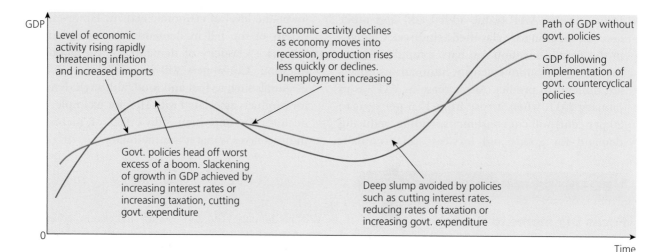

Figure 21.4 Government economic policies at work

Supply-side policies

These are a range of measures intended to improve the operation of free markets and the amount that is produced by the economy. They can take a number of forms.

Labour market measures

In recent years UK governments took a range of measures intended to allow labour markets to operate more effectively. In the 1980s and early 1990s successive Conservative governments reduced the power of trade unions to permit labour markets to operate more freely. By reducing the power of trade unions businesses were enabled to implement policies to allow them to use labour more flexibly and efficiently. For example, employees were able to carry out a range of duties, rather than a limited role to avoid demarcation disputes. Disputes and confrontations became less common as a consequence of a series of laws.

Other policies have been implemented to encourage the effective operation of the UK's labour markets. The unemployed have been encouraged back into the labour force through the provision of training programmes designed to equip them with employable skills, by limiting the availability of unemployment benefit to those in genuine need and the cutting of income tax rates on low earners to encourage people into the labour force. Currently the Coalition Government is seeking to reduce the EU's powers over UK labour markets. In particular it wishes to remove restrictions over the number of hours that employees can be required to work each week to allow businesses to respond flexibly to changes in demand for goods and services.

Privatisation

This is the process of transferring organisations from the state to the ownership and control of individuals and other businesses. In the 1980s and 1990s many major state enterprises were sold into the private sector and the policy has continued in recent years, although it has slowed as the state now owns relatively few enterprises. Since 2000 the London Underground system has been partly privatised as has air traffic control and the port of Dover. In 2011 the Government announced the privatisation of some of the UK's prisons.

The arguments in favour of privatisation are formidable.

- By removing potentially inefficient monopolies privatisation offers consumers the possibilities of lower prices and better-quality products. Businesses in competitive markets cannot afford to be inefficient. The policy is based on the unshakeable belief in the superiority of private enterprise.
- Private businesses are more likely to pursue long-term policies to increase the prosperity of the businesses, to the benefit of all in society. In contrast, the objectives of the former nationalised industries were unclear and inconsistent – often little more than breaking even.
- The process of privatisation has provided huge sums of revenue for the government. This has and will continue to assist the government to reduce its deficit as part of its spending revenue. The proceeds from privatisation played an important part in creating a society in which enterprise was valued and rewarded.

In recent years governments have tended to move away from the policy of full privatisation, preferring to see the public and private sectors cooperate on a range of projects. Two systems have been used.

- Public–Private Partnerships (PPP). This is collaboration on relatively small-scale projects using private- and public-sector money.
- In contrast, a Private Finance Initiative (PFI) relies entirely on funding from the private sector. This approach is used for major capital projects such as building schools and hospitals. The building of the Norfolk and Norwich hospital is a well-known example of the operation of PFI in the UK. This policy has been called into question in 2011, as many analysts consider it to be an expensive way of providing public services.

However, the drawbacks of privatisation have become increasingly apparent.

- Critics have argued that privatisation has not, in fact, resulted in more efficient industries. The establishment of watchdogs such as OFGAS and OFTEL have highlighted that left to their own devices the newly privatised companies might exploit consumers through excessive prices and poor-quality products. Furthermore, the well-publicised problems facing the UK's railways have provided further ammunition for those opposed to privatisation.
- Some economists have argued that having thousands of UK citizens as shareholders in privatised businesses has not encouraged long-term strategies to be implemented by the businesses. Shareholders, having limited understanding of business, have looked for a quick return. This has encouraged managers to maximise short-term profits – a policy not necessarily in the long-term interests of the company or the economy.

The perceived shortcomings of privatisation have led to a mild backlash against the policy. Countries such as New Zealand have created new nationalised industries, and even California has taken steps in this direction. Government proposals to privatise the UK's forests encountered much opposition and the plans were abandoned.

Other supply-side measures

Governments have tried to make other resources more freely available by removing controls on the operation of markets that provide capital and land. The negotiating of the free movement of capital throughout the EU has been a major factor in

Figure 21.5 Government plans to privatise the UK's forests were abandoned

increasing the funds available to UK enterprises. Similarly the removal of rent controls has made the property market operate more effectively.

Government intervention

The issue of privatisation is at the forefront of the debate about the extent to which the government should intervene in the economy. The Conservative governments of the 1980s and 1990s argued that the state's role in the economy should be minimised to allow markets and businesses to operate with the maximum degree of freedom. In part this was achieved through the policy of privatisation, but also by the reduction in government subsidies and grants to industry and by legislation limiting the state's role in business matters. For instance, wages councils (responsible for setting the wages of many low-paid workers) were abolished and regulations governing markets such as telecommunications and financial services were relaxed allowing new suppliers and greater competition. This approach to managing the business environment is described as laissez-faire and puts faith in a greater degree of self-regulation by businesses. The current Coalition Government is committed to reducing the administrative burden placed on businesses by the state.

There are, not surprisingly, advantages and disadvantages to businesses arising from trading under a government that takes a laissez-faire approach to economic management.

Businesses benefit through less interference in their activities. Government intervention tends to raise costs (insisting on the employment of safety officers, for example) reducing the competitiveness of UK businesses. This can be a major handicap for firms operating in highly price-competitive markets where small cost differentials can lead to substantial loss of sales. By removing the requirement to pay national rates of pay, wages may fall in poor regions such as the north of England and Wales attracting new businesses and making existing businesses more competitive. Supporters of the laissez-faire approach argue that the UK has been extremely successful in attracting overseas producers because of the lack of regulation of businesses. They contend that governments cannot prevent the operation of global market forces, and that it is a waste of money to try. Finally, the laissez-faire approach helps to promote an entrepreneurial society in which individuals take responsibility for their own economic welfare and are more creative and hard working as a result, to the benefit of all in society.

However, many individuals and groups oppose the laissez-faire style of economic management.

They argue that it is vital that governments support struggling industries in poor regions to prevent heavy unemployment and poverty. The government is considering how best to intervene in the telecommunications market to ensure that all regions of the UK have access to fast broadband services. This is seen as essential in generating economic growth in more remote areas.

Governments should recognise that economic change is inevitable, and attempt to soften the blow of economic restructuring of this type. Allowing businesses to regulate their own activities with minimal interference from the authorities is likely to result in unscrupulous businesses exploiting workers (through low wages and poor conditions) and consumers – by charging excessive prices. Some controls, it is argued, are essential to prevent this happening, particularly where a business faces little competition and exploits its monopoly power.

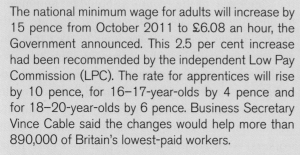

BUSINESS IN FOCUS

National minimum wage to rise 2.5 per cent

The national minimum wage for adults will increase by 15 pence from October 2011 to £6.08 an hour, the Government announced. This 2.5 per cent increase had been recommended by the independent Low Pay Commission (LPC). The rate for apprentices will rise by 10 pence, for 16–17-year-olds by 4 pence and for 18–20-year-olds by 6 pence. Business Secretary Vince Cable said the changes would help more than 890,000 of Britain's lowest-paid workers.

The LPC was unanimous in its recommendations 'despite all the economic uncertainties' according to its chairman, David Norgrove.

The complete set of changes are:

- over-21s: up 15 pence (2.5 per cent) to £6.08
- 18–21-year-olds: up 6 pence (1.2 per cent) to £4.98
- 16–17-year-olds: up 4 pence (1.1 per cent) to £3.68
- apprentices: up 10 pence (4 per cent) to £2.60.

With consumer prices inflation at 4.4 per cent, the Unite union said the wage increase was not enough to help low-paid workers keep up with rising food and fuel prices. 'This small increase in the minimum wage is completely outstripped by the current rate of inflation,' said Unite general secretary, Len McCluskey.

The British Chambers of Commerce (BCC), however, said the wage increase risked pricing young people out of work at a time when youth unemployment was at a record high. 'The change to the national minimum wage rates announced today is the wrong increase, at the wrong time,' said the BCC's David Frost. 'These changes will be a barrier to job creation, and ultimately economic recovery,' he said.

(*Source: Adapted from* BBC News, *7 April 2011*)

Question:

Does the apparent success of the minimum wage suggest that the government should play a larger role in determining pay rates for other groups of workers, such as company directors?

Political decisions affecting trade and access to markets

The trend towards the globalisation of markets has been encouraged by a series of decisions by governments. In this chapter we shall consider two key decisions.

Greater freedom of trade

The World Trade Organisation (WTO), which we profiled in the previous chapter, has played a prominent role in developing increased freedom to trade. The economic case for an open trading system based on multilaterally agreed rules is simple enough and rests largely on commercial common sense. But it is also supported by evidence: the experience of world trade and economic growth since the Second World War. Tariffs on industrial products have fallen steeply and now average less than 5 per cent in industrial countries. Reducing tariffs is intended to increase world trade and to promote economic growth and development.

Lowering trade barriers is one of the most obvious means the WTO uses to encourage trade. The barriers concerned include customs duties (or tariffs) and measures such as import bans or quotas that restrict quantities selectively. From time to time other issues such as red tape and exchange rate policies have also been discussed at WTO meetings.

The General Agreement on Trade and Tariffs (GATT) was the WTO's predecessor and existed until the end of 1994. Since GATT's creation in 1947–48 there have been eight rounds of trade negotiations. A ninth round, under the Doha Development Agenda, is now underway – and has been for 11 years! At first these focused on lowering tariffs (customs duties) on imported goods. As a result of the negotiations, by the mid-1990s industrial countries' tariff rates on industrial goods had fallen steadily to less than 4 per cent.

Although the actions of the WTO have attracted much opposition from pressure groups it has encouraged nations to take political decisions aimed at freeing trade and promoting economic growth. The current round of talks at Doha have lasted for more than 11 years without a clear and agreed outcome, but this should not detract from the WTO's achievements and those of its predecessor GATT.

Extending the European Union

The European Union currently has 27 member states constituting a market of over 475 million people – larger than the markets of Japan and the US added together. In 2004, the EU expanded to 25 states with the entry of Cyprus, the Czech Republic, Estonia, Hungary, Latvia, Lithuania, Malta, Poland, the Slovak Republic and Slovenia. In 2007, Bulgaria and Romania joined taking the total to 27. Despite the ongoing financial difficulties in the eurozone countries, Turkey has made an application to join the EU, while Iceland and some former Balkan states such as Croatia are engaged in discussions.

The enlargement of the EU offers businesses considerable opportunities. Since 2004 there have been 100 million extra consumers freely available to businesses in the UK and other established EU member states. Firms expect to achieve increased sales and perhaps to benefit from economies of scale in supplying this enlarged market. High-technology and service industries (such as telecommunications and banking) are likely to face relatively little direct competition from these countries.

Furthermore, firms have chosen to locate in countries such as Poland and Hungary to benefit from lower costs and, initially at least, fewer controls on business activity. The states of eastern Europe have proved particularly attractive to manufacturers seeking to expand or transfer their European productive capacity.

There is, of course, a downside to the expansion of the EU. Greater competition is likely to appear in some industries where the relatively undeveloped economies of eastern and southern Europe have an advantage. Analysts fear that western Europe's agricultural industry may be threatened by a surge of cheap imports from the new member states. The productive potential of Poland's agricultural industry alone is awesome. Jobs may also be lost in economies where labour is relatively expensive as the competition from the east increases.

Pan-European strategy

The increasing size of the EU market will place firms under greater pressure to develop strategies to sell their products successfully in 27 diverse countries. A single strategy is unlikely to suffice.

Managers responsible for developing strategies to sell products throughout Europe will need to consider a number of issues.

- The acceptance that Europe is not a single market, not even 27 countries, but a series of localities all of which are different in some way and need different products and different approaches to marketing. This means that differences in products and marketing campaigns are essential, making it more difficult to achieve economies of scale.
- Increasing Europe's borders has made it bigger, more varied and more difficult to sell to successfully as languages and cultures become more diverse.
- Market intelligence becomes less available as one moves east and south. This makes it more difficult for managers to assess market and production potential within the proposed new member states of the EU. For example, pricing can be a difficult issue: firms wish to generate the highest sales possible, but to avoid allegations of dumping cheap goods.

The legal environment

The law is a framework of rules governing the way in which our society operates. These rules apply to businesses as well as individuals. The legal framework affects businesses in a number of ways affecting almost all areas of business activity. Marketing, production, employment, relationships with customers and competitors and even the establishment of the business itself are examples of business operations influenced by the law.

Employment legislation

Individual labour law

This aspect of employment legislation refers to the rights and obligations of individual employees. The amount and scope of individual labour law has increased in recent years, in part encouraged by the growing influence of the European Union on business matters in the UK.

A number of the most important Acts relating to individuals in employment are explained as follows.

- Working Time Regulations, 1998. This European Union legislation (hence the term regulation) set a limit on the hours that employees could be required to work each week of 48 hours. Employees can opt to work longer hours if they wish, but employers cannot insist that they do so without inserting an appropriate clause in their contract of employment. The regulations also gave employees an entitlement to four weeks' paid annual leave.
- The National Minimum Wage Act, 1998. This highly publicised act came into force on 1 April 1999. The key features of this legislation are:
  a general hourly minimum wage rate – £6.08 an hour from October 2011
  a minimum level of £4.98 for 18–21-year-olds
  all part-time and temporary workers must be paid the minimum wage.

The Equalities Act 2010

The Equalities Act replaced a number of earlier anti-discrimination laws (such as the Disability Discrimination Act) to simplify legislation in this area.

The Act relates to nine protected characteristics, which cannot be used as a reason to treat people differently or unfairly. Each person in the UK is protected by this Act, as everybody has one or more of the characteristics. The protected characteristics are:

1 Age
2 Disability
3 Race
4 Gender reassignment
5 Marriage and civil partnership
6 Religion or belief
7 Pregnancy and maternity
8 Sex
9 Sexual orientation.

This Act established the different ways in which it is illegal to treat someone, including victimisation and harassment.

The Act makes unfair treatment unlawful in the workplace, in education, when supplying goods and services, and in private clubs.

Collective labour law

This group of laws apply to the operation of industrial relations and collective bargaining as well as the activities of trade unions. For many years the law did not play a significant role in employer–employee relationships. However, this philosophy was changed when the Conservative governments of the 1980s and early 1990s passed a series of Acts intended to restrict the power of trade unions.

- Employment Act, 1980. Under this Act employers were no longer obliged to negotiate with unions – many unions were derecognised as a consequence. It also restricted picketing to employees' own place

Employment protection

Individual labour law	Collective labour law
This legislation relates to the rights and obligations of individual employees	This body of law covers the activities of trade unions and the conduct of industrial relations.
Examples include: • Disability • National Minimum Wage Act, 1998 • Working Time Regulations, 1998 • Equalities Act, 2010	Examples: • Employment Acts,1980 and 1982 • Trade Union Act, 1984 • Trade Union Reform and Employment Rights Act, 1993 • The Employment Relations Act, 1999

Figure 21.6 Employment legislation

BUSINESS IN FOCUS

UK employee loses discrimination case

A UK worker has lost his case against a Chinese telecoms company that he sued for race discrimination after claiming that 49 workers in Basingstoke were axed and replaced with Chinese nationals.

Judeson Peter, a customer support engineer who was paid £48,000 per annum by Huawei Technologies, accused the firm of making him redundant because he was British. But a Southampton-based employment tribunal ruled that he had not been unfairly dismissed and that the company had followed a fair and legal process. Huawei said in a statement that the firm was a 'responsible and fair' employer that was committed to the 'equal treatment of all our employees, providing the same career opportunities to all our employees globally. We are committed to expanding our business both in the UK and across Europe. Currently 75 per cent of our 650 UK workforce is recruited locally and we will continue with growth plans to attract new talent to the company'.

According to the *Daily Mail*, Peter had told a Southampton-based employment tribunal earlier in the week that there was 'clearly' an increasing number of Chinese staff working at the company. He claimed that it had transferred 342 workers to the UK over the last three years, while 49 British and non-British employees had lost their jobs over the same period. Peter, who alleged unfair dismissal, breach of contract and discrimination on the grounds of race and age, said: 'A large number of Chinese employees were joining the workforce in 2009 at the same time that I was being made redundant. I believe I could have done these roles.'

Huawei has its headquarters in Guandong, China, employs 110,000 personnel worldwide and made a profit of £2.36 billion last year.

(*Source:* Equality Law, *23 November 2011, www.equalitylaw.co.uk*)

Question:

Although the company won this case, how might it have suffered as a result of it?

of work, thereby outlawing 'secondary picketing'. Closed shops were only permitted if supported by at least 80 per cent of the workforce in a secret ballot.
• Employment Act, 1982. This Act increased the support for closed shops to 85 per cent to make their continuation legal. It also made trade unions liable for damages if the union supported illegal industrial action.

• Trade Union Act, 1984. This legislation made a secret ballot of employees a legal requirement before industrial action was lawful.
• Employment Act, 1988. This protected union members from disciplinary action by their union for refusing to take part in strike action or picketing, despite a ballot in favour of industrial action.

- Employment Act, 1990. Closed shops were finally outlawed by this piece of legislation. Employees taking part in unofficial strike action could be dismissed without being able to make a claim of unfair dismissal.
- Trade Union Reform and Employment Rights Act, 1993. This Act required unions to give employers a minimum of seven days' notice before taking official industrial action. It also abolished wages councils and minimum pay rates.
- Employment Relations Act, 2000. Under this Act a trade union with a membership exceeding 50 per cent of the employees in any particular business can demand union recognition and the right to introduce collective bargaining.

Unfair dismissal

Unfair dismissal is the termination of a worker's contract of employment without a legal reason. Legislation relating to unfair dismissal only relates to workers once they have been in a particular job for one year or more. There are a limited number of reasons why an employee might be dismissed:

- where a job no longer exists – this is redundancy
- gross misconduct – examples of this reason include theft from the employer or behaving violently at work
- failing to carry out duties in 'a satisfactory manner'
- another substantial reason (for example, the ending of a temporary contract).

All other reasons for dismissal are considered unfair. Employees who think they have been unfairly dismissed can claim compensation by taking their case to an employment tribunal.

Health and safety legislation

Health and safety legislation has been enacted to discourage dangerous practices by businesses and to protect the workforce. The legislation is designed to prevent accidents in the workplace, and has developed steadily over the last 30 years.

The main Act in the UK is the Health and Safety at Work Act of 1974. This is an example of delegated legislation whereby Parliament gives responsibility to government departments to update the scope of the legislation as necessary. This process avoids any particular aspect of legislation taking up too much of Parliament's time.

BUSINESS IN FOCUS

HSE prosecutes council

Castle Point Borough Council has been prosecuted by the Health and Safety Executive (HSE) following an incident where a seven-year-old girl was trapped by a water outlet at the Waterside Swimming Pool on Canvey Island.

The girl was using the swimming pool with her great grandfather at Waterside Farm Leisure Centre. Her hair was sucked into the water sampling outlet on the side of the pool, trapping her underwater for 2 minutes and 36 seconds. Her great grandfather had to pull a clump of hair from her head in order to free her. She was unconscious when she was finally taken out of the water, limp and blue in colour, but came round once laid on the poolside.

HSE told Basildon Magistrates' Court today that Castle Point Borough Council, which owns and runs the swimming pool, had not managed the risks to members of the public using it. Castle Point Borough Council from Kiln Road, Benfleet, Essex pleaded guilty to breaching section 3(1) of the Health and Safety at Work etc. Act 1974 and was fined £18,000 and ordered to pay costs of £7,500.

(*Source: Health and Safety Executive, 15 June 2011, www.hse.gov.uk*)

Question:

Is the damage to the Council's reputation a greater penalty than the fine?

The Health and Safety at Work Act gives employers a legal obligation 'to ensure that they safeguard all their employees' health, safety and welfare at work'. The Act covers a range of business activities:

- the installation and maintenance of safety equipment and clothing
- the maintenance of workplace temperatures
- giving employees sufficient breaks during the working day
- providing protection against dangerous substances.

Businesses are required to protect the health and safety of their employees 'as far as it is reasonably practicable'. This means that the business concerned must have provided protection appropriate to the risks. Thus, a chemical manufacturer would be expected to provide considerable protection for its employees.

The Act also requires employees to follow all health and safety procedures and to take care of their own and others' safety. The Health and Safety Executive (HSE) oversees the operation of the Act and carries out inspections of businesses' premises. The HSE also carries out investigations following any serious workplace accident.

The impact of employment and health and safety legislation on businesses

It is easy to assume that employment legislation simply constrains business activities and therefore has a purely negative effect on businesses. However, this is not the case. Employment legislation can have positive and negative effects on businesses and their activities.

Employment legislation can help to motivate the workforce. Employees who work in a safe and secure physical environment will be more contented and probably more productive. Employers will also avoid the costs, delays and bad publicity caused by accidents at work or employee complaints about poor conditions. Furthermore, freedom from arbitrary dismissal may encourage a more cooperative, flexible and productive workforce enhancing the performance of the business.

Employment legislation restricting the powers of trade unions has encouraged the development of more flexible workforces. The ending of closed shops and the requirement for union recognition in many circumstances made it easier for businesses to implement changes in working practices improving the productivity and competitiveness of UK businesses. Firms were able to adopt single-union deals, making collective bargaining simpler and ending damaging and costly demarcation disputes (disputes between unions concerning the respective roles of their members in the organisation).

Following the legislation of the 1980s and 1990s, the UK has some of the most employer-friendly employment legislation in the western world. This has helped the country to attract the lion's share of foreign investment entering Europe. The UK is an attractive site for overseas businesses because its favourable employment legislation helps to minimise labour costs. The UK is the major recipient of inward investment into the European Union.

However, in spite of the employer-friendly approach in the UK, employment legislation does increase costs above the level that would exist if no legislation were in place. To take an example, the national minimum wage, introduced in 1999, raised the wages of an estimated 3 million employees. It is estimated to have added approximately 1 per cent to the nation's wage bill. Similarly the requirement (under the Disability Discrimination Act) to make 'reasonable' alterations to the working environment to enable the employment of disabled employees adds to costs of production.

Employment legislation also requires firms to employ greater numbers of non-productive workers such as human resource managers and safety officers. These employees add to the costs of production without making any direct contribution to the output of the business. Inevitably, costs increase as a consequence.

The effects of legislation may be greater on small firms who have fewer resources and are less able to keep up with changes in employment laws and may not be able to afford to respond in the appropriate manner. Larger firms have expert human resource specialists and are more likely to be geared up for change. They may also be able to afford specialist employment lawyers to advise them on avoiding some of the effects of a new piece of employment legislation.

Consumer protection legislation

Consumer protection is a term used to describe a series of acts designed to safeguard consumers against:

- businesses charging excessively high prices or rates of interest
- unfair trading practices, for example selling quantities less than those advertised
- unsafe products such as children's toys with sharp objects or toxic paint
- having insufficient information on which to take purchasing decisions.

Since 1973 the Office of Fair Trading (OFT) has overseen consumer protection in the UK. The OFT's Consumer Affairs Division seeks to improve the position of consumers by giving consumers information to allow them to make better choices when purchasing goods and services. It also protects consumers by prosecuting offenders against consumer legislation and negotiating voluntary codes of practice with producers.

Consumers in the UK have become more informed and less accepting of poor products or unscrupulous trading practices by businesses. Consumers often conduct research (aided by organisations such as *Which?*) before making major purchases. This trend is known as consumerism.

There is a considerable quantity of consumer protection legislation in the UK. The Acts listed below represent some of the highlights.

- Sale of Goods Act, 1979. The basic requirement of this Act is that the goods sold should be:
of merchantable quality – must be undamaged and unbroken and must work properly
fit for the particular purpose.
as described by the manufacturer.
- Consumer Protection Act, 1987. Under this Act producers are liable for any harm to consumers caused by their products.
- Weights and Measures Act, 1986. This Act states the weights and measures to be used in trading. Weights and measures must be guaranteed in terms of accuracy.
- The Consumer Credit Act, 1974. This Act lays down that consumer credit can only be given by licensed organisations. It also sets out the terms under which credit may be given.
- The Trade Descriptions Act, 1968. This Act makes misleading descriptions of goods and services an offence.
- The Consumer Protection from Unfair Trading Regulations 2007. These were introduced from May 2008. They specifically ban a number of practices which have been deemed to be unfair to the consumer. An example of a practice that is banned is aggressive selling by businesses. The Regulations have also amalgamated a lot of the consumer harms under previous legislation, such as Trade Descriptions Act, 1968, as well as keeping pace with new scams which are continuously being evolved and developed by scammers and rogue sellers.

The Advertising Standards Authority. This body supervises the operation of this code of practice. It is an independent body; its members are not in the advertising industry. The ASA protects the public interest and deals with complaints from the public.

The impact of consumer protection legislation on businesses

Increases in the scope of consumer protection have had a number of implications for businesses. Meeting the requirements of consumer credit regulations, for example, entails additional processes and personnel thereby increasing costs. Under this legislation, consumers expect firms to supply products that are safe and of consistently high quality. They expect the processes used in production to avoid any pollution and raw materials to be from sustainable sources. All of these expectations mean that production costs are greater, partly owing to additional costs of materials and employing extra workers to carry out the necessary checks.

Consumerism has resulted in higher expectations on the part of consumers, in areas not necessarily covered by legislation. They require firms to provide advice and technical support and effective after-sales service and to behave in a socially responsible manner.

Environmental protection

The government has passed a series of Acts of Parliament designed to protect the environment. Two acts are of particular importance.

1 The Environmental Protection Act, 1991 introduced the notion of integrated pollution control recognising that to control only a single source of pollution is worthless as damage to one part of the environment means damage to it all. This Act requires businesses to minimise pollution as a whole.
2 The Environment Act, 1995 established the Environment Agency with a brief of coordinating and overseeing environmental protection. The Act also covered the control of pollution, the conservation of the environment and made provision for restoring contaminated land and abandoned mines.

The government imposes fines on firms who breach legislation relating to the protection of the environment. These are intended to force firms to bear the full costs of their production (including external costs) although environmental pressure groups and other critics believe that the sums are not sufficient to deter major businesses with annual budgets of billions of pounds. The government also attempts to encourage 'greener' methods of production through the provision of grants. It created the Carbon Trust, which since April 2001 has given capital grants to firms who invest in energy-saving technologies. The intention is to slow the onset of global warming by reducing emissions of carbon dioxide. In a similar vein, government funding is also supporting the development of environmentally friendly offshore wind farms to generate 'clean' electricity.

The EU has also passed hundreds of directives relating to environmental protection. The UK is also a signatory to a number of international agreements intended to provide environmental protection on a global scale. For example, the UK government has attended a number of Earth Summits at which targets for reducing the production of carbon dioxide have been agreed.

Strategic responses to changes in the political and legal environment

The political and legal environment can have a major impact on the way in which businesses operate and also their costs of production. Because of this, businesses may adopt a variety of strategies in response to changes in this aspect of their external environment.

- **Relocation**. If a government implements new legislation which increases costs or raises taxes, perhaps on company profits, business may respond by relocating to another country with more favourable corporate tax regimes and business laws.
- **Changing production methods.** This might be an appropriate response to changes in laws on environmental protection or to new employment laws. In the latter case a business might seek to reduce the number of employees in its workforce. However, such changes can be costly, especially in the short term. However, changing production methods to a more environmentally friendly approach may offer the business additional benefits in terms of improving corporate image.
- **Producing new products.** A new product range may be necessary to meet environmental laws. For example, furniture manufacturers may only use wood from sustainable sources and need to

change the products they manufacture to meet this requirement. This strategy may also be necessary due to changes in the law. For example many pubs have created outdoor smoking areas following the ban on smoking in public places in England in 2007.

The precise strategic response taken by any business will depend upon a range of factors including the nature of the product that the business sells, the financial position of the business and the extent of the change in the political or legal environment. Changes in health and safety legislation for example are likely to have significant effects on businesses involved in construction, agriculture or manufacturing, but may be less significant for some businesses in the service sector.

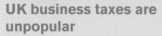
UK business taxes are unpopular

Over a quarter of businesses in the UK could be relocated due to unpopular tax policy, according to new reports. A study by Tenon Group found that 26 per cent of business owners are thinking about relocation due to the UK's high tax levels. The figure rose to 30 per cent for business owners who had previously experienced a recession.

Some 37 per cent of respondents admitted that high corporation tax (on company profits) was the primary reason for possible relocation, with 16 per cent citing capital gains tax as a cause.

Andrew Jupp, head of tax at Tenon, said: 'Entrepreneurs are genuinely struggling in the current legislative and economic environment and the Government must heed this call for help in order to avoid losing some of the country's most talented business people.'

(*Source: GAAP, 27 October 2008, www.gaapweb.com*)

Question:

What problems might a business experience when relocating to another country during a period of slow economic growth in the UK?

Key terms

Economic policy: a series of actions (such as changing interest rates and altering rates of taxation) through which the authorities attempt to create the best possible economic environment for businesses and individuals.

The economy: the complex interaction of millions of consumers, thousands of businesses, and governments in supplying a wide range of goods and services.

Balance of payments: a record of a country's trade and employment occurring in an economy at a given point in time.

Balance of payments (current account): a financial record of a nation's trade in goods and services with the rest of the world over a specified period of time, normally a year.

Laissez-faire – a policy in which governments reduce taxes and spend less on supporting the activities of businesses.

Supply-side policies are designed to improve the free operation of markets and therefore the total amount that is produced (or supplied) by the economy.

Direct taxes – taxes on income and wealth, for example, income tax, corporation tax and inheritance tax.

Indirect taxes – taxes on spending, for instance value added tax.

Interest rates – the price of borrowed money.

Fiscal policy – the use of taxation and public expenditure to manage the level of economic activity.

Monetary policy – controlling the amount of money and/or interest rates within the economy in order to achieve the desired level of economic activity.

Privatisation – the process of transferring organisations from state to the ownership and control of individuals and other businesses.

Consumerism is an approach that places the interests of the consumer at the heart of discussions about business decisions or activities. This could be contrasted with trade unionism, which places the interests of workers first.

Consumer protection is a term used to describe a series of Acts designed to safeguard consumers against:

- businesses charging excessively high prices or rates of interest
- unfair trading practices, for example selling quantities less than those advertised
- unsafe products, such as children's toys with sharp objects or toxic paint
- having insufficient information on which to take purchasing decisions.

This chapter only includes some examples of political decisions that have contributed to the shaping of the environment in which businesses operate. Many others have taken place and you should be prepared to use them to support your arguments as necessary.

It is easy to just think of laws as constraining business activity. Of course this is true, but legislation also offers opportunities to many businesses. For example, health and safety laws requiring firms to provide safety clothing and equipment provides sales for businesses supplying such equipment. Legislation requiring food products to have 'use by' dates created a small industry supplying specialised ink jet printers for use on production lines.

The list of strategic responses in this chapter is not exhaustive – there are others that a business may adopt. It is important that you consider the possible responses in the context of the scenario with which you are presented. This will assist you in selecting and justifying the most appropriate response in any circumstances.

Progress questions

1 Outline the difficulties a government may encounter when attempting to achieve its economic objectives simultaneously. *(7 marks)*
2 Distinguish between monetary and fiscal policy. *(4 marks)*
3 Outline the possible effects of a fall in interest rates on a multinational business manufacturing consumer durables such as televisions and freezers. *(8 marks)*
4 Explain how a government might use fiscal policy to increase the level of economic activity. *(7 marks)*
5 Outline the implications for businesses of one supply-side policy that a government may use. *(6 marks)*

6 Explain **two** possible employment laws that might increase the costs of UK businesses. *(4 marks)*
7 How might UK Health and Safety legislation help to make a workforce more productive? *(6 marks)*
8 Outline **two** ways in which business activities might be constrained by consumer protection legislation. *(6 marks)*
9 Explain **two** ways in which employment legislation might make the UK a less attractive location for footloose multinationals. *(6 marks)*
10 Explain **two** implications for UK businesses of the operation of the National Minimum Wage Act. *(6 marks)*

Essay questions

1 British Aerospace (BAE), a major international manufacturer of aircraft and other military equipment, reduced the size of its UK workforce by 3,000 people in 2011, while the Arcadia Group announced plans to close up to 260 of its Topshop and BHS stores by 2014. Throughout 2011 the base rate of interest in the UK was 0.5 per cent, the lowest level ever set by the Bank of England. Does this mean that interest rates have little effect on strategic decisions taken by businesses? Justify your answer with reference to BAE, Arcadia and/ or other businesses with which you are familiar. *(40 marks)*

Candidate's answer:

Interest rates are the price of borrowed money. The level of interest rates can influence businesses in two ways. If interest rates are low it is cheaper for businesses to borrow money and thus it is more likely that they will invest in new non-current assets because there will be a better chance of new projects resulting in a profit. Interest rates at 0.5 per cent make it very cheap to raise capital and should encourage businesses to do so. Secondly low interest rates should help to persuade consumers to buy more goods and services, especially more expensive products like cars which are often paid for through loans. Low interest rates should make it cheaper to repay the loans and will encourage consumers to spend money, especially when their savings are earning little interest.

But the level of interest rates might not be totally relevant to BAE as it makes weapons for the government. Low interest rates will help the company to raise capital to build new factories as it is a manufacturer but since it sells its products to governments, the rate of interest on loans may be less relevant. Low interest rates will help the company to succeed in export markets. Low UK interest rates mean that the demand for pounds on international markets will be reduced and this will reduce the pound's exchange rate. As a consequence the price of UK exports will be reduced and imports from overseas will rise. This will help international businesses like BAE to compete in global markets for military equipment and thus it will benefit from interest rates at 0.5 per cent.

Retailers like Topshop and BHS can also benefit from low interest rates. They may operate store cards and will be able to offer lower rates of interest on these cards helping to attract more customers giving higher levels of sales. The Arcadia Group may also be able to offer interest free loans on large purchases as a means of persuading customers to purchase its products helping to boost its sales and profits. However, these low interest rates and benefits are also available to the other major UK retailers so this does not offer a competitive advantage.

Retailers will benefit in other ways too. Many purchase expensive high-street property to enable them to attract large numbers of customers and to maintain prestigious sites in well-known locations. This requires heavy investment in capital and long-term borrowing to finance this. Low interest rates will reduce the cost of interest on these loans and will improve the company's profits by reducing its finance costs on its income statement. This may help to improve profit margins.

To conclude it is important to have low interest rates at a time when the economy is not performing well to boost the sales and to reduce the costs of all businesses. This can lead to more employment and spending and can assist recovery. It can also aid businesses competing globally by reducing their costs and causing a fall in the exchange rate which makes it easier to compete. Interest rates do therefore have a big impact on strategic decisions taken by businesses.

Examiner's comments:

This is not a good quality answer to this essay question. Although it is clear that the candidate has a fair amount of knowledge of the topic of interest rates and knows a little about the two companies mentioned in the title, they have not really answered the question. This is a danger when tackling essays – it is easy to drift into a line of argument that bears some relation to the title, but does not really answer the question. This answer focuses on how interest rates might affect businesses operations, rather than their importance to decision-making. The candidate did not have to illustrate their answer with reference to these two companies – they could have chosen any company.

The candidate did not pick up on the tension in the question. It provided two examples of companies who are scaling down the size of their operations at a time of record low interest rates in the UK. A strong answer would have explored the reasons for this (falling government spending and very low consumer confidence are obvious points) and used this to develop an argument about the importance of interest rates in strategic decisions in different circumstances. Of course, the importance of interest rates in strategic decisions depends on the circumstances and the nature of the decision.

Question:

2 The European Union has 27 members and nearly 500 million consumers. Several countries, including Turkey and Croatia, are in negotiations to become members. Do you think that further enlargement of the EU can only offer benefits to businesses? Justify your answer with reference to businesses with which you are familiar. *(40 marks)*

22 Businesses and the social environment

> Businesses are a part of society and are affected to varying extents by social change. The factors arising from changes in society change and, at the time of writing, factors such as migration and the increasing need to protect employment may be argued to be important social factors affecting the activities of businesses. The chapter also considers ethical behaviour by businesses. This has become a more important influence on the activities of businesses over time, and represents a distinctive USP for a number of organisations.
>
> **In this chapter we examine:**
> - social responsibility and changes in the social environment
> - the ethical environment and developments that have taken place
> - how businesses respond to changes in the social environment.

Introduction

Stakeholders are individuals or groups within society who have an interest in an organisation's operation and performance. Stakeholders include shareholders, employees, customers, suppliers, creditors and the local community. The interest that stakeholders have in a business will vary according to the nature of the group.

Over recent years businesses have become much more aware of the expectations of stakeholder groups. In the past managers were expected to operate businesses largely in the interest of the shareholders. A growing awareness of business activities and the rise of consumerism has complicated the task of the management team. Today's managers have to attempt to meet the conflicting demands of a number of stakeholder groups.

Social responsibility

Social responsibility is a business philosophy that emphasises that firms should behave as good citizens. They should not merely operate within the law, but should consider the effects of their activities on society as a whole. Thus, a socially responsible business attempts to fulfil the duties that it has towards its employees, customers and other interested parties. Collectively these individuals and groups are termed a business's stakeholders.

Figure 22.1 Examples of a business's stakeholders

Meeting social responsibilities has many implications for businesses, including:

- taking into account the impact of their activities on the local community – protecting employment and avoiding noise pollution, for instance
- producing in a way that avoids pollution or the reckless use of finite resources
- treating employees fairly and not simply meeting the demands of employment legislation
- considering the likely sources of supplies (and whether they are sustainable) and the ways in which suppliers meet their social responsibilities.

Stakeholder group	Possible nature of stakeholder's interest
Shareholders	Expectation of regular dividends Rising share prices Preferential treatment as customers – for example, lower prices
Employees	Steady and regular income Healthy and safe working conditions Job security Promotion and higher incomes
Customers	Certain and reliable supply of goods Stable prices Safe products After-sales service and technical support
Suppliers	Frequent and regular orders A sole supplier agreement Fair prices
Creditors	Repayment of money owed at agreed date High returns on investments Minimal risk of failure to repay money owed
The local community	Steady employment Minimal pollution and noise Provision of facilities (for example, scholarships, arts centres or reclaimed areas) for local community

Table 22.1 Stakeholders' interests

Some businesses willingly accept these responsibilities partly because their managers want to do so, partly because they fear a negative public image. It can be argued that socially responsible behaviour can pay off for businesses in the long term, but may entail additional short-term expenditure.

Areas of social responsibility

The nature of a business's social responsibility will vary according to the nature of the business. A petrochemicals company is more likely than a bank is to be concerned with polluting the environment. On the other hand, in an age of rapid developments in information technology, banks may see their social responsibility to be the maintenance of employment. We can identify a number of key elements of social responsibility, beyond the responsibilities a business has to its shareholders.

1 **Responsibilities to consumers**. The consumer has become a force to be reckoned with over recent decades and this has been reflected in the development of consumerism. Increasingly, consumers have been better informed about products and services and prepared to complain when businesses let them down. The rise of consumerism has meant that businesses have been required to behave more responsibly by looking after the interests of the consumer.

2 **Responsibilities to employees.** Businesses have a variety of responsibilities to their employees that are not a legal requirement. For example, firms should provide their employees with training to develop their skills as fully as possible and make sure that the rights of employees in developing countries (where employment legislation may not exist) are protected fully. This may mean paying higher wages and incurring additional employment costs.

3 **Responsibilities to the local community**. Firms can benefit from the goodwill of the local community. They can encourage this by meeting their responsibilities to this particular stakeholder group. This may entail providing secure employment, using local suppliers whenever possible and ensuring that the business's operation and possible expansion does not damage the local environment.

4 **Responsibilities to customers**. Customers are critical to businesses. Offering high-quality customer service, supplying high-quality products that are well designed and durable and at fair and reasonable prices should create satisfied customers and quite possibly generate repeat business.

5 **Responsibilities to suppliers**. Businesses can promote good relations with suppliers by paying promptly, placing regular orders and offering long-term contracts for supply. These are not legal requirements, and might result in higher prices for materials and components, but may also assist suppliers to meet their own responsibilities, for example in the maintenance of employment.

Business and social responsibilities

Stakeholder and shareholder concepts

The importance of social responsibility to businesses is a matter of considerable debate. Businesses accept the need to make a profit for their owners and the need to operate within the law. More contentious is the expectation that a competitive business will take into account the obligations it may have to society in general. This is known as the stakeholder concept whereby a business considers the needs of its stakeholders – and not just its shareholders.

In spite of the growing popularity of the stakeholder concept, there are opponents to the philosophy. A school of thought exists that supports what is known as the shareholder concept. This view advocates the management of businesses to meet their responsibilities to shareholders, by maximising profits. This should result in increasing share prices and higher dividend payments. The needs of other stakeholders are regarded as of secondary importance.

In what ways can businesses accept their social responsibilities?

Businesses can take a variety of decisions and actions allowing them to meet their responsibilities to their stakeholders in general.

- For manufacturing businesses the impact of their sources of supply can be considerable. Using sustainable sources for resources means that future generations will have access to the same materials. Body Shop International's refusal to use any materials that are unsustainable or any components that have been tested on animals reflects a sense of responsibility to many relatively poor communities in developing countries and to animals.
- Many manufacturers have considerable potential to pollute the environment. Altering production processes (sometimes at considerable cost) can reduce or eliminate many forms of pollution. A report by the Environment Agency in 2011 revealed that many rivers in England and Wales have shrugged off their industrial past to become havens for wildlife, walkers and anglers.
- Socially responsible firms put employees before profits. Maintaining employment, even when the level of sales is not sufficient to justify this, is an important means of fulfilling social responsibilities, as is the continuation of unprofitable factories to avoid creating high levels of localised unemployment. These types of policies are only really sustainable in the short term, unless the business in question is earning handsome profits elsewhere.
- Choosing suppliers is an increasingly important issue for firms who are keen to confirm that their raw materials and components come from socially responsible firms. Many firms operate a code of conduct for suppliers, including restaurant chain McDonalds. The fast-food company operates a code of conduct prohibiting suppliers from using child labour and insisting upon basic health and safety standards. The company has a contractual right to inspect suppliers' premises to ensure the code of conduct is implemented.
- Supporting the local community is an important way of fulfilling social responsibilities. It can provide the public with a clear perception of the 'caring' side of modern businesses. BT, one of the largest telecommunications companies in the world, received an award for its support of the children's charity, Childline. BT donated £1 for every customer who signed up to the company's 1571 call minder service. This action improved the company's reputation and increased sales of the 1571 service by 25 per cent.
- Over 70 per cent of the UK's best-known companies (those making up the FTSE 100) are members of Business in the Community. This organisation exists to assist member companies in 'continually improving, measuring and reporting the impact that their business has on their environment, workplace, marketplace and community'. However, the state of the economy can influence the level of charitable donations given by businesses. *Corporate Giving*, which provides guidance for corporate funders in their charitable giving, says that giving by companies fell from £808 million in 2008 to £762 million in 2010 – a fall of 5.7 per cent.

Unilever adopts a sustainable business model

Consumer products manufacturer Unilever has unveiled a 'new business model' making sustainability central to all its global operations. It pledged to halve the environmental impact of its products while doubling sales over the next 10 years.

Chief executive Paul Polman said the new model was 'the only way to do business long term'.

The company said it would report on its progress towards achieving these goals annually. Unilever makes a number of well-known brands, such as Persil, Dove, Flora, PG Tips and Ben & Jerry's. It has made three overarching commitments to achieve by 2020:

- to cut by 50 per cent the environmental impact of its products in terms of water use, waste and greenhouse gases
- to obtain 100 per cent of its agricultural supplies from sustainable sources
- to improve the health and well-being of 1 billion people across the world.

Polman continued: 'There is a compelling case for sustainable growth – retailers and consumers demand it and it saves us money.'

The company plans to deliver these commitments by doubling its use of renewable energy to 40 per cent of total energy use; reducing its water consumption by 65 per cent from 1995 levels; reducing the waste sent for disposal by 70 per cent on 1995 levels; and reducing the levels of salt, fat and sugar in its food products.

The company admitted these were difficult goals, but said they could be achieved with the help of non-governmental organisations (NGOs), governments and suppliers.

(*Source: Adapted from Richard Anderson, BBC News, 15 November 2010*)

Question:

How might Unilever's shareholders react to the launch of the company's 'new business model'?

Environmental threats and opportunities

The media take a great interest in business activities in relation to the environment. When firms are found to be guilty of some act of pollution adverse publicity is likely to follow. Society expects higher standards of environmental performance than in the past.

There are many potential causes of damage to the environment. The major environmental concern identified by the government is global warming. This is caused by the release of a concoction of industrial gases (principally carbon dioxide) that has formed a layer around the earth. This layer allows the sun's rays in but prevents heat escaping causing the so-called 'greenhouse effect'. Other problems include the pollution of rivers and land and the dumping of waste, some of which is toxic and harmful to wildlife and humans alike.

Businesses contribute in many ways to the creation of environmental damage.

- The emission of gas through production processes.
- Pollution caused by transporting raw materials and products, particularly using road vehicles which emit noxious gases and create congestion and noise. A report by the EU suggested that pollution from vehicles in the UK could be responsible for up to 40,000 deaths among elderly people each year.
- The pollution of the sea by businesses using it as a 'free' dumping ground. The North Sea is one of the most polluted stretches of water in the world.
- Destruction of natural environments as a result of activities such as logging (cutting down trees for commercial purposes as in the Amazon rainforest) and the building of homes on greenfield sites.

Despite engaging in activities which damage the environment there is evidence that businesses are improving some aspects of their environmental performance. Figure 22.2a illustrates that the contribution to greenhouse gas emissions by the non-household sector (UK companies and the public sector) fell by 26.9 per cent between 1990 and 2009. However, average temperatures in the UK, and across the globe, continue to rise, with a rapid increase since 1990, as shown in Figure 22.2b.

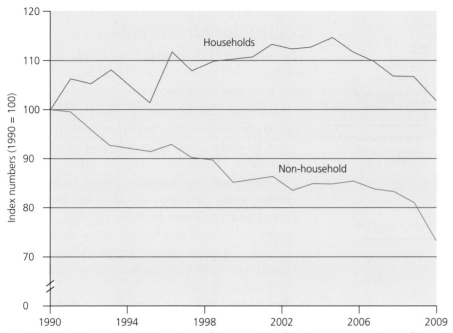

Carbon dioxide, methane, nitrous oxide, hydroflurocarbons, perflurocarbon and sulphur hexaflouride

Figure 22.2a The contribution of businesses (non-household) to greenhouse gas emissions has declined since 1990

(Source: Social Trends 41, National Statistics website: www.statistics.gov.uk)

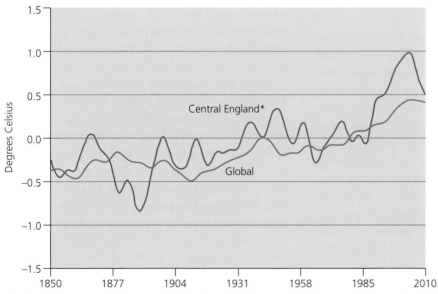

Data have been smoothed using a 21-point binomial filter to remove short-term variation from the time series and to get a cleaner view of the underlying changes.

*Central England temperature is representative of a roughly triangular area of the UK enclosd by Bristol, Lancashire and London.

Figure 22.2b Global warming

(Source: Social Trends 41, National Statistics website: www.statistics.gov.uk)

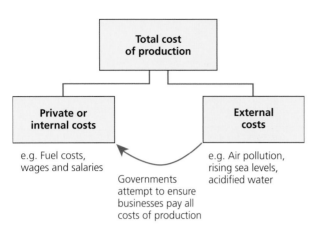

Figure 22.3 Internal and external costs of production

Costs of polluting the environment

Businesses are acutely aware of their private costs (the costs of production they have to pay themselves, such as expenses for raw materials and wages). These are easy to calculate and form part of the assessment of profitability. However, environmental pressure groups and others have pressed for businesses to acknowledge the costs they create for other groups in society – the external costs of production.

Noise, congestion, air and water pollution all impose costs on other individuals and groups in society. A firm extracting gravel from a quarry may create a number of external costs. These could include congestion on local roads caused by their lorries. This would impose costs in terms of delay and noise pollution on local residents. The destruction of land caused by the quarrying could create an eyesore for people living nearby and may reduce the value of their properties. Dust may be discharged into the atmosphere. The quarrying firm will not automatically pay for these costs. It requires government action to ensure that they pay these external costs as well as their internal ones.

Thus, the total costs of production equal internal or private costs plus external costs borne by third parties. By ensuring that firms pay all the costs associated with the production of a product, governments can avoid what is termed market failure. Market failure could occur as a result of pollution because suppliers may not be charged the full costs of production and oversupply might result, as profits are high.

Implications of environmental control for businesses

The need to alter business practice to take account of environmental protection has implications for most aspects of business activity.

- **Production**. Firms face pressure to redesign products to use less materials and packaging and to make these materials biodegradable or recyclable. These requirements affect all types of businesses. For example, house builders are under great pressure to build on brownfield sites (land previously used for building, often in cities and towns) and to protect the countryside by minimising the use of greenfield sites. Strict controls on production techniques are intended to minimise pollution.
- **Purchasing**. Businesses are encouraged to seek sources of supply that are sustainable and do not damage the environment or to use recycled materials. For example, the paper industry makes a great deal of use of recycled materials and uses this as part of its promotion.
- **Marketing**. Businesses use their 'green credentials' as an important component of their marketing strategy. Adverts will make reference to environmental protection and even projects to improve the environment. Packaging will confirm the company's concern to avoid pollution. This is particularly important to firms that are seen to have great potential to pollute (BP and Shell, for example) or for those who use this aspect of their operations as a USP – Body Shop International is an example of the latter. The Business in Focus item on Unilever on page 308 shows the importance some managers place on an environmentally friendly business model.
- **Human resources**. New processes and procedures in manufacturing make some jobs and skills obsolete creating a need for redundancies or retraining. Environmental management has resulted in many businesses needing employees with new skills requiring a retraining programme or recruitment. Environmental managers seek to minimise the effects of the business's activities on the environment and to ensure that the firm meets new legislative requirements as they emerge. Businesses may also seek to hire employees skilled in resource management and having the ability to influence corporate decisions to ensure the development of management strategies designed

for the most efficient use of scarce natural resources.

The implications of environmental protection are profound, especially for the so-called polluting sector (for example, chemicals and oil extraction and refining). They require a corporate response from senior managers within a business. But as with many external influences the environment provides opportunities for businesses as well as constraints.

New markets have been created for businesses supplying training in environmental management. Firms also offer to supply environmental control equipment to adapt production processes to minimise the possibility of environmental harm. Equally a market exists for testing equipment to monitor emissions or the toxicity of waste products. Finally, businesses can use environmental policies as a means of obtaining a competitive advantage. BMW, for example, promotes itself as a manufacturer of cars that are almost entirely recyclable. This could prove attractive to environmentally aware consumers.

Why should businesses accept social responsibilities?

It is easy to argue that by meeting their social responsibilities businesses are likely to reduce profitability. Providing workers with ongoing training, investing in facilities for the local community, trading with suppliers who do not use cheap child labour and only engaging in non-polluting production techniques will all increase costs, reducing a business's profitability and limiting its international competitiveness.

However, this is a relatively simple view and there are more subtle arguments in favour of businesses fulfilling their obligations to society.

- Some businesses have a high profile with regard to issues of social responsibility. Thus the public sees Shell and BP as having enormous potential to pollute. The directors of these companies have recognised this and regard socially responsible behaviour as an important competitive weapon. As an example, Shell supports education and produces much valuable material for use in schools and colleges. In particular the company gives information on environmental matters. Clearly both Shell and BP hope that being seen to be socially responsible will improve their sales.
- Sometimes behaving in a socially responsible manner may reduce costs. Treating employees with respect and paying slightly above the going rate may improve motivation and performance and reduce labour turnover. For businesses where labour represents a high proportion of total costs (banking and insurance, for example) this could represent an important saving.
- In markets where little product differentiation occurs, adopting a socially responsible stance may improve sales and profits. The Co-operative Bank is alone in the banking sector in promoting its ethical and socially responsible views. In recent years its profits have risen significantly.

It may be that social responsibility might reduce profits in the short term, but over a longer timescale the marketing advantages may dominate and profits could increase.

Corporate social reports

Analysts do not assess businesses solely in terms of profits, even during difficult financial times, such as those the UK is experiencing at the moment. It can be argued that businesses should also be judged in terms of their records on pollution, consideration of their employees and support for the community. A growing proportion of businesses are engaging in social responsibility reporting. This form of reporting includes the costs to the business of acting in a socially responsible manner (charitable donations for example) and the benefits received, which are usually difficult to quantify in monetary terms. A few businesses include their social reports within their annual reports. A 'successful' business might not be the most profitable, but the one of most value to all sections of the community in which it operates.

Apple is the world's most admired company

Apple has topped the Forbes Magazine list of the world's most admired companies for the fourth straight year. Despite worries that the company would start to suffer without its iconic front man Steve Jobs, who is taking some time at home to recover from a recent liver transplant, Apple has continued to set the bar for tech companies throughout the world.

The latest innovative product to be launched by the company is the second generation of the iPad, a device which has changed the way we all think about computers and has left the rest of the industry struggling in its wake.

In purely financial terms, Apple is now the biggest and richest technology company in the world, beating Microsoft into an ignominious second place. The maker of reassuringly expensive, beautifully designed and irritatingly compelling gadgets has doubled its profits over the last year.

(*Source: Adapted from Thinq.co.uk, 8 March 2011*)

Note: Steve Jobs sadly passed away just seven months after this article was written.

Question:

To what extent is this result important for the management team at Apple?

The trend for social and environmental reports continues with most of the UK's largest firms producing some form of social and environmental report. However, while the quality of the reports is improving, some do not cover all the relevant issues. Many companies do not have their Corporate Social Reports (CSR) independently audited to confirm their accuracy. A further criticism is that some firms do not analyse their supply chains. This means that suppliers could engage in practices such as employing children without it being revealed in the CSR. It is possible that the impact of the 2008–2009 recession might reduce the number of businesses prepared to devote resources to producing a CSR, or to improving its quality and extent.

Extracts from Morrisons corporate social report

Morrisons is the UK's fourth largest food retailer and publicises the fact that it takes its responsibilities to the environment and society in which it operates very seriously. The company is large and:

- has 455 stores throughout the UK
- in 2011 its annual sales revenue exceeded £1,475 million
- employs 132,000 staff.

The following extract from Morrison's Corporate Responsibility Review summarises the company's commitments to its stakeholders.

Stakeholder engagement is vital to ensuring our approach to sustainable business is both relevant and effective. It enables us to identify issues and opportunities, respond to changing needs and adhere to best practice by incorporating different views and feedback into our business operation.

All of our stakeholders recognise the importance of sustainable business. Each group has their own particular focus.

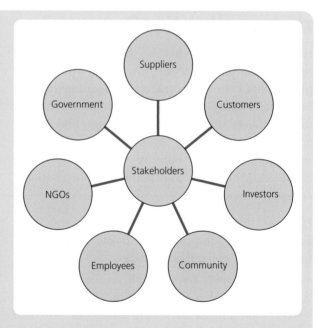

Figure 22.4 Morrisons stakeholders

(*Source: Morrisons Corporate Responsibility Review, 2011*)

Customers want quality products at a fair price with good service.

Communities are where our operations have the most immediate impact. They require us to be a good neighbour and bring employment and investment.

Investors expect a good return on their money and that we grow, find opportunities and mitigate risks.

Employees want good working conditions, job security and satisfaction and opportunities to develop a career.

NGOs (Non-Governmental Organisations) ask us to follow their advice, change or adapt the way we operate.

Government sets the rules and regulations but also asks for support to deliver government policy.

Suppliers want our custom, a reliable trading relationship and the best price.

Question:

What competitive benefits might Morrisons receive from publishing a CSR each year?

The changing social environment

At any time there are a number of factors of work which promote change in the social environment in which businesses work and require socially responsible businesses to respond in certain ways. Current issues may include the following.

The increasing threat of unemployment

Since the recession in the UK which started in 2008 there has been a significant rise in the level of unemployment. By December 2011 the number of people unemployed in the UK had risen to over 2.62 million, or 8.3 per cent of the working population. This posed a challenge for businesses seeking to act in a socially responsible manner and to protect employment. At a time when sales are falling along with profit margins, it is increasingly difficult to maintain employment levels within a business when a real improvement in the economic situation appears to be some way off.

The increasing importance of the environment

Many UK consumers are increasingly aware of, and concerned by, the threat that the activities of businesses pose to the environment. This concern has manifested itself in two main ways. Some people have protested against the activities of businesses such as airlines and energy companies, which are deemed to be responsible for substantial amounts of pollution. For example, in 2011 protesters stopped work at the Cuadrilla shale gas site in Banks, near Southport, after climbing on to a drilling rig. Drilling for shale gas is believed by some to pollute water supplies and to cause earthquakes, albeit minor ones. The protesters' actions received much publicity. This can result in affected businesses receiving adverse publicity and may have negative effects on sales. Other businesses whose activities are considered to be damaging to the environment may experience falling sales and revenues.

BUSINESS IN FOCUS

The environment remains important to consumers

Consumer spending on 'green' goods from Fairtrade food to eco-friendly travel grew by almost a fifth over two years despite the economic downturn, figures reveal today. The ethical market in the UK was worth £43.2 billion in 2009 compared with £36.5 billion two years earlier – an increase of 18 per cent – according to the Co-operative Bank's annual Ethical Consumerism Report.

Some sectors enjoyed huge growth, including Fairtrade goods, which pay a premium to farmers and producers in poor countries to help them work their way out of poverty. Fairtrade food grew by 64 per cent to reach sales of £749 million, while sales of the RSPCA-backed Freedom Food products tripled in two years to reach £122 million. However, sales of organic foods declined.

Ethical personal products, including clothing and cosmetics, was the fastest growing sector, increasing by 29 per cent to reach £1.8 biilion. The market ➝

for green home products such as energy-efficient appliances grew by 8 per cent in two years to reach £7.1 billion.

(*Source: Rebecca Smithers in* The Guardian, *30 December 2010*)

Question:

Why would any business opt to ignore the environmental and ethical values of its consumers?

Changes in the composition of the UK population

The UK is subject to large migrationary flows. There have been substantial inflows of migrants from parts of Asia and also eastern Europe, leading to the UK's population size passing 62 million in 2010 and a rate of increase at its highest since the 1960s. This has led to a demand for different types of products (as well as offering new sources of labour supply). In 2011 545,000 Polish passport holders lived in the UK, compared with just 75,000 in 2003. This development has led to a new market niche, and suppliers of Polish products such as foods and books have appeared. It is not just small businesses that have responded to the creation of this niche market. Tesco has launched a Polish language website to enable it to supply homesick Polish migrants in the UK with products from 'home'.

The UK's ageing population

The population of the UK is steadily ageing with larger numbers of people in the older age groups. In 2005, 34 per cent (20 million people) of the UK's population was over 50. In 2025 it will be 40 per cent, about 25.5 million people. In 2005 16 per cent of UK citizens were over 65 – this is expected to rise to 21 per cent in 2025 – as many as 13.5 million people. There are expected to be 4.5 million people in the UK aged over 85 in 2025. Figure 22.5 illustrates the main trends in the age structure of the UK's population until 2041. The older age groups represent substantial segments of markets for many products and businesses have responded to the increased spending power of older groups. Firms supplying products including holidays, clothes, insurance and housing have designed products for the older age group.

The rise in the number of single-person households

People in the UK are increasingly living alone meaning that the country is comprised of more, smaller households. This has significant implications for businesses of all types. Table 22.2 illustrates how the number of single person households in the UK is expected to rise until 2026. This trend has implications for businesses supplying houses, consumer durables and even food, where smaller packet sizes may be more commonly purchased.

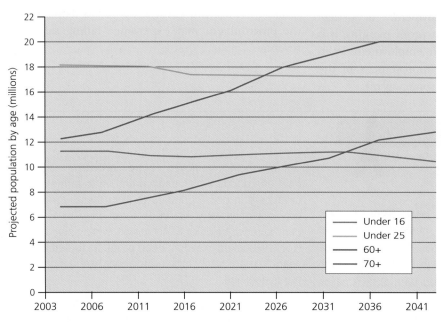

Figure 22.5 The age structure of the UK's population 2003–2041

(*Source: Government Actuary's Department*)

	2003	2026	Average annual increase
Under 25	226,000	254,000	1,000
25–34	797,000	1,048,000	11,000
35–44	923,000	1,460,000	23,000
45–54	834,000	1,415,000	25,000
55–64	947,000	1,792,000	37,000
65–74	1,061,000	1,559,000	22,000
75 and over	1,659,000	2,359,000	30,000
Total	**6,447,000**	**9,886,000**	**150,000**

Table 22.2 One-person households by age in the UK, 2003–2026

(Source: News Distribution Service)

Business ethics

Business ethics can provide moral guidelines for decision-making by organisations. An ethical decision means doing what is morally right; it is not a matter of merely calculating the costs and benefits associated with a decision. Individuals' ethical values vary. Ethical values are shaped by a number of factors including the values and norms of parents or guardians, those of religion, and the values of the society in which a person lives and works. Most actions and activities in the business world have an ethical dimension.

What are ethical decisions?

Ethical behaviour requires businesses to operate within certain moral guidelines and to do 'the right thing' when taking decisions. What exactly is ethical behaviour? This is a tricky question. An ethical decision would take into account the moral dimension, but not everyone would agree about what is ethical. Some may argue that it is not ethically wrong for supermarkets to charge high prices for basic foodstuffs; others would disagree. Different moral values make a decision as to whether a business is behaving ethically a tricky one to reach.

The following scenarios arguably illustrate examples of diverse businesses taking moral decisions.

- Starbucks, the world's largest coffee retailer, has donated £100,000 to a development programme run by the UK charity Oxfam in the East Hararge region of Ethiopia. In this region farmers struggle to produce high-quality Arabica coffee because of poverty and a hostile climate. The money will be spent on improving irrigation as well as providing seeds and tools. Starbucks experts will also offer advice on improving coffee yields and quality, and on strengthening the growers' marketing co-operative. Starbucks and Oxfam also plan to pool ideas on alleviating rural poverty in Ethiopia.
- Primark, the high-street discount retailer, sources much of its clothing in Bangladesh. The company regularly conducts unannounced inspections of its suppliers' factories. Primark pays for these audits and provides training for its suppliers' employees.
- A Work Study Foundation report complimented McDonald's, the fast food chain, for creating jobs in deprived areas within the UK. The report also noted that many of McDonald's managers worked their way up within the company and, when initially recruited, had few qualifications.

Each of these decisions could be judged to be financially disadvantageous to the business in question. It is therefore possible to argue that they

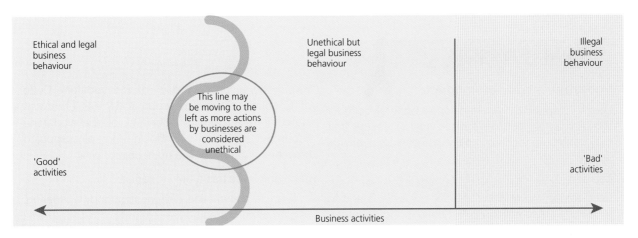

Figure 22.6 Legal and ethical behaviour

Nike faces further allegations of 'sweatshop labour'

Nike is one of the world's top sports clothing brands, but for years it has been troubled by allegations of dealing with suppliers who operate sweatshops and use child labour. The latest allegations relate to workers making Nike's Converse shoes at a factory in Indonesia who say they are being physically and mentally abused.

Workers at the Sukabumi plant, about 60 miles from Jakarta, say their supervisors frequently throw shoes at them, slap them, kick them and call them dogs and pigs. Nike admits that such abuse has occurred among the contractors that make its fashionable high-tops but says there was little it could do to stop it.

Interviews by The Associated Press, and a document released by Nike, show the company has not yet met the standards it set for itself a decade ago in an attempt to end its reliance on sweatshop labour.

One worker at the Pou Chen plant in Sukabumi said she was kicked by her supervisor last year after making a mistake while cutting rubber for soles. 'We're powerless,' said the woman, who like several others interviewed spoke on condition of anonymity out of fear of reprisals. 'Our only choice is to stay and suffer, or speak out and be fired.'

The 10,000 workers at the Pou Chen plant make around 50 cents an hour.

(*Source: Adapted from* The Daily Mail, *13 July 2011*)

Question:

Why might it be difficult for a large multinational such as Nike to operate ethically?

---

have been taken because the businesses believe that it is the morally correct course of action. However, some may contend that there are 'hidden' commercial benefits from each of the decisions.

Ethical codes of practice

As a response to consumer expectations and, in many cases, competitive pressures businesses have introduced ethical codes of practice. In 2008 over 85 per cent of the UK's major businesses (the FTSE 100) operated an ethical code of practice.

They are intended to improve the behaviour and image of a business.

Common themes in ethical codes of practice may include:

- promoting products with integrity and honesty
- minimising possible damage to the environment by, for example, using sustainable sources of raw materials
- competing fairly and avoiding collusion or other anti-competitive practices
- taking into account the needs of the business's stakeholders.

An ethical code of practice states how a business believes its employees should respond to situations that might challenge the values of the business. The first part of an ethical code of practice sets out the values in which the business believes.

The nature of the code will depend on the business concerned. Banks may concentrate on honesty, and chemical firms on pollution control.

Vodafone's code of conduct

Below is an extract from Vodafone's Code of Conduct in which employees are advised how to ensure that they contribute to the company maintaining its ethical standards.

'For Vodafone to maintain its reputation we each need to assume responsibility for our actions and to take action if something is not done in the Vodafone way. If you suspect a breach of The Vodafone Code of Conduct you should report it. Unless otherwise stated in this Code of Conduct or the Vodafone Group Security Policy you should report all suspected breaches first to your line manager.

Each employee has a duty to report:
- financial malpractice, dishonesty, money laundering, corruption or fraud

- failure to comply with a legal obligation that may result in criminal liability or damage to Vodafone's reputation
- a serious breach of Vodafone policy relating to any criminal activity
- any breach or potential breach of data privacy or unlawful disclosure of sensitive and confidential information
- a serious breach of competition law (such as fixing prices in agreement with other suppliers)

- endangering health and safety of employees or the public or serious environmental issues, including threats and assaults involving any Vodafone personnel
- any other suspected criminal activity
- serious conflict of interest without disclosure
- any attempt to conceal any of the above.'

(Source: Adapted from Vodafone plc's Code of Conduct)

Companies normally publicise ethical codes of practice, as in the case of the Vodafone plc above. Being seen to behave ethically is an important element of the marketing strategy of many businesses.

Ethics and profits

A conventional view is that if a business behaves ethically, its profits are bound to suffer. Any of the following ethical actions is likely to increase costs of production and possibly reduce profits:

- using more expensive resources (perhaps recycled or from sustainable sources)
- training employees to behave in an ethical manner
- treating animals with respect
- implementing safety systems beyond the legal requirements.

However, the argument is not as simple as it might appear at first.

The Co-operative Group is an example of a business that has its ethical stance as a central part of its marketing strategy. Its businesses includes food, funerals, pharmacy and farming. The Group's ethical position is promoted strongly within the UK and has assisted it in recording an improved performance by the business. In 2011, despite the problems facing the UK economy, the Co-operative Group's sales increased by 6.3 per cent to £11.2 billion, while profit was £459.3 million, an increase of 34.7 per cent.

This example highlights that there are marketing advantages from being seen to behave ethically. Businesses may attract new customers and (as in the case of the Co-operative Group) customers with more money to spend. A reputation for ethical behaviour can provide a business with a USP. This can be particularly valuable when products provided by rivals are similar and may explain some of the success of the Co-operative Group's approach. A positive corporate image may also assist businesses by allowing them to charge higher prices and enjoy increased profits on each sale.

Benefits also exist in terms of recruiting the best employees. A business that is successful and has a good reputation is attractive to potential employees. High calibre employees may be recruited in these circumstances and valuable employees will be less likely to leave. Ethical behaviour can help to develop a talented workforce.

However, a high profile ethical stance is not a guarantee of profits. For example, Body Shop, despite its strong ethical stance characterised by its opposition to testing products on animals, experienced several years of financial problems before it was purchased by L'Oréal.

Businesses introducing ethical practices for the first time may face other costs leading to reduced profits. Training is an obvious cost – for a company to be ethical all employees must carry out their everyday activities in the right ways. Firms may also need to spend heavily adapting production processes to reduce the possibility of pollution. These factors make it probable that profits will be lower, at least in the short run.

Creating an ethical business culture

An ethical business culture exists when all employees in a business behave in a moral manner as a normal part of their working lives. This offers businesses a number of advantages in terms of marketing, particularly in relation to corporate image. Furthermore, businesses with a reputation for ethical behaviour may be more successful in attracting high-quality employees.

However, although senior managers may appreciate the benefits of changing the corporate culture to enable the adoption of an ethical stance, it may be less apparent to employees further down the organisational hierarchy.

The first issue to be resolved is the introduction of an ethical policy into the organisation. The Institute of Business Ethics offers advice to managers seeking to make this change. This information is highlighted as follows.

Six key stages in implementing an ethical culture within a business:

1 Find a champion – make sure that the change has the public support of the chief executive.
2 Discover the issues – discover the ethical issues employees are likely to encounter.
3 Benchmarking – look at the policies introduced by other firms and copy good practice.
4 Test the idea – try the new approach out on a small part of the business first. This will help to iron out teething problems.
5 Code of conduct – issue this to everyone to make sure that all employees, suppliers and interested parties are aware of what is expected of them when taking decisions.
6 Make it work – ethical elements should be introduced into training programmes and especially into induction programmes.

Some businesses have enjoyed great success in developing ethical values within their organisations. Texas Instruments (better known as TI) took the approach of ensuring the organisation behaved ethically by encouraging each individual employee to be ethical in all aspects of their work. This extended to issuing individual employees with cards offering advice on what to do when faced with ethical dilemmas and identifying more senior staff able to offer support.

Introducing ethical approaches and codes of conduct can conflict with existing policies. In some senses a democratically led organisation with high-quality, two-way communication lends itself to implementing change. Such an organisation might be more responsive to a new culture, although there is potential for conflict in a business managed in this way. First, in a democratically managed business employees are unlikely to respond well to a new culture imposed upon them without consultation. Indeed, they may wish to play a substantial role in shaping the new culture, which might conflict with the objectives of the senior managers.

Second, in an organisation with a high degree of delegation employees take responsibility for some decisions and may, if empowered, have considerable responsibility for controlling their daily work. Imposing a new and uniform culture in such an environment may prove difficult. Employees may resent any loss of independence in how they conduct their working lives. This can be a tricky dilemma for even the most highly skilled managers.

Is ethical behaviour simply another form of public relations?

Certainly businesses would like to be perceived as more ethical. There is little doubt that some businesses have adopted a more ethical stance that is genuine. Companies such as Unilever have increasingly based their marketing on their strong moral principles. This can prove to be a profitable decision as well as a moral one. Ethics is seen as good business by many firms at a time when a more informed public demands moral behaviour by firms.

The danger for businesses adopting token ethical stances is that the attentions of the media and pressure groups might reveal the superficial nature of their principles. This could be a public relations nightmare causing substantial damage to the business's public image and profits. However, for firms in the tertiary sector, the temptation to pay lip service to ethical behaviour may prove irresistible.

For many firms however, the decision on their ethical position will depend upon an assessment of the potential costs and benefits. If the costs of ethical behaviour exceed the benefits, a superficial adoption of moral principles is the most likely outcome. However, if a commercial advantage can be gained without incurring too many additional costs, then a complete change of corporate philosophy might result.

Responses to changing social and ethical environments

We have already identified a number of strategies that businesses might adopt in response to changes in the social and ethical environments, notably developing an ethical culture to persuade consumers of the strong moral principles underlying the business. There are other actions that businesses can adopt in response to changes in the social and ethical environment.

- **Adopting new techniques of production.** This may entail using sustainable resources, or reducing carbon emissions that are the by-product of the production process. In contrast it could mean using different resources in production, perhaps, for example, relying heavily on migrant labour. As we saw earlier, such decisions are likely to increase production costs but can form the basis of a distinctive marketing campaign.

- **Developing a new corporate image.** This may involve publicising genuine actions that the business has taken to meet the needs of its stakeholders more fully or to operate throughout the organisation in the most ethical fashion. In part this may require the business to implement an ethical code of conduct and to train its employees. Alternatively it may be based on a marketing campaign to change stakeholders' perceptions of the business. As we saw above it may depend upon the extent to which the ethical stance is genuine.

- **Developing a new product range or entering new markets.** The ageing of the UK's population, for example, may mean that house builders adjust their product ranges to build more bungalows and developments including sheltered housing. The growing size of the market may persuade holiday companies to provide products simply aimed at the 50+ age group. Other businesses may decide to target all their products at this age group.

The precise strategic response taken by any business will depend upon a range of factors including the strength of the competition that the business faces, the financial position of the business and the type and extent of the change in the social or ethical environment. Businesses may be most likely to react strategically to changes that they believe to be long-term. Thus the fashion amongst many consumers towards thrift at the time of writing may prove to be short-term and not worthy of developing new product ranges.

Key terms

Shareholder concept is the view that the main responsibility of managers is to the shareholders (or other owners) of the company.

Social responsibilities are the duties a business has towards employees, customers, society and the environment.

Stakeholders are individuals or groups with a direct interest in an organisation's performance.

Stakeholder concept is the view that the managers of businesses are responsible to a wide range of groups including their customers, employees, suppliers and society in general.

Corporate Social Reports (CSRs) are documents setting out a business's targets for meeting its social obligations and the extent to which previous social targets have been achieved. These may also be called Corporate Responsibility Reviews.

Ethics are the shared attitudes and principles held by the employees within a business.

An **ethical code of practice** states how a business believes its employees should respond to situations that might challenge the values of the business.

An **ethical stance** refers to a business that has introduced an ethical policy.

Examiner's advice

Figure 22.1 shows the primary stakeholders for businesses, although others exist. When writing about stakeholders it is important to develop answers fully. This is impossible if you attempt to cover too many stakeholder groups – just concentrate on two or three.

The factors considered in this chapter are only a small selection of ways in which society is changing. It may be that new factors will emerge during your course of study and you should consider the implications that these have for businesses and how they may respond.

The list of strategic responses presented in this chapter is not exhaustive – there are others that a business may adopt. It is important that you consider the possible responses in the context of the scenario with which you are presented. This will assist you in selecting and justifying the most appropriate response in any circumstances.

1 What is meant by the term 'social responsibility'? *(3 marks)*

2 Identify the interests that consumers and employees may have in a business. Why might these interests clash? *(7 marks)*

3 Outline the responsibilities that a retailer such as Tesco might have to its suppliers. *(7 marks)*

4 Explain **two** advantages that a business may receive from operating in a socially responsible manner. *(6 marks)*

5 Explain the possible ways in which a multinational manufacturing business might fulfil its social responsibilities. *(7 marks)*

6 Outline the possible reasons why the business above might want to fulfil its social responsibilities. *(7 marks)*

7 Explain the differences between a business that operates legally and one that operates ethically. *(6 marks)*

8 What difficulties might a large multinational business face when trying to implement an ethical code of conduct? *(8 marks)*

9 Explain why ethical behaviour by businesses is increasingly important as a competitive weapon. *(8 marks)*

10 What factors might prevent an ethical business from being highly profitable? *(6 marks)*

Essay questions

1 In 2010 BP was responsible for a major oil leak in the Gulf of Mexico while at the same time, Marks & Spencer was judged to be one of Britain's most ethical and environmentally friendly businesses. To what extent do you believe that it is impossible for some businesses to be genuinely social responsible because of the nature of their products? Justify your answer with reference to the BP, Marks & Spencer and/or other businesses with which you are familiar. *(40 marks)*

Candidate's answer:

BP's oil leak into the Gulf of Mexico was very damaging to the company. Millions of gallons of oil leaked into the sea causing immense damage to many of the company's stakeholders. Fishing businesses around the Gulf were hard hit as the oil polluted their waters and the local tourist industry suffered greatly as pollution put off visitors. There were effects on other of the company's stakeholders too as the company's profits fell heavily because of the heavy clean up and adverse publicity in the US hitting sales. Employees in America and shareholders across the world suffered as the business failed to meet its social responsibilities. To a great extent these problems occurred because of the type of business that BP is in. As world oil supplies become more scarce the company has to attempt

to retrieve oil from more difficult locations (such as from deep in the sea) making accidents like this more likely as new and untried methods of extraction are used and mistakes are more likely to occur. A more fundamental reason is that using BP's products pollutes the environment and in this sense it is very difficult for the company to be genuinely socially responsible. Using oil products contributes heavily to the release of carbon into the atmosphere resulting in global warming. This has negative effects on the environment and people throughout the world and does make it more difficult for BP to be socially responsible.

In contrast it is easier for a retailer such as Marks & Spencer or the Co-operative Group to be socially responsible. The Co-operative Group promotes itself as an environmentally friendly business. It sells a wide range of fairtrade products, provides training and advice for young people when unemployment is high and uses 'green' energy. But selling groceries and similar products does not directly cause oil spills and so it is simpler to be socially responsible. However, despite the Co-op's good intentions it does adversely affect the environment in some ways by, for example, operating huge lorries across the UK to distribute its goods and sometimes Co-op stores are closed causing unemployment in certain areas. So, despite the nature of its products it can damage society through its actions.

But there are other factors which impact on a business's ability to be socially responsible. The finance available determines a business's ability to be socially responsible. Following the oil leak in the Gulf, BP established a £13 billion fund to compensate the victims of its oil leak. This huge amount of money could go some way to cleaning up the environment and paying fishing businesses for the loss of earnings they suffered. Most businesses would not be able to finance such a huge scheme and BP's profitability in previous years meant that it was able to do this. If the fund was sufficient and spent properly it could offset many (but obviously not all) of the costs that the company had imposed on society and enable it to be socially responsible. The clean up process could create positive effects too, which would enhance BP's degree of social responsibility. It may have created jobs around the Gulf, and generated trade for existing businesses involved in the clean up. However, despite this spending, people, businesses and the environment will have suffered.

A key factor apart from the nature of the business's products is the attitude and objectives of the business's senior managers. BP has been a highly profitable business for several years, much more so than the Co-op Group. If its senior managers had been completely committed to social responsibility through, for example, protecting the environment, it should have been possible to use more resources in testing the new equipment used in extracting the oil from the Gulf to reduce the chance of problems and therefore protect society. Managers possibly decided to move quickly to extract the oil to improve cash flow, and less testing and development of new production equipment (or perhaps using other firms') would control costs and increase profits. A focus on profits and shareholders rather than all stakeholders would not promote social responsibility, no matter what the product. In contrast the Co-operative Group has what looks like a genuine commitment from its senior managers to be environmentally friendly. Its legal structure places less emphasis on profits and it does not have shareholders to consider. This means that the organisation is able to devote more of its resources to actions to be socially responsible without coming under pressure from shareholders. It is also possible that over time senior managers, committed to a socially responsible approach have created a culture which assists them in maintaining and extending the socially responsible approach to business.

Examiner's comments:

Many aspects of this answer are good. The candidate has maintained a good focus on the answer throughout which is essential to achieve high marks when responding to relatively open questions such as essays. Their use of real-world businesses to support their answer is pleasing. They obviously know a little about the Deepwater Horizon oil spill in the US (although it wouldn't matter as other examples would serve just as well). They also wrote well on retailing, although they chose a different business. Indeed, their choice of the Co-operative Group was sensible as it allowed them to bring in the impact of the legal structure of the business as a line of argument.

The structure of this essay had much to commend it. The candidate recognised that although the nature of the product is important, there are other factors which may affect a business's ability to be socially responsible. This was a wise choice, suggesting that this answer was planned before writing. Using the finance available to the business and linking this to BP's compensation fund was good technique and provided an effective line of argument. However, there was one key element missing from this answer. The candidate did not write a conclusion pulling together the arguments and providing an overall response to the question, thereby restricting the marks awarded for evaluation. You might like to consider how you would have concluded this answer.

Question:

2 Sir Richard Branson has argued in favour of ethical business behaviour and Unilever, one of the UK's major manufacturers of consumer products has announced a new ethical and environmentally friendly business model. Do you think that it is impossible for a business to be successful if it is not considered to be ethical? Justify your answer with reference to the Virgin group, Unilever and/or other businesses with which you are familiar. *(40 marks)*

23 Businesses and the technological and competitive environment

This chapter commences by considering changes in the technological environment and the ways in which this can affect the products that businesses and consumers require and the production process itself. The chapter also covers the factors which cause change in the competitive environment in which businesses trade. This is strongly influenced by topics that we have already considered such as globalisation and the emergence of economies such as China. As with all the chapters looking at external causes of change, they should be seen as creating opportunities as well as posing threats.

In this chapter we will examine:

- the factors that cause technological change
- the competitive environment and developments that have taken place
- how businesses respond to changes in the technological and competitive environment.

Technological change

In the eighteenth century news of technological developments spread at the rate of one mile per year. In the first few years of the twenty-first century people and businesses throughout the world learn quickly of technological changes and the rate of technological progress is increasingly rapidly. The last few years have seen a number of technological advances having significant implications for businesses. The internet has probably been the biggest single technological factor leading to change in business behaviour, but other sources of technological change such as bio-technology are also having and will continue to have substantial effects on business behaviour.

Technology and marketing opportunities

Technological advances have created new markets for new products and new ways to sell them.

Technology and new products

New technology can open up new markets for businesses. In 1990 mobile telephones were unheard of by most people. By November 2011 there were an estimated 5,250 million in use across the world. Companies such as Nokia and Vodafone have grown as a consequence of the developments in this field of communications technology. Markets for MP3 players, satellite navigation systems and, more recently, tablet computers have been created as a

consequence of technological advances. Today they are multi-billion pound markets selling products to millions of consumers. Smaller, niche businesses have also developed, based on technological products, and we consider two very different examples below.

- **Electric motorbikes.** Zero Motorcycles is a California-based company that designs and produces electric motorcycles that can be used on or off-road. Established by a former NASA engineer, Neal Saiki, the company describes its products as: 'high performance electric motorcycles that are lightweight, efficient, fast off the line and fun to ride'.

- **Glasses to help correct the vision of the world's poorest people.** Professor Josh Silver of Oxford University has used simple technology involving fluids, syringes and special hollow lenses to create glasses that wearers can adjust themselves to correct their own vision. This removes the need for specialist advice from an optometrist. Over 40,000 people in 20 countries are already using his glasses. However, Silver is ambitious for his project, and not to make money, but to help the needy. He hopes to supply 200 million pairs of spectacles to children in Africa who have eyesight problems. He is negotiating with the World Bank to make his vision a reality. In 2011 Silver was shortlisted for the European Patent Office's Inventor Award at a ceremony in Budapest.

Using technology in the products themselves, rather than in the production process also offers great advantages to businesses. Firms possessing a technological lead over rival producers are frequently able to charge a high price for their products – at least until the competition catches up. This technique of price skimming is likely to boost profits. Possessing a technological edge may attract new customers to a business. Toyota's Prius hybrid car offered environmentally aware consumers the chance to buy a vehicle that switched off its petrol engine at low speeds and used a self-charging electric motor in its place. Toyota's hybrid car was first on the market and recognised to be of high quality. The company had a waiting list for this product despite its premium price.

Technology and promoting and selling products

One of the world's largest businesses – the Microsoft Corporation – has developed alongside the technological revolution in software and computing. Microsoft has benefited from technology not only in terms of being able to develop new products, but also from using technology to promote and market its products. Technological advances have allowed the company to produce new products such as its software, and gaming equipment such as the Xbox, as well as providing a means to promote and sell its products online as consumers can download the company's software at any time.

It has also used technology as a basis for product development and to encourage consumer loyalty. Microsoft's Office product (Word, Excel, etc.) is designed to be used with its Windows operating system but is also highly compatible with the company's internet browser (Explorer). Thus technology has offered the company the opportunity to develop and sell a suite of products, rather than a single one.

Other businesses rely entirely on technology to distribute their products. Apple is famous for producing innovative technological products such as the iPad2, but the company also uses technology to distribute its products. Its iTunes store allows purchasers to download music, music videos, television shows, applications, iPod games, audio books, various podcasts, feature length films and movie rentals. It is also used to download applications for the iPhone and iPod touch.

Using technology in this way offers substantial cost advantages. Apple does not have to pay to distribute its products nor does it have to pay retailers commission on each sale. This increases the company's profit margin and increases its flexibility in pricing decisions.

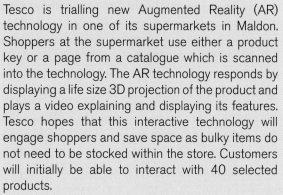

The company also receives marketing benefits in that it can easily collect large amounts of data about its customers and their preferences, enabling it to target its future marketing effectively.

Technology and production processes

Technology and communications

Technological advances also affect the ways in which businesses operate. Communications within businesses have been transformed by technology. Businesses can communicate simply, cheaply and (most importantly) quickly across the globe. Developments such as video conferencing have allowed employees in a business to see and talk with one another while at different locations.

This offers considerable benefits in terms of use of time and reduction of costs to multinational businesses, or even those operating more than a single site in the UK. Similarly, email allows employees and organisations to communicate immediately and messages can be sent to many recipients at the same time.

The development of extranets has created closer links between businesses, helping to improve efficiency. Companies like the giant American retailer Walmart share sales data through an extranet with suppliers such as Proctor & Gamble, to enable production and deliveries to match demand in the stores. Walmart estimates that this improved its stock control enormously when introduced and saves it $2 billion in costs each year.

Technology and production

New technology offers a range of benefits to businesses and consumers. Perhaps the major advantage of technology to businesses is that it allows the development of new methods of production resulting in lower costs. This permits the firm to enjoy higher profits on each sale. However, in an increasingly competitive global market firms seek to improve their market position by offering high-quality and sophisticated products at low prices. Using ever-more sophisticated technology in planning and producing products is one way of achieving lower costs.

Figure 23.1 Computer-aided manufacture (CAM)

The process of manufacturing in many industries has been transformed by automation whereby machines do jobs previously carried out by people. The most dramatic aspect of this has been use of computer controlled technology on the production line. The use of computer controlled technology is an integral part of lean production. Its use allows businesses to control the production line to supply variants on a standard product to meet the precise demands of consumers. Thus Vauxhall's car factory at Ellesmere Port uses computer-aided manufacturing systems to produce different colours and styles of cars in succession in response to customers' orders. This is part of the company's JIT (or 'pull') manufacturing system.

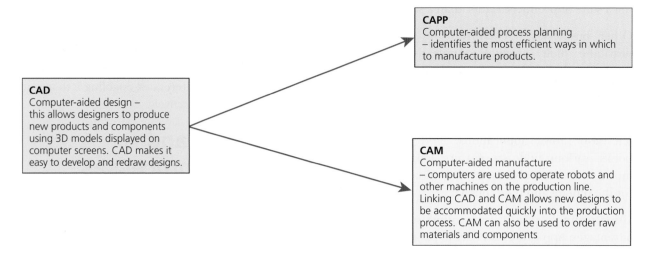

Figure 23.2 Computer-aided design (CAD), computer-aided manufacture (CAM) and computer-aided process planning (CAPP)

Virtual design at Boeing

Before the first 787 Dreamliner entered service in 2011, designers at the American aeroplane manufacturer, Boeing, had created a virtual aeroplane to test and check their ideas before production of the aeroplane started.

Using a French software system, the American designers assembled an entire virtual Boeing 787 Dreamliner to check that the several hundred thousand parts that make up the airliner fitted together. Every component will have been modelled in 3D geometry, milled and shaped on digital machine tools, assembled several times in virtual factories, and maintained by people who have 'crawled' into digital equipment bays. Any parts that did not meet tough standards were redesigned to overcome problems.

The benefits of this approach were seen when the first Dreamliner was built: the model was assembled with few difficulties occurring. The costs of this process were also much cheaper than the traditional technique of actually constructing a prototype airliner to discover the potential problems.

The use of CAD and CAM has assisted in improving productivity levels in many manufacturing industries helping to keep costs down and enhance productivity. Because of this its use has spread to many industries including food processing and the manufacture of pottery.

Technology is not only used in production processes in the manufacturing sector. It is also widely used by businesses that supply services. For example, companies such as Aviva supply insurance policies using the internet. Policyholders enter their requirements onto the company's website and complete their personal details. Avivia's technology computes the price and deducts the appropriate sum from the customer's credit card before downloading the policy to the customer's computer. The whole production process is based on technology.

Driverless trains under consideration for London Underground

Mike Brown, managing director of London Underground, has a clear vision in which fully automatic, driverless trains will hurtle down the Victorian-era tunnels of London's underground railway early in the 2020s.

His vision is not shared, however, by the unions. They reacted, in November, in a typically robust manner to a leaked discussion paper outlining how new technologies could change the shape of the capital's underground system.

Bob Crow of the RMT labelled it an 'ill-conceived ... finance-led document' that 'ignores reality in favour of austerity'. He painted a bleak picture, predicting that the proposals would leave 'passengers stranded in tunnels with no means of evacuation and would turn the platforms and stations into a muggers' and vandals' paradise'.

Along with driverless trains, the document envisages that the increasing use of swipe-card technology for debit and credit cards will make ticket offices all but redundant other than at the biggest interchanges.

These two developments, the RMT claims, will lead to the loss of 1,500 jobs and leave passengers with almost no staff to interact with on their journey.

(Source: Mark Odell in Financial Times, 14 November 2011)

Question:

Why might some employees (or trade unions) view new technology more positively?

Technology and human relations

Humans within businesses are always affected by technological change. This is particularly true when new technology is introduced onto the production line. Such change may simply lead to some minor changes in the duties of employees. On the other hand, technological developments can result in enormous changes for a business's workforce. For some it may be redundancy: replaced by technology as part of the process of automation. Many high-street banks have made workers redundant owing to advances in technology. Other employees may be required to undertake duties dramatically different from those with which they are familiar as a result of the increasing use of technology in the banking sector.

Employees' reactions to technological change can be equally diverse. For some employees it may represent an opportunity. They may have a chance to acquire new skills, to make their jobs more secure and enjoy higher wages or salaries. The new working practices may offer great benefits. Technology can allow employees greater control over their working lives leading to increased responsibility and possibility of achievement. This can result in greater motivation.

Others may fear technological change as it increases job insecurity. This is likely to be true of those with few skills and carrying out tasks that may be easily automated. Fear of unemployment may lead to industrial action as workers seek to protect their jobs. In such circumstances the introduction of new technology may be awkward and expensive. Redundancy payments may be expensive and corporate images may suffer.

New technology-based products create jobs and unemployment at the same time. For example, automated telephone switchboards have resulted in a loss of jobs for telephonists. Direct dial numbers and electronic answering systems have made telephonists obsolete in many firms. Simultaneously, employment has been created in industries manufacturing and maintaining the automatic telephone systems.

The reaction of employees to technological change may depend upon the culture of the business. Businesses operating with a traditional culture placing great emphasis on bureaucracy and convention may experience difficulties in adapting to technological change. The existence of a task culture may make the process less difficult. It may be most appropriate if the managers of businesses that are affected by technological change develop a culture that is responsive to change and one where employees' attitudes are to embrace change rather than to resist it.

BUSINESS IN FOCUS

Google's culture

Though growing rapidly, Google still maintains a small company feel. At the Googleplex headquarters almost everyone eats in the Google café (known as 'Charlie's Place'), sitting at whatever table has an opening and enjoying conversations with Googlers from all different departments. Topics range from the trivial to the technical, and whether the discussion is about computer games or encryption or ad serving software, it's not surprising to hear someone say, 'That's a product I helped develop before I came to Google'.

Google's emphasis on innovation and commitment to cost containment means each employee is a hands-on contributor. There's little in the way of corporate hierarchy and everyone wears several hats. The international webmaster who creates Google's holiday logos spent a week translating the entire site into Korean. The chief operations engineer is also a licensed neurosurgeon. Because everyone realises they are an equally important part of Google's success, no one hesitates to skate over a corporate officer during roller hockey.

Google's hiring policy is aggressively non-discriminatory and favours ability over experience. The result is a staff that reflects the global audience the search engine serves. Google has offices around the globe and Google engineering centres are recruiting local talent in locations from Zurich to Bangalore. Dozens of languages are spoken by Google staffers, from Turkish to Telugu. When not at work, Googlers pursue interests from cross-country cycling to wine tasting, from flying to frisbee. As Google expands its development team, it continues to look for those who share an obsessive commitment to creating search perfection and having a great time doing it.

(*Source: Google, www.google.com/corporate/culture.html*)

Question:

In what ways does Google's culture assist the business in embracing technological change?

Threats and technological change

However, technological change can be threatening as well as providing opportunities for businesses. The impact of technological change has been profound on one of the UK's most familiar organisations: the Royal Mail. In 2010 the company saw its volume of business fall by 4 per cent as its average daily postbag declined by over 4 million letters. The major reason for this change is increasing competition from email and digital delivery of information. Royal Mail expects the volume of letters it handles to continue to decline over the next few years. The company has estimated that the decline in its volume of business has reduced its operating profit by £500 million annually.

The threats of rapid changes technology are considerable. Firms in high-technology markets will face demands to research new products and to implement more efficient methods of production. Thus commercial pressures may exist to improve technology used in products and processes. New technology, in whatever form, can be a major drain on an organisation's financial resources. Installing new technology on the production line will involve a heavy capital outlay and disruption to production while the work is completed. Thus, a business may lose sales revenue at the time its expenditure rises significantly. Some firms may experience difficulty in raising the funds necessary to purchase new technology. Costs of research and development can be huge and many years may pass before any return is received on them.

Businesses operating in markets experiencing rapidly changing technology can be left behind – or find it too expensive to keep up with other producers. Small firms can be particularly vulnerable even if they are well managed. This is one factor leading to mergers and takeovers in markets supplying high-technology products. The series of mergers and takeovers in the world car manufacturing market has been brought about, in part, by the high costs of developing new products, especially environmentally friendly ones. Sir Alex Trotman, the former chief executive of Ford, has forecast that the global market for car manufacture will eventually comprise just three large companies and the extent of investment in technology is one factor driving this change.

New production methods do not always work effectively from the start. Some sort of teething problems are inevitable following the introduction of state-of-the-art technology onto production lines. Workers will take time to adapt to what is required of them and the technology may not behave as expected. This may result in lower levels of productivity and higher production costs.

Changes in the competitive environment

A business's competitive environment is made up of a number of factors. It includes the power of rivals and the potential rivals that the business faces in a battle to win customers and market share, but it also includes its customers and its suppliers and the influence that they wield.

The competitive environment faced by a business can change in a number of ways.

New competitors

The arrival of a new business into a market poses an obvious threat to existing firms. A new business is likely to take at least some customers from the firms already trading on the market and this becomes more likely if the market is not growing. In this case the only way a new business can gain sales is at the expense of businesses that are already trading. Such a situation is a 'zero-sum' game in that the total number of customers lost and gained must total zero.

Li Ning's performance raises concerns for Chinese brands

In the latest rankings of the richest people in China, Li Ning − founder of one of the country's most famous retail brands − has tumbled from 64 last year to 291.

The decline in fortune mirrors that of the Olympic gymnast's brand (named after him), which last year had overtaken Adidas for second place in the Chinese sportswear market. At that time, the chief executive was predicting it would be a top-five global sportswear brand by the end of the decade.

But Li Ning has since seen its profits and share price plunge and is rethinking its ambitious branding strategy. Is this a temporary setback, or is there a bamboo ceiling that stops Chinese brands from becoming truly competitive even in their own market? The question is whether Chinese companies are strong enough in branding, marketing, innovation, design and quality to become something more than just copycats.

Li Ning, who lit the flame at the opening ceremony of the 2008 Beijing Olympics, is not only one of China's top athletes but also among its most renowned entrepreneurs. His appearance at the Bird's Nest stadium − which instantly linked the powerful nationalism of the event with his brand − must rank as one of the marketing coups of the decade. But those days seem long gone: Li Ning's net profits fell 50 per cent in the first half year-on-year, and its share price has fallen 57 per cent since the beginning of the year.

With many Chinese consumers unwilling to follow a local brand upmarket, Li Ning appears to be returning to its cheap-and-cheerful roots. It still holds a slight advantage over Adidas in the China market led by Nike, but market analysts expect it to slip back to third place soon. Chinese customers in general do not want to spend extra for a domestic brand if they can afford a foreign one.

'Li Ning has done really well to challenge Adidas, but it has done it by copying the model,' says Andy Edwards, head of planning at BBH, the advertising agency, in Shanghai. 'Now Li Ning needs to build greater value, stop copying and find its own unique voice … and drive this through everything the brand does, especially the product.'

(*Source: Adapted from Patti Waldmeir, FT.com, 10 October 2011*)

Question:

What actions might Nike and Adidas have taken in response to the threat posed by Li Ning?

The extent of the change in the competitive environment will depend upon the scale of the new competitor, and whether its products will be appealing to customers in the market. A large business that is diversifying into a new market may pose a major threat to established producers, especially if its product is differentiated. In contrast, a small business seeking to gain a foothold in a small segment or niche of the market may hardly represent a change in the competitive environment. In November 2011, Nokia, the global mobile phone manufacturer announced over 3,500 job losses in factories across Europe as it cut back its production. One reason for this, the company admitted was tough competition from Apple and its hugely successful iPhone.

Dominant businesses

A dominant business is able to have a substantial influence over market prices and in some cases may determine them with other, less powerful firms, following its lead. A dominant firm is likely to be the largest in an industry and to hold the greatest market share. As a consequence it will probably be highly profitable, though it may not be highly efficient and innovative, especially if its supremacy is not immediately challenged.

Dominant businesses may emerge through internal or organic growth as in the case of Microsoft. Other firms may achieve dominant positions in their markets as a result of a strategy of takeovers and mergers. It is this approach that Vodafone has used to create its market power.

Competition policy

Competition policy is intended to create free and fair competition within markets in the UK and throughout the European Union. The aim is to provide consumers with quality products at a fair price allowing producers the opportunity to earn reasonable profits. Unfair competition can arise in a number of ways.

- The abuse of monopoly power. Lack of competition means that monopolies have the power to exploit consumers by charging high prices and supplying outdated products. In 2011 the Competition Commission came under pressure to investigate the UK's energy market (for gas and electricity) which is dominated by six large suppliers. Critics of the structure of this industry have argued that the profit margins of these companies have risen at the expense of consumers.

- Mergers and takeovers can create monopolies with the power to exploit consumers. In August 2011 Thomas Cook and the Co-operative Group received approval from the Competition Commission to merge their high-street travel agent businesses.

- Restrictive practices exist when businesses interfere with the free operation of markets. Restrictive practices may take the form of producers making agreements to share out a particular market between them or forcing retailers to stock all of a firm's products by threatening to withdraw all supplies. Such practices make markets less competitive.

The UK's approach to competition policy is described as 'pragmatic'. This means that the authorities do not believe automatically that monopolies or mergers are damaging and anti-competitive. Each case is investigated by the Competition Commission and a decision is taken on whether the monopoly or merger is 'against the public interest'. Only if it is judged to be so will any action be taken. Restrictive practices are viewed differently: they are considered to be against the public interest unless the firms concerned can prove otherwise.

A famous example of a dominant business is Microsoft. Microsoft was established by Bill Gates in 1975 and operates in a number of markets including computer hardware (the Microsoft mouse), home entertainment (Xbox) and cable television (it has its own American channel). However, it is in the global computer software market that the company is dominant. Its Windows operating systems and Microsoft Office suite of products are sold in every country in the world. The company was estimated to hold 78.6 per cent of global sales of desktop operating systems at the end of 2010.

Diet Coke and Coca-Cola dominate Pepsi

Diet Coke has become so popular, it has overtaken Coca-Cola's rival, Pepsi Cola, for the first time. This means that Diet Coke has become the second most popular soft drink in the US, behind Coca-Cola – which emphasises the market domination the brand enjoys. This change reflects a long-term trend toward diet sodas.

Coca-Cola sold nearly 927 million cases of its diet soda in 2010, compared to Pepsi's 892 million, a report by trade publication *Beverage Digest* released Thursday said. Regular Coke remains far and away the most popular soda, selling 1.6 billion cases.

Overall, US soft-drink sales have fallen for six straight years as consumers switched to healthier alternatives such as juices and tea and cut back on spending in the recession.

While both Diet Coke and Pepsi sold less soda in 2010, the decline was more pronounced for Pepsi. The downward trend in US soda sales puts more pressure on the beverage companies to compete. Coca-Cola has pumped up its traditional advertising, including online ads. PepsiCo, which has lost market share in recent years, maintained some traditional ads but also steered dollars toward its Pepsi Refresh Project, an online donation programme meant to build brand awareness.

(Source: Adapted from David Hope in The Online Journal, *18 March 2011)*

Question:

Are there any advantages from having a company dominate a market in the way that Coca-Cola does in the United States?

If a business is becoming more dominant in a market this represents a threat for its competitors. The growing power of a single business may lead to its rivals losing sales and market share and a decline in profitability. The dominant business's competitors may have to invest in new products, new marketing campaigns and cut prices to protect their market positions. This may become increasingly difficult to do if the dominant business uses its market power ruthlessly to increase its power within the market.

Changes in the buying power of customers

The major feature of the competitive environment for some businesses is the scale and power of their customers. An increase in the power of a single large buyer can pose difficulties for a business, particularly if it is relatively small and the dominant customer purchases a large proportion of its output.

In such circumstances the change in the competitive environment could have a range of adverse consequences for the business.

- The customer will have increased bargaining power and may be able to negotiate substantial reductions in the price at which products are supplied. The customer may use the threat of transferring to another supplier to achieve its ambitions. Being forced to sell at lower prices could reduce, or in extreme cases, eliminate the supplier's profit margins.

- Customers may request changes in the specifications of products to be supplied or may impose tough conditions in terms of delivery dates or the quality or appearance of products. Such outcomes are likely to put the supplier under pressure and to increase costs of production. Once again the ultimate effect could be to reduce profits.

- A dominant customer may ask for generous trade credit terms. Thus the customer may request a 60-day trade credit period. This can cause liquidity problems for suppliers, not least because the size of the order will mean that the sums involved are substantial. In such circumstances the supplier may have to negotiate expensive overdrafts with its bank.

Most of the UK's large supermarkets have come under a great deal of criticism for the way they deal with their suppliers. The Business in focus featured here considers this is more detail.

BUSINESS IN FOCUS

Supermarket watchdog lacks the power to fine, MPs say

Government plans to crack down on supermarkets who treat their suppliers unfairly do not go far enough, a committee of MPs said. Ministers are creating an adjudicator to resolve disputes in the sector, but the cross-party business committee said it should have the power to impose fines.

It also suggested that there should be more protection for suppliers who may be afraid of making a complaint against a major supermarket. Business Minister Ed Davey said he would consider all the recommendations.

The new independent Groceries Code Adjudicator (GCA) will investigate alleged breaches of the grocery industry code of practice. The code was created to prevent supermarkets from using their size and power to impose unfair terms on suppliers. Small suppliers often complain that their profit margins have been squeezed as supermarkets have driven down prices.

Under the draft legislation, the GCA's only sanction will be to require supermarkets to publish the results of its investigations. Ministers will consider granting it the power to impose fines if this does not not work well.

Business committee chairman and Labour MP Adrian Bailey said: 'We disagree with the government on the introduction of fines. We propose that fines be an available penalty from the start, not least so that the adjudicator's performance can be judged on the basis of a full package of remedies.'

(*Source: Adapted from* BBC News, *28 July 2011*)

Question:

What benefits might small suppliers receive from dealing with large supermarket chains?

Changes in the selling power of suppliers

In contrast to dominant customers, some businesses find that a major influence on the competitive environment in which they trade is the power of their suppliers. Powerful suppliers who hold a dominant position in a market have control over prices and this power is increased if the product they sell has few or no substitutes.

The implications for businesses can be severe, especially if the supplier provides a large percentage of the resources used by the business. In this event, a policy of increasing prices as the supplier's market power increases can squeeze the business's profit margins.

In 2010 and 2011 many small businesses in the UK complained about the actions of their energy suppliers. Even tiny micro-businesses were facing energy bills amounting to over £10,000 a year.

Responding to changes in the technological and competitive environments

Changes in the technological and competitive environments provide opportunities as well as posing threats. A business may respond to a change in the technological environment by embracing the change. If it is a technological change in relation to the products the industry supplies a business may attempt to be a market leader and to supply the most technologically advanced products possible. This offers benefits in terms of developing a valued brand image and making demand for products less price-elastic, or sensitive to price changes as the products become more desirable. Such an approach may boost profits.

Equally, a business may adopt the most up-to-date technology in its production processes. This can permit a highly efficient service and can reduce costs. In either case the performance of the business may be enhanced. Budget airlines such as easyJet use technology which allows them to adjust their online prices if a surge in demand occurs. Thus, if a particular flight is proving popular the company's website technology responds to this by raising prices to improve profit margins in the face of increasing demand.

An alternative approach may be to emphasise the traditional element of a business's products. This involves operating in a niche market to attract consumers who wish to avoid some aspects of the technological age in which we live. Some pubs present themselves as refuges from the latest technology and ban mobile phones and do not have electronic gaming machines or piped music.

The ways in which businesses may respond to changes in their competitive environment may be equally diverse and will clearly depend upon the nature of the change. The entry of a new competitor to a market or the emergence of a dominant business may provoke a number of strategic reactions. Affected businesses may seek new markets or develop new product ranges. Alternatively they may seek alliances or mergers with other businesses in the same industry to increase their own market power in response to these changes in the competitive environment.

Changes in the competitive environment which manifest themselves as increasing power of suppliers can create major difficulties for businesses, especially if no alternative suppliers exist. In this situation managers may consider the production process and ways in which the business may adapt to reduce its reliance on the products sold by the supplier in question. Other strategies in this situation could include taking over the supplier (in what may be a hostile action) or negotiating favourable deals with smaller rival suppliers in the hope of fostering greater competition.

One step further: Porter's five forces model

Michael Porter's famous 'five forces of competitive position' model provides a simple framework for assessing and analysing the competitive strength and position of a corporation or business. It can be used to good analytical effect alongside other models such as the SWOT and PEST analysis tools.

Porter's five forces model suggests points under each main heading, by which you can develop a broad and sophisticated analysis of competitive position, as might be used when creating strategy, plans, or making investment decisions about a business or organisation.

Five forces analysis looks at five key areas, namely the threat of entry, the power of buyers, the power of suppliers, the threat of substitutes, and competitive rivalry.

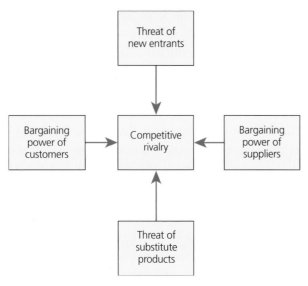

Figure 23.3 Porter's five forces

1 **Competitive rivalry.** Competitive rivalry is a major force. If entry to an industry is straightforward then competitive rivalry is likely to be high. If it is easy for customers to move to substitute products, for example from oil to gas as a fuel, then again rivalry will be high. Generally competitive rivalry will be greater if:
  ● there is little differentiation between the products sold between customers
  ● competitors are approximately the same size of each other
  ● the competitors all have similar corporate strategies
  ● it is costly to leave the industry and so businesses do not do so.

2 **Power of suppliers.** Suppliers are a vital element of an effective organisation. Raw materials are needed to complete the finished product of the organisation. Suppliers can be highly powerful. This power arises from:
  ● the number of suppliers that are operating – fewer suppliers means more powerful suppliers
  ● the cost involved in changing suppliers – if it is difficult suppliers have greater power
  ● if there is no other substitute for their product.

3 **Power of buyers.** Buyers or customers can exert influence and control over an industry in certain circumstances. This happens when:
  ● the products are similar and it is easy to find substitutes
  ● products have a high price-elasticity of demand (customers are sensitive to price)

  ● switching to another supplier's product is cheap and straightforward.

4 **Threat of substitutes.** A substitute is an alternative product that offers purchasers similar or the same features and benefits. The threat of substitute is high when:
  ● the price of that substitute product falls
  ● it is easy for consumers to switch from one substitute product to another
  ● buyers are willing to substitute.

5 **Threat of a new entrant.** The threat of a new organisation entering the industry is high when it is easy for an organisation to enter the industry (when entry barriers are low). An organisation will look at how loyal customers are to existing products, how quickly they can achieve economy of scales, whether they would have access to suppliers, whether government legislation would prevent them or encourage them to enter the industry.

Key terms

- **Competition Commission** – the Commission's function is to monitor proposed mergers and to prevent monopolies operating against the public interest.
- **Computer-aided design (CAD)** and **manufacture (CAM)** use computer programs to design new products and control production. Used together, they can create a highly efficient method of production.
- **Extranets** link the computers of a business to those of suppliers and retailers, allowing the effective exchange of information between key commercial partners.
- **Intranets** link computers within an individual business, allowing employees to use email and access a range of online services.
- In theory, **a monopoly** is the only supplier of a particular product. The law considers a firm with 25 per cent or more of a market to be a monopoly.
- **The Office of Fair Trading** is a government organisation established to ensure that firms are complying with relevant legislation.
- **Restrictive practices** are actions by producers that prevent the free working of markets.

Progress questions

1 Outline **two** major technological changes that have affected UK businesses since 2004. *(4 marks)*

2 Technological change can affect products and processes. Carefully distinguish between these **two** types of technological change. *(4 marks)*

3 Examine the ways in which technological change can result in opportunities for businesses offering services. *(6 marks)*

4 Explain the difficulties a business might face if trading in a market subject to rapid changes in technology. *(6 marks)*

5 Explain what is meant by a business's 'competitive environment'. *(4 marks)*

6 Why might the entry of a new firm into a market change the competitive environment for established producers? *(6 marks)*

7 How does the existence of a small number of large supermarkets in the UK affect the competitive environment of small suppliers to the UK grocery market? *(8 marks)*

8 In what ways might the UK government influence the competitive environment in which businesses operate? *(6 marks)*

9 What possible effects might a dominant and large supplier have on a small manufacturing business? *(8 marks)*

10 What factors make the UK airline market highly competitive? *(8 marks)*

Essay questions

1 In 2011 it was reported that Foxconn, the Taiwanese electronics manufacturer, is to introduce 300,000 robots onto its production lines, which may threaten thousands of jobs. This decision will help to control rising labour costs and maintain the company's competitiveness in a global market. Do you agree that shareholders always benefit from technological change while employees suffer? Justify your answer with reference to Foxconn and/or other businesses with which you are familiar. *(40 marks)*

Candidate's answer:

Foxconn is a large business making electronic components, such as circuit boards, for a range of well-known businesses such as Apple and Nokia. Foxconn is under considerable pressure to minimise its labour (and overall) costs to keep winning large contracts from customers such as Apple. This has resulted in reports that it does not treat its workers well and that some have committed suicide. As a large manufacturer operating in a price-elastic market achieving all possible economies of scale is vital if the company is to continue to succeed in winning contracts against rival suppliers. Using technology to its fullest possible extent in a basic manufacturing context is a good decision for a business seeking to maximise its long-term profits. Manufacturing robots bring long-term benefits in that they will not ask for pay rises or improved working conditions (as some Chinese workers have been doing) and thus costs will be more controllable and more easily predicted. This means that the business can be more competitive and profit margins may be higher, boosting potential dividends as well as having positive effects on share prices. Thus, in the long run shareholders will benefit from this example of technological change. Equally, ➡

it is likely that employees will be disadvantaged in that, if reports are true, thousands of jobs may be lost.

However, this situation could be interpreted differently. Some low-skilled jobs that are easily replaced by technology may be lost, but, at the same time, new jobs will be created. More skilled employees will be required to install and maintain the new technology and by reducing costs (and possibly) prices, sales may increase. These jobs may attract higher wages improving the financial position of employees while offering more interesting and less monotonous employment. Cutting the price of consumer technology may bring it within reach of many consumers in developing countries, especially in Asia and thus employment opportunities may be generated.

Technological change also occurs under other circumstances. Technological change has created many new markets. The development of mobile phones (including the latest 4G systems) has led to many thousands of jobs being created in the UK and overseas. British companies such as Vodafone and Orange have grown on the back of this development, while manufacturers such as Nokia have expanded dramatically as they have supplied a rapidly growing global market with handsets and other equipment. Until the recession of 2008 this had proved to be a profitable industry offering the prospect of shareholders receiving good returns. In a similar way, the technology that allows the world's major car manufacturers to create electrical cars will generate new jobs for employees (although conventional car manufacturing positions may be threatened). In both the cases – of the electric car and the 4G mobile phone systems – the job opportunities may come before any significant returns for shareholders. These projects are likely to require very heavy investment by the companies concerned and sales may take a long time to generate profits, if they ever do, in what are very competitive global markets.

At a simple level it may be true to say that technological change benefits shareholders while employees suffer from job losses. However, even this may only be true in the long run as the investment and the cost of job losses (if they are in countries with strong employment protection laws) may be high. But the situation is more complex. Technological change can create jobs, sometimes on a large scale and also create more interesting and more highly paid jobs, thereby benefiting employees. Equally the effects on shareholders depend upon the circumstances. Although technological change can offer opportunities to generate high profits, risk certainly accompanies this. High technology companies do not always succeed – Nokia has faced financial problems recently. The answer depends on many factors but especially whether the technology relates to processes or products. It is possible to argue that technology that results in new products may generate new jobs and benefit employees as well as shareholders, while technology that is used in production could replace jobs and disadvantage employees, though this is not always the case.

Examiner's comments:

An interesting opening to this answer in which the candidate shows that they have been following business news as they make reference to the reports of suicides at Foxconn's factories. Overall this is a good quality answer. The candidate has a clear focus on the question throughout and makes effective use of examples to support their arguments. They also introduce business studies concepts effectively as part of their arguments.

The structure of the answer is good recognising that there are two (or more) sides to this argument and seeking to draw out the factors which affect the likely implications for two key stakeholder groups. The final paragraph is thoughtful and interesting and arrives at a sensible and well-supported judgement.

Question:

2 Tesco is the dominant business in UK grocery retailing with around 32 per cent market share. The Co-operative Group has presented itself as an ethical retailer while ASDA (which is owned by Walmart) has promised lower prices. What do you think is the best strategy for a business to adopt when faced by a dominant business in its market? Justify your answer with reference to Tesco, Asda, the Co-operative Group and/or other businesses with which you are familiar. *(40 marks)*

SECTION 6 *Managing change*

At AS you have been faced with many situations where a business decision was needed, such as starting up a business or raising finance but you have not been asked to think through some of the issues that occur when actually implementing some of these decisions and changing the way things are done. At A2 we examine the possible causes of change and think about the best way for managers to prepare for and cope with change.

24 Introduction to change

Change is the one predictable element of business. You may not know what is going to change, but you know something is! These changes may be due to internal or external causes (they can come from within the business or from outside) or both. Just watch or listen to the news tonight and you can appreciate how much change occurs – new laws, changes in the economy, new products being launched and new entrants into markets. The problems managers have is making sure they are ready for change and turn it into an opportunity.

In this chapter we consider:
- the causes of internal change
- the causes of external change.

Introduction

The one constant in business is change. All businesses are constantly undergoing change. Just think of your school or college and the many changes it will have experienced in recent years: new qualifications will have been introduced, exam questions may have changed in their style, some staff will have left and some will have joined, there will have been new investment in facilities, new students, changes to the timetable and changes to what other local schools and colleges are providing and how well they are doing. Similarly, businesses will experience new laws, new taxes, changes in customers' tastes, changes in technology, changes in staff and changes in the activities of competitors. Standing still is not an option – change will happen whether you like it or not (although the rate may be faster in some markets than others), so it is better to be prepared if possible, rather than to find yourself having to react. The ability to survive and prosper depends on your ability to be ready for, to respond to and to adapt to change. As Charles Darwin wrote: 'In the struggle for survival, the fittest win out at the expense of their rivals because they succeed in adapting themselves best to their environment.'

External change

Some change will be external. It happens *to* you. For example, change may come from any of the PEST (political, economic, social, technological) factors you studied earlier in this book or changes in the competitive environment (such as suppliers, distributors and competitors). Change is happening all the time in the external environment and your job as a manager is to anticipate such change and prepare for it; hopefully preparing to exploit the opportunities it creates and/or minimise the threats it generates. Of course, the nature of the change and the significance of any particular change will depend on the industry we are examining. Technological change is clearly vitally important in the computer games console market; economic change may be more significant in the construction industry; political regulations may be critical in the banking sector following massive government intervention in the banking crisis of 2008; the ageing population has major implications for the health care sector.

The significance of change for any business will depend on the particular circumstances of the business: an economic recession may hit health clubs and leisure centres but benefit takeaway pizza companies and tent manufacturers. A global business may be less sensitive to changes in the UK than one that operates solely within this country. What may be an opportunity for one business may be a threat for another.

The rate of change may also vary over time. The UK economy underwent a period of relative stability in the late 1990s and early 2000s; inflation stayed relatively constant around 2 per cent, the economy grew each year and unemployment was relatively low. Then in 2007 and 2008 came the global credit crisis. Suddenly businesses could not borrow, the UK economy went into a recession, the Government had to step in to save several banks and share prices fell dramatically. This became a time of very radical change and unpredictability, making planning incredibly difficult. Who would have predicted in early 2007 that the UK Government would have to nationalise banks, that the UK would enter a recession, that interest rates would be slashed, VAT increased and the Government would pump billions of pounds into the economy to try and preserve growth? The whole business environment, not only in the UK but globally, was shaken up and managers were operating in a whole new world. Even as we come out of the recession there is massive uncertainty about the economy which is limiting investment and demand. And then in 2011 the eurozone went into crisis as many governments such as Greece and Italy struggled to pay their debt; this placed enormous pressure on the whole euro system and threatened the stability of the European Union. Meanwhile the continued growth of emerging markets such as China and India offers growth opportunities for businesses such as Unilever which are changing their strategies to target customers there.

The effects of change can be seen in many different industries. The travel industry, for example, has undergone major reorganisation in recent years due to the growth of the internet. Customers are searching around more and often going direct to the hotels and resorts, bypassing travel agents. The music, newspaper and television industries have been transformed by online media. The fast-food industry has had to change in response to customers' greater concerns about health. By comparison, industries such as clothes production, art galleries and garden seeds may have experienced less change, although even in these sectors there will undoubtedly have been differences over time in the issues facing the businesses involved, and there will still be many examples of innovation often due to external factors such as new technology. Think of how developments in fabric have led to washable suits, non-iron shirts and permanent-crease trousers.

Other sources of external change come from the competitive (or micro-) environment. This includes the organisations that a business is dealing with on a regular basis, such as:

- **Competitors** – new competitors into the market can pose a new threat to the existing providers of a product. Just think of Branston launching its beans to attack Heinz, Cadbury launching Trident gum to attack Wrigley, Amazon challenging the iPad with the Kindle Fire or Google buying Motorola to enter the mobile phone market.
- **Suppliers** – all business have to buy in some supplies. Suppliers may try to increase prices, may have quality problems or may change their terms and conditions, all of which will force a business to reconsider its own decisions. In the airline market, for example, there is a very limited number of aircraft producers

(such as Boeing and Airbus) which gives them a great deal of power over the airlines.

- **Buyers** may also try to negotiate new terms or change the price paid. The buyers of a product may be the end-users or intermediaries such as wholesalers and retailers. The majority of cereal in the UK is sold via supermarkets, so producers such as Kellogg's have to negotiate and bargain with them.
- **Providers of substitute products** and their marketing actions may affect your own business. Better marketing of laser eye treatments will affect sales of spectacles, for example. Greater use of email may reduce the demand for a postal service. The rise of tablet computers means more people get their news online rather than in print.

These changes in the competitive environment are happening close to the business and can create favourable or unfavourable landscapes in which to compete.

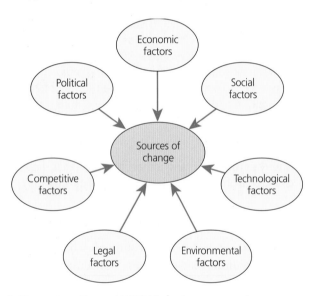

Figure 24.1 External PESTEL and competitive forces as sources of changes

Internal change

Change can be internal as well as external. Staff may want higher rewards or to be more involved in decision-making, for example. They may want better facilities at work or want more training. These internal developments require changes in the way a business is managed. Similarly, there may be changes in other aspects of the business such as poor cash flow, falling sales or quality problems which require action to be taken.

The changes that affect a business can therefore come from within (internal change) or from outside (external change). In many cases external change will bring about internal change as the firm has to respond and react given the altered environment.

Analysing change

When analysing any development in a market we should take account of the nature and the rate of the change. The UK's population is ageing, for example, but this has not happened suddenly; managers could have and should have expected this and planned accordingly. Other changes are more rapid and less predictable. Twitter was only launched in 2007 and yet it is difficult to think of any large organisation that does not use it to communicate about itself. Gradual change is called 'incremental change'; dramatic change is called 'transformational change'. Although we tend to think of fast change as the most disruptive (think how ebooks have upset the publishing industry in a very short space of time), slow change can also cause problems. Businesses may not appreciate that their markets are disappearing around them (for example, the Royal Mail may have a long-term issue as email continues to grow in popularity). Charles Handy, a business writer described how if you left a frog in a pan of cold water and gradually heated up the pan the frog would stay there and be boiled to death. Not a pleasant image but one which highlights that slow change can be deadly as it creeps up on you. If the water was heated up quickly the frog would notice and react, but the fact it gets hotter slowly is the killer in this instance.

Change can create undesirable outcomes (threats) for business or desirable outcomes (opportunities). In fact, the same change will be a threat to some businesses and an opportunity for others. Hot weather can boost sales of barbecues, lemonade and beer and reduce sales of overcoats.

In part the effect of any change depends on what it is, but also it depends on the internal position of each business, the quality of the management and the extent to which the change has been expected and prepared for. For example, the recession in 2008 depressed the share price of many companies. This may have been a threat to some businesses because there was a danger of takeover by competitors, but an opportunity for other companies to buy rivals for a lower price. In this case whether it is an opportunity or a threat depends on the funds each business has, their strategies for the future and their ability to combine with rivals.

Proactive v reactive approaches to change

Proactive managers look ahead and anticipate change wherever they can. A reactive approach waits for change to happen and then responds. Obviously a proactive approach is better in terms of planning ahead and having the resources to identify and exploit opportunities. To be proactive managers must be scanning their environment, undertaking research and watching their existing and potential future competitors. However, in some cases the change may be unexpected either because it could not be easily anticipated and/or because the managers were not looking properly. Kodak was slow to respond to the rise of digital cameras because it did not see companies such as Sony and Fujitsu as real competitors; instead it was still watching traditional producers of cameras such as Nikon and did not see the long-term threat of digital cameras. Even Microsoft has been guilty of not anticipating change – it took several years of the growth of the internet for the company to realise its potential and divert resources to online-focused products. More recently, Nokia lost its hold on the smartphone market as Apple took it over (and eventually the investors reacted by appointing a new chief executive). Studies of management have highlighted how much of managers' time is spent firefighting — fixing problems and solving day-to-day problems. This can eat up so much time and energy that bigger movements in the business's markets get missed or there simply is not the time to plan properly for them.

BUSINESS IN FOCUS

Alvin Toffler

Alvin Toffler is a business writer who coined the phrase 'future shock' in an article that was first published in 1965. The term is now quite commonly used. It refers to what happens to society when too much change happens in a very short time, causing confusion and chaos. His first book was also called *Future Shock*, and was followed by *The Third Wave* and *Powershift*. All of these books are about change: the first focuses on how it affects organisations; the second about where it is taking them; and the third is about who can control change. Toffler was the first to point to the acceleration of change in business. He also highlights the significance of the information revolution we have experienced. 'The advanced economy,' wrote Toffler, 'could not run for 30 seconds without computers'. His book *Revolutionary Wealth*, written with his wife, discusses the growth of the 'prosumer' – a consumer who is also part-producer of what they consume, for example, the person who designs their own kitchen or bathroom using a store's software, buys from the store and then assembles it themselves.

Books:

1 *Future Shock*, Bantam Books, 1970; Pan Books, 1979
2 *The Third Wave*, Morrow, 1980
3 *Powershift: Knowledge, Wealth, and Violence at the Edge of the 21st Century*, Bantam Books, 1990
4 *Revolutionary Wealth*, with Toffler, H., Alfred A. Knopf, 2006

Question:

Can you think of any other examples of a prosumer?

Summary

Change cannot be avoided in business and in many cases you will not want to avoid it because it can bring opportunities – just ask investors in eBay, iTunes, X Factor, Ryanair, Sky and Nintendo. However, it can bring threats as well and challenge or cause dramatic upheavals in an industry (think of music, broadcasting and education). Of course, the shape and nature of change can differ significantly; it may be internal or external, slow or rapid, predicted or unexpected.

Key terms

PEST analysis is a way of analysing the external macro-environment of business. It examines political, economic, social and technological factors. It can also be known as PESTEL analysis, referring to political, economic, social, technological, environmental and legal factors. Changes in these factors create opportunities and threats.

The **macro-environment** refers to external factors, generally beyond the control of a business, which will affect its success such as new laws, the economy, the level of technology and social factors. Businesses mainly have a one-way relationship with factors in the macro-environment because they are affected by it but cannot easily influence it (for example, one firm will be affected by a recession but on its own will not be able to help boost the economy significantly).

Marketing myopia is a term that was introduced by Theodore Levitt and describes organisations that are short sighted and miss the trends developing within their markets, such as Kodak and digital cameras.

Examiner's advice

Remember that change is happening all the time in many different areas. For any business, what matters is identifying which are the critical changes and how well positioned the organisation is to exploit opportunities and protect against threats. In an exam you may want to weigh up the relative importance of different factors – is economic change the key to success? It may be, but what about technology, social change and political change for example?

Progress questions

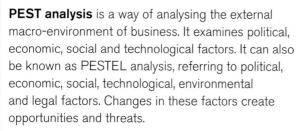

1. Identify **two** changes that have occurred at your school or college in the last few years. What changes have senior staff had to make as a result? *(6 marks)*

2. Outline **one** way in which *you* have personally changed in the last year. What do you think caused the change? *(5 marks)*

3. Outline **one** change in the UK economy in the last year. Explain, with examples, how this is an opportunity for business. Explain how it may be a threat. *(8 marks)*

4. Outline **one** change in the UK social environment in the last decade. Explain, with examples, how this is an opportunity for business. Explain how it may also be a threat. *(8 marks)*

5. Identify **one** possible cause of internal change within a business. Explain the possible impact on the business this change might have. *(6 marks)*

6. Explain **two** factors that might determine whether any given external change was an opportunity or a threat. *(6 marks)*

7. Explain the difference between a proactive and a reactive business. *(3 marks)*

8. Explain **two** ways that a business might prepare for change. *(6 marks)*

9. Explain **two** possible changes in the competitive environment of a business and explain how they might affect the business. *(8 marks)*

10. Identify **two** recent changes in the legal environment and explain how they might affect a business. *(8 marks)*

1. Many businesses in the UK suffered a decline in sales in the recession. To what extent is external change inevitably bad for business? *(40 marks)*
2. Many changes in the external environment such as the growth of the European Union have created opportunities for UK businesses. To what extent do external changes always create opportunities for business? *(40 marks)*
3. In recent years there has been a recession in the UK, and then high inflation and a weak pound. To what extent do you think that changes in the economic environment are the most important factors in the external environment for businesses to prepare for? *(40 marks)*

Candidate's answer:

The economic environment involves factors such as the exchange rate, interest rates, inflation and GDP. Changes in these economic factors create opportunities and threats for businesses. In recent years the economy has been very unpredictable with the recession and the euro crisis – neither of which was anticipated. This makes the economic environment even more dangerous. When the UK was in a recession this meant that there was negative GDP growth. This hits the sales of many businesses, especially those with income-elastic products such as construction firms. Their sales may fall and this can reduce profits and affect the ability and willingness to invest which causes a negative knock-on effect on demand in the economy. Business plans were based on false assumptions because the recession had not been anticipated, which meant businesses had overcapacity, too many staff and liquidity and cash-flow problems. Some business gained as customers switched to lower price items, such as own-label products, but even then it was unexpected and meant that the necessary investment and workforce plans were not necessarily in place. Interest rate changes affect the cost of borrowing and thereby costs and also demand. Exchange rate changes affected the price of imports and the overseas price of export again affected costs and demand. Economic factors are clearly an important macro-influence on business success. This is especially true when they can change unexpectedly.

However, there are other factors that are also very important. In the consumer electronics industry, for example, technology is absolutely key. New products can almost destroy markets – think of digital cameras' impact on traditional film camera, the impact of mobile phones on watches and calculators and the impact of tablets and netbooks on PCs at the moment. Technological change can radically alter an industry and when groundbreaking changes occur, such as the launch of the iPad, this is more significant than economic factors. In industries such as tobacco the legal factors are incredibly important, with legislation on how to advertise products (most recently one country has said all cigarettes must be sold in plain packaging). The ongoing effect of legal changes increasing the price and reducing advertising and promotional opportunities is extremely important in this industry. So is social change – the greater awareness of the health effects of the product has made it more difficult for tobacco producers to sell more. Social change such as birth rates and crime rates can be very important for markets such as baby products and security products, highlighting that it is not just the economy that matters. The macro-environment involves many different factors not just the economy, and different elements of these will be important at different times for different businesses. At the moment in the public sector government cuts may be the most important issue to consider, in the banking system issues such as regulation may be the priority and in the communications sector it may be technology. This does not mean the economy can be ignored and the unfavourable economic climate at the moment with high levels of uncertainty, high inflation in the UK, low growth and a lack of confidence are extremely important. However, this does not always mean it is the most important for all businesses. Even within the economic environment, different factors will matter. For a global business such as McDonald's exchange rates could be vital; they may be less important to a local taxi business. To a business or government (such as Italy) with huge debts, interest rates are very important; they matter slightly less if borrowing is low. Overall, the economic environment is part ➡

of the landscape in which businesses compete; it must be understood and if possible planned for, but it is not the only or not necessarily the most important factor. Each business situation needs examining uniquely.

Examiner's comments:

A superb answer. It shows a sound grasp of economic issues and analyses the effect of changes in economic variables on a business. Relevant examples are used well to support the analysis. The candidate appreciates that the significance of different economic factors will depend on the business and will vary from business to business. They also highlight the importance of other factors apart from the economy, again using examples well to support the arguments. Overall a very focused answer and a clear grade A.

25 Internal causes of change

Internal change can occur as a result of the challenges and opportunities that growth provides. Managers report to investors and often these investors will want evidence that something is happening and the business is progressing. Growth may be one way managers can keep shareholders happy with their performance and there is often pressure to deliver growing sales, profits and/or dividends.

In this chapter we will consider:

- changes in organisational size
- the impact of new owners/leaders
- poor business performance.

Changes in organisational size

Internal change can occur as a result of the challenges and opportunities of growth. Many owners and managers will want their firms to grow. There are several reasons for this:

- Larger firms may benefit from economies of scale (see Chapter 11). This may mean lower unit costs and can result in higher profit margins or lower prices making the business more competitive. Economies of scale can arise for many reasons such as bulk buying or specialisation.
- Larger firms have more power over their markets, for example, they may be able to negotiate better deals with their suppliers and distributors; they may also be able to bargain for better positioning for their advertisements in the media. Bigger scale increases buying power (Porter's five forces).
- Larger firms tend to be safer from takeover simply because they are more expensive to buy up. With more assets the shares of the business are likely to be more expensive, giving the company a higher market value (this is called its 'market capitalisation'). Managers who are interested in their own job security may therefore have an incentive to make their firms bigger and as a result protect their own jobs.
- Larger firms have more status. Managers will often want the praise and recognition that comes with building up a business. This relates to the ego needs and self-actualisation in Maslow's hierarchy of needs. Managers may want to be in charge of a bigger business because it makes them more important and/or because it means they feel they

have achieved more when in charge.

A business may grow internally or externally. Internal growth occurs when the firm sells more of its products – for example, by launching new products or undertaking more extensive promotion its sales increase. External growth occurs when a firm acquires or joins up with another.

Internal growth is often slower than external growth – it may take some time to penetrate a market further and increase sales. External growth is naturally faster and more sudden because a firm acquires another organisation's sales in one go.

However, all forms of growth bring about changes because there are more people to organise, more products to provide, more markets to operate in and more decisions to be made. This can lead to changes in the structure of the business and its culture.

Adjustment during the growth of a business

As an organisation grows, its managers must examine the firm's structure and the roles of people within the business. Many firms start off as sole traders (in fact over 60 per cent of businesses in the UK are sole traders). The founder is the boss and they make all the major decisions. This type of enterprise is able to respond quickly to market conditions and the founder has complete control. They can make decisions without having to consult others and they have a clear overview of the business situation. This is a very flexible business form because decisions do not involve long processes of consultation and negotiation.

The next stage, as a firm continues to grow, usually involves more people being hired to deal with the additional business. At this stage there may well be a good team spirit. Individuals share out tasks among themselves and can still communicate easily with each other to sort out any problems. Employees feel they are all working towards the same goals. Individuals share jobs, help each other out and generally deal with things as and when they come up; there may not be formal job descriptions at this stage.

If, however, growth continues it may be necessary to develop a more formal structure within the organisation. To avoid too many people doing the same thing, or to avoid things not getting done at all, it usually becomes necessary to clearly define what each job involves. More rigid job descriptions become the norm and a more formal structure evolves with defined lines of accountability. At this stage processes are becoming more formalised and systematic. There may be more forms to fill in, more rules and procedures, more committees and more policies in an attempt to coordinate and control what people are doing,

At this point the people at the top of the organisation are less directly involved with the day-to-day work. Their approach must be less hands-on simply because they cannot do it all themselves; senior managers must learn how to delegate and let others do the frontline work for them. In larger organisations managers have to focus on the overall planning, coordinating and controlling rather than the actual doing.

For some managers the transition from the 'boss' (the people who do things themselves) to 'manager' or 'leader' (the people who focus on the overall direction of the business and delegates day-to-day tasks to others) can be a very difficult one; they can find it hard to remove themselves from direct contact with the job and their customers. In some firms the senior managers continue to intervene too much, even though the business has grown, because they cannot 'let go'; the danger of being too interventionist is that this undermines subordinates. Furthermore, managers who cannot relinquish control inevitably place a block on the size of the firm – if they always want to know exactly what is going on, the business as a whole cannot grow very big.

Keeping control of a growing business

As an organisation grows it naturally becomes more difficult for managers to keep control of all of its activities. There are more people to manage, more products to oversee and more things to do. The internal and external environments become more complex. Managers must therefore develop ways of keeping everyone informed and focused, and ensuring that employees know exactly what is happening and how their actions contribute to the success of the organisation as a whole.

To help coordination and maintain control within the firm managers often introduce procedures such as budgeting, appraisal systems and management by objectives. Budgeting helps managers to plan and monitor what is being spent, appraisals provide a good opportunity to review what has been happening and set new targets for the future, while a system of management by setting clear objectives helps to ensure everyone is working towards the same goals. Without such systems running throughout the organisation, there may be no clear direction.

Good communication is of course also essential to effective growth. Employees, suppliers and investors must be kept informed so they are clear about what is happening at the moment within the firm and where the business wants to go next. Good communication is also needed to keep the organisation in close contact with its customers so it can meet their needs precisely. However, the introduction of committees, rules and procedures can stifle innovation and creativity – the very things that made the business successful in the first place. The challenge for many big organisations is how to keep the spirit of a smaller business in terms of a can-do attitude, a flexible approach and an environment that welcomes new ideas. To achieve this the business may be split into many smaller units that operate relatively independently and/or the managers must foster an approach that continually questions and challenges. Steve Jobs once called Apple the largest start-up in the world, highlighting how he felt the business had retained its youthful nature.

The changes in the role of the founders of a business are shown in Figure 25.1. As the business expands the owner's ability to actually do the job himself or herself becomes less significant. At the beginning they are very hands-on and have to actually provide the service, but over time others can do this for them. What they have to do is delegate and assume the role of a manager. To do this successfully they need good people around them, effective plans to show where the business is going and what everyone else has to

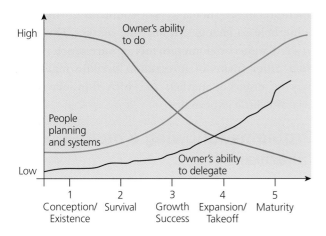

Figure 25.1 As a company grows, the owner's role changes

do to contribute to this, and they need to ensure that systems are in place to control performance.

Growth therefore requires changes in the role of managers and changes in the style and structure of the business.

External growth

External growth occurs when one firm decides to expand by joining together with another. This may occur either by a takeover (also called an acquisition) or a merger. A takeover occurs when one firm gains control of another by acquiring a controlling interest in its shares. A merger occurs when one firm joins together with another one to form a new combined enterprise. Mergers and takeovers are both forms of integration.

If one business wants to take over another it must buy up 51 per cent of the other firm's shares so that it has a majority vote. It may buy these shares either by using cash or by offering its own shares in return (this is known as a paper offer). The attacking company will make an offer to the shareholders of the victim company. The directors of the targeted company will decide whether or not they think the bid is fair and whether or not to recommend to their own shareholders that they should accept it; if they reject the offer the takeover becomes a 'hostile bid'.

If there are not enough shareholders willing to accept the offer, the attacking company may decide to increase the amount it offers for each share. There is, however, a strict timetable that the attacking company has to follow, so it cannot keep increasing its offer indefinitely.

In a merger the two (or more) firms agree to form a new enterprise; shares in each of the individual companies are exchanged for shares in the new business.

Key issues

The way a business is organised and managed has to change as it changes in size. What works for a business of four or five people does not work for a business of 4,000 or 40,000. Systems and processes have to be reviewed, new structures and reporting mechanisms need to be created and the way the business is run must adapt. The shape, the rules and the style will change at different stages in the development of an organisation.

Types of integration

There are three types of integration:

1 horizontal
2 vertical
3 conglomerate.

Horizontal integration

Horizontal integration occurs when one firm joins with another at the same stage of the same production process. For example, when Ford took over Volvo this was an example of horizontal integration because they are both car manufacturers.

The possible reasons for this type of integration include:

- **greater market share** – by combining together the two firms will have a greater share of the market and, as a result, they are likely to have more power over other members of the supply chain, such as suppliers and distributors
- **economies of scale** – larger-scale production may bring a reduction in unit costs due to managerial, production or purchasing economies
- **the opportunity to enter a different segment of the market** and thereby spread risks to some extent. For example, you may be strong in Europe while the other business may be strong in Asia, so by integrating you both get access to each other's markets. This is what happened with the merger of Nippon Glass and Pilkington Glass.

Vertical integration

Vertical integration occurs when one firm joins with another at a different stage of the same production process. Forward vertical integration occurs when one firm joins with another business at a later stage in the same production process. Backward vertical integration occurs when one firm joins with another business at an earlier stage in the same production process. Some businesses are very vertically integrated controlling the key stages of the production process: for example, Zara and American Apparel both manufacture and also have retail outlets for their clothes, BAT owns tobacco plantations as well as producing the cigarettes, Morrisons owns many of the farms producing the food it sells in its supermarkets. Part of the success of IKEA is also due to its control of the whole process from design to the retail outlet; this means that design is undertaken not only with the end-customer in mind, but it also takes account of the manufacturing process, the transportation process, storage and display – thus making the business leaner.

Firms may undertake vertical integration for various reasons.

- **In order to gain control over supplies**. This may be important for a firm to ensure it can maintain its suppliers (for example, in times of shortage) or if it is essential to maintain the quality of its supplies. By gaining control of its inputs a firm may also be able to deny competitors the supplies they want. By controlling supplies businesses can also ensure that appropriate environmental processes are used and staff are treated fairly. In recent years companies have come under greater scrutiny from consumers in relation to the behaviour of the suppliers they use; it may be safer to control the process than rely on external suppliers.
- **In order to guarantee access to the market**. By buying up retailers, for example, manufacturers may ensure that their products actually get to the market and are displayed and promoted in the way they want.

Conglomerate integration

Conglomerate integration occurs when firms in different markets join together, for example, if a chocolate company joins with a paint company. Tomkins plc was one of the last big conglomerates in the UK and at one time sold guns, Mother's Pride bread and bicycles! Tata is a large Indian conglomerate whose interests include Jaguar cars, Tetley tea and Corus Steel, as well as numerous other businesses in other product markets. A firm may become a conglomerate in order to spread its risk. By operating in several markets or countries a firm is less vulnerable to changes in any one market. However, in some ways conglomerate mergers are much riskier than other forms of integration because managers may be entering markets in which they may have relatively little experience.

Problems following a merger or takeover

Although, in theory, integration can offer many potential advantages such as economies of scale, many mergers and takeovers are relatively unsuccessful. One of the main problems following integration is coping with the different beliefs and ways of doing things in the organisations involved. Employees are likely to have different values regarding key areas such as customer service, quality, investment and training and this can cause conflict. Employees from one organisation may find that behaviour that was praised and rewarded in the past is now criticised. There will also be adjustment problems regarding pay and conditions, for example, employees in one of the organisations may have a significantly better remuneration scheme than in the other – creating discussions over fairness and possibly resentment.

Many firms also find that they experience diseconomies of scale following integration (for more on diseconomies of scale see page 139). Despite improvements in information technology, communication can be a problem as organisations join together and become bigger, and there can be a lack of a common sense of purpose. The result can often be demotivation as employees' status may have changed in the organisation and they may fear redundancies; there may also be a lack of coordination due to the increased scale and complexity of operations.

Furthermore, many of the anticipated benefits of integration often do not appear – computer systems turn out to be incompatible, employees do not cooperate and share information and the business lacks focus or control. As a result, integrated companies can find that their costs increase and that the returns generated are lower than would have been expected if they had remained single. Studies often show that over 60 per cent of mergers and takeovers actually destroy shareholder value (the companies combined end up being worth less than they would if they had remained separate).

Handy (1998, pp. 107–8) offers this perspective: 'Businesses can grow more profitable by becoming better, or leaner, or deeper, or more concentrated, without growing bigger. Bigness, in both business and life, can lead to a lack of focus, too much complexity and in the end, too wide a spread to control. We have to know when big is big enough.'

It is surprising, therefore, how many large-scale deals continue to occur. In many cases this is because the big deals are driven by a demand by managers for greater scale – they want to show that under their leadership the business grew and they acquired more power. Growth may be pursued for personal rather than business reasons. In addition managers may feel they can do better than anyone else – the data may show that mergers and takeovers in general are unsuccessful, but managers looking at a particular deal may be convinced they can succeed.

The cost of a firm being taken over

The amount paid by one firm for another will ultimately depend on its perceived value. This in turn depends on the assets of the target firm and how the attacker believes these can be utilised. A starting point in a bid may be the target company's balance sheet – this shows the 'book value' of a company. However, the book value will not necessarily reflect the actual value of the firm for several reasons:

- Some assets may not be valued, for example, the value of brands may not be included. In the case of many companies such as Microsoft, Sony, Apple or McDonald's the brand is clearly worth millions but is usually not listed in the accounts. The balance sheet will also fail to value the quality of the employees – a very important asset in many organisations (think of the importance of the skills and ideas of employees for companies such as Manchester United, Oxford University and the advertising agency Saatchi and Saatchi).
- Some assets – such as property – may be valued at historical cost (the price paid for them) rather than their current value.
- The firm may have used window-dressing techniques (such as changing the depreciation policy) to flatter the accounts.
- The published accounts are only published annually, so are not up to date.

These other factors may well be reflected in the current share price, which is why the market value (market capitalisation) of a business is different from its book value (the value in the published accounts).

To make sure that the victim company's shareholders are willing to sell their shares the attacker is likely to have to pay a premium (offer more than the existing share price). The amount of premium the bidder is willing to pay will depend on the extent to which it believes there will be gains such as economies of scale or synergy; the bigger the perceived gains the more it is likely to pay.

When deciding what a firm is worth there is inevitably a degree of risk. The risk involved will depend partly on whether it is a hostile or a welcome bid. If the bid is welcomed by the directors of the target company they will be willing to share information with the bidder. If the bid is hostile the attacking company will have no inside knowledge of the target firm and so may or may not be paying more than it should.

BUSINESS IN FOCUS

RBS and ABN Amro

According to most commentators, Sir Fred Goodwin of Royal Bank of Scotland paid far too high a price to take over ABN Amro. RBS beat Barclays in the bidding battle for the Dutch bank with an offer of £47 billion in the world's biggest ever bank takeover. The Barclays chief executive said: 'We weren't prepared to secure a win at any price. I think the consortium has overpaid. We made a very clear commitment to our shareholders that we would not be irresponsible in this transaction and we have been faithful to that'.

The Scottish bank denied suggestions that its promised synergies of €1.8 billion were over-ambitious, claiming they were more conservative than those envisaged by Barclays, but in fact it used up huge amounts of cash in a deal that did not bring the returns that had been expected by Goodwin. It is widely recognised, in retrospect, as an ill-advised deal. Goodwin seemed desperate to take over ABN and make RBS a global player; far too little research seems to have been gone into whether it would really work and whether the businesses would work well together.

Questions:

1 Discuss the possible reasons why RBS bought ABN Amro.
2 Discuss the factors that might have determined how much RBS paid for ABN Amro.

Going international

As well as growing within their domestic market, firms can also grow by expanding overseas. The benefits of this are that it provides new market opportunities. If, for example, the domestic market is saturated, selling overseas can provide new growth. Imagine you sell mobiles phones; the UK market is fairly saturated so the majority of the sales which now occur are when people upgrade or replace their phones. In other countries with a lower standard of living the mobile phone market may still be in the growth phase of its life cycle. Nokia has recently been upgrading its smartphones to regain market share from Apple, but it continues to target emerging markets where it has a huge market presence with its more basic models. Alternatively, it may be that further expansion in the domestic economy may be difficult due to market conditions or potential government intervention. Given its high market share in the UK Tesco cannot easily grow more because it may create competition (monopoly) issues for itself; further growth overseas is, therefore, one option.

The decision to sell overseas can be a difficult one to take. Along with all the usual problems of expansion a firm may face additional challenges, such as dealing with exchange rate fluctuations and coping with new legislation. A firm will also have to familiarise itself with market conditions and consumer behaviour, which can vary radically from one country to another.

Typically, firms begin to sell abroad by exporting. They continue to produce in the UK but sell some of their products to overseas customers. If, however, demand from abroad continues to grow a firm may extend its operations by using an overseas agent. An agent will represent the business overseas and try to generate more sales on its behalf. An agent is likely to have more insight into the market than the UK firm and this should help to boost sales. Agents do not take ownership of the goods or services – they are paid on commission.

Instead of using agents, a firm may join up with a local producer and either give or sell a licence to allow the products to be made there. The advantage of this approach is that the firm can benefit from local knowledge and skills as well as having lower distribution costs by producing in the region. In some cases, linking up with a local firm may be the only way to enter a market because the foreign government may insist that local businesses are involved.

Alternatively, a business may set up its own factory abroad and produce for itself. This is likely to involve high levels of investment and so will only be undertaken by firms if they are sure that demand will be sustained and profitable.

However, the risks of overseas expansion should not be ignored. Many businesses have failed to fully understand the business environment abroad or customer demands, and have had to withdraw or have performed badly.

The decision about how to enter a market will depend on how much risk a business is prepared to take, how much it is prepared to invest and whether it perceives the market as having long-term potential.

BUSINESS IN FOCUS

Tata

The Tata group is a conglomerate. This means it is a collection of companies operating in many sectors, such as cars and consulting, software and steel, tea and coffee, chemicals and hotels. Tata Consultancy Services (TCS) is Asia's biggest software company. Tata Steel is India's largest steelmaker and number ten in the world. Taj Hotels Resorts and Palaces is India's biggest luxury hotel group by far. Tata Power is the country's largest private electricity company. Tata Global Beverages is the world's second-largest maker of branded tea.

Under the leadership of Ratan Tata, who became chairman in 1991, the group has been transformed. He took over an uncoordinated, and badly managed company and made it leaner and more competitive. He increased the power of the head office over the divisions to make sure they were run properly. He also embraced globalisation with a policy of rapid acquisition abroad. In 1995–2003 Tata companies made, on average, one purchase a year; in 2004 they made six; and in 2005–06 more than 20. In 2000, Tata Tea's took over Tetley Group, a British company, for $450 million. In 2007, Tata Steel bought Corus, Europe's second largest steelmaker for $12.1 billion. In 2008, Tata Motors paid $2.3 billion for Jaguar Land Rover (JLR). Today, the company earns over 60 per cent of its revenue abroad and employs more British workers than any other manufacturer.

Why do you think the Tata group has expanded overseas?

Business is becoming more global these days. Markets are more open, with free trade agreements reducing the barriers to trade. The World Trade Organisation (WTO) is an organisation with over 150 member countries, which aims to reduce protectionist barriers. Other drivers of increased international trade are lower transportation costs and cheaper communication methods.

BUSINESS IN FOCUS

Coca-Cola

In 2008 Coca-Cola announced it wanted to buy Huiyuan, China's largest fruit juice company, for $2.4 billion (£1.35 billion) in the biggest foreign takeover of a Chinese company. This was the second-largest acquisition in Coke's 122-year history.

The deal was intended to consolidate the soft-drink maker's position in China where it already dominated the carbonated and diluted drinks markets.

Coke, which was an official sponsor of the Beijing Olympics, sells more than a billion bottles of Coke in China. According to its Chinese website, Coke has invested $1.25 billion since making its first entry in 1979. Analysts expect the Chinese fruit juice market to grow by more than 10 per cent in the next few years as the country's growing middle class become increasingly health-conscious.

'Though it's a relatively small market in the beverages space, it's a high-growth market because of the growing personal income in China and increased health awareness,' said Coca-Cola president and chief executive Muhtar Kent. 'Huiyuan is a long-established and successful juice brand in China and is highly complementary to the Coca-Cola business in China. This is further evidence of our deep commitment to China and to providing Chinese consumers with the beverage choices that meet their needs.'

Figure 25.2

State dominance of the corporate sector and strict red tape have made foreign moves into the country notoriously difficult.

Huiyuan, which has about a 46 per cent share of the pure-juice market exports drinks to about 30 countries, including Japan and the US.

Source: BBC News

Questions:

Analyse the reasons why Coca-Cola may have wanted to buy Huiyuan.

Discuss the factors likely to determine whether this takeover is successful.

Financing growth

In order to grow, a firm will need to have the finance necessary to acquire resources such as new premises or equipment or to hire new staff. This finance can come from internal and external sources.

Internal sources of finance include:

- **retained profits**: the firm can invest its profits into stocks and new equipment. This assumes it has the finances to do this; a poorly performing business may lack the finances to grow and may need to focus on improving its existing operations.
- **the sale of assets**: if firms have assets which are not being used (such as land) they may sell these to raise cash.

External sources include:

- **overdrafts**: this is a short-term form of finance which can be called in at any time by the bank. This would not usually be used for a major expansion project because funds will be tied up for some time.

- **mortgages**: this is finance acquired using property as collateral
- **loans**: this is long-term borrowing in which a firm agrees to pay back the borrowed money over a set period of time. Increasing loans will increase the gearing of the business and the manager must be sure that the extra rewards generated through growth cover the additional interest costs of a loan.
- **Share issue**: to raise finance managers may approach investors for more funds. Gaining these funds will obviously require an effective plan of how the money will be used and what returns the investors can expect.

Growth may therefore lead to changes in ownership and/or changes in the amount of debt the business has. This in turn can influence the decisions that are made and the impact of external change such a change in interest rates.

Growth and cash flow

The expansion of a business may bring many benefits in the long term, but can also lead to cash-flow problems in the short term. As a firm expands it will be buying new fixed assets, purchasing stocks and investing in areas such as new product development. These all lead to cash outflows. Over time this investment should lead to more sales and cash inflows, but in the short term the business may have to plan carefully to avoid cash-flow problems. Its options may include:

- arranging a loan (if this is available and financially feasible)
- ensuring debtors pay on time (but this may cause issues with customers switching to competitors with longer credit periods)
- delaying payment to suppliers as long as possible (but this may lead to a loss of goodwill).

If a firm does grow too fast and fails to manage its cash flow effectively this is known as 'overtrading'. Overtrading occurs when a firm has too much money invested in building up stocks or has spent too much acquiring bigger premises and, as a result, has liquidity problems.

Imagine you have a successful idea for a cafe. The business does well so you decide to open two more. This requires investment and drains your cash flow, even though the first one is successful. The two new cafes eventually open and the first few months are promising. To exploit your idea as quickly as possible (and before others do), you decide to open another five cafes. Once again this leads to a drain on your cash. The business idea is a good one, but rapid growth can place an enormous strain on your cash-flow position – if you run out of cash you will experience overtrading.

Growth, therefore, will require careful planning to ensure that liquidity does not become a problem. Some organisations grow at a very fast rate (for example, Whitbread was opening one Costa Coffee shop a week in recent years) and this means its cash flow needs careful monitoring.

Retrenchment

Although businesses may want to grow there will be times when the managers decide to shrink the business – this is called retrenchment. This may be because of a lack of demand and/or problems controlling a large-scale business. Retrenchment occurs when managers withdraw from some markets. This may involve the closure or sale of different divisions, or redundancies. Many firms had to retrench (or rationalise) during the 2008–9 recession when the UK economy was shrinking and demand for some products fell.

A company may pull out of a market because:

- the demand is no longer there so it does not generate sufficient returns
- it cannot manage operating on a larger scale (for example, diseconomies of scale)
- it no longer has competitive advantage in that market (perhaps because of competitors)
- it wants to raise money by selling the business.

When scaling down the business managers should consider:

- How this decision is communicated to investors and the media. Is it planned and can the reason be explained as part of an overall strategy rather than seeming like a business in trouble? If there is a high level of uncertainty this can damage the share price.
- Consultation with employees to ensure they understand the reasons why the business is shrinking and how they will be affected. If redundancies are to be made can the business help employees find new jobs? If employees do not understand the reason for or the need for change they will resist, making change more difficult to bring about.

Key issues

Retrenchment became a key issue in the UK in 2008 when the economy went into a recession. This led to a drop in profits for many companies and a delay in investment plans. Some businesses also started to close parts of their operations because they were not profitable enough. This was retrenchment caused by external factors.

The impact of new owners and leaders

Internal change may occur because of growth, which will alter the way the business is managed and organised. Another key driver of change is the impact of the owners and managers wanting to alter the way that the business is run.

New leaders in a business often want to make changes. This may be because they have a different vision of where the organisation is headed from the previous leaders, or because they have a different view of how to achieve particular goals. They may have different experiences, different values, different personal styles of leading and therefore they want to change the way things are done. In some cases managers might want to make change simply to show they have arrived and that they can and will make changes. Changes made soon after their arrival, for example, may change some key personnel to mark a change of approach.

In fact, new managers are often brought in precisely to bring about change because of the failure of a previous strategy. For example, faced with falling sales or rising costs the owners may seek new leadership to bring about better solutions to the problems. Stephen Elop was brought in at Nokia in 2011, for example, because the company's performance had been in decline. He was recruited from Microsoft to turn the business around. Stephen Hester was appointed as chief executive at RBS in 2008 when the government took control of the struggling bank.

BUSINESS IN FOCUS

Hewlett–Packard

Hewlett–Packard (HP) has lost six chief executives since 1999. These include Carly Fiorina who was dropped in 2005 when HP's share price fell by 50 per cent and Mark Hurd who stood down in 2010 after an expenses scandal. On 22 September 2011 the board sacked Léo Apotheker after just 11 months in office. The sense is that HP keeps reaching out for a corporate saviour – it is still looking for the right leader to save them. This strategy can work. Jack Welch at General Electric transformed the business in the 1980s increasing its market value by 4,500 per cent! And many other companies look to bring in outsiders to save them. In the 1970s only around 15 per cent of chief executive positions in leading companies were filled externally. Now it is over 30 per cent.

However, Jim Collins, the author of *Good to Great*, argues that great companies nearly always recruit CEOs internally. Rakesh Khurana of Harvard

Business School claims that looking for a saviour outside actually damages the business internally as it is demoralising. Recently, Cazier and McInnis studied 192 chief executives who were externally recruited and found that there is negative correlation between what they are paid and the performance of the business! (The more expensive the recruit, the worse the business performs.) This could be because the incomers overestimate their ability or are taking credit for the success of their last business when in fact the success it was due to others. It will be interesting to watch HP's success in the future.

Questions:

Why do you think HP has changed its chief executives so often?

What do you think the consequence of this might be for the company?

Differing expectations of employees

Change can also come from within the workforce. In the UK the nature of the workforce has changed in many ways in the last 20 years. For example:

- employees are getting older due to demographic change
- employees are better educated than they were as more people have stayed on at school and gone to university
- there are more families where both parents work
- there is greater concern about a work–life balance
- the workforce is more diverse in terms of gender and ethnic groups.

This will affect employees' expectations, how they want to be treated, how they need to be motivated. For example, a better-educated workforce may want more involvement in decision-making and more opportunities to make decisions. This may require a change in management style and/or structure.

Poor business performance

According to Lewin, at any moment a business will be in a temporary equilibrium where the forces for change are exactly balanced by the forces resisting change. There may be pressures to change (either internal or external) but, at the same time, there are forces pushing against this.

For example, managers may not want to bring about change due to:

- the cost
- the likely opposition from some staff
- the extra work involved.

For change to occur there must be greater pressure for change or the resistance to change needs to decrease (for example, it becomes cheaper to install new equipment; employee relations improve). Greater pressure to bring about change is often caused by poor business performance because the owners want something done about it. Not surprisingly, a fall in sales and/or a decline in profits is likely to lead to pressure from investors for better performance. The existing managers are likely to feel pressurised to improve matters or they may fear they will lose their jobs. This may help managers to bring about changes they may have wanted to make anyway, but now

they have the incentive and the justification. When asked why these changes are necessary they can point to a disappointing financial performance. The disappointing results can therefore be a factor for change and also help employees to understand why it is necessary, thereby reducing opposition to change.

Typical changes following poor business performance include:

- **Replacing some staff**. Specific employees may be held responsible for the firm's problems. In 2011 Carol Bartz was sacked from Yahoo as she was held responsible for the company's poor performance. There may also be redundancies in an attempt to cut costs.
- **Restructuring**. The managers may look at the structure of the business and decide that some parts are no longer necessary or are over-staffed. They may also feel the structure hinders the efficiency and effectiveness of the business; perhaps a functional structure limits communication between functions and therefore a matrix approach may be better.
- **New processes and systems**. New ways of doing things, new ways of organising work and new technologies may all be introduced to reduce waste and improve quality. As a business moves operations overseas, for example, this may mean a loss of jobs domestically.

- **Mergers or takeovers.** Change will also be common following a merger or takeover. To make the deal worthwhile the managers must have seen some hidden value in the victim business; once they have control they need to bring about changes to generate this value. This is especially true given that they may have paid a premium to gain control of the business, and this spending needs to be recovered before extra profits are generated.

Summary

Internal change may come from the growth of the organisation. This may be internal (through greater sales) or external (through mergers or takeovers). Expanding the size of a business brings many management challenges to maintain control and direction effectively. Changes are likely to the structure of the business and how it is managed.

Change may also be prompted by new managers in the business who may have their own ideas of how things should be done. New managers may be brought in because of poor business performance – given disappointing results managers are appointed to turn around the business by making changes.

One step further: Greiner's stages of growth

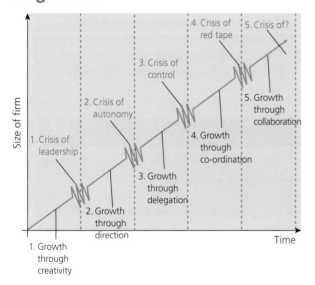

Figure 25.3 Greiner's stages of growth

According to Greiner (1998) the key stages of growth for a business are as follows.

1. Creativity

This is common with a start-up business when there are new ideas. Entrepreneurs may have created a new product or process and the business structure is fairly informal. Communication between employees is regular and frequent, typically employees work hard at this stage, often helping to do a range of jobs. They may not be paid particularly well but may be hoping to continue to be part of the business as it grows.

As the business grows there are more jobs to be done, there is greater complexity and there are more decisions to be made. The informal creative approach no longer works and there is a leadership crisis.

2. Direction

Typically, a traditional functional structure is adopted at this stage, clarifying who does what and avoiding the overlap of jobs and decisions that was happening before as the business grew. Roles become more defined, budgets are set to determine how much can be spent, appraisals are introduced to review progress. Generally, systems are introduced to control the direction of the business.

However, if the business continues to grow with more products, more division and more regions then a centralised approach with one set of rules and systems may not be appropriate. In this situation there may be an autonomy crisis. The senior managers need to delegate.

3. Delegation

This occurs when a business decentralises and lets local regions or divisions make more decisions and react to local market conditions. Business units are likely to be run as profit centres, with reviews of progress and more independence.

The problem with this approach is that if the business continues to grow and be successful each section of the business may see itself as a separate unit and then there is a lack of control of what they are doing. This is a control crisis. To overcome this problem managers may enter phase four.

4. Coordination

This occurs when there is formal planning for the business as a whole. Key functions, such as human resources and purchasing, are centralised. The danger of this approach is that a large number of centralised forms and controls develop, causing a red tape crisis.

5. Collaboration

In this system teams work independently but collaborate. Cross-functional teams provide a common sense of purpose and work on projects the different units have in common. While this may work there is always the danger of another crisis requiring some restructuring or some change of management style.

Key terms

Economies of scale occur when a change in the capacity of a business results in lower unit costs. These can be technical, financial or managerial.

External growth occurs when a business grows by merging with or taking over another business.

Horizontal integration is between organisations at the same stage of the same production process.

Vertical integration is between organisations at different stages of the same production process.

Conglomerate integration is between organisations involved in different production processes.

Progress questions

1 Identify two reasons why managers might want a business to grow. Explain these reasons. *(6 marks)*

2 Distinguish between a merger and a takeover. *(3 marks)*

3 Explain two possible problems of a takeover. *(6 marks)*

4 Explain, with an example, what is meant by horizontal integration. *(3 marks)*

5 Explain, with an example, what is meant by vertical integration. *(3 marks)*

6 Why do new bosses often make changes? *(5 marks)*

7 Explain why poor business performance is often an effective trigger for change. *(4 marks)*

8 Explain two difficulties firms may face when entering overseas markets. *(6 marks)*

9 Explain how the role of the founders might change over time as the business grows. *(6 marks)*

10 Explain two factors that might affect how much a firm pays to take over another. *(6 marks)*

Essay questions

1 A few years ago Nippon Sheet Glass took over Pilkington Glass to expand into Europe. To what extent do you think taking over another business is a good way to grow? *(40 marks)*

2 Google has recently moved into the mobile phone handset market. Why is it important for businesses to keep changing what they do? *(40 marks)*

3 General Electric has grown very rapidly over the last 20 years and now produces many different products, from light bulbs to fridges to engines. To what extent do you think it is better for a business to be bigger rather than smaller? *(40 marks)*

Candidate's answer:

By being bigger a business may benefit from economies of scale. This means that the unit costs may fall due to the larger size. This could be due to technical economies of scale – for example, mass-producing cars is cheaper per car than producing more by hand (for example, Ford v Aston Martin). This is what was achieved by Ford with the Model T when Ford was one of the first to produce using production line techniques; this enabled him to reduce the cost per car and then the price per car, which made the cars affordable to the masses and enabled Ford to dominate the industry. Economies of scale include bulk buying – businesses such as Walmart buy on such a scale that they can drive suppliers' prices very low because of their power, and then pass this on to customers in the form of lower prices. Another economy of scale is financial, which means that businesses such as BT have so many assets that they pose less of a risk and may be able to borrow at lower interest rates. This reduces their fixed costs and makes it easier to generate a good rate of return on projects.

However, getting bigger can lead to diseconomies of scale, which means the cost per unit rises. This can be due to problems with communication. Multinationals such General Motors operate in many different countries which means it can be more difficult to communicate; there are fewer face-to-face meetings, and even time differences can make it more difficult to exchange messages. There are more opportunities for messages getting distorted and for miscommunication. There can also be demotivation because employees feel they are just a small part of a big organisation and

that no one really cares. Organisations such as the National Health Service are huge, with staff in many different locations and departments and specialisms. Employees may feel loyalty to their specific part of the organisation but not feel much of a link to the very senior bosses. This can result in less productivity, more mistakes and higher unit costs.

Overall then, getting bigger can be good and bad. It depends how it is handled and how big.

Examiner's comments:

This has the potential to be a very good answer, but it does not evaluate enough. The candidate outlines the potential economies of scale and diseconomies of scale well. They clearly understand the case for and against large size and apply that knowledge well to a number of scenarios. However, the judgement about whether being bigger is better is limited. The candidate has something of a throwaway and undeveloped comment at the end. The answer remains limited in terms of evaluation which lets it down. Why does it depend on how it is handled? How big is too big? What does this depend on? It is important to develop and defend your judgements.

26 Planning for change

According to the management writer Peter Drucker, 'The greatest danger in times of turbulence is not the turbulence; it is to act with yesterday's logic'.

Managers should be looking ahead to anticipate change. Much better to be ready for what might happen than to have it happen to you. By anticipating change and planning ahead managers have more chance of being in control of their own destiny. The central plan of the business is known as the corporate plan.

In this chapter we examine:

- the purpose of corporate plans
- the internal and external influences on corporate plans
- the value of corporate plans.

Introduction

A corporate plan sets out what the business as a whole is trying to achieve and how it intends to achieve this. It will include the corporate objectives and the overall business strategy to be pursued. These overall targets and plans must then be turned into specific objectives and strategies for each of the functions.

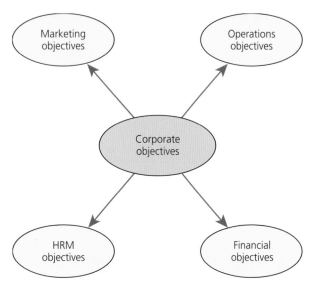

Figure 26.1 Corporate objectives lead to functional objectives

A corporate plan may be derived from a process of analysing the internal **S**trengths and **W**eaknesses and comparing these with the future external **O**pportunities and **T**hreats. This process of strategic planning is known as SWOT analysis.

Figure 26.2 SWOT analysis

SWOT analysis

The strengths and weaknesses of a business are internal. They relate to the present situation. Strengths include qualities such as a well-known brand, a strong cash-flow position or a broad portfolio. Weaknesses might be poor quality processes, demotivated staff or high costs.

The opportunities and threats facing a business are external and in the future. Opportunities might include expansion overseas, going online or launching new products. Threats could include a worsening economic climate, new competitors entering the market or increasing input prices.

A SWOT analysis for Toyota

Strengths	Opportunities
Strong brand name, helping the company charge premium prices	Increasing demand for hybrid electric vehicles
Good at research and development	The Asian market
Strong distribution network	New product launches likely to maintain customer interest
Production system uses lean production	Car industry recovering after the global recession
Keeps costs relatively low	
Weaknesses	**Threats**
Problems with product quality in recent years have negatively hurt brand image and sales	Greater competition in the global automotive market
Cash-flow problems due to high pension costs	Tightening emission standards increasing production costs
	Appreciating Japanese Yen against the US Dollar

Question:

Based on the SWOT analysis above what would you recommend Toyota include in its corporate plan?

When forming a corporate plan managers will consider:

- how to build on the strengths of the business to exploit its opportunities and protect itself against the threats. A good plan will use the competences of the business as a starting point so the business is competing in ways that enable it to win. These could be its ability to innovate, its links with suppliers or its distribution system.
- how to protect the business against the dangers from its weaknesses.

The value of corporate planning

The value of planning is that it makes sure that managers are looking ahead and thinking about what they want to achieve and how to achieve it, rather than just drifting along. Producing the plan is also a useful exercise because it forces managers to consider the organisation's strengths and weaknesses in relation to its environment and to think about how all the different elements of the firm interrelate. By planning you may be able to anticipate what might happen more effectively.

All other plans within a business can also be derived from the corporate plan. Each function can decide what it has to do to contribute to the overall plan.

Then, within each department, plans can be developed to contribute to the functional targets. Here are some examples.

Corporate plan:

- Corporate target: grow the business by 15 per cent over three years.
- Corporate strategy: open new stores in the UK.

Operations plan:

- Open 20 new stores over the next three years.
- Open five stores this year, ten stores the following year, then 15 in year 3.
- Focus on the south-east.
- Open three stores in London this year, one in Oxford and one in Cambridge.

However, corporate planning can have drawbacks. A plan which sets out what a firm is going to do for, say, the next five years can easily become out of date. If managers keep pursuing the original plan when all around them has changed there is a danger that they will actually be doing the wrong thing. It may be necessary, therefore, to ensure that the firm has a flexible approach to planning and keeps revisiting the original plan to ensure it remains viable and relevant.

Emergent plans

The end results of planning are often different from those initially intended. Businesses often end up with a different strategy from the one that was intended as conditions change. Talk to your parents – did their careers end up the way they had initially planned, or did they take different turns along the way? The same is true for businesses – they often reassess their plans and alter objectives and strategies. When Honda wanted to enter the US motorbike market it set up a series of shops selling high-powered motorbikes. Staff moved between stores on small mopeds. Although demand for the bigger bikes was poor many US customers were intrigued by the Japanese mopeds and wanted to buy them. Sales of these small mopeds became high and over time this established the Honda brand in the US. Customers gradually traded up to the bigger motorbikes and this strategy of entering at the lower end of the market became quoted as a superb strategic decision by Honda; in fact it was luck!

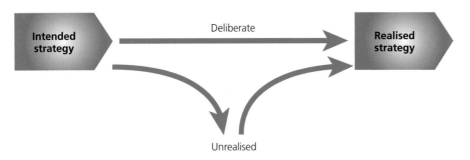

Figure 26.3 Emergent strategy versus planned strategy

Although plans can (and often do) go wrong this does not mean that planning is not worthwhile – on the contrary, it makes it all the more important. Without planning and review you will not know where you are headed and where you are at any moment. You may wander from the chosen track at any point and indeed may even change your destination, but without planning you do not know where you have come from, what resources you have, what your strengths are and what your options are. Imagine you set off travelling on a gap year without a map. By planning ahead you think about:

- where you might want to visit
- how long you have
- how much money you have
- how you prefer to travel.

You may end up staying somewhere a bit longer than you originally intended, or add a destination, or are delayed by some problems with the travel arrangements. However, because you have a plan you can estimate the knock-on effects, amend your arrangements without necessarily disrupting your overall plans and notify everyone of the consequences.

Planning needs reviewing

Management is the 'process of getting things done through others' (Stewart). It involves:

- planning where the organisation is heading (this may be expressed in the mission statement and in its corporate objectives)
- organising the resources needed to achieve its targets
- coordinating these resources to ensure everything is running on schedule
- controlling by reviewing progress and, if necessary, changing the plan (this may be achieved via systems such as budgets and appraisals).

Planning is therefore only part of the management process. A plan may fail because it is not implemented correctly and/or because progress is not reviewed properly meaning that the right actions are not taken for the plan to be successful.

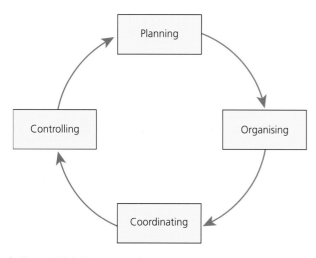

Figure 26.4 Management processes

The success of a corporate plan also depends on the resources available. Setting a plan is all very well. But effective management means you have to have the staff, money, equipment and materials required to implement it. Managers must organise these resources and ensure that the targets, the standards, the means by which they should be achieved and how they are to be achieved are all communicated effectively.

It is also important to assess the progress of the plan at regular intervals. Where are we compared with where we expected to be? Reviews may occur informally or using formal mechanisms such as budgets and variance analysis and employee appraisals. By reviewing, changes can be made to get things back on track. You may plan to get the top grades in all your subjects; to help make sure you are on the way to achieving this it is helpful to have regular feedback (via mocks and reports) to let you know how it is going. If there are problems in one subject you can devote more energy to this or review your targets. If you never reviewed your progress you might get to the end of your two-year course before realising that your university and career plans were not going to be fulfilled.

Levels of planning

The problems of keeping to a given plan were highlighted by Carl von Clausewitz, a great Prussian military strategist, in his book, *On War* in 1832. He argued that detailed planning necessarily failed due to chance events, problems in executing the plan and the actions of the opposition. Any grand strategy you have for a battle falls apart as soon as the opposition is met because they do not react the way you want and the battle conditions are never quite what you expect, and so you have to change the plan. What matters at times like these is leadership, good morale and the instinct of generals to react to the chaos of the battlefield. Clausewitz argued that it is vital to set broad objectives, but that you also need to be ready to seize opportunities as they evolve rather than stick rigidly to some plan drawn up away from the battlefield.

The same may be true of business; managers must rely at times on their feelings, on what needs to be done quickly, and must be prepared to jettison a plan that is no longer appropriate. However, it is still important to know the broad objectives and ways you want to compete because this will determine what you do overall. What Clausewitz's experience suggests is that some of the detail of any plan may be changed in the heat of battle as conditions turn out to be different from those you expected and because they change during the battle. So you need good generals (managers) who understand the overall strategy and objectives and know your resources so they can make the right decisions at any moment. This would suggest that getting the right staff and drawing the broad strokes of the plan are essential to success, but so is being prepared for details to change along the way and being flexible.

Contingency planning

Businesses operate in uncertain and risky environments. Managers are always making decisions about the future and inevitably are not sure of exactly what the future will be like. This makes planning even more important; planning for a situation that is expected but also reviewing the plan regularly to assess where the business is compared with where it is expected to be and to decide what to do next to get back on track if necessary. This type of planning is known as contingency planning. This occurs when a firm prepares for unlikely events, such as:

- a fire
- the bankruptcy of a major customer
- the closure of an important supplier
- a major computer virus attacking the database
- an epidemic causing illness among staff.

Contingency plans might include:

- using two suppliers for the same part or component in case there are problems with one of them; this can safeguard supply
- paying a fee to be able to use computer facilities or office space elsewhere in case of flooding, earthquake or a terrorist attack
- training employees in several tasks so they can take over from others if there are major absences, illnesses or strikes
- ensuring new products are in development so that if there is a problem with existing products they can be replaced.

However, you cannot afford to have a contingency plan for every possible event that might happen. Managers must therefore decide exactly which events are worth preparing for and how many resources to put into contingency planning. Should the firm have back-up plans in case there are problems with suppliers? Should it have a plan for what to do if there is a safety problem with one of its products? What about planning for a situation where a competitor makes a takeover bid? Decisions must be based on the likely risk and damage of any event.

A contingency plan should provide a sense of direction and enable each element of the business to see how it should contribute. It should help managers set their priorities and allocate their resources.

The greater the likelihood of an event and the greater the potential damage if it does occur, the more likely a firm is to plan for it. Food manufacturers, for example, are likely to plan for a situation where their products are contaminated and they have to recall them. An airline will plan for a crash. An oil transportation business will prepare for a spillage. A prison will plan for a breakout.

BUSINESS IN FOCUS

Lehman Brothers

After the terrorist attacks on 11 September 2001 Lehman Brothers, an investment bank which had offices just across the road from the World Trade Centre, was able to restart its business in New York almost immediately. This was thanks to careful advance planning which meant its computer systems allowed many of its staff to work from home, and others to set up in hotel rooms as a temporary measure. As a result, it came through the period after 11 September better than some of its competitors that suffered much less physical damage and disruption. (Despite such contingency planning Lehman Brothers later collapsed in the financial crisis of 2008, showing that no business is ever completely safe.)

Question:

To what extent is planning for terrorist attacks a good use of resources?

The need for contingency planning highlights the dynamic nature of business and the need to be prepared for the unexpected. Obviously a firm cannot prepare for every emergency but it is worth highlighting the biggest risks and preparing for these. Firms must continually examine their own operations and their environment to check that they are prepared for possible changes in the future; in this way managers will be proactive (anticipating and preparing for change) rather than reactive (having to react to crises as they develop).

Of course this does not mean that companies that have contingency plans are safe from disaster; unfortunately managers often do not or cannot foresee what events will occur. In 2008, for example, there was a major global financial crisis that few had predicted. This led to a problem gaining credit and lower customer spending which damaged many businesses, very few of whom would have had any form of plan for this scenario.

BUSINESS IN FOCUS

Disaster planning

Every few years over 5 million Southern Californians agree to simultaneously drop to the floor on a given day and huddle face down under tables and desks for two minutes of imagined seismic turmoil in the biggest US earthquake drill ever.

The Great Southern California ShakeOut drill was organised by scientists and emergency officials as part of a campaign to prepare the region's 22 million inhabitants for a catastrophic quake that experts say is inevitable and long overdue.

The exercise is based on the premise of a magnitude 7.8 tremor striking the San Andreas Fault, similar in strength to a devastating quake that had hit China recently.

At precisely 10 a.m. on a given day people in classrooms, offices and homes throughout the region 'drop, cover and hold on' for two minutes, the duration of the hypothetical quake. They are guided by a public service message distributed to businesses and schools and played over the airwaves by radio and TV stations.

Question:

To what extent would disaster planning be useful for all businesses?

The impact of a crisis

When a disaster does occur, such as a fault in the product or a fire at the factory, this can cause panic. It is hoped that the firm will have a contingency plan which it can put into action, but even so this is likely to be a stressful time. It is easy to rush into a decision at times like these because of the pressure to do something and be seen to be doing something – this can lead to rushed and inappropriate decision-making. On the other hand, if you delay too long the crisis may get worse. As well as sorting out the crisis itself, the firm may have to handle the press as well. When managing a crisis it is important to:

- identify the 'facts' as soon as possible. What is the scale of the problem? How many people are likely to be affected?
- establish good communication systems. Managers must make sure that everyone is 'on line' and reacting in the same way. If, for example, different managers are giving the press different information following a scare about the safety of the product, this will create the impression they are not in control and the public may lose faith.
- have the authority and resources to make decisions quickly, rather than having to consult endless committees.

BUSINESS IN FOCUS

Johnson & Johnson

Tylenol is a headache cure (like aspirin) produced by Johnson & Johnson. In 1982 it had 35 per cent of the US over-the-counter market and accounted for around 15 per cent of the company's profits. That year someone interfered with some of Johnson & Johson's Tylenol products and added cyanide. Seven people died as a result and there was widespread panic about how many products had been contaminated. The same situation occurred in 1986 but this time the company had learnt its lessons. It acted quickly, ordering that Tylenol should be recalled from every outlet, not just those in the state where it had been tampered with. Not only that, but the company decided the product would not be re-established on the shelves until something had been done to provide better product protection. As a result, Johnson & Johnson developed the tamperproof packaging that would make it much safer in future. The cost was extremely high. The share price fell, there was lost production and millions →

of packets of Tylenol were destroyed as a result of the recall.

However, the company won praise for its quick and appropriate action. Having sidestepped the position others have found themselves in – of having been slow to act in the face of consumer concern – they achieved the status of consumer champion. Within five months it had regained 70 per cent of its market share. By comparison, companies such as Cadbury and Perrier have been criticised for the way they handled crises when their products were contaminated. They were slow to react and accept there was a problem and lost customer goodwill which took longer to recover.

Johnson & Johnson reacted very quickly in 1986 because of its previous experience of how serious it could be and because everyone in the business knew that its mission statement (called 'Our Credo') stated that the business was there to serve the doctors, nurses, mothers and patients – so they had to take action and did not need to hesitate. This reaction is often quoted as evidence of how important the values of a company are and how they influence behaviour. A different business might have hesitated to act, might have tried to keep the incident quiet and might have tried to do as little as it could get away with.

Question:

To what extent would disaster planning be useful for all businesses?

Scenario planning

This is another technique to help managers plan ahead. In this approach managers try to imagine three or four possible scenarios that might develop in the future in their industry. Scenario planning does not assume the future will be like the past, but asks managers and experts to think of what the world might look like in the future. This could be very different from the past. This technique has been used widely by Shell, where managers work with experts to create possible visions of what the world might look like in the future. For example, one scenario might include a stable political position in the Middle East, high levels of oil production and a low oil price. Another might focus on high levels of intervention by the government to reduce car usage, leading to high taxes and low levels of demand. Managers then work on how these scenarios might affect the business and the implications for their strategy. Schwartz describes scenarios as: 'Stories that can help us recognise and adapt to changing aspects of our present environment. They form a method for articulating the different pathways that might exist for you tomorrow, and finding your appropriate movements down each of those possible paths.'

BUSINESS IN FOCUS

Gary Hamel

Working with CK Prahalad, Gary Hamel developed the concept of core competences in 1990. 'They wrote that core competences are the collective learning in the organisation, especially how to coordinate diverse production skills and integrate multiple streams of technologies' (they are the things that an organisation does extremely well and therefore its strategy should be based on this). If an organisation is not good at something it should consider outsourcing it to others that have competences in these areas (businesses should concentrate on what they are good at). Hamel saw strategic planning not as a series of logical steps but as moments of dramatic change. He said that 'Strategic innovation will be the main source of competitive advantage in the future'. He believed great strategies come from challenging the status quo. He quoted Anita Roddick, the founder of Body Shop: 'I watch where the cosmetics industry is going and then walk in the opposite direction.'

'Management was designed to solve a very specific problem – how to do things with perfect replicability, at ever-increasing scale and steadily increasing efficiency. Now there's a new set of challenges on the horizon. How do you build organisations that are as nimble as change itself?'

In his book *The Future of Management* Hamel says: 'Management is out of date. Like the combustion engine, it's a technology that has largely stopped evolving, and that's not good … My goal in writing this book was not to predict the future of management, but to help you invent it'. Businesses need to think about their purpose, seek out ideas from the fringes, and embrace the democratising power of the internet.

Gary Hamel's books:

- *Competing for the Future*, with Prahalad, CK, Harvard Business School Press, 1994
- *Strategy as Revolution*, Harvard Business Review, July–August 1996
- *Leading the Revolution*, Harvard Business School Press, 2000
- *The Future of Management*, with Breen, B, Harvard Business School Press, 2007

(*Source: Adapted from* The Economist, *26 September 2008*)

Question:

How do you think a business can become better at innovation?

Summary

Planning is an important part of the management process; it is then followed through by coordinating, communicating and controlling. The corporate plan is the overall plan of the business; this then influences the functional plans. The corporate plan should be linked to the external environment, the culture and the strengths and weaknesses of the business. Contingency planning is a particular form of planning which tries to prepare for dramatic unwelcome change. Scenario planning may also be used to try and see what the future might hold and how the business should compete in different landscapes.

Key terms

Competences: these are activities and processes which use resources in a way that gains the organisation a competitive advantage because others cannot easily imitate them.

A **corporate plan** sets out where the business as a whole is aiming over the coming years and how it intends to get there.

Examiner's advice

You need to consider the plan of any business in relation to its strengths, the market opportunities and the alternatives available. Does the plan make sense and fit with the strengths of the business? Having a plan is, of course, not enough – the success of the business will also depend on factors such as the quality of the leadership, the resources invested into fulfilling the plan and the commitment of employees to making it work.

Progress questions

1. Explain what is meant by a corporate plan. *(2 marks)*
2. State **three** items likely to be in a corporate plan. *(3 marks)*
3. Explain **two** factors likely to influence a corporate plan. *(6 marks)*
4. Explain the links between a corporate plan and functional plans. *(5 marks)*
5. Explain **two** factors that might influence a corporate plan. *(6 marks)*
6. Explain the difference between a corporate plan and a mission statement *(2 marks)*
7. What is meant by scenario planning? *(2 marks)*
8. Explain **two** reasons why a corporate plan might go wrong. *(6 marks)*
9. What is meant by an emergent plan? *(3 marks)*
10. Explain why a plan needs to be reviewed. *(3 marks)*

Essay questions

1. Under the leadership of Justin King, J Sainsbury plc has successfully pursued a corporate plan called 'Making Sainsbury's Great Again' (MSGA). To what extent is corporate planning useful? Justify your answer with reference to Sainsbury's and/or other organisations that you know. *(40 marks)*

→

2 Many government organisations such as councils and government departments produce corporate plans. To what extent do you think the success of a corporate plan depends mainly on the external environment? Justify your answer with reference to government organisations and/or other organisations that you know. *(40 marks)*

3 Vodafone has a corporate plan that focuses a great deal on expansion in emerging markets. To what extent do you think having a corporate plan guarantees business success? Justify your answer with reference to Vodafone and/or other organisations that you know. *(40 marks)*

Candidate's answer:

A corporate plan sets out what a business wants to achieve and how to get there. It refers to the business as a whole as opposed to functional plans. The functional plans are derived from the corporate plan. The plan is usually long term and focuses on where the business is going. It can be looked at by any of the stakeholders to understand more of what the managers want to achieve and how they plan to achieve it.

Having a plan can be useful because it tells other managers what to do. Marks & Spencer is hoping to expand overseas, which means that its HR team need to think about the skills (for example, language skills) that may be needed, and operations and marketing will have to find suitable sites. On the other hand, if the business is reducing its operations (such as BAE recently) this may involve redundancies for HR and the sale of some sites for operations. A plan will also be useful to investors. If a company undertakes a share issue the potential investors will want to know what will happen to their funds and how they will be used. The plan, if published, can show that managers and directors know what they are doing and this can help raise funds and boost share price.

A plan also means employees know what the priorities of the business are, for example, whether Barclays bank is keen to push its retail side or investment arm, and this helps to allocate resources and make appropriate decisions. This can coordinate activities and help to ensure that the business as a whole works together and fulfils its overall mission as opposed to being a collection of separate parts. These factors all help the business to be more successful because the parts are not fighting against each other.

However, whether this guarantees success is another matter. For example, it depends on whether the plan is the right one. Sainsbury's focused on the UK rather than going overseas (unlike Tesco) which may have slowed its growth. Woolworths operated in many markets with no clear proposition, meaning customers were unsure where it was positioned in the market and switched elsewhere. Saab focused on a narrow product range and didn't offer enough models for customers, causing bankruptcy. It also depends on how the plan is implemented – if the finances are badly managed it may lead to too much debt or cash-flow problems. A good plan needs to relate to the strengths of the business, for example, customer service for Whitbread, consistency for McDonalds, design for Apple and exploit opportunities in the market. The external environment will change and therefore the plan of the business must change as well. A static plan will fail. Many years ago Lyons tea houses were a very well-known brand but it disappeared because the business did not adapt; other businesses also go out of fashion such as Tie Rack and Athena posters. This is because their plan did not adapt to a new world. However, many retailers such as Sainsbury's realise that as the business environment changes so must their plans and they do adapt their product mix, their prices and their overall approach to new situations.

So, no a corporate plan does NOT guarantee success because it depends on how good it is and how well it is implemented. A plan may seem good but be blown off course by competitors or the external environment. This is why businesses have to continually scan the environment.

Examiner's comments:

This is an excellent answer. It analyses the benefits of corporate planning while recognising its limitations. It directly answers the question arguing that a good corporate plan can help but it certainly does not guarantee success. It is well argued and makes good use of relevant examples. Excellent. Notice that the candidate has not used the context of Vodafone and emerging markets – although this stem provides plenty of opportunity for application and evaluation you can use your own examples instead.

27 Key influences on the change process: leadership

How a business reacts to change and whether it is able to successfully bring about change in its market will depend in part on its leaders. Strong leaders may take a business in a new direction, may revitalise it and may bring about major change.

In this chapter we examine:

- the meaning and significance of leadership
- the range of leadership styles
- the internal and external factors influencing leadership style
- the role of leadership in managing change
- the importance of leadership.

Leaders and managers

A leader is someone who has followers who want to follow their direction. At the top of an organisation is the chief executive or managing director. At head of other departments are numerous other managers. This means they have been appointed to run their parts of the business. However, this does not mean they are automatically leaders. Many business writers draw a distinction between managing and leading. According to the view of writers such as Kotter:

- a manager is someone who gets things done. Managers tend to focus on the present and the short term and are responsible for implementing the decisions of others. They manage but they also follow. Their role in many ways is to maintain things the way they are.
- leaders are people who are followed, who have a vision of the future and a clear sense of where they are taking the business. A leader decides what needs to be done and is prepared to shake things up to get them done. According to a significant writer in this area, John Adair, 'Leadership is the process of motivating others to act in particular ways.'

Leaders	Managers
Look to the future	Focus on the present
Are willing to break the mould and innovate	Maintain the status quo
Have vision	Are implementers

Table 27.1 Leaders and managers

According to Kotter (2001), 'leadership and management are two distinctive and complementary systems of action. Each has its own function and characteristic activities. Both are necessary for success in an increasingly complex and volatile business environment'. Whereas management is about coping with complexity (making sense of a complex environment), leadership is about coping with change (coping with moving from one complex environment to another). A leader may be important therefore in moving the business forward and helping it to cope with change by providing a vision for the future. It is possible then that someone is appointed as a manager but does not actually lead. Equally, it is possible and desirable that your chief executive is a leader who looks to where the business is heading and helps inspire others to get it there.

Similarly, Drucker (1985) argues that a leader has the ability to generate a commitment and is capable of the 'lifting of people's vision to a higher sight, the raising of their performance to a higher standard, the building of their personality beyond its normal limitations'.

A leader should understand where they want to take the business. They should be able to provide a clear direction for the business and motivate and inspire others. A leader is often brought in to make changes. The leader will know what needs to be done and is responsible for making it happen. Leaders may or may not always be liked but should be pushing (or pulling) the business forward.

What makes a great leader?

Given the importance of leadership in determining the direction (and therefore the success or failure) of a business it is not surprising that there have been many studies to try and identify what makes a leader. Some of these theories are examined below.

Trait theories

Early studies of leadership tried to identify qualities (or traits) that successful leaders possessed. They tried to identify exactly what it is that makes someone a leader (for example, self-confidence, extroversion).

According to this approach if we can identify a set of traits that all leaders have then we should be able to identify future leaders by looking at what they are like. However, despite numerous trait studies no common set of qualities has yet been identified. Some leaders seem to be loud, some seem quiet; some seem very confident, others less so. This difference in the qualities of leaders means that in practice trait theories have not been very useful. Even so according to Stodgill (1974) the most common traits that leaders seem to have include being:

- adaptable to situations
- ambitious and achievement oriented
- assertive
- decisive
- dependable
- dominant
- energetic
- persistent
- self-confident
- tolerant of stress
- willing to assume responsibility.

Unfortunately, this does not mean all leaders are like this!

Behavioural theories

These theories focus on how a leader behaves, trying to identify the right way of leading rather than what a leader is like as a person. Once again there have been many studies looking at styles of leadership. For example, researchers at Ohio State University used questionnaires to ask employees to describe the behaviour of their managers. They identified two dimensions: 'consideration' and 'initiating structure'.

- a **considerate style** focuses on the well-being of subordinates. Are they comfortable at work? Do they feel at ease? Do they feel well treated? This style listens to employees, encourages them and treats them with respect. This type of manager is approachable and rewards good performance. However, staff may feel looked after and cared for without necessarily completing the task effectively.
- an **initiating structure** focuses on defining and planning work. The leader concentrates on getting the work done. They allocate the tasks, inform subordinates of their task and monitor what is happening.

Another study by researchers at Michigan University called the relevant dimensions 'task orientation' and 'relationship orientation'. These different styles can be analysed using the Blake Mouton grid (1964 – see Figure 27.1). The vertical scale on this grid reflects a leader's concern for people. The horizontal scale reflects concern for the task.

If a leader focuses on getting the job done no matter what then they are 'task focused'. The danger here is that you lose the goodwill and support of your team; this can cause problems over time. If the leader is more concerned about keeping people happy this can lead to a pleasant environment in which to work but may mean the task is not completed effectively. This is called 'country club management'. The best style of leadership is to inspire your staff so that they want to get the job done.

Leadership styles can also be analysed in terms of the extent to which managers 'tell' or 'listen to' their employees.

- An **autocratic (or authoritarian) leader** is one who tells employees what to do. This may make sense in some circumstances, for example if:
  - a decision needs to be made quickly
  - employees lack the skills and training to decide
  - the leader wants to keep control.
- However, it can:
  - demotivate staff who do not feel involved
  - mean that the leader does not benefit from the ideas and skills of subordinates.
- A **democratic approach** involves more consultation with employees. The leader asks for the views of subordinates and discusses the options with

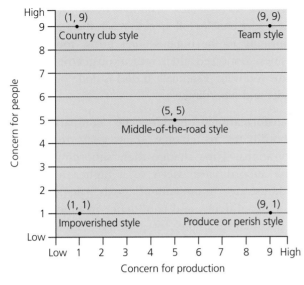

The Blake Mouton grid examines management styles in terms of their concern for production and their concern for people. You can plot a manager's style on the grid. Different styles of management include:

Country club leadership – this places a lot of focus on people and very little on the task itself. This type of leader is most concerned about the needs and feelings of members of the team. The work environment is likely to be relaxed and fun but the work may suffer due to lack of control and supervision.

Produce or perish leadership – this places a great deal of emphasis on the task and little on the people. It is likely to be very authoritarian. Employees are a means to an end; getting the job done is the key, regardless of the implications for the people.

Impoverished leadership – this has a low concern for the task and the people. The type of leader is ineffective. He or she does not focus on getting the job done or creating an environment where people want to work. The result is both work and people are neglected.

Middle-of-the-road leadership – this has some focus on the task and on people but not a great deal. It is a compromise between meeting people's needs and getting the job done but neither is fully met. The result is an average performance.

Team leadership – this approach has a high focus on the task and people. Employees are involved in the task and want to get it done. They are involved in the process and their needs are met by doing a good job.

Figure 27.1 The Blake Mouton grid

them. This can be a slower decision-making process but may lead to better quality results because:

- it utilises the talents of more people
- ideas are discussed so better solutions may be found and flaws may be uncovered
- employees feel more committed to the decision because they were part of it.

In fact there are a range of different styles of management, which are shown on the Tannenbaum Schmidt continuum in Figure 27.2. These vary in the extent to which the leaders are making the decisions

or whether subordinates have a significant input into the decision-making.

The contingency approach to leadership

The contingency approach recognises that the 'right' leadership style may depend on a variety of factors, such as:

- The nature of the leader – Do they like to keep control? Do they like to know what is happening at all times? Has an autocratic approach worked for them in the past? If the answer is yes to all of these then an autocratic style is likely to be adopted.

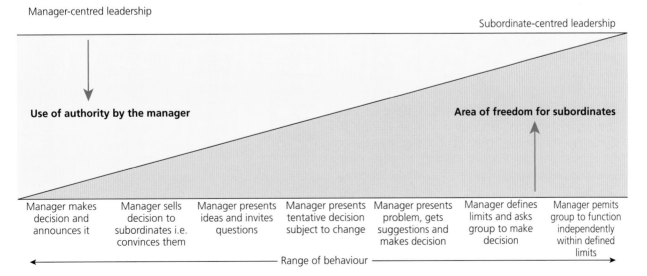

Figure 27.2 The Tannenbaum Schmidt continuum

- The nature of the subordinates – Do they have the skills and experience to make decisions for themselves? Do they expect and want to be involved?
- The nature of the task – Is the task simple (in which case employees may be able to decide for themselves)? Does a decision have to be made rapidly (in which case an authoritarian approach might be appropriate)? Would the decision benefit from debate and different perspectives?

This approach stresses that the style of leadership needs to be adapted at different times according to the situation. This either means leaders themselves must adapt or that different leaders are appropriate in different circumstances. It also highlights there is no 'right' approach to leading; unfortunately it is not as simple as learning a rule book – you have to be able to read the situation and adapt.

Transactional and transformational leaders

James Burn (1978) distinguished between transactional and transformational leadership. Transactional leaders influence subordinates' behaviour by way of a bargain. The leader enables followers to reach their goals if they contribute to the organisation's goals. You help the business to succeed and in return you get the salary and status you want. Essentially a deal is done between the leader and subordinate.

Transformational leaders, by comparison, get subordinates to change their goals, needs and aspirations. They change their subordinates. They raise subordinates' views to a higher level. They demonstrate 'transcendent goals, demonstration of self-confidence and confidence in others, setting a personal example for followers showing high expectations of followers' performance and the ability to communicate one's faith in one's goals' (Fiedler and House, 1994). In 1976 Steve Jobs founded Apple; in 1983 he hired John Sculley from Pepsi saying 'do you want to sell sugar for the rest of your life or do you want to come with me and change the world?' This sounds like a transformational leader!

BUSINESS IN FOCUS

Whitbread plc

Whitbread plc has transformed itself in just over ten years. The business was originally set up in 1742 as a brewer, and in 1750 established the first purpose-built mass-production brewery in Britain. Over the next 200 years, Whitbread & Co introduced many brands to the UK market, such as Stella Artois and Heineken alongside its own brands. However, the company decided that the alcohol market was not going to be a fast growing market, with rising concerns about people's health and increasing taxation on alcohol.

In 2001 Whitbread sold all its breweries and brewing interests to Interbrew, and in 2006 sold 239 of its 271 Beefeater sites to Mitchells & Butlers. Under the transformational leadership of Alan Parker the company reinvented itself by building the budget hotel business with Premier Inn and the coffee shop business with Costa. Parker said 'When Whitbread began changing, it created a vacuum in the company. Why would people want to work for Whitbread when they weren't sure what it stood for? We had to spend some time on creating that vision and purpose and building up the brand again and communicating that to people. You have to sell the vision, to get people to understand what you're trying to do and not debate every decision'.

The company now employs over 35,000 people and serves more than 10 million customers every month, with brands that include Premier Inn, Beefeater Grill, Brewers Fayre, Table Table, Taybarns and Costa Coffee.

Question:

What skills might Parker have needed to bring about successful change?

Howard Stringer

Sir Howard Stringer became chief executive at Sony in 2005 and retired in 2011. While in charge he radically changed the company by outsourcing operations, shifting production overseas, selling off parts of the business and developing new ones (such as the smartphone). He was hired to make difficult and painful decisions and it was felt that an outsider might be able to do this more easily than an insider. However, he has suffered from many unwelcome external factors (for instance, in 2010 the earthquakes in Japan damaged many Sony factories, and the company was also the victim of cyber attacks).

In 2005 Sir Howard inherited a company that was bloated and badly run and had missed the technology shift to flat-panel televisions. In his first few years Sir Howard removed a number of managers who opposed his changes and promoted talented individuals who owed their success to him.

(*Source: Adapted from* The Economist, *26 May 2011*)

Questions:

1 What does the experience of Howard Stringer show us about the extent to which a leader alone can make a business successful?

2 What does it show us about how a leader can bring about change?

Why do we follow leaders?

A leader is someone who is followed voluntarily rather than someone who makes others follow them or someone who simply tells people what to do. Why do we follow others? Because they have power over us. According to French and Raven (1959) there are a number of different sources of power that a leader might have. These are:

- **Legitimate power** is the authority that flows from their position in the organisation; for example, they are the chief executive and are recognised as 'the boss'.

- **Reward power** is power that comes from the leader's ability to give out benefits. For example, you may do as you are told because someone can decide whether you get a pay increase or a promotion.

- **Coercive power** occurs if someone has the power to force you to do something; perhaps they threaten you with redundancy? This is not a positive source of power – it may lead people to do as they are told but it does not mean they are willing followers.

- **Referent power** occurs when you follow someone because you respect them. You admire them and want to be like them. Philip Green, who owns Top Shop, Next, Burton, Wallis and Evans, is said to be a forceful and impressive character who is very impressive for those who come into contact with him.

- **Expertise power** occurs when you follow someone because you respect their intelligence, their knowledge of an issue and their expertise.

Of course, a leader may have several of these sources of power. Employees may follow a chief executive because they are the chief executive, because they have a superb grasp of the direction the business should move in, because they have a brilliant personality, because they decide on your bonus and because they have the power to sack you – that would be a very powerful leader!

Why do leaders matter?

Leaders provide the vision that takes a business forward. They take the difficult decisions and bring about the difficult change. They can inspire or push through change. Leadership may not always be in the hands of one person – the leaders may be a team – but the direction needs to come from somewhere. Particularly in a crisis people look to a leader for guidance and to show them what to do; this is why, when an organisation is in trouble, a new leader is often brought in. Of course, leaders cannot by themselves save a business – they need the support and help of others, and great leadership may not in itself be enough if the external environment is too harsh or the weaknesses of the business too great. However, the ability of great leaders in business, in sport, in politics and in all aspects of life to achieve great things is inspiring. Just think of someone like Nelson Mandela who helped bring about the end of the division between blacks and whites in South Africa and made this a peaceful process through leading by example.

Limitations of leadership

Leaders may have to work hard to change the culture of the organisation they work for. They may have been specifically brought in to change the way a business works and may face resistance from employees who fear they will be worse off. Employees may try to block or disrupt the change. A leader's ability to bring about change will therefore depend on how much support they can gain from those within the organisation. It will also depend on factors such as:

- the resources available to implement changes; in some cases the leader will be required to revitalise the business but it could be that resources are in short supply, which in itself may make change difficult
- the extent to which people understand the need for change
- the support from the board of directors.

Key issues

All organisations need a direction. This may be expressed on paper in the form of a mission statement, but someone (or a group of people) needs to lead the business forward. A key issue is where to find such people. Should they be recruited internally or externally? Can we train people to become leaders or are people born leaders? Should we always look for someone in our industry or would someone with a different set of experiences be better? How can we prepare someone for the role? And if we get them, what determines how they should lead and what determines whether they are actually successful?

Summary

A leader drives a business forward. This may be important to push the business through a period of change or indeed bring about change in the industry. A manager is more of an implementer; someone who gets things done but does not necessarily inspire or have vision. Businesses need leaders and managers and these individuals are an important element of success. Managers are the ones who plan, organise, coordinate and control and, as such, they determine how the business performs.

One step further: Mintzberg and management

In the 1970s Henry Mintzberg undertook a great deal of research into the nature of managerial work. From his studies he concluded that:

- senior managers are very busy and have heavy workloads! There is little free time and trying to get away from work is difficult.
- the work is fragmented; you are moving from one task to another. You need to focus on what really matters and what really makes a difference (80 per cent of results usually come from 20 per cent of the effort, so try and work out what that 20 per cent is). Interruptions are common and there is little time to sit back and think.
- managers focus on short-term immediate problems. They are often fire-fighting, dealing with the problem in front of them; this pushes them away from long-term planning and thinking.
- managers seldom get out and about; walking around is useful because it makes you visible and makes you more aware of the issues within the business.
- managers actually control little of what they do day to day – things happen *to* them!

It is all too easy to have a vision of calm logical planning by senior managers who are looking years ahead. In reality they are pushed and shoved by day-to-day emergencies.

Examiner's advice

The leader or leaders within an organisation are often the ones to determine strategy and lead the business forward. They may well have been brought in to turn the business around. They can be a strong internal force. In exam questions we are interested in the extent to which leaders can indeed bring about change.

What is interesting to consider is the role of leaders within the business. How much can they change? What determines their power? What makes successful change more or less likely? In reality there will not be one leader but many different ones throughout the organisation so it depends how they work together. Also there are many other factors to consider when examining business success such as the strategy itself, the strengths of the business and the external environment.

1   What is a leader? *(2 marks)*

2   Distinguish between a leader and a manager. *(4 marks)*

3   What is meant by transformational leadership? *(2 marks)*

4   Outline **three** sources of power for a leader. *(6 marks)*

5   What is meant by trait theory? *(2 marks)*

6   Explain **two** factors that might influence the leadership style adopted. *(6 marks)*

7   Explain what is shown by the Tannenbaum Schmidt continuum. *(4 marks)*

8   Distinguish between people-oriented and task-oriented leadership styles. *(4 marks)*

9   Outline the key features of the Blake Mouton grid. *(5 marks)*

10 Explain **two** ways in which a leader can affect the success of a business. *(6 marks)*

Essay questions

1   Some leaders (such as Steve Jobs when he was chief executive at Apple) are said to have been autocratic in their approach. To what extent do you think this is the best leadership style to adopt? Justify your answer with reference to Jobs and/or other leaders that you know. *(40 marks)*

2   When he was at Marriott plc, Alan Parker is said to have been a transformational leader. To what extent can the leader of a business guarantee its success? Justify your answer with reference to Alan Parker and/or other leaders that you know. *(40 marks)*

3   HP has tended to appoint its chief executives from outside the business to improve the performance of the business. Is it better to appoint leaders from outside when bringing about change? Justify your answer with reference to HP and/or other organisations that you know. *(40 marks)*

Candidate's answer:

External recruitment means that you recruit from outside the organisation. This is good because you get more ideas and a fresh approach. It also means you get more choice than recruiting internally and therefore should be able to appoint a better person with more skills. This means the job should be done better and more effectively which helps the organisation to succeed. However, there is more risk recruiting externally because you do not know the people as well and therefore may get it wrong which can be disastrous. If you recruit internally you know the person already and so have records on them and can talk to people to see how they do. Internal recruitment may motivate staff internally because they have something to aim for; this can increase productivity and lead to better performances. However, internal recruitment limits your options because you may not have the person you want and they may lack the skills that you need, especially if you are moving into new areas of business. Also if you promote someone upwards then you need to replace them and so you have to start recruiting again.

So external and internal recruitment both have their advantages and disadvantages and it is a matter of choosing the right approach in any given situation.

Examiner's comments:

This is a very limited response. It demonstrates knowledge of internal and external recruitment but never discusses this in the context of leadership or change. The response does not engage with the question set. There is no real evaluation except that they both have advantages and disadvantages. Overall this is a very basic response that does not address the question set.

28 Key influences on the change process: culture

Just as every person has their own personality, their own values and their own attitudes to things, so every business is different. There are, of course, obvious differences between, say, a car manufacturer and a software design business just in terms of the types of resource used, the working environment and the nature of the work. However, even if you visit two businesses in the same sector, such as two insurance firms, two clothes retailers or two banks, you will find enormous differences in the way they do things and the attitudes and beliefs of the employees. This is because the culture of businesses varies.

In this chapter we examine:

- the meaning and significance of organisational culture
- types of organisational culture
- the reasons for and problems of changing organisational culture
- the importance of organisational culture.

What is culture?

The culture of a business can be described as the values, attitudes and beliefs of the people working for it. It describes 'the way we do things around here' (Ouchi, 1981). Hofstede (1991) describes it as 'the collective programming of the mind', which perhaps highlights how individuals' own values may change as they become accustomed to the established ways of doing things when they join a business.

In reality, there is not just one culture in a business – different departments, different levels within the business, different groups of employees may all have their own way of doing things; nevertheless there may be some key areas where people generally agree and this can therefore help to define 'the overall culture' of a business. In some organisations the values and beliefs are very clear and reinforced by the reward systems and appraisal system – this is a strong culture. In weak cultures the values are not as clear.

How can cultures differ?

The culture of businesses can be tremendously different. For example, organisations may be:

- entrepreneurial (encouraging ideas and initiative)
- bureaucratic (involving many rules and procedures to define and control behaviour)
- customer focused (emphasising the importance of understanding customer needs)
- long term (managers are willing to invest in training and research and development for long-term rewards even if it is expensive in the short term).

Entrepreneurial

In entrepreneurial organisations you are highly valued if you try something, even if it does not necessarily work. The fact you had an idea and tried to make it work is regarded as worthwhile and commendable. This type of organisation may value people who 'think outside the box', try new approaches and show initiative. They are willing to take risks and accept that some projects will fail. This approach may be critical in markets that are fast changing or where there are high levels of product development. WL Gore is a highly entrepreneurial and innovative business. To help bring this about it says it has a 'team-based organisation that fosters personal initiative'. It has no organisational charts, no chains of command, nor predetermined channels of communication. 'We communicate directly with each other and are accountable to fellow members of our multi-disciplined teams.'

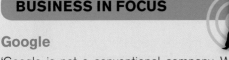
Bureaucratic

This type of business may want people who stick to the rules and who do not make decisions for themselves. In some organisations you may not want people to start making up their own rules. At the Inland Revenue you would want all the tax forms processed in the same way, for example. The risks of letting people use their initiative could be too high in some organisations or some parts of organisations; for example, you may want nursing staff to concentrate on administering the treatment doctors have prescribed and not diagnosing people themselves or making decisions on the medication for themselves.

Customer focused

Some organisations clearly value their customers (most would, we hope, but in reality not all do!). This means getting it right for the customer – staff are expected to put themselves out to make sure the customers' expectations are met. Employees are not expected to find reasons why things cannot be done. While a customer-focused approach seems sensible and certainly advisable in competitive markets, some businesses have been much more inward looking and have focused on what they could do and what they wanted to do rather than what customers wanted. British Airways had a terrible reputation in the 1970s because it placed too much emphasis on flying planes and not enough on the customer experience. Money was being invested in engines, landing gear and pilots' uniforms but not into improving the in-flight entertainment or the cleanliness of the planes. A big push to refocus on customer needs led to a change in approach (which culminated in the rebranding of the business as the 'world's favourite airline'), training all staff to place the customer first. More recently, McDonald's has been accused of being too inward looking and not appreciating the change in the market demand towards wanting healthier food. Similarly the major American car manufacturers, such as General Motors and Ford, spent too long producing big, oil guzzling cars and did not appreciate that customers wanted more fuel efficient, smaller vehicles that were being provided by producers such as Toyota.

Conservative

In these businesses there is a tendency to avoid risks. Relatively safe decisions are taken and before any new ideas are accepted there is extensive, possibly overly extensive, research. At the other extreme are high-risk organisations where decisions are made without enough thought about the resources and the dangers involved. In 2008 the global banking system underwent major shocks due in part to high-risk lending – bank managers had taken undue risks in their attempts to increase their lending and this had damaged them in the long run when borrowers could not repay.

Short run and long run

Some businesses are very focused on the short term (perhaps because of pressure from investors for dividends); they look for quick pay backs. Businesses focusing on the short term may not be willing to invest much in training and development or new product development or brand building. Businesses that look

	Risk Low	**Risk** High
Feedback and reward Rapid	Work-hard, play-hard culture	Tough-guy macho culture
Feedback and reward Slow	Process culture	Bet-the-company culture

Figure 28.1 Risk, feedback and reward

more towards the long term on the other hand, might plan 15 years ahead and be willing to sustain losses in a market in order to build brand awareness.

Types of culture

There are many ways of categorising the culture of an organisation. For example, Deal and Kennedy analysed businesses in terms of the speed of reward and feedback and the risk involved. They identified four types of culture that relate directly to the nature of the businesses they are in.

Tough-guy macho culture is an environment in which there is rapid feedback and rewards but also high risk, such as the operating theatres of hospitals, or the police.

Work-hard, play-hard culture is a rapid feedback/reward and low-risk environment such as estate agents. There are lots of deals to be done but any one deal is unlikely to break the bank.

Process culture is a slow feedback/reward and low-risk environment such as the civil service.

Bet-the-company culture is a slow feedback/reward and high risk, such as pharmaceuticals; you plan ahead for years and then launch the product and hope it succeeds.

Another famous model of business (or corporate) culture is that of Charles Handy (1993). Handy's model outlines four types of culture. These are:

BUSINESS IN FOCUS

A risk culture may be necessary for long-term success. To gain rewards you need to take risks. Thomas Edison performed 9,000 experiments before coming up with a successful version of the light bulb.

When Alan Mulally became chief executive of the Ford Motor Company in 2006 (when it was making huge losses) one of the first things he did was demand that his colleagues admit to their failures. He was amazed at the start that everyone seemed to think everything was going well despite losses of billions of dollars. When someone finally admitted they had made mistakes he clapped!

Companies are trying harder to encourage people to try things out even if they fail. India's Tata group awards an annual prize for the best failed idea and Intuit, a software business, and Eli Lilly, a pharmaceutical company, both have 'failure parties'. Proctor & Gamble encourages employees to talk about their failures as well as their successes during performance reviews.

Question:

Why do you think failure is important?

1. power culture
2. role culture
3. task culture
4. person culture.

Power culture

This type of culture is most common in relatively small, owner-run businesses. There is one dominant person (or a few key people) who makes all the major decisions and all employees refer to them if they want to know what to do. The 'boss' is in charge of all the operations of the business and its success depends very much on them. This can be very positive because it can lead to decisive leadership, quick decision-making and a consistent approach. However, if the business starts to grow the person or people at the centre may become overloaded and cannot cope with the number of decisions that need to be made. This can bring decision-making to a halt as employees wait to get a response. It also encourages employees to become reliant on the boss and not learn how to make decisions for themselves.

Role culture

This is very common in businesses as they begin to grow and adopt a more formal structure and culture. The importance of someone begins to be defined by their position in the hierarchy and their job title. This type of culture relies quite heavily on rules and procedures. To do well you need to follow the systems that are in place and do what is expected of you, rather than using your initiative to define your own job boundaries. Communication is via established channels of communication rather than through, say, informal conversation. This leads to very predictable outcomes in terms of performance. Senior managers know what is going to happen because employees do what they have been told to do. This has the value of certainty. However, the danger is that the organisation is inflexible to change and is not prepared for unexpected challenges.

Task culture

This is relatively common in businesses such as design agencies or management consultancies, where the value of an individual to a project depends on their expertise rather than any formal title. In this approach teams are formed for particular projects and individuals brought into these as and when they can contribute. Your value depends on what you can add to the team rather than your age or how long you have been working there. This approach can bring together expert teams to help solve different problems; however, coordinating this approach can be difficult.

Person culture

This is not a very common culture but occurs in an organisation or part of an organisation where there are groups of well-qualified individuals who respect each other's skills and knowledge. This may occur in a university or a doctors' practice, for example. Each individual is fairly self-reliant and can make decisions for themselves. They collaborate with each other and share their expertise and skills when needed but operate independently. This works well if the business can function with relatively independent units, but the danger is that the approach lacks consistency and may overlap (for example, university lecturers designing their own courses independent of each other and the student finding that elements of these courses overlap). Unfortunately, sometimes the individuals will resist if a more centralised approach is needed, because they are used to their independence.

BUSINESS IN FOCUS

Walmart

Walmart is currently trying to shift its corporate culture across the world from one based on rules to one based on values.

The aim is to ensure that employees will feel empowered and have the right values so they can make the right decision in any situation and whatever problem they face. To bring about this change the business has to look closely at its recruitment policies, its reward policies and its appraisal systems.

Question:

Why might it be better to have a culture based on values rather than rules?

The significance of national culture

In 1966 Geert Hofstede undertook what has become some of the most famous research on national cultural differences. Around 116,000 employees at all levels of the multinational, IBM, across 50 countries were involved. The result was a massive amount of data on employees within the same organisation but in different countries. This took Hofstede 15 years to analyse. He concluded that there were five major dimensions that can describe a national culture:

- **Power distance**. This is the extent to which there is a difference between who has the power within a business (for example, a difference between the boss and the subordinate). A low power distance means that power is distributed fairly equally and there are few obvious differences in a meeting between the manager and the junior – the junior can express their views, question and challenge; a high power distance means there are big differences in power – for example, there may be many levels of hierarchy in organisations and big status differences from top to bottom. In a high power distance culture there will be clear rules for example, on what order people walk into a room, who sits down first, who speaks when and who is allowed to question.
- **Uncertainty avoidance**. This is the extent to which employees need to know exactly what they are supposed to do and how success is measured. A high uncertainty avoidance means employees want clear guidelines on what to do; a low

uncertainty avoidance means employees are willing to be given general guidelines but do not need a high level of detail on what to do and when.

- **Individualism v collectivism**. This measures the extent to which employees feel they are supposed to be part of a team, part of the business 'family', or whether they want to work and look after themselves and their own performance. In an individualistic culture you are expected to look after yourself and try to be a star performer even if the team as a whole suffers; in a collectivist culture the team matters more than one member of it.
- **Masculinity v feminity**. This measures the extent to which employees feel they need to be dominant and assertive (which Hofstede referred to as 'masculine') or whether they feel that concern for others is more important ('feminine'). If the management style is to push for decisions and getting things done this is a masculine approach, according to Hofstede.
- **Long-term orientation**. This measures the extent to which individuals plan ahead. Is the long term five years or 20 years? This may affect whether a business is willing to enter a market and how it judges success along the way.

There can be significant differences between societies in terms of how they score on these scales, and managers need to be aware of these differences when having meetings, making decisions and working with overseas partners. The differences that exist can be because of their history, society, traditions and politics. Look Hofstede's findings on the UK and China in Figure 28.2, for example.

The UK is strong on individualism – people recognise and reward individual performance rather than team players; the UK is low on long-term orientation, tending to be short-term planners. China, by comparison, tends to plan for the long term but place less emphasis on the individual. In China the idea of a hierarchy is accepted much more than in the UK. You can imagine how these differences could cause problems in business. Chinese managers might be interested in projects that generate a return in the long term; UK managers might not. In the UK junior managers might be asked for their opinion in meetings even if it contradicts the senior managers; in China they might not.

BUSINESS IN FOCUS

Olympus

In 2011 after just a few months in post, Michael Woodford resigned as chief executive of the Japanese company Olympus because his leadership style clashed with the prevailing culture of the business. Tsuyoshi Kikukawa, the former chief-executive and current chairman complained that Mr Woodford 'made decisions entirely on his own judgment'. Worse, he 'ignored our organisational structure', by giving orders directly to staff rather than via the division heads.

Question:

Do you think Woodford's approach sounds desirable? Why do you think it caused problems?

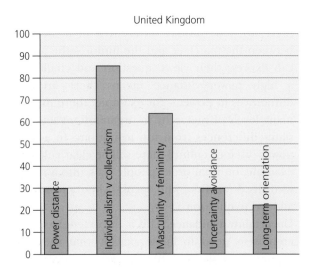

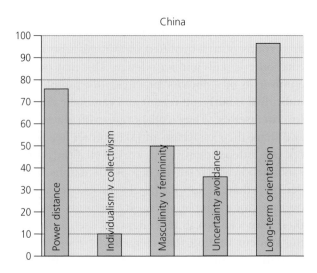

Figure 28.2 National cultures: the UK and China

Of course, these findings do not represent every individual and every business in a given country (in fact, with increasing globalisation and greater diversity among staff it becomes difficult to talk of a 'British' or 'Chinese' company), and these features will change over time. Nevertheless, they highlight that there can be significant differences in cultures between regions and this needs to be remembered when doing business with foreign partners. An understanding of Hofstede's cultural dimensions can help managers to understand the way business is done in different countries and try to avoid potential conflict in their business dealings with others.

BUSINESS IN FOCUS

W L GORE

Whenever business experts make lists of the best American companies to work for, or whenever consultants give speeches on the best-managed American companies, W L Gore is high on the list. It has a rate of employee turnover that is about a third of the industry average. It has been profitable for 35 consecutive years and has growth rates and an innovative, high-profit product line that is the envy of the industry. Gore has managed to create a small-company ethos so infectious and sticky that it has survived their growth into a billion-dollar company with thousands of employees. And how did they do that? By (among other things) adhering to the Rule of 150.

Bill Gore, the founder of Gore Associates, a privately held, multimillion-dollar firm, understood from the start that smaller is often better and designed his organisation according to the Rule of 150 – each facility is limited to 150 associates. The size limitation enables this organisation to grow; yet it continues to behave like a small entrepreneurial start-up. This has not only proven to be a profitable strategy, but also it has created a culture of highly committed employees. Gladwell (2002, p. 182) comments:

'This organisational strategy is not unique to Gore and Associates. Semco, a Sao Paulo, Brazil-based manufacturer of industrial machinery, has a similar size strategy and, like Gore and Associates, Semco has experienced remarkable success (Semler, 1993). Semco has, in fact, grown 24 per cent annually for the past ten years – without an organisational chart or headquarters facility. Ricardo Semler, chairman of the board, reflecting on the decision to forego a traditional corporate structure, comments that traditional organisational hierarchies are "a source of control, discrimination, and power mongering" (Colvin, 2001, p. 60). The fact that Semco operates in a South American culture with patriarchal national values that are quite different from this company's participative organisational values, makes this a particularly noteworthy example of the paradoxical nature of successful organisations.'

Question:

Discuss the ways in which the decisions made regarding the structures of their business might affect or reflect the cultures of WL Gore and Semco.

Key issues

The culture of a business, or the cultures within it, are not easy things to define or understand. They are also difficult to change. However, this does not make them less important. The culture influences the way everything is done and should not be underestimated as a force that determines the success or failure of a business. Making a failing school successful for example, involves changing the culture so that staff, pupils and parents want it to win. It is not just a question of new rules or new funding. This can be difficult and take time.

How can we tell the culture of a business?

The answer is, you cannot! Not unless you actually spend time working there and realise what matters by working with other employees. And even then you may only be understanding the culture of a particular part of the business. The way the UK division works could be very different from the French division; the way the marketing department works could be very different from the operations department. So, you need to be careful when discussing the culture when you have only experienced a part of it. You must be careful not to base your decisions on a one-off visit. Imagine trying to explain the 'rules' of your family: what is and is not allowed, what your parents value, what you would be praised for and what you would be criticised for, the 'family view' of sport, religion, charity, the death penalty, government intervention and education. Understanding the culture of a family would take a long time; understanding the culture of a business is just as difficult.

Whether or not you actually work in a business there are a few indicators that can help you understand its culture.

According to Johnson and Scholes's cultural web you will get some idea by looking at six interrelated elements:

1 **Stories:** What stories do employees tell about the business? What do these reveal about the attitudes of people within the business? Who are the heroes of the business and who are the villains? This will tell you something about who the managers value and what behaviour is rewarded.

2 **The rituals:** All organisations have rituals. Think about your school. Does it have assembly every day? Does it have a sports day? Does it celebrate certain occasions? Is there a school song or uniform? These are all rituals and all businesses have them, each one revealing something about what is valued. At Honda the day may start with group meetings (highlighting the importance of the team compared with the individual); these meetings involve all employees, all of whom wear overalls (highlighting that everyone has a contribution to make and there is no 'us' and 'them'), and there may even be a company song (highlighting the loyalty to the company which is returned by company loyalty to the individual).

3 **The symbols:** What is on the wall of your school? Is it student artwork highlighting the importance of students and art to the life of the institution? Is there a list of sporting achievements or prefects or scholars? Who has the biggest office? What does the school look like? What investment has occurred in recent years? What do these developments tell you about priorities? The symbols of an organisation such as the brand can reveal a lot about its beliefs.

4 **Organisational structure:** How are things organised within the business? Who reports to whom? Is it traditional hierarchy with small spans of control, suggesting long lines of authority and tight control over individuals? Or is it a flatter organisation in which spans are wider?

5 **Control systems:** How is control kept within the business? What is measured and monitored? This

tells you what is regarded as important. Is the emphasis on reward for positive performance or punishment for poor performance?

6 **Power structures:** Who has the power to make decisions? Who really decides what happens? How much authority do individuals have?

Having analysed these six features of culture you should be able to summarise the key elements of an organisation's culture, which can be called its 'cultural paradigm'.

What determines the culture?

The culture of an organisation is originally derived from the attitudes and values of its founders. They often have a very strong influence on the business's

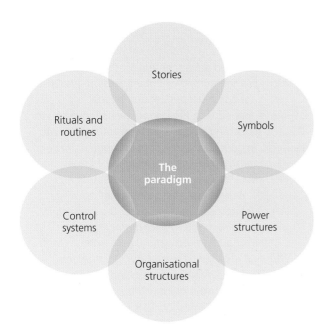

Figure 28.3 The cultural web

values for many years, not least because of the people they employ, and then the people these people employ, and so on. The culture comes from the views of those who are already there and this then influences who is selected to join the business. Once you have joined an organisation you are likely to adjust even more to become one of the 'insiders'. You will see what those at the top are doing and are likely to want to emulate them – leadership is therefore a key element of forming a culture. Those who do not 'fit in' may be ignored, punished or may be removed. Those who do fit in are likely to be rewarded, to get promotion and to receive praise. In this sense culture can be self-fulfilling.

But newcomers into the business will also be able to bring about change, as their own ideas will affect the thinking that goes on within the business. As society's values change, for example, this will influence what employees want and expect, and influence the values within the business. We can see this with the increasing concern for environmental issues in recent years.

Employees will also be affected by investors who will demand certain forms of behaviour and by what is happening elsewhere and their own experiences. Seeing that a more cooperative approach with suppliers is benefiting competitors may change their own attitudes, and they may look for more ways of working with suppliers rather than always trying to beat them down on price. Realising that their customers

really do value greater ethical behaviour may make them reconsider their own attitudes on these issues.

The culture will also be shaped by the reward systems within the organisation. People tend to do more of the things they are praised for and rewarded for and less of the things they are criticised for. If a business seems to value someone who wins deals even if this is at the expense of other members of their team, then that person will tend to want to go it alone and be highly competitive; sharing information and contacts with others in their team will not be on the agenda. If promotions go to those who 'don't rock the boat' people will tend to keep their heads down and follow orders rather than question.

Culture will also be shaped by experience – if what you believe in and how you behave seems to get you what you want then why change? If, however, it does not work and the performance of the business is poor then the need for change becomes more compelling.

Culture and mission statements

The mission statement of a business (if it has one) sets out what the main purpose of a business is (that is, why it exists). This will obviously be influenced by the culture of the business. An organisation that sets out to reward the owners clearly values investors more than other stakeholder groups. A business that values the environment is likely to include this in its mission statement.

BUSINESS IN FOCUS

Premier Farnell plc

Premier Farnell plc is a leading UK business selling components to electronic engineers. Its values are to be 'driven to deliver results by being:

- totally reliable (we deliver our promises)
- resourceful (we look for innovative ways to provide solutions)
- customer focused (we understand our customers and suppliers, anticipating their needs)
- with integrity (we are honest and trustworthy).'

(Source: Premier Farnell, www.premierfarnell.com)

Question:

How might these values affect the behaviour of employees in the business?

Johnson & Johnson: our credo

The mission statement of Johnson & Johnson highlights the importance of the customer to the business.

Our credo

We believe our first responsibility is to the doctors, nurses and patients, to mothers and fathers and all others who use our products and services.
In meeting their needs everything we do must be of high quality.
We must constantly strive to reduce our costs in order to maintain reasonable prices.
Customers' orders must be serviced promptly and accurately.
Our suppliers and distributors must have an opportunity to make a fair profit.
We are responsible to our employees, the men and women who work with us throughout the world.
Everyone must be considered as an individual.
We must respect their dignity and recognise their merit.
They must have a sense of security in their jobs.
Compensation must be fair and adequate, and working conditions clean, orderly and safe.
We must be mindful of ways to help our employees fulfil their family responsibilities.
Employees must feel free to make suggestions and complaints.
There must be equal opportunity for employment, development and advancement for those qualified.
We must provide competent management, and their actions must be just and ethical.
We are responsible to the communities in which we live and work, and to the world community as well.
We must be good citizens – support good works and charities and bear our fair share of taxes.
We must encourage civic improvements and better health and education.
We must maintain in good order the property we are privileged to use, protecting the environment and natural resources.
Our final responsibility is to our stockholders.
Business must make a sound profit.
We must experiment with new ideas.
Research must be carried on, innovative programmes developed and mistakes paid for.
New equipment must be purchased, new facilities provided and new products launched.
Reserves must be created to provide for adverse times.
When we operate according to these principles, the stockholders should realise a fair return.

(Source: Johnson & Johnson, www.jnj.com)

Question:

Discuss the impact 'Our credo' might have on the performance of Johnson & Johnson.

Why does culture matter?

The culture of a business or a part of a business matters because it determines how employees will behave in any given situation. This can work in an organisation's favour. Companies such as Google have a culture that recognises and rewards creative talent and technological skills. Bright computer programmers will go far in this organisation regardless of their age and, to some extent, regardless of their formal qualifications; if they can do it and prove they can do it they will probably be promoted. This encourages ideas and new thinking which helps keep Google ahead of its rivals. A culture of accuracy and attention to detail, by comparison, may ensure your firm of accountants does not make any mistakes.

On the other hand, a culture can limit a firm's success. In some retail organisations the customer seems to be almost an unwelcome visitor! Customers are not truly valued and employees do not make the effort to provide good customer service. This will lose business over time.

In other organisations, the unwillingness to take risks may mean market opportunities are missed. In Marks & Spencer in the 1990s the culture became one of unquestioning agreement with the chief executive's decisions; this meant that when the wrong products were ordered and the wrong approach to displays was chosen no one dared to question. The culture did not encourage a questioning approach which meant that even though staff may have seen the iceberg ahead they did not shout out the dangers because they simply followed the course the captain set for them. Equally, a culture of risk-taking can be dangerous – just think of the excessive high-risk lending of many banks in the last ten years that almost led to financial meltdown in 2008.

The importance of culture in terms of business success (or failure) should not be underestimated. Is the business full of ideas, encouraging initiative, stressing the value of working hard and working effectively? Are new projects met with open arms? Do individuals take care to get it right and show commitment to a project? All these issues depend on the culture of a business. It determines what people do, how they work together, how much effort they make, what they strive for, and basically determines how the business 'ticks'. Whatever plans you bring in, whatever ideas you have, the culture of the business will influence whether they are implemented, how they are implement and the level of commitment to them by employees.

Often the underlying problem in a business is its culture; the attitudes and behaviours of staff are not appropriate. In this situation new leaders are often brought in to bring about cultural change.

BUSINESS IN FOCUS

Daimler Chrysler

The Daimler Chrysler merger in 1998 turned out to be a disaster because the companies operated in such different ways. A simple example illustrates the problems: in one meeting the German Daimler executive could not understand why a particular issue was being discussed when he felt that it had already been decided. He produced his minutes from the meeting which he had circulated. His American counterpart said he had received these but had assumed they were just some notes from the meeting and did not constitute a decision having been made. The Germans found the American style too informal; the Americans found the Germans too inflexible. One observer said, 'Germans analyse a problem in great detail, find a solution, discuss it with their partners and then make a decision. It is a very structured process … Americans start with a discussion, and then come back to it with new aspects after talking with other people. Eventually – after a process which they call creative – they come to a conclusion'. In America it is common to pop into your boss's office and get an instant decision without having to explain it to everyone else. In Germany there tends to be more data analysis then formal recommendations and the involvement of all those affected.

These business differences mirror deeper differences in the societal values of the US and Germany. According to Hofstede's study of global cultural differences, Germans are less individualistic than people in the US. They also tend to feel more uncomfortable with uncertainty and ambiguity, and they have a longer-term time orientation. Germans are also found to be significantly more indirect in their communication styles and more respectful of title, age and background connections. These societal values are reflected in businesses from these countries. This is particularly apparent in preferred leadership styles. German managers frequently prefer a more autocratic style than their US counterparts and their employees expect to be treated accordingly. Research on obedience to authority indicates that a higher percentage of Germans are obedient to their managers than are US employees. For example, employees in a US organisation often feel comfortable challenging their managers, perhaps even giving them advice. German employees, on the other hand, expect their managers to give them specific instructions and they typically follow them unquestioningly.

There are differences in employment practices as well. For example, many Europeans view US hiring and firing practices as unnaturally brutal. In European companies, employees are protected by much stronger labour laws and union rules. Organisations in France and Germany are more concerned with protecting and nurturing the workforce than are US organisations. For example, in France and Germany, the average manager and worker get at least six weeks of paid vacation each year (most US employees get two weeks). French and German employees also enjoy a much wider range of benefits, such as paid maternity leave and layoff payments where the value increases as the number of years a person has worked for an organisation increases. Indeed, both France and Germany regard the US system of hiring and firing as harsh and exploitative.

The US-based Chrysler Corporation and German-based Daimler-Benz mirrored these cultural differences. Chrysler had a reputation for having a more freewheeling, open culture, in contrast with the more traditional, top-down management style practised at Daimler. Daimler-Benz was synonymous with words like conservative, efficient and safe. Chrysler, on the other hand, was known as daring, diverse and creative. In fact, these cultural differences in many ways were the foundation for the mutual attraction between the two companies. However, like many marriages of opposites, the differences led to disaster. →

No one seemed to know how to discover common ground.

(*Source: Dorothée Ostle, 'The culture clash at DaimlerChrysler was worse than expected' in* Automotive News Europe, *22 November 1999, Vol. 4, Issue 24*)

Questions:

1 Explain the possible benefits of centralised decision-making at Daimler.
2 Analyse the cultural differences at Chrysler and Daimler.
3 Discuss the factors that might have led to the merger of Chrysler and Daimler.
4 To what extent was the merger of Chrysler and Daimler bound to fail?

BUSINESS IN FOCUS

Enron

Enron was one of the biggest corporate collapses ever. Once regarded as an amazing success story, it turned out that figures had been manipulated and there had been false reporting of profits (profits were being reported that did not exist). This happened on an extraordinary scale. This seemed to happen because there were no proper mechanisms in place to question employees' behaviour or check what they were doing. They were able to make up numbers without anyone asking where they came from. The culture of the business encouraged this behaviour. Each year in the company, poor performers were sacked and good performers were rewarded massively – the pressure was to deliver good figures, whatever it took. The company recruited very able MBA graduates straight from university; these employees lacked experience and did not really know what was and what was not allowable behaviour. With unbelievable bonuses on offer all the incentives encouraged them to do what everyone else seemed to be doing and make up some profits. The example from the top seemed to further encourage this approach. The culture of Enron led to its collapse and the loss of thousands of jobs and millions of dollars for investors.

Figure 28.4 Enron

A special report commissioned to investigate the cause of the collapse found that the cause was 'A combination of self-enrichment by employees, inadequate control from the board and outside auditors, and an aggressive and overreaching corporate culture'.

Question:

How do you think Enron's culture contributed to its decline? Why was the culture so bad?

How can you change culture?

With difficulty. To change the culture of an organisation you need to change what people value and what they believe is important. This can happen but often takes time. Imagine you were someone who does not like sport, who sees no point in taking part in it if you do not like it and who likes the freedom your sixth form gives you to choose whether to participate. If the school headmaster suddenly decides that your views on the importance of sports at school are wrong and that from now on it will be compulsory you would probably argue about this. It is possible that over time you could be convinced that compulsory sport at school would help your academic performance or help you feel better in yourself, but simply being told that this is true would not necessarily work. You would want to see some evidence or try it out for a while to see for yourself, or be talked through the arguments for and against until you were convinced and agreed with the arguments being made. Unfortunately, businesses do not always have time to go through this process with every member of staff. Sometimes culture needs to be changed faster than a process of education and discussion allows; sometimes leaders may think it is better to push on and let people see the benefits rather than spend the time trying to convince them in advance.

To achieve cultural change quickly managers may:

- offer incentives for those who agree to the changes and start adopting them (for example, higher marks for those who participate in sport); this is the 'carrot' approach
- punish those who do not adopt the changes (for example, lower marks for those who do not participate in sport); this is the 'stick' approach.

Neither the carrot nor the stick approach will in itself change people's attitudes. They are simply changing behaviour. They do not change what you believe, simply what you do. This means people may not be very committed to the changes. However, in the long run if the changes are proved to be beneficial people may change their attitudes as well.

Other approaches to managing cultural change and overcoming resistance include:

- educating people about the benefits of the change; people are likely to be more open to change if they understand the reason for it. Culture change may be easier if the business is in trouble because employees understand things have to be done differently.
- reassuring people about the change, to reduce fears
- providing resources to enable people to prepare and train for change
- focusing on key people to get their support; once they are won over others will follow.

Summary

The culture of a business reflects 'the way things are done around here'. The culture within a business will influence the priorities set by individuals, the way they treat stakeholders, the way they plan and behave. The culture in some organisations clearly encourages and promotes innovation, it expects people to 'go the extra mile' and it puts customer service at the top of its agenda. In other organisations employees seem more interested in their own aims, and the culture permits complacency and waste. Changing culture can be a major managerial task to help improve performance. This can be a difficult task because it may involve trying to get employees to change long-standing attitudes and approaches.

One step further: Schein

Schein (2004) identified three levels of culture, as follows:

1 **The artefacts**. These represent the visible level of culture – for example, what the buildings look like, what is displayed on the walls, what people wear, what stories are told within the business. Within minutes of walking into any business we immediately get a sense of what it is like from the artefacts we see around us, although we may not always understand the significance of them (do you have a school crest or motto? What does this say about your school? What about an awards board – what is being rewarded?). Within a business are the offices open plan? (This might suggest an environment where everyone is able to contribute.) Are there separate dining facilities for managers and other employees? What does this say about the business? What sort of furniture and fixtures and fittings are there? Is it very modern or traditional?

2 **The stated beliefs and values**. This refers to the beliefs of employees about the work they are doing and the issues they face, for example:

- how much quality matters; is it regarded as important to get it right first time or is it seen as acceptable to fix it later if anyone complains?
- is teamwork more important than individual performance? Is someone who works well on their own but does not mix well with others and sometimes focuses on their own work at the expense of the team a good employee or not?
- how much freedom are people given to try out their ideas? In some organisations it is seen as important to let employees try things out for themselves; in other businesses this may be seen as risky or possibly unnecessary if the belief is that managers should make the decisions.

Sometimes these values and beliefs will be written down in a mission statement that sets out key values of the organisation.

3 **Underlying assumptions**. This refers to the assumptions that are deeply held by employees; these will determine the stated beliefs. For example:

- satisfied customers are essential for survival (that's why the customer comes first)

- people work better in teams (that's why we like teamwork)
- we employ capable people (that's why we can give them room to try things out)
- assumptions about what matters, what needs to be done, how to behave, what is expected of staff, what is a 'normal' effort level or what is meant by 'good' performance can vary significantly from one organisation to another.

Examiner's advice

You can probably see by now how interlinked many Unit 4 topics are. The culture of a business will be shaped by its leader and at the same time the culture will influence the appropriate leadership style. The culture will be influenced by the external environment such as social attitudes and at the same time it will affect the ability of a business to react to change in the environment.

Progress questions

1 What is meant by 'organisational culture'? *(2 marks)*

2 How can the culture of a business help its success? *(5 marks)*

3 Explain **two** influences on the culture of a business. *(6 marks)*

4 Why might it be wrong to try and describe 'the' culture of a business? *(4 marks)*

5 Outline **four** different types of culture according to Handy. *(8 marks)*

6 Explain **one** reason why the culture of an organisation matters. *(3 marks)*

7 Hofstede identified five dimensions on which national cultures can differ. Outline these dimensions. *(5 marks)*

8 Why might changing the culture of an organisation be difficult? *(5 marks)*

9 Why is it difficult to identify an organisation's culture from the outside? *(3 marks)*

10 Undertake a cultural web analysis of your school or college. *(12 marks)*

Essay questions

1 The culture of an organisation such as Virgin seems very closely related to its founder's values. To what extent is the culture of a business determined by its founders? Justify your answer with reference to Virgin and/or other organisations you know. *(40 marks)*

2 Some organisations such as Intel, the microprocessor manufacturer, seem to have an innovative culture. To what extent is an innovative culture the right one for a business? Justify your answer with reference to Intel and/or other organisations you know. *(40 marks)*

3 Some people say the culture of a business such as W L Gore is the main reason for its success. To what extent is the success of a business due to its culture? Justify your answer with reference to WL Gore and/or other organisations you know. *(40 marks)*

Candidate's answer:

The culture of a business refers to the way that we do things around here. It refers to the values, attitudes and beliefs of the employees in an organisation. There are many different types of culture.

A power culture is one where everyone looks to the leaders to make decisions. Ideas are referred to the centre all the time; this is where the power is held. This is good because decisions are made fast but can be bad because the leaders can become overloaded.

A role culture is where everyone has a role in the organisation and they know how they fit in. They have a clear position in the hierarchy. This can be good because it means everyone knows who to talk to or who controls who, but it may mean people stay in their own section and do not mix enough with others.

A task culture is one where your importance depends on what you can bring to the organisation regardless of age, experience or job title.

A culture will influence what people do, how they behave and how they react to things. This could help them to make the right decisions or it may mean they are slow to respond to change or they do not listen enough to comments about where they are going wrong. Some businesses have made some wrong decisions in the past, and this is sometimes because their culture was too inward looking and therefore they missed the information that would have told them how to change. A culture may also be too risk taking,

encouraging people to take risks and possibly endangering the business. People may invest too much in a project that does not pay off and does not deliver the payback, the average rate of return or the net present value expected. This can cause problems for the business in terms of the profitability of the business and the likely dividends to investors. This means the success of the business does depend on the culture.

A culture that is open to change and that encourages change means the business will be able to adapt to its environment and change strategy to match its strengths to market opportunities. It will be looking for new options and finding ways to improve and increase its competitiveness. This will help the business succeed.

Examiner's comments:

This essay has some strengths – the candidate understands the meaning of culture and can highlight some of the reasons why the success of a business is linked to its culture. However, the answer has no application to W L Gore or any other business; the candidate is not supporting their ideas with relevant examples. Also, the argument is one sided – the candidate is arguing that culture does matter for success but is not providing the counter argument – for example, is success actually due mainly to other factors? Is it possible the culture has very little effect on success? The candidate also needs to focus more on analysis – the section on types of culture is descriptive and not needed unless it is used to answer the question by showing how it links to success.

29 Making strategic decisions

Over time businesses are likely to face major decisions about what they offer and how and where they compete. These are strategic decisions. As technology changes, competitors enter the market, or when there are other external and internal changes managers may need to consider what the business is and what they want it to be in the future. This requires strategic change.

In this chapter we examine:

- types of decisions
- the significance of information management
- different approaches to decision-making
- influences of decision-making.

Decisions

Management involves making many decisions. What to do, how to do it, who to do it with and when to do it all have to be decided. A decision involves a specific commitment to action (Boddy 2002). Making a decision will involve:

- knowing what you are trying to achieve
- considering the next-best alternative (the opportunity cost)
- committing resources to a course of action
- uncertainty about what will actually happen.

Types of decision

There are different types of decision that have to be made. Simon (1960) analysed types of decision in terms of programmed and non-programmed decisions.

Programmed decisions (Simon 1960) deal with problems that are familiar and where the information required to make them is easy to define and obtain. The situation is well structured and there are often established procedures, rules and policies. For example, reordering components is often a programmed decision. Employees know what has to be ordered, who to order from and how to order it. They simply decide issues such as when to order and how much to order. These are short-term decisions likely to be made by junior managers.

By comparison, non-programmed decisions deal with situations that are unstructured and require a unique solution. These are unusual decisions that may be risky, such as a major investment. These decisions are more likely to be made by senior managers.

Decisions may also be categorised in terms of whether they are tactical or strategic. The strategy of a business is the long-term plan to achieve the business's objectives. For example, if a firm's target was to increase profits it might try and do this by reducing costs or by increasing revenue; these would be two strategies to achieve the same goal. Similarly, if a business was trying to boost overall sales the managers might take a strategic decision to do this by trying to sell more of its existing products or by investing into new products; again these would be two different ways of achieving the same end goal.

Strategic decisions tend to be long term, involve a major commitment of resources and be difficult to reverse. For example, the decision to invest in new product development is likely to involve a high level of finance and take several years. Strategic decisions also tend to involve a high level of uncertainty. Over time market conditions often change significantly and so firms must change their strategies to cope with unfamiliar conditions. Given that strategic decisions often involve new problems and challenges they tend to be non-programmed decisions.

The value of producing a clear strategy is that it sets out the firm's overall plan; this helps employees develop their own plans to implement the strategy. If you know the firm wants to diversify, for example, you know that it is realistic to consider market opportunities in new segments of the market. If you know the strategy is to boost the firm's market presence in a particular region, you will know it is worth putting more resources into this area.

The decisions made about how to implement the strategy are called 'tactical decisions'.

Compared with strategic decisions, tactical decisions tend to:

- be short term
- involve fewer resources
- be made more regularly and involve less uncertainty.

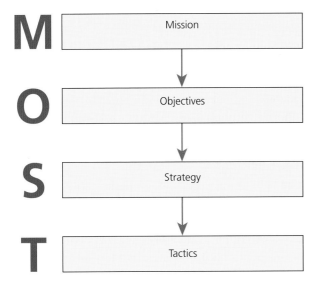

Figure 29.1 The relationship between strategy and tactics

Scientific decision-making

There are many different ways of making a decision: in some cases managers will research the decision thoroughly – they will gather data and analyse it before deciding what to do; in other cases they may rely on their own experience from the past or on their gut feeling. It depends on what the decision is, the risk involved, their own personality and what information is available. If, for example, the decision concerns the purchase of new production equipment and involves hundreds and thousands of pounds, a manager will probably research the decision very carefully; with an unfamiliar decision involving high levels of resources, managers would not want to risk getting it wrong. However, because it is an unfamiliar decision getting information may not be as easy compared to making more tactical decisions and so managers may have to fall back on experience and intuition. On the other hand, if the decision simply involves ordering some more supplies of pens for the office, an employee might be more inclined to use their experience. The same is probably true of your own decision-taking – if you are spending a few hundred pounds on a new PC you will probably research the decision much more than if you feel thirsty and want to buy a soft drink, when you will rely on experience.

When you gather data and analyse it before making a decision, this is known as a scientific approach to decision-making. It is scientific because it is rational and logical and is based on data. Many of the mathematical topics you have studied are to help managers analyse the data as part of scientific decision-making. Break-even analysis, ratio analysis, investment appraisal and correlation analysis, for example, are all ways in which managers analyse the data to try and make the right decision.

Scientific decision-making should reduce the risk of error because decisions are based on information. On the other hand, the usefulness of this method will inevitably depend on the quality of the data. The better the information the more likely it is the right decision will be made; this is why market research is important and why managers need to ensure they have effective ways of gathering, analysing and circulating information within the organisation to ensure each manager has the information they need at the right time.

The scientific decision-making process involves:

- recognising that there is a problem or opportunity (recognising that a decision has to be made)
- setting objectives for what you want to achieve
- setting decision criteria and deciding how important each one is
- developing and identifying alternatives
- comparing the alternatives
- choosing and implementing a course of action
- reviewing the effectiveness of the decision.

Decision-making is a dynamic process with continual review and assessment of what has been done and what needs to be done.

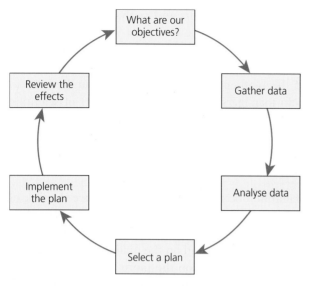

Figure 29.2 Decision-making is a dynamic process

A scientific approach to decision-making

A scientific approach to decision-making is rational and logical. Decisions are made based on information, not hunch (or intuition). This approach is likely if there is high risk which managers are seeking to reduce.

If a scientific approach is adopted then managers try to understand the environment in which they operate. They consider the macro-environment and the micro-environment to identify opportunities and threats.

The macro-environment

This comprises factors that are not easily influenced by any one business. These are often analysed using the PESTEL framework (political, economic, social, technological, environmental and legal factors). Managers need to try to identify which factors in the macro-environment are most significant for the future. These will vary from business to business. In the cigarette industry the threat of even more legal restrictions on smoking must be a concern, as well as legal action by those whose health has been damaged by smoking. In the computer industry technological advancement is a concern if a business fails to keep up with the changes. In the healthcare market demographic changes may be a key factor. Managers must identify which factors are most significant for their business. Of course they may operate in many product markets and many regions across the world and so there are different macro-factors for different parts of the business.

The micro- or competitive environment

This relates to factors within a business's environment which firms are more likely to be able to influence than those in the macro-environment. These include:

- competitors' actions
- suppliers
- buyers (customers).

The importance of market and competitor intelligence is clear in terms of strategic planning. You have to understand the markets and the business environment you are competing in. This data may be gathered through many sources such as secondary research, your own databases or your own sales force.

SWOT analysis

Once the external environment (macro and competitive) has been analysed, managers should, in theory, be able to identify relevant opportunities and threats. An opportunity is a course of action that may provide benefits for a business. What is an opportunity for one business may not be an opportunity for another. GlaxoSmithKline may see an opportunity in a cure for the common cold; the managers of Cadbury may not see the same opportunity because they lack the skills and resources necessary to exploit this because their experience lies in other markets. A threat is a possible action that could cause harm to the business. A threat to one business may not be a threat to another. Changing legislation to insist cars are made more environmentally friendly may be a threat to some car manufacturers because of the potential costs. However, it may be an opportunity to the developers of environmentally friendly engines and bicycle manufacturers.

To identify the relevant opportunities and threats we must therefore look at the specific circumstances of a particular business. This involves an examination of the firm's strengths and weaknesses. The strengths of the business may relate to any of the functions. For example, it could have a strong brand (marketing), good cash flow (financial), well-trained staff (human resources) or a good track record of research and development (operations). Equally, the weaknesses of a business could refer to any aspect of the business, such as falling sales (marketing), low profit margins (finance), high labour turnover (HRM) or a poor quality record (operations).

SWOT analysis for BP

Strengths	Opportunities
Dominant market position	Takeovers/mergers
Vertically integrated controlling each stage of the process	Investments in alternative energy activities
Wide geographical presence	
Weaknesses	**Threats**
Oil spill in the Gulf of Mexico	Saturation of resources in the North Sea
Explosion at its Texas refinery	Instability in some oil-producing regions
	Environmental regulations
	Risks related to exploration and production business

Question:

How do you think the above SWOT analysis might affect the strategy of BP?

Decision trees

In order to make logical decisions, managers may use different approaches to help them organise their information and think through the various problems. These include decision-tree analysis. Decision-tree analysis tries to estimate the possible outcomes of different courses of action and work out the likelihood of these occurring. A decision tree is a mathematical model which can be used by managers to help them make the right decision. By combining possible outcomes with the probability of them happening, managers can compare the likely financial consequences of different decisions. The aim is to make a logical decision based on the numbers. However, it involves estimating the likelihood of different outcomes which can be difficult. Decision trees also require managers to give everything a financial value; in reality there may be all kinds of factors in a decision that are difficult to value in this way, such as the impact on the brand image of the business, the ethics of a decision and the reaction and support of stakeholders.

The value of the technique will therefore depend on managers' ability to accurately estimate the options and their likelihood and whether some factors can be valued financially, but decision trees do stress the key issues in decision-making of risk and anticipated rewards.

Influences on corporate decision-making

The influences on the way that decisions are made will include:

- **The success of a particular style of decision-making in the past.** A risk-taker who 'follows their instinct' and who has been successful so far may assume they have luck on their side and that they will continue to win (a dangerous assumption); they may be more likely to trust their instincts until it goes wrong, when it may be too late to change.
- **The nature of the industry and business.** In the film business great films sometimes break the mould and, on occasion, are successful despite initially poor feedback. Simply following research findings may lead to many films being similar and imitating the last blockbuster. Film makers may therefore decide to ignore or not even find out film goers' opinions and make the film they want to make. Having said this, film companies often show films to focus groups to get their feedback and amend the endings or the story line in response to this. The 'director's cut' is often the film the directors wished they had released but were not allowed to.
- **The risk involved.** If it is a high-risk decision, managers may want to reduce the risk or at least take steps to reduce the risk by gathering data on which they can base decisions. If it is a low-risk decision they may be more inclined to trust instinct. This links with the type of decision being made. With

a small tactical decision you may rely on what you have always done; with a major strategic decision you may want to be more scientific because much may be unfamiliar.

- **The corporate culture, mission and objectives.** Whether a particular decision is suitable will depend on whether it helps a business to do what it is there to do. A takeover may make sense if rapid growth is the objective. Giving suppliers longer to pay may make sense if you value suppliers. Trying to delay any redundancies may be essential if you are trying to treat your employees well. What is the 'right' decision for one business may be the wrong decision for another. Relocating to cut costs may be right for profit-driven business and wrong for a business trying to look after existing staff.

- **The ethics of a decision.** This is linked with the point above in that the importance of ethics in decision-making may depend on the business. Some organisations want to try and do the right thing (Innocent Drinks founders say, 'we are not perfect but we are trying to make the world a bit better'); others may show less interest in social responsibility. What matters is what the owners and managers believe in and this will influence what they might or might not go ahead with. How important is the environment? What about suppliers? What about 'fair treatment' of customers (for example, should we pass on a fall in our costs in the form of lower prices)? The 'supreme purpose' of John Lewis (which also owns Waitrose and Peter Jones) as stated in its constitution is 'the happiness of our Partners' (its employees); the managers here will take into account the partners' views when it comes to making decisions. More and more companies are taking their stakeholders into account when it comes to decision-making and showing an interest in Corporate Social Responsibility (CSR).

  A CSR approach recognises the impact that a business can have on its staff, its suppliers, the community, the government, the environment and various other stakeholders; the impact on such groups is considered when setting objectives and making decisions. Several companies now produce CSR reports alongside their financial accounts to measure their progress in relation to the treatment of stakeholders. Greater commitment to reducing global warming, better treatment of staff or helping the community will affect the decisions managers take.

  What also matters is the customers' and media's perception of a company's actions (do *they* think it

is ethical?). Ryanair may think it is fine to refuse a refund if you are late for a flight for reasons totally beyond your control, but if there was enough media pressure it might change its approach. In some cases managers may consider the perception of their actions as much as what they actually believe – they may do something (give money to charity, sponsor an event or reduce emissions) because they want to be associated with this and think it will help their public image regardless of whether they believe in it.

- **Resources.** What you decide to do may depend on what is feasible, which in turn depends on your resources. When choosing a university you have to consider your likely results – there is no point applying to places that will not give you an offer. There may be many universities you would like to go to, but are they realistic options? Similarly there may be many decisions a manager wants to make, but how much money is available? How many staff? How much time? What is actually chosen will have to be what is feasible.

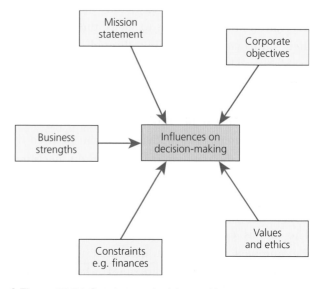

Figure 29.3 Influences on decision-making

Problems making decisions

Making decisions in business is not easy, not least because you will be dealing with many different stakeholders. A business is a political system (Pfeffer 1992) and made up of people with different opinions, and sometimes very different views on what they want to achieve and how they think it should be achieved. Any major decision is likely to make some better off and others worse off; it is therefore likely to meet with opposition.

Every decision will involve different stakeholders and you will consider their objectives and their relative power. Do you want to listen to them? Do you need to listen to them? What will happen if you ignore them? This means you need to think about their relative power. A well-organised workforce that is unionised, for example, may be able to negotiate for more consultation and participation in decision-making than individual employees could on their own. You may want to pay more attention to an investor who owns 65 per cent of the company compared with one who has 1 per cent. A key supplier of your major component will have more influence than the supplier of a component which can be bought in thousands of stores. So the more you need a particular stakeholder, the more you like or agree with them and their objectives, the more they are likely to influence your decision.

Decision-making can also be difficult because:

- the data you have gathered may be insufficient or inaccurate (it depends how you gathered it). Alternatively, the data may be valid but there may simply be so much of it that managers may not be able to identify the underlying patterns or they spend so much time making sense of it that by the time a decision is reached it is too late (this is called 'paralysis by analysis').
- the data may be incomplete; however much data you gather you often find you want more or you want it in a different format. Also it is possible that you have overlooked some key data. Managers may have a particular view of the world based on their own experience and when they are presented with data that conflicts with this they may ignore it. The managers of McDonald's took some time before realising the need for the business to become healthier because they assumed their usual burgers would always be in high demand.
- the data may have been relevant when it was collected, but given the rate of change in some markets it can quickly become out of date; you may well produce a plan that is designed for a particular competitive landscape that has now changed.

The limitations of scientific decision-making

Scientific decision-making is logical and rational. If the data is available, is relevant and is not too expensive to gather, then it makes sense for it to

BUSINESS IN FOCUS

Jim Collins in his book *How the Mighty Fall* looks at the failure of big businesses and considers why they end up making bad decisions. Collins identifies different stages that a business can go through that can end in the closure of the business. These are closely linked with problems with the culture of a business that may have become too big and overconfident.

- **Stage 1: hubris born of success**. In this stage managers feel they are unbeatable and are likely to overestimate their skills. They focus on what to do next and lose sight of whether it is actually worth doing or worrying about why they are doing it.
- **Stage 2: undisciplined pursuit of more**. In this stage the business is still growing and keeps seeking to do more. Managers want the business to get even bigger and they start expanding into areas where they do not have the right competences. Increasingly, there is a shortage of good staff, and personal ambition starts to override what is good for the business.
- **Stage 3: denial of risk and peril**. In this stage there are some warning signs that the business may have lost focus, but managers ignore them. Staff argue that these signs are temporary or not important. More focus is put on positive data and the belief remains that nothing is fundamentally wrong.
- **Stage 4: grasping for salvation**. In this stage the problems become obvious and managers desperately look for a solution. They sometimes try to bring in a new leader or they adopt an untested radical shift in strategy or rush through what they hope is a blockbuster product.
- **Stage 5: capitulation to irrelevance or death**. In this stage leaders accept that the business is in fundamental trouble. In some cases, they sell out; in some cases the business dies.

feed into your decision-making. When big high-risk decisions are being made you often want to feel you have done all you can to make sure you get it right, and gathering and analysing data is part of this. However, data is not always reliable (political predictions of who will win an election are sometimes wrong, for example, despite fairly sophisticated ways of researching). Also there may not be the time or money for a scientific approach or information may not be readily available. In this case you may fall back

Kodak cash crisis

Eastman Kodak warned in 2011 that it must raise new funds to survive the next year.

The 131-year-old US photography firm said it might raise the cash through patent sales or by taking on additional debt.

The firm revealed that its cash balance at the end of September 2011 totalled $862 million (£537 million) after it ran up a $222 million operating loss over the preceding three months. Industry commentators said Kodak took too long to move from its traditional film business into digital cameras.

The firm's inkjet printer and inks unit was still performing well with recent sales up 44 per cent higher than the previous year. But Kodak warned it might need to slow investment in the printing business 'if liquidity needs require'.

The firm announced in July 2011 that it was exploring selling or licensing around 1,100 of its digital imaging patents – around 10 per cent of its library. The company said it had no intention of filing for bankruptcy, but it seemed that a great deal depended on the sale of its innovation rights.

One former executive of the firm called for more radical change.

'I think you are going to see Kodak getting broken up and the various parts of the company will go to where they add the most value and therefore Kodak captures the most value for creditors and stock holders,' the firm's former vice president Don Strickland told the BBC.

Mr Strickland left the company in 1993 after he failed to persuade Kodak to release a digital camera. He claimed the firm's current problems could have been avoided.

'We developed the world's first consumer digital camera and Kodak could have launched it in 1992. We could not get approval to launch or sell it because of fear of the cannibalisation of film … a huge opportunity missed.'

(*Source: Adapted from BBC News, 3 November 2011*)

Note: Early in 2012, Kodak did file for bankruptcy protection and made plans to phase out some parts of its business.

Question:

Kodak was slow to move into digital cameras. Why do you think this was?

on your intuition. In some instances you may think this is a better way of deciding anyway, for example, in the worlds of fashion, art and music it may be difficult to scientifically analyse what will work. Steve Jobs, who founded Apple, said that customers did not know what they wanted – he knew before they did. If this was true then this might limit the value of market research.

Even if there is enough data, at the end of the day you are likely to be influenced by your gut feeling (your intuition); you can research universities as much as you want but people often have a feeling about a course or place. A decision to do business with someone often depends on your feelings about them. So, however scientific your approach, intuition will often play a part in decision-making, whether we like it or not. We need to be aware of this (for example, when interviewing people we sometimes let our feelings about whether we like them or not override whether they would be good at the job), but also appreciate that not everything is quantifiable (for example, whether two business could easily work well together, whether an advert which sets out to break the mould will immediately be appreciated by a focus group, whether a new logo works or not).

Henry Mintzberg identifies three types of decision-making: thinking, feeling and doing. Some people in some situations prefer to analyse and think through problems if they can. Some have a gut feeling about what will work. Some like to get on and do things and see what happens and then learn from this.

BUSINESS IN FOCUS

Styles of decision-making

The style of decision-making can vary considerably from organisation to organisation depending on the culture and management style. Some organisations are far more consensus based than others – they want the people involved to agree before going ahead. In other organisations the senior manager decides and will insist it goes ahead. This is often linked to the culture of different countries. In Japan, for example, the decision-making process is known as 'ringi'. Decisions go round and round for consultation. Everyone involved has a chance to input and their view is listened to, debated and taken into account; if someone raises an objection then the debate continues until a solution is found that is acceptable to all. This leads to a much slower decision-making process than in the US or the UK. However, everyone affected has seen how the decision has been made, they have all made a contribution and the chances are that it is a better decision than one person on their own would make. It may take longer but once made it probably works.

Question:
What is the best style of decision making?

Corporate and functional strategies

The overall strategy of the business (for example, to launch its products in new countries) is the corporate strategy (which is part of the overall corporate plan). This will then have to be implemented by the different functions of the business; this requires functional strategies. For example, imagine that an airline decided to target the low-cost segment of the short-haul market – this is the corporate strategy. To achieve this each function must play its part. For example, the operations managers must work out how to keep costs down (for example, by finding low cost airports to take off from and land at, keeping services offered to a minimum and speeding up turnaround time). Meanwhile the marketing function must promote this in a way that is cost effective (for example, via the internet rather than mainstream advertising). The functional strategies, therefore, are developed to implement the corporate strategy.

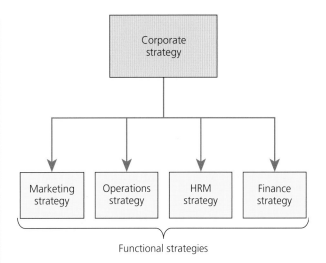

Figure 29.4 Functional strategies implement the corporate strategy

What types of strategy exist?

Strategies can be analysed in different ways. One way of categorising these is the Ansoff matrix. This examines strategies in terms of the products offered by a business and the markets in which it competes.

- **Market penetration** occurs when a business chooses to fight on its home ground. It is trying to sell more of its existing products. This may be achieved by more promotions, price cuts or greater efforts to get the product distributed. The aim is to gain more share of the existing market.

- **Market development** occurs when a business aims at a new segment; for example a business may try to sell in new countries or to a different target group. The product is familiar but the way in which it is marketed may be new.

- **New product development** occurs when a business develops new products for its existing customer base. This involves risk because many new products are dropped before they are developed or fail when they are launched. Developing a new product can be very expensive and take time, only to flop when it hits the market (for instance, Wrigley's thin ice strips, and Coca-Cola's vanilla Coke).

- **Diversification** is the most difficult strategy to manage because it involves new products and new markets. Therefore this strategy involves a high degree of risk in terms of making it successful. However, if it does work it means the business is operating in more than one market and so may be less vulnerable to change in any one of them.

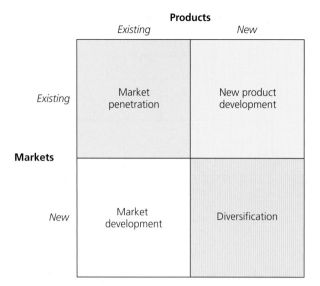

Products

	Existing	New
Existing	Market penetration	New product development
New	Market development	Diversification

Markets

Figure 29.5 The Ansoff matrix

The Ansoff matrix highlights where firms are fighting – with which products and in which markets. We are also interested in how firms compete, which depends on the value they offer relative to their rivals.

The value of a product to a consumer depends on the price paid and the benefits offered. Is a £2,000 holiday better than a £200 holiday? It depends on what you get for it. If you get a luxury hotel, the flights, car rental, free food and entertainment in a premium resort then £2,000 may be good value. If you get a leaky caravan next to a busy motorway £200 may be bad value. The combination of price and benefits therefore determines whether something is good or bad value. To be competitive a business may:

- offer more benefits than the competition; it may then be able to charge for more for this, the same or (if it is possible to provide it a lower price) less. Mont Blanc pens have a well-established brand that people will pay more for, for example. The Lexus entered the luxury car market trying to offer more for less.
- offer the same benefits as competitors but at a lower price, for example own-label products competing against well-known brands
- offer lower benefits but at a much lower price, for example Ryanair and Poundland.

For any of the strategies above to be successful a business must understand the benefits customers want and, if it decides to offer lower prices, it must find ways of being more efficient than competitors.

Strategies that focus on offering more are called differentiating strategies by Michael Porter. Strategies that aim to offer benefits at lower prices are known as low-cost strategies.

What businesses must not do is offer a similar range of products and services at a higher price than rivals. This would be to get 'caught in the middle'. They must focus on differentiation or low costs, according to Porter.

Why can strategies go wrong?

Strategies often do not turn out the way we want them to. This is because:

- It can be difficult to estimate what is going to happen in the future. In 2007, how many of us would have guessed that share prices worldwide were about to fall, that banks would be nationalised and governments would pour in billions of dollars to make funds available for lending? In such volatile circumstances as these it is no surprise that a firm's expansion plans may be put on hold or its decision to launch new products delayed. Even now as we write it is unclear what the future holds in terms of the euro or UK GDP growth.
- The implementation may prove far more difficult than you imagined; there may be technical problems, greater resistance to change than you imagined or costs may escalate.

BUSINESS IN FOCUS

Why businesses fail

In 2011 Cass Business School published a study called *Road to Ruin*, identifying the key reasons why businesses failed. These were:

1 inadequate board skills and inability of non-executive members to exercise control (non-executives are directors who sit on the board but do not work day-to-day within the business. The purpose of non-executives is to provide an outside check and perspective on what is happening in the business)
2 blindness to inherent risks, such as risks to the business model or reputation
3 inadequate leadership on ethos and culture
4 defective internal communication and information flow
5 organisational complexity and change
6 inappropriate incentives, both implicit and explicit.

Question:

Research and find a business that has failed recently; explain the possible reasons for this failure.

- You may not have the resources to see the plan through.

Information management and decisions

Managers are in charge of various resources (such as people, money, machines and materials) and must decide how to use these most efficiently and most effectively. This involves hundreds of decisions every week. Every decision has an opportunity cost – this means managers must consider what they are sacrificing when they make a decision. They must also measure the success of any decision: Did it work? How effective was it? This highlights the importance of gaining feedback; whenever a particular course of action is taken data is needed to assess how well it is working so it can be corrected along the way and/or a different decision is taken next time. Imagine that you decide to write an essay using a different style. Does it work? Was it a good idea to change your style? You can only tell if you see what mark you get and read the comments on your work so you can assess the impact of your decision. Information, then, is at the heart of decision-making: you need information to decide what the present situation is, information to decide what your options are and information to assess whether a given decision worked or not.

Information therefore helps managers decide: what to do, how to do it and decide whether it worked.

No manager will get everything right all of the time, but good managers are ones who get it right most of the time and who make sure the big decisions are correct. Getting it right matters because:

- you have limited resources and cannot afford to waste them
- there is always an alternative; you do not want to choose the wrong course of action
- there are competitors and if you get it wrong you are leaving it open to them to get it right.

To help get it right the management of information is important. Information can be used as a resource to help the business compete more effectively.

What is information?

Data consists of raw unanalysed facts, figures and events. Information comes from data that has been processed so that it has meaning for the person receiving it. £100,000, £200,000, £300,000 are just a series of numbers; if, however, you know that these numbers represent the turnover of a business they begin to have more meaning. If you know that this increase is following an increase of £15,000 on advertising then the figures begin to be very significant. As you know, in business studies we stress the importance of context. This means turning data into information – turning raw numbers into something meaningful by considering their context.

What is good-quality information?

The quality of information depends on its:

- reliability (accuracy): to be useful information must be accurate
- timeliness: information needs to be available at the right time to help make the decisions; it is no good if it arrives too late
- quantity: the amount of information must be appropriate – having too much information may mean that it cannot be digested and made sense of; most managers suffer from information overload and so do not process it all effectively
- relevance: good information is relevant to the user – it must not be too detailed nor too general but related directly to the needs of the user.

Information management (IM) involves the collection and management of information from one or more sources and the distribution of that information to different individuals. The management of information has, of course, been revolutionised by the growth in information technology. The amount of data that can now be transferred, the faster speed and lower costs of transferring and analysing data have significantly

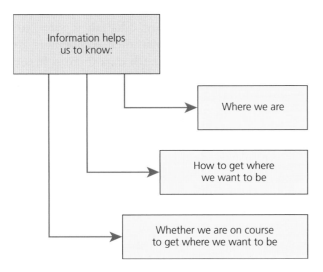

Figure 29.6 The importance of information

changed the way information is managed and the importance of information management.

According to the Carnegie Mellon School, information management (an organisation's ability to process information) is at the core of organisational and managerial competencies.

How can managing information help a business to compete?

Better management of information can help businesses to be more competitive in many areas. For example:

- It should provide better insight into the nature and behaviour of customers. Companies use loyalty cards, for example, as a way of tracking customer purchases and linking this to information held about the customers, such as their age, socio-economic group and home address. The effects of more promotional spending, price cuts or a changed store layout can all be measured directly.
- Stock management (information on the level of stocks held at any moment) can be useful to be able to tell customers quickly what is in stock, and good links with suppliers can help a just-in-time production approach to be developed. With good information passing between a business and its suppliers, the delivery of supplies can occur just when they are needed and they can be delivered in the order they will be used.
- Information is essential to know what resources are being used, how they are being used, what they cost and how effective they are. Systems such as budgeting and appraisal rely on information.

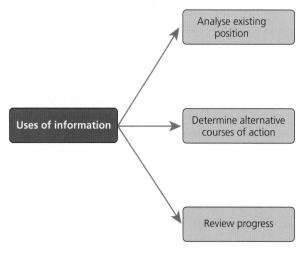
Figure 29.7 The uses of information

BUSINESS IN FOCUS

How businesses are using information

Tesco collects 1.5 billion pieces of data every month and uses this to adjust its prices and promotions. Williams-Sonoma, an American retailer, uses its knowledge of its 60 million customers (which includes such details as their income and the value of their houses) to produce different versions of its catalogue. Amazon has stated that 30 per cent of its sales are generated by its recommendation engine which states 'you may also like'. The mobile phone revolution creates even more opportunities for using information – companies are now developing programmes to enable businesses such as Starbucks to send you offers when you get close to one of their stores.

Question:

Analyse how better information management can lead to more profits.

Information helps a business to:

- identify where it is at the moment (for example, an internal and external analysis)
- evaluate different strategies to take
- review the results.

Information systems

Managers need to understand the importance of information and look at how they are managing it. Some organisations nowadays have knowledge managers, highlighting how significant they think the management of information is to the business. Organisations gather lots of data all the time, such as who their customers are, what their sales are, what their costs are and what their competitors are doing. Just think of how much data there is in any organisation, often stored in different places and known by different people – often this information is not shared or analysed effectively.

Imagine if the information that exists in many different places about you could be made easily available in the right formats to those who need it: teachers, exam officers, parents, personal tutors, UCAS advisers. This would enable those involved to provide you with better information and help you more effectively in your studies.

Far too many organisations have very valuable information but keep it in all sorts of places where it cannot easily be found; some of it is on the marketing managers' shared drive, some on the operations director's memory stick, and some in the chief executive's brain. The information is stored in a way that does not make it very accessible.

An information system is a set of people, procedures and resources that collects and transforms data into information and disseminates this information. Some of these systems are formal (for example, computer systems); some are informal (for example, gossip).

How do we manage information?

When developing a system to manage information we need to:

- **decide what information we need.** There is sometimes a danger of collecting too much data and losing sight of the key issues, so it is important to be clear why you want something gathered.
- **decide how to store the data.** In what format will it be stored? How and where will it be saved?
- **decide who can access it and how.** For example, how do we keep managers up to date? How do we get information to them in a manner they can understand and that will inform their decisions?

Uses of information systems

There are many different types of information systems, such as:

- enterprise resource planning systems which aim to coordinate activities and decisions across many functions by creating an integrated platform that integrates them into company-wide business processes. When an order is received, for example, this triggers decisions throughout the business in terms of ordering more materials.
- customer relationship management (CRM) is intended to build and sustain long-term business with customers. It represents a move from mass markets and mass production to customisation and focused production. It helps to:
  - gather customer data quickly
  - identify valuable customers and less valuable ones
  - increase customer loyalty and retention
  - reduce the costs of meeting customers
  - make it easier to acquire similar customers.

Information systems can enable managers to:

- identify changes in conditions more quickly
- respond more quickly to change
- make better, more accurate decisions
- make fewer mistakes
- review their progress and identify what has and what has not worked in order to make better decisions next time.

Summary

Making decisions is an important part of management. Strategic decisions are non-programmed and long term. They often involve a high degree of risk. These are difficult decisions to make because they involve forecasting, dealing with unfamiliar scenarios in the future and a high degree of pressure because these decisions may be difficult to reverse. To help reduce the risk of such decisions managers are likely to take a scientific approach, which involves gathering and analysing data. They may also use techniques such as decision trees. Decision trees involve quantifying outcomes and risk to try and make the most rational decision on financial grounds. Of course there may be other motives driving the decision apart from the highest financial reward.

1. What is meant by scientific decision-making? *(3 marks)*

2. What is meant by a decision tree? *(2 marks)*

3. Explain **two** benefits of using decision trees. *(5 marks)*

4. Explain **one** limitation of decision trees. *(2 marks)*

5. Explain **one** limitation of a scientific approach to decision-making. *(3 marks)*

6. What is the difference between a strategic decision and a tactical one? *(2 marks)*

7. Explain **two** reasons why strategies can go wrong. *(6 marks)*

8. Explain **two** reasons why information management can help a business compete. *(6 marks)*

9. What is meant by a management information system? *(2 marks)*

10. What is good quality information? *(3 marks)*

Essay questions

1. Steve Jobs at Apple is said to have ignored market research and gone with his gut instinct because 'customers do not know what they want'. Is this the best way for managers to make decisions? Justify your answer with reference to Steve Jobs and/ or other organisations or individuals you know. *(40 marks)*

2. Before entering the market in the US Tesco invested heavily in market research. Is this the best approach to making a strategic decision? Justify your answer with reference to Tesco and/or other organisations or individuals you know. *(40 marks)*

3. Businesses such as Mont Blanc pens and BMW focus on differentiating their offering from their competitors. To what extent do you think this is the best strategy for a business to pursue? Justify your answer with reference to Mont Blanc, BMW and/or other organisations or individuals you know. *(40 marks)*

4. Some companies such as Marks & Spencer plc generate most of their sales in the UK. To what extent do you think that a strategy of focusing on the UK market is desirable for stakeholders? Justify your answer with reference to Marks & Spencer and/or other organisations or individuals you know. *(40 marks)*

Candidate's answer:

A strategy is a long-term plan. It is used to help a business achieve its objectives. It is usually high risk and involves a long-term commitment of resources. It is then implemented by tactics.

Stakeholders are groups that have an interest in the organisation and its activities.

A strategy focusing on your own market, like Marks & Spencer has, is one of market penetration or new product development according to Ansoff. Market penetration occurs when existing products are aimed at existing markets; for example if Marks & Spencer used more promotional campaigns to push sales and try to gain a bigger market share of the clothing and food market in the UK. This has great appeal in that it deals with markets that you know; Marks & Spencer is a well established brand and therefore well accepted by customers; it can use this brand to open new stores relatively easily and cheaply, and quickly gain a customer base in any part of the UK. It understands UK laws such as employment and planning, and so the process of growth may be relatively easy. If the business then launches new products (whether this be new foods or a more dramatic move into new product categories such as electronics) but still targets existing customers this is known as market development. It can, for example cross-sell its new products to new customers using its store card lists. New product development can go wrong – it can be expensive to undertake and new products are not always accepted (for example, the famous disaster of New Coke being launched in the mid 1980s). However, given you know your customer base (for example, its demographics and possibly even its shopping habits if it uses your cards) it may mean your promotion can be more focused and more efficient.

Whether focusing on the UK market is desirable for a business depends on the alternative. Marks & Spencer did go abroad for many years but found they did not understand the market needs well enough. This strategy of taking products to new markets is called market development (if you take new products as well this is called diversification); this is quite risky because you are less familiar with market conditions – you may not be fully aware of marketing regulations, the significance of symbols, words and signs culturally, the best way of promoting your product or the likely reaction of customers. In the world of food retailing the types of foods people buy vary significantly globally meaning that companies such as Tesco change their product mix a great deal in different countries. Even then, even big firms can get it wrong. B&Q, for example found that in China there was not the demand expected for do-it-yourself as people tended to employ local builders to do the work for them. The dangers of entering a foreign market can be quite great and so it may well be more desirable to stay in a market you know. However, this means you might miss out on a great number of opportunities.

The desirability also depends on who you are asking. A business has many stakeholders and so these different groups may be considered. A move overseas may mean more access to markets and potentially more profits for investors but it may mean fewer jobs in the UK compared to a situation when the business focused on this country; it might also mean less demand for UK suppliers and more for overseas suppliers. The desirability may therefore relate to which stakeholder group is considered.

Overall a strategy of focusing on the UK may be safer and therefore desirable. It may also benefit some stakeholder groups such as UK employees and suppliers more than expansion overseas. However, if you are looking for fast growth and more profits and you are an investor the overseas market may be more desirable.

Examiner's comments:

This response has potential but does not focus enough on the stakeholder issue. It basically analyses the advantages of operating in the UK and the dangers of overseas marketing but does not relate this to stakeholders much until the end paragraph. The analysis and application is not good because it lacks sufficient reference to the specific context of the desirability of the UK versus overseas markets in relation to stakeholders. Similarly, while the last paragraph makes an attempt to start considering the different perspectives it does not do this in any depth.

30 Implementing and managing change

Change is a constant in business but that doesn't make it any easier to manage. Given that change is going to occur, managers must consider the best way(s) of managing it.

In this chapter we examine:

- techniques to implement and manage change
- the factors that promote and/or cause resistance to change.

Why is change necessary?

Open the newspapers and you will see how much change there is happening in almost every market you can think of. Managers must try to prepare for this change and ensure they adapt to it when it has happened. Standing still is dangerous and may lead to competitors exploiting market opportunities more effectively than they do. To play to their strengths and to avoid threats organisations must continually review what they are trying to achieve and how to do this. Businesses are constantly repositioning themselves and redefining themselves as conditions change.

Bringing about change

Why is a business doing what it is doing? According to Lewin (1951) it is because at any moment in time there are some forces pushing for change and some forces resisting change. A business is in equilibrium when these forces are balanced (they offset each other). To bring about change managers need to increase the forces that would promote change (called 'driving forces') or reduce forces preventing change (called 'restraining forces'). The equilibrium 'can be changed either by adding forces in the desired direction or by diminishing the opposing forces' (Lewin).

Figure 30.1 Managing change

Imagine a situation in which managers want to introduce new technology. To bring about change managers must try to increase the pressure for it; this means they increase the drivers for change. For example, they might stress to employees:

- the dangers of holding on to old technology (for example, loss of competitiveness and the possible loss of jobs)
- the benefits of new technology (in terms of boosting competitiveness)
- the threats from competitors who are already using this technology.

Alternatively, managers might focus on reducing the resistance to change and perhaps:

- educate employees on the benefits of the change
- offer incentives to those willing to change
- threaten or intimidate those who resist
- guarantee jobs to reduce this insecurity
- offer training to those who need to re-skill.

This would reduce resistance to change and make it more likely to happen.

Why do people resist change?

Some people embrace change – they pioneer new ideas and new ways of doing things, but almost inevitably any innovation will meet resistance. Where there is a pioneer there is likely to be someone who does not want the change to happen.

According to Kotter and Schlesinger (1979) the main reasons why people resist change are:

- Self-interest – they do not want the effort of change or are better off as they are (for example, their status or importance might be less after the change).

- Misunderstanding and lack of trust – they do not understand why change is necessary and/or are suspicious about why the change is happening.
- They prefer the status quo – they would rather keep things as they are because they feel comfortable with it.
- They do not think the new idea will work – they think there are flaws in this and therefore it would be wrong to pursue it.

Resistance to change may come in many forms, such as:

- a lack of effort to learn the necessary new skills or a general lack of cooperation
- a demand for more pay
- a refusal to use the new systems
- a demand for extended discussion to slow down the process of change.

Figure 30.2 highlights the different states that employees might be in when managers are introducing change. This model by Zeira and Avedisian highlights that the openness and readiness for change will depend on how dissatisfied employees are with the present situation and the extent to which they think they will suffer from change. The more dissatisfied they are and the less they think they will personally suffer as a result of it, the more open they will be to change.

Why else might change not happen?

Change may not happen because there is resistance to it. Also, it may be that the business lacks the resources to bring it about. We may know we need to update our database systems, improve our website or refurbish our stores but lack the resources to do so. Often the very time when change is needed (when a business is doing badly) is when a business is short of resources to bring it about.

The lack of resources may involve a lack of:

- **money**, for example, a business may not have the cash or access to credit to invest
- **skills**, for example, a business may not have the talents, experience and abilities within its organisation to manage a change or bring about change effectively. This may be due to the recruitment policy, a lack of training and/or a new situation arising which requires new skills it does not have.

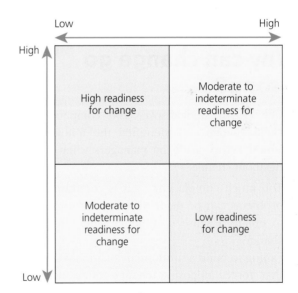

Figure 30.2 Employee readiness for change

- **time** – you should never underestimate time as a resource. There may be many changes managers want to bring about but they may be so busy fire-fighting that they cannot implement all the changes they would like to.

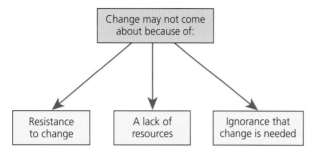

Figure 30.3 Unsuccessful change

Another problem that can occur is that managers simply do not recognise that change is needed. They may be too inward looking and not appreciate that their market has changed. A manager like this is a reactive rather than a proactive manager.

What happens if you do not change?

If you ignore or fail to identify the need for change, the danger is that you will be left behind: you are the only typewriter shop on the block (and not for much longer); you have a lovely collection of cameras using photographic film but no customers. Change can, of course, go wrong but standing still is often dangerous.

Why can change go wrong?

Kotter (1990) studied over 100 companies going through change and identified the following most common errors made by managers when trying to bring about change:

1 Too much complacency – it is common to think problems can be dealt with later. Managers need to create a sense of urgency when introducing change.
2 Failing to build a substantial coalition – this means that forces opposing change often undermine the changes that managers are trying to bring in. Managers need to build a coalition to gain support and help push the change through.
3 Underestimating the need for a clear vision – without a clear vision of where you are headed you may end up with a series of initiatives that are rather disconnected.
4 A failure to communicate the vision – a vision needs to be shared.
5 Permitting roadblocks against the vision; allowing things to get in the way and delay change – managers

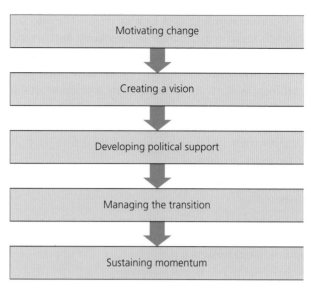

Figure 30.4 Successful change

need to empower people to clear obstacles.
6 Not planning or achieving short-term wins – it is important to sustain momentum. Managers need to secure short-term wins to show they can succeed.
7 Declaring victory too soon – managers need to keep moving.
8 Not anchoring changes in corporate culture – managers need to anchor change and make sure it is part of the culture (for example, by rewarding those who have helped bring it about).

Kotter stressed the importance of using the sequence in the order shown in Figure 30.4 to bring about effective change.

Successful change

Change is most likely to be successful if:

- those affected by the change were involved in bringing it about (rather than having it imposed on them)
- those involved in the change feel they have an opportunity to air their views
- the benefits of the change are made clear to those involved
- individuals feel able to cope with the change; they feel they have the resources and skills to deal with it
- the people involved agree with the reasons for the change.

To bring about successful change managers may:

- try to educate employees to explain why it is necessary, what the benefits are if they change and the dangers of not changing. In 2003 Samsung underwent major change reinventing the way it did business. To make change easier to bring about its chief executive said, 'I'm the chaos maker. I have tried to encourage a sense of crisis to drive change. We instilled in management a sense that we could go bankrupt any day'

- try to reassure employees that it will work and provide training to help it work
- try to win support from key people
- reward those who agree to change and penalise those who do not
- if necessary, force the change through; if the change works people will eventually stop resisting.

SARAH

When a change is announced it often generates the following reactions from those involved:

- **S**hock: people may be surprised that the change has to occur or has occurred.
- **A**nger: people may be annoyed, perhaps because they did not know or expect the change and/or because they may be worse off.
- **R**ejection: people try to deny the change is really going to happen; they think if they ignore it, it may go away.
- **A**cceptance: eventually people accept that the change is going to happen.
- **H**elp: at some point people decide to ask for help.

Managers need to recognise these stages and help people to move through them as fast as possible to get to the stage when they will recognise the need for change and show a willingness to accept help.

Project management

In many cases change may be ongoing; however, in some instances there may be a distinct project to manage (for example, restructuring the business, undertaking a takeover or launching a new project). This requires particular skills to make sure that a project is completed on time, on budget and to the standards required. The process of ensuring these targets are met is known as project management.

What is a project?

A project occurs when an individual or team attempts to accomplish a specific objective by completing a set of interrelated tasks.

A project has:

- an objective
- a series of interdependent tasks
- resources that will be used up
- a specific timeframe by which it has to completed
- a degree of uncertainty.

Examples of projects are:

- launching a new product
- a takeover of a competitor
- entering a new market overseas
- moving offices.

Any project may face unforeseen circumstances such as delays from suppliers, difficulties completing some stages of the process on time and achieving quality targets on time. The challenge facing project managers is to prevent, anticipate and/or overcome such circumstances. This will involve planning to anticipate where possible and to set targets which will help define what is and is not possible. For example, you will need to estimate:

- the different stages of a project
- the order in which the stages must take place
- who is in charge of each stage
- the costs involved and the time allowed for each stage.

Project managing will involve a range of skills. These include the ability to:

- communicate to everyone what has to be done when and how
- organise and plan ahead
- set financial targets
- deal with and resolve conflict if necessary
- negotiate
- lead and inspire others to get the job done
- build a sense teamwork and common purpose.

Projects go through successive stages, and results depend on managing the project through these stages in an orderly way, such as to:

1 define the objectives
2 allocate responsibilities (define who is in charge of what)
3 fix deadlines and milestones (what has to be completed by when)
4 set budgets (how much can be spent on any aspect or part of the project)
5 monitor and control (set targets and deadlines to review along the way; make sure action is taken if the project is not on target).

Terminal 5

When Heathrow's $4.3 billion Terminal 5 finally opened there were terrible delays. Flights had to be cancelled and there was a backlog of over 15,000 bags which were stuck in transit.

Despite months of preparations at T5, its problems began almost immediately as staff arrived for their morning shifts. Many employees could not actually get to work on time because there was not sufficient space in the staff car parks.

Once inside the terminal building, workers also faced problems getting to the restricted 'airside' via security checkpoints. According to the GMB union, workers had not been familiarised with the new terminal and many simply did not know where to go.

The disastrous opening was a severe embarrassment for BA and BAA, the Spanish-owned company that operates Heathrow. Both had spent five years claiming that the new terminal would transform passengers' experience of Heathrow and work efficiently from day 1. Last night they blamed each other for the chaos inside Britain's biggest free-standing building, which was opened by the Queen in a lavish ceremony two weeks ago.

BAA claimed that the baggage system was working properly but had become clogged with bags because BA had too few staff to unload them from conveyor belts. BA said that BAA had provided too few security staff to process its baggage handlers as they arrived for work. BAA had claimed that the baggage system was the most advanced in the world, with belts travelling at 23mph and capable of handling 12,000 bags an hour. The system had been operating in test mode with thousands of dummy bags for the past 18 months.

BA had been preparing for the switch to Terminal 5 for three years and claimed that it had trained thousands of staff on the new systems. But many were delayed after being unable to park their cars or to find their way to their work stations. Several lifts were also out of action and screens were wrongly showing that gates had closed when no one had yet boarded.

That was not the end of the problems, as *The Guardian* reported:

'Simultaneously, BA baggage teams struggled immediately with an automated system that, via handheld devices, told them which flight to unload and which flight to put bags onto. According to staff, the devices told handlers to sort bags for flights that were already cancelled. This meant they turned up to load flights that were not there while, in other parts of the sorting area, bags piled up unattended.

'Without managers on the ground to allocate work, there appeared to be a communication breakdown between handlers and their supervisors in the BA control centre elsewhere in the terminal. By midday, 20 flights were cancelled as handlers frantically tried to reduce T5's inaugural baggage mountain.'

(*Source: Dan Milmo in* The Guardian, *28 March 2008*)

Questions:

1 Explain the possible costs of the problems experienced when Terminal 5 opened.
2 Analyse the reasons why people might have objected to Terminal 5.
3 Discuss the possible reasons why the opening of Terminal 5 may have gone wrong.
4 With reference to organisations or industries that you know, to what extent is effective project management a key element of the success of a business these days?

To bring about a successful completion of a project you may need internal support. This can be helped by finding people who will champion the cause (these are called project champions). They are the ambassadors telling others of the benefits of the project, enthusiastically pushing its benefits, explaining its value. If you can identify such champions in advance (or appoint them as project leaders) this can help overcome resistance to the plan.

Project groups can also be helpful to identify possible problems. You may, for example, put together a multi-functional team with people from all the different areas of the business that might be affected by the project to get different perspectives on possible difficulties. This helps to flag issues before they occur and also helps to get people onside early because they have been involved in the planning. Without this people may feel that change is being forced on them, and they may automatically resist because of this. Constructive criticism and debate is good in project teams because you are trying to flesh out problems, incorrect thinking and assumptions, and flawed logic. This probably will not be highlighted if everyone agrees with everyone else out of politeness or if everyone has a similar background and training. In some organisations someone is specifically given the role of being 'the devil's advocate' to try to find flaws with the idea. However, disagreement and debate must be managed to ensure that progress is made and the whole project does not deteriorate into name-calling!

Summary

Given that change is constantly occurring both within and outside the business, managers must learn how to cope with it and to manage it. This includes overcoming resistance to change. Resistance can occur for a number of reasons, not least because people think they will be worse off. To overcome resistance managers can use a number of techniques such as offering rewards for changed behaviour, training, education or even using punishments to force change through. Managers will also have projects to lead – to do this they need to plan carefully and be prepared to deal with delays and problems as they emerge, especially with major and new projects.

Web link

To watch Kotter talk about change go to these You Tube videos.

Dealing with resistance to change:
www.youtube.com/watch?v=Wdroj6F3VlQ&feature=related

Communicating a vision for change:
www.youtube.com/watch?v=bGVe3wRKmH0&feature=related

Key terms

A **project** is a 'unique set of coordinated activities, with definite starting and finishing points, undertaken by an individual or team to meet specific objectives within defined time, cost and performance parameters' (Office of Government Commerce).

Examiner's advice

You can see how project management links to leadership – who pioneers the project and helps push it through? It also links to the management of change – who is likely to oppose the change? Why? What can be done to overcome this resistance?

Progress questions

1 Outline Lewin's model of the drivers and restraining forces of change. *(5 marks)*
2 What might increase the forces for change? *(4 marks)*
3 Explain **two** reasons why employees often resist change. *(6 marks)*
4 Explain **two** reasons, apart from employee resistance, why change may be difficult to bring about. *(6 marks)*
5 What is meant by project management? *(3 marks)*
6 Explain **two** features of effective project management. *(6 marks)*
7 Explain **two** reasons why change might go wrong. *(6 marks)*
8 Explain **two** ways of overcoming resistance to change. *(6 marks)*
9 Using an example, explain why one stakeholder group might welcome change while another might resist change. *(6 marks)*
10 Explain **two** factors that might help make employees open to change. *(6 marks)*

Essay questions

1 When Qantas Airways announced its strategy was going to focus more on Asia than Australia its employees took industrial action. To what extent do you think that strategic change will always be resisted? Justify your answer with reference to Qantas and/or other organisations you know. (40 marks)
2 Some organisation such as Timpsons, whose activities include shoe and watch repairs, key cutting and engraving, seem to reinvent themselves as market conditions change. To what extent is the ability of an organisation to reinvent itself essential to long-term business success? Justify your →

answer with reference to Timpsons and/or other organisations that you know. (40 marks)

3 Leaders such as Alan Parker at Whitbread plc seem to have played an important role in bringing about change for their organisation, moving it out of pubs and into coffee shops and budget hotels. Does the success of any change process rely on having a good leader? Justify your answer with reference to Whitbread and/or other organisations that you know. (40 marks)

Candidate's answer:

A leader is someone who has vision and is followed by others. A leader sets out where the business should want to go. People like Steve Jobs at Apple, Richard Branson at Virgin, Lou Gerstner at GE, Alan Parker at Whitbread and Sergey Brin at Google inspire others to want to go where they want to go. They have power based perhaps on their expertise, their charisma, their power as founders and managers or their ability to give rewards. This enables them to bring about change. A leader plans, organises, coordinates and controls, and this helps to ensure change can happen. Change may be resisted because people think they will be worse off, fear change or do not understand it. A leader can help make this easier by winning over hearts and minds, by making clear the direction and by reassuring the employees that the business is in safe hands. There are different types of leader. A transformational leader is one who inspires and can provide a figurehead for change; a transactional leader is someone who gets what they want by offering something in return; an autocratic leader tells people what to do; a democratic leader discusses more. Some leaders focus on the task. Others focus on the people more. Some try to get people motivated on the task. The style of leadership has to be appropriate to the environment, people and nature of the task. There is no one right way. So the style needed to bring about change will have to take account of this. In a time of major resistance, for example, a leader may have to force through change and to get things done quickly an autocratic approach

may be required. If employees are more willing to contribute, have more training and have the skills to contribute and are open to change then greater discussion may be possible and may help bring about more effective change.

It is important also for the leader to think about how change can be brought about. Do they need to educate staff? Is training required? Are there enough resources? Is it necessary to bargain with key people to win them over to your side? What about threatening people to get them to agree? There are many ways of getting change to happen and a good leader will select appropriate ones to get the change to happen.

A leader therefore is a very important part of change and a good leader will select the right style and techniques. Get it wrong and this can hurt the business. When Willie Walsh was trying to change things at British Airways he forced it through but this led to some very damaging strikes and hurt the brand. Get it right, such as Alan Parker did when refocusing Whitbread to get out of pubs when this market was stagnant and into coffee shops (Costa) and budget hotels when they were booming and you lead change successfully.

Examiner's comments:

A good answer in many ways. There is a clear understanding of the role of the leader and how a good leader can make change easier. There is a recognition also that it depends how the leader goes about change and that it can depend on factors such as the resources available. However, the response could have been more applied – perhaps developing further the example of British Airways or Whitbread or other organisations they knew. It also needed to develop other factors influencing the success of change in more detail – it is not just the leader but also managers throughout the organisation, the employees' attitudes and skills, the pace of change and whether in fact it is the right change and whether it is seen as such. This answer has potential but is reasonable rather than good.

REFERENCES

This is a list of selected references from the books and articles mentioned throughout this textbook.

Ansoff, I. (1957), 'Strategies for Diversification', *Harvard Business Review*, Vol. 35 issue 5, Sept–Oct, pp. 113–24.

Boddy, D. (2002), *Management: An Introduction*, Financial Times Prentice Hall.

Deal, T. E. and Kennedy, A. A. (1982), *Corporate Cultures: The Rites and Rituals of Corporate Life*, Penguin Books.

Drucker, P. (1985), *The Effective Executive*, HarperBusiness.

French, J. and Raven B. (1959), *Bases of Social Power, Studies in Social Power*. Ed. Dorwin Cartwright, University of Michigan, Ann Arbor.

Gladwell, M. (2002), *The Tipping Point: How Little Things can Make a Big Difference*, Abacus.

Handy, C. (1990), *Understanding Organisations*, Penguin.

Herzberg, F. (1968), 'One more time, how do you motivate employees?', *Harvard Business Review*.

Hofstede, G.(1991), *Cultures and Organizations: Software of the Mind: Intercultural Cooperation and its Importance for Survival*, McGraw Hill.

Johnson, G. and Scholes, K. (1997), *Exploring Corporate Strategy*, Prentice Hall.

Kotter, J. (1990), *A Force for Change, How Leadership Differs from Management*, Free Press.

Kotter, J.P. and Schlesinger L.A. (1979), *Choosing Strategies for Change*, Harvard Business Review.

Lewin, K. (1951), *Field Theory in Social Science*, Harper and Row.

Maslow, A. (1943), 'A theory of human motivation', *Psychological Review*, Vol. 50.

Mayo, G.E. (1977), *The Social Problems of an Industrial Civilisation*, Ayer Co.

Mintzberg, H. (1973), *The Nature of Managerial Work*, Harper Collins.

Office for National Statistics (2011), *Labour Force Survey*, Vol. 2.

Ouchi, W. (1981), *Theory Z: How American Business Can Meet the Japanese Challenge*, Avon Books.

Porter, M (1980), *Competitive Strategy Techniques for Analysing Industries and Competitors*, Free Press.

Simon, H.A. (1960), *The New Science of Management Decisions*, Harper and Row.

Tannenbaum, R. and Schmidt, W.H (1957), *How to Choose a Leadership Pattern*, Harvard Business Review.

Note: page numbers in **bold** refer to keyword definitions.